AF580070

Praise for

FUNGI

Creatures & Cultures

"A beautifully crafted network of fungal threads. This book is a generous and imaginative invitation into the world of fungi, not just as organisms, but as cultural, historical, and creative forces. Full of insight, practical activities, and playful curiosity, which encourages engagement with mycology as a living, evolving relationship. A genuinely inspiring read."
Rich Wright, Senior Conservation Officer (Fungi) at Plant Life

"This is a great book. I love the vibe; it's playful and easy to read. Gonna help a lot of younguns learn about the culture."
William Padilla-Brown, Multidisciplinary Citizen Scientist and Founder and CEO of MycoSymbiotics

"A profoundly insightful and personal overview of the fungal kingdom, and how it has myceliated Human civilization. It's visually stunning, thought provoking, factual, packed with humor and quirky recipes which make this book unlike any other on this topic."
Marc Violo, Founder and CEO of MycoStories

"An absolutely superb foray into Kingdom Fungi!"
Lawrence Millman, author of Fungipedia

"The infectious enthusiasm and love for fungi splashes from each page. This is the type of fungal contamination to embrace!"
Yasmine Ostendorf-Rodríguez, Curator and Researcher on art and ecology, and Author of Let's Become Fungal!

"A fabulously insightful journey through the vast kingdom of fungi."
Jem Purry, Student and Young Mycologist of the Year 2025

"*Fungi: Creatures and Cultures* is a beautifully crafted ethnomycological exposition that poetically weaves the eons of association between humans and fungi. With its stunning images and Kit's punchy writing style, it's the perfect centerpiece for your coffee table. Aspiring mycophiles are going to have their minds blown on nearly every page, but even veteran funginauts will have to put the book down from time to time to look up into empty space and just sit in the wonder of what they've just read. I know I certainly did."
Jasper Degenaars, Hyphae Headmaster of Fungi Academy

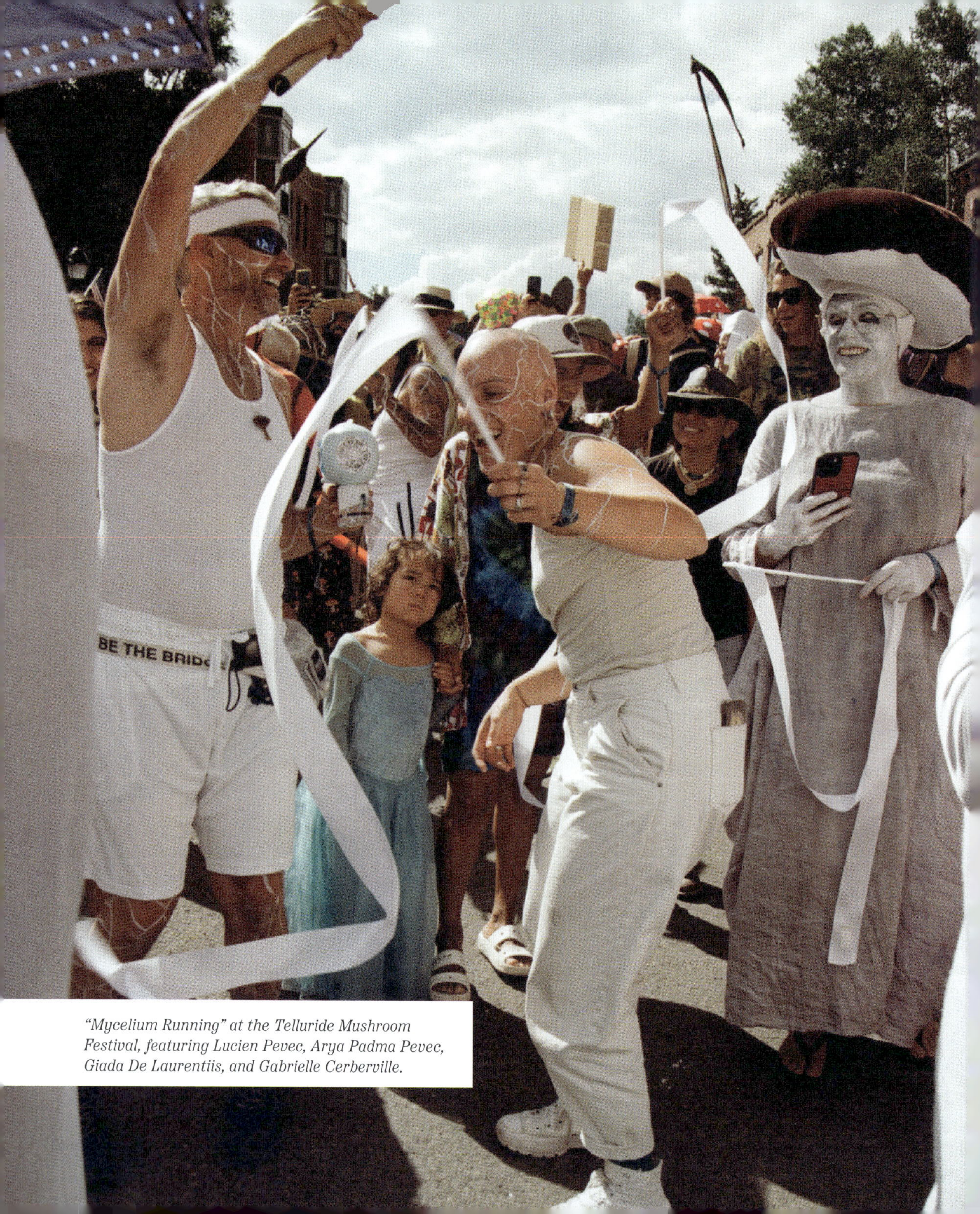

"Mycelium Running" at the Telluride Mushroom Festival, featuring Lucien Pevec, Arya Padma Pevec, Giada De Laurentiis, and Gabrielle Cerberville.

FUNGI

Creatures & Cultures

Unearthing the Ancient Wisdom and Modern Wonders of the Mycological World

Kit Ondaatje Rolls

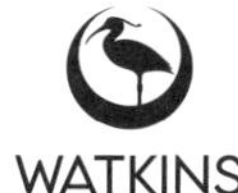

WATKINS

Fungi: Creatures & Cultures

Kit Ondaatje Rolls

First published in the UK and USA in 2026 by
Watkins, an imprint of Watkins Media Limited
Unit 11, Shepperton House,
83–93 Shepperton Road
London N1 3DF

enquiries@watkinspublishing.com

Editorial Director: Ella Chappell
Managing Editor: Brittany Willis
Development Editor: J. D. Halcro
Content Editor: Charles Rolls
Copy Editor: Emma Hill
Mycological Editor: David Satori
Editorial Assistant: Caitlin Nolan
Designer: Francesca Corsini and
Alice Claire Coleman
Picture Research: Emma Thackara
Production: Uzma Taj

A CIP record for this book is available from the British Library

ISBN: 978-1-78678-972-3 (Hardback)
ISBN: 978-1-78678-973-0 (eBook)

10 9 8 7 6 5 4 3 2 1

Printed in China

The manufacturer's authorised representative in the EU for product safety is: eucomply OÜ - Pärnu mnt 139b-14, 11317 Tallinn, Estonia,
hello@eucompliancepartner.com,
www.eucompliancepartner.com

www.watkinspublishing.com

Publisher's note: This book intends to educate but does not prescribe treatment for any ailments. Be self-aware, self-respectful and conscious of all risks associated with these powerful fungi. While every care has been taken in compiling the activities for this book, Watkins Media Limited, or any other persons who have been involved in working on this publication, cannot accept responsibility for any errors or omissions, inadvertent or not, that may be found in the recipes or text, nor for any problems that may arise as a result of preparing one of these recipes. The information in this book is not intended as a substitute for professional medical advice and treatment. If you are pregnant or are suffering from any medical conditions or health problems, it is recommended that you consult a medical professional before following any of the advice or practice suggested in this book. Watkins Media Limited, or any other persons who have been involved in working on this publication, cannot accept responsibility for any injuries or damage incurred as a result of following the information, exercises or therapeutic techniques contained in this book.

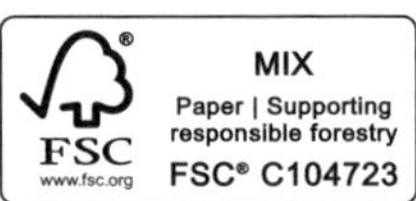

CONTENTS

FOR ALL BEINGS, SLIMY AND UNUSUAL

A young Icelandic puffball splitting open to reveal its white interior, which will later mature into spore-bearing tissue.

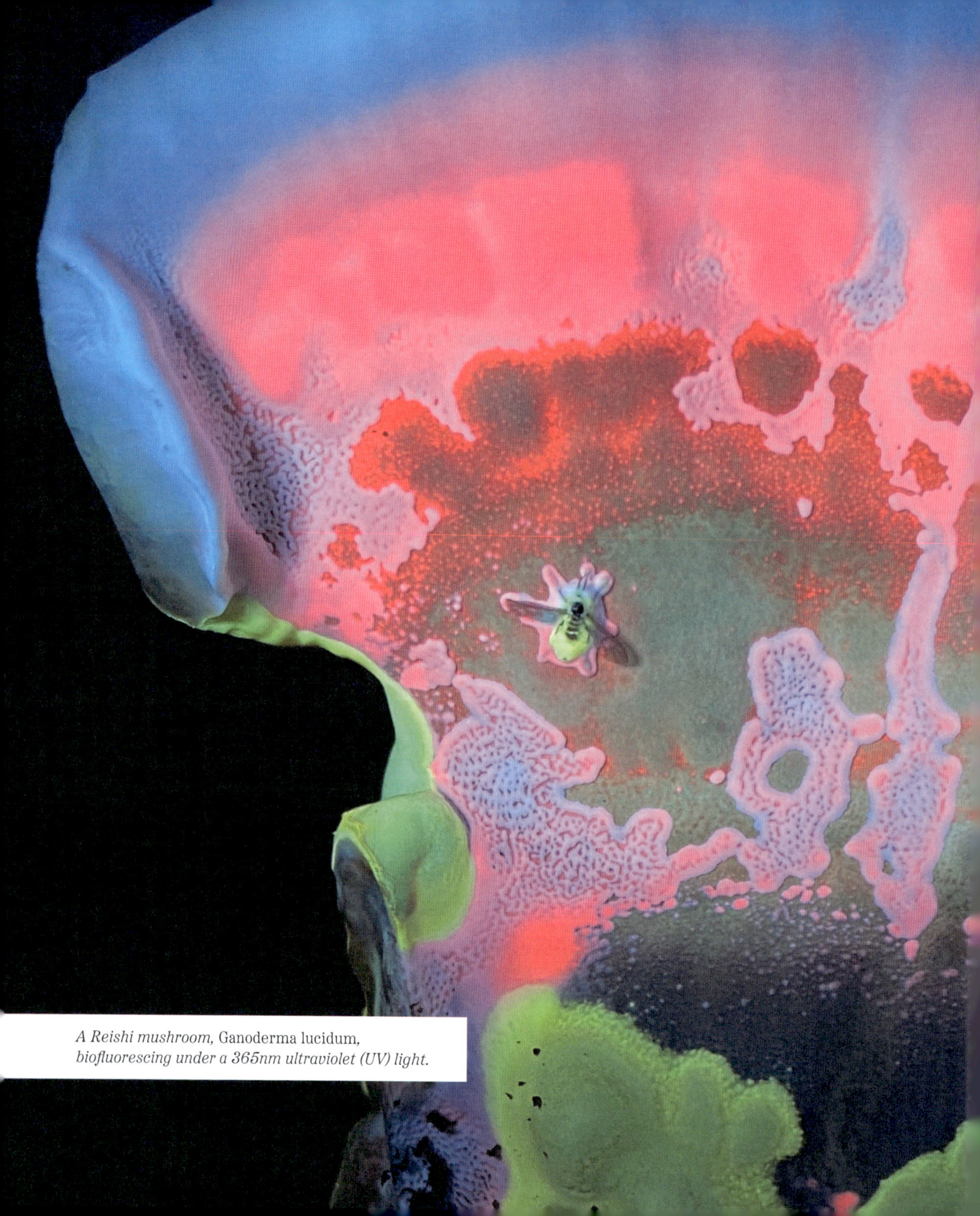

A Reishi mushroom, Ganoderma lucidum, *biofluorescing under a 365nm ultraviolet (UV) light.*

Prologue

This is not a mushroom cookbook.

In fact, you can't exactly *cook* many of the recipes in this book, and its contents spans far beyond just mushrooms.

Instead, *Fungi: Creatures & Cultures* is an interdisciplinary journey through the cultural history of fungi. It bridges art and ecology, science and spirituality, myths, madness, and medicine – revealing the countless ways fungi shape our lives and influence us, whether we're aware of it or not.

This book presents a collection of roughly 30 stories, each entangling the life of a human and a fungus to explore a certain theme – death, disease, sex, seduction, immortality, and microbial intimacy. Every story ends with a recipe or activity that brings these ideas and organisms to life.

Through archival records, macro- and micro-photography, and just *one* AI-generated image, this book takes us backwards and forwards in time. We peer down microscopes into hidden mycorrhizal entanglements, trace the movements of intoxicated molluscs, and recreate the hostile and alien landscapes of Mars – in an attempt to grow a Martian Mushroom Garden. This book takes us on a journey to the origins of life on Earth, showing how fungi have been crucial to evolution for billions of years,[1] if not from the very beginning. Along the way, you'll learn how to forage for mushrooms, cook them, and appreciate their rich ecological significance through ancient wisdom and modern science – and *modern* wisdom and *ancient* science. As you explore these fungi-fuelled adventures, you'll uncover how mushrooms and their kin may be the key to addressing global challenges like climate change and health crises.

A recurring theme throughout this book is how fungi help to bridge and expand the arts and sciences, touching consciousness, psychedelics, indigenous knowledge, dreams, ecological crafts, nutrition, and mental health. By weaving together the voices of friends and experts from diverse fields, this book illustrates how cross-pollination across disciplines and cultures can lead to fresh insights and offer a richer, more interconnected perspective on the world.

Hopefully, this isn't just a book to read – it's a book to engage with. The activities within invite you to approach fungi in a hands-on way, getting down to their level and asking you to think and be like a fungus: interconnected, collaborative, and adaptable. Expect to get weird, wet, and messy as you explore fungal worlds, from painting and brewing to growing and cultivating microbial cultures. Whether it's building a living psychedelic sanctuary, swabbing yourself for culinary samples, or extracting medicinal mushroom tinctures, the experiences in this book seek to inspire creativity and wonder.

Importantly, don't worry if your experiments don't go as planned. I've had my fair share of failures: unintentionally mouldy cheeses, weak mushroom dyes, contaminated mycelial sculptures, and many, many more. It's all part of the experience. I hope you'll find joy in the process, no matter the outcome, and be inspired to join me in collaborative workshops where the real magic happens anyway. Some activities will require specialised equipment, but many can be tried at home with whatever materials you have available.

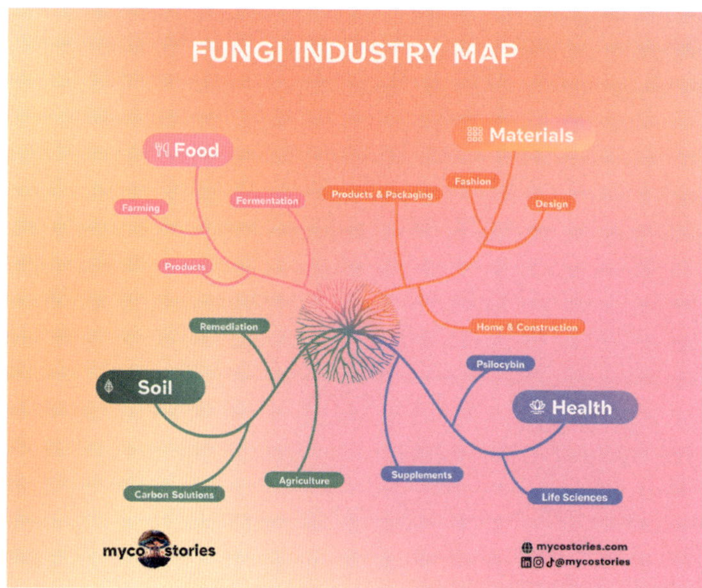

Mycostories' Fungal Industry Map – An overview of the sectors shaping the global fungal economy, from biotech and food to materials and medicine.

This is a fascinating time to study fungi. Interest in fungi is rising, and this book reflects this growing wave of enthusiasm. From the subcultures of Japan to "fungiculture" in Africa and the Middle East, fungi are taking centre stage in various fields, across material sciences, climate policy, urban design, and fashion design. Around the world, people are embracing fungi as powerful tools for innovation and healing. This book introduces you to the individuals and movements behind this fungal renaissance.

There's still so much to discover about fungi, and this book is just my addition to a burgeoning bibliography. It's designed to spark your curiosity, inspire your imaginations and encourage you to embark on your own mycelial adventure. You can dive in from the beginning or jump to the chapters that interest you most – each story stands alone, so you can engage with the book however you like.

Initially, my vision was for each copy to come with a syringe of native Oyster mycelium, to be grown from the pages and transform into a living experience. While that proved logistically challenging, I encourage you to try it yourself (ideally once you've finished the book!) – see the epilogue for more details. Also, if you bought a copy of this book as a mycelium-leather-bound volume, remember to treat the material with a leather conditioner every six months or so. Further, for legal reasons, the publishers redacted several of the psychedelic stories and activities; perhaps one day a raw version of this text might be released.

One final caveat: Mycology is a dynamic, rapidly evolving field, with discoveries emerging even as you read this. Some of the information here may have shifted since publication, and I'm sure that what I learn in the coming months will build upon what you're reading now. This keeps us on our toes, and I'm excited to see where these future fungal findings will take us next. You may well be a part of that story.

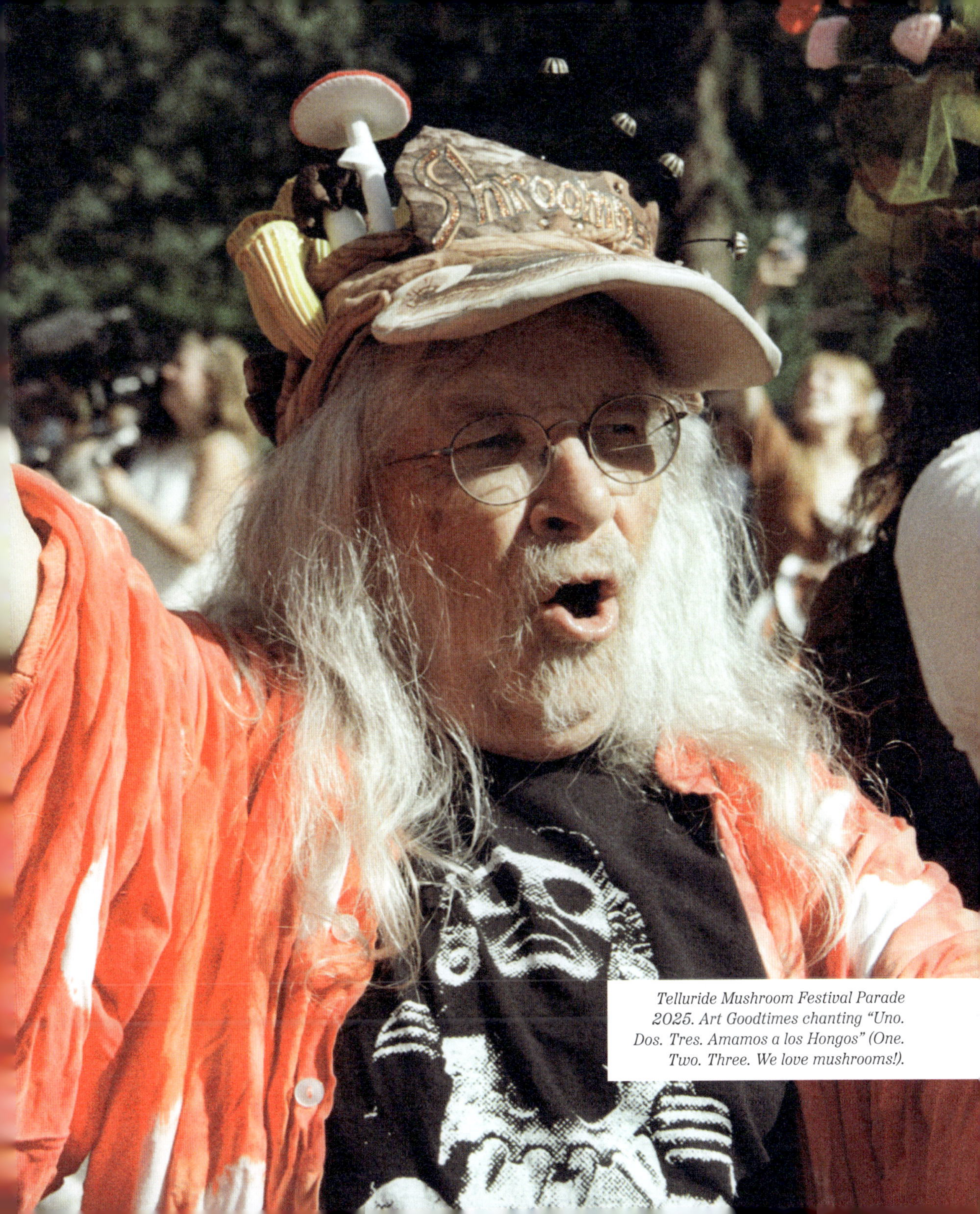

Telluride Mushroom Festival Parade 2025. Art Goodtimes chanting "Uno. Dos. Tres. Amamos a los Hongos" (One. Two. Three. We love mushrooms!).

INTRODUCTION TO FUNGI

"Just stop now, and devote the rest of your life to mushrooms."

- Gary Lincoff (1942–2018)

Our view of fungi has undergone a massive metamorphosis in recent years. Once reduced to the occasional forest mushroom or the unwelcome mould on leftovers, fungi are now recognised as a vast, distinct kingdom – neither plant nor animal – that is strange, mysterious, and indispensable.

What we do know is already astounding. Fungi decompose matter, recycle nutrients, and form such intricate partnerships with plants that the plants seem more fungal than vegetal. Some species can zombify insects, regenerate neurons, yield medicines and poisons, replace plastics and pesticides, and, of course, alter human consciousness. Yet our understanding is still in its infancy. With millions of species yet to be identified, and their behaviours only beginning to be studied, fungi remain one of the great frontiers of biological and cultural discovery.

Conservative scientific estimates suggest that there are 2–3 million fungal species. Other methods give higher numbers: global eDNA data indicates around 6.3 million species, while soil DNA and plant-fungal ratios suggest 3.5–5.1 million.[2] Some outliers even propose 110 million – though this is likely an overrestimate! Whatever the exact number, fewer than 155,000 have been formally described[3] and over 95 per cent of the fungal kingdom remains undescribed. The "known unknowns" are fascinating enough, but it's the "unknown unknowns," the roles we cannot yet imagine, that make the study of fungi so urgent and exciting.

Fungi occupy every continent and every conceivable habitat, from the seafloor to volcanic ash. They have survived five mass extinctions and continue to adapt to Earth's harshest environments. After the meteorite impact that likely ended the dinosaurs – when dust blocked out the sun and photosynthesis became ineffective – fungi flourished.[4] They were among the first to reclaim the darkened Earth. As mycologist Paul Stamets has suggested, those who partnered with fungi were rewarded. In fact, such partnerships began hundreds of millions of years earlier. Mycorrhizal symbiosis – from the Greek *mykos* ("fungus") and *rhiza* ("root") – evolved around 460–480 million years ago, before plants had even taken root on land. Lichens, composite organisms formed from fungi and a cyanobacteria, may have appeared even earlier.[5] This long history of collaboration and adaptability is encoded in fungal genomes and expressed in their extraordinary diversity, from extremophilic moulds to single-celled yeasts.

Today, mycorrhizal fungi form symbiotic relationships with over 90 per cent of terrestrial plants. The fungi extend root systems downwards and outward, dramatically enhancing water and nutrient uptake in exchange for sugars from their plant hosts. These underground networks, popularly known as the "Wood Wide Web", link trees and plants in ways that appear cooperative, competitive, and even

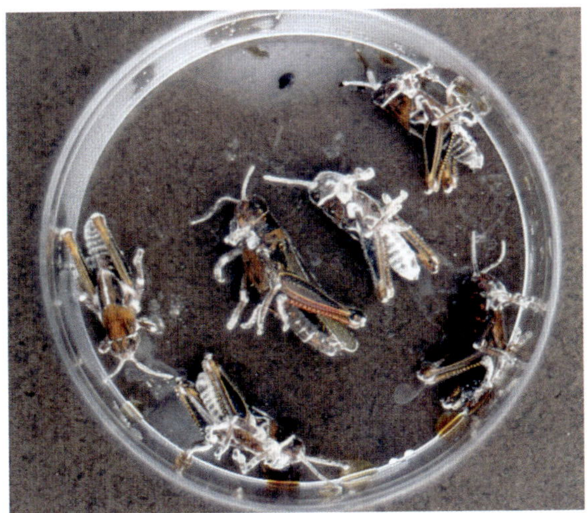

Grasshoppers, Melanoplus sp.*,
digested and killed by the fungus*
Beauveria bassiana.

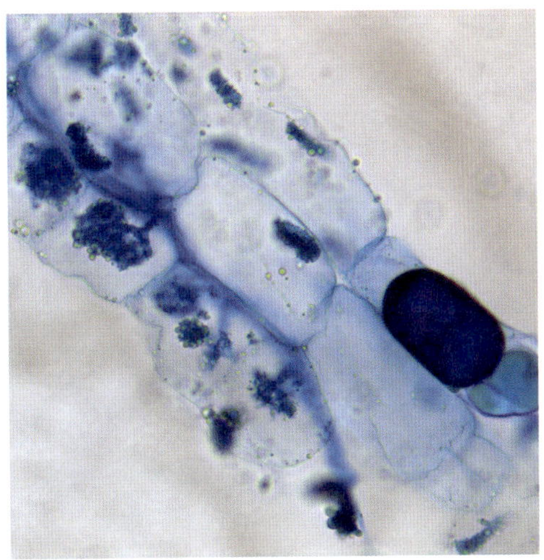

Microscopic mycorrhizal *filaments show the hidden, relationships between fungi and plants – one of the foundational natural symbioses on Earth.*

communicative. In some cases, older trees serve as central hubs, distributing nutrients to younger seedlings or stressed neighbours through these shared fungal pathways. This system has been likened to a biological internet, complete with signals, resource exchange, and defence mechanisms.

Yet, how fungi maintain internal coordination across vast distances – up to 9.65 kilometres in the case of the Earth's largest organism, the Honey Fungus, *Armillaria* spp., – is still a mystery. So is their exact role in soil microbiomes, where they interact with bacteria and viruses in a three-dimensional web of life so complex our current instruments can scarcely capture. Scientists, like ecologist Toby Kiers and her team at SPUN (Society for the Protection of Underground Networks), are now racing to map and protect these fungal networks before they're lost to deforestation, agriculture, and climate change.

Speaking of climate, fungi play a crucial role in regulating the carbon cycle. When fungi die, they can lock carbon into the soil. Likewise, living mycorrhizal networks absorb approximately 13 billion tons of carbon dioxide annually, about one-third of global energy-related emissions.[6] Saprotrophic fungi, on the other hand, release carbon dioxide by breaking down dead matter, supporting photosynthesis in plants, and continuing a beautiful ecological loop. Mycorrhizal fungi's involvement in carbon sequestration is only beginning to be quantified, but it could be a game-changer in climate science and policy.

Fungi also hold vast potential in biotechnology and sustainability. Mycoremediation, the use of fungi to clean up pollutants such as oil spills and heavy metals, is an emerging field. Researchers are even studying psychedelic species for their potential to remediate chemical weapons and neurotoxins.[7] Further, mycelium (the thread-like structures of many fungi) is being developed into biodegradable packaging, building materials, and even fashion items as an eco-friendly alternative to plastics and leather.

Yet fungi are fickle. Many can switch roles – from friend to foe, symbiont to pathogen, medicine to poison – based on context.[8,9] Some mushrooms considered edible in one region may be poisonous in

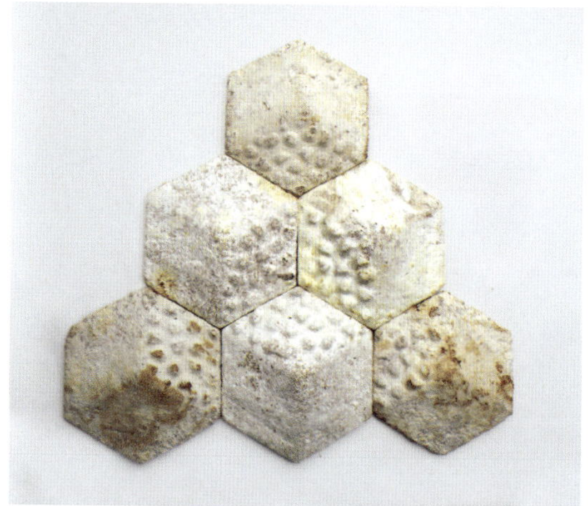

Mycelium-based acoustic panels. Fungi are shaping sustainable innovation, revolutionising how we build, dress, and consume.

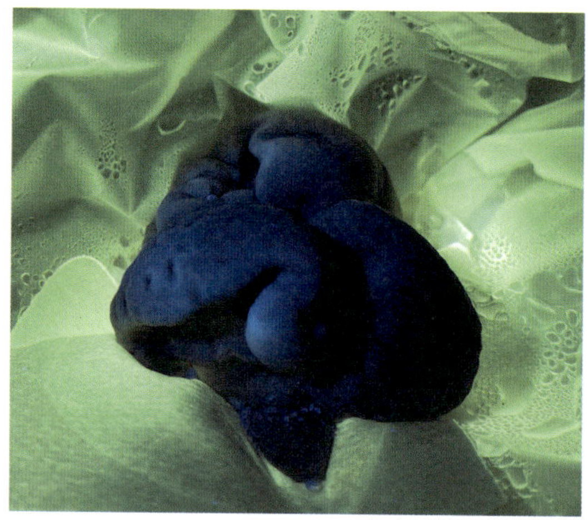

Biofluorescent Maitake, Grifola frondosa, *fruiting from a grow bag.*

another, and toxicity levels can vary between ecosystems and throughout lifecycles.[10] Similarly, while certain *Aspergillus* species produce powerful antimicrobials, others cause disease and food spoilage. This plasticity makes fungi both indispensable and potentially dangerous. For example, the Rice Blast Fungus, *Magnaporthe oryzae*, destroys enough crops annually to feed over 60 million people.[11] Meanwhile, fungal diseases are increasingly on the rise, especially as more people become immunocompromised or face antimicrobial-resistant pathogens.[12]

Fungal infections also affect wildlife, especially amphibians who inhabit moist environments. The Chytrid Fungus, *Batrachochytrium dendrobatidis or Bd*, has wiped out entire frog populations across Europe, Africa, Asia, North and South America, and Australia. Likewise, a bizarre case in India in 2014 saw a frog sprout a mushroom from its hind leg – a still-unexplained biological anomaly.[13]

Human cultures around the world have interacted with fungi in an extraordinarily diverse number of ways, both expected and unexpected. The Maasai in Kenya and the Ahnishinaubeg in North America burned skewered Common Puffballs, *Lycoperdon perlatum*, to produce spore-bearing smoke that anaesthetised bees before honey harvests.[14] *Psilocybe* species were revered as deities and consumed ceremonially by the Mazatec, Mixtec, and Zapotec peoples to "bemushroom themselves" and achieve a heightened state of consciousness. The Peeling Puffball, *Lycoperdon marginatum*, is used by the Gi'-i-Wa of southern Mexico to induce "half sleep" and auditory hallucinations, while various *Boletus* species contribute to the "mushroom madness" of the Kuma people in New Guinea – though chemical analysis of both mushrooms reveals no substances that would explain these effects.[15,16] Meanwhile, penicillin, the first antibiotic, was derived from the *Penicillium* mould frequently found on mouldy bread.

Closer to our daily lives, fungi have been cultivated and collected for culinary purposes. From the prized truffles of Europe to the Shiitake and Matsutake mushrooms of Japan, fungi have long influenced diets, economies, and traditions. In Africa, mushrooms like *Termitomyces,* which grow in

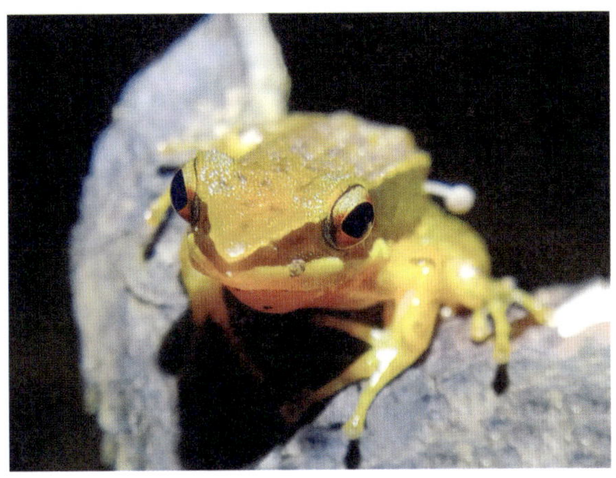

An Indian frog with a mushroom sprouting from its leg – a rare case likely caused by opportunistic fungal colonisation on injured tissue in a moist environment. While such visible fungal growths are extremely uncommon, frogs more typically suffer from chytridiomycosis, a deadly skin infection caused by the Chytrid fungus, Batrachochytrium dendrobatidis, *which has devastated amphibian populations worldwide. However, since 2024, Australian scientists have been using "frog saunas" to protect green and golden bell frogs from infection, as the warmer temperatures help fight the disease.*

association with termite mounds, are highly valued for their protein content. They rank among the largest mushrooms in the world, with a single specimen capable of feeding a family for up to a week. In Scandinavia and North America, Chanterelles are part of community identity, while culinary staples like cheese, bread, and beer – all partially fermented by fungi – dominate the Western diet.

Still, despite all this, fungi remain marginalised in public education and awareness. School curricula and media rarely mention them – unless, of course, it's a headline-making poisoning. This lack of fungal literacy may turn out to be more dangerous than the most toxic known mushroom. As the climate shifts and ecosystems destabilise, fungi could either help us adapt or blindside us with new diseases and agricultural crises. We urgently need more fungal research, funding, and education to keep pace with their complexity and the implications for the environment in which we live.

Fortunately, a renewal in fungal appreciation is already underway. Books like Merlin Sheldrake's *Entangled Life* and documentaries like *Fantastic Fungi* are bringing fungi into the spotlight. DNA sequencing and imaging technologies are revealing fungal forms and functions we never knew existed. New species, such as the spider-parasitising *Gibellula attenboroughii,* are being discovered almost daily and are reshaping our understanding of this kingdom. Just shine a UV light on a mushroom, and you may witness fungal biofluorescence; science understands *how* it works, but not exactly *why*.

Every question we answer about fungi seems to open many more. How do they interact with our immune system? What language do their electrical signals represent? Could fungal networks possess some primitive form of consciousness? What role might they play in planetary-scale processes that we have yet to understand? These and countless others are the questions that make fungi so compelling, not just as subjects of study, but as mirrors to our ignorance.

Fungi are not just quirky natural oddities; they are essential, dynamic, and powerful forces that sustain life on this planet. They are endless and often ridiculous sources of myth and metaphor. They decompose, heal, poison, nourish, and connect. They are deeply entwined with our past and, increasingly, our future. To ignore them is to miss a massive piece of the planetary puzzle. To learn about them is to know how the world truly works.

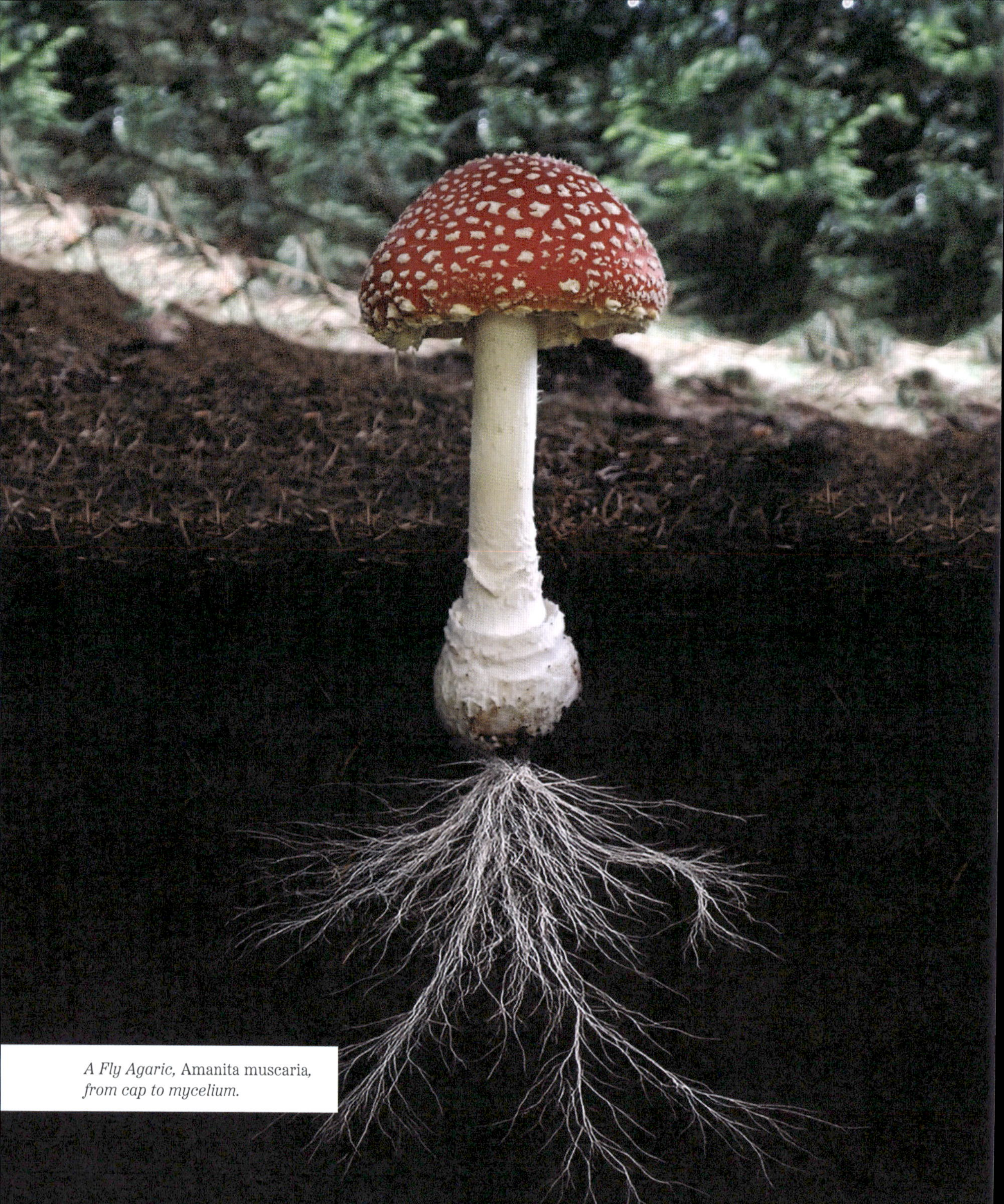

A Fly Agaric, Amanita muscaria, *from cap to mycelium.*

THE ANATOMY OF A MUSHROOM

A mushroom is the reproductive structure of a fungus, and emerges from the below-ground mycelium. Let's look at the different parts.

The **cap** is the top of the mushroom structure. It is often umbrella-shaped and protects the gills beneath.

The **gills** (lamellae) are thin, blade-like structures on the underside of the cap where spores are produced, held, and released.

The **universal veil** is a membrane that completely encloses the young mushroom; remnants may remain as patches on the cap or a cup-like structure (volva) at the base of the stipe.

The **partial veil** is a protective layer that covers the gills in immature mushrooms; it breaks as the mushroom matures, often leaving a ring (annulus) on the stipe.

The **stipe** is the stalk that supports the cap and elevates it to aid spore dispersal.

The **spores** are microscopic reproductive cells released from the gills to allow the mushroom to reproduce. They disperse widely and germinate into hyphae in suitable conditions.

The **hyphae** are thread-like filaments that make up the body of the fungus, growing through soil or organic matter.

The **mycelium** is the underground network of hyphae that breaks down matter, absorbs nutrients, and anchors the mushroom, often forming symbiotic relationships with plants.

Note: Most mushrooms don't look like the common cap-and-stem toadstool. Instead of gills, many have teeth, like Lion's Mane, or pores, like Boletes. Others come in a mind-boggling variety of shapes and sizes: eggs, mosaics, octopuses, nests, phalluses, stars, shelves, cups, and clubs.

These shapes have evolved in response to Fungi's diverse methods of spore dispersal. For example, Puffballs, *Lycoperdon* spp., use the momentum of falling raindrops to launch their spores into the air, carried away by wind currents. Stinkhorns, *Phallus* spp., secrete a mucousy *gleba* – a dark, spore-bearing goo – that emits a foul odour to attract flies that spread the spores. Many *Basidiomycete* fungi use a surface tension catapult to eject spores; a fluid drop forms at the base of each spore and, after reaching a critical size, fuses with the spore and launches it from the gill surface.[17] The underground variety rely on chemical signals to attract animals such as the Tasmanian potoroo, which eats at least 60 mushroom species! Most remarkably, the *Pilobolus* fungus uses light to shoot its spores away from its bed of faeces. They track the sun and eject their spores in the morning to maximise distance.[18] Fungi are endlessly ingenious.

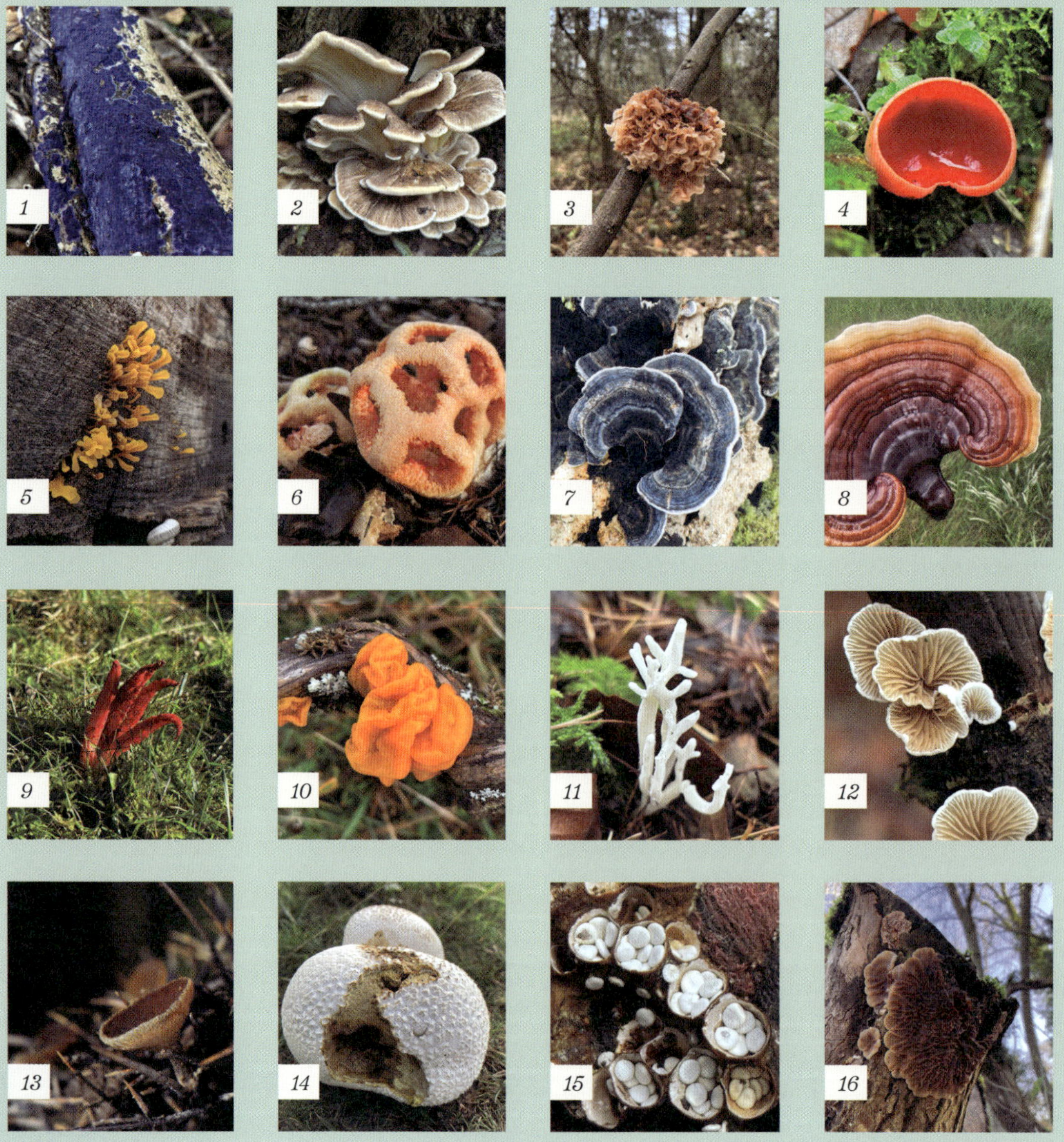

1. *Cobalt Crust Fungus,* Terana caerulea; 2. *Blackening Polypore,* Meripilus sumstinei; 3. *Leafy Brain,* Phaeotremella foliacea; 4. *Scarlet Elf Cup,* Sarcoscypha coccinea; 5. *Fan-shaped Jelly Fungus,* Dacryopinax spathularia; 6. *Red Cage Fungus,* Clathrus ruber; 7. *Turkey Tail,* Trametes versicolor; 8. *Reishi,* Ganoderma lucidum; 9. *Octopus Stinkhorn,* Clathrus archeri; 10. *Witches' Butter,* Tremella mesenterica; 11. *Fairy Fingers,* Clavaria fragilis; 12. *Variable Oysterling,* Crepidotus variabilis; 13. *Hairy Nuts Disco,* Lanzia echinophila; 14. *Mosaic Puffball,* Handkea utriformis; 15. *Bird's Nest Fungus,* Nidulariaceae spp.; 16. *Tripe Fungus,* Auricularia mesenterica.

A NOTE ON STRUCTURE

Homo sum, humani nihil a me alienum puto

I am a human, therefore nothing that is human is alien to me

– Publius Terentius Afer, 170 BCE

When you look at the creatures and cultures of the world, one thing becomes clear: the ways we can live are endless. There are countless possibilities for how we relate to nature, to one another, and to ourselves.

Yet, globalisation and colonialism are rapidly homogenizing societies and ecosystems eroding bio-cultural diversity, stifling resilience, and narrowing the scope of our imaginations. We no longer see the full range of human potential or the diverse "normals" that once existed.

My instinct tells me there are far more ways we could inhabit this world. For all its achievements, Western culture allows only a narrow fragment of what it truly means to be human.

Fungi, however, in all their strange and magnificent forms inject creativity back into our lives. They help us reconnect with the depth and breadth of the human experience. As trusty guides and malleable metaphors, fungi take us into deep time. Their relationship with humanity predates *Homo sapiens,* shaping our evolution and continuing to influence cultures and consciousness, in both visible and invisible ways.

Fungi are unique in their ability to access parts of our psyche, showing us that other ways of living, thinking, being, moving, loving – ways of relating – are not only possible, but desirable and inherent within us. Fungi destabilise, and in that destabilisation, things become slippery. But they also help us to reorganise. What has emerged for me is a compass, reflected in the structure of this book, one that guides us into long-neglected parts of ourselves.

DOWN

We start down – in the underground – where fungi decompose the dead and recycle it back into life. Here, fungi reconnect us to the subconscious, the wild, the suppressed, and the animalistic parts of ourselves. With them, we journey inward, confronting decay and returning with insight. Damp, dark, and visceral, DOWN embodies ecofeminism in its most elemental and raw form.

UP

Next, we look up, daring to behold, and even consider, the spiritual world. Fungi are known to elevate consciousness, cleanse the spirit, and reveal visions of geometric perfection. Seen as sacred, intelligent beings, they lift us towards the divine. UP is light, reverential, and symbolic, a space where science and spirituality converge.

CENTRE

Perhaps what we need most today is our centre – to move with love from the heart, to find ecological balance both inside and out. Mycelium acts as a stabilising force, dynamically holding life between growth and decay. CENTRE anchors us, drawing from the past and the future to find a steady point of gravity.

IN & OUT

Finding our centre is crucial, but sometimes we must shift. IN & OUT is about transformation – primal release, understood to be an essential part of being and becoming by ancient cultures across the globe. As masters of transformation, fungi ferry us across thresholds – between worlds, states of being, and selves. Linked to the fae, they open portals to the mystical, the altered, and the imagined. IN & OUT is dynamic, swift, and world-bending.

INTER

We are increasingly learning that everything is interconnected – both living and non-living. To understand this is to see how we fit into this network. Fungi show us how life is woven together across scales, from the macrocosm to the microcosm. Mycelial networks interlace plants, animals, viruses, bacteria, and environments into intricate, relatively cooperative webs. INTER is exploratory and expansive, fuelled by new technologies that highlight our ecological interdependence.

INTRA

In times of crises, we turn to the values that matter most: love and community. Essential to our well-being, we reconnect with the Earth and all her inhabitants. Fungi are cultural allies, fermenting food, healing illnesses, preserving knowledge, and enabling survival across generations. INTRA is intimate and personal, honouring tradition, family, and, above all, love.

INCONSISTENCIES

Order is magnificent, but at the edges of order, there is chaos. Mystery, uncertainty, and unpredictability are forces we all must reckon with. Fungi help us navigate these unknowns. They resist neat categorisation, thriving in paradox and ambiguity. They remind us to embrace the unknown. INCONSISTENCIES strips away certainty and binaries, reaching the core of things and leaving us open to the uncertainty and possibilities of new forms.

Fungi, our wisest and cruellest companions, guide us through these directional metaphors. They challenge us to expand our vision and embrace the many ways life can be lived.

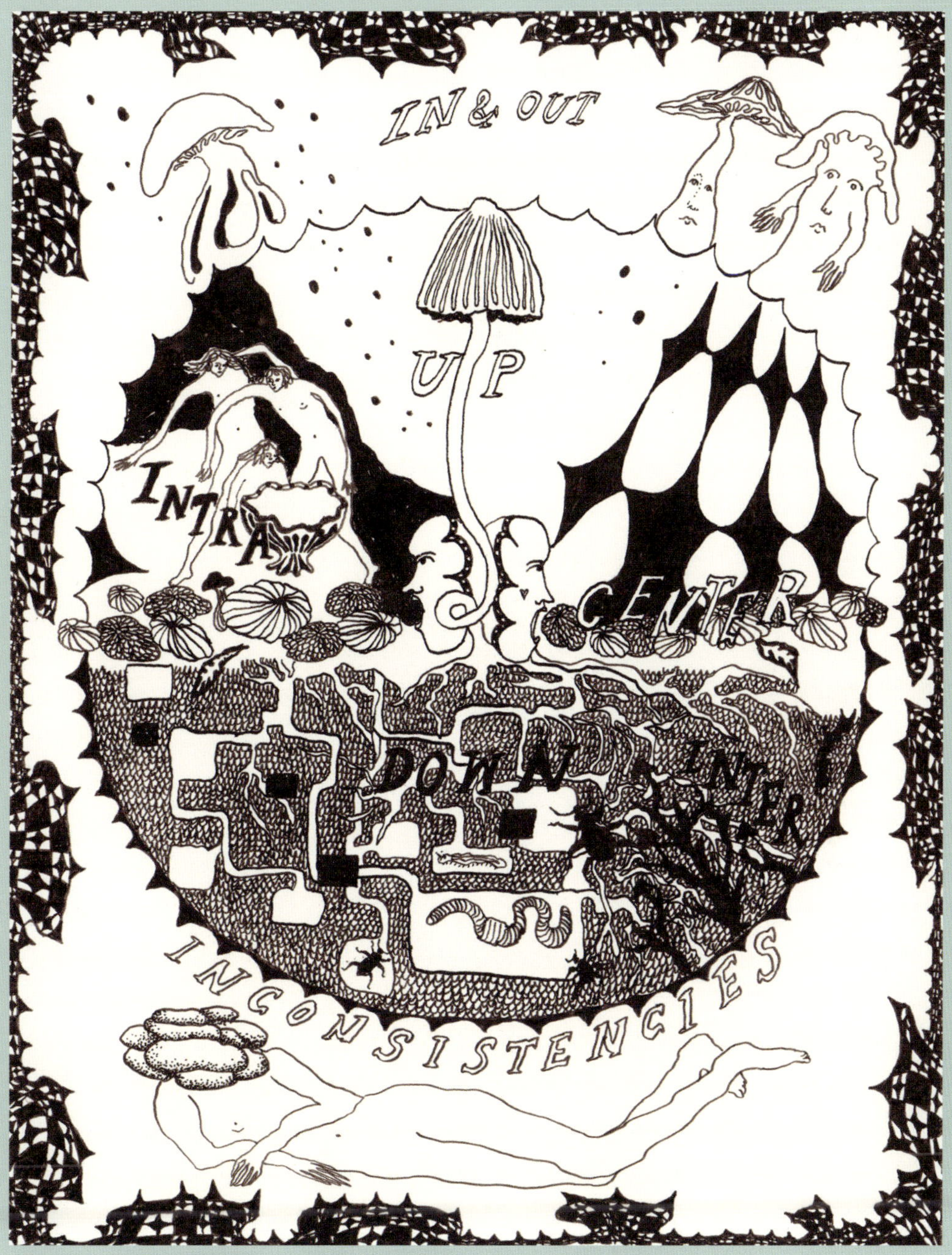

Creatures & Cultures Compass. *Illustration by Helen Robinson.*

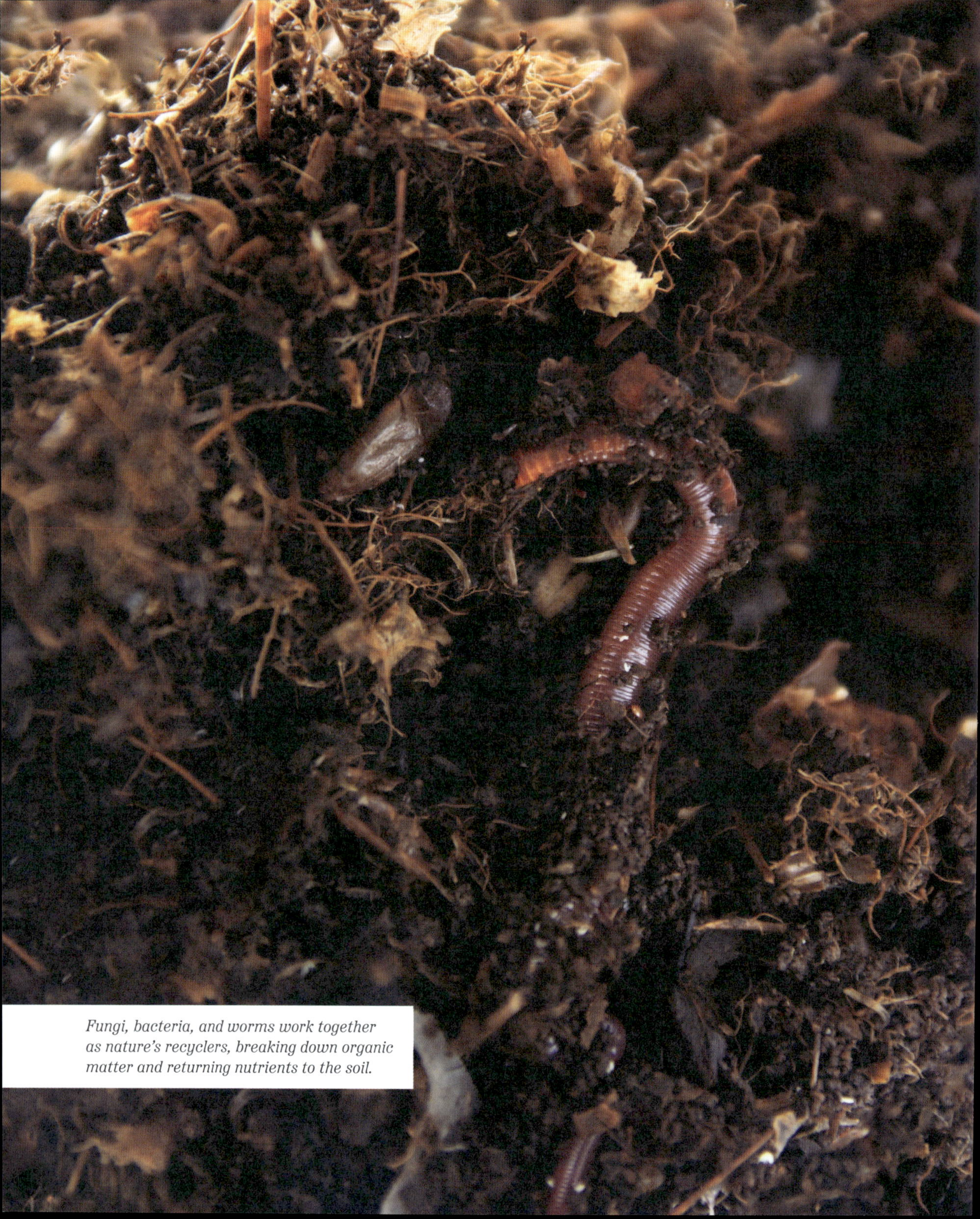

Fungi, bacteria, and worms work together as nature's recyclers, breaking down organic matter and returning nutrients to the soil.

1

DOWN: Revolting Revolutions

"Fungi are the evil ferment of the Earth."

– Nicander 2 BCE, Greek poet and physician[1]

Dirt is miraculous; the dark matter from which all life springs. Yet it remains paradoxical: revered for its fertility and reviled for its filth. We call it soil, mud, excrement, waste. The word "dirt" stems from Old Norse *drit*, meaning "shit" – and the Norse were not wrong. Much of the Earth's most nutrient-rich soil comes from the excretions and secretions of animals, us included. For centuries, we scattered our waste across fields to grow crops. While this might sound grotesque to modern, sanitised ears, our disgust reflects a deep alienation from the regenerative cycles of nature, where death is not an end but a reconfiguration.

At the heart of this reconfiguration is the kingdom of fungi. Masters of decay, fungi are nature's recyclers, converting death into new life. They thrive in what we discard. Consider the humble Cremini mushroom, *Agaricus bisporus,* grown in beds of horse manure. Coprophilous, or dung-loving fungi, consume waste, sprouting fruiting bodies that feed us in turn. Here, nothing is wasted. In the fungal worldview, rot is not ruin but renewal.

To a culture obsessed with linear progress and purity, this truth is deeply unsettling. We've been taught to separate life from death, body from soil, food from filth. But fungi defy these divisions. They reveal that life, death, nourishment, and excrement are entangled in a constant, creative dance. Inspired by Earth's closed-loop metabolism, they offer us a different model of existence: one where decomposition is sacred, and waste is a misnomer.

This understanding is ancient. Egyptian Goddesses Isis and Nephthys presided over death and rebirth alike. Alchemists spoke of *prima materia*, the raw, base matter from which all things emerge. Before gold could be created, matter had to be blackened, broken down in a stage called *nigredo*. Fungi embody this principle. They dwell in the "As Below" – the symbolic underworld, where chaos reigns and transformation brews.

Carl Linnaeus, father of modern taxonomy, once classified all microbes under the genus Chaos. These invisible organisms were unpredictable, disorderly, and impossible to categorise – just like the realms they inhabit. Microbes ferment, rot, infect, and awaken. They undo the boundaries we cling to and remind us that life is built on cycles, not hierarchies.

Descent, then, is not metaphorical – it is lived. We descend into the soil, into dreams, into our guts. Transformation happens in the dark. The Kogi people of Colombia raise their children in darkness for nine years,[2] symbolising gestation within the Earth itself. Darkness becomes a teacher, a womb, a crucible for inner vision. Psychedelics like ergot and *Amanita muscaria* serve a similar purpose: dragging us into the chaotic depths of the subconscious, only to return us to the surface changed – often with insight.

This descent has long been associated with the feminine. Patriarchal traditions, particularly Christianity, have moralised darkness, decay, and the body – casting them as sinful and impure. Heaven was upward, pure and ordered; hell was downward, carnal and chaotic. The underworld became a place of punishment rather than one of transformation. But in many mythologies, the underworld is not evil, it is essential. It is the source, the place of becoming. Wombs, tombs, and underground caverns all speak to this mysterious process of breakdown and rebirth.

Creatives, lovers, mothers, witches, gardeners, and mycologists understand this magic. All beginnings start in darkness. Seeds germinate in soil. Foetuses grow in the womb. Artistic ideas ferment in silence before emerging into form. Night, dreams, and trance sharpen our senses, allowing us to commune with the unseen. Psychedelics – often called "eyes of the underworld" – dissolve boundaries and inject the chaos necessary for transformation.

Jungian analyst Mackenzie Amara calls this realm "the soup" – a place where categories dissolve and everything connects. In the underground, distinctions like male–female, human–animal, real–unreal begin to blur. We enter a mycelial state of mind: interconnected, porous, and wild. But myths warn us: descent requires discernment. Like Psyche sorting seeds in the underworld, we must retain our ability to differentiate, even in chaos. Otherwise, we risk dissolving completely.

Today, we are collectively descending. A renaissance in psychedelia, ecology, shadow work, and mythology is underway. Feminine wisdom is re-emerging, not just for or from women but for everyone, as we seek to restore balance and remember what has been buried. Indigenous and ancestral traditions, once dismissed, are now being reclaimed as essential guides in this journey downward.

And so, this chapter digs in the dirt. We follow witches, shamans, midwives, and herbalists – custodians of the underworld – who work with fungi and plants to navigate darkness and transformation. We crawl into the forest's understory, where mycelium tangles with roots and rot. We dissolve, decay, and remember ourselves through microbes and metaphors. Finally, we feast with pigs in a fungal celebration that rejects purity and embraces pleasure, power, and instinct. This is the Revolting Revolution.

To work with fungi is to confront death, decay, and regeneration. They pull us down – into the dark, the damp, the unseen. For centuries, we've feared this descent. But perhaps now, we are ready to follow the fruiting body back to its hidden source, to become part of the cycle once again.

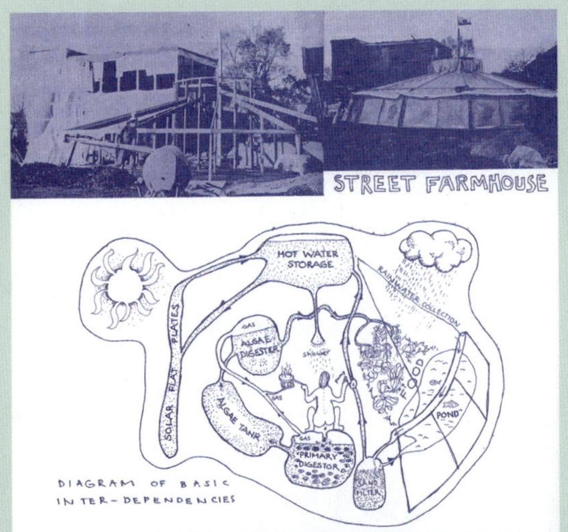

Street Farmhouse Diagram of Basic Interdependence. *This diagram illustrates how humans and microbes can work together to create a closed-loop metabolic system, cycling waste into resources and sustaining mutual life.*

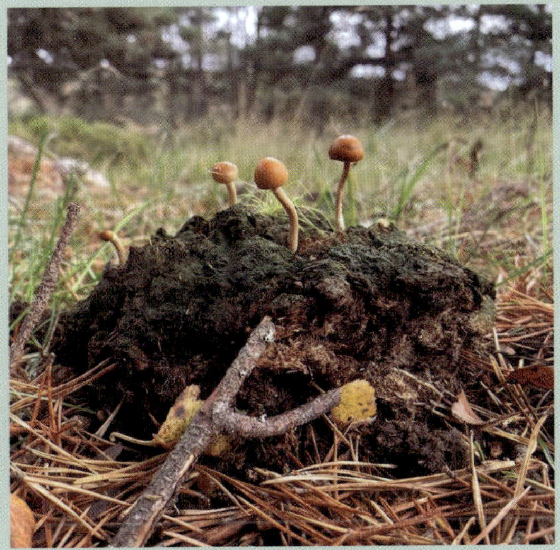

Dung Roundhead, Protostropharia semiglobata. *As its name suggests, this fungus fruits from animal dung – particularly that of herbivores like cows, horses, and deer – rich in nitrogen and organic matter, which it transforms into its golden-yellow-orange fruiting body.*

WITCHES & ALKALOIDS

Witches are often recognised for their skills as herbalists. Yet, the archetype of the witch is far more complex and multifaceted. Witches, by definition, are provocateurs – challengers of societal norms and boundaries. We commonly hear of the hag or crone, but many people overlook a fourth archetype: the wild witch or enchantress. This archetype, often disregarded, is intricately tied to the post-ovulation phase, autumn, and the waning Moon. Both the wild witch and the crone embody the essence of the archetypal witch – unconventional, fearlessly interacting with unearthly forces that defy reason. Their wisdom and power come from the depths: whether that be the underworld, the inner world, the wildwood, or the profound and erotic realms of the unconscious.

Their craft was magic, and their materials were taboo: found objects, bodily excretions, remnants of decay, poisonous creatures, weeds, bones – items considered "abject" or unclean. Through these, witches created their magic, making use of what society deemed unspeakable. Born of necessity and defiance, their craft was an act of resistance, wielding the ambiguous powers of taboo that both oppressed and empowered them.

Witches embody the Earth's regenerative abilities and have always revered darkness, death, and delirium in equal measure to light, life, and lucidity. Both witches and mushrooms are depicted as enchanting sources of magic and divination,[3] possessing powers to intrigue and intoxicate. Consider the quintessential red-and-white-spotted Fly Agaric, *Amanita muscaria,* for example. Its genus name is derived from the Greek *aman* (poison), likely due to the toxic nature of many *Amanita* mushrooms. But the *Amanita muscaria* has been used in folk remedies across the world and can be either poisonous, medicinal, or hallucinogenic depending on the dose and preparation. This delicate balance is known as the Narrow Therapeutic Index. As the age-old toxicology adage goes, "*Sola dosis facit venenum*": "The dose makes the poison".

"Mycophobia" and a cultural distrust of fungi stems from a combination of ignorance and years of adverse experience. Given the sudden appearance of toxic toadstools, mushrooms rotting much-loved trees, moulds contaminating our food, rusts parasitising flowering plants, and pathogens invoking foul bodily infections, it's unsurprising that our recent ancestors feared these seemingly horrific agents. Mushrooms were often carelessly categorised as toadstools, a term laden with contempt, possibly derived from the German words *tode* (death) and *stool* (seat), or because toads – often associated with magic and toxins – could frequently be found resting on them, thus lending their malevolent reputation to their perch. Although only a mere 0.5 per cent of mushroom-producing species are truly poisonous and pose a significant risk, it's enough to have sparked centuries of widespread distrust.

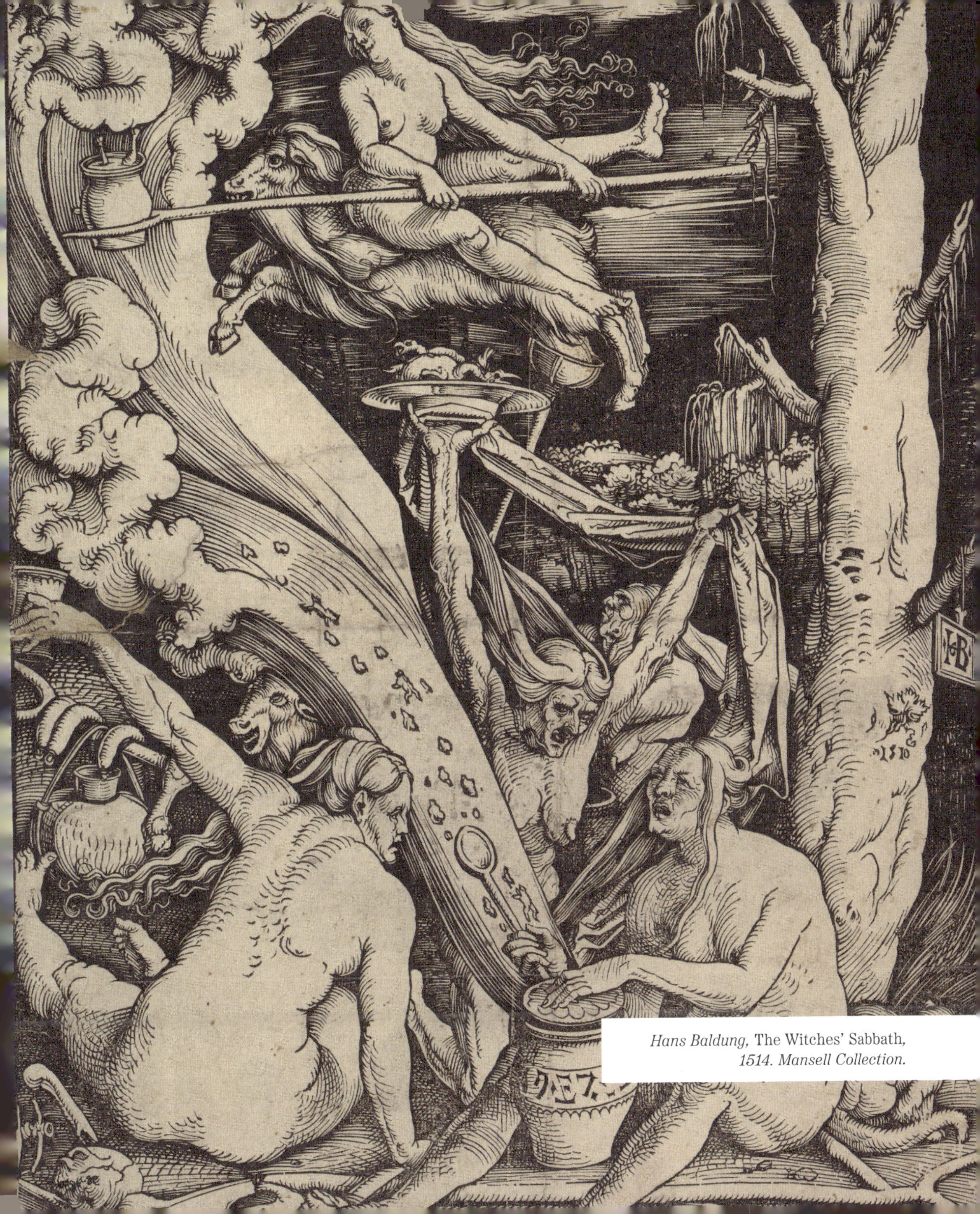

Hans Baldung, The Witches' Sabbath, *1514. Mansell Collection.*

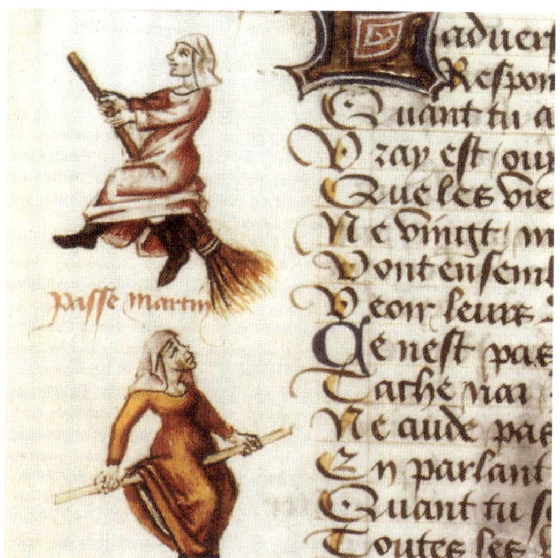

Champion des dames Vaudoises. *An illustration depicting two witches on broomsticks in Martin Le Franc's "Ladies' Champion", 1451.*

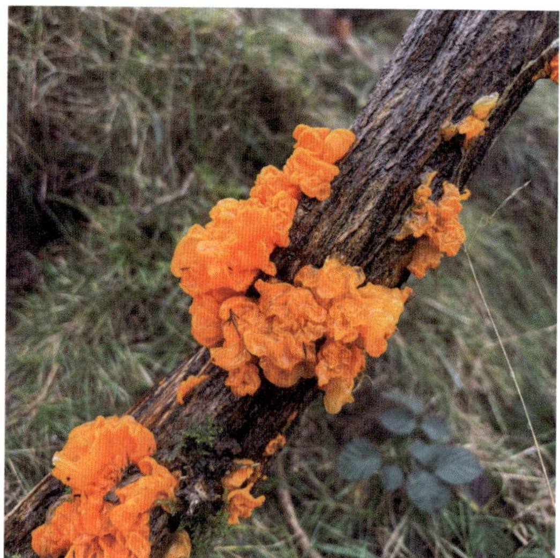

Witches' Butter, a bright yellow, gelatinous parasitic fungus. In Swedish folklore, it was said to be spit from witches' feline familiars; in Eastern Europe, a sign that a witch was about to cast a spell on a household.

Among the 0.5 per cent, a surprising number are pure white. While white traditionally symbolises light, innocence, and goodness, it also carries darker connotations of poison and death in many cultures. This is especially true since creatures of the dark, like larvae (which means "spectre" in Latin), often glow with a ghostly white luminescence. The deadly Destroying Angel, *Amanita virosa*, is a prime example of this danger. In fact, one of the first rules for foragers is to avoid mushrooms with pure white caps, stems, and gills, because much like green and occasionally red, pure white often serves as nature's indication of toxicity.

Anarchists at heart and herbalists by trade, witches dismissed any coarse, customary advice, discerning the magical toads from the toadstools. So, into their cauldrons the frogs' legs and fungi flew and, in turn, facilitated the witches' flight. More than a mere Halloween stereotype, witches genuinely flew – not physically, but psychologically, buoyed by the psychotropic effects of these alkaloid-rich plants, fungi, and animals. Vividly experiencing "all the pleasures and delights in the world", witches were high and infused with the delightful cosmic giggle, sent sideways and cackling to the Moon. Broomsticks, symbols of womanly domestic life, were used as tools to mix the hallucinogenic brew and allegedly, as dildos to effectively administer and absorb the psychotropic alkaloids – hence the imagery of witches ecstatically riding their broomsticks.

The compounds responsible for such diverse pharmacological effects are alkaloids, which are present in various plants, bacteria, animals, and fungi. Many are used in both traditional and contemporary medicine as narcotics with antimalarial (e.g., quinine) and analgesic (e.g., morphine) properties. Other alkaloids exhibit psychotropic (e.g., psilocin, muscarine, and ibotenic acid) and

"Bitter to me as death."

– William Shakespeare, Cymbeline, Act 5, Scene 5

stimulant activities (e.g., cocaine, caffeine, nicotine, and theobromine), and continue to be used in entheogenic rituals or as recreational drugs. Toxic alkaloids, such as atropine, hyoscyamine, and scopolamine, almost universally elicit a bitter taste.

There are, of course, many natural compounds used by human beings. But among them all, says chemist Ayushi Rajput, "Alkaloids are quite special."[4] Alkaloids play a vital role in defence and are often secreted as insecticides. The very name "Fly Agaric" was born not from its effects on witches, but from its ability to kill flies if left out in a pale of milk. Interestingly, the tobacco hornworm caterpillar has evolved a protein that allows it to consume alkaloid-dense, nicotine-rich tobacco leaves. The caterpillar then secretes and exhales the nicotine to deter predators, effectively co-opting the plant's chemical defences. This "Mother of Tobacco" caterpillar inspired Lewis Carroll's hookah-smoking caterpillar in *Alice's Adventures in Wonderland*. (We'll get to that in chapter 4).

A surprising number of alkaloid-rich botanicals are derived from creatures traditionally associated with witchcraft and shamanism, including the *Solanaceae* family, ergot fungus, cocoa beans, coffee, tobacco, frogs, toads, and toadstools. Are alkaloids the magical compounds through which we engage with the metaphysical realm? If so, how did these spirit practitioners become aware of these herbs' (general term for plants and fungi) mind-altering abilities? The answer is: not through the reductionist lens we often employ today, but through direct communion. These entities communicate with them through the physical body (via ingestion or topical application) or through the spirit body (via dream work and intuition). Witches and shamans might not understand the chemical content of the alkaloids per se, but they know how to navigate and work with these plants, fungi, and now also lichen.[5] Theirs is a well-informed craft almost impossible to fathom.

Just as fungi reemerge year after year, the culture of the witch fruits time and again. The US and UK, including Bristol, my home, are alive with esoteric Wiccan communities and neo-pagan witches. While ancient crafts of tarot and crystal magic are largely unfamiliar to me, I am, technically, a witch. As an initiated member of the Bioart Coven, a community of ecofeminist artists and biotechnologists, we use biotech tools for counter-hegemonic purposes. We gather monthly on the New Moon to share our magic and methods, led by pioneering artist WhiteFeather Hunter, PhD. We are the witches in lab coats.

Like many DIY biotech witches, our practices began in the kitchen with experimental herbalism and microbiology: brewing, fermenting, sharing SCOBYs (Symbiotic Cultures of Bacteria and Yeast), distilling essential oils, creating medicinal tinctures, dyeing with food waste, cultivating spirulina, and even "growing" mycelium-based clothes. At our core, we seek self-empowerment through community. In a time of profound isolation and externalisation, the very act of gathering as women (no warlocks allowed) to laugh, share, and cultivate our own food and medicine rather than buying them from shops is radical.

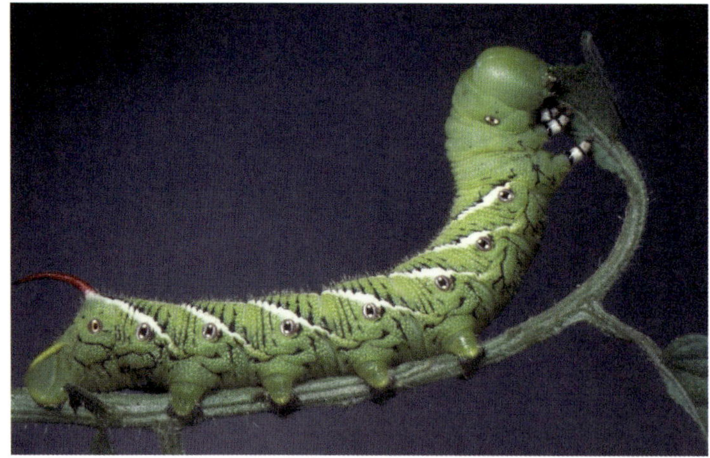

Tobacco Hornworm caterpillar. Evolved to feed on nicotine-rich tobacco leaves, this caterpillar absorbs the plant's toxins and exhales nicotine to deter predators, turning the plant's defence into its own.

Our work embraces slow fermentation – a form of "ancestral tech" that contrasts today's sterile, mechanised technologies. These messy, interspecies practices continue women's long history as healers and medicine carriers through nature-based wisdom and intergenerational knowledge.

"The birthplace of magic is the land around us."

India Rakusen, Witch: The Spark in the Fire

Many biotech witches, including those in the coven, still embrace these principles, collaborating with organic materials and transgressive biological systems. WhiteFeather Hunter, with over a decade of bioengineering expertise, shocked the scientific community by proposing lab-grown meat might thrive in women's menstrual blood – her own, no less – rather than the traditional foetal calf serum.[6] Meanwhile, Josie Rayner, a former NASA biochemist and genetic designer, hacked their microbiome by consuming a "healthy normal's" stool in capsule form for two weeks, conducting a revolutionary, unregulated home-science experiment to heal their gut. Speculative artist Alexandra Daisy Ginsberg genetically engineered bacteria to secrete pigments to colour one's stool in the presence of specific pathogens, enabling inexpensive, personalised disease monitoring. Though these practices defy cultural norms, many interdisciplinary creatives (whether witches or self-identified "mad pirate queens") embrace the radical feminist ideals of Silvia Federici to reframe disgust, centre the body as a site of scientific and feminist innovation, and reclaim cultural power.

These biotech practices challenge the three types of disgust: core disgust (bodily fluids or contaminants), animal-nature disgust (reminders of our creaturely nature), and moral disgust (acts like genetic modification). Yet, people marvel at how Oyster mushrooms can remediate cigarette butts or how algae can turn urine into drinking water – well, not everyone. "Your pee is disgusting and doesn't

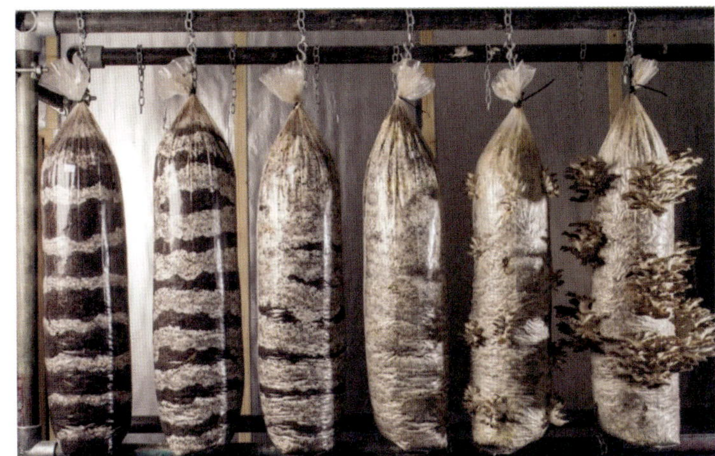

Oyster mushrooms growing on hanging tubes of used coffee grounds. Biodesigners and mushroom farmers harness fungi's power to break down waste – turning materials like cotton, cardboard, cigarette butts, and food scraps into valuable and delicious resources.

belong in the fridge!" my mum exclaimed when she finally kicked me out of the house, along with my bags of Reishi mushrooms and half-grown mushroom chair!

Orifices hold special significance in witchcraft, symbolising the blurred boundary between self and other, offering both promise and vulnerability. Take the belly button: once the connection between mother and foetus, it marks our first act of individuation. Regarded as an important source of magical power, it represents the initiation into life.[7] Similarly, the vulva can act as a portal for physical, spiritual, and psychological transformation. Witches remind us that the body holds wisdom beyond reason – deep, wild, and rich with sensory knowledge.

THE SEED SISTAS

Reimagining sacred sexuality and ritualistic masturbation, the Seed Sistas – a remarkable wild-witch-come-clinical herbalist duo – create hallucinogenic lubricants to be applied topically. They engage in acts of untamed pleasure under the Moon, merging momentarily with the universe. "Enjoying the sensuality of nature is a taboo", says Kaz, the elder Sista. "We're pushing against sex-negative culture and seeking to heal the deep shame wound surrounding female pleasure, self-exploration, and eco-sensuality." Kaz explains that the Fly Agaric, with its vibrant beauty and aura of danger, is the mushroom that can re-story individual and cultural narratives. The thirteenth witching herb in their "Flying Ointment" (also known as "Hallo-lube"), the Fly Agaric is transforming our relationship with sex, spirit, and the underworld.

Sensual, rebellious, and delightful, the Seed Sistas continue to reclaim and subvert the judgements cast upon women throughout history, empowering and liberating not only themselves but perhaps also you, me, and the creatures of this Earth.

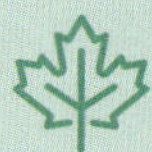

ACTIVITY

PREPARING FOR THE FLYING OINTMENT
THE SEED SISTAS

Preparing the flying ointment demands deep care and commitment. It's a year-long process aligned with the seasonal rhythms of nature and the celestial cycles of the Moon. The details regarding herbs, their histories, mythologies, and preparation would fill an entire book – indeed, the Seed Sistas have created such a masterpiece. Their book takes us step by step through this ancient preparation.[8]

Their recipes and practices hark back to the old grimoires. In magic of this nature, the significance lies in your mindset; how you dedicate your attention to the process is just as important as the outcome. Performing these rituals or exercises without proper focus is a fool's errand. This principle echoes the practices of alchemists, who would recite prayers before, during, and after their procedures.

The Seed Sistas advocate for the reintegration of medicine and magic, dedicating their lives to increasing awareness of the healing potential found within the botanical realm. They celebrate the evolution of human-herb relationships through sensory engagement and intuitive guidance, reminding us that one need not ingest a herb to experience its medicinal properties.

Their first guidance on connecting with herbs is to grow and harvest them yourself. Only then can you begin to understand their powers. Fi, the younger Sista, shares, "Datura has such potent alkaloid fragrances that if you place her in your room or under your pillow, she will enter your dreams. You can converse with her or set an intention for the night, and she will visit you."[9] However, the lying ointment's final ingredient, the Fly Agaric, cannot be cultivated at home, so the best way to become acquainted with her is to seek her presence in the woods.

Fly Agarics are mycorrhizal, forming intimate underground relationships with coniferous trees such as pines and silver birches. They also tend to grow near other woodland herbs, so you'll likely find them between heather and bilberries, or with fireweed and rosebay willowherb nearby.

Your task is to immerse yourself in the *umwelt* of the Fly Agaric – the world as experienced by the mushroom. Be patient with her seasons. Cultivate a sense of peace with the fact that her emergence cannot be coerced or predicted; this is part of her magic. Slow down and engage with her in every possible way. Listen. Observe. Touch. Smell. Though abstain from tasting just yet . . . Ground yourself. Sit or lie beside the mushroom: meet her at her level. Allow her time.

If you feel safe enough, stay with the Fly Agaric until the evening; the forest feels different at night. As your eyes adjust to the dark, observe how everything becomes more vivid. Try to stay present. The value in witchcraft lies in the process and the inner transformations that resonate throughout your being and manifest in the world around you. Submerge yourself in the earth and allow yourself to be wholly and unpredictably encountered by the enigmatic Fly Agaric mushroom.

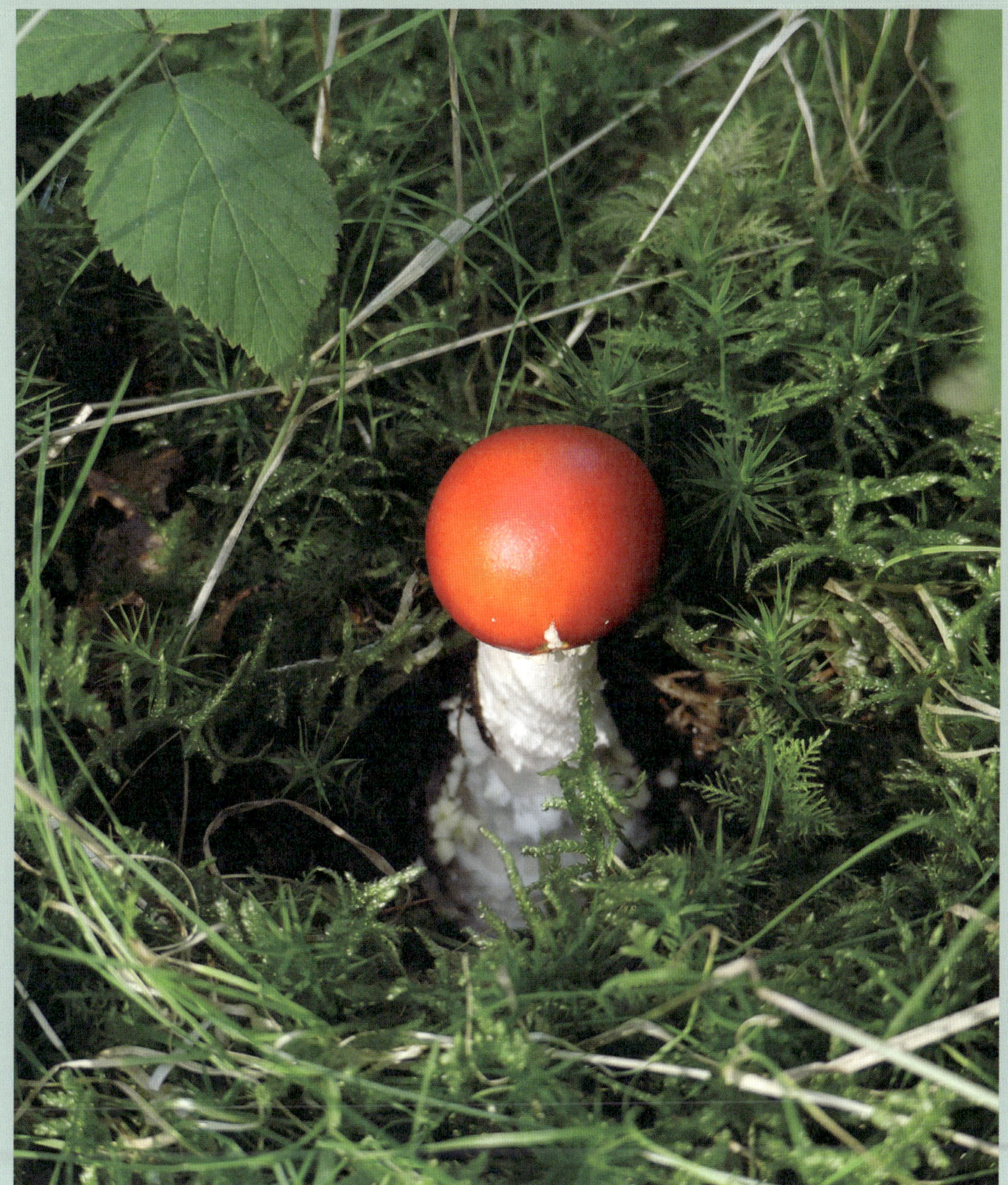

Fly Agaric, Amanita muscaria, *without remnants of its universal veil.*

BIRTH, DEATH, & LSD

"Moments after giving birth to my wonderful baby boy, the midwife offered me an injection of ergotamine – a common practice to help prevent bleeding. I agreed, until my husband, a fungus expert, jumped in. Angrily, he asked whether this was ergotamine *from the Ergot fungus, known for producing LSD. The midwife said she didn't know but assured us they were not drugging their new mothers. But, always irritatingly, my husband was right; they were in fact offering me a sister alkaloid to LSD."*

– Lily, New York State mushroom farmer, 2021

Before the accidental synthesis of LSD by Swiss chemist Albert Hofmann in 1937, Ergot, *Claviceps purpurea,* – a parasitic fungus that infects rye and grasses – had been used for centuries in traditional midwifery. In Europe, especially in Germany, Ergot was known as *Mutterkorn*, or "mother's corn," and was used to accelerate childbirth, manage postpartum haemorrhaging, and induce abortions.

Ergot contains two active alkaloids, ergometrine and ergotamine. Correct dosage and preparation were context-dependent and crucial, as the line between life-saving intervention and fatal poisoning was often perilously thin. This invaluable herbal knowledge, passed down through generations of women, was suppressed by Christian patrons during the Middle Ages and largely forgotten. It was "rediscovered" in the early 19th century when a physician happened upon an "old wives' tale" recounting its use in obstetrics, reigniting medical interest in this extraordinary fungus.[10]

We can assume that midwifery is as old as our hominid ancestors. While some suggest we may have learned the practice by observing other mammals – such as elephants, primates, and hyenas, all of which display "midwifery"-like behaviours – it's more likely that such practices emerged instinctively: a helping hand, healing herbs, or protection from predators.

Across cultures, midwives continue to integrate spiritual and physical practices to navigate pregnancy and the transformative experience of childbirth. Among the Guarani people of Brazil, for example, midwives prepare herbal remedies as well as sacred bamboo tools for cutting the umbilical cord, and they approach the process with the most sincere reverence and ritual.[11] Similarly, the Triqui midwives of Central America interpret the mother's dreams as essential guides.[12] Nightmares, I am told, are particularly important to heed, as they are thought to reflect a mother's fears and anxieties, the health of the child, or even serve as omens. Likewise, the Māori people of New Zealand, Aotearoa, typically burn the birthing spot after labour and bury the umbilical cord to connect the child to the Earth.

European midwives also developed their own distinct rituals. They harvested said Ergot growths from standing grains, then dried and ground them to create potent aqueous extracts.[13] It is likely they

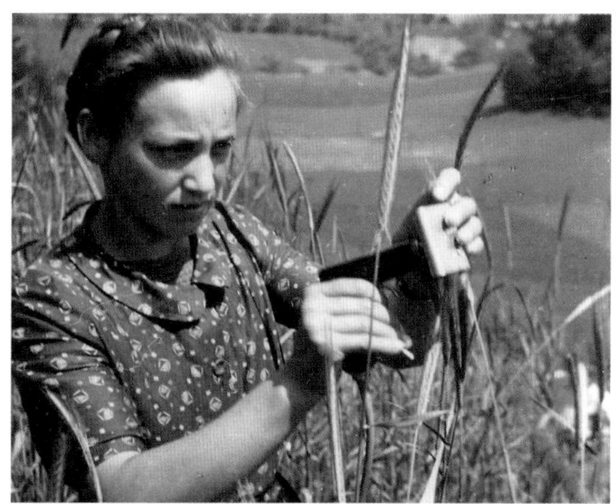
A woman uses a handheld device to inoculate rye seed heads with ergot in 1943.

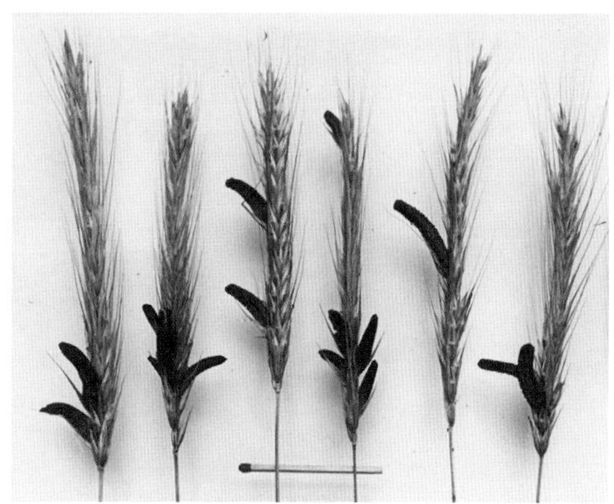
Rye seed heads infected with Ergot fungus, Claviceps purpurea*, historically cultivated by Sandoz AG. Ergot produces potent alkaloids that have served as deadly poisons, lifesaving medicines, and the precursor to LSD.*

were used alongside other medicinal herbs, such as mugwort, sage, chamomile, and yarrow, depending on the region and specific needs of the mother.

Ergot grows primarily on rye and other cereals. In the late spring and early summer, cool, moist weather facilitates the germination of Ergot spores, which then infect the plants. The spores land on the stigmas of grass flowers via rain, wind, or insect exploration. They then send out hyphae, which penetrate the plant's ovary, turning it into a black, elongated mass known as an Ergot sclerotium, which contains high concentrations of ergotamine alkaloids.

Throughout history, there have been infrequent yet unforgettable episodes of Ergot poisoning, also known as ergotism. As late as 1951, the town of Pont-Saint-Esprit in France suffered mass poisoning from tainted bread made from infected rye flour.[14] This poisoning caused horrific symptoms of nausea, vomiting, burning sensations, convulsions, hallucinations, gangrenous growths, and even death. Sensational newspaper articles decried "Monsters and flames haunt the brains of those addicted to the Holy Spirit", blaming flour mills – and the Devil – for "Le Pain Maudit" or "The Cursed Bread".

This "cursed" phenomenon was not without artistic legacy. Hieronymus Bosch's "Temptation of St Anthony" famously depicted the nightmarish effects of ergotism in Medieval Europe, with burning bodies, grotesque deformations, and cities in ruin.

While Ergot and LSD aren't the same, they both contain lysergic acid, the precursor to LSD. So, as you would imagine, the psychosis induced by ergotism bears striking resemblance to the hallucinatory experiences or "bad acid trips" brought on by LSD. In fact, between the 1930s and 60s, LSD was initially used as a "psychotomimetic"– a drug that mimicked psychosis. Nurses and doctors were encouraged if not required to take LSD to help them better understand their patients' disturbed experiences and ultimately, to better care for them.

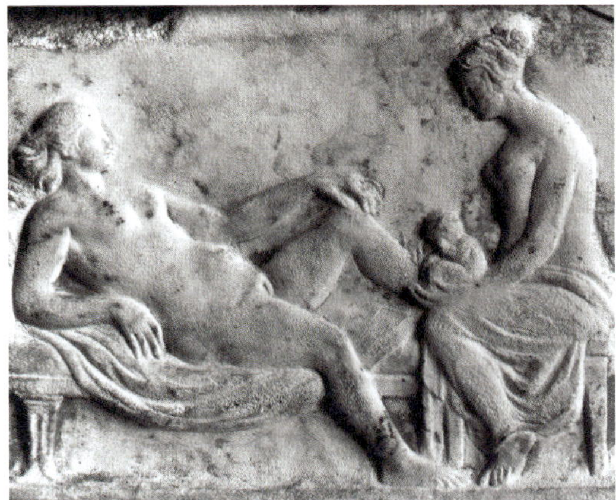

An ancient Roman relief of a woman giving birth, assisted by a midwife.

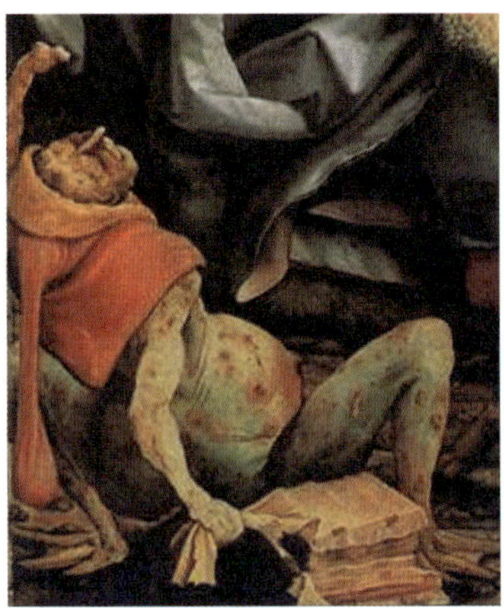

Detail from Matthias Grünewald's Temptation of St Anthony *(1512–1516), depicting a patient suffering from advanced ergotism – named after St Anthony, the protector of those afflicted by this disease.*

This government-endorsed LSD was introduced to the world in large quantities by Sandoz, a Swiss pharmaceutical company. Sandoz granted access to the compound to over 1,000 research groups, sparking an explosion of scientific inquiry. The US government, captivated by the potential of the substance and its research, funded nearly 140 separate grants to support LSD studies. By the early 1940's, Sandoz had launched an experimental programme for large-scale Ergot cultivation, developing new techniques and machinery to meet the rapidly-growing global demand for LSD.[15]

Therapeutically, LSD was a challenge to work with, as the psychedelic experience is very long lasting – between nine and ten hours.[16] But its effects were profound. It was used to treat a range of psychological conditions, including depression, anxiety, alcoholism, and neuroses. [17] The idea was that LSD could "unlock" the subconscious mind, allowing individuals to process traumas and gain insight into their psychological issues.

The psychedelic movement, however, gained traction outside of clinical settings. LSD became a cornerstone of countercultural movements in the 1960s, with figures like Timothy Leary advocating for its mind-expanding properties and its potential for spiritual awakening. As its popularity spread, however, government regulation tightened, especially with the war on drugs and the criminalisation of psychedelics in the late 1960s and 1970s.

The social stigma around LSD was further fuelled by the sensationalised and often negative portrayal of the drug in media campaigns. The "This is Your Brain on Drugs" commercials in the 1980s, for example, contributed to the fear that LSD could cause brain damage, lead to psychosis, or result in dangerous behaviour. These widespread misconceptions still permeate public understanding today.

Despite the stigma, many psychonauts and spiritual seekers have used LSD for profound spiritual experiences. It has long been associated with ego death, a transformative experience where the boundaries between the self and the universe dissolve. This experience, while initially terrifying, often leads to feelings of oneness and unity with the cosmos, providing a profound sense of rebirth.[18]

The depth-psychology practitioner Mackenzie Amara aptly scribes this phenomenon: "We're having such an incredible time exploring the infinite expanse of space out here, but as the Hermetic adage goes, 'As above, so below; as without, so within; as the universe, so the soul.' So, this spaciousness is also true of our inner universe. Just as we require tools for outer exploration, we need them for inner journeys. The analogy of LSD as a microscope for the psyche is perfect." LSD can assist in self-discovery, providing an opportunity to explore the unconscious mind and confront fears of death and the unknown.

Ergot's role as a psychopomp, a guide for souls, can be seen in the Eleusinian Mysteries of ancient Greece.[19] The Mysteries, which were held annually to honour the goddesses Demeter and Persephone, are thought to have included the use of *kykeon*, a barley-based drink that some scholars believe contained Ergot alkaloids. Participants in the Mysteries would undergo a process of spiritual initiation, which involved fasting, darkness, and the consumption of the psychotropic beverage.

This initiation was believed to provide the initiates with insight into the afterlife and the mysteries of death and rebirth. It took place at the site where Hades was said to have abducted Persephone into the underworld, from which she would return each spring, symbolising the cyclical nature of life and the impermanence of death.[20] As echoed in an inscription at St Paul's Monastery on Mount Athos: "If you die before you die, you won't die when you die," an allusion to the expansive experience of ego death and the dissolution of the self.

Today, the roles of midwives and death doulas continue to intersect with the ancient tradition of guiding souls through transitions. While midwives assist in the birthing process, death doulas offer spiritual, herbal, and emotional support to those nearing the end of life, ensuring that the journey out of this world is as meaningful as the one into it.

Death doulas, like midwives, often incorporate the use of medicinal and psychedelic fungi in death care practices and to help ease the transition from life to death.

In Papua New Guinea, for example, *Ganoderma* mushrooms with finger-like projections were worn as necklaces by doctors to treat the sick and dying.[21] Agarikon mushrooms were placed on the graves of shamans in the Pacific Northwest to guide souls into the afterlife. The Ainu people of northern Japan burned dried Birch Polypore to expel evil spirits around the dead and dying. Medicinal mushrooms, such as Turkey Tail and Chaga, are still used for their antimicrobial and anti-tumour effects. Likewise, psychotropic mushrooms like the Fly Agaric, are thought to facilitate communication with spirits and help guide the soul across the threshold.

Baiba Baika is a contemporary heir to Latvia's rich tradition of herbal healing. A mythologist, mycologist, and death doula, she researches how fungi can assist consciousness in its final moments. For Baiba, mushrooms hold profound mystical powers essential for a peaceful death.

Latvia, known as the "motherland of mushrooms," is my grandmother's homeland, where mushrooms transcend their role as mere sustenance, shaping cultural identity and folklore. *Sēņu māte,* or "Mother Mushroom" stands as one of many revered mother figures in Latvian mythology. Likewise, Baltic *völvas* were female practitioners of magic divination, said to have used Fly Agarics in their shamanic rituals.

Baiba tells me that the further north you go, the stronger the mushrooms become. The rare Brown Fly Agaric, *Amanita regalis,* for example, is up to four times more psychoactive than the common Red

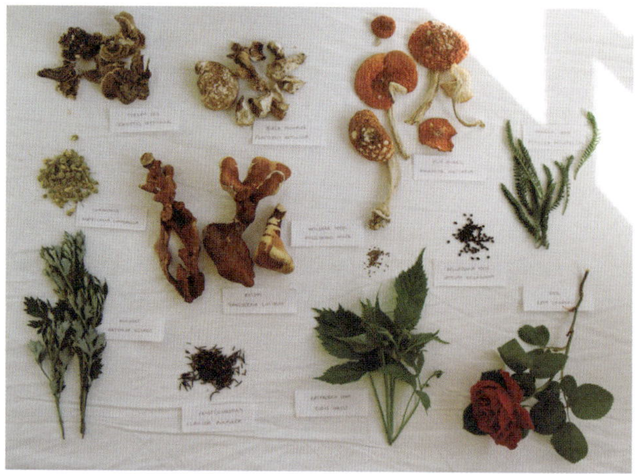

A Death Doula's Key Herbal Allies: ***Nervous System:*** *Chamomile, Lavender, Lemon Balm, Peppermint, Oat Straw, Rose, Rosemary.* ***Restful Sleep:*** *Hops, Valerian, Opium Lettuce, Wood Betony, Lime Blossom.* ***Cleansing & Purifying:*** *Mugwort, Rosemary, Lavender, Seasonal fruits (quince, apple, strawberry).* ***Skin Issues:*** *Plantain, Yarrow, Pine, Spruce, Juniper Needles, Calendula.* ***Transformative Perception:*** *Henbane, Fly Agaric.*

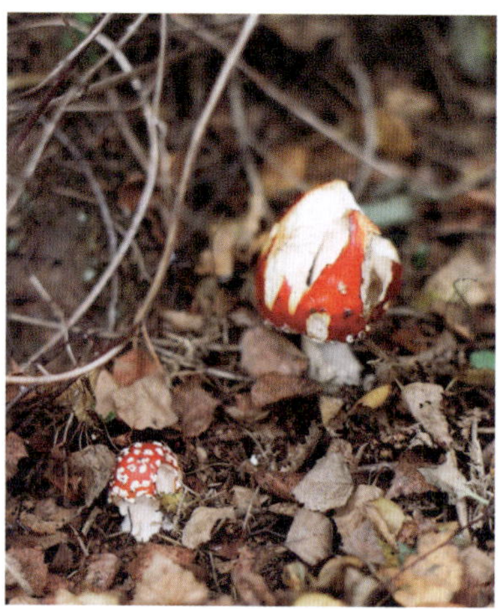

Encountering Fly Agarics in Latvia, where they are used in traditional saunas, or pirts, *to guide souls through life's transformations and face the mysteries of death and rebirth.*

Fly Agaric, *Amanita muscaria*. Both species fruit from volvas (eggs) to reveal their rosy caps. And both are integral to Latvian bathing rituals, where mushrooms are dried into crackers, brewed as teas, or made into scrubs that are rubbed on the body.

Traditional Latvian saunas, or *pirts*, are sacred spaces where pivotal life events unfold – births, transitions, and even death.[22] Enhanced by the subtle psychoactive properties of Fly Agarics, these saunas help to guide souls through life's transformations and face the mysteries of death and rebirth.

Baiba continues the legacy of Baltic *völvas,* using Fly Agarics to help patients ease their fear of death. In the wild, Fly Agarics are symbiotic with birch trees, symbolic of new beginnings and "deathlessness." Fly Agarics, for their part, are known by many names, including "the mushroom of immortality", "the eyes of the underworld", and "the blood of wisdom."

"It takes an entire lifetime to learn how to live, and—what will perhaps make you wonder more—it takes an entire lifetime to learn how to die."

– *Seneca,* De Brevitate Vitae, *c.1 CE*

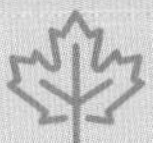

RECIPE

A DEATH DOULA'S ESSENTIAL PHARMACOPOEIA

BAIBA BAIKA

In plant medicine traditions, the Fly Agaric is revered as a "Master Plant" for its ability to expand perception and calm the spirit. Chemically, it supports GABA production, soothing the nervous system. Baiba's Fly Agaric balms provide natural relief from pain, muscle tension, and anxiety.

PART 1: OIL

EQUIPMENT

- Jar with a lid
- Towel or blanket
- Tea strainer or cheesecloth

INGREDIENTS

- 1 part dried Fly Agaric (*Amanita muscaria*) cap skins
- 5 parts base oil (any oil of your choice. Baiba's preference is coconut oil.)
- Optional Essential Oils: Clove, Chilli, White Willow

METHOD

1. Harvest several Fly Agarics. Peel off the skins while they are still wet.
2. Immediately dry the skins in a dehydrator at 40–45°C/104–113°F until cracker dry.
3. Put the dried *Amanita* skins in a jar.
4. Add warm oil and cover the jar with a lid.
5. Place a blanket around the jar and let it cool.
6. Store the blanketed jar in a dark place for one lunar cycle, shaking it occasionally.
7. When the extraction is ready, strain it. Then bottle, label, and store in a cool, dark place.
8. Apply topically as a massage oil for pain, or use it to make salves, creams, or balms.

PART 2: BALM

EQUIPMENT

- Double boiler
- Glass jars with lids for storing

INGREDIENTS

- 100ml/3¼fl oz/½ cup of Fly Agaric oil
- 7g beeswax

METHOD

1. Put the oil in the double boiler. Warm it up gently and add the wax.
2. Wait till the wax melts. Take off the heat and whisk well, adding several drops of essential oils if desired.
3. Pour the mixture into a jar and let it sit until cool and firm. Cover the jar and label. Apply topically as a massage oil for pain.
4. Note: This has a one year shelf-life in the fridge.

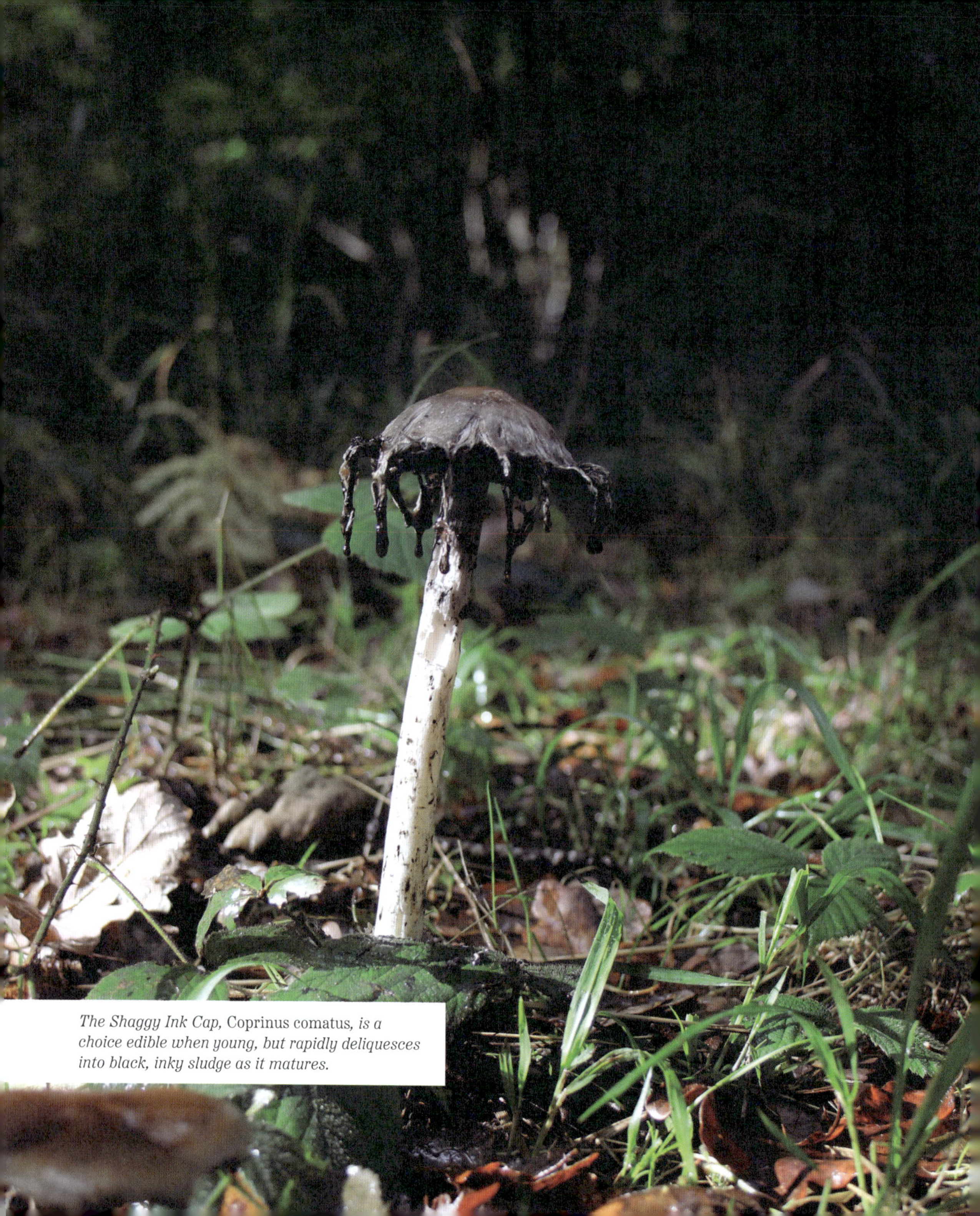

The Shaggy Ink Cap, Coprinus comatus, *is a choice edible when young, but rapidly deliquesces into black, inky sludge as it matures.*

DECOMPOSITION & SELFHOOD

Last year, I came weirdly close to eating my grandmother. My dad sent me an image of some beautiful Shaggy Ink Caps, *Coprinus comatus,* that I encouraged him to harvest and sauté for dinner. He replied promptly, "Not this time. These were growing on Ginny's grave". Clearly, my dad wasn't into the idea of eating his mother in whatever way, shape, or form she was taking in the afterlife. Fair enough. I was glad, at least, that my grandmother had partially transformed into these ochraceous mushrooms, glistening with minuscule droplets in the late-summer sun. The following morning, I visited her grave, shaking my head at the universe's cruel sense of humour: she hated mushrooms. I whispered my words of love and good fortune and bid her adieu.

Fungi symbolise regrowth, rejuvenation, and regeneration. Their role in the cycle of life is to decompose and decay, returning vital nutrients to the earth and facilitating new growth. Their association with death and mould often evokes fear, which makes sense. They are the saprobes – the despoilers and the rotters – capable of breaking down virtually anything organic, from plastics and pollutants to cigarette butts and corpses. They're at the end of life, but they're also at the very beginning.

Graveyards elegantly exemplify this duality, nurturing the transformation of nutrient-rich human remains into gourmet gastronomic delights, overflowing with wild edibles and herbal medicines. This makes them an ideal, albeit disarming, spot to begin a fungi foray.

So in early autumn of 2023, I did just this, amid the chalky South Downs in southern England. Breath held in anticipation, we passed around a chunk of Chicken of the Woods, *Laetiporus sulphureus*, carefully harvested from the sprawling yew tree in the churchyard, its great branches sheltering countless graves. Yews protect our churches and are associated with death and the underworld, symbolising everlasting life and rebirth. I watched as my fellow foragers reacted to this strange fusion of corpse, tree, and mushroom. Responses varied widely: an involuntary sneeze, a flicking away of an insect, and one participant who vanished into the church. Reactions oscillated between intrigue, disgust, fear, laughter, fascination, distrust, and outright refusal to engage with the mushroom. And yet, when you think about it, this manifestation of constant reincarnation is beautiful: heartwood of yew, nurtured by countless years of sunlight and water, supported by a rich diet of decomposed remains, now reincarnated as a stunning fungal mass: a jewel of sulphurous chicken.

Humour can serve as an effective vehicle to broach ostensibly uncomfortable truths about mortality. By entertaining the idea of foraging from – and feasting in – a graveyard, we can engage with alarming possibilities in a more approachable manner. While there are clear spiritual and linguistic connections between us and the soil (human, humus, humility, and humour share a common Latin root, *solum*, meaning "soil" or "ground"), culturally, we tend to suppress such associations. We fear "others", "monsters", and "creatures" because we fear them in ourselves. So, society fosters an exaggerated

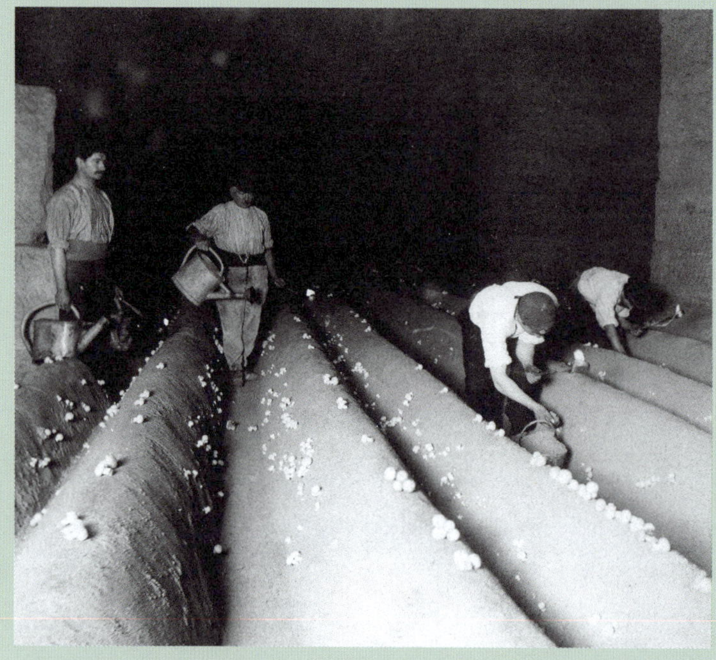

Mushroom cultivation in "Les Champignonniéres", France.

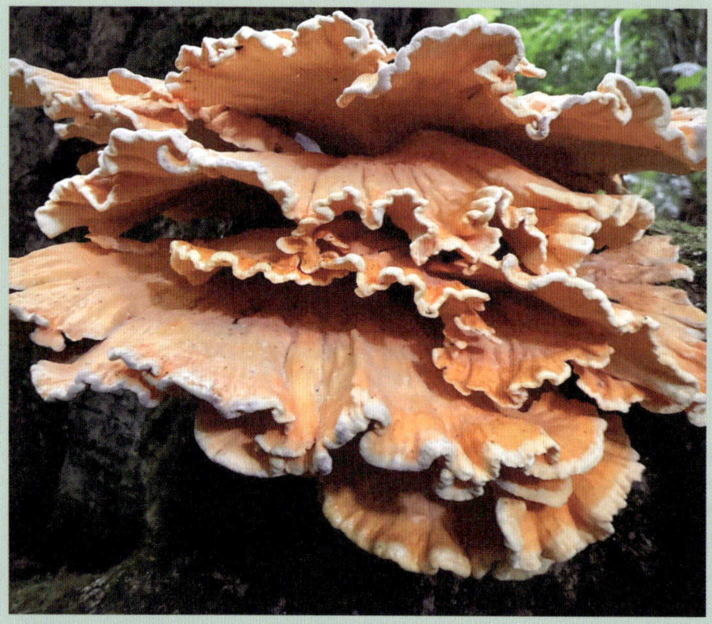

Chicken of the Woods, Laetiporus sulphureus, *growing on a yew,* Taxus baccata, *in a graveyard. Foragers often caution against eating mushrooms grown on yew trees as they may accumulate taxol – a deadly poison present in yews. Likewise, while graveyards poetically symbolise the cycle of life and decay, it's advised not to forage from graveyards as human remains contain various toxins, and fungi are skilled toxin-accumulators.*

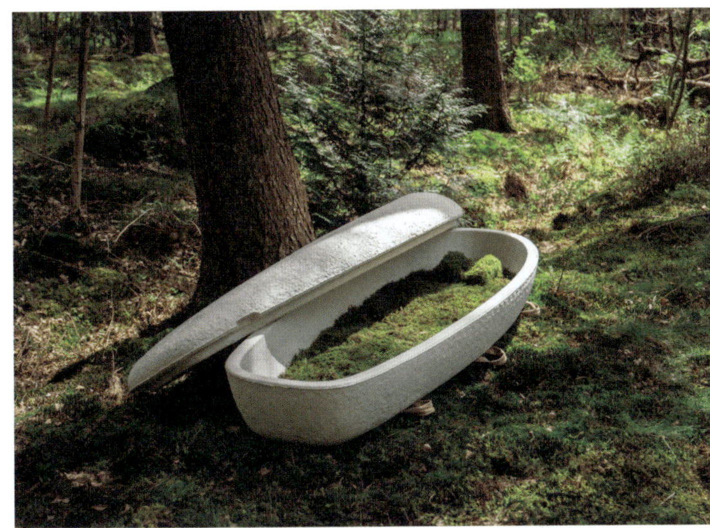

Loop Biotech's Mycelial Cocoon integrates fungi into ecological burials. Certified for traditional, natural, and cremation services, the company celebrates mycelium as nature's recycler, key to nutrient sharing and soil regeneration.

divide between "us" and "them", "human" and "non-human", "clean" and "dirty", "alive" and "dead", sharpening boundaries of separation that might otherwise be hazy or indistinct. We epitomise this tendency by isolating graveyards from the bustle of city life in the name of safety and sanitation.

But if the differences can't be exaggerated, they are best ignored. Consider, for example, the Parisian Catacombs. In the late 18th century, as Paris expanded and outgrew existing cemeteries, the former subterranean quarries beneath the City of Light became a burial site for over six million bodies! This practice continued into the 19th century, and by 1820, a new subterranean industry had emerged: mushroom farming. The consistent temperature, humidity, and darkness proved ideal for fungi, as they thrived in rows of nutrient-rich horse manure. The mushrooms of choice were Button mushrooms, *Les Champignons de Paris,* that gained fame far beyond the city limits. Mushrooms absorb the characteristics of the space and substrate in which they grow, and although it may seem somewhat revolting, people believed the flavour of these mushrooms surpassed all others!

While these tales might spark your curiosity to seek edible fungi, it's important to say that graveyards (and catacombs!) should serve strictly educational purposes, as their soils are often heavily contaminated. Over a lifetime, our bodies accumulate various toxins, differing in severity and substance across generations. In Victorian England, for example, lead poisoning was a common mortality cause. Later, asbestos claimed lives, and today, residues from tobacco, cleaning chemicals, pesticides, fungicides, flame retardants, heavy metals, preservatives, pollution, microplastics, and, most notably, formaldehyde used for embalming, contribute to our toxic legacy. After we pass, many of these trace elements and chemical substances leach into the soil, and fungi – masters of ecosystem remediation – absorb and concentrate these contaminants into their fruiting bodies, rendering them both fascinating and perilous inhabitants of cemeteries. (We'll explore "mycoremediation" further in chapter 7).

"As I Was, So Are Thee
As I Am, So Wilt Thou Be"

Written upon a gravestone at St Nicholas' Church, Wiltshire, UK

In a positive spin on the intersection of life and death, you may be familiar with Jae Rhim Lee, an artist and scientist who created the Mushroom Burial Suit. Her full-body suit was infused with mushroom spores and microorganisms designed to decompose the body, neutralise toxins, and return our nutrients to the soil. Similarly, Loop Biotech's mycelial cocoons exemplify innovative collaborations with fungi in ecological burial practices. This Dutch company is now certified for both traditional and natural burials, as well as cremations. "Mycelium", they explain, "is nature's greatest recycler. Its unique ability to share nutrients, communicate with forest ecosystems, and improve soil quality makes it a driving force in life's cyclical processes." While this is true, their mycelial cocoons are dehydrated and dormant, therefore not actively transmitting nutrients. Still, no doubt, this mycelial necromass will nourish hungry soils.

These are just a few examples of intriguing innovations already in progress, and there is so much opportunity to collaborate with fungi in death care practices. But nothing compares to being decomposed by the mushrooms native to the burial environment, as was the case with the Ink Caps sprouting from my grandmother's grave. Even if the fruiting bodies remain hidden from sight, microscopic fungi and intricate networks of mycelium diligently thrive beneath the surface.

As death approaches, our microbiomes shift, altering many things, including how we smell to others. Once we die and our life systems shut down, our microbes begin to decompose our tissues. They spread through the body from the gut into capillaries and lymph nodes, breaking down tissues and even bone.[23] The food we eat, the people we cuddle, and the environments in which we spend our final days all significantly influence what is called our "necrobiome": the microbial communities associated with decaying remains. Underground, our internal microbes intermingle with soil microbes to decompose the body further and reintegrate us into the ecosystem.[24,25]

My greatest fear about dying is the prospect of being buried in winter. The cold ground could slow the activity of creatures and microbes, which I romantically imagine feasting on my body, breaking me down, and remoulding me into new forms. Instead, in a frozen winter, they might be dormant, rendering those of us who die in winter (statistically a larger number) stiff as stale bread, packed into stagnant soil, and caught in an unsettling wait for the summer sun. Though we may be dead, and fair to say untroubled by such musings, I still think it's worth contemplating while we remain vertical. Death is the only certainty; perhaps if we engage with it more openly in life, we might find the fear dissipating.

Armed with both apprehension and curiosity, I conducted some experiments to understand decomposition and the sluggishness of winter soils. A friend gifted me a badger skull, still adorned with remnants of flesh. I buried it to see whether the insects and beetles would clean the skull throughout the sparse winter months. After precisely marking its location with a large stone and noting its depth at approximately half a metre, I returned six months later in March, anticipating a bleached white skull. To my surprise, I found no skull at all. Digging a little wider, I unearthed the skull roughly 30 centimetres from where I'd originally placed it. The soil had moved my skull! Indeed, the slow but

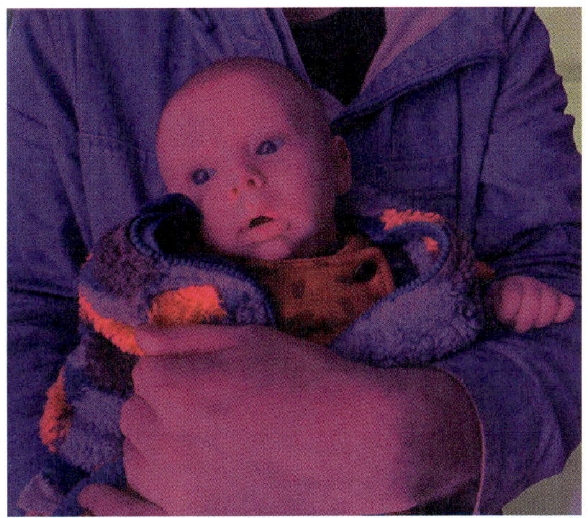

I swabbed my colleagues' palms, armpits, bellybuttons, and toes to create the "Staff Cheese Profiles". There was unanimous agreement as to who tasted the best.

steady actions of worms, woodlice, beetles, bacteria, fungi, roots, and other small organisms thriving in darkness were in motion: the true march of death. Even in the "dead of winter", life in the soil was far from dormant. (Phew!)

Time and culture shape what a community chooses to do with its dead. For example, 15,000 years ago in Cheddar Gorge, just around the corner from my former workplace, evidence suggests that ancient humans consumed their kin. Far from being an "uncivilised" grotesque violation of nature, this endocannibalism was believed to have been an expression of compassion and respect towards ancestors: eating the dead to honour the dead. Needless to say, cannibalism has fallen out of favour in Somerset, and any concept of self-consumption – whether of oneself, one's family, or even one's microorganisms – is firmly regarded as taboo.

This backdrop makes the collaborative efforts of synthetic biologist Christina Agapakis and smell artist Sissel Tolaas seem both brilliant and provocative. Their work probes our instinctive revulsions surrounding self-consumption, death, and microbial decomposition, resulting in the creation of "Selfmade Cheeses". Many of the world's most pungent cheeses are home to bacteria and fungi akin to those that produce the odour of human armpits, belly buttons, and feet. Delving into the physicality of cheesemaking, they speculated about the origins of the microbiota in cheese, ultimately creating cheeses with cultures isolated from the human body: Farmer's cheese from journalist and professor Michael Pollan's belly button and Comté from chef Heston Blumenthal's armpit. Astonishingly, both were reported to be quite tasty!

Eager to experiment with these fascinating yet slightly repulsive ideas, I swabbed various parts of my colleagues' bodies, inoculated pasteurised milk from The Courtyard Dairy Farm's cows, and – in somewhat of an homage to our cannibal ancestors – crafted "Staff Cheese Profiles". While some were more hesitant to sample their creations than others, there was, rather interestingly, unanimous agreement as to whose tasted the best.

RECIPE

SELFMADE CHEESE
CHRISTINA AGAPAKIS

Many cheeses crafted in Cheddar are cave-aged, transported by hand down into the Wookey Hole Caves in the Mendip Hills, where they mature for 18 months. During this time, they absorb the distinctive characteristics of their subterranean surroundings, developing a uniquely metallic flavour and dense texture that sets them apart from ordinary Cheddar (so I'm told).

Cheese production involves milk and a complex interplay of microbes (bacteria and yeasts) that determine the scent and taste of the final product. Milk is acidified, and rennet enzymes derived from cattle intestines are added to coagulate the protein-rich caseins. Solid curds are separated from liquid whey and pressed into cheese. The longer cheese matures, the more solid the final product becomes, with some varieties culturing aromatic fungal moulds on the rind (as with Camembert and Brie) or throughout (such as Roquefort, Blue, Gorgonzola, and Stilton).

Creating your personalised fungus cheese at home is surprisingly straightforward. If you're interested in trying this hilarious experiment yourself, here's a simple guide:

EQUIPMENT

- Cotton swab
- Cooking pot
- Cheesecloth

INGREDIENTS

- Carton or bottle of organic whole cow's milk (250ml/8½fl oz/1 cup)
- Body microbes

METHOD

1. Thoroughly swab any of the following areas: hands, feet, belly button, or armpits with a sterile cotton swab.
2. Introduce the microbes to the milk by cutting the swab head into the carton. (I swabbed my bellybutton and used a 250ml carton).
3. Bring a pot of water to 60°C/140°F.
4. Submerge the inoculated carton(s) in the pot of water and incubate at this temperature for 3 hours.
5. Allow your milk carton to remain in the water bath as it cools to room temperature.
6. Remove it from the water and let it sit in a warm room for 3–5 days. Loosen the lid slightly for air exchange.
7. Eventually, the milk will curdle (separate into solid curds and liquid whey). Some microbes act faster than others; my bellybutton cheese formed quickly, while Aubrey's foot-derived microbes were slightly slower.
8. Strain the curds through a cheesecloth to release the whey. Don't squeeze the cheesecloth.
9. Keep the cheese in the cloth to support its surface and allow for moisture and gas exchange. Allow it to age for 2–4 weeks in a humid room at 12°C (54°F). Label the cloth with the date, body part, and creator's name – best not to make any mistakes of identity here.

A cautionary note: most people prefer to eat others' than their own.

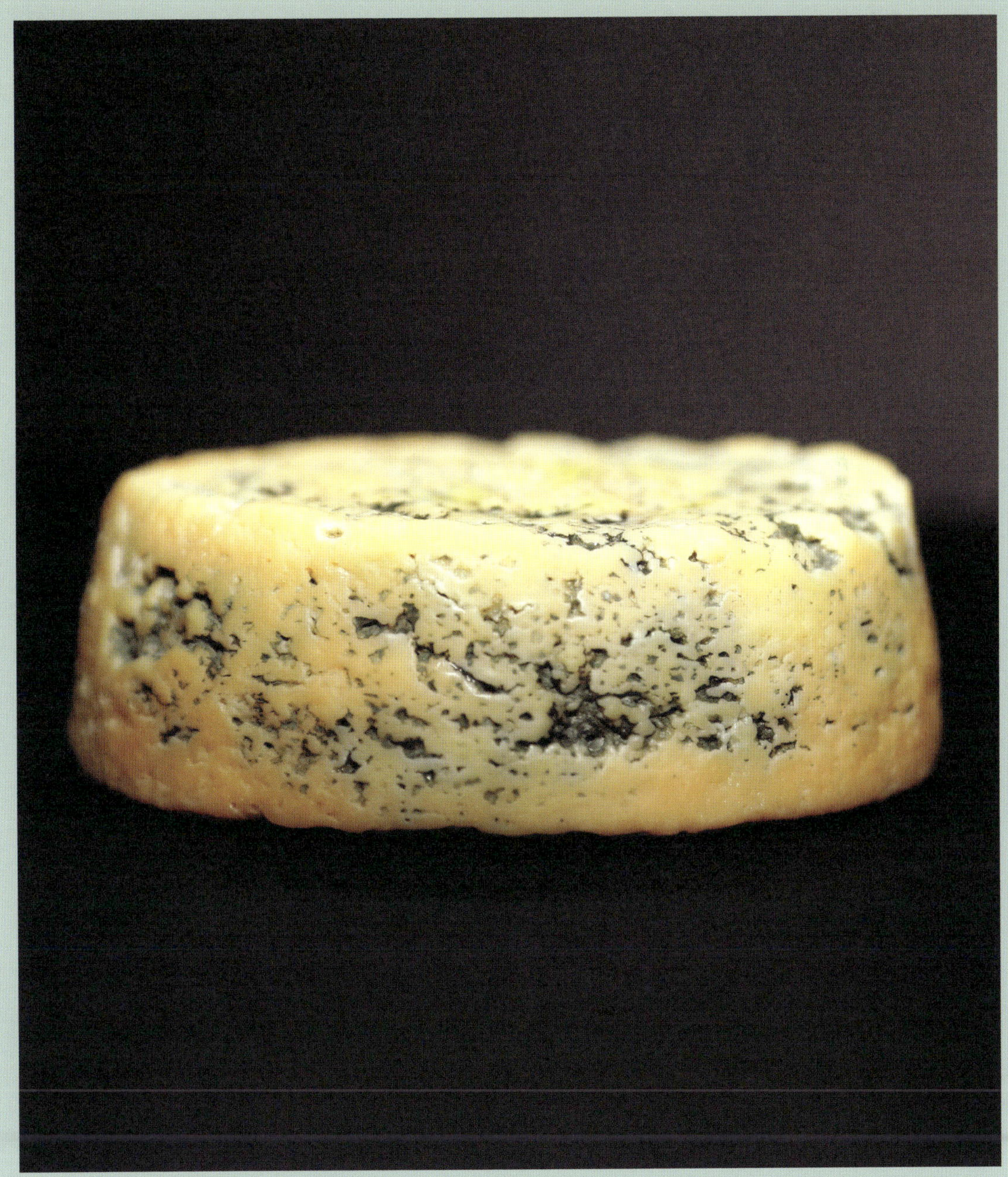

Selfmade cheese.

SIN, SEDUCTION, & SCENT

"It is absolutely delicious, but then again, so is everything sinful."

– Jans Ondaatje Rolls

Cynically speaking, the human experience can be reduced to three primal drives: sex, food, and power. Truffles have embedded themselves deep within this tangled web, seducing our senses in ways we are still struggling to fully understand. These subterranean delicacies, particularly prized for their ability to trigger intense culinary pleasure, also hold a deeper allure – one that intertwines with our most basic instincts of attraction, desire, and indulgence.

Yet, as climate change reshapes weather patterns and delicate microbial ecosystems, wild truffle populations are largely in decline. The situation is compounded by a familiar foe: human greed, which fuels a dangerous underground world of truffle trafficking. Analysts project that the global truffle market will be worth over $1.5 billion by the end of 2025,[26] and much of this trade is now controlled by the so-called "agromafia".[27] With this comes violence, territorial disputes, kidnappings, and a black market flooded with fakes. Still, truffle hunters persist, lured by the mystique of this elusive underground fungus.

Truffles are the underground descendants of above-ground mushrooms, having gradually adapted to life beneath the soil. In losing their exposure to air, they also lost the ability to disperse spores through wind, instead evolving to depend on animals for reproduction. This subterranean shift turned truffles into olfactory wizards – masters of scent who must seduce eager "fungivores" to dig them up and spread their spores.

Truffles play critical roles in the ecosystems they inhabit. They form ectomycorrhizal relationships with the roots of specific trees – a symbiotic connection where the truffle's mycelium surrounds the tree's roots, providing vital nutrients in exchange for carbohydrates. This relationship is highly species-specific, meaning each type of truffle can only grow in association with certain tree species, such as beech, oak, birch, or hazel. These fungi promote drought tolerance for their host trees, enhance soil structure, and aid in nutrient recycling.

Truffles are surprisingly resilient. Though they prefer warm, well-drained, alkaline soils, enriched with chalk and limestone, they have been found north of the Alps in southern Germany, and in the deserts of North Africa and the Middle East.

The *Tuber* genus includes approximately 180–230 species of truffles worldwide.[28] Of these, there are 38 "true truffles";[29] the rest are "false truffles", though still hypogeous (fungi with underground fruiting bodies). Despite the diversity, only a few species shine in the culinary world, particularly the Summer Truffle, *Tuber aestivum*, and its autumn counterpart, *Tuber aestivum var. uncinatum.*

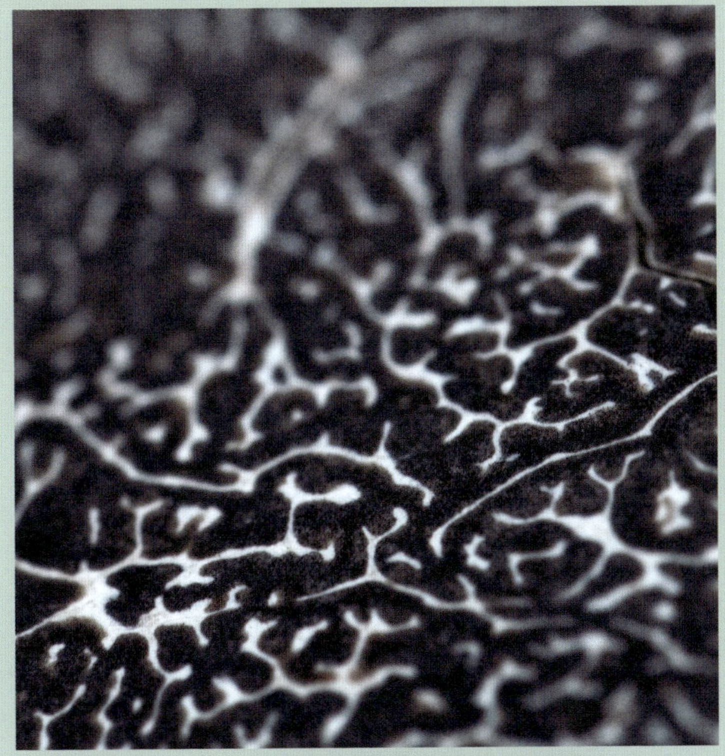

Winter Truffle, Tuber melanosporum, *a subterranean fungus prized for its intense flavour and aroma, as well as its ability to tap into deep instincts of attraction, desire, and indulgence.*

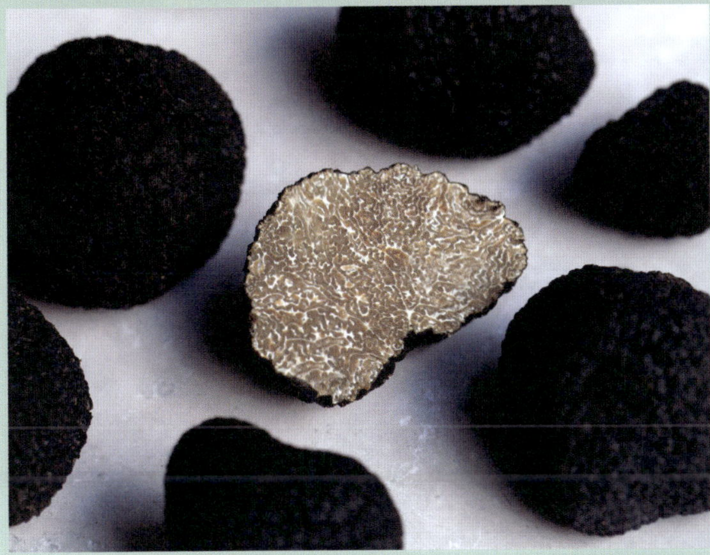

The Summer Truffle, Tuber aestivum, *adorned with pyramidal warts. Though distinct in aroma and flavour, both summer and autumn truffles are the same species, harvested in different seasons.*

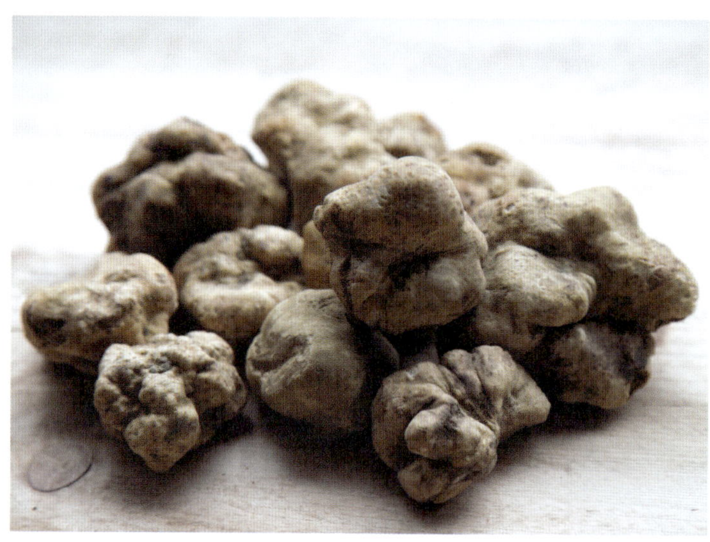

Alba White Truffle, Tuber magnatum, *also known as the Italian white truffle,* Tartufo Bianco d'Alba *– one of the rarest and most expensive truffles in the world.*

The Summer Truffle, with its light brown flesh and white veins, offers a mild aroma. In contrast, the Autumn Truffle is darker, with marbled grey-black flesh and a more powerful aroma.

While the UK and US may be home to a modest selection of edible truffles, the true treasure trove lies in Europe, particularly Spain, Italy, Croatia, Romania, Serbia, and Greece. At the pinnacle of the truffle market lies the White Truffle, *Tuber magnatum*, notably the Alba White Truffle from the Piedmont region of Italy. These truffles are among the rarest and most expensive on the planet, often fetching over €10,000 per kilogram. Their elusive nature – difficult to locate and almost impossible to cultivate – adds to their mystique, making them the ultimate culinary prize.

In 2014, a record-breaking 1.89 kilogram White Truffle was flown to Sotheby's in New York, escorted by a security guard, and sold at auction for $61,000. Many insisted that it could have reached as much as $1 million, had the auction not been rigged.

The allure of truffles is not just culinary; they are also thought to possess mood-enhancing and aphrodisiac properties. This reputation is primarily due to the presence of compounds such as anandamide, known as the "bliss molecule".[30] Anandamide activates cannabinoid receptors in the brain, promoting feelings of euphoria, happiness, and social pleasure.[31] Truffles also contain serotonin and dopamine. Dopamine plays a pivotal role in sexual arousal, enhancing reward pathways in the brain, while serotonin regulates inhibitory pathways in the brain.[32] Together, they create a complex neurobiological response that contributes to heightened sexual desire and emotional engagement upon eating said truffle.

During the Middle Ages, the Catholic Church even deemed truffle consumption inappropriate, fearing that indulgent monks would stray from their vows. Nineteenth century French Gourmand John Evfeln wrote, "Whoever says truffle utters a great word, which arouses erotic and gastronomic memories among the skirted and bearded sex."

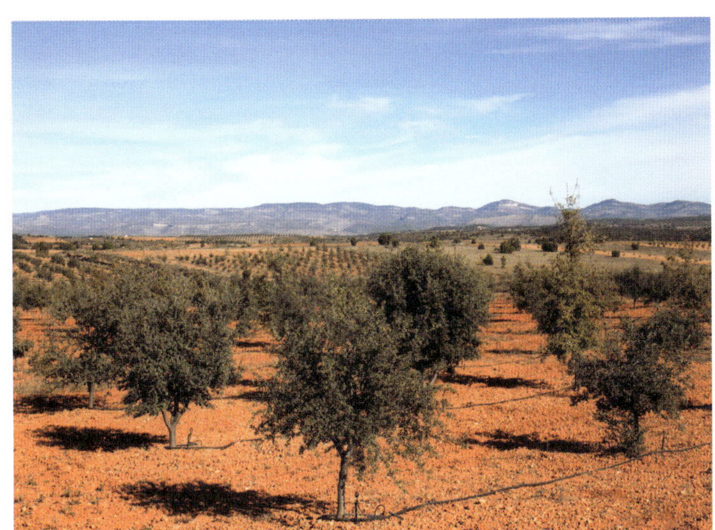

Truffle cultivation site. Truffles derive much of their character from their surrounding ecosystem – the weather, terroir, and microbiome. The truffle's microbiome is especially important in shaping its distinctive aroma.

Truffles owe much of their allure to their scent. Variously described as earthy, oaky, nutty, beetrooty, oniony, musky, sexy, or even likened to the "sticky sweat between your ball sack and leg" – gross – opinions on truffles and their aromas vary widely. Some adore them, others feign interest, and a resolute few detest them.

Like the wine-growing terroir of France's Champagne, truffles derive much of their character from the ecosystems in which they grow. But truffles are ecosystems in and of themselves. The truffle microbiome is a dynamic community of bacteria, yeasts, filamentous fungi, and even viruses. These microbes colonise the truffle, inside and out, and change throughout the truffle's lifecycle. Much like the human gut microbiome, these microbes play a crucial role in the truffle's growth and overall health, and contribute to their ability to attract animals and insects. Together, these form what is known as a holobiont – a dynamic and symbiotic ecological unit comprising the host (the truffle) and its microbial companions.

A study titled "The Role of the Microbiome of Truffles in Aroma Formation" suggests that the truffle's aroma – so central to their culinary value – arises from a blend of truffle and microbial origin.[33] Together, they create a complex mixture of volatile organic compounds (VOCs), including alcohols, esters, ketones, and sulphur compounds. One such compound is the steroidal pheromone androstanol, which mimics the sex pheromones found in a male boar's saliva during mating season. The scent drives female pigs into a wild frenzy – precisely as the fungi – or their microbial counterparts – intended. Taking the idea of symbiosis further, an Italian study found that when Summer Truffle spores passed through the digestive tracts of pigs, they had enhanced germination rates and were more successful at establishing mycorrhizal relationships with oaks.[34] Research also suggests that when given the choice, sows preferentially select the full truffle aroma over the sex pheromone. This leaves us with two options: either fungi are more delicious than sex, or truffles have pulled off the ultimate evolutionary con – convincing female pigs that digging them up is more urgent than making piglets.

Sows have accompanied truffle hunters since at least the Roman times, though their enthusiastic digging often results in a damaged truffle – or human. As such, Italians banned truffle hunting with pigs in 1935 and modern truffle hunters found companions in dogs (especially the Lagotto Romagnolo breed) or even goats, both of which are easier to control and more gentle on the fungi.

But there are radicals and purists in the mycological world who instead, train themselves to hunt for these elusive treasures. Like any skilled predator, they must get to know their target organism, learning its optimal fruiting season (summer and autumn), terrain (alkaline soils), symbiotic partners (oak, hazel, beech, or birch trees), and microclimate (south-facing, well-drained, and aerated soils with minimal undergrowth). Yet, if all else fails, the truffle hunter will do as we've always done, and look to the ways of other creatures.

Truffles are epicurean delights for countless species. Mycophagous animals, including squirrels, mice, voles, rabbits, and larger creatures like badgers, deer, and bears, all seek out this underground fungus and leave untidy traces of their truffle digs. Insects, like the truffle fly, *Suillia tuberiperda,* both feed on and lay their eggs in the soil just above the truffle, giving their offspring easy access to a nutritious first meal. But the absence of life can also be a telltale sign for the truffle hunter. Truffles secrete bitter antimicrobials and herbicides to outcompete plant and fungal rivals, creating barren zones on the forest floor known as "brûlées".

Once hunters master these visual techniques for finding truffles, they then, like a loyal Lagotto Romagnolo, learn to follow their nose – literally. Comedian and musician the FUNgi guy popularised this method when he announced he had undergone intensive olfactory training with "Dr Ollie Fakchray" (@liberate.your.nose). He shared that his training had enabled him to detect even the faintest truffle scent, finding them in obscure places like car parks and roundabouts. While his training turned out to be an April Fool's prank, he and mycologist Jesper Launder have since refined the technique, and nose-training is in high demand. So, if you spot someone with a spade in hand and nose to the ground, it might be worth sticking around to see what they dig up.

The final unconventional tactic for increasing one's truffle finds is to hunt after a thunderstorm. What was once dismissed as folklore has since garnered scientific backing. A study by Japanese scientists at Iwate University has revealed that lightning strikes can significantly boost the yield of various fungi, including truffles.[35] By artificially inducing electrical storms, researchers found that fungi shift from a vegetative to reproductive state (from mycelium to fruiting bodies), likely triggered by a perceived environmental change or threat. The storms may also break nitrogen bonds in the atmosphere, releasing essential nutrients like nitrates that fertilise the soil and stimulate truffle development.

The connection between truffles, thunder, and lightning has endured for millennia. Ancient texts describe how nomadic tribes linked seasonal thunder to truffle abundance, and Pliny the Elder observed that truffles seemed to thrive after rain and lightning. In Māori, the word *harore* means both thunder and mushroom, and Bedouins even refer to Desert Truffles as "thunder fungus". This striking natural phenomenon led to associations with Zeus, the Greek God of sky and lightning, known for both his thunderbolts and his infamous libido, further cementing truffles' ties to sensuality and desire.

Lacking a suitable pig, dog, or goat, my fungi-loving friends and I arranged a truffle hunt in the chalky South Downs, guided by the UK's foremost truffle expert, Melissa Waddingham. She brought her trained dogs; I, my discerning nose, while our group contributed boundless enthusiasm and determination.

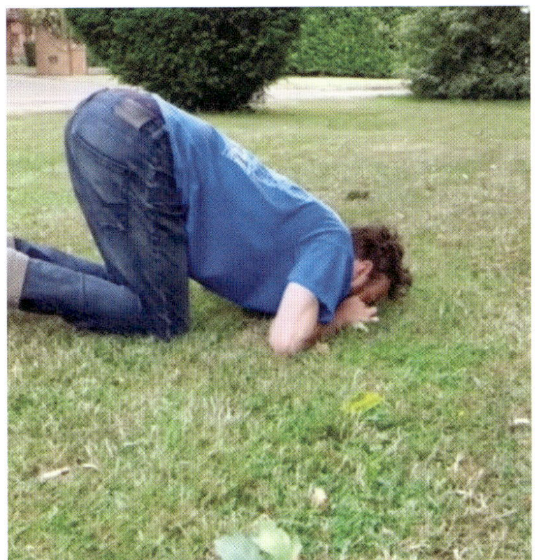

The FUNgi Guy truffle hunting during olfactory training to sharpen his sense of smell for locating elusive underground truffles.

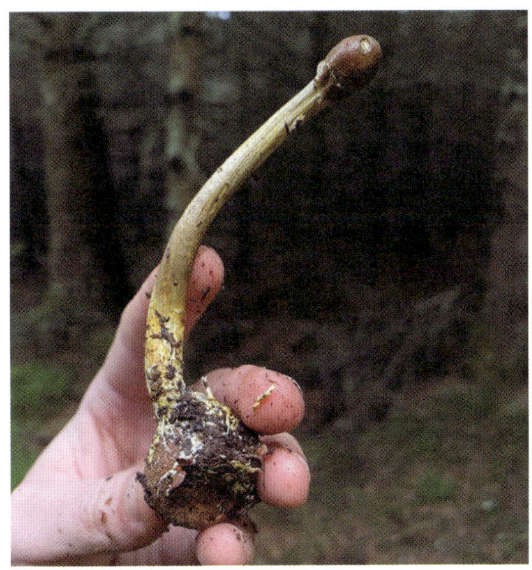

The parasitic Drumstick Truffleclub, Tolypocladium capitatum, *growing from a false truffle. A foolproof way of finding truffles!*

Earlier that month, an eight-year-old with an encyclopaedic knowledge of fungi (also called Kit) informed me that some false truffles are parasitised by the Drumstick Truffleclub – a Cordyceps species, cousin to the "zombie" fungus. "Below ground", Kit explained, "the truffle and its mycelia are entangled with the roots of a nearby conifer, often a spruce. But sprouting from the top of the truffle lies a yellow stipe (stem) crowned with a shiny brown, egg shaped cap. A foolproof way of finding a truffle!"

This union is the epitome of interspecies fungal intimacies: false truffles, parasitic Cordyceps, spruce rootlets, their respective microbial companions, and human animals on the hunt for a treat. It appears almost sensual: Microbes, playing an intrinsic role in indulgences like bread, wine, and cheese, symbolise pleasure and excess. Cordyceps, dubbed "Himalayan Viagra", take this story of sensuality to new heights. Spruces, long symbolic of friendship, nurture these interspecies connections, while truffles add their aphrodisiac allure. We were desperate to find the Drumstick Truffleclub.

Roald Dahl gave me an idea. While best known for his whimsical children's tales like *Matilda* and *Charlie and the Chocolate Factory*, he also wrote provocative fiction for adults. My favourite is *Switch Bitch*, a collection featuring his outrageous Uncle Oswald – hedonist, opera lover, expert in Chinese porcelain, and self-proclaimed world's greatest fornicator. In one story, Oswald hunts the mythical Sudanese Blister Beetle, whose powdered essence becomes an irresistible aphrodisiac perfume – powerful enough to seduce any lover. It worked, to various degrees.

But if only Oswald knew of the seductive powers of Zeus' truffles and the infamous Drumstick Truffleclub! Inspired by Oswald's absurd adventures, I felt compelled to find this parasitic alliance and

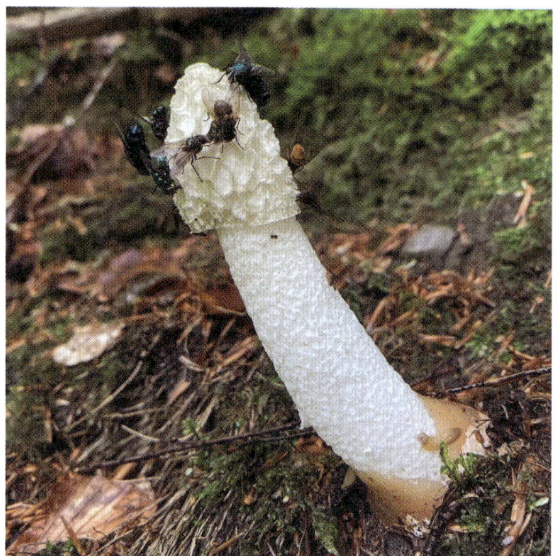

Common Stinkhorn, Phallus impudicus. *Recognisable by its foul odour and the buzzing of flies drawn to the mushroom.*

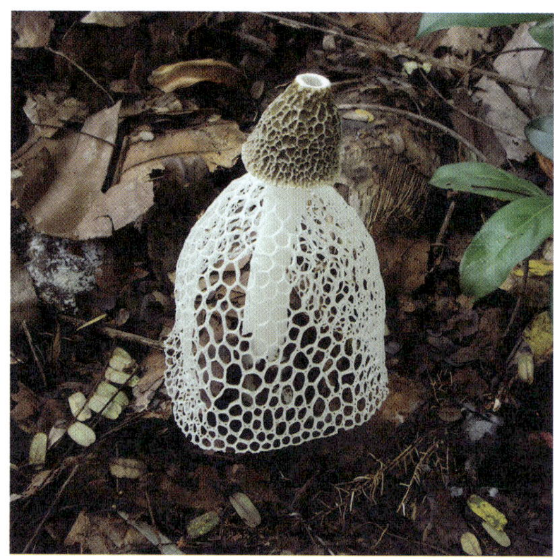

Skirted Stinkhorn, Phallus indusiatus.

create a perfume to rival his aroma. The universe seemed aligned; we ventured out following a storied thunderstorm, a team of eager fungal enthusiasts in tow.

Yet fungi, like romance, can be capricious. Despite our best efforts, we didn't find them. But before the end of the day, in a nearby woodland, we found an extraordinary number of Common Stinkhorns, *Phallus impudicus*, a surprising bounty that transformed our venture.

Phallus impudicus translates as "shameless phallus," and for good reason. Stinkhorns begin as an egg and produce an undeniably phallic-shaped mushroom, capped with a rancid-smelling, dark green, spore-laden gleba that attracts flies for spore dispersal. Prudish Victorians were said to attack and burn these fungi to shield impressionable young women. Still, we tramped through the pungent atmosphere, dodging stinkhorns that jutted obscenely from the soil.

Despite returning empty-handed in terms of our desired truffle–Cordyceps union, my basket was piled high with the putrid stinkhorns. Unable to create the desired love potion, I shifted focus. Together with myco-perfumer Bee Evans, I spent an unconventional October afternoon attempting to extract the stinkhorn essence, strong enough to repel any suitor. The resulting perfume had a lingering, sickly-sweet aroma. Ironically, and perhaps we should have known, the Romans once brewed love potions from these stinkhorns to boost sexual potency, and in parts of France and Germany, they are still used as aphrodisiacs for livestock. The symbiosis is inescapable. Despite our best efforts, we *had* made a love potion: sweaty, vegetal, and sulphurous, for pigs, perverts, and the bold but misguided.

RECIPE

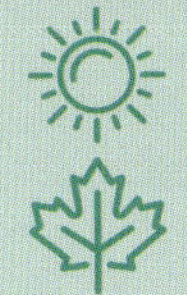

STINKHORN PERFUME
ONLY FOR THE BRAVE!

EQUIPMENT

- Glass jar
- Cheesecloth
- Small glass vial
- Optional: 500ml/17fl oz/2 cups of glass jar with lid (see Truffle Tip)
- 200ml/7fl oz/¾ cup of spray bottle (or an old perfume container)

INGREDIENTS

- Stinkhorns (Forage anywhere from 1–10 stinkhorns. If you only find eggs, pick them by the "rule of thirds" (take no more than a third of what you can see) and store them in a Tupperware container in your fridge. They'll eventually fruit within the Tupperware and release a *very* strong aroma).
- 40ml scentless jojoba oil
- Optional: 80ml/2¾fl oz/⅓ cup of perfumer's alcohol (SD-40b)
- Optional: Cordyceps and Truffles

METHOD

1. In a glass jar, submerge the fully fruited stinkhorns in the jojoba oil, ensuring they are completely covered.
2. Allow the mixture to steep for 3 months.
3. If possible, periodically replace the stinkhorns with fresh specimens throughout the year. (They can be found from May through October).
4. After the 3 months, use a cheesecloth to filter out the stinkhorns. Don't squeeze the stinkhorns or your golden yellow oil will turn a revolting grey green! This is your central perfume heart note. Pour it in to a small glass vial to store.
5. When the occasion is right, dab some stinkhorn oil perfume onto your wrists and rub together.

Note: Oil-based perfumes are often more intense and longer-lasting than alcohol-based perfumes.

OPTIONAL ALCOHOL BASE PERFUME

1. Pour 80ml of perfumer's alcohol into your spray bottle or old perfume container.
2. Add 20ml of your stinkhorn fragrance oil.
3. Gently shake or swirl the bottle to ensure the ingredients are well combined.
4. Let the mixture sit for a few hours or overnight to allow the fragrance to meld fully.

*MELISSA WADDINGHAM'S TRUFFLE TIP

To capture as much of the truffle's scent as possible, place them at the base of a glass jar and rest a small bowl with jojoba oil on top. Put a lid on the glass jar. The VOCs from the truffles will rise and infuse into the oil. If you'd rather create a truffle-infusion for food, you can do this same method with olive oil or boiled eggs!

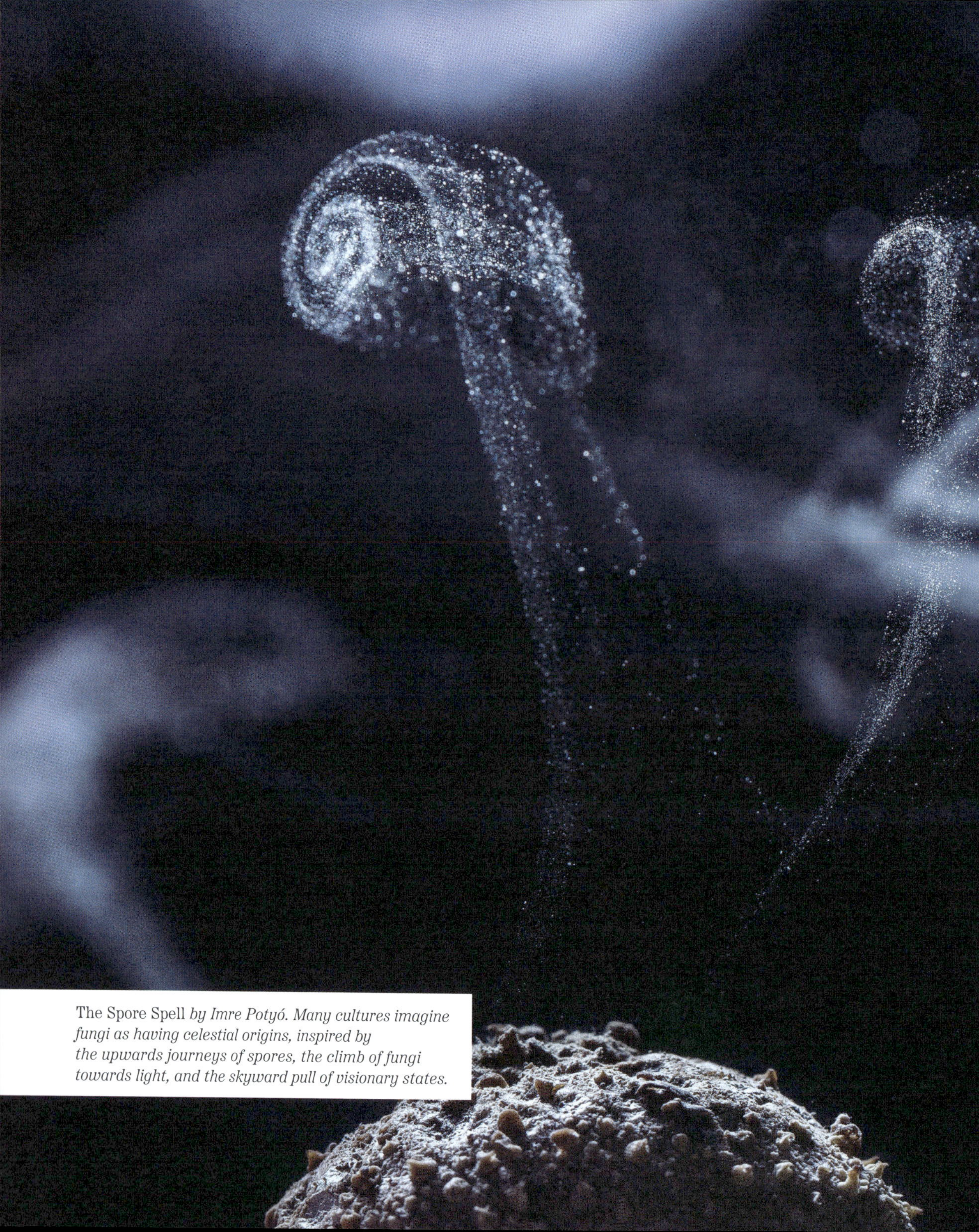

The Spore Spell *by Imre Potyó. Many cultures imagine fungi as having celestial origins, inspired by the upwards journeys of spores, the climb of fungi towards light, and the skyward pull of visionary states.*

2

UP: Spirit & Subjectivity

"He who eats many, many things sees."

Bernadino de Sahagún, Historia General de las Cosas de Nueva España, *c.1577*

We often think of fungi as belonging to the underworld, creatures of soil, shadow, and decay. Yet, many cultures have imagined a celestial origin for fungi. Among the Tungus of Siberia, fungi are thought to be reincarnated ancestors, flung to Earth by the Moon. Star jelly, a gelatinous fungus that appears mysteriously on grass, is believed to fall from the sky in the wake of meteors. The Greeks believed mushrooms were shocked into life by Zeus's lightning, and for the Aztecs, psychedelic *Psilocybes* were divine gifts from the Gods.

Such myths hint at something fundamental: Fungi are in a constant, subtle dialogue with their surroundings. Though they lack eyes, ears, or brains, they are highly sensitive to shifts in chemicals, pressure, vibration, and electromagnetic fields.[1] Why mushrooms appear where and when they do remains largely unknown. Beneath our threshold of perception – and understanding – lies a vast, dynamic interplay of signals and stimuli that guide fungal life.

Every day, fungi release billions of electrically charged spores into the atmosphere.[2] Hyphae (the branching filaments that make up the fungal body) navigate the world through chemotaxis, moving and fusing in response to chemical cues.[3] Some fungi even glow in the dark or exhibit biofluorescence, though what they're communicating remains unclear. As we begin to observe and listen more closely to these organisms, our understanding of communication and cognition starts to soften. Slime moulds navigate mazes without brains. Plants like *Mimosa pudica* appear to "speak" through touch and movement. Fungi, too, seem to possess complex vocabularies – some researchers suggest their electrical signalling rivals the complexity of spoken language.[4]

From Indigenous perspectives, these organisms are regarded as "beings": animate, relational, and intelligent. In Brazil's Mata Atlântica, plants and fungi are known collectively as *ervas*, or "herbs", and honoured as the "Masters of Masters." They serve as guides, connecting shamans (spiritual leaders and healers) to both ecosystems and supernatural realms. Animist communities believe every form –

animal, vegetable, mineral, and fungal – carries a unique essence, a spirit with which one can engage. Some *ervas* act on subtle, energetic levels, altering biochemistry below the threshold of perception. Others, especially psychedelic *ervas*, are powerful spiritual allies, "*mestres mais potentes*", that heal the body, expand awareness, and inspire the soul.

Many believe that the geometric patterns often seen in psychedelic experiences reveal an underlying universal order. Sacred geometries, based on the Golden Ratio (phi, φ), emerge in everything from sunflower seeds and seashells to galactic spirals and the human inner ear.[5] These self-similar, fractal forms also appear in cymatics – the visual patterns created by sound – as well as in ancient temples, cathedrals, and pyramids, each a vertical axis linking heaven and Earth.[6]

So too do they appear in fungi. The raised patterns of Mosaic Puffballs, the honeycomb structures of the Basket and Red Cage Fungus, and the radial, almost lotus-like mycelial growth of certain *Psilocybe* species, all approximate the golden ratio.[7]

These patterns bridge science and spirit. They render the abstract tangible, weaving maths and mysticism into a shared language of structure and meaning. Brazilian *pajé* (healer and spiritual leader) Carlos Papa advocates for a dialogue between shamans and physicists, suggesting their methods, though distinct, arrive at similar metaphysical truths.

Yet over time, science and spirituality split. The soul was abstracted from matter, and the divine lifted skyward. Earthly gods, represented by wind, rain, and storms, became celestial, distant, and immaterial. Spirit came to be associated with light, with reason, and the upper parts of the body – the head, the eyes, the cortex. "Up" became a metaphor for clarity, elevation, and perfection.

But fungi complicate this linear ascent. Chilean psychedelic neuroscientist Chris Timmerman suggests that fungi help us reweave the spirit back into matter. "Our wonder at mushrooms reflects our growing re-enchantment with the natural world", he explains. A shift from an objectified universe to one alive with intention and, perhaps consciousness.[8]

So in this chapter, we look up and around. We trace the upwards journeys of spores, the climb of fungi towards light, and the skyward pull of visionary states. We seek Lingzhi, "Queen of Mushrooms", said to restore vitality and extend life, and prepare Magu's sacred wine for a sip of immortality. We watch biofluorescent snails ascend fallen trees, drawn to glowing mycelium in a luminous exchange of energy. We interface with researchers building bio-hybrid electronics with slime moulds – shapeshifting entities that "compute" through stimulus and response.

We hike Oregon's peaks and learn of those who microdose on wild, indigenous psychedelics. Honouring the dainty Liberty Cap mushroom, a symbol of cognitive liberty and the right to explore our inner space, we track its sporulation as both a scientific and political act. Following this gradual lift-off, we are shot into the abyss, journeying through the world's religions, where sacred mushrooms are believed to bridge dimensions, texts, and truths. Inspired by San Francisco's Living Psychedelic Church, we envision a mycelial House of God; a holy structure that reminds us: the divine does not always come down from above. Sometimes, it rises from below, then reaches up.

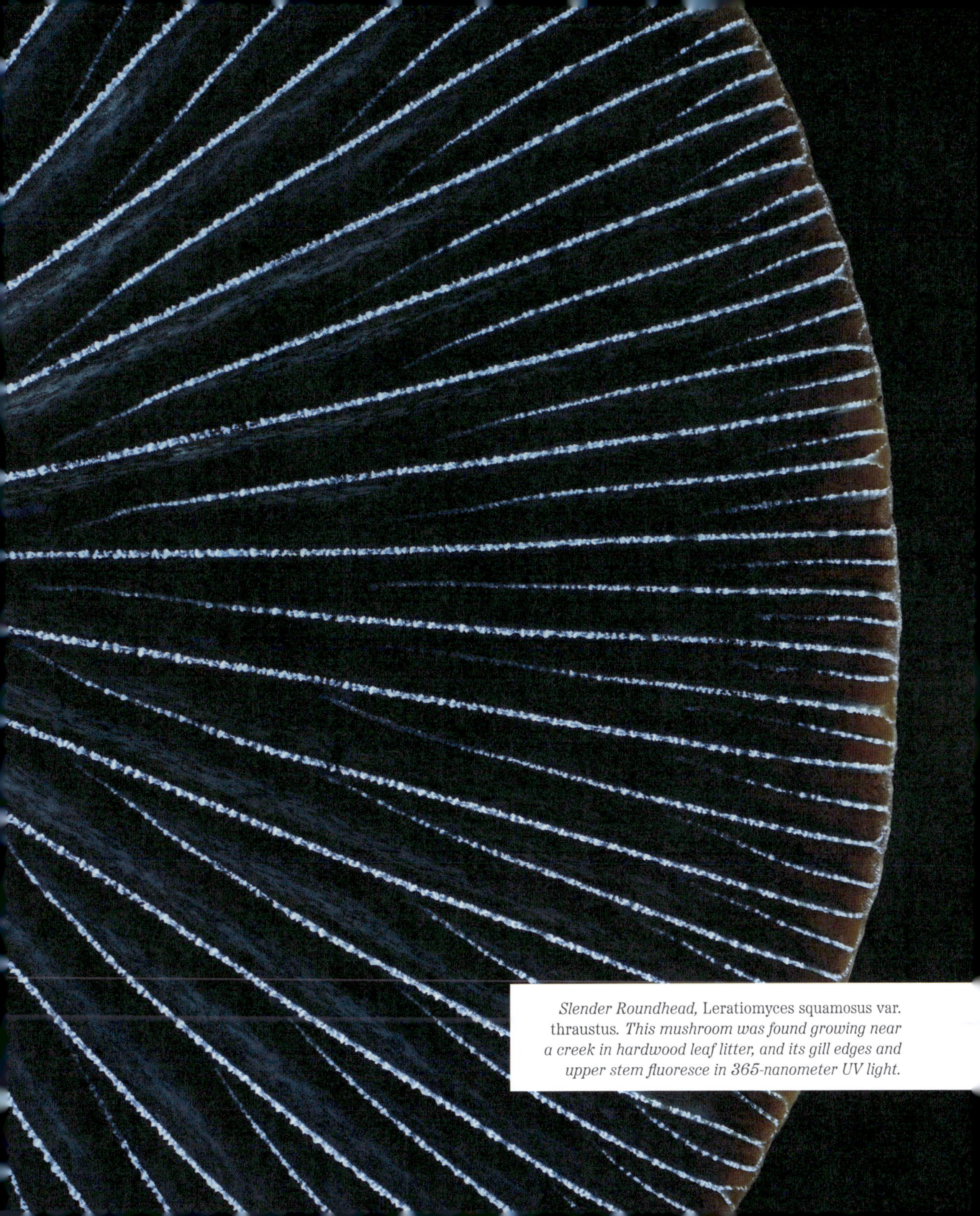

Slender Roundhead, Leratiomyces squamosus var. thraustus. *This mushroom was found growing near a creek in hardwood leaf litter, and its gill edges and upper stem fluoresce in 365-nanometer UV light.*

THE MUSHROOM OF SPIRITUAL POTENCY

"They dose themselves with the germ of gold and jade,
Eat the finest fruit of the purple polypore fungus.
By eating what is germinal, their bodies are lightened,
And so they are capable of spiritual transcendence."
– First-century philosopher Wang Ch'ung, describing Daoist practices

When foraging for mushrooms, I often have to remind myself to look up: up off the forest floor and into the canopies where another kind of mushroom grows: the Polypores. Unlike the familiar toadstools, Polypores produce large, leathery fruiting bodies called conks, brackets, or shelves, with pores or tubes on their undersides instead of gills. Some, like Reishi, *Ganoderma lucidum*, fruit annually, while others, like Artist's Brackets, *Ganoderma applanatum*, are perennial and grow larger each year.

Cultures around the world have used Polypores for practical, medicinal, and spiritual purposes. Ötzi the Iceman, who died over 5,000 years ago on a European Alpine glacier, was discovered with a necklace carrying Birch Polypore, *Fomitopsis betulina*, an effective anti-parasitic, along with true Tinder Bracket, *Fomes fomentarius*, a fire starter and medicinal mushroom. The Tsimshian people of North America called the latter the "bread of ghosts", appreciating its unrivalled healing properties. Similarly, Chaga has been respected for thousands of years in Russia, Korea, and Eastern Europe, and is celebrated as the "King of Medicinal Mushrooms" – a title it still holds as one of the world's most nutrient-dense superfoods.[9]

If Chaga is the King, Reishi is rightly the Queen. Known as Reishi (pronounced RAY-shee) in Japan and Lingzhi (pronounced Ling-jrr) in China (which I will continue to call it from here on in this chapter), both names mean "divine mushroom" or "mushroom of eternal youth", as extracts from this fungus are believed to add years to one's life. While Lingzhi's medicinal use dates back at least to Neolithic China, it is still an essential remedy in modern Chinese medicine, valued for its warming, detoxifying, and calming properties. Rich in polysaccharides and triterpenes, Lingzhi is a renowned adaptogen, believed to regulate cortisol levels and promote restful sleep. Chinese pig thieves even used it as an anaesthetic to quieten their stolen herds.[10]

Ancient Chinese alchemists sought the "elixir of life" by crafting potions from an extraordinary array of ingredients, including plants, fungi, lichen, insects, reptiles, fossils, gems, minerals, and even

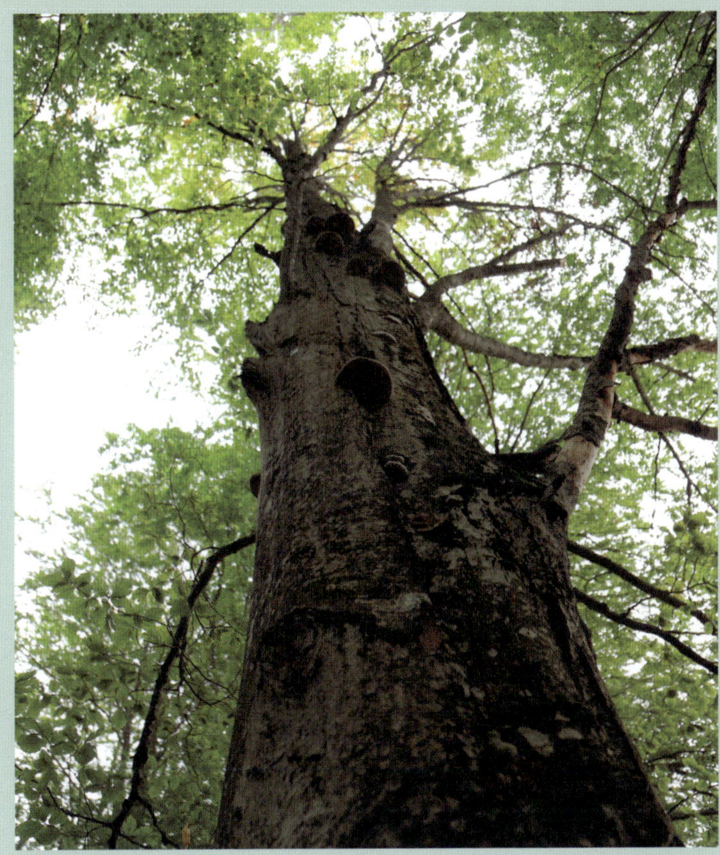

Polypores climbing a tree trunk. These bracket fungi grow in stacked, shelf-like formations and have been used in traditional medicine for millennia.

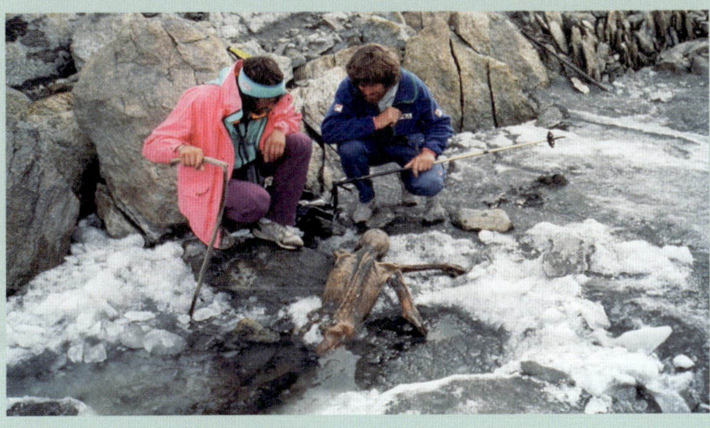

Two Swiss hikers observing the skeleton of Ötzi the Iceman, who died over 5,000 years ago on a European Alpine glacier. Ötzi was discovered with a necklace carrying Birch Polypore, an effective anti-parasitic, and True Tinder Bracket, a fire starter and medicinal mushroom.

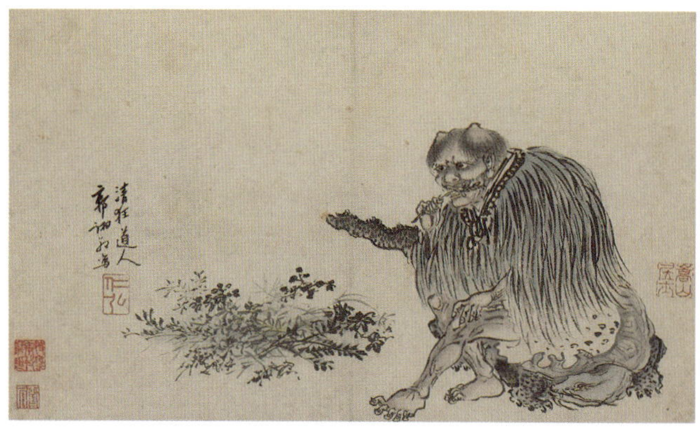

The Immortal Shen Nong Chewing a Branch, *painting by Guo Xu, 1503. A central figure in Chinese medicine and mythology, Shen Nong is revered for having tested hundreds of medicinal herbs.*

heavy metals like mercury and arsenic. They believed distillation extracted the spirit of a substance, and drinking distilled extracts would imbue or intoxicate one with its very essence. The words *sprite* and *spirit*, meaning both a strong alcoholic drink and an ephemeral being, derive from the Latin *spiritus*. This dual meaning reflects how these spirits embody both the physical substance and its intangible, elusive nature, seen in figures like Absinthe's Green Fairy or the Immortal Spirits, or *Xian*, of Chinese myth.[11]

The search for spiritual enlightenment often intertwines with mystical practices, including those of the Daoist sage King Shen Nong, who is said to have tested countless herbs for the public good. He was known as the Divine Farmer, and his *Shen Nong Ben Cao Jing* (*Materia Medica*) praises Lingzhi, claiming it "lightens the body and youthens the spirit". Lingzhi was so revered that Emperor Qin Shi Huang Di (The First Divine Emperor of Qin) was presented with this mushroom of immortality as a gift, leading to the exclusivity of all Lingzhi species for his use alone.

Legend has it that the Divine Farmer guided the emperor to the Isles of the Blessed, only accessible to those of great virtue who can find the elixir of immortality.[12] These paradisiacal islands were said to be populated by translucent immortals riding on clouds, half-human beings, and feathered dragons, lush with magical trees, jewelled fruits, and stone-like mushrooms. Enigmatic priestesses even transform into psychedelic mushrooms upon death,[13,14] and spirits renew their youth each day by eating branches of Lingzhi.[15]

Without immortal sages or elixirs, these mythical lands are cruelly fleeting. Upon the emperor's return to the mortal realm, he obsessively pursued the elixir that might grant him eternal life. Ultimately, his quest led to his early demise while he sent out virgins in a nationwide search, called for expeditions to the East China Sea, and consulted with alchemists and magicians. Some accounts claim he poisoned himself by overindulging in hazardous concoctions, and that he was buried with his Terracotta Army in a tomb said to contain underground rivers of mercury.[16] While this may be a myth, archaeologists have found evidence of high mercury levels near the emperor's tomb and in his body.[17]

In Daoist belief, the sacred Lingzhi grows where heaven and Earth meet, on misty mountain slopes and in liminal zones between worlds. The ancient medical text *Huang Di Nei Jing* (*Yellow Emperor's Classic of Medicine*) describes Lingzhi as thriving in deep mountains, nestled at the base of giant trees

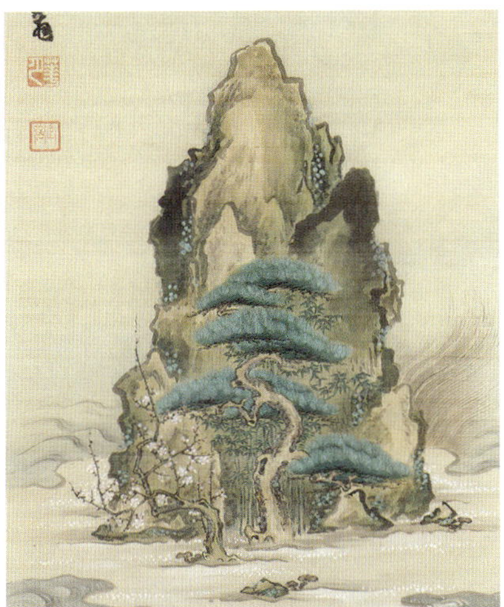

Mount Penglai, or the Isles of the Blessed – a mythical paradise where immortals reside, found in both Chinese and Japanese traditions.

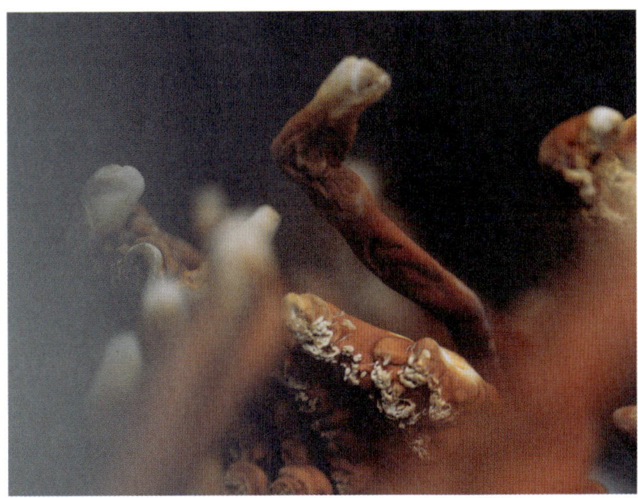

Lingzhi mushrooms, admired in Traditional Chinese Medicine, are said to take forms like dragons, birds, or human hands. Classical texts claim they induce "spirithood", enhancing vitality and spiritual well-being.

or by springs. They are said to resemble buildings, palanquins, horses, dragons, tigers, humans, or airborne birds[18] and when consumed by the spoonful, they induce "spirithood". Among the lower and intermediate varieties are the Yellow, Black, White, Purple, and Green Lingzhi, each boasting distinct medicinal properties. Yet none could surpass the sacred Red Lingzhi, associated with the blood and the soul, categorised as a "divine" herb capable of conferring several thousand years of life. More pragmatic enthusiasts take Lingzhi to support high blood pressure, elevated cholesterol levels, cardiovascular diseases, and respiratory issues.

Although Lingzhi is most valued in its wild form, growers now cultivate many species commercially, fuelling a multi-million-dollar industry, projected to reach approximately 13.6 billion USD by 2030.[19] The finest Lingzhi comes from China's Longquan district, where it is grown on native Duanwood logs, the same trees they occupy in the wild. This prized mushroom is now available in various forms, including whole Duanwood Lingzhi mushrooms and Lingzhi spore oil, which may boast a higher concentration of therapeutic sterols, triterpenes, and fatty acids.[20] These spores, released from the mushroom's pores, have electrostatic properties that cause them to "jump" and land on the upper surface of the mushroom.[21] The spores are produced in staggering quantities and form a dense layer on the mushroom's shelf, aptly described in Japanese as *kofuki-saru-no-koshikake* (powder-covered monkey's bench). These spores are harvested using meticulous techniques to preserve their delicate bioactive compounds and are typically taken orally as a supplement, either in capsule form or by using the oil directly on the skin. Today, Lingzhi is cultivated on an increasing scale, offering the promise of eternal youth to anyone willing to pay.

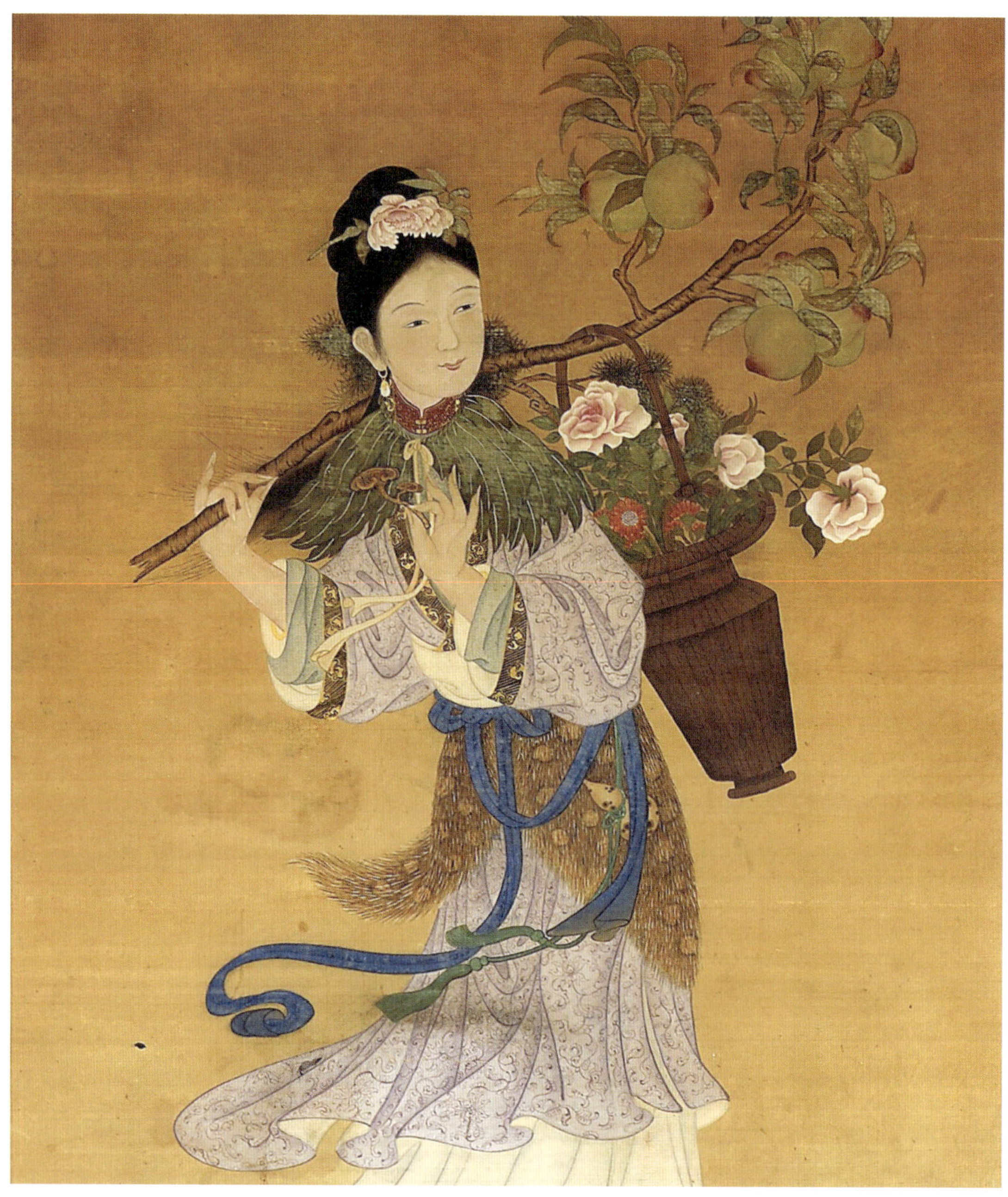

Magu, a mythical figure of longevity in Chinese and Korean cultures. Magu is credited with sharing healing herbs like Lingzhi and cannabis with the world.

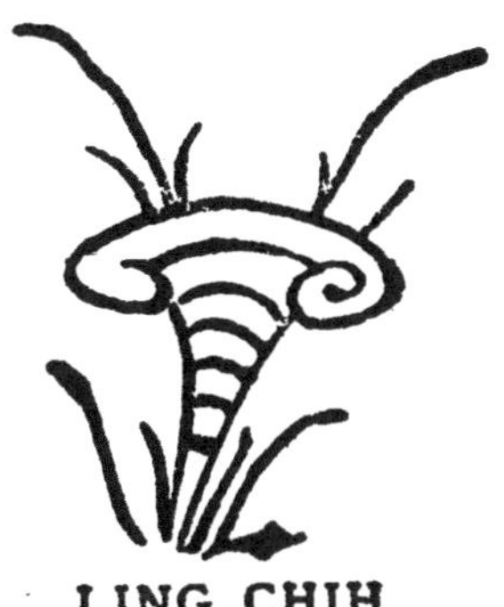

The "sacred fungus", used as an emblem of longevity.

FORAGING FOR LINGZHI IN THE V&A

Lingzhi's symbolism extends beyond its medicinal properties to its cultural significance. In Chinese art, it often represents protection for the body, mind, and spirit. Lingzhi motifs appear on silk robes worn by emperors and on the doors of Beijing's Forbidden City. Traditionally, Lingzhi was carried as a talisman to ward off evil spirits or crafted into ornate necklaces to soothe infants. To appreciate such artistry, mycologist and globally recognised Lingzhi specialist Martin Powell and I visited the Victoria and Albert Museum in London, which houses one of the most significant collections of Chinese art outside East Asia. We wandered through the Chinese Hall, where one of the most celebrated artworks depicting this mushroom can be found, a painting by Chen Hongshou (1598–1652) featuring a "fully realised" Daoist figure sitting on a cloud and holding a branch of Lingzhi.

After Martin left to teach a class, my curiosity was drawn to the vast section dedicated to wine, which detailed its significance in Chinese culture. In antiquity, Chinese wine, made from fermented rice, was esteemed for its ability to stimulate creativity and was often consumed by poets and calligraphers, including the "Eight Immortals of Wine". Many believed wine possessed medicinal properties and commonly offered it to deities and ancestors during rites of worship. The museum's collection includes extraordinary Chinese wine drinking vessels, including jade cups believed to preserve the body, as well as exquisite chalices carved with motifs of cranes and butterflies – also symbols of long life.

These motifs recall the myth of Magu, the Daoist Goddess of longevity, who is said to have created Lingzhi wine using water from the sacred Guyu Mountain. The wine, which combined fermented rice and dried Lingzhi, took 13 years to mature, ultimately granting her immortality. Artists and sculptors often depict Magu holding Lingzhi in one hand and cannabis in the other, symbolising the powerful healing alliance between these two sacred herbs. Visitors can admire a miniature sculpture of Magu with her revered herbs in the V&A's Chinese Hall.

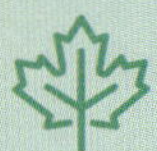

RECIPE

MAGU'S SACRED LINGZHI WINE
MARTIN POWELL

Due to its leathery texture and bittersweet taste, Lingzhi cannot be eaten directly. Instead, it is prepared as an infusion or tincture, or consumed in powdered form – encapsulated, or blended into teas, smoothies, and broths. Lingzhi contains highly active polysaccharides, particularly beta-glucans, which support immune function and gut health. The most effective way to extract these polysaccharides is with hot water, as a slow-brewed tea.

But Lingzhi also contains triterpenes, naturally bitter compounds produced for antimicrobial and insecticidal purposes. Beyond these roles, they show therapeutic potential, contributing anti-inflammatory, antioxidant, sedative, and antihypertensive effects. Lingzhi is especially rich in them, with over 130 identified. As triterpenes are water-insoluble, alcohol is needed for extraction.

During our V&A excursion, Martin explained that while hot-water extraction was the most common way of preparing Lingzhi in Traditional Chinese Medicine, it was also often used alongside other herbs in medicinal wines. Chinese herb shops still display colourful jars containing a variety of herbs and even animal parts, soaked in rice wine or grain alcohol. Martin's words and the V&A's display of Chinese medicinal wines inspired me to try making my own version of Magu's sacred Lingzhi wine. This simple process, though long, captures the essence of traditional practices, blending Lingzhi's therapeutic qualities with the rich, symbolic history of Chinese alchemy.

EQUIPMENT

- Mason jar

INGREDIENTS

- 150g/5¼oz sun-dried Lingzhi (Reishi) (*Ganoderma lucidum or lingzhi*) fruiting bodies (sliced, conks, or antlers)
- 3l/100fl oz Shaoxing rice wine (fermented from glutinous rice)
- Optional: Honey for sweetness, rose hips for added vitamin C, or any other of Magu's sacred herbs of choice.

METHOD

1. Harvest your homegrown or foraged Lingzhi mushrooms.
2. Sun-dry them cap-side up for at least 30 minutes to boost their vitamin D2 levels.
3. Place the dried Lingzhi in a sterile mason jar and cover them completely with Shaoxing rice wine.
4. Allow the brew to steep for as long as possible, ideally the full 13 years. If time is limited, let it steep for at least 3 weeks, then consume 1–2ml daily.

Note: Lingzhi mushrooms have contraindications for certain individuals, especially those with bleeding disorders, low blood pressure, or those taking medications that affect blood clotting or blood pressure. Due to lack of research, they're also generally not recommended for pregnant or breastfeeding women.

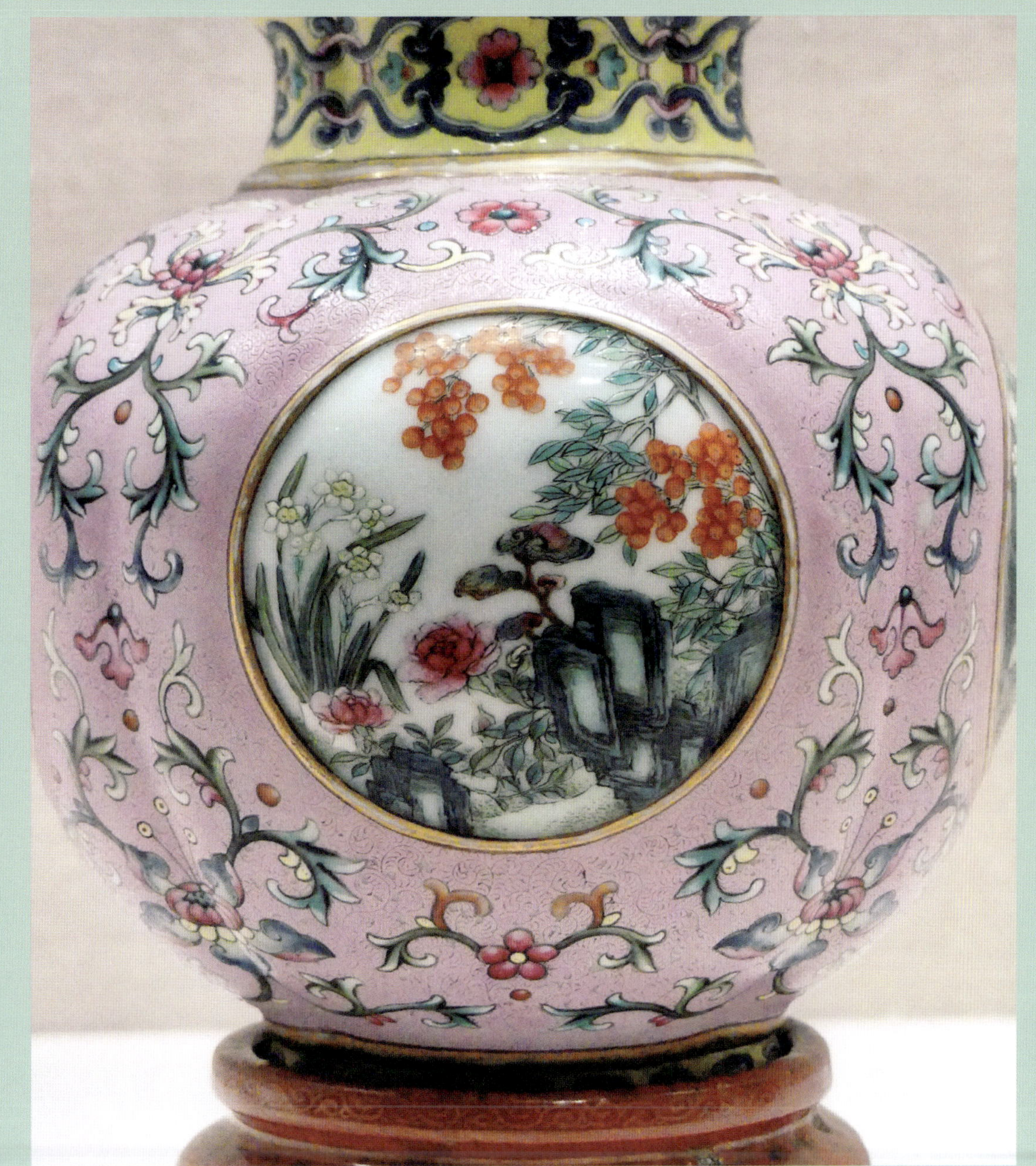

A Chinese vase at the Metropolitan Museum of Art, New York decorated with Lingzhi, a symbol of longevity and spiritual power in Chinese culture.

FUNGAL COMMUNICATION

"Mycelium is a way of life that challenges our animal imaginations."

– *Merlin Sheldrake,* Entangled Life

Humans perceive the world through a limited sensory spectrum – sights, sounds, and smells tailored to our biology. Yet countless other organisms communicate through channels we barely comprehend or cannot detect at all. From molecular signals to bioelectrical pulses, nature hums with invisible dialogues that shape ecosystems. Fortunately, technology can help us bridge these gaps and glimpse the remarkable complexity of non-human communication.

Take, for example, the phenomenon of biofluorescence. Under ultraviolet (UV) light, many seemingly mundane organisms reveal dazzling hidden colours. Snails and slugs, often overlooked in the forest understory, glow with incredible blue-green hues that echo their aquatic ancestors. Alongside dragonflies, woodlice, frogs, flowers, and fungi, these gastropods transform UV light into luminous displays, showing us a secret world of light and colour.

One unforgettable night in a mushroom fruiting chamber revealed this spectacle firsthand. Crawling on hands and knees beneath the purple glow of a UV torch, a group gathered around a vibrant Reishi mushroom. Its fruiting body shimmered with a kaleidoscope of hues: bright green, electric blue, soft pink, vivid fuchsia, and warm yellow, each shade corresponding to different growth stages. The "leading edge", or outermost rim, was dark and non-fluorescent; the sporulation surface glowed pink, active mycelial zones radiated yellow, shifting to lime-green as they aged, and mature bodies settled into a deep forest green. This biofluorescence was not universal; only Reishi *mushrooms* and Maitake *mycelium* exhibited such vivid colours. Why? Fungal fluorescence experts still don't know.

Fungi can shine through two distinct processes: bioluminescence and biofluorescence. Bioluminescence is an internal glow created by enzymatic chemical reactions that generate photons, the fungus's own lantern. Biofluorescence, on the other hand, is a response to external illumination; fungi absorb UV or other wavelengths and re-emit light at longer, visible wavelengths. I think of it as the difference between the Sun and the Moon: The Sun generates its own light, while the Moon shines by reflecting the Sun's rays.

In the UK and US, *bioluminescent* fungi are rare and faint, though certain species, such as the Honey Fungus and Candlesnuff, glow more brilliantly in North America. Yet, when equipped with UV lights, nighttime forest walks unveil an astonishing array of *biofluorescent* fungi: Russulas, *Cortinarius* sp., Sulphur Tufts, among others, explode into whites and blues. Many insects, birds, fish, and even some mammals perceive ultraviolet light naturally, advantageous adaptations that humans lack or never needed. When illuminated, chlorophyll-rich leaves shift from green to red, while pale lichens glow

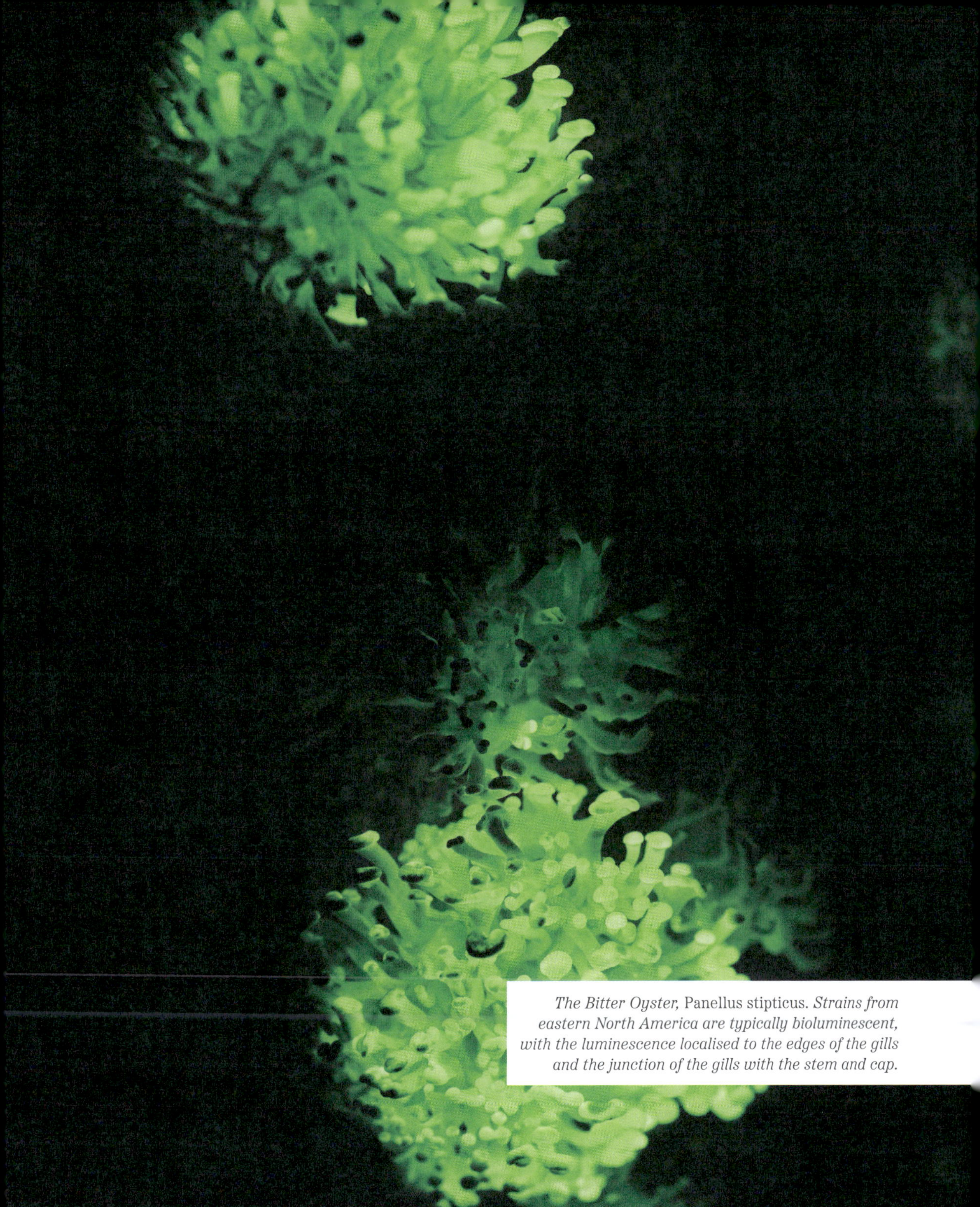

The Bitter Oyster, Panellus stipticus. *Strains from eastern North America are typically bioluminescent, with the luminescence localised to the edges of the gills and the junction of the gills with the stem and cap.*

purple and orange, and muted fungi burst into glowing gems that sprout from the forest floor and thread through decomposing logs.

Despite considerable research into fungal luminescence, fungal fluorescence remains poorly understood. Oregon-based mycologist Sidnee Ober-Singleton suggests that aerial fungi and lichens may use fluorescence as natural "suncream", protecting cells from UV damage.[22] Others speculate biofluorescence enhances visibility in dim environments, attracting spore-dispersing insects or deterring predators. Whether this light show constitutes deliberate communication or an incidental evolutionary byproduct is still debated.

Given nature's economy, it seems improbable that fungi would expend energy on meaningless signals. Instead, this glowing magic likely serves ecological or communicative functions still beyond our grasp.

MIT Technology Review explains, "As organisms living in complex relations to other life forms, fungi could not exist without communicating."[23] Though lacking brains or nervous systems, fungi continuously sense their environments and integrate this sensory data with a response. Fungi respond to tactile, chemical, optical, and electrical stimuli by altering the patterns of their electrochemical activity, suggesting a form of adaptive reaction to environmental changes. The authors explain that they "are like polyglots: they both 'speak' and understand a wide range of signals".

Within a single fungus, information spreads throughout networks of branching structures. Fungal biologist Merlin Sheldrake explains that fungi use a combination of liquid flows, chemical, and electrochemical modalities to regulate their growth and behaviour. Chemicals transmit slow and non-urgent signals, whereas electrochemical signals enable faster responses. Early studies have shown that filamentous fungi generate action potential-like signals and electrical currents at hyphal tips – the leading edges of mycelial networks – suggesting that their continuous plasma membranes, specialised septal pores, and insulating cell wall structures could support electrical signalling over long distances.[24]

"When we think of fungal networks", Merlin explains, "we often think in terms of threads or wires, but these metaphors make invisible the *space* within these fungal cells! They are tubes, and within these tubes, material moves around." [25] These flows are complex, bidirectional, and finely controlled. "We don't know exactly how they control these flows yet . . . But we're learning."[26,27]

The Kiers Lab at VU Amsterdam, run by evolutionary biologist Toby Kiers, is at the forefront of this research. Using neuroscience tools adapted to fungi, Kiers and her collaborator Professor Tom Shimizu, study electrical excitability in underground mycorrhizal networks. Moreover, their custom robotic imaging system, known as Prince, monitors the growth of 50 petri dishes simultaneously, capturing hundreds of thousands of cytoplasmic flow trajectories.[28] What they're finding is that fungi can solve problems, without a brain, through the very architecture of their networks.

When fungal networks grow, they do so in several different ways. Some of the exploratory tips grow outwards in fine lines, like scouts exploring the area. But other parts of the fungus proliferate behind this wave of exploratory tips, forming a lace-like network structure that allows the fungus to extract nutrients from its surroundings. However, it could very easily grow into a highly branched structure in such a way as to be inefficient. Therefore, it needs to balance long-distance exploration with short-distance proliferation, and it does this via simple local rules. One such rule is that they simply fuse with each other, creating the lace-like structure rather than the exploratory, wiry threads.

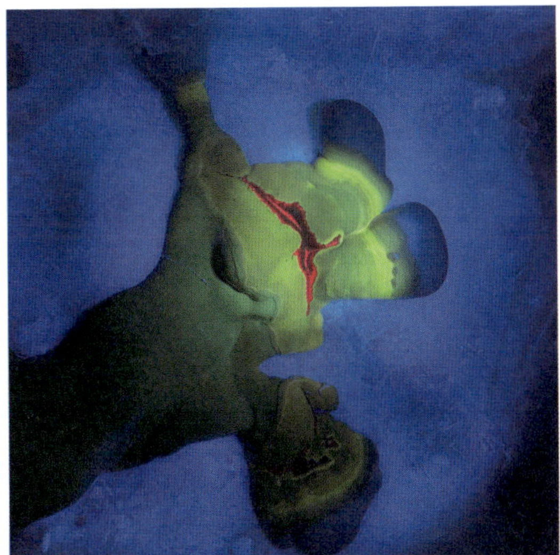

Biofluorescent Reishi, Ganoderma lucidum. *Each colour marks a different growth stage: the dark, non-fluorescent leading edge; pink sporulation surface; and bright yellow mycelial zones that shift to lime-green with age.*

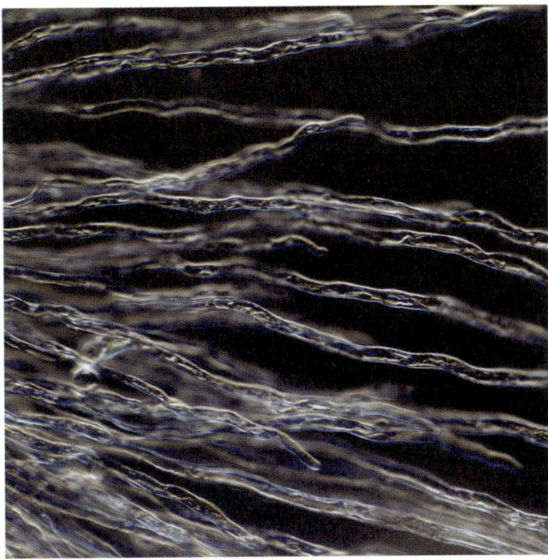

We often think of mycelial networks as microscopic threads or filaments, yet zooming in we see that they are tubes–ferrying water, nutrients, minerals, and electrochemical signals across their networks.

Merlin, who works at the Kiers Lab, explains, "Solving problems without a brain often looks like that: simple local rules that, when added up over a network in a dynamic way, multiply into statistically meaningful behaviours."

In a 2025 paper published in *Nature*, Loreto Oyarte Galvez and colleagues from the Kiers Lab offer a groundbreaking look into these dynamic mycorrhizal networks. It revealed that these networks operate as self-regulating "travelling waves" that stretch, recede, and adapt to optimise resource distribution.[29] The exploratory branches reach into new territories, prioritising future trade opportunities over immediate gains, and solving complex spatial problems via decentralised growth strategies.

Fungi do not only communicate within individual networks; they also interact with other fungi through chemical signalling and physical contact. They even use information from others to help orient themselves or to decide whether to branch, fuse, retreat, or defend.[30] Like snails emitting pheromones, or wolves scent-marking their range, fungi release signals to attract mates or negotiate territory. Others secrete mycotoxins, powerful chemicals that kill or inhibit fungal competitors, clearing space and resources. Interactions vary widely: some display cooperation, others antagonism, while many coexist with indifference. This "fungal diplomacy" influences ecosystem dynamics and mirrors social relationships in animals, albeit through biochemical channels.

Beyond the fungal kingdom, fungi "talk" to a great many other organisms – plants, insects, nematodes, and humans – via chemical cues that modulate behaviour. Mycorrhizal fungi, as we have seen, establish relationships with plant roots, boosting their immune system, drought tolerance, and even blocking

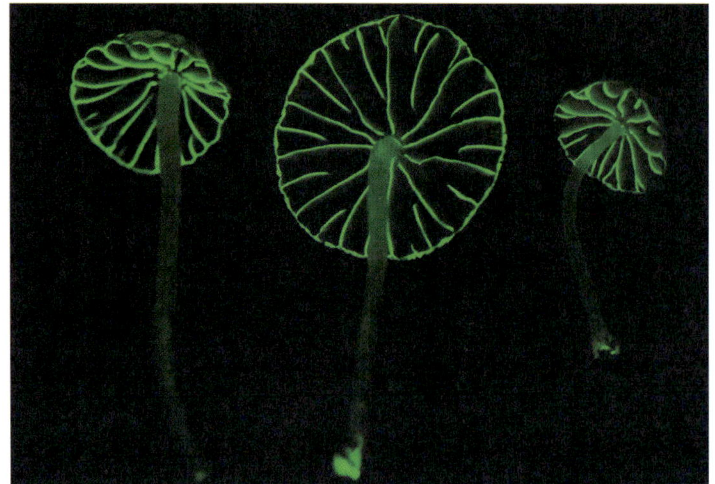

Bioluminescent Mycena globulispora *mushrooms in Veracruz, Mexico, growing on a moss-covered fallen tree near the river. Very few mushrooms can sustain bioluminescence, as it quickly depletes their metabolites. One close relative,* Mycena luxaeterna, *also known as the "Eternal Light" mushroom, is able to constantly bioluminesce.*

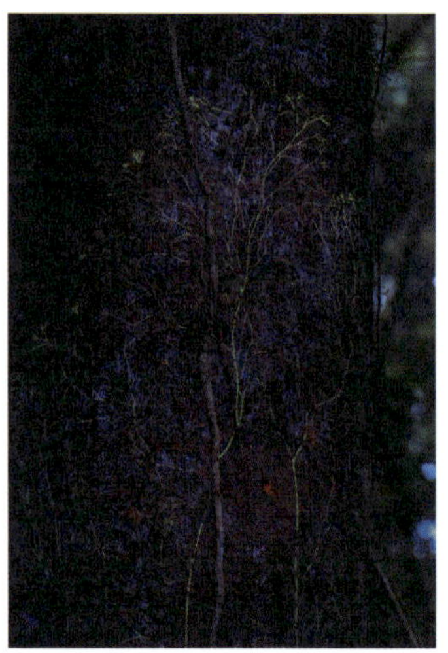

Bioluminescent Laternea pusilla *mycelium climbing a tropical hardwood tree trunk in San Jose, Costa Rica. Surprisingly,* Laternea *is a genus of fungus in the Stinkhorn family* Phallaceae.

pathogens from entering their roots.[31] Parasitic fungi can manipulate their host to their advantage, like the rust fungus *Puccinia monoica* that infects mustard plants, causing them to grow false flowers that attract pollinators, which then carry fungal spores instead of pollen.[32] Some fungi are preyed upon by nematodes and produce defensive compounds to ward them off, while others, like carnivorous Oyster mushrooms, hunt these poor creatures with toxin-filled poison darts.[33] These darts are microscopic toxocysts, lollipop-shaped structures that burst on contact, releasing a nerve gas (3-octanone) to paralyse their prey before digestion. One paper even compares fungal strategies for killing nematodes to medieval weapons (diagrams included!). And then, of course, fungal hallucinogenic compounds dazzle and distract those who eat them, human or otherwise. These are all forms of inter-kingdom communication.

In life, all organisms are presented with problems: finding food, avoiding harm, and reproducing. The organism's task is to solve them, and if they can't, they won't survive for very long. Fungi have evolved to solve very different problems to me and you. Flows of information, mycelial architectures, and decentralised decision making are some of the different ways that fungi process information to solve the problems that life throws at them. And they're good at it.

Biochemist Dr Gordon Walker notes that "fungi display network intelligence, albeit not in the way that we know it."[34] This idea aligns with the emerging field of basal cognition – *basal* meaning "foundation" or "step", from the Latin *basis*. Researchers study cognitive-like processes in organisms that lack nervous systems or brains focusing on how basic forms of perception, memory, learning, and decision-making emerge in simple life forms.

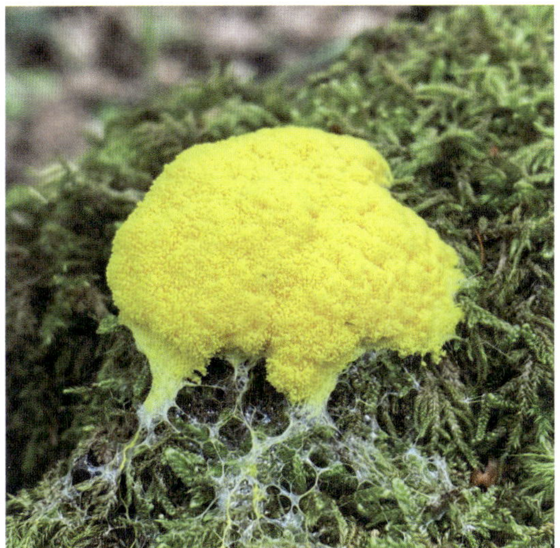

Dog Vomit Slime Mould spreading over moss on the forest floor, leaving behind an iridescent slime trail as it moves in search of nutrients.

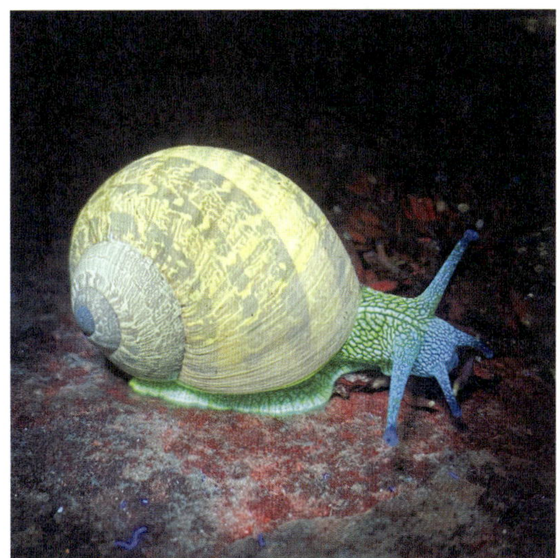

Biofluorescent Garden Snail, Cornu aspersum, *revealing an unexpected glow under ultraviolet (UV) light.*

Sheldrake explains that we marvel at the power of the human brain, and rightly so. It's powerful, complex, busy. "But we sometimes forget that brains are a relatively recent development in the story of life." The very traits that make them effective – electrical excitability, networked structures, the capacity to integrate sensory input and generate a response – are not unique. "These features appear across life, even in single-celled organisms."

Enter slime moulds. Often found on forest floors amid leaf litter, slime moulds are nobody's idea of a genius. And yet, they fascinate scientists.

The slime mould *Physarum polycephalum* forms expansive "protoplasmic networks" to forage efficiently for bacteria, fungal spores, and organic matter. When faced with a maze and a food incentive (like an oat flake), it spreads its tendrils exploring all possible paths. They mark dead ends with slime trails that discourage further growth, and reinforce promising routes, resulting in an optimised network without any central control.[35]

Researchers have expanded upon these experiments by arranging oat flakes to represent major cities on maps of real-world transport networks. Many are familiar with the 2010 experiments where *P. polycephalum* recreated efficient analogues of Tokyo's railway system,[36] and later, the national road networks in Canada,[37] Britain,[38] Portugal, and Spain.[39] In several cases, they even outperformed human-engineered design in hypothetical cost efficiency, fault tolerance, and optimal redundancy.[40]

While slime mould navigation does not make them "intelligent" per se, their emergent behaviours have caught the world by storm, and might, at least, help us improve transport networks and inspire novel biotechnologies. For example, Andy Adamatzky is the director of the Unconventional Computing

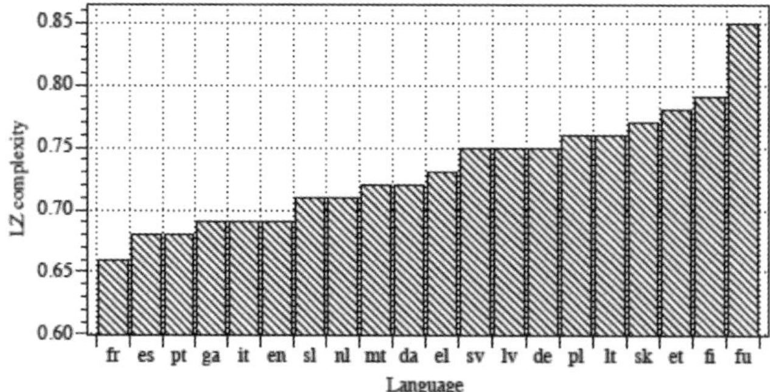

Fig. 16: Lempel-Ziv complexity of European languages (data from [58]) with average complexity of fungal ('fu') electrical activity language added.

Fungal language complexity, Mohammad Mahdi Dehshibi and Andy Adamatzky, University of the West of England. Adamatsky explores communication systems within fungal networks, revealing how fungi might "speak" through electrical signals, chemical exchanges, and complex growth patterns.

Laboratory at the University of the West of England, Bristol, and explores "biocomputing" with slime moulds.[41] His team has shown that slime moulds can behave like Boolean logic gates – responding to stimuli such as touch, chemicals, heat, and light by opening or closing electrical pathways. These responses produce simple binary outputs (yes/no or 1/0), suggesting that living networks could one day become components in bio-electronic devices.

In fact, Adamatzky has already developed several fungal devices, such as mycelial wearables, load detectors,[42] and sensing skins, [43] along with components for fungal computers – capacitors, memristors, and even reservoir computer prototypes. Basal cognition researchers imagine "wetware" machines – living, self-growing systems that respond to stimuli – offering potential breakthroughs in medicine, agriculture, art, and environmental monitoring.[44] The USDA (United States Department of Agriculture) has even funded research into fungal biohybrid robots, [45] developing a model that uses mycelial voltage spikes to guide locomotion. By stimulating the mycelia with UV light, the trajectories of their robots can be modified, enabling dynamic, real-time responses to environmental conditions.

Integrating living materials into electrical systems allows researchers to combine biology's adaptability and complexity with engineering's precision and control. Living tissues can grow, self-organise, regenerate, and respond in real-time to environmental changes – traits often hard or impossible to replicate synthetically. Furthermore, living systems are energy-efficient, operating at ambient conditions without high power needs.

But unlike inert metals or silicon, these organisms have agency. As basal cognition researcher Michael Levin explains, fungi and slime moulds "have billions of years of evolution behind them; they have goals, they have preferences, and they are not just going to sit where you put them."[46] Slime moulds escape petri dishes, mycelia refuse to cooperate, agar gets contaminated, and sometimes things just don't grow. Working with biology demands patience, humility, and a certain degree of respect for these primitive lifeforms.

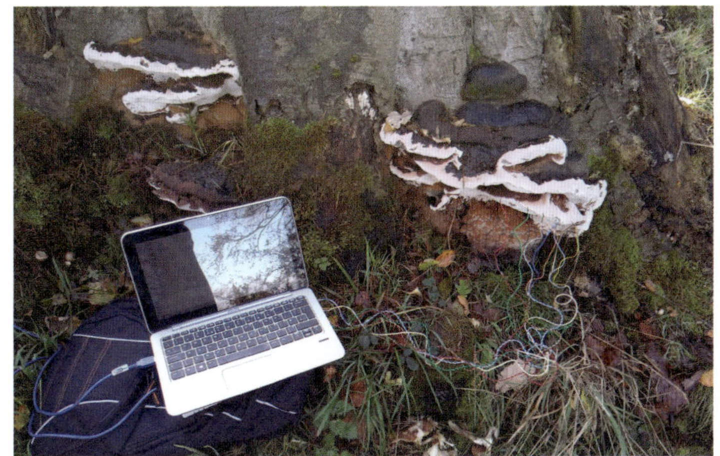

Adamatzky's computer plugged into a mushroom. By attaching electrodes, he measures fungi's electrical signals, exploring how they may process information and communicate through bioelectric impulses.

Despite the enticing talk of fungal computers and robots, Adamatzky avoids calling fungi "intelligent". "Intelligence", he notes, "does not have a formal definition, so I prefer not to use this word."[47] Instead, he sidesteps labels, focusing on traits often considered uniquely human (like problem-solving and complex language) probing traditional notions of intelligence, just without saying so explicitly.[48]

His 2022 study, *"Language of Fungi Derived from Their Electrical Spiking Activity",* attracted international interest (and much scepticism) for its bold interpretation of fungal communication. [49] His team recorded and analysed the electrical spiking patterns of four species: Ghost fungi (*Omphalotus nidiformis*), Enoki (*Flammulina velutipes*), Splitgills (*Schizophyllum commune*), and Caterpillar fungi (*Cordyceps militaris*). Each generates species-specific electrical spikes within their mycelium networks, which appear to serve as a form of communication and information processing. By categorising these spikes into "words", Adamatzky's team is beginning to decode a potential fungal "language". They found that the fungal lexicon can contain up to 50 "words", though the core vocabulary of the most frequently used words typically ranges between 15 and 20.

Adamatzky explains, "While it's plausible that mushrooms' electrical activity carries information, proving it remains difficult. The key question is whether these signals are simply reactions to stimuli or whether they encode meaningful data." While definitive proof is lacking, circumstantial evidence from plant electrophysiology and lab experiments continue to offer promising clues.

Imagine a future where we interface with fungi! [50] Where we tap into their natural communication networks and converse with them, much like artist Helene Steiner did with plants in Microsoft's *Project Florence*. [51] What would you say to a fungus? And what might it say back?

As researchers decode the electrical spiking patterns of fungi, they're revealing unexpected forms of communication and problem-solving that push us to reconsider the nature of cognition itself. Could intelligence lie beyond brains and neurons? These ancient networks hint at forms of computation and creativity embedded in living systems. As Michael Levin puts it, "There is no indivisible diamond of intelligence."

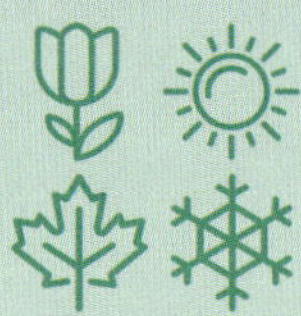

ACTIVITY

BIOELECTRIC SLIME MOULD CIRCUITS

ANDY ADAMATZKY

We will create a simple biohybrid circuit using slime mould, electrodes, and a multimeter. By placing oat flakes as food to encourage slime mould growth between two electrodes, we will harness the slime mould's natural (albeit weak) electrical conductivity. By applying environmental stimuli like light and heat, we can observe how the slime mould responds by altering its electrical activity. These changes will affect the amp's meter reading, demonstrating how living organisms can interface with electronic devices. This hands-on experiment explores concepts of bioelectronics, living sensors, and unconventional computing.

INGREDIENTS

- Slime mould culture (*Physarum polycephalum*) (lab sourced or wild-collected)
- ~25 oat flakes
- 2g agar powder (to prepare ~5 plates)
- 100ml/3¼fl oz/½ cup of distilled water

EQUIPMENT

- 3V battery or low-voltage DC power supply
- 4 wires with alligator clips
- Multimeter (to measure voltage/current)
- Digital scale (accurate to 0.1g)
- Microwave-safe beaker or jar
- Microwave
- Measuring jug
- Heat-resistant gloves
- 5 Petri dishes (or shallow plastic containers)
- Tweezers
- Timer or stopwatch
- Heat source (warm water bath or low-wattage heat lamp)
- Light source (lamp or torch)
- Notebook for observations

METHOD

PREPARE GROWTH MEDIUM (WATER AGAR)

1. Mix 2g agar into 98ml/3¼fl oz/½ cup of the water.
2. Microwave in short bursts, swirling between each wearing heat-resistant gloves.
3. Repeat until the mixture comes to a rolling boil and appears clear (no powder or cloudiness). Careful not to let it overflow.
4. After cooling slightly (~20 minutes), pour into Petri dishes to ~0.5cm depth.
5. Place the lids on top, slightly ajar to prevent condensation.
6. Let the agar solidify at room temperature (approximately 30–60 minutes).

INOCULATE SLIME MOULD

1. On each plate, place 4–6 sterile oat flakes in a pile.
2. Position a piece of slime mould roughly 2cm away and allow it to grow towards the oats.
3. Incubate (in the dark with high humidity) for several hours to days until it bridges the gap.

SETUP CIRCUIT

1. Connect the wires to the battery/power supply and include the multimeter in the series.
2. Touch the ends of the wires to either side of the slime mould's pathway. Don't touch the agar.
3. Record baseline voltage and current (before stimulation).

APPLY ENVIRONMENTAL STIMULI

1. Light: Shine a lamp or torch onto one side.
2. Heat: Gently warm one side using a heat lamp or warm water bath.
3. Observe slime mould behaviour: growth direction, tube thickening, or withdrawal.

MEASURE ELECTRICAL RESPONSES

1. Use the multimeter to monitor voltage/current changes during stimuli application.
2. Log stimulus type, timing, intensity, and corresponding electrical change.

REPEAT & COMPARE

1. Repeat stimuli with different intensities and durations.
2. Test control cases (no stimuli).
3. Compare results to see if slime mould adjusts conductivity or signal patterns.

NOTES & TIPS

- Slime mould grows slowly, so allow hours to days for network formation.
- Use a low-voltage power supply to avoid harming the slime mould.
- Keep the Petri dish moist but avoid excess water.

Alternatively, you could set up a simple experiment with slime mould and oats on water agar. Add salt or chilli to test chemotaxis (its response to chemical gradients) or introduce physical barriers to observe its mechanoception (how it senses and responds to touch or pressure).

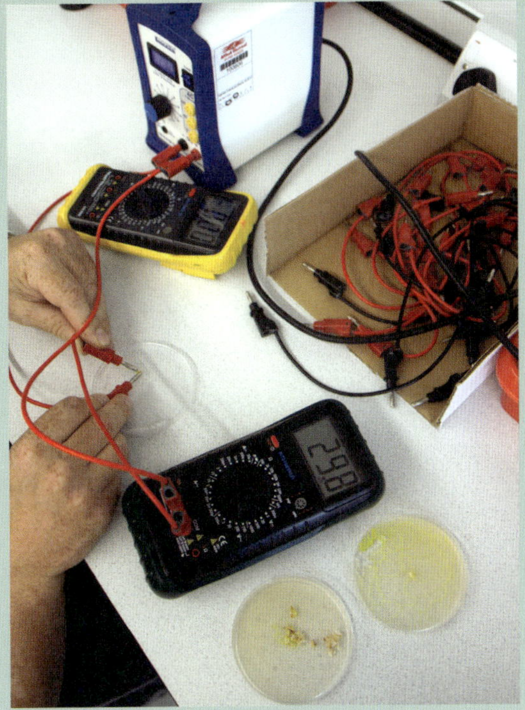

Testing slime moulds' electrical conductivity by plugging it into a series circuit.

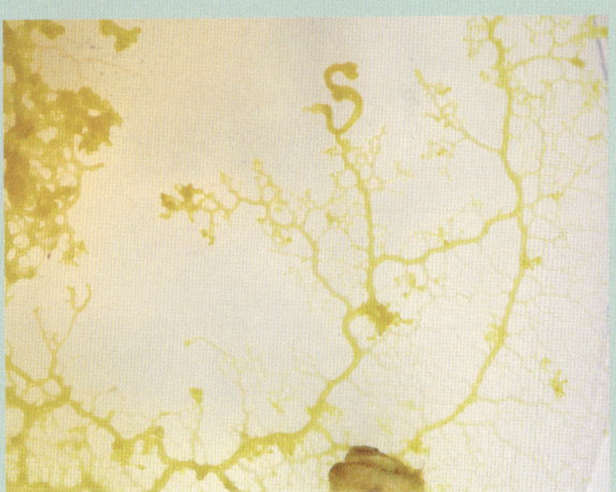

Slime Mould in a Petri dish. Slime Moulds can detect mechanical pressure, chemical cues, light, gravity, temperature, and texture, all of which help them move and grow towards optimal conditions.

MICRODOSING: THE CAP OF LIBERTY

Important legal disclaimer: *This story and the following guide are for educational and identification purposes only. Possession or consumption of psilocybin mushrooms is illegal in many countries and states. Do not collect or consume them without understanding your local laws.*

Britain's first well-documented encounter with the mind-altering powers of wild mushrooms happened by accident. On the morning of 3 October 1799, a man remembered only as "J.S." gathered mushrooms in London's Green Park and served them to his wife and four children.[52] Within an hour the family were in disarray: the youngest, eight-year-old Edward, burst into fits of laughter before collapsing into discomfort and confusion, while the rest of the household soon reported dizziness, distorted vision, and overwhelming unease.

As luck would have it, the physician Everard Brande was nearby and treated the family with the standard medicines of the day, including tartar emetic and castor oil. By late afternoon their alarming symptoms had faded. Brande sent specimens to notable botanists for study, but at the time no one recognised them as hallucinogenic. Today, the culprit is understood to have been Liberty Caps, *Psilocybe semilanceata*, the small, conical "magic mushrooms" that still fruit across Britain's fields and pastures each autumn.

What's striking is that before the 19th century, Liberty Caps were not connected with magic at all, but with freedom.[53] Their name recalls the *pileus*, the soft felt cap given to freed slaves in the Roman Republic, later worn as a symbol of liberty by revolutionaries in France and America. The cap appeared on medals, satirical caricatures, and banners as shorthand for emancipation and defiance. Only much later did its meaning shift from political freedom to psychological liberation.

Brande's report remained a curiosity for decades, but the Liberty Cap itself wasn't definitively identified until 1958.[54] That year, Gordon and Valentina Wasson returned from Mexico, where they had met the curandera (healer) María Sabina, who introduced them to the ceremonial use of psilocybin mushrooms.[55] The Wassons' widely publicised account reframed these fungi not as hazards of the English hedgerow but as keys to visionary states. The mushrooms gathered in Green Park in 1799 and the ones used in Oaxaca belonged to the same genus: Psilocybe, now known to encompass over 200 species worldwide.

Across cultures, names for these fungi reflect their qualities and habitats. In Brazil they are called "blue mushrooms," for the vivid staining reaction that follows a bruise. In Mexico they are revered as *los niños santos* – "the sacred children." In China they are known as "laughing mushrooms," while

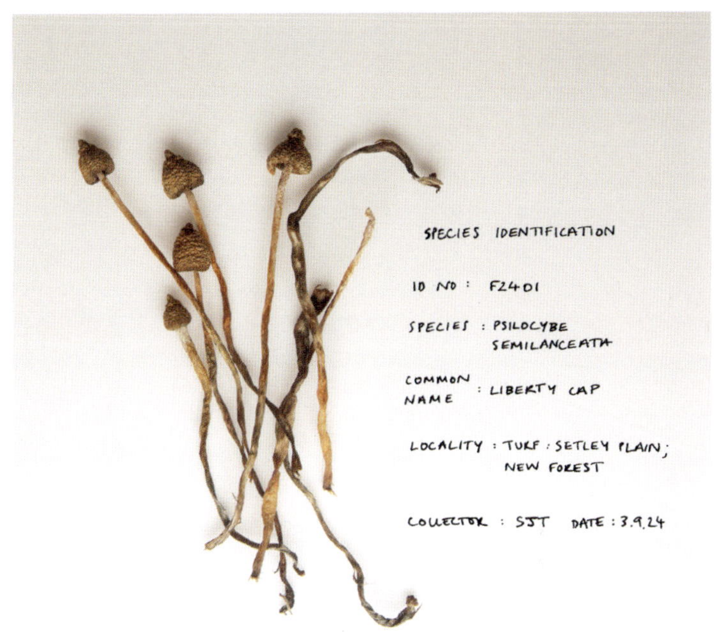

The Liberty Cap, Psilocybe semilanceata, *is easily recognised by its distinctive conical cap and potent psychoactive properties. One of the most widespread psilocybin-containing mushrooms in nature, it grows abundantly in the UK – where it has become a symbol of rebellion and cognitive freedom. In the United States, however, it is found almost exclusively along the West Coast in northern California, with only rare occurrences in Maine and also in eastern Canada.*

in Thailand their earthy name, *hed keequai*, translates as "the mushrooms that grow after the water buffalo defecates."

All Psilocybe species contain psilocybin, which the body converts into psilocin upon ingestion. Psilocin closely resembles serotonin, one of the brain's key neurotransmitters, and binds to the same receptors, particularly the 5-HT2A receptor associated with perception, imagination, and learning.[56] This simple substitution is enough to alter the brain's chemistry in profound ways: collapsing habitual patterns, amplifying sensory input, distorting time, and prompting states of deep reflection or transcendence.

Liberty Caps are unusual within the Psilocybe family because, alongside psilocybin and psilocin, they contain high levels of baeocystin, another tryptamine alkaloid whose effects remain largely mysterious. We know it interacts with serotonin receptors, but its role in shaping the psychedelic experience is unclear. Mycologist Paul Stamets has described taking 10mg of pure baeocystin and simply feeling "different and good." For now, this is little more than a clue that much more research is needed.

Laboratory studies of pure psilocin have begun to reveal how it interacts with the Default Mode Network (DMN), a web of brain regions that governs self-reflection, memory, and the stories we tell ourselves about who we are. Under psilocybin, the DMN temporarily quiets, allowing the brain to forge new connections across previously segregated areas.[57] Psychologists often liken this to shaking a snow globe: entrenched tracks of thought give way to fresh patterns as the flakes settle in new

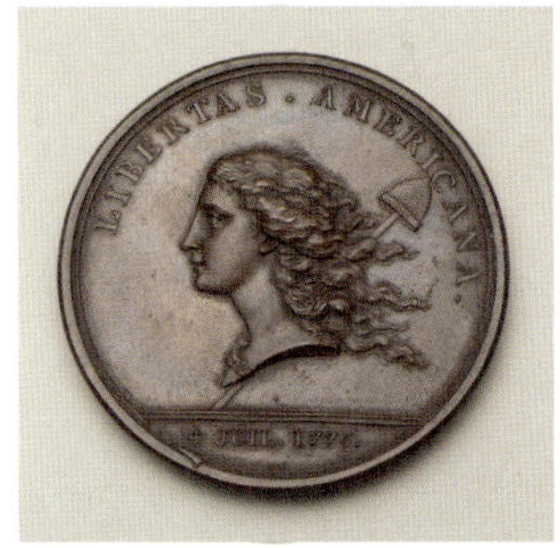

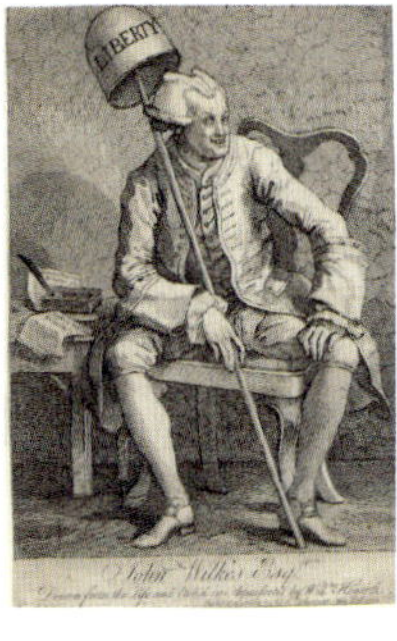

Benjamin Franklin's commemorative medal "LIBERTAS AMERICANA," 1782. William Hogarth's 1763 caricature of John Wilkes with a Liberty Cap on the end of a pole as a sign of defiance and rebellion.

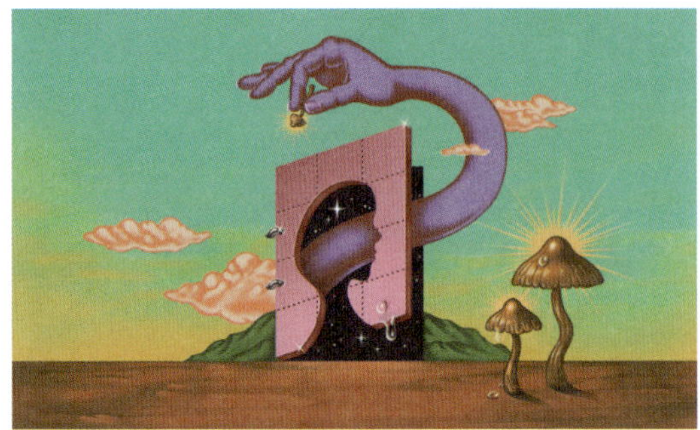

Microdosing *illustration by River Cousin*

configurations. Neuroimaging confirms this "enhanced global connectivity," showing how psilocybin briefly frees the brain from its usual constraints.

This neurological reset is what makes psilocybin promising for conditions marked by rigid mental loops, such as depression, OCD, PTSD, addiction, anorexia, or end-of-life anxiety. Clinical trials at Johns Hopkins University,[58] Imperial College London,[59,60] and NYU[61] have consistently shown that a single guided session can produce rapid and lasting improvements in mood, perspective, and behaviour. The US Food and Drug Administration (FDA) has designated psilocybin a "Breakthrough Therapy," expediting its development for treatment-resistant depression.[62] Since 2023, psychiatrists in Australia have been able to prescribe it; in the US, Oregon and Colorado now permit its use in licensed centres, with other countries cautiously exploring similar pathways.[63]

While clinical research focuses on controlled doses, underground culture has long explored psilocybin in two very different ways: the "heroic dose" and the microdose. The former, around five to ten dried grams, plunges users into overwhelming experiences often described as ego-dissolving or mystical. Microdoses, in contrast, are roughly a tenth of that – sub-perceptual yet still physiologically active. Users claim benefits ranging from enhanced mood, focus, and creativity to reduced anxiety and menopausal symptoms. Though some scientists argue many of these effects may be placebo,[64] anecdotal enthusiasm has fuelled widespread adoption, particularly in Silicon Valley. Steve Jobs, Doug Engelbart, and a particularly vocal engineer have been linked to the practice.[65,66] A popular version, the "Stamets Stack," combines psilocybin with Lion's Mane mushroom and niacin to promote neurogenesis and circulation.

Despite its popularity, rigorous research on microdosing is still scarce, hampered by regulatory hurdles. As neuropsychopharmacologist David Nutt points out, current laws require researchers to treat a microdose with the same security protocols as a full psychedelic dose, making long-term trials prohibitively expensive and logistically difficult.[67] For now, much of what we know about microdosing comes from citizen science, surveys, and self-reports rather than controlled experiments.

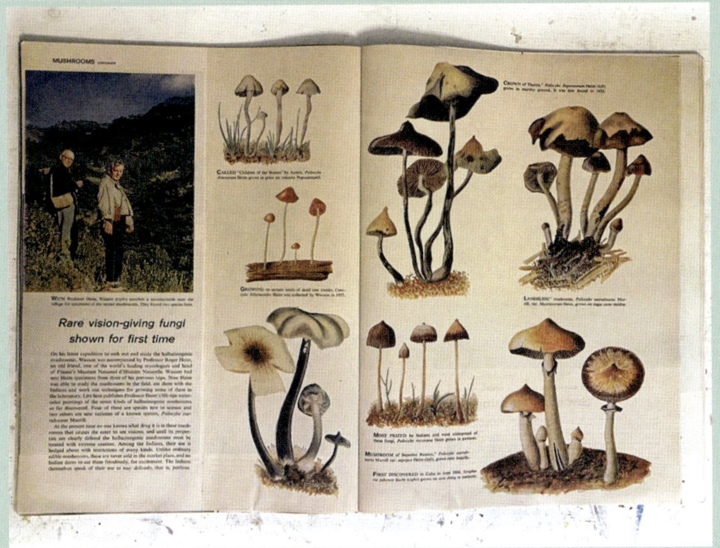
MUSHROOMS

Rare vision-giving fungi shown for first time

Seeking the Magic Mushroom *(1957): A long-form* Life *magazine feature chronicling Gordon and Valentina Wasson's trip to Oaxaca, Mexico, where they met the* curandera *(healer) María Sabina and took part in a "magic mushroom" ceremony. Although they had promised to keep the experience private, the article's publication marked the moment psychedelic mushrooms were first introduced to the United States – and, inadvertently, to the wider world.*

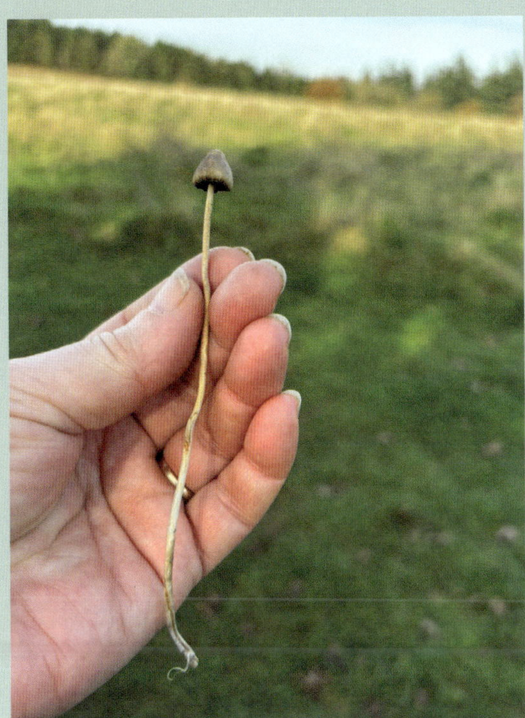

Foraging for Liberty Caps in the wild. These mushrooms are saprotrophs, feeding on decaying grass, and are commonly found in meadows and pastures.

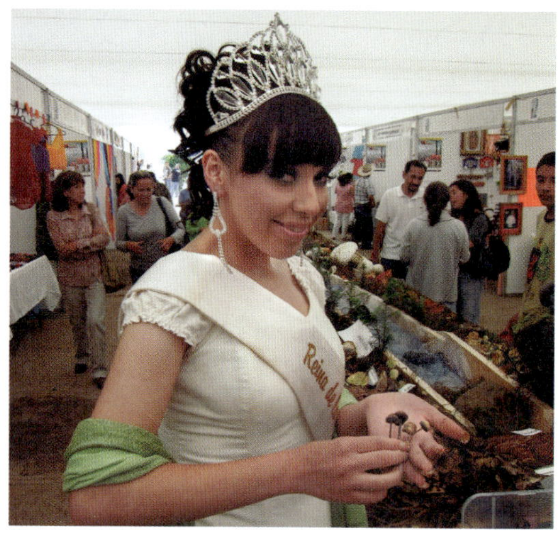

Mexico is home to one of the richest diversities of Psilocybe *species in the world, with around 50–60 documented species. Many of these mushrooms, including* Psilocybe mexicana *and* Psilocybe caerulescens, *have been used for centuries in traditional ceremonies in regions such as Oaxaca and Veracruz. Here, the Queen of the Senguio Fungus Fair holds a native* P. caerulescens *species.*

Meanwhile, the legal status of psilocybin mushrooms remains fraught. In the UK, they have been Class A drugs since 2005, carrying the harshest penalties despite their relatively low physical risks. Before this ban, Liberty Caps were openly sold in markets and at raves, where they became entwined with the countercultural ideals of the 1980s and '90s – blending psychedelia, environmentalism, and cognitive liberty. In the US, cities like Denver, Oakland, San Francisco, and Washington D.C. have decriminalised possession, though psilocybin remains federally illegal. Around the world, laws are slowly shifting as medical evidence accumulates, but progress is uneven and contested.

Beyond legality, foraging itself has become a quiet act of resistance. Seeking Liberty Caps on misty hillsides each autumn is, for some, not only a way of sourcing medicine but also an assertion of independence and connection to land. Open-source tools like the Magic Mushroom App and online databases curated by figures such as Alan Rockefeller have made the locations and identification of Psilocybe species more accessible than ever. Rockefeller has mapped thousands of finds but, mindful of conservation, withholds exact coordinates for the largest patches. For him, these mushrooms are the only medicinal fungi that "really, definitely work."[68]

From Green Park in 1799 to the therapeutic clinics of the 21st century, Liberty Caps have travelled a remarkable path: from accidental poisonings to symbols of liberty, from underground gatherings to mainstream medicine. They have shaped not only individual states of consciousness but also broader cultural movements, bridging science and spirituality, politics and ecology.

And yet, their story is still being sown. With wild numbers dwindling in many locations, radical mycologists and passionate foragers have begun to cultivate Liberty Caps in inventive ways, practising "guerrilla mushrooming" to ensure they endure for future generations. One underground cultivator described producing three litres of Liberty Cap liquid in a jar of honey-water, then hiking into the hills to release a living shower of fresh mycelium into the wind: a quiet act of resistance, a gift to the land, and a way of ensuring that Britain's most unassuming psychedelic continues to grow wild.

ACTIVITY

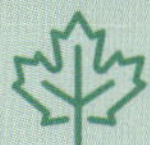

LIBERTY CAP SPECIES ID & SPORE MICROSCOPY

In the US, UK, and many European countries, it is legal to buy and possess magic mushroom spores because they do not contain psilocybin or psilocin – the compounds largely responsible for the mushroom's psychoactive effects. These substances only develop after the spores germinate and form mycelium. At that point, under most drug laws, you've crossed into illegal territory.

So, this activity invites you to meet Liberty Caps in their natural habitat and later, in their dormant form as spores. Informed by the radical mycologist Alan Rockefeller, we identify, photograph, and – without harvesting – collect spores for closer observation under a microscope.

PART 1: HOW TO IDENTIFY LIBERTY CAPS

1. IDENTIFY & FIND

- Common Names: Liberty Cap, Magic Mushroom, Shroom
- Scientific Name: *Psilocybe semilanceata*
- Season: Late September to December in temperate climates (peak in October).
- Conditions: After consistent rainfall and cool temperatures (10–15°C/50–59°F). Early morning is best.
- Regions: Common in Europe, parts of North America, and the Pacific Northwest.
- Habitat: Unfertilised grasslands, fields, moors, and animal-grazed meadows.
- Soil: Damp, but not waterlogged.
- Elevation: Low to moderate. Often on slopes or countryside hills.
- Ecological Role: Saprotrophic.
- Food Source: Decaying organic matter, predominantly dead grass roots.
- Frequency: Common.

ID CHECKLIST

Possible Lookalikes:

- Some Mottlegills, *Panaeolus* spp., can resemble Liberty Caps, but none display both a pronounced umbo (nipple) and a distinctly curved or wavy stem.
- Mature specimens of Grassland Bonnets, *Mycena* spp., may also appear similar, but their striated caps (with fine radial lines) are usually a clear distinguishing feature.[69] Also, *Mycena* mushrooms produce white spore prints, whereas Liberty Caps have dark, almost black spore prints so you can quickly find out if you've got a *Mycena* instead.

Scan for Alan Rockefeller's phenomenal compendium of global Psilocybe *species.*

FEATURE	DESCRIPTION
Cap	Conical to bell-shaped, often with a distinct nipple (umbo) on top. Darker to black bottom edge, which tucks under.
Gills	Mottled. Dark grey to purple-brown with whitish edges.
Stem	Long, thin, off white to brown, often curves and is rarely straight.
Spores	Dark purple-brown, elliptical to ovoid in shape, and typically measure around 10–14 × 6–8 microns.
Colour (wet)	Tan to light brown, hygrophanous (changes when drying).
Colour (dry)	Pale beige or straw-coloured.
Size	Cap: 0.5–2cm across; Stem: 4-10cm long.
Bruising	May turn blue or bluish-green, especially on stem base.
Smell	Slightly earthy, possibly flour-like – but not particularly distinctive.
Touch	Cap is viscid (slippery) when wet. Stem is tough and elastic; it can bend without snapping.

2. DOCUMENT

- Take multiple photos of the following:
  - In habitat (showing surrounding environment)
  - Underside (showing gills)
  - Side profile of cap and stem
- Use a ruler or coin for scale.
- Record GPS location, date, weather conditions, and growth pattern (single or clustered).
- Optional: Upload to an online database such as iNaturalist or Mushroom Observer.

3. COLLECT SPORES

Do **not** harvest the mushroom. Instead, find a mature specimen and gently tap or flick the cap with your finger to release the spores onto a small sheet of foil held beneath. If you have a small pen knife or something sharp, you could also lightly scrape the gills or upper stem to dislodge spores and keep them in the foil.

Carefully fold the foil to protect and contain the spores for later ID.

PART 2: SPORE MICROSCOPY

EQUIPMENT

- Sterile needle or tweezers
- Compound microscope (400x or higher)
- Glass slides and cover slips
- Pipette

INGREDIENTS

- Spores
- A drop of water
- Optional: Stain (Melzer's reagent for clearer visibility)

METHOD

1. Add a drop of water on a glass slide.
2. Drag a needle across the foil to collect spores, then gently touch the top of the needle onto the water droplet and the spores immediately separate out into the water.
3. Cover with a slip.
4. Examine at various magnifications.

WHAT TO LOOK FOR

- Shape: Elliptical to oblong
- Size: Length: ~10–15μm; Width: ~5-7μm
- Colour: Purple-brown
- Surface: Wrinkled and warty

WHAT TO DO

- Document: Take notes, draw, or photograph what you see, and compare with spore images from field guides or academic mycology references.
- Reflect: Though ungerminated, these spores hold the latent potential to transform consciousness. Bound by law and culture, they nonetheless carry the blueprint for cognitive liberty and therapeutic insight.

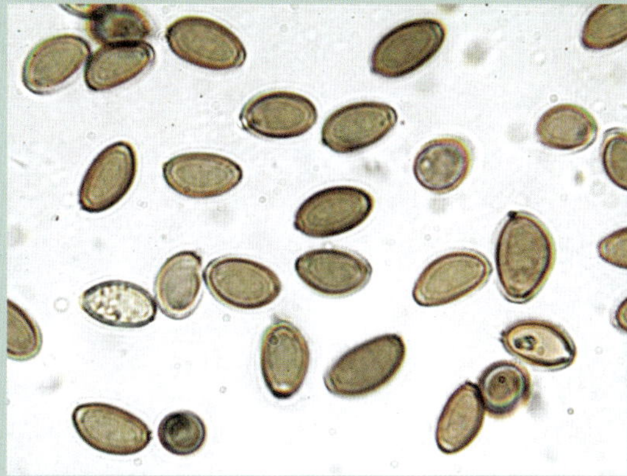

Liberty Cap, Psilocybe semilanceata, *spores.*

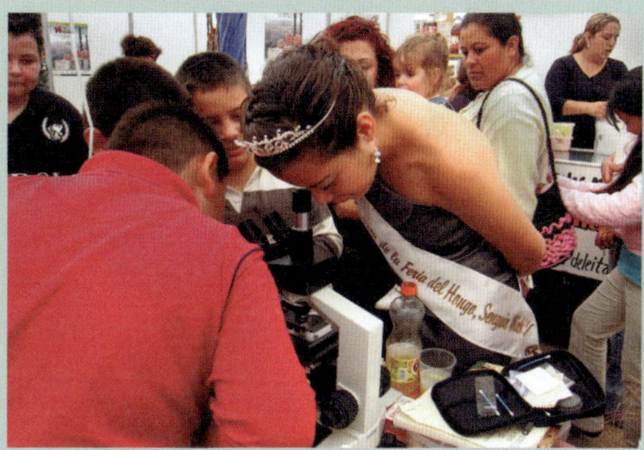

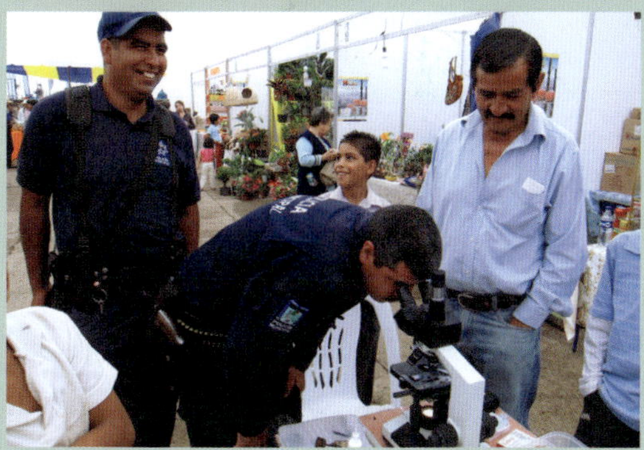

Though psilocybin-containing mushrooms remain illegal in Mexico outside regulated contexts, here, Psilocybe caerulescens *are on display at the Senguio Fungus Fair and looked at by several kids, police officers, and the Fair's Princess.*

MACRODOSING: ARCHITECTURES OF IMMORTALITY

"I assume that psychedelics somehow change our channel from the evolutionarily important channel giving traffic, weather, and stock market reports to the one playing classical music of an alien civilization."
– Terrence McKenna[70]

Richard Millar, a scholar at Northwestern University, suggests that "the earliest major use of psychotropic substances was likely in the context of religion." He even proposes that these substances may have played a pivotal role in the very genesis of religion.

The word "psychedelic" comes from the Greek *psyche* (mind or soul) and *delia* (to reveal), expressing their capacity to unveil hidden dimensions of consciousness. Large doses can trigger powerful mystical states, often described as encounters with the divine, marked by feelings of awe, bliss, and unity. Similarly, the term entheogen, coined by ethnobotanist Carl Ruck, means "generating the divine within". The Entheogenic Theory posits that many of the world's major religions were shaped by psychedelic substances. Terence McKenna even went further, proposing in his "Stoned Ape Theory" that early human consciousness evolved through symbiosis with psilocybin mushrooms found in the dung of grazing animals in ancient Africa.[71]

Psychedelic plants and fungi grow widely in nature and would have been easily accessible to early cultures. Evidence suggests psychotropic use dates back at least to 7000 BCE.[72] In ancient India, the *soma* described in Vedic texts is said to have been a psychoactive fungus.[73] Sufi mystics used Syrian rue,[74] Siberian communities consume the Fly Agaric, and Australian tribal elders ingested *pituri* to enter altered states.[75] Pre-Incan civilizations revered the mescaline-containing San Pedro cactus; Amazonian tribes still brew ayahuasca, a DMT-rich tea; and the Maya and Aztecs ritualised psilocybin mushrooms, calling them *teonanácatl* or "divine mushroom". Cannabis-infused bhang remains common in India, and Zulu warriors may have used hallucinogenic fungi during warfare and rites of passage.[76] Some even speculate that the Biblical manna[77] and the wine of early Christian sacraments contained psychedelic compounds.[78]

Psychedelic experiences often demand expression. It's as if this "seizure by the tremendum"[79] propels people to shape matter – stone, wood, pigment – into artefacts that convey visions of divine or

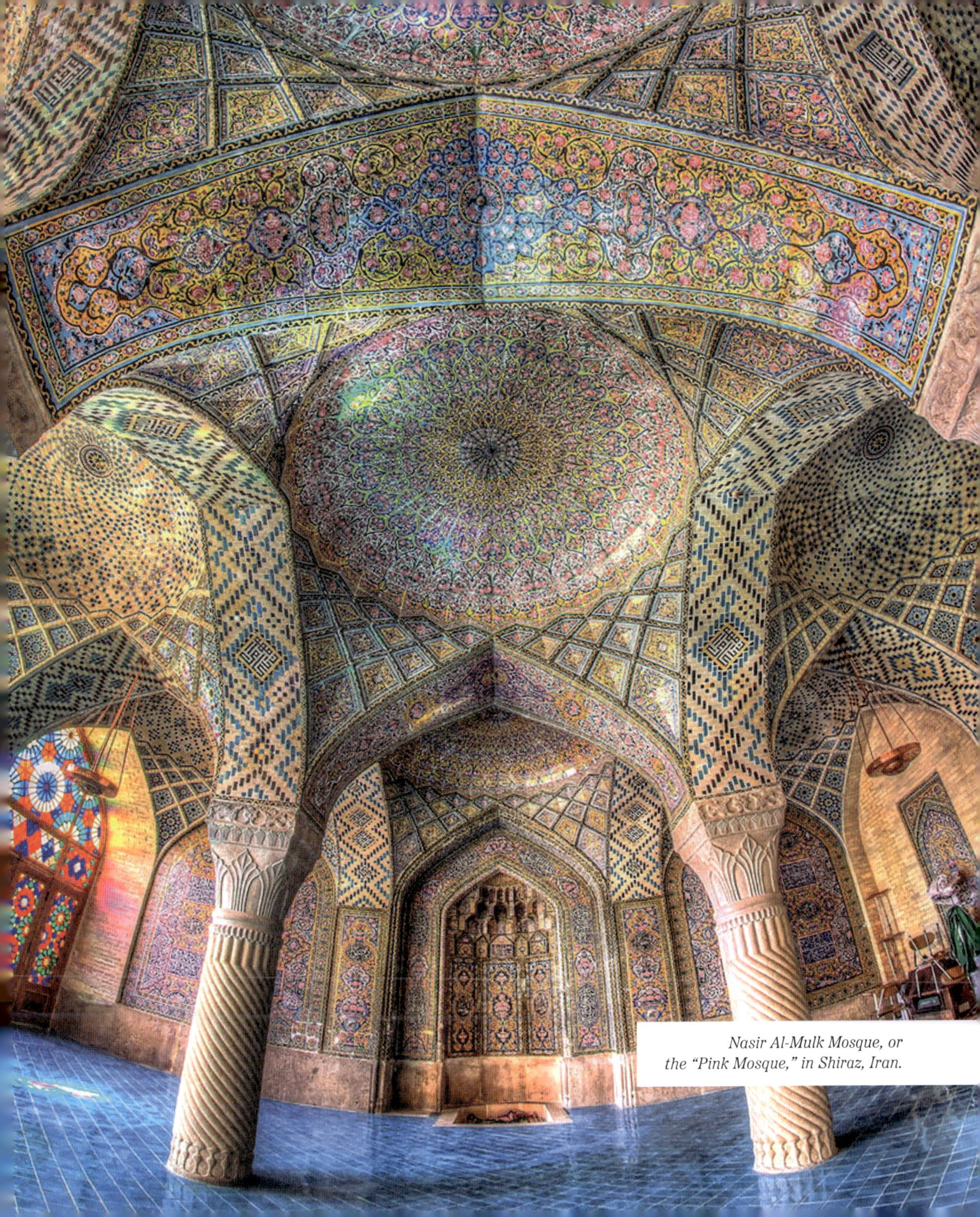

Nasir Al-Mulk Mosque, or the "Pink Mosque," in Shiraz, Iran.

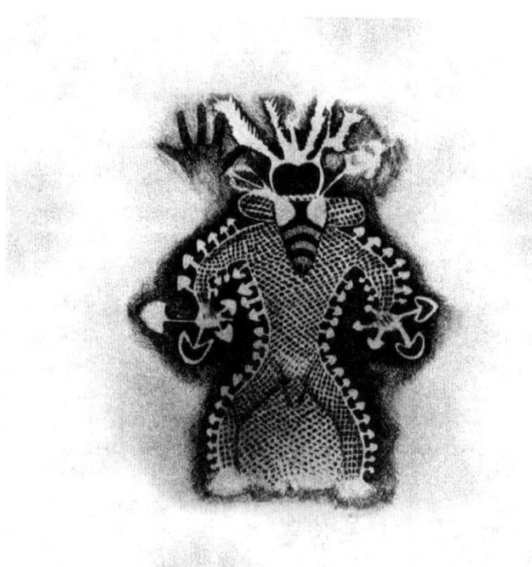

The "bee-faced mushroom shaman" of Tassili n'Ajjer. A mysterious figure depicted in ancient rock art from the Saharan caves of Algeria, believed to represent a shaman associated with psychedelic mushroom use.

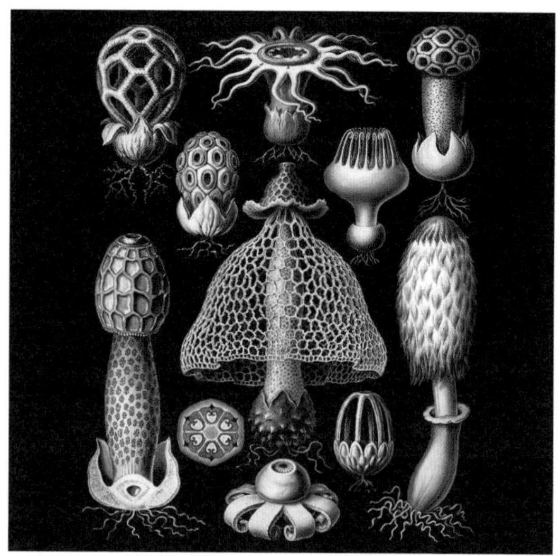

Ernst Haeckel, Art Forms in Nature, *Plate 63, illustrates the recurring geometric patterns found in nature, offering a visual testament to the mathematical harmony in biological forms.*

cosmic order. These creative surges have influenced sacred art and architecture throughout history.[80]

The Tassili Mushroom Figure, or "bee-faced shaman", painted in the caves of Tassili n'Ajjer in Algeria around 4700 BCE, is believed to be one of the earliest known depictions of psychedelic experience. The figure's body is painted with geometric patterns reminiscent of fractals and insect-like symmetry, common motifs in altered states of consciousness. Similarly, Aztec statues such as that of Xochipilli, the "Prince of Flowers", may show figures enraptured in entheogenic trance. He sits upon a temple-like base carved with sacred plants, including mushrooms, tobacco, and possibly *cacahuaxochitl* – the "flower of cacao".

These intricate geometric patterns reflect the mathematical principles behind the Golden Ratio ($\Phi \approx 1.618$), also known as the Divine Proportion. This ratio has fascinated mystics, scientists, artists, and philosophers, who believe it unlocks a universal code that reveals deeper cosmic truths.

The Golden Ratio underpins essential mathematical concepts such as Pythagorean Triples and Fibonacci's sequence. These principles have been used for millennia to construct monumental architecture. The ratio appears not only in nature but also in the human body, from embryonic development to the proportions of the "ideal" human figure, as depicted in Da Vinci's *Vitruvian Man*. Ancient Greeks, who regarded Sacred Geometry as central to understanding the divine, saw humans as reflections of divine harmony. This belief extended to personal conduct, where physical strength and dignity (being literally and metaphorically "upright") were not just about aesthetics but a moral responsibility, symbolising the transmission of sacred knowledge through the spine.

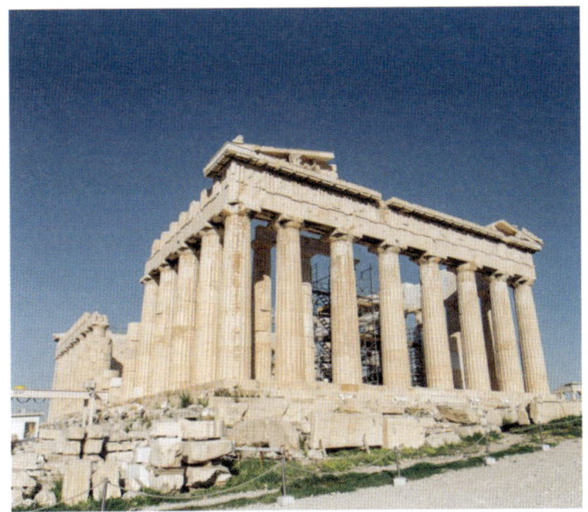

The Parthenon, Athens, Greece. Believed to embody the Golden Ratio, the Parthenon represents divine order in stone. Its columns mirror the human spine, merging art, anatomy, and cosmic harmony.

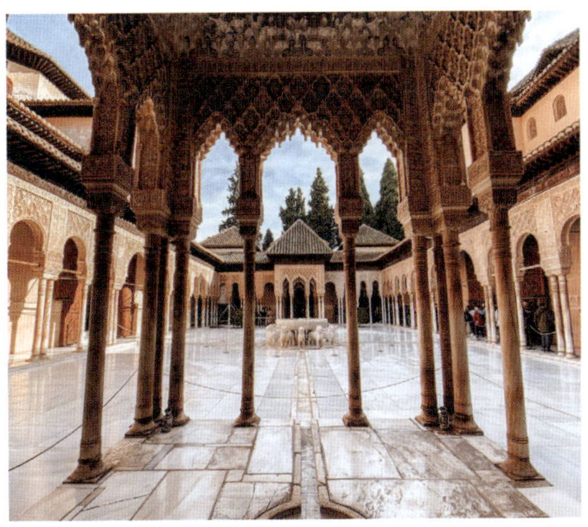

The Alhambra Palace, Granada, Spain. Built 1238–58, the Alhambra showcases vegetal motifs, muqarnas (stalactite ceilings), and fluid light patterns.

One striking, yet debated, example of the Golden Ratio in architecture is the Parthenon. Its columns, designed to echo the human spine, feature slight variations from one to the next, mimicking vertebrae.[81] The columns' subtle zigzag pattern and hollow core enhance their flexibility and endurance. Just as the human form mirrors the divine, sacred structures like the Parthenon reflect the divine proportions of the universe.

Early architecture around the world, from Egyptian pyramids and Hindu temples to African settlements,[82] mosques, and European cathedrals, embodies humanity's attempt to mirror the divine. These structures symbolise our effort to translate celestial grandeur into Earthly forms, facilitating a connection with the heavens. In Islamic art, particularly in Iran and Pakistan, intricate geometric designs are often described as psychedelic.[83] Without representational images of God, Islamic artists use tessellating patterns and Arabic calligraphy to evoke divine perfection, symbolising transcendence and celestial order.

Islamic architecture's enduring masterpieces, such as the Nasir al-Mulk Mosque in Iran and the Alhambra Palace in Granada, Spain, exemplify this. The Alhambra, a stunning fusion of Moorish, Christian, and Iberian ideals, left me speechless when I visited at age 14. Its tranquil gardens, flowing water, and sacred geometry create a visual language of divine allusion. The palace's three-dimensional stalactite ceilings, with their shifting shadows, offer visitors an immersive experience of a unified vision of paradise.

The use of psychedelic mushrooms has followed a winding path from their supposed African origins to global spread, marked by recurring cycles of reverence and repression. Bill Richards, a psychologist specialising in psychedelic-assisted therapy (even amid the War on Drugs), notes that

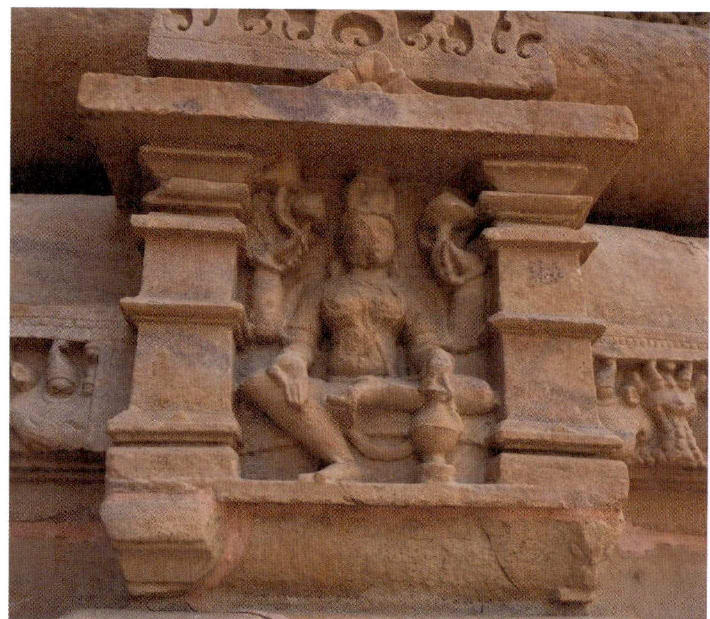

Some researchers suggest that the Khajuraho Temples of northern India encode entheogenic mushrooms and shamanic themes. In the Lakshmana Temple (c. 1000 BC), a figure is framed by mushroom-like carvings – interpreted as lotus buds, sacred umbrellas, or psychedelic psilocybe mushrooms.

psychedelics often thrive "above ground" before facing inevitable suppression. This ebb and flow parallels the natural rhythms of mushrooms themselves. Within this rhythm, architectural forms that encapsulate sacred psychedelia have been constructed, and later destroyed, leaving few traces of their psychedelic connections.[84]

But the Vishwanath Temple in India holds a relic: a carved mushroom at the entrance to the temple's sanctum, standing more than a foot high. This placement is significant as it marks the threshold between the phenomenal and transcendental worlds. One has to step on the mushroom's cap to enter the sanctum, leading scholars to suggest that the mushroom was once regarded as the "stepping-stone" to the spiritual realm.[85]

While Europeans often look to other cultures for examples of ancient psychedelic use, many believe that native practices also left their mark on sacred sites. Ronald Hutton, a scholar of pagan religions, suggests that world religions often succeed not by extinguishing preceding beliefs but by integrating elements from them. This process of assimilation explains why certain practices in Buddhism resemble indigenous rituals or why Christianity adopted pagan deities as saints.

Notre-Dame Cathedral in Paris offers a striking example of architectural confluence. Originally a Celtic worship site, the Romans transformed it into a temple dedicated to Zeus, after which it became a Christian Basilica. Similarly, the Church of St Mary and St David in Kilpeck, England, blends Saxon, Romanesque, and Celtic influences in its design. Its ornate tympanum features carvings of snakes with heads swallowing tails, green men, and mystical beasts. Likewise, grotesque Sheela-na-Gigs are figurative carvings of a female figure, often found on medieval churches and castles, depicting a

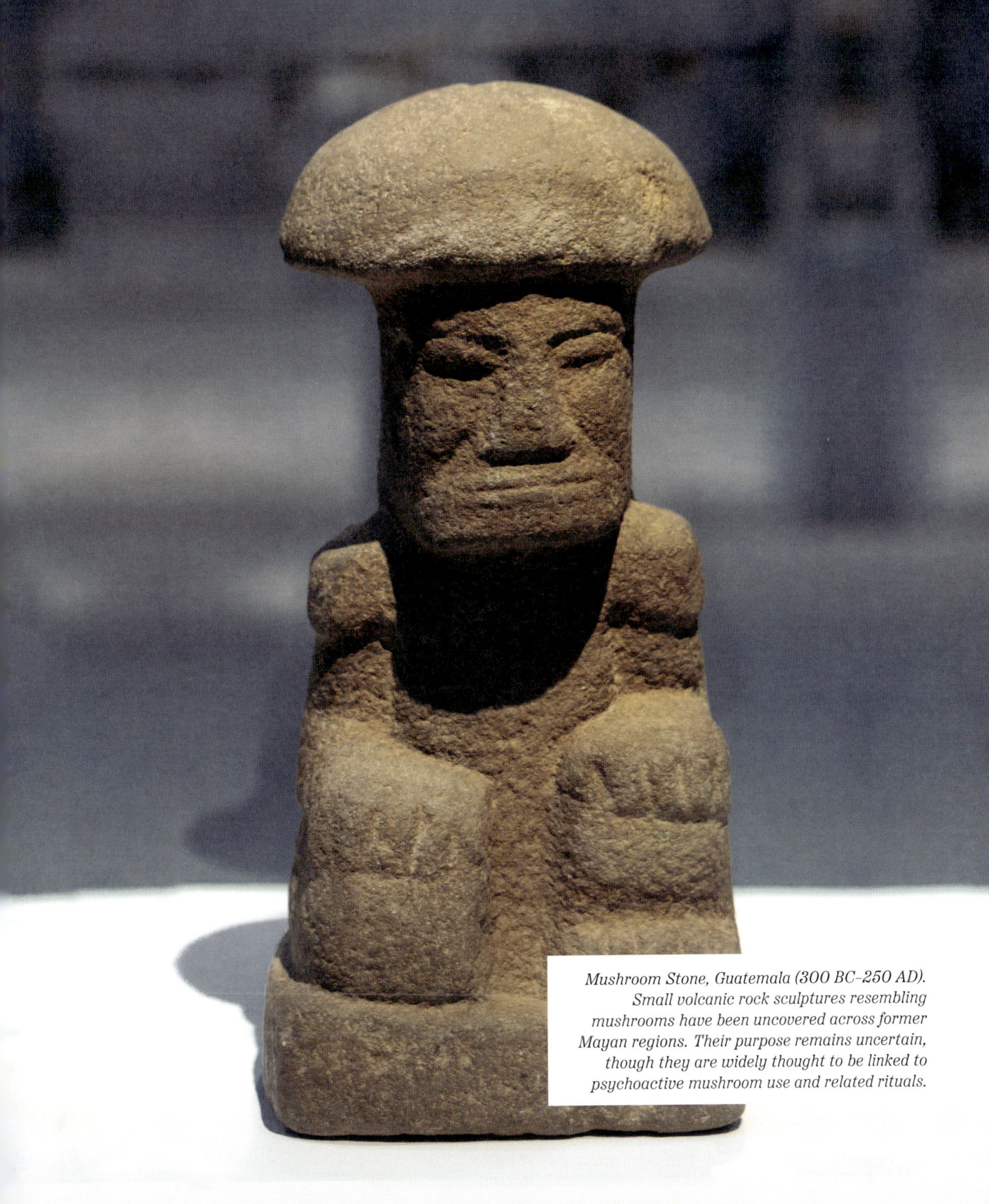

Mushroom Stone, Guatemala (300 BC–250 AD). Small volcanic rock sculptures resembling mushrooms have been uncovered across former Mayan regions. Their purpose remains uncertain, though they are widely thought to be linked to psychoactive mushroom use and related rituals.

squatting woman with an exaggerated vulva. With their bulging eyes and hands pulling apart giant vulvas, Sheela-na-Gigs stand as remnants of a pagan past, playfully engaging with the spirit world. These motifs also bear a resemblance to Māori patterns: swirling ferns, eternal knots, bulging eyes (*pūkana*), and protruding tongues (*whetero*). These similarities are suggestive of universal symbols, often envisioned during psychedelic experiences. This came into focus during a conversation with my friend, writer and historian Sam Dalrymple. As we toured Delhi's sacred sites during Holi – an Indian festival alive with colour and cannabis – the sacred and the surreal began to blur. Echoing Terence McKenna, we were struck by the idea that "the psychedelic tradition is part and parcel of humanity's universal religious heritage." Though it may sound radical, our experience made it feel self-evident.

In *The Doors of Perception*, Aldous Huxley describes "animated architectures, rich with gems and fabulously lovely", often seen during psychedelic experiences.[86] These visions reflect archetypal sacred forms across cultures: symmetrical Buddha heads, endless Arabic tessellations, kaleidoscopic Hindu Kovils, gold-domed Buddhist stupas, the hypnotic whorls of Celtic and Māori design, and pagoda rooftops tapering like genie shoes, their pointed tips multiplying into infinity. As journalist Graham Hancock has argued – though I am aware, with much resistance – these forms may indicate that religion and sacred sites were originally, and universally, inspired by psychedelic experiences.[87]

But psychedelics also have a shadow side. As Huxley wrote, "To fathom hell or go angelic, take a pinch of psychedelic." I wonder if gargoyles, like Sheela-na-Gigs, are part of this infernal visionary realm. Unlike the orderly beauty of sacred geometry, these grotesques are chaotic, open-mouthed, and raw. Positioned on the exterior of churches, they may represent creaturely impermanence or act as spiritual guardians to ward off evil spirits. Their gaping orifices evoke what some theorists call the "mouth-anus vortex" – a self-forming and self-consuming donut-like form frequently reported in deep psychedelic states.

But bringing it back down to earth, psychedelic mushrooms and their visions vary considerably by geography. Different Psilocybe species grow in specific ecosystems and seem to reflect their local environment. In Wales, Liberty Caps, *Psilocybe semilanceata*, are said to produce sombre, misty Celtic motifs. In contrast, people often report that *Psilocybe mexicana*, native to Central America, evokes radiant, colourful visions shaped by its vibrant cultural and ecological context.

It was from *Psilocybe mexicana* that Dr Albert Hofmann first extracted and identified psilocybin and psilocin, two decades after he synthesised LSD. In a supervised experiment in Switzerland, Hofmann described how the familiar forms and colours of his environment dissolved into vivid Mexican imagery. In *The Botany and Chemistry of Hallucinogens* (1977), he wrote:

"As I was perfectly aware that my knowledge of the Mexican origin of the mushrooms would lead me to imagine only Mexican scenery, I tried deliberately to look on my environment as I knew it normally. But all voluntary efforts . . . proved ineffective. Whether my eyes were closed or open, I saw only Mexican motifs and colours . . . When the doctor supervising the experiment bent over me to check my blood pressure, he was transformed into an Aztec priest . . . In spite of the seriousness of the situation, it amused me to see how the Germanic face of my colleague had acquired a purely Indian expression."[88]

This suggests a dynamic feedback loop between ecology and culture. The mushroom's origin (Mexico) may shape the resulting visions – plumed serpents, skulls, gods, and colourful geometries – which feed into art, festivals, and collective memory. But, of course, the loop spins both ways: our cultural

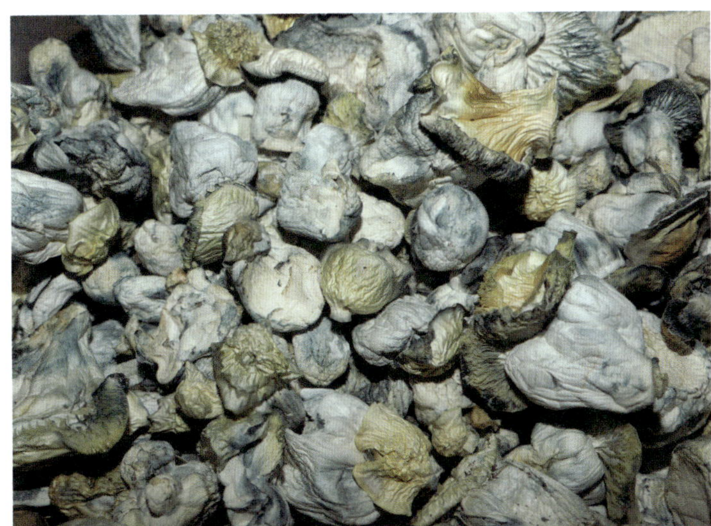

Golden Teachers, Psilocybe cubensis. *This psilocybin mushroom is central to Terence McKenna's "Stoned Ape" theory. Several Psilocybe species bruise blue due to the oxidation of psilocin, a key psychedelic compound.*

frameworks shape what we see under the influence, reinforcing familiar symbols and mythologies. The result is a living dialogue between land, culture, and spirit.

Mushrooms remind us that even gods grow from roots, or more precisely, hyphae. While mainstream narratives often downplay or completely disregard the role of nature and psychedelics in religious history, many are now reclaiming these ancestral threads.

San Francisco stands as a buzzing epicentre of psychedelic restoration, where the legacy of the 1960s countercultural movement continues its evolution. With both cannabis and psilocybin decriminalised, vendors openly sell their wares, even in areas dense with police presence. Near Dolores Mission Park, the most "colourful" green space in the city, I finally visited the Church of Cosmic Consciousness, a sister to the Living Church of Psychedelics. I'd long imagined it as a grand, sanctified space for communal psychedelic exploration – perhaps echoing the psychedelic cathedrals of the past. Instead, it was delightfully low-key: a pop-up table displaying neatly packaged magic mushroom capsules, adorned with geometric designs. With a huge smile, the "divine vendor" guided me through the strains: Albino, Golden Teachers, Mexican Dutch King, Hawaiian, Mazatapec, YAKS, and McKennaii; they had it all.

Humbled and mildly high, we shared a delightful cosmic giggle, the kind where sacred revelation meets street-level reality. A roaming vendor walked me back to the park, then vanished on his mission.

Despite the cosmic revelations these fungi reveal, they are deeply, resolutely terrestrial. Psychedelics may launch us into visions of divine symmetry and universal perfection, but they always begin with the quiet, earthy presence of a mushroom. In every journey, no matter how far I travel, I am brought back to this grounded truth: mushrooms are my umbilical cord connecting me to the Earth.

Still inspired by my misfired expectations of the Living Church, I decided to create a structure that would honour psychedelic traditions across time – light and dark – and embody the mysteries of the long-neglected underground fungal world. I collaborated with a sculptor, and together we began a

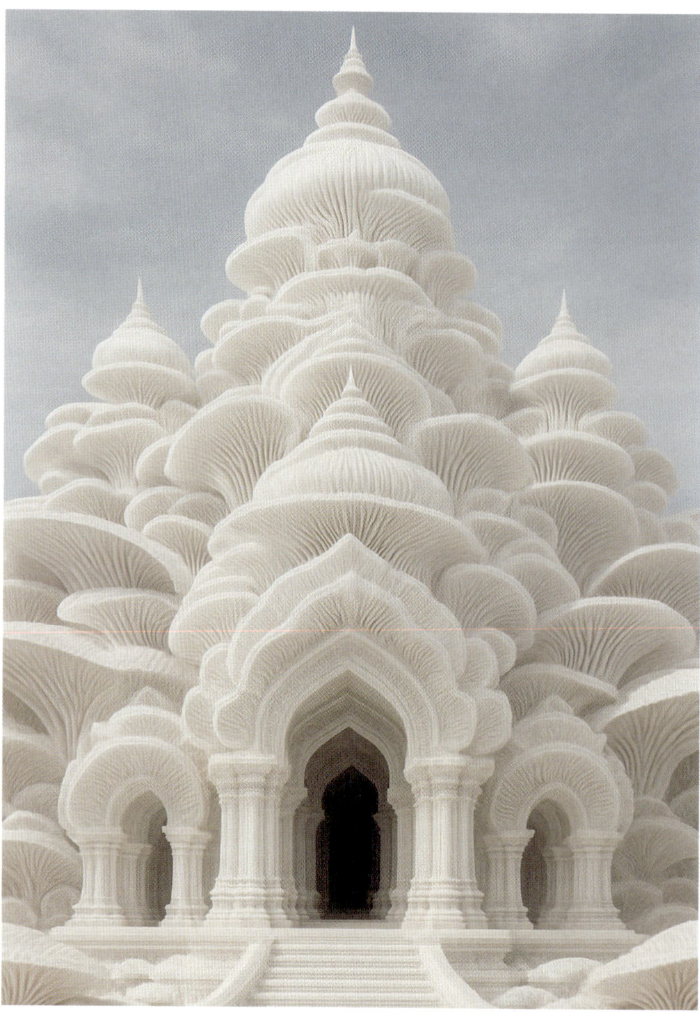

Visions of a Sacred Psychedelic Structure *- the model for our creation.*

process of co-creation: tripping, sketching, downloading cosmic visions, and building. Like McKenna suggested, we invited the mushrooms to reveal something new, and they did.

We translated our insights into a sculpture, a tangible form reflecting the boundless heights and unfathomable depths encountered in visionary space. To make it truly alive, we inoculated the carved wood with native (unfortunately, non-psychedelic) mushrooms. We allowed the mycelium to run through the sculpture; fusing the pieces together from the inside out. Although the sculpture is yet to bear fruit (it may take another year or two) we will soon have one mighty, multi-species, multi-kingdom, multi-dimensional celebration. And I cannot wait.

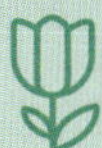

ACTIVITY

BUILDING A LIVING PSYCHEDELIC HOUSE OF GOD

Engage in this activity in early spring (the optimal time for log inoculation).

MATERIALS

- Hardwood logs (oak or beech)
- 1x 1kg/2¼lb native Turkey Tail mushroom fruiting block
- Drill and drill bit (12mm)
- Beeswax
- Metal pan
- Paintbrush
- Log inoculation tool (to deliver a 10mm x 28mm pellet of sawdust spawn into a 12mm diameter drilled hole)
- Elastic band

Note: As a general guide, 1kg of sawdust spawn will inoculate around 10 x 1m/40in logs.

METHOD

1. Source and cut logs to approximately 1m/40in in length and 15cm/6in in diameter.
2. Leave them in a dry place for 2 weeks.
3. Use sandpaper to scrub any mosses and lichens off the logs.
4. Carefully carve the logs into your desired structure in a relatively clean environment.
5. Once a log has been carved, immediately inoculate it.

INOCULATION PROTOCOL

1. Drill holes of 28mm (1 inch) depth in a diamond pattern along the length of the log. Leave roughly 11cm between each hole and take care to avoid any intricate or detailed areas.
2. Fill each drilled hole with Turkey Tail substrate from your fruiting block. Use gloves, your fingers, or a stick for this process, or for convenience, use a "log inoculation tool", widely available online. Fill the holes in a linear fashion for consistency.
3. Melt some beeswax in a pan. Generously cover the filled holes with wax to seal them from air exposure and external microbes. Be sure to paint over any exposed or recently carved areas as well, to enhance the chances of successful mycelium growth (though you might need a lot of wax!).
4. Arrange the logs in a Jenga-like formation, 3–5 logs across, alternating each layer's orientation by 90 degrees. Store the stacked logs in a shady, well-ventilated location, such as a shed, for 1–2 years (depending on the thickness of the log).
5. After the year has passed, submerge the logs in cold water for 1–2 days to stimulate the mycelium and initiate fruiting.
6. Assemble your final structure using the prepared logs, securing each part by hammering it into place. Interestingly, the vibrations are known to encourage logs to start fruiting!
7. Finally, offer a hopeful prayer for lighting, also to help stimulate fruiting.

As you begin this journey, remember that our built environments reflect our deepest questions – each structure shaped by our ongoing search for meaning and the divine.

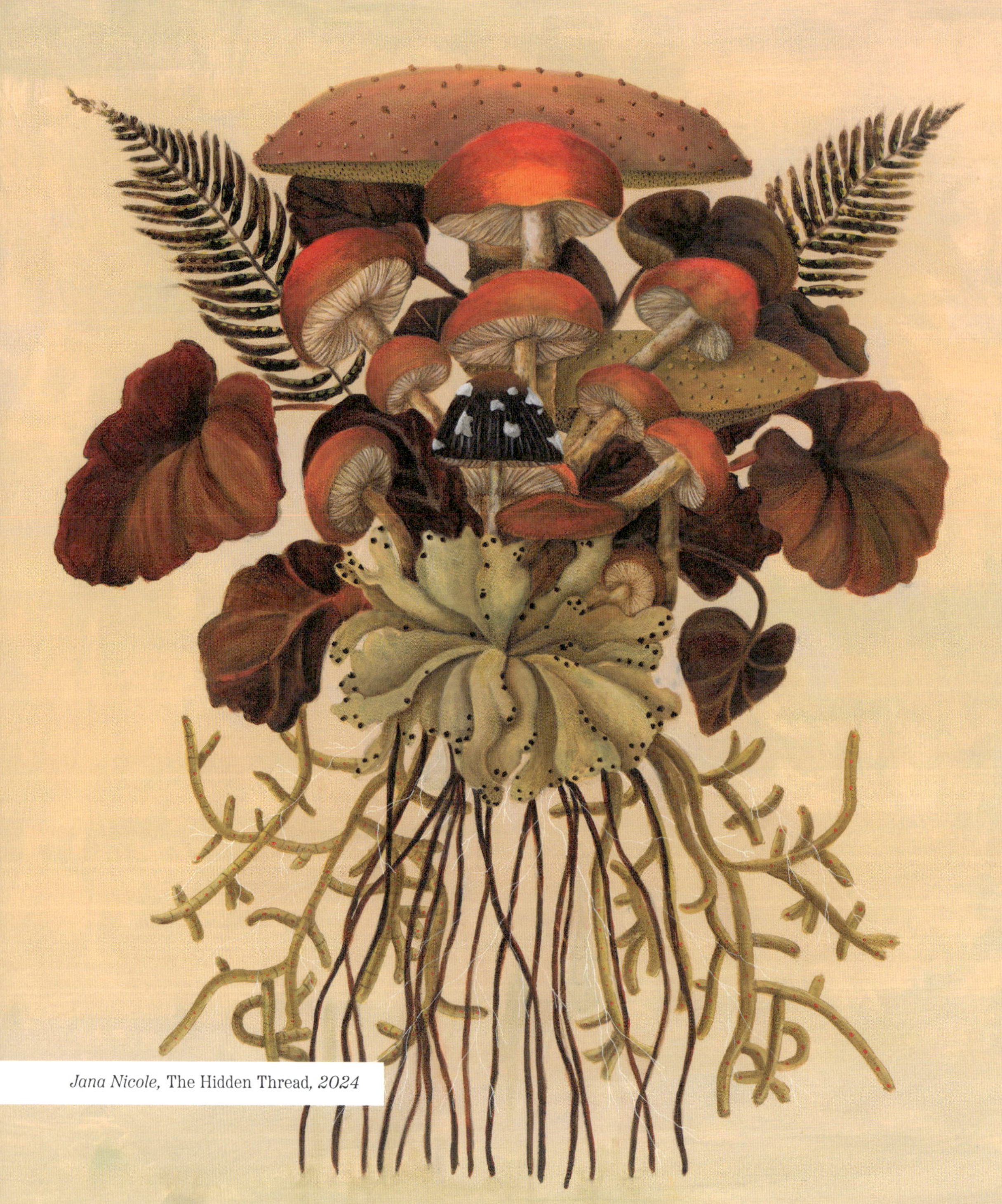

Jana Nicole, The Hidden Thread, *2024*

3

CENTRE:

Flow & Balance

According to the Haida people of the northern coast of British Columbia, creation emerges not from a single source, but through the tension and interplay of opposites.[1] Central to their origin story is Raven, the trickster-creator, who seeks the help of Fungus Man, a humble, mushroom-bodied figure.[2]

Though strange and unassuming, Fungus Man guides Raven to the island where female genitalia exist. Only he has the power to steady the canoe against the force of the *tsaw* (orgasm) that had caused all previous voyagers to fail. Fungus Man is the sacred mediator, a bridge between light and shadow, surface and depth, physical and spiritual. He embodies the contending energies of creation and dissolution: the surge towards complexity and the tidal pull that draws it back.

Many creation myths begin in polarity: male and female, sky and earth, water and fire. The creative spark is forged in the meeting of opposites. From the Primordial Egg of many cosmologies to the Yin and Yang of Daoist philosophy, we see this principle echoed. Yin, the receptive, creative source, and Yang, the active, expressive force, are not rivals but partners in flow. True creativity arises when these polarities are harmonised.

The Haida tale of Raven and Fungus Man is not unique. The Siberian "Birth of Amanita" myth shares similar themes and characters: once again, Raven and Fungus (known as *V'apaq*)[3] conspire to restore harmony in a disrupted world.[4] These stories have flowed across oceans and centuries, adapting, connecting, and evolving. This example reminds us that indigenous cosmologies are not frozen in time; they are alive, contemporary, and responsive. As Inuit Canadian artist Noah Kelly puts it: "The great flow of life reminds us that we [Inuits] can't be what we were before. We're revising how we place ourselves in the world and the dialogue with ancestral knowledge in light of current realities."

Fungi mirror this message. They are neither plant nor animal, but a third kingdom altogether – intermediaries that dismantle rigid categories and thrive in-between. Their lives are defined by movement: beneath our feet, their mycelial networks ferry water, nutrients, and information across huge terrains, connecting nearby trees, regulating decay, sustaining life. They are nature's supreme stabilisers.

In forests, fungi orchestrate nutrient flow, decomposing matter to nourish the soil and the next generation of organisms. In our bodies, they regulate internal ecosystems; some mushrooms even modulate our immune systems, promoting homeostasis – that elusive but essential internal equilibrium.

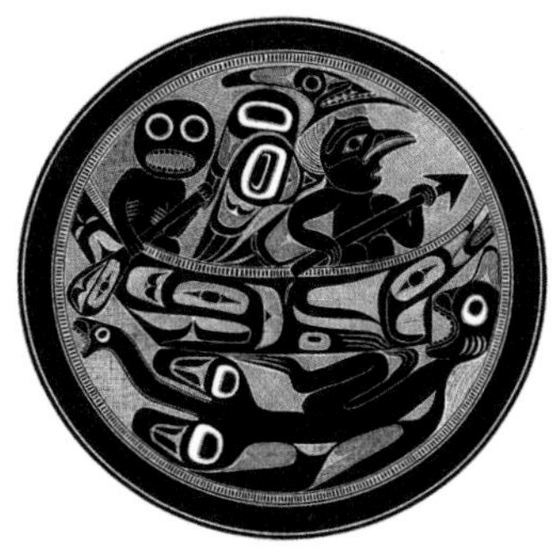

An argillite carving by Charles Edenshaw depicting the Hadia Creation Myth. Raven seeks Fungus Man's aid to reach the island of female genitalia, as only Fungus Man has the power to cross its sacred barriers. He sits securely in the back, protected from the overwhelming force that had thwarted all previous voyagers.

Medicinal mushrooms, such as Reishi, Lion's Mane, and Turkey Tail, support hormonal, emotional, and microbial balance. They restore flow where things have become blocked or chaotic.

To live is to oscillate. The human body is in constant negotiation, adjusting temperature, managing inflammation, digesting, regenerating, and healing. Homeostasis is not a fixed point but a dynamic wave. To be alive is to sway and correct, inhale and exhale, break and mend. We are rhythmic beings in an ever-flowing world.

And yet, so often, we feel dislodged from that rhythm. I have felt it – a yearning for stillness, an uncomfortable sense of being unmoored from life's flow, lost in past or future, out of step with the present. But physical movement brings me home. I walk daily; long, slow, attentive walks. I find my footing in the act of moving. This book was written through walking, spoken aloud as my feet traced the land in search of fungi. Through this motion, I found creativity, balance, and presence.

Even in our earliest days, we instinctively seek our centre. Infants must find balance in their bodies to rise and walk. As we age, we continue the search, seeking an inner core to guide us through life. Fungi can help. They show us how to ground down and reach upward, how to die to old forms and be reborn anew. Their existence helps us to understand that to centre is not to fix, but to flow.

Fungi are at the heart of a renewed interest in nature and intuition. They offer a living metaphor for balance: at once ancient in origin and revitalising in function. Their complex chemistry influences mood, immunity, and cognition. Their vibrant colours, extracted into dyes by artists like Miriam C Rice, speak to the emotional spectrum. Her palette, drawn from wild mushrooms and lichens, echoes the internal landscape: no emotion exists in isolation; each flows into another, often counter-balancing the previous. Lichens themselves are a perfect expression of union, a conjunction of variance: fungi and algae, merged into a singular adaptive organism.

We can see this principle of reconnection mirrored everywhere. Wildlife crossings are built to reunite fragmented ecosystems, letting animals reclaim migratory paths blocked by highways. Initiatives like Woven Science[5] aim to bridge Indigenous wisdom and contemporary science – and *indigenous* science and *contemporary* wisdom – facilitating reciprocal learning and ecological restoration. Across art, science, and activism, we are learning how to build bridges, some literally made from living roots,[6] others made from mycelium.

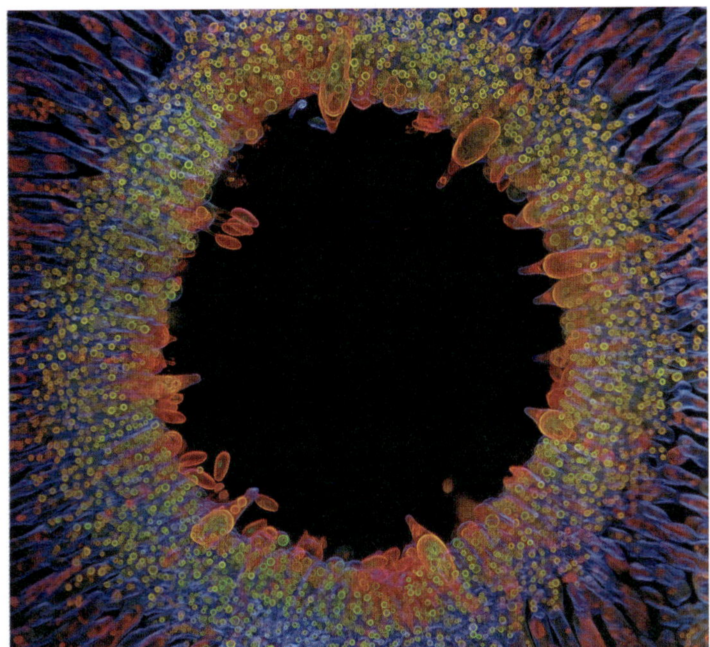

A Bitter Bolete under 40x magnification, stained with chitin-binding dyes. Unlike gilled mushrooms, Boletes release spores from tiny pores on the underside of their caps. This image shows a single microscopic pore in cross-section, with four spores developing on a basidium – ready to drop and continue the fungal life cycle.

And perhaps the most vital bridge we must rebuild is within ourselves. In a world saturated with external noise, we are often disconnected from the inner dialogue that keeps us whole. Listening deeply – to our bodies, our breath, our intuition – is an act of rebalancing. Flourishing Diversity's Listening Sessions remind us that there are things on Earth that depend entirely on what the human heart has to offer.[7] Fungi teach us to listen – to the quiet transformations, the unseen processes, and the slow revolutions within.

So, I invite you now to pause. Close your eyes. Reflect on the word "centre". What does it stir in you? What does it mean to feel centred? What does it mean to flow?

This chapter is a journey back to the centre. We begin in the heartwood of veteran trees, where rot and regeneration coalesce. Here, we discover the essential symbiosis between tree and heart-rot fungus. We then shift to the inner ecosystems of the human body, exploring the scarcely understood effects of fungi on immunity and hormonal balance. We turn to fungal pigments and the emotional resonance of colour, then wander into the anaerobic conditions of ancient bogs: those strange, preserved worlds of ancient offerings and suspended decay.

Through it all, we return to the lesson that fungi whisper again and again: balance is not stasis. To be in flow is to move in rhythm with life's opposites: death and birth, stillness and movement, dark and light, up and down. To find your centre is not to be at the centre of everything. It is to recognise that nothing is.

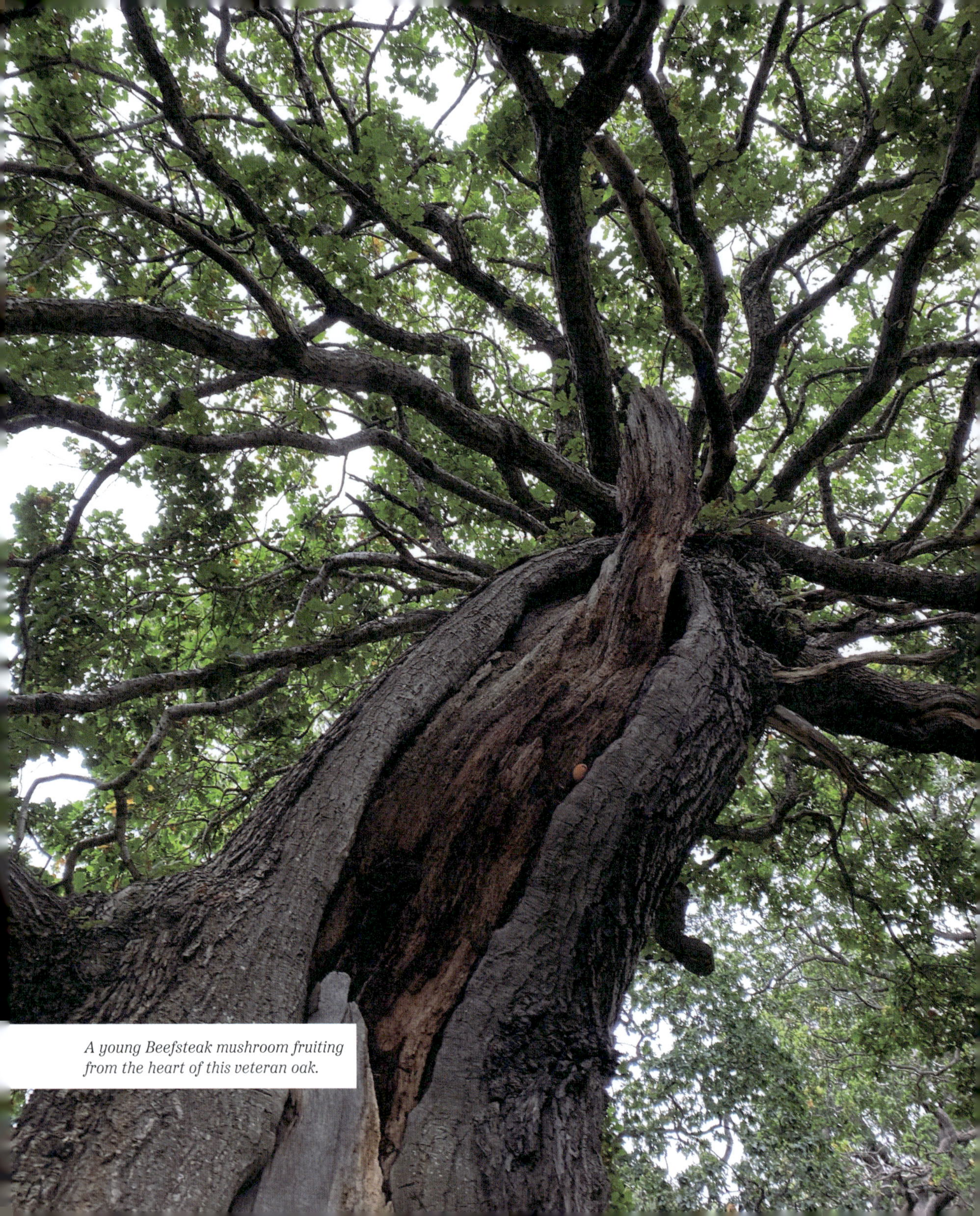

A young Beefsteak mushroom fruiting from the heart of this veteran oak.

STANDING DEAD TREES

"The oak took on a beauty all its own; a kind of sculptural, metaphysical grandeur. Death became a different kind of living."

– *Isabella Tree,* Wilding[8]

Trees are the Earth's most powerful symbol of longevity: of life. Their roots plunge deep into the soil, forming the veins and arteries of nature. Branches reach skyward, fractal bronchi that renew the air we breathe, releasing oxygen vital for life on Earth. The trunks serve as channels for nutrients and information, as xylem transports water from roots to leaves, while sugars and nutrients flow down the phloem, nourishing the tree and the fungi below them. Majestic and lush, trees embody the principles of flow, natural balance, and cosmic harmony.

Many cultures represent the universe as a tree. With roots that anchor into the underworld and leaves that stretch into the skies, trees have long been revered as mediators between the above and below.[9]

"World trees" are prominent in mythologies across the world and have served as timeless symbols of connection, linking all creatures with the great creator. These world trees formed the heart of cultural beliefs, connecting societies to the spirits, gods, ancestors, and landscapes that shape identities and nurture souls. The Mayan Tree of Life, depicted as a sacred ceiba, upholds the sky while uniting all realms of existence. Similarly, Hindu texts describe the topsy-turvy, cosmic banyan tree, with its aerial roots in the heavens and branches that caress the earth.

We descended from trees and later formed living connections among them. They provide shelter and a place of refuge, while their leaves, roots, and bark serve as seasonal medicines. We feast on their nourishing fruits, berries, and associated mushrooms and hunt the animals that roam in their shadows. We warm ourselves by burning the wood they provide. The essence of trees flows through every aspect of our being. In their splendour, they are an infinite source of sustenance.[10]

World trees are often depicted in full bloom: vibrant, sturdy, and abundant. However, we're also awakening to the ecological richness of what arborists term "standing dead trees" – those with thinning branches, weakening roots, and hollow cores. Although dead, or more accurately dying, they are in fact biodiversity hotspots, hollowed by heart-rot fungi. To understand their ecological significance, we must journey back in time, to an era predating trees as we know them today.

Around 450 million years ago, plants evolved lignin, an exceptionally complex compound constituting 30 per cent of the Earth's organic carbon. This crucial component of plant cell walls provides structural strength, waterproofing, and protection from pathogens, allowing terrestrial plants to flourish.[11] For nearly 300 million years, this was botanical checkmate; no organism could decompose lignin. During

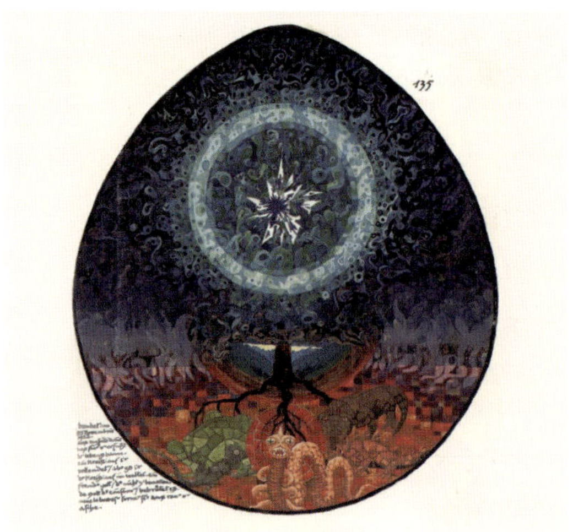

Carl Jung World Tree*, 1922, Yggdrasill, the tree that connects the nine worlds in Norse mythology.*

this time, trees soared to great heights. Fallen trees piled upon one another, succumbing to nothing but gravity, and slowly transforming into carboniferous coal. As Merlin Sheldrake explains, "Coal provides a negative of fungal histories: it's a record of fungal absence, of what fungi could not digest."[12]

Eventually, fungi evolved the ability to break down lignin. With this breakthrough, these saprotrophic, or decay-loving, organisms allowed carbon-dense lignin to re-enter the nutrient cycle, reshaping geology, topography, and biodiversity in profound ways.

Fungi associate with trees in numerous ways, but always in the pursuit of carbon, particularly in the form of carbohydrates – or sugars. Fungal saprotrophs feast on carbon sourced from the deadwood, while mycorrhizae – deemed "collaborators" by natural historian Richard Forte – tap into the tree's roots for carbon, exchanging minerals for nourishment. Fungal parasites, on the other hand, are carbon scavengers who steal without benefit to their host. Parasitic fungi can devastate tree populations and even threaten entire species, as seen with Dutch Elm disease and the European ash tree, respectively. The interplay among these fungi – saprotrophic, mycorrhizal, parasitic – varies throughout a tree's life cycle; they shift dramatically, adapting to the tree's age and health.

Consider oaks: majestic rulers of the forest. They take 300 years to mature, live for 300 more, and take another 300 to decline.[13] In their youth, early mycorrhizal partnerships establish between, within, and throughout the sapling's roots, forming an enduring network that enhances the survival of both. These fungi provide sugars and nutrients to the young tree, while receiving little immediate return. As the oak matures into a hyperconnected Mother Tree, communicating with other trees and plants via underground mycelium networks, exchanges of carbon and sugars rise. The subsequent succession of fungal decomposers begins to break down carbon from the tree's heartwood into fertile nutrients that underpin woodland food webs.

The manner of a tree's death also significantly impacts its fungal relationships.[14] A tree that falls suddenly, chopped down or uprooted by a storm, creates moist, shaded conditions ideal for fungi and

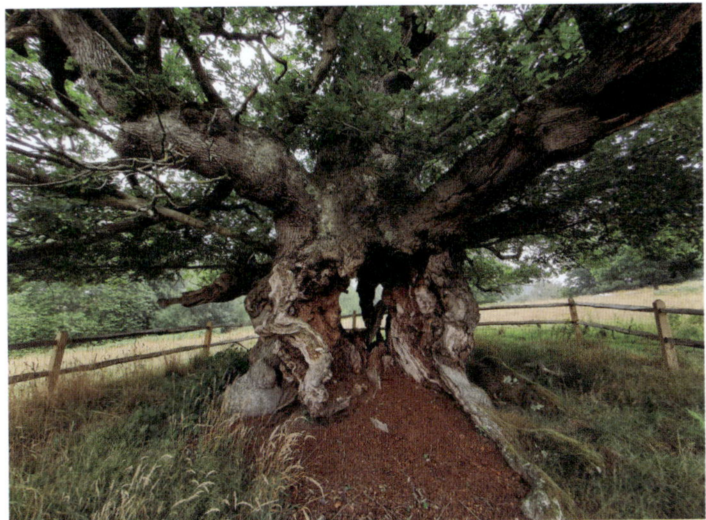

Lady in Waiting Oak, Cowdray Estate. "Standing Dead Trees" are ecological hotspots – home to heart-rot and mycorrhizal fungi, lichens, mosses, insects, birds, and small mammals, while also providing shelter and scratching bark for larger animals like deer.

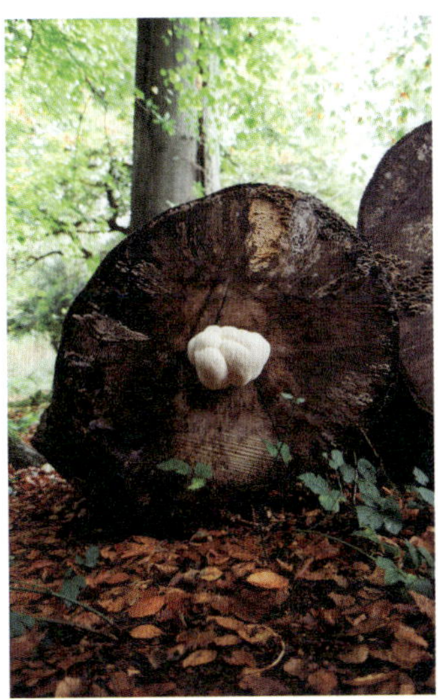

Lion's Mane fruiting from the heart of a beech tree.

insects adapted to lying wood. In contrast, a standing dead tree – naturally senescent or cut as a high stump – receives more sun and dries quickly, attracting a different suite of species. While artificial deadwood can mimic some features of natural death, it often lacks the complexity of gradual decay. Naturally dying standing trees, or "kelo" in Finland, release nutrients over time and support diverse, slow-colonising fungal communities.[15] A diverse mix of deadwood – standing, fallen, natural, and artificial – is essential to a forest's health and resilience, fuelling biodiversity and sustaining life at every stage of decay.

To fully appreciate the life cycle of British oaks, the mycologist David Satori and I explored his favourite just outside Edinburgh, in Dalkeith Country Park. When we first visited in 2021, we scanned the ground for multicoloured Waxcaps peeking through the grass. This time, however, our focus shifted skyward to the jays: the brightest members of the crow family and avid acorn foragers. Surprisingly, it's jays, not squirrels, that bear the primary responsibility for planting acorns and nurturing the next generation of oaks.

Britain boasts more ancient oaks than the rest of Europe combined.[16] Our two native species are the English (or Pedunculate) Oak, *Quercus robur*, and the Sessile Oak, *Quercus petraea*. Under the right soil conditions, fallen or forgotten acorns will germinate in spring. These seedlings become saplings, fortifying and growing over time. The form of an oak is shaped not only by its genetics and habitat, but also by the creatures that graze or wander nearby. A single nibble from a deer or an errant footstep by a human can profoundly influence its growth. Shoes might carry unfamiliar or disease-bearing spores,

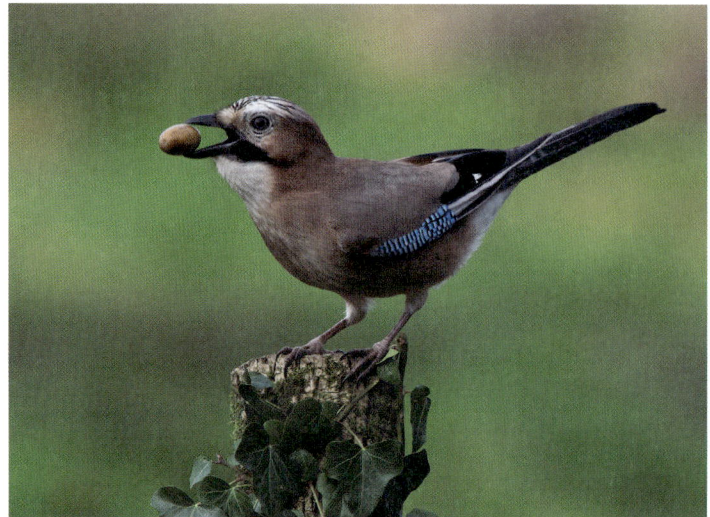

Eurasian Jay, Garrulus glandarius, *with an acorn. Jays are more vital in then squirrels in planting acorns – seeding subsequent generations of oak forests.*

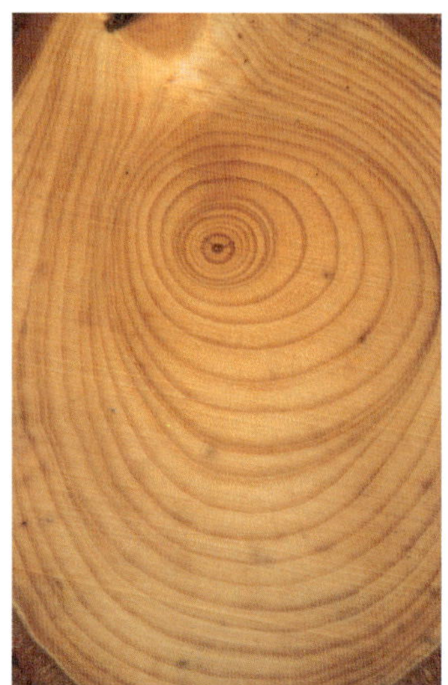

Tree rings: Each light and dark ring pair represent one year of a tree's life, offering insights into past climate, seasonal patterns, and ecological conditions – including surrounding flora, fauna, and funga.

or they might simply stamp upon a young sapling underfoot. Environmental conditions also play a critical role, as seen when comparing the towering oaks of Sussex to their stout counterparts on Welsh hillsides, where harsh weather and poor soils prevail. Within British folklore, regardless of shape and size, all oaks are revered for their wisdom and strength.

Oaks grow radially from their centre, an organic process reminiscent of mycelial growth. Tree rings speak a history, recording a tree's age and the climate and microbes it has endured. Light-coloured rings signify growth during spring and early summer, while darker rings indicate growth in late summer and autumn. Wide rings denote access to ample resources, while narrow rings hint at stress or scarcity.

But tree trunks don't always survive to tell the tale. As trees age, the heartwood, the dense core of the trunk, dies off; only the cambium, the outer layer beneath the bark, remains alive and active. As a tree grows taller, the weight of its dead heartwood may risk instability. This is where the heart-rot fungi enter, paradoxically providing balance, both physically to the tree and ecologically to the entire ecosystem.

Heart-rot fungi are vital. They thrive primarily when trees are mature, feeding off the dead wood at the core while preserving the living tissue on the exterior. Heart-rot fungi can hollow out living trees over centuries without causing immediate harm, even coexisting for 600 or 700 years![17] White rot fungi, like Lion's Mane (*Hericium* sp.), Turkey Tail (*Trametes versicolor*), Maitake (*Grifola frondosa*), and

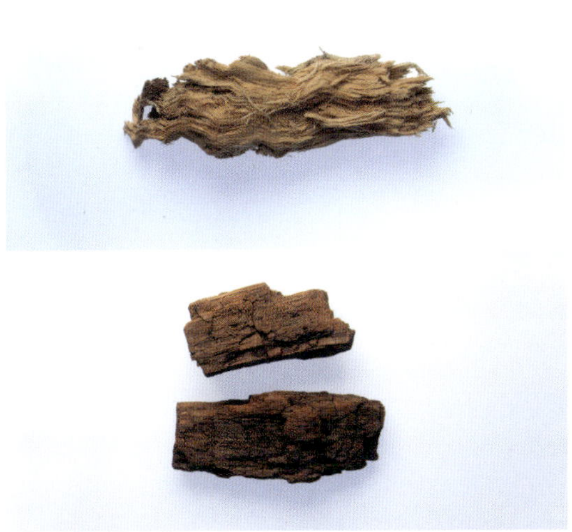

Top: White-rot fungi break down lignin, creating linear, streaky textures. Bottom: Brown-rot fungi decompose cellulose, leaving behind rectangular patterns in the dead wood, signalling residual lignin.

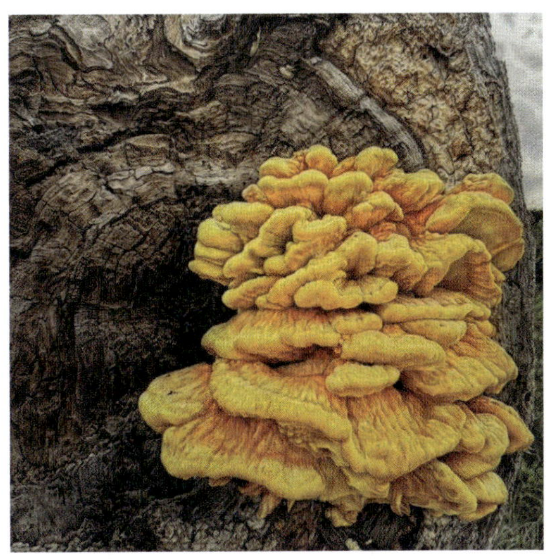

Chicken of the Woods, a brown-rot fungus growing from the heart of deadwood and leaving complex, telltale patterns in the wood.

Oyster (*Pleurotus sp.*), are enzymatic biohackers capable of breaking down stubborn lignin, resulting in streaky, pale, and crumbly wood. On the other hand, brown rot fungi, including Artist's Bracket, Chicken of the Woods, and Beefsteak, decompose the tree's cellulose, leaving typical rectangular formations in the reddish-brown wood, indicative of the residual lignin they cannot metabolise.

These primary and secondary decomposers soften the tree's heartwood, allowing insects and other creatures like woodpeckers to excavate the wood further and create cavities where insect larvae can develop. Over time, this hollowed trunk collects decomposed wood that forms a delicious-smelling, nutrient-rich mulch, providing sustenance for the soil and, in turn, the tree's roots, which channel vital nutrients back into the living branches. They feed off their own decay. Together, oaks and their fungal allies form a stable, self-sustaining partnership, oscillating nutrients that keep both alive and thriving.[18]

Dead or alive, oaks offer refuge to an astonishing array of wildlife. They act as guardians for forest inhabitants, supporting more life than any other native tree in the UK.[19] Their limbs provide sanctuary for birds; their hollows house owls, mice, voles, and other small mammals. The intricate fissures in their bark sustain a rich diversity of lichens and mosses, while their roots nurture microbial communities throughout the changing seasons. Oaks can endure for over a millennium, serving as habitats for a staggering 2,300 species, furnishing vital resources for nourishment, shelter, rest, and reproduction. Yet, within these remarkable ancient trees, numerous microhabitats face the threat of extinction.

David explains, "At the end of the last Ice Age, when most of Britain was an expansive tundra, some of the earliest woodlands established in the North would've been along the west coast of Britain."[20]

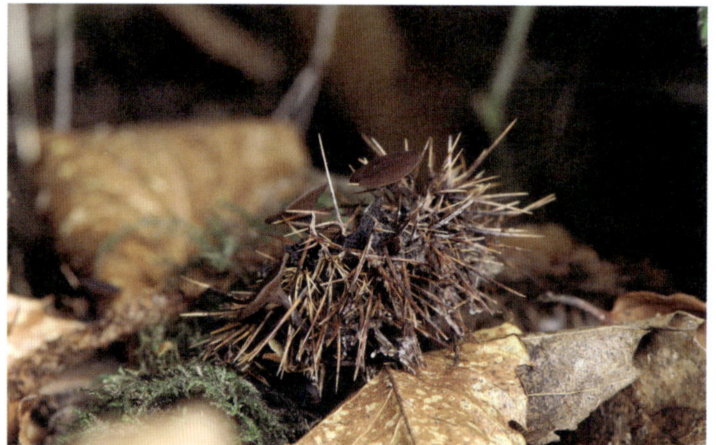

Hairy Nuts Disco, Lanzia echinophila, *a cup-shaped fungus found on beech, acorn, and hazel casings. Likely travelling from the Iberian Peninsula around 10,000 years ago, this fungus arrived hidden within hazelnuts, colonising UK soils as hazel trees thrived in Britain's Celtic rainforests.*

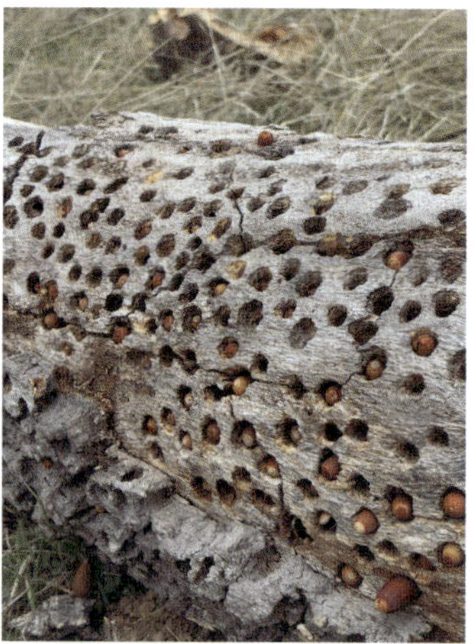

The unmistakable handiwork of the Acorn Woodpecker: rows of neatly drilled holes in tree trunks, each precisely sized to hold a single acorn.

He describes a time when temperate rainforests may have covered up to one-fifth of Britain, inspiring the imaginations of Neolithic wizards, Celtic druids, Roman poets, and Viking warriors. Today, remnants of these extraordinary woodlands persist, distinguished ecosystems of hazel, oak, birch, pine, and holly can be found across the Western Highlands, Lake District, and down through the temperate rainforests of Wales, Devon, and Cornwall.[21] DNA sequencing has revealed connections to mainland Europe, detailing how the Iberian Peninsula's hazelnuts, accompanied by a host of fungal companions, primarily travelled across seas and oceans to establish deep roots.[22,23]

However, centuries of deforestation have led to a fragmented network of woodlands, resulting in a decline in the number of veteran trees. In response, mycologists Lynne Boddy and Matt Wainhouse from Natural England are inoculating younger trees with wood-decay fungi to "veteranise" them, initiating early decay processes. The goal is to encourage habitats typical of older trees to develop more quickly, allowing rare fungi and insect species to reestablish themselves and thereby rebuild biodiversity and resilience within the ecosystem.

This is a beautiful idea to wrap our heads around and invites us to reshape our understanding of thriving trees. We often envision an ideal tree with a luscious green canopy, robust roots, and a strong trunk. Yet, standing dead trees broaden this view, representing ecological vigour in their own right. These veteran trees continue to stand tall, with rotted stag heads, swollen burls, and crumbling trunks. They harbour rare communities and form the very bedrock of healthy ecosystems. Perhaps it's through the slow processes of decay and transformation that we can truly appreciate ecological resilience.

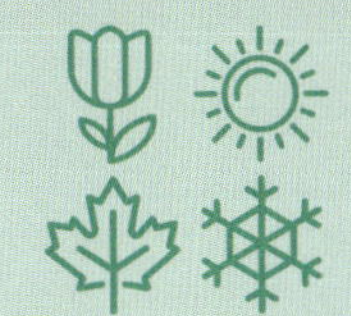

ACTIVITY

WORKING BACKWARDS TO TELL THE TALE OF A TREE

DAVID SATORI

"Trees tell a story, but only to those who know how to read it."

- Tristan Gooley

The art of reading a tree lies in noticing its shapes and patterns. Soil, weather, water, light, disturbance, animals, competition, and climate all influence its form. Each variation reflects that particular place and time, as no two trees are alike.

Begin by finding a veteran tree, ideally upright though dying. Breathe in its essence, perhaps step into its hollow (mind the bats). The stature of a tree, particularly an oak, tells an unhurried life story of its relationships within the local ecosystem.

ORIENT

Branches tend to grow longer on the sunny side (south-facing in the northern hemisphere). Use this as an indicator to find direction. Rusty-red crust lichen, *Trentepohlia umbrina*, favours the cooler, damp northern aspects, as do moss and algae. Bark is also often thicker and more weathered on the north side.

STUDY THE TREE'S FORM

Tall with a narrow crown suggests woodland competition, while gnarled, twisted branches reveal a veteran in harsh conditions. Foliage may lean away from prevailing winds. Hollows hint at fungal activity: rectangular patterns from brown rot, streaks from white rot. Look for mycelial strands, or mushrooms sprouting from soil (mycorrhizal) or from the tree's heart or base (saprotrophic or parasitic).

YOUR TASK

Retrace the tree's life. Imagine how a seed matured into this giant. Write it down or speak it to the wind. Did hares nibble its tender leaves, coaxing offshoots that shaped its trunk? Did lightning scar a limb? Did a bird drop spores into a crevice, birthing heart-rot fungi? Perhaps centuries ago, a child planted a lone acorn with whispered hopes.

Construct a story as vivid as you wish, weaving in jays, fungi, owls, deer, humans – even weather and wind – that have left their mark.

This practice builds eco-literacy. To do it well, learn the oak's companions and the meanings of its forms. What is a bulge? A burl? How do white and brown rot differ? Why do holly trees sprout from the base of ancient oaks, their lower leaves spiny but smooth above? The answer may lie in the presence of deer. Tristan Gooley writes, "Many patterns in nature are invisible to most, but easy to spot, then hard to miss." So look closely, listen deeply, and let your informed imaginations run wild.

LICHENS: HYPHAE HUES

Toes are so important to life and movement. But sometimes I can't see mine. Sometimes I forget they're there. Every moment, walking or standing, our toes actively help us find balance. I love the idea that balance is an active pursuit. Bio-architect Rachel Armstrong draws an enlightening parallel between balance and metabolism: all living beings exist in constant flux, tipping off balance to achieve balance. In nature, she explains, true stasis equals death.

Homeostasis is the process by which our bodies maintain equilibrium. I visualise homeostasis as an oscillating wave: just like our emotions, just like the outline of my toes.

In 2018, I self-published *Homeostatic Toes*,[24] a book that embraces the full spectrum of emotion. It celebrates the rawness of feeling and channels it through creative process. Whether the outcome is a masterpiece or just a stepping stone to an indistinct goal, the act of creating becomes a kind of catharsis – an emotional release.

But between 2019 and 2021, I was thrown off balance by the weight of biodiversity loss and ecological collapse. It felt like a pathetic fallacy: as the Earth's temperatures climbed and fell to greater extremes, so too did my emotions. And the more overwhelmed I became, the more rigid I grew, desperately seeking stability.

So I turned to my toes. I prescribed myself daily walks in the woods. Step by step, I dropped into a moving meditation, shedding stagnant energy. My body slowed, softened, and attuned to something deeper as the rhythmic movement steadied me.

That's when I noticed the lichens. Quiet, slow-growing, clinging to bark, brick, and stone. Their name, from the Greek *leichein*, to lick, is whimsically apt. They thrive in harsh environments, adapting slowly and subtly. They don't rush.

Lichens became a mirror for me. In their patient resilience, I found my own. Balance, like them, is quiet, persistent, and always in motion.

Lichens are epiphytes; they grow on other organisms without parasitising them. Once considered primitive plants, they are now understood as a symbiotic union between a fungus (mycobiont) and a photosynthetic partner (photobiont) – an alga, a cyanobacterium, or both. The fungus benefits from the sugars produced by the photobiont, while the photobiont receives a secure habitat, physical protection, and improved access to minerals. Lichens are so deeply fused that they were historically studied as one single organism. Today, we recognise that nearly one-fifth of all known fungal species form lichens.[25] This relationship is intimacy in the most astonishing form, so striking that many have described it as an erotic biological partnership.[26]

These organisms are among the oldest and slowest-growing life forms on Earth, advancing just one to two millimetres per year. As pioneering colonisers, lichens are often the first to reappear after ecological disturbances like volcanic eruptions or landslides. Today, lichens cover between six to eight per cent of Earth's land surface and play a vital role in ecosystems, capturing carbon, fixing nitrogen, preventing soil erosion, and providing food and shelter for countless tiny lives. Because they absorb

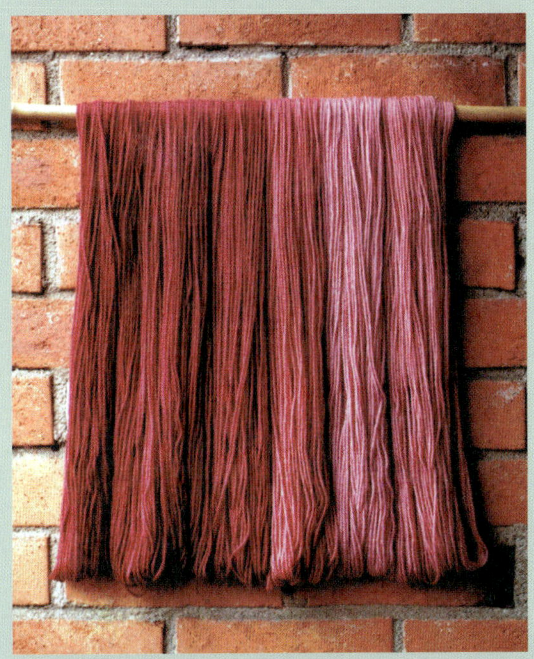

Lichen-dyed fibres. This ancient craft produces a surprising range of colours – soft golds, mossy greens, deep purples, and rusty reds – depending on the lichen species and dyeing method.

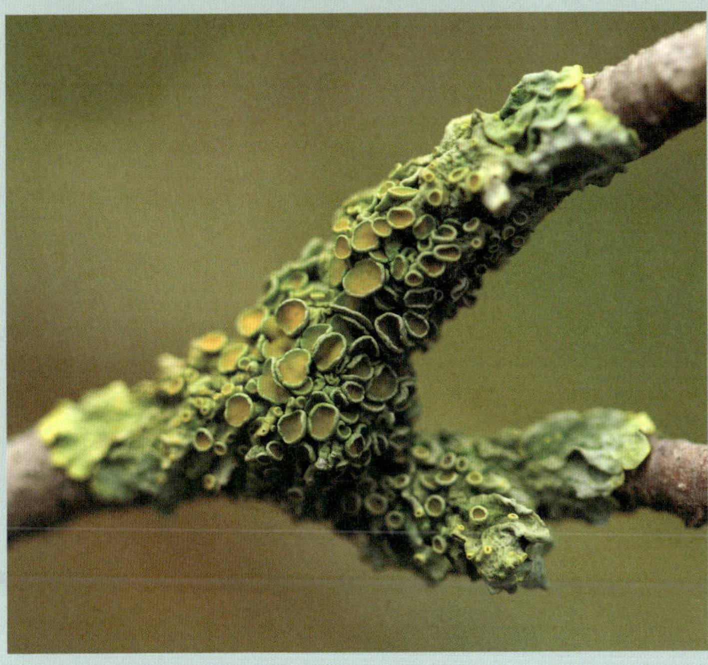

Lichens are symbiotic organisms made up of a fungus (mycobiont) and a photosynthetic partner (photobiont). They are important indicators of environmental health, particularly sensitive to air pollution.

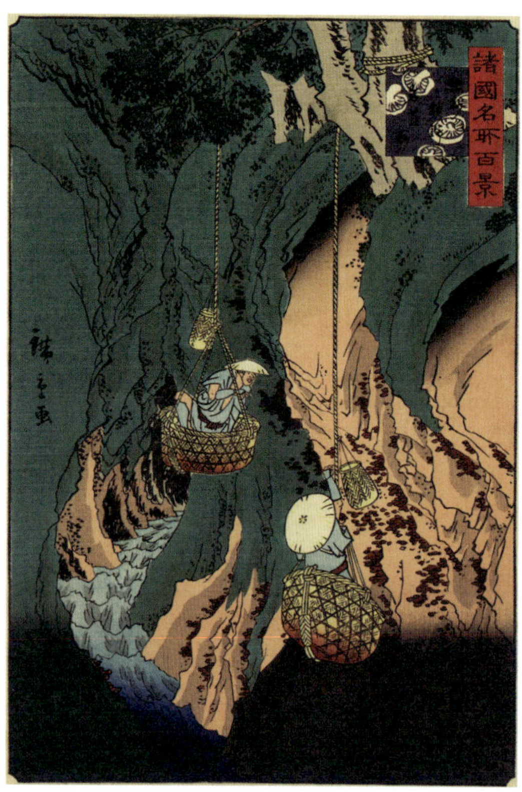

Harvesting the rock tripe lichen Umbilicaria esculenta, *known as* Iwatake *in Japan, from cliff tops. Shokoku meisho hyakkei, (100 famous views of Famous Places in the Provinces), Hiroshige II.*

everything from the air directly into their tissues, lichens are highly sensitive to pollutants and serve as excellent indicators of air quality and environmental health.

Lichens are ecological generalists. While many prefer ancient, unspoiled forests, others are extremophiles, thriving in harsh environments from tundras and deserts to rocky coastlines. Like trees, they are environmental storytellers, offering subtle clues about their surroundings – chemical composition, moisture levels, light exposure. For example, only certain lichens can grow on acidic birch bark, while others prefer the alkaline surface of ash.

They also have a rich yet often overlooked cultural history. The rock tripe *Umbilicaria esculenta*, also known as *Iwatake* in Japanese, is much prized in Japan, China, and Korea where foragers have been known to scale cliff faces to collect it. In Iceland and Russia, certain lichens are still brewed into traditional therapeutic teas. Following the medieval Doctrine of Signatures – the belief that a herb's appearance reveals its healing properties and medicinal uses – lungwort's lobed shape was once thought to cure respiratory issues. In early modern Europe, Dutch dyers made a lichen dye called Lac or Litmus, sold as small, dark blue cakes. Since lichens are highly sensitive to pH, doctors would grind up various species to test the acidity of a patient's urine, hence the term "litmus test." [27] In ancient Egypt, lichens

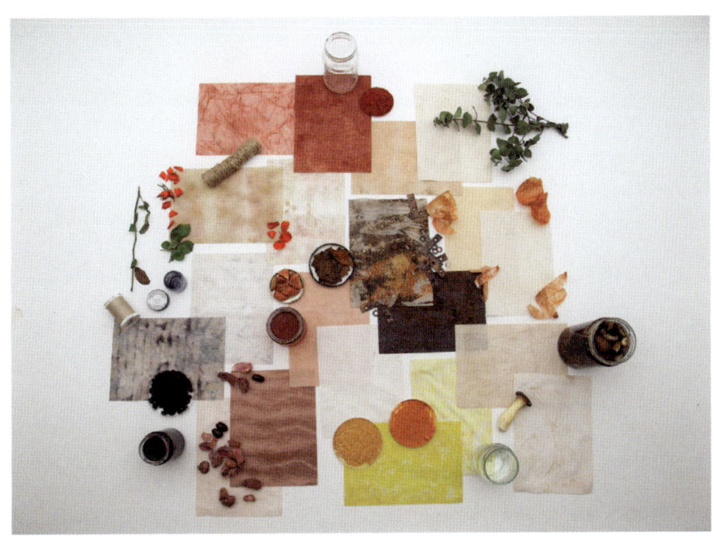

MA Biodesign Natural Dyeing. Ochre, Oyster mushroom, Rust, Lychee shells, Turmeric, Onion skins, Indigo, Eucalyptus.

were used for embalming and today, oakmoss remains a key ingredient in perfumery, prized for its earthy, musky scent.

During my woodland walks, lichens had a quiet medicinal effect on me. The sheer diversity of colours, shapes, and poetic taxonomies[28] – crustose, foliose, fruticose, squamulose – made me feel delightfully dizzy and wonderfully fungal. They helped shift my attention outwards and beyond my mammalian preoccupations. My growing interest led me to niche Facebook groups[29] of hobbyists and amateur lichenologists. Some harvested lichens for medicine, others for cooking. All practised "salvage botany", collecting lichens only from fallen branches after storms, preserving their delicate populations. I soon began brewing lichen dyes and using colour to express my emotional states, making small colour wheels to map my inner world.[30] Colour became a language, a form of gentle self-inquiry and catharsis.

Natural dyeing opened up a whole new world. Since prehistory, people have turned to the natural world not just for nourishment, but for pigment and creative expression. In Indonesian caves, early humans used ochre and charcoal to paint the walls. Māori adorned their skin with soot, charcoal, and burned Cordyceps mushrooms. Explorers pursued exotic dyes like indigo and turmeric for clothing and décor, symbols of status and power. Each colour carries its vibration and story, shaped by time and culture. In the West, pink, for example, has symbolised everything from strength and masculinity to femininity and softness, while in Japan it represents spring, cherry blossoms, and renewal, and in India, celebration and joy.

In my Biodesign Master's we explored both traditional dyes from the past and innovative, future possibilities. We grew purple pigment-producing bacteria and foraged for the blue-green spalting effects of the elusive Turquoise Elf Cup fungus, used for decorative wood working since the 14th century.[31] We went "colour foraging", collecting natural materials by hue and arranging them into spontaneous palettes. This playful, intuitive exercise revealed surprising combinations: subdued, brilliant,

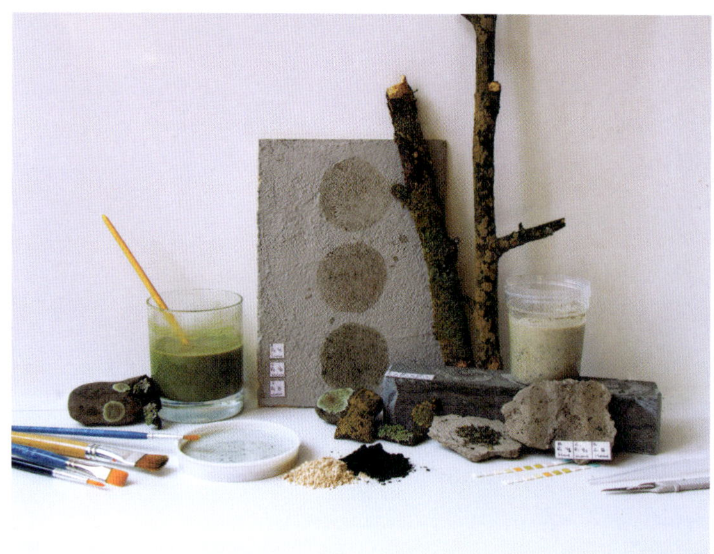

Eleonora Rombolà's Within the Surface *project transforms urban walls, rocks, and statues into living habitats using lichen-based paints.*

harmonious, dull. The Living Colour Database was especially useful. This online resource links organisms to their natural pigments, detailing each by chemical and molecular structure and biological classification. Pigments are indexed by colour codes, including HEX, RGB, and Pantone, offering a comprehensive view of colour across the tree of life.

From there, we experimented with various dyeing methods: solar, ammonia, ice, water bathing, and boiling. I started using vegetable waste and foraged materials, and later sourced unsellable, misshapen mushrooms from local farmers' markets to make delicate creamy brown tones.

My wonderful Italian friend, Eleonora Rombolà, took these early experiments even further. Turning to the microscopic worlds of algae and lichens, she developed Algalip, an award-winning lipstick made entirely from algae pigments and housed in 3D-printed biodegradable algae-based packaging. It was phenomenal. But her next project, "Within the Surface", pushed the boundaries of biodesign even more boldly.

"Within the Surface" is a visionary exploration of lichen-based paints that turn urban surfaces – walls, rocks, statues – into living habitats. Eleonora's lichen patterns address the growing loss of urban biodiversity and worsening air pollution, forming part of a wider climate adaptation strategy for future cities. These living paints purify the air while creating micro-environments for insects that rely on lichen ecosystems to survive. Her work challenges us to reimagine aesthetic value, to see the grey, inert surfaces of cities as potential habitats for new life, and to celebrate the quiet resilience of lichens as agents of transformation.

One of the rarest and most historically significant colours in nature is purple. So when archaeologists uncovered an entirely purple robe from a Chinese tomb dating back to 2000 BCE, it caused a stir. The garment had been dyed using molluscs, whose glands produce a sticky yellow fluid that oxidises into

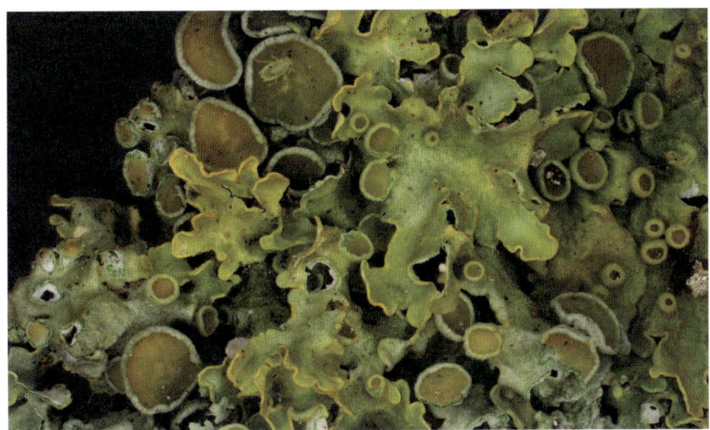

Lichen with a tiny insect moving across its landscape.

vivid purple. This was one of the earliest methods for achieving purple dye – a colour long associated with royalty, mysticism, religion, and prestige.

Lichen-based purples came next.[32] Dye houses thrived in Norway, Iceland, and Canada, but none more famously than in 14th century Florence. There, a merchant named Alemanno del Giunta travelled to the Levant and learned that the lichen *Roccella tinctoria,* also known as Orchil, produced a dark-red purple dye when mixed with urine. He began importing the lichen to Florence where the dye became immensely popular and earned the nickname "poor man's purple".

Del Giunta's family soon dominated the industry, sourcing lichens from Scotland, the Canary Islands, and Cape Verde, with annual earnings approaching $200,000. In a bid to solidify their prestige, they renamed themselves the Rucellai, after the very lichen that made their fortune. Their precise recipe, however, was kept secret for nearly a century, during which time they built the Palazzo Rucellai, the Orti Oricellari gardens, and even forged marital ties with the Medici family.

Scotland, though more modest in scale, developed its own thriving lichen dyeing tradition throughout the 18th and mid-19th centuries. Using native Orchil species, collectively known as "Cudbear" from the lichen-dyeing Cuthbert family, artisans produced deep purples, crimsons, golds, maroons, and reddish-violet hues, used to dye traditional tartan fabrics. This crottle-based cottage industry still lingers in the Outer Hebrides, where visitors can still see lichens being gathered, cleaned, and fermented in urine-filled stoneware or iron vessels. While recipes are now shared openly, the Cuthbert family, like the Florentines, guarded their methods closely, employing only Gaelic speakers to protect their trade secrets and ecological knowledge.

Yet all these industries shared a fatal flaw: lichens grow too slowly to support large-scale harvesting. As demand soared, natural populations declined, and the once-flourishing crafts collapsed under their own success. Fortunately, a professor at Imperial College developed mauveine in 1856, which gave humans unlimited amounts of purple dye. While no longer in widespread commercial use, mauveine marked the beginning of the synthetic dye industry, which now produces countless dyes and pigments, including many shades of purple.

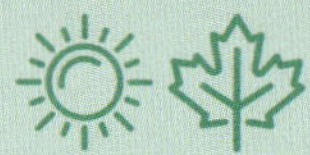

RECIPE

BIOFLUORESCENT MUSHROOM DYE FROM THE DYER'S MAZEGILL

In November 2024, the British Lichen Society released an article on the use of lichens for dyeing. They had one clear message: "Please leave lichens alone!"[33] Lichenologists, they explained, are deeply concerned about the conservation of lichens across the UK and Ireland, and for good reason. Many species are in steep decline nationwide due to habitat losses from farming, land development, and climate change.[34]

So rather than dyeing with lichens, we'll dye with faster-growing, more abundant mushrooms.

This is an incredibly ancient craft. The Indian Paint fungus, *Echinodontium tinctorium*, hidden beneath its dull grey crust, reveals a vivid brick red highly valued by Native Americans like the Tlingit of Alaska, who ground it into powder and mixed it with deer grease to make sunblock paint. Similarly, the rare Black Tooth fungus, *Phellodon niger*, produces a grey-blue or green dye when combined with ammonia or soda ash, which darkens over time. The Scaly Tooth mushroom, *Sarcodon squamosus*, sometimes growing in fairy rings, yields a striking blue pigment as it matures.

But above all, the Dyer's Mazegill has been prized for centuries in Europe and North America as a natural dye, offering an astonishing spectrum of colours – from luminous golds and deep greens to hues that stretch beyond visible light. During a biofluorescent night walk at All Things Fungi Festival 2024, mycologist Sidnee Ober-Singleton revealed a skeletal-fungal pattern inked onto his hands with biofluorescent henna derived from this magnificent, slightly hairy fungus. The following recipe is inspired and informed by Sidnee's experiments.

EQUIPMENT

- Stainless steel or enamel pot (non-reactive)
- Wooden spoon
- Strainer or cheesecloth
- Optional: Spice grinder
- Paintbrush
- Optional: Gloves
- UV light (blacklight) for testing fluorescence
- Small glass bowls or jars

INGREDIENTS

- 100g/3½oz Fresh Dyer's Mazegill (*Phaeolus schweinitzii*) (10g dried and finely ground)
- 500ml/17fl oz/2 cups of distilled water
- Optional: Mordant (Alum 10–15% weight of fibre (WOF)), Iron (2–5% WOF), Copper (2–5% WOF))

METHOD

1. Collect Dyer's Mazegill from fallen pine or spruce logs. Ensure correct ID (always cross-reference a field guide or consult a mycologist). The best time to pick and dry this mushroom is when its outer edge is bright yellow, with yellow-green pores underneath. Chop into small pieces to maximise dye release. (If dry, grind into a powder.)
2. Place the chopped mushrooms in the pot and add enough water to submerge them fully. (Again, if dry, place the powder into the foot of an old pair of tights and tie a knot at the end. This prevents it from sticking to the bottom of the pan). Slowly bring to a simmer then maintain this low heat for about 1 hour, making sure to stir occasionally.

3. While the mushrooms simmer, soak your natural fibres in warm water for at least 20 minutes to thoroughly wet them out and prepare them for dye absorption. (Optional: Soak and simmer fibres in a mordant solution for 1 hour to alter colours and improve colourfastness. Alum brightens and enhances yellows and golds. Iron deepens tones, shifting yellows towards olive, green, or brown shades. Copper adds greenish or bluish hues and can boost fluorescence.)
4. After simmering, add the pre-soaked fibres directly into the mushroom dye bath. Maintain a gentle simmer, stirring occasionally to ensure even dyeing.
5. Let the fibres simmer in the dye bath for 30 minutes to 2 hours, depending on the desired of colour.
6. Remove the fibres carefully, rinse in cool water until the rinse water runs clear, then gently squeeze out the excess water. Hang or lay flat to dry away from direct sunlight to preserve fluorescence.
7. Shine a UV light over the fabric to witness natural fluorescence! It will likely be green or blueish, depending on the materials.
8. Alternatively, use the dye as a paint. I painted my hands and feet and danced with joy for my homeostatic and biofluorescent toes!

NOTES

- Not all Dyer's Mazegill mushrooms fluoresce strongly. Environmental factors like substrate, age, and region affect pigment content.
- Always patch-test for skin sensitivity before application.
- This dye leaves faint golden marks on skin. It is non-permanent and will fade naturally in a few days.
- Store in the fridge and use within a week, or freeze to preserve.

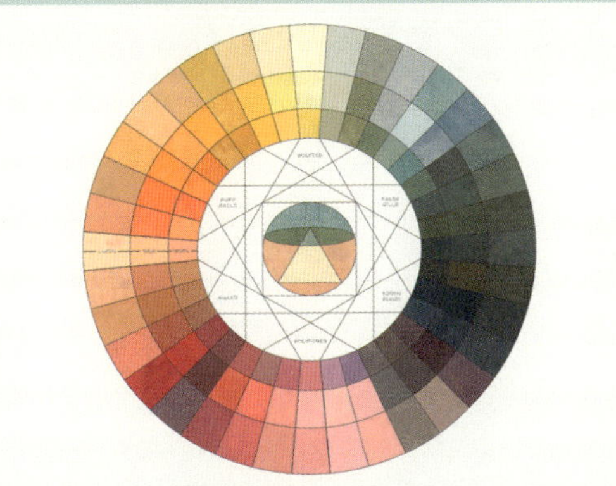

Mushroom Colour Atlas, A Chromatic Guide to the Fungi Kingdom.

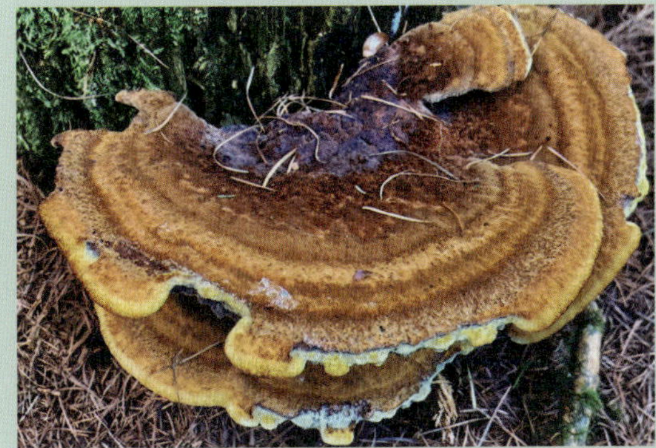

Dyer's Mazegill.

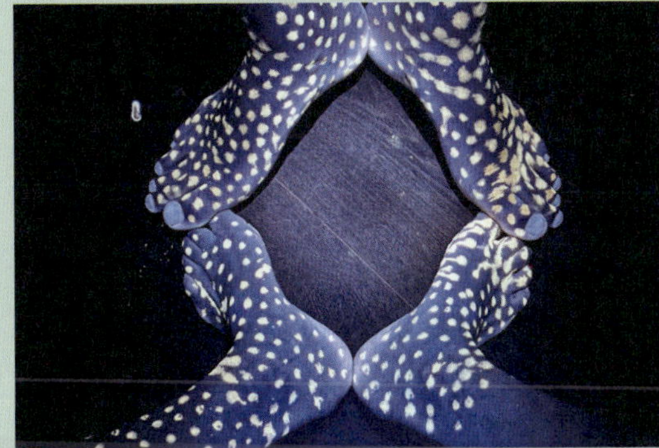

Feet painted with biofluorescent dye made from the Dyer's Mazegill.

MEDICINAL MUSHROOMS

For many, the idea of medicinal mushrooms still feels paradoxical. Western culture has long been shaped by mycophobia – a deep seated fear and mistrust of fungi – leaving many unaware of the remarkable health benefits mushrooms can offer. But that mindset is shifting. A growing mycophilia – a renewed love and appreciation for fungi – is steadily gaining ground. People are discovering the cognitive-enhancing effects of Lion's Mane, the immune-boosting powers of Turkey Tail, and the growing popularity of medicinal mushroom teas and coffees, now common in many households.

Mycotherapy refers to the use of medicinal mushrooms as nutritional supplements to support the immune system and promote well-being. Once considered fringe, it is now a well established practice, embraced by millions worldwide. In 2025, the mycotherapy market was valued at $37 billion USD and is projected to reach $65 billion by 2032.[35]

At the forefront of this "medicinal mushroom boom" are companies like MycoNutri, DIRTEA, Hifas da Terra, Four Sigmatic, Bristol Fungarium, and Fungi Perfecti. They offer a range of products – capsules, powders, tinctures, and gummies – all functioning as adaptogens: substances that help the body adapt to stress and maintain balance.[36]

The most widely recognised functional mushrooms include Lion's Mane (*Hericium erinaceus*), Reishi (*Ganoderma lucidum or lingzhi*), Cordyceps (*Cordyceps militaris*), Turkey Tail (*Trametes versicolor*), Chaga (*Inonotus obliquus*), Oyster (*Pleurotus* spp.), Shiitake (*Lentinula edodes*), Maitake (*Grifola frondosa*), and Tremella (*Tremella* spp.). Some companies create blends; others focus on single species, allowing consumers to connect with the unique properties of each mushroom.[37] For example, Tremella is known for hydrating the skin, while Chaga is linked to gastrointestinal health and liver protection.[38]

Even within a single species, different parts of the mushroom can hold distinct therapeutic effects. For example, the Poria fungus, *Wolfiporia extensa*, is divided into four parts in Chinese medicine. The sclerotium (*Fu Ling*) aids digestion and fluid metabolism. The inner core (*Fu Shen*) is used for its calming and neuroprotective effects. The outer peel (*Fu Ling Pi*) promotes urination and reduces swelling, while the flesh just under the skin (*Chui Fu Ling*) supports circulation and spleen function.[39]

Unlike conventional pharmaceuticals, medicinal mushrooms work holistically, supporting the body as an interconnected system. For example, Button mushrooms, *Agaricus bisporus*, are believed to support spleen function and reduce "dampness" – helping to regulate mucus in the lungs. Maitake can help balance insulin levels by influencing the gut microbiome, which in turn affects progesterone production.[40] This makes it particularly useful for those managing Polycystic Ovary Syndrome (PCOS), a condition marked by hormonal imbalance, irregular periods, and blood sugar fluctuations.

Personally, I saw dramatic improvements after adding both Cordyceps and Maitake tinctures to my routine. After ten years without a menstrual cycle, mine returned within a month. A Japanese study found similar outcomes: of 26 women with anovulation (a condition where ovulation does not occur) given Maitake extract, 20 began to ovulate. Of the eight women who hadn't responded to other treatments, 6 did after Maitake – and all three who wished to conceive became pregnant.[41]

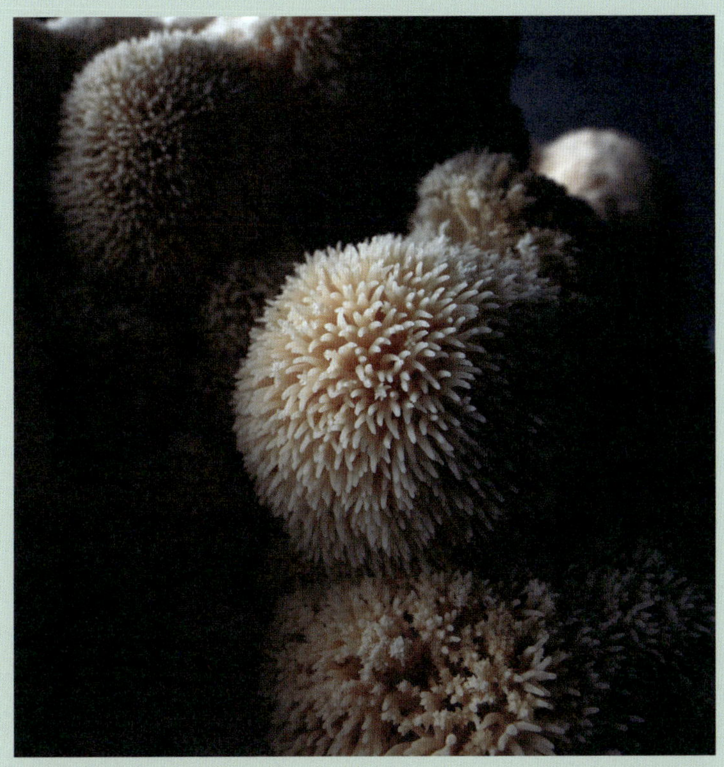

Young Lion's Mane mushroom, also called "Pom Pom" or "Monkey Head mushroom" due to its distinctive shaggy spines.

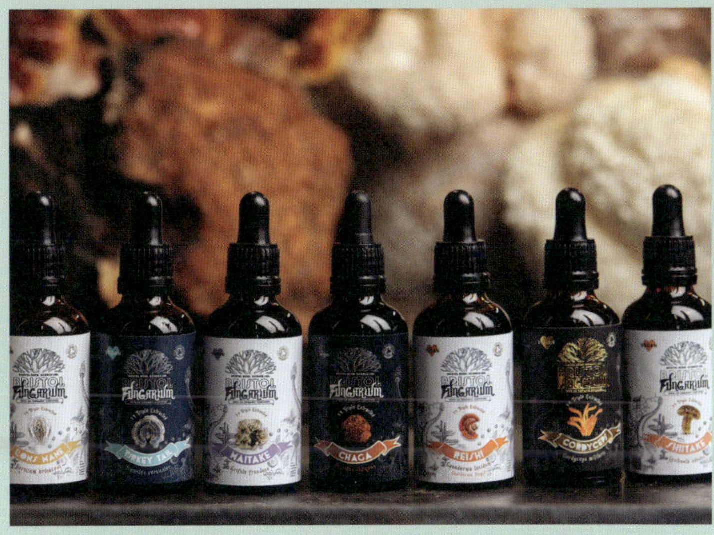

Bristol Fungarium's tincture range as of 2024, featuring Lion's Mane, Reishi, Cordyceps, Turkey Tail, Chaga, Shiitake, and Maitake. Tinctures are concentrated liquid extracts, created to draw out the bioactive compounds from medicinal mushrooms.

IMMUNOMODULATION

At the heart of medicinal mushrooms' therapeutic potential is immunomodulation – the ability to regulate and rebalance the immune system. I think of this as a waveform: when the immune system is overactive, as in allergies or autoimmune conditions, mushrooms can act as immune suppressants, down-regulating activity. On the other hand,, when the immune system is underactive, as with chronic illness or chemotherapy, they function as immune stimulants, up-regulating immune response. In both directions, mushrooms help restore dynamic balance.

This adaptive intelligence is extraordinary. It makes medicinal mushrooms uniquely personalised – two people can take the same dose of the same mushroom and experience completely different effects based on their individual physiological needs.

Amazing. But how do they do this?

The answer lies in their cell walls, primarily composed of beta-glucans and chitin – long-chain polysaccharides that maintain fungal structure. [42] Because fungi are evolutionarily closer to animals than plants, their bioactive compounds are uniquely compatible with the animal immune system.

When ingested, beta-glucans bind to immune receptors in the gut, triggering a cascade of responses: increased activity of natural killer cells, enhanced dendritic cell function, and elevated antibody production. These effects strengthen the body's defences against viruses, pathogens, and even cancer cells.[43,44]

Some beta-glucans also mimic hormonal activity, binding to receptors and exerting anti-inflammatory or immune-enhancing effects. For example, Reishi-derived beta-glucans have been shown to stimulate anti-inflammatory molecules when natural hormone levels are low, an elegant way of modulating immune response and reducing chronic inflammation. The specific structure of each beta-glucan determines its specific immunological action. [45]

And this isn't limited to humans. In a landmark study by mycologist Paul Stamets, bee colonies fed *Ganoderma resinaceum* mycelium extract saw a 79-fold reduction in Deformed Wing Virus and a 45,000-fold decrease in Lake Sinai Virus compared to controls.[46] A 2025 study using *Fomes fomentaris* showed increased bee activity, healthier brood development, and more stable hive temperatures.[47] Across species – dogs, fish, horses, cattle – the immunomodulatory effects of beta-glucans are being recognised and explored.

Some beta-glucans bind directly to gut-associated immune cells, while others pass through the digestive tract and act as prebiotics, feeding beneficial bacteria like Bifidobacteria and Lactobacilli. This promotes a diverse microbiome and increases short-chain fatty acid production that helps maintain the integrity of the gut lining – critical for reducing inflammation.

Beyond beta-glucans, medicinal mushrooms contain an array of therapeutic compounds, including:

- Triterpenoids – anti-inflammatory and anti-cancer
- Cordycepin – anti-tumour, antiviral, immune-enhancing
- Ergothioneine – antioxidant and neuroprotective
- Lentinan – a potent polypeptide that stimulates immune function

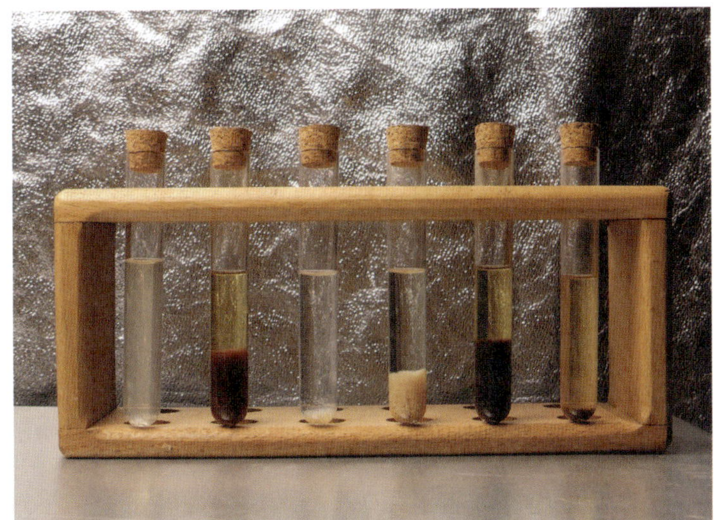

Crude Polysaccharide Test, comparing the beta-glucan composition of Lion's Mane, Chaga, and Turkey Tail. With over 20,000 published studies, fungal beta-glucans are among the most extensively researched mushroom-derived compounds for their potential immunomodulatory effects.

- Phenolic compounds – antioxidant, anti-inflammatory
- Fatty acids – anti-inflammatory
- Sterols – known to support cardiovascular health and lower cholesterol [48]

These compounds often work synergistically, creating effects greater than the sum of their parts. Each mushroom species brings a unique biochemical profile and therapeutic emphasis.

That said, rigorous scientific validation is still catching up. While in vitro and animal studies are promising, large-scale, placebo-controlled human clinical trials remain scarce. Much of the current enthusiasm comes from personal testimonials (mine included), which, while compelling, can fuel hype and overstatement. This is one reason why, under the EU's Novel Foods Regulation, several medicinal mushroom products, like Turkey Tail and Cordyceps, have faced sales restrictions as of 2025, due to insufficient documented evidence of long-term safe use.[49]

This is ironic because much of what we know about medicinal mushrooms comes from centuries of traditional and indigenous use. These fungi have been central to healing practices across Siberia, Africa, Asia, America, and beyond for centuries. In Traditional Chinese Medicine (TCM), mushrooms are used to cultivate and harmonise Qi, the vital energy that flows through the body. Infused into teas, wines, and tonics, they are believed to nourish organ systems, balance elemental energies, and promote free flow of life force.

Each mushroom corresponds to a different organ and energetic function. Cordyceps, for example, is linked to the lungs, kidneys, and reproductive system – organs associated with water metabolism and the yin principle in TCM.[50]

In contrast, Western medicine tends to compartmentalise the body into isolated systems. But TCM recognises the interdependence of these systems – a perspective now echoed in emerging research.

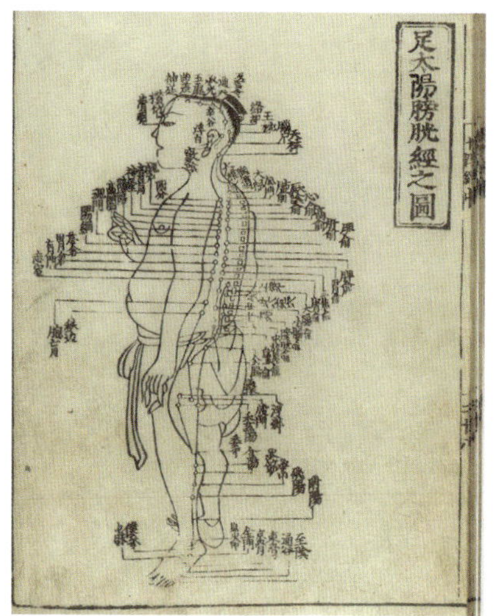

Traditional Chinese Medicine (TCM) embraces a holistic approach to health, using mushrooms to cultivate and harmonise Qi – the vital energy flowing through the body.

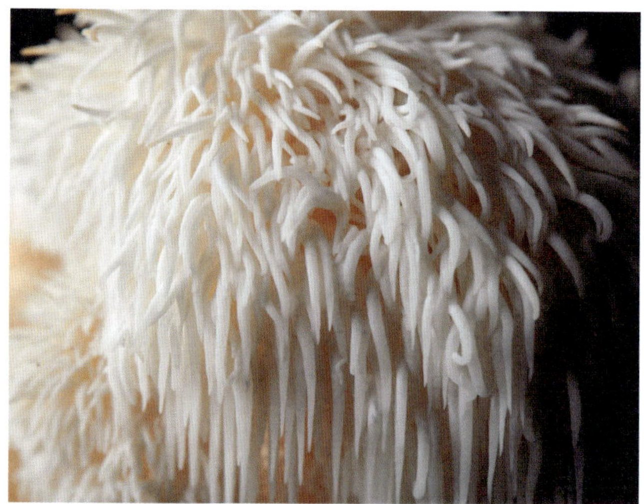

Lion's Mane. In Traditional Chinese Medicine, Lion's Mane is used to support the immune system, improve digestive health, and balance mood. Recent research is exploring its potential neuroprotective properties, highlighting its promise for both gut and brain health.

Consider Lion's Mane: in the West, it's known as the "Smart Mushroom", celebrated for boosting nerve growth factor (NGF), improving memory, and protecting against neurodegeneration.[51,52] But in TCM, Lion's Mane is used to support digestion, calm the nervous system, and regulate mood – reflecting an understanding that gut and brain health are inseparably linked.

The gut-brain connection is increasingly validated by modern science. The vagus nerve acts as a communication superhighway between the gut and the brain, influencing mood, memory, and cognition.[53] The enteric nervous system (ENS), often called the "second brain", sits within the gut wall and directly impacts immune and neurological health. There's also growing evidence linking gut health to Alzheimer's disease, highlighting how gut imbalances can potentially influence cognitive decline and underscoring the systemic reach of mushrooms like Lion's Mane.[54]

Lion's Mane contains two key compounds: erinaceines and hericenones, which stimulate the production of NGF, a protein for neuronal growth, plasticity, and repair.[55] Research suggests these compounds exert their effects via the gut, reinforcing the holistic, integrated perspective of traditional medicine.

At the forefront of this research is my former workplace, Bristol Fungarium, now partnering with the University of the West of England on the first human clinical study into Lion's Mane's neuroprotective potential.[56] Led by Dr Tim Craig and neuroscientist Katie Turk, the study explores how this mushroom may reduce inflammation, slow neurodegeneration, and encourage cellular regeneration. Their findings could reshape how we understand the immune, gastrointestinal, and neurological benefits of functional fungi.

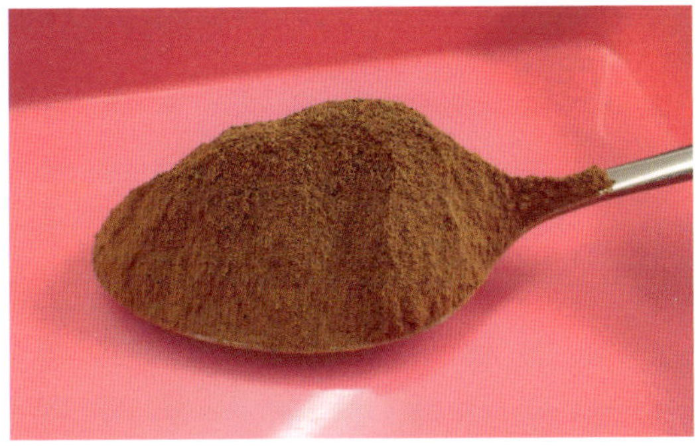

Cordyceps extract powder from The Fungi Folks.

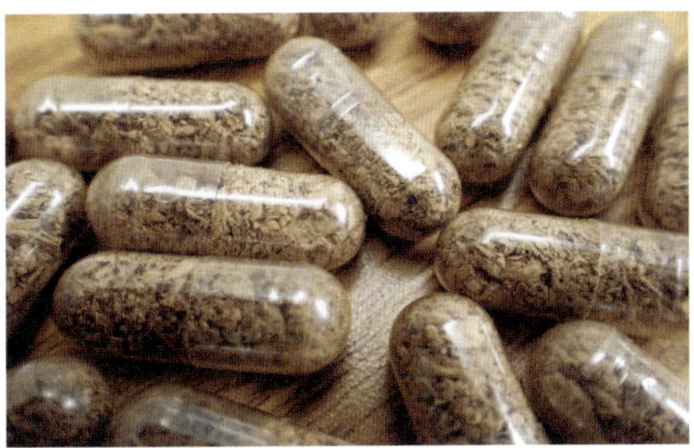

Reishi extract powder in capsule form from The Fungi Folks.

TINCTURES VS. POWDERS

When it comes to incorporating medicinal mushrooms into a wellness routine, tinctures and powders are by far the most popular options. Both have their strengths, and each offers distinct advantages depending on the user's goals, preferences, and physiology.

Tinctures are concentrated liquid extracts designed to deliver a potent dose of bioactive compounds. The highest-quality tinctures are made using a triple-extraction method – water, pressure, and alcohol extraction – ensuring a wide range of therapeutic compounds are preserved. Because they're rapidly absorbed, tinctures are often chosen for their faster-acting effects. (That said, most medicinal mushrooms work slowly – it's consistency, not quantity, that matters.) They're particularly helpful in acute cases or when a more targeted, immediate intervention is needed.

That said, some argue that tinctures may act too quickly, bypassing the gut – where so much of the body's immune and neurological magic actually happens. Since many medicinal mushrooms work through gut-mediated mechanisms (like the microbiome, vagus nerve, or gut-associated lymphoid tissue), there's a case to be made for slower, more sustained absorption.

This is where powders come in.

Powders are typically made from dried, ground fruiting bodies and are often praised for their versatility and nutritional breadth. Easily stirred into teas, coffees, smoothies, soups, or broths, they're a gentle yet effective way to build up the body over time. In addition to beta-glucans and other bioactives, powders offer dietary fibre, amino acids, and micronutrients, supporting the body's systems in a more holistic, food-like way.

While powders may be less concentrated than tinctures, their cumulative effects can be profound when used consistently. For many, they become a staple part of a nourishing daily routine – subtle, steady, and grounding.

Whether you lean towards the precision and potency of tinctures or the everyday nourishment of powders, medicinal mushrooms offer something rare: a form of plant – or rather fungal – medicine that bridges the wisdom of ancient practices with the cutting-edge discoveries of modern science.

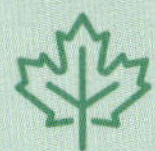

RECIPE

LION'S MANE TINCTURE

Lion's Mane mushrooms, *Hericium erinaceus*, are well-known for supporting cognitive function and gut health. While wild Lion's Mane is rare and illegal to harvest in many places, you can grow your own or source it from a local market. Informed by my time at Bristol Fungarium, this recipe uses a roughly 1:4 triple-extraction process to create a tincture that combines both alcohol and water-based extracts for maximum effectiveness.

EQUIPMENT

- Dehydrator
- Grinder
- Mason jar
- Large pot
- Thermometer
- Cheesecloth
- Pressure cooker

INGREDIENTS

- 500g/17oz fresh Lion's Mane (*Hericium erinaceus*) (50g dried)
- 350ml/11¾fl oz/1½ cups of high-proof ethanol
- 3l/100fl oz/12½ cups of distilled water

METHOD

- **Dehydrate and Grind Mushrooms:** Dehydrate 500g/17oz of Lion's Mane mushrooms at 45°C/113°F in a dehydrator or oven until brittle, and grind into a coarse powder (not too fine or it can go gloopy in the extraction process). You should end up with approximately 50g/1¾oz of dried mushrooms.
- **Alcohol Extraction:** Place the mushroom powder into a mason jar, covering it with 350ml/11¾fl oz/1½ cups of high-proof ethanol (add more alcohol if necessary to fully cover the mushrooms). Seal the jar and let it sit for 3 months, shaking occasionally to help with extraction.
- **Filter Alcohol Extract:** After 3 months, decant and keep the alcohol extract. Then dehydrate the post-alcohol mushroom substrate to prepare it for the second extraction.
- **Hot-water Extraction:** Wrap the dehydrated mushroom powder in cheesecloth and simmer in 1l of distilled water at 70°C/158°F for 12 hours. Afterwards, remove the cheesecloth and squeeze out any remaining liquid.
- **Pressure Cooker Extraction (Optional):** For a stronger extract, place the cheesecloth in a pressure cooker with 2l/67⅔fl oz/8⅓ cups of water. Cook at 121 PSI for 5 hours. This will extract more beneficial compounds from the mushrooms.
- **Combine Water Extracts:** Combine both water extracts (hot-water and pressure cooker) in a large pot, and reduce the mixture to about 145ml/5fl oz/⅓ cup.
- **Mix Alcohol and Water Extracts:** Combine 55ml/1⅔fl oz/¼ cup of alcohol extract with the concentrated 145ml/5fl oz/⅔ cup of water extract, aiming for a final tincture with 26% alcohol content. This yields roughly 4 x 50ml/1⅔fl oz bottles of 1:4 triple-extracted Lion's Mane tincture.

Directions for use: Take 1-2ml daily, as consistently as possible. Get busy with some crosswords and see if you notice any improvements!

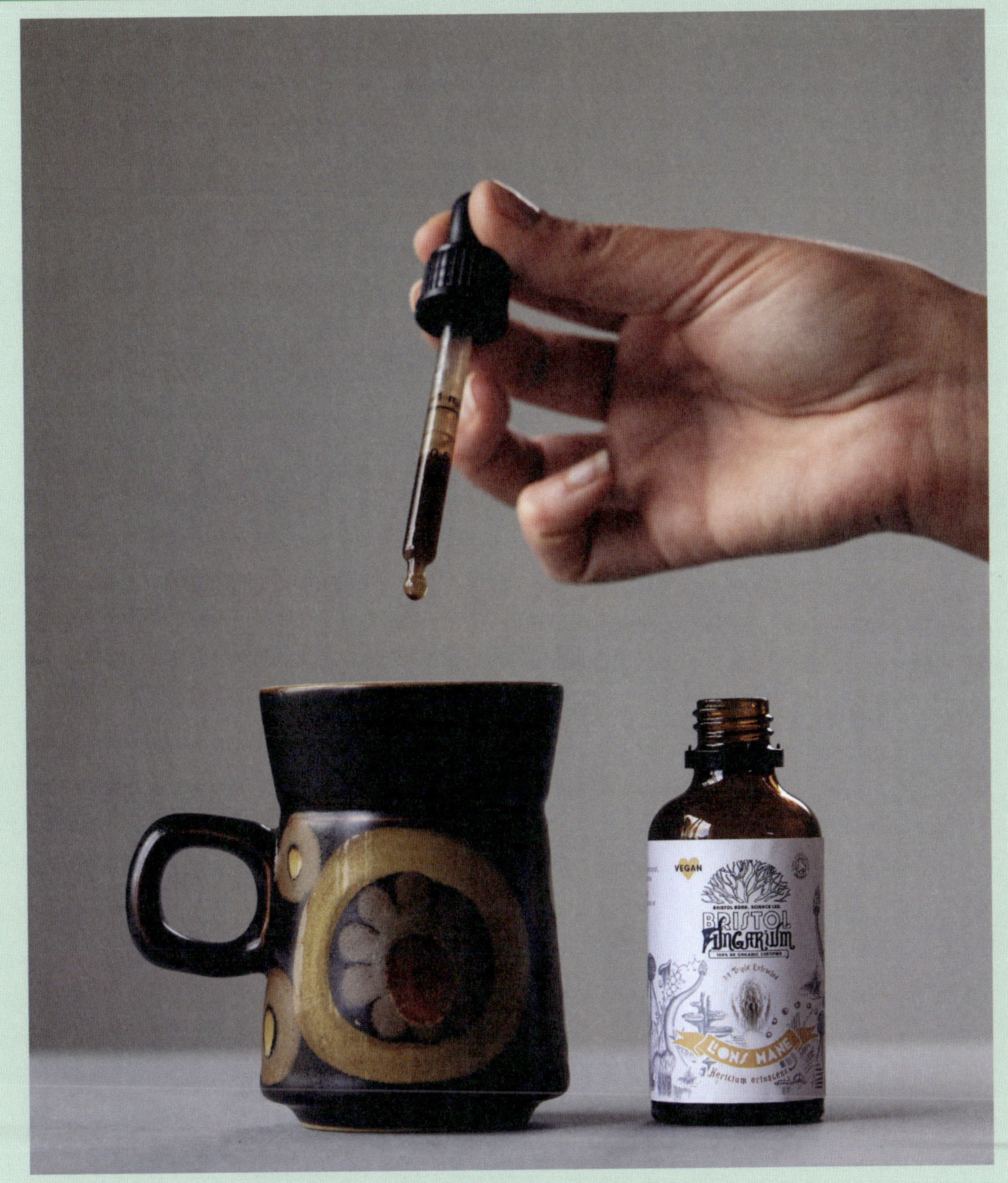

Bristol Fungarium's Lion's Mane tincture.

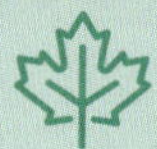

RECIPE

TURKEY TAIL EXTRACT POWDER

Turkey Tail, *Trametes versicolor*, is the most extensively studied medicinal mushroom, renowned for its polysaccharopeptides (PSPs, or sugar-protein complexes). Two well-known commercial extracts, PSP and PSK, have demonstrated significant immune-enhancing effects in both preclinical and clinical studies.[57] PSK, in particular, has been shown to boost the production of immune cells, help reduce the side effects of chemotherapy and radiotherapy, and improve survival rates in cancers of the stomach, colon, oesophagus, nasopharynx, uterus, and lungs.[58]

That said, the UK's novel foods regulations are beginning to prevent the sale of *Trametes versicolor* extracts. (A loophole is to use the less medicinally potent *Trametes hirsuta* instead.) So, this is a DIY recipe for making your own Turkey Tail extract powder, which can be easily added to teas, soups, smoothies, or taken as a supplement.

EQUIPMENT

- Blender
- Pot
- Dehydrator
- Spice grinder
- Silica gel packs
- Airtight glass jar

INGREDIENTS

- 100g/3½oz Turkey Tail mushrooms (*Trametes versicolor*)
- 1l/33¾fl oz/4¼ cups of distilled water

METHOD

1. Harvest Turkey Tail mushrooms from decomposing logs or buy from a trusted supplier. (You can't now sell these independently, only *Trametes coliorus*.) Be sure to identify them correctly as False Turkey Tail is similar but lacks the medicinal benefits of true Turkey Tail.
2. Clean the mushrooms with a brush or knife to remove debris. Cut them into small pieces or blend them for a finer material.
3. In a large pot, simmer the mushrooms in 10 times as much water for 2–3 hours to extract the compounds. Maintain a low temperature to preserve the beneficial compounds.
4. After simmering, let the mixture cool, then blend it to achieve a smooth consistency. This helps release additional compounds from the mushrooms.
5. Let the mushrooms sink to the bottom of your blender and pour off the remaining liquid – keep and drink as a tea!
6. Spread the blended mixture on a tray and dehydrate at 45°C/113°F in a dehydrator or oven. Once dried, it should be brittle and easy to grind.
7. Use a spice grinder to turn the dried extract into a fine powder.
8. Store the powder in an airtight glass jar with a silica gel pack to keep it dry.

Directions for use: Take a heaped spoonful of the powder and add it to your chosen medium! The flavour is delicious.

BOG BODIES & BUTTER

BOGLAND

For T.P. Flanagan

We have no prairies
To slice a big sun at evening –
Everywhere the eye concedes to
Encroaching horizon,
Is wooed into the cyclops' eye
Of a tarn. Our unfenced country
Is bog that keeps crusting
Between the sights of the sun.
They've taken the skeleton
Of the Great Irish Elk
Out of the peat, set it up
An astounding crate full of air.
Butter sunk under
More than a hundred years
Was recovered salty and white.
The ground itself is kind, black butter
Melting and opening underfoot,
Missing its last definition
By millions of years.
They'll never dig coal here,
Only the waterlogged trunks
Of great firs, soft as pulp.
Our pioneers keep striking
Inwards and downwards,
Every layer they strip
Seems camped on before.
The bogholes might be
Atlantic seepage,
The wet centre is bottomless.

– Seamus Heaney, Door into the Dark, *1969*

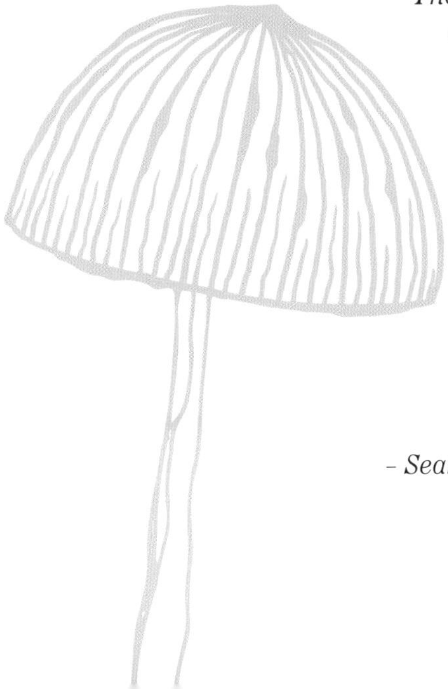

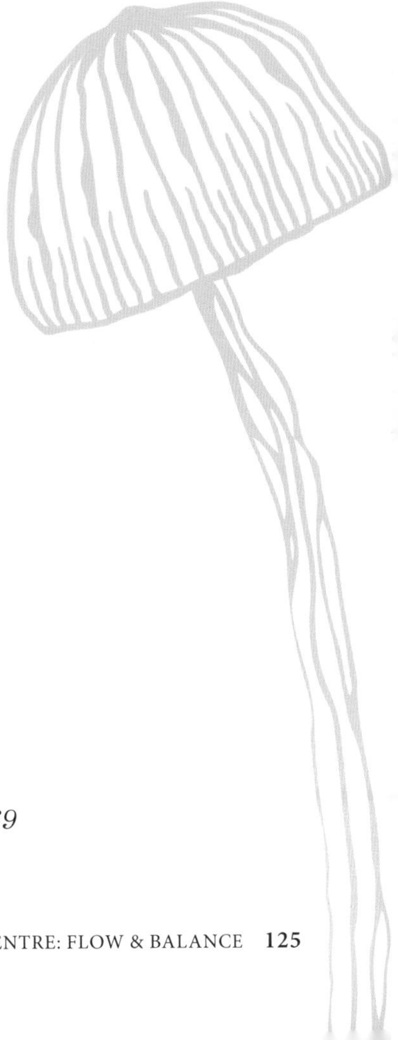

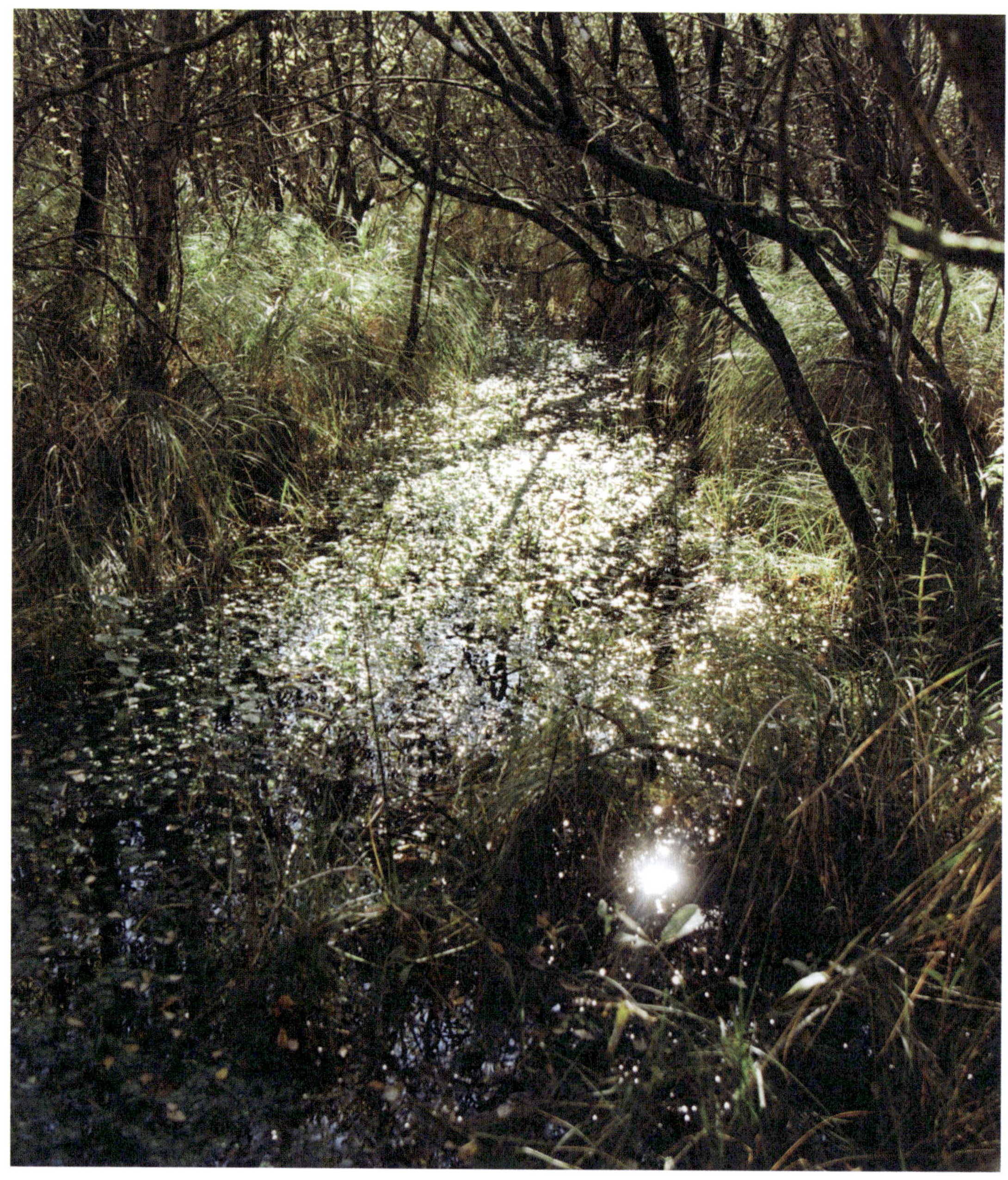

Ancient willow trees in South Wales' Rhos Goch National Nature Reserve – a raised peat bog and Site of Special Scientific Interest (SSSI).

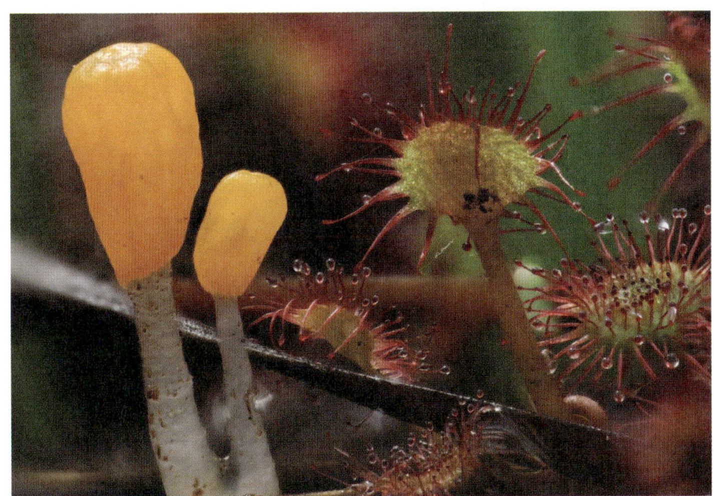

Bogland ecosystems host rare birds, invertebrates, mosses, lichens, and fungi, creating extraordinary biodiversity hotspots. Here, rare Bog Beacon Mushrooms, Mitrula elegans, *and Round-leaved Sundews sprout from a Californian bog.*

Water is essential to life, that much we know. But few would look to the common bog, with its acidic pools and spongy ground, to further that idea.

Bogs are wetland ecosystems characterised by waterlogged, oxygen-poor, and nutrient-deficient conditions. Over thousands of years, dead plant material, mainly mosses like *Sphagnum*, accumulates to form peat. The lack of oxygen slows down decomposition, creating a unique and stable environment. Despite their harsh conditions, bogs support a surprising variety of lifeforms, from insect-eating plants to specialised fungi and insects. In these slow-moving ecosystems, survival depends on adaptation, making them an important reservoir of biodiversity.

Bogs form in different geographical conditions. Raised bogs, some of the oldest on Earth, develop in ancient lake basins. Blanket bogs form over waterlogged soils in areas with high rainfall, while frozen bogs lie beneath permafrost in Arctic regions.

These ecosystems are strange; they evolve incredibly slowly. In places like Scotland's Loch Squad in Wester Ross, a single foot of peat represents around a thousand years of accumulation. Though still incredibly slow, the pace of growth far outstrips the rate of decay.

This is, in large part, because fungi, the great decomposers of the natural world, find peat bogs challenging places to thrive. The highly acidic and oxygen-poor conditions limit most fungal activity, resulting in slow, decomposition and surprisingly low fungal diversity compared to other habitats. Within bogs, fungal communities often show vertical stratification: surface layers are dominated by Ascomycota and Basidiomycota, while Zygomycota species tend to thrive deeper in the peat.[59]

At the bog's surface lies the acrotelm, a dense, fibrous mat often more than a foot thick, interwoven with the roots of mosses and small plants that stabilise the ecosystem. Unlike forests where plants form rich mycorrhizal networks with fungi, bog mosses lack true roots, preventing typical mycorrhizal associations. This absence forces bog fungi to rely on alternative survival strategies rather than the nutrient exchanges common in more fertile soils.

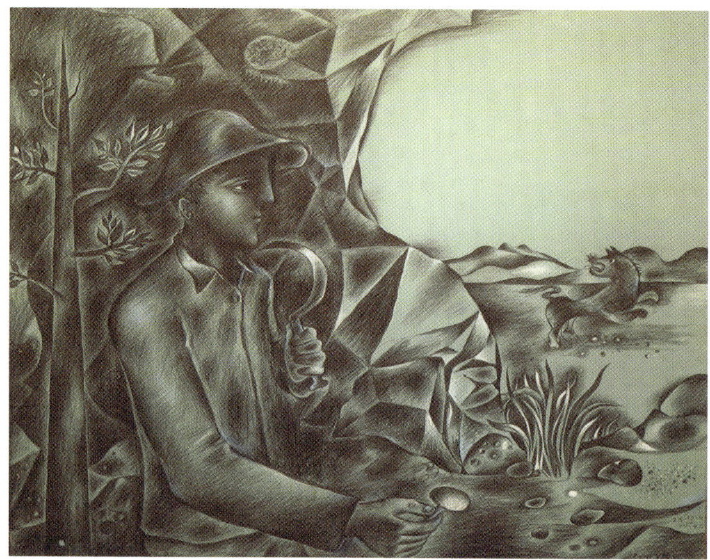

John Craxton, Reaper with Mushroom, *1944–1945. Bogs have long been linked to mystery, murder, and danger, with their still waters symbolising stagnation.*

For example, beneath the acrotelm is the catotelm, a water-saturated, anaerobic layer where oxygen is scarce and decomposition slows almost to a halt. Only specialised anaerobic bacteria and a few resilient fungi eke out a living here, slowly breaking down organic matter and releasing methane gas that bubbles to the surface if you sink too deeply into the peat.

Some fungi, like aquatic chytrids and acid-tolerant species, manage to survive in this waterlogged environment, but the robust fungal decomposers common elsewhere are mostly absent or greatly reduced. The Bog Beacon, *Mitrula elegans*, is an exception. It primarily decomposes dead leaves, twigs, sphagnum mosses, and other plant debris such as sedge and grass litter, playing a vital role in releasing nutrients back into the bogland ecosystem.

Since nutrients from below are hard to access, fungi such as the Willow Glue, *Hydnoporia tabacina*, have evolved a clever alternative: they catch fallen branches from above, "gluing" them to the stable branches on which they perch. Likewise, lichens and wood-decaying fungi like delicate Green Elf Cups cling to weathered tree branches, avoiding the swamp below. Alternatively, mycorrhizal fungi such as russulas and milkcaps form partnerships with plants along the *edges* of bogs, surviving in these slightly less hostile conditions.

While these resilient species remind us that fungi can take root even in the most hostile environments, bogs offer a haunting glimpse of a world where fungi – and decay – are largely absent: where biological accumulation exceeds decomposition.

Throughout history, bogs have held deep cultural and spiritual significance. Dante's *Divine Comedy* immortalised the River Styx as a bog, a symbol of moral stagnation and spiritual decay, where souls of the damned endure eternal punishment. Likewise, waterlogged wetlands have served as natural boundaries between kingdoms and civilisations. European and North American folklore often casts

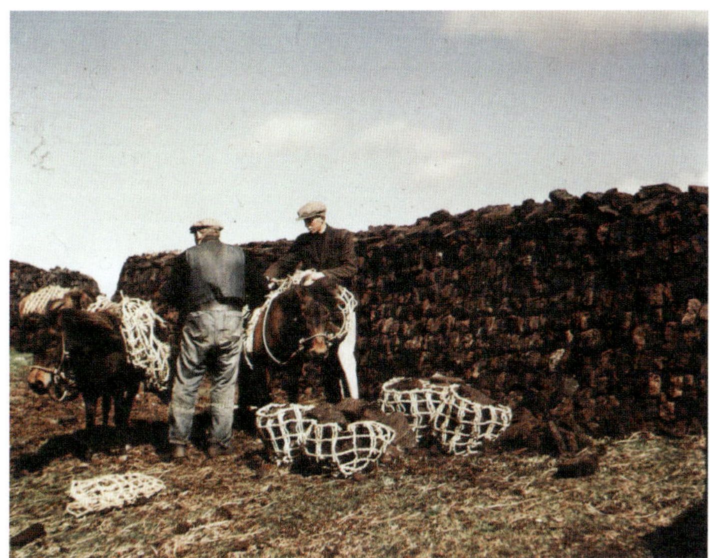

Shetland Ponies transporting cut peat. In the Hebrides, peat production involved one person (typically a man) cutting, and another (usually a woman) laying-out. Though peat has been harvested for fuel since the 1700s, they are vital carbon sinks. Their slow organic decay, due to limited fungal activity, helps regulate the global climate.

bogs as mysterious and dangerous places, haunted by glowing will o' the wisps that lure travellers into swampy depths and shape-shifting spirits like the Irish *púca*.

In Irish mythology, bogs (like springs, rivers, and wells) are portals to the Otherworld, places where spirits and ancestors dwell. The amber-coloured peat was revered as a place of power, where costly offerings – trees, treasures, and animals – were cast into the depths to appease deities and ensure prosperity.

Seamus Heaney, one of Ireland's greatest poets, described bogs as "dark caskets" preserving the ancient past, like geological memory banks. Each peat layer connects us to history, offering fragments of the past and cultures long gone. T P Flanagan echoed this reverence, calling bogs the "fundamental Irish landscape", rooted in a mysterious history that was at once sacred and violent.

Bogs also preserve some of the most gruesome and fascinating relics of past rituals: bog bodies. These remarkably intact human remains, found across Europe but especially in Ireland and Denmark, are preserved by the sphagnum moss and the bog's acidic, oxygen-poor environment. The humic acids effectively tan the skin, halting decay and turning bodies into leathery time capsules.

Many of these individuals appear to have met violent ends, leading scholars to believe they were part of ritual sacrifices, possibly linked to kingship or fertility rites. In ancient Ireland, rulers were seen as stewards of the land, and their failure to ensure prosperity might warrant a ceremonial death. One of the most striking examples is Oldcroghan Man, discovered in 2003 near Croghan Hill, County Offaly. His mutilated body – missing limbs and nipples – suggests a symbolic dethroning. In early Irish tradition, sucking a king's nipples signified submission; to have none meant disqualification from kingship itself.[60]

Elsewhere, Koelbjerg Man of Denmark, dating back to around 8000 BCE, is one of the earliest known bog bodies. As bogs embody a liminal realm between life and death, preservation and decay, these

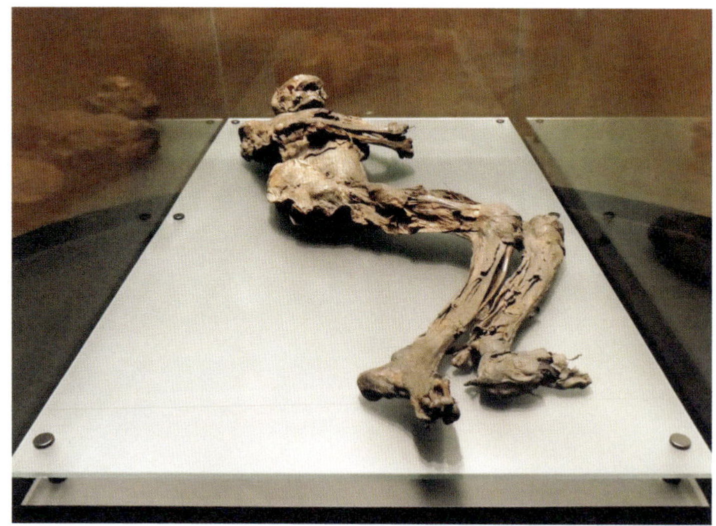

"Bog bodies" have been discovered across Ireland, Scotland, Norway, and Denmark. Harsh bog conditions preserve them remarkably well, as seen with Old Croghan Man, whose scarred torso reveals his brutal death, believed to be linked to an ancient fertility rite.

remains blur the line between punishment and reverence. Were these burials acts of reverence, granting the dead a form of immortality? Or were they sentences to eternal punishment – bodies suspended in time, trapped in the half-life of incomplete decomposition? Were these people condemned criminals, royal hostages, sacrificed kings, or revered offerings to appease the gods of earth and sky?

The picture grows murkier with dietary and biochemical analysis. Some bodies were fed humble meals of gruel and buttermilk, typical of lower-status individuals, while others had a protein-rich diet, though always with a vegetarian "last supper". Curiously, several bodies contain traces of Ergot, a hallucinogenic and toxic fungus found in damp rye. Was this accidental, medicinal, or part of the ritual? [61]

As Frodo says in *The Lord of the Rings*, gazing into the Mirror of Galadriel:

"They lie in all the pools . . . grim faces and evil, and noble faces and sad. Many faces proud and fair, and weeds in their silver hair."[62]

The bog holds them still – between death and decay, honour and horror.

Even more curious treasures emerge from bogs, like bog butter – a waxy, often dairy-based substance buried and preserved in anaerobic peat for millennia. These butters, found in Ireland, Scotland, and Norway, speak to ancient agricultural practices and possibly spiritual offerings, much like the human sacrifices.

In ancient Ireland, butter was a symbol of wealth, power, and sacred connection to the land. When Count John de Perilhos visited in 1397, he remarked, "They have excellent butter", noting how closely people lived alongside their cattle.[63] Cows, which produced milk in spring and provided butter throughout the seasons, formed the backbone of medieval Irish society. As the renowned archaeologist and bog butter expert Karen O'Toole aptly notes: "In Ireland, cows were King."[64]

Hundreds of lumps of bog butter have been unearthed, clearly buried with intent, yet many questions lie unanswered. Who made these butters and why? Did the bogs enhance their flavour, as is practised

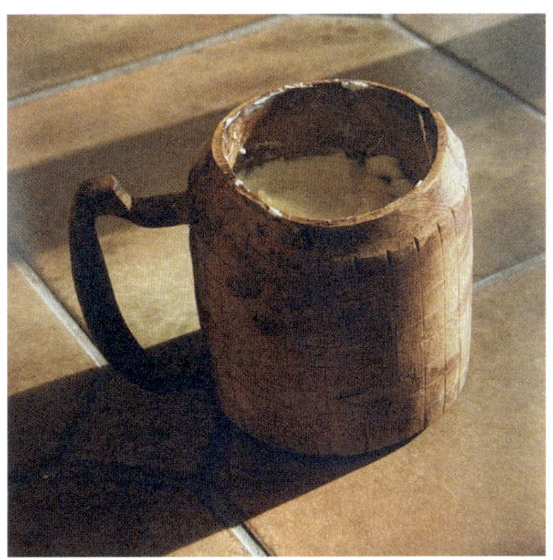

"Bog butters" have been uncovered in boglands, some dating back to 1500 BC. Over 700 samples of bog butter have been found, including a 47-kilogram piece discovered in 2025 that still faintly smells of dairy.

in certain Indian traditions with ghee? Were they salted? Could butter have served as currency, like in Norway, stored in bogs like ancient vaults? Or was burial a method of preservation, keeping surplus butter cool and free from spoilage for later use. Many scholars believe these butters were offerings to water deities like Boann, Goddess of the River Boyne – dedications made from up to a year's worth of milk to secure fertile fields, healthy herds, and divine favour.

Surprisingly, most excavated bog butters from the 19th and 20th centuries no longer exist. We know of them only through newspaper reports and Ordnance Surveys[65] because many were repurposed – used as candles, shoe polish, joint pain remedies for humans and livestock, and even, occasionally, in cooking, though details remain vague. In contrast, modern discoveries are often stored in museums as cultural relics – further preserving the bog-preserved butters.

This fate raises important questions about how we preserve cultural heritage. While museums play a vital role in safeguarding artefacts, some argue for more active, participatory approaches. Irish artist Gareth Kennedy, for example, advocates engaging with bog butter through contemporary practice, reviving ancient traditions in ways that feel relevant today.[66]

An example of this living connection is the 3,500-year-old Blanket Bog Oak found in northwest Ireland. Inside the ancient tree, 180 acorns were discovered and replanted into Irish soils.[67] Preserved for millennia, these seeds now bridge past and present. They are both archaeological treasures and ecological gifts: bearers of ancient DNA with the potential to enrich genetic diversity and promote future forest resilience. As craftsman Dominic Trimble, who discovered the acorns, said, "It matters what story we tell with these."

Of course, museums are invaluable for education and conservation. But I can't help feeling grateful that none of these acorns ended up behind glass. All of them were returned to the land – living and growing once again in an Irish landscape changed by time, people, and culture.

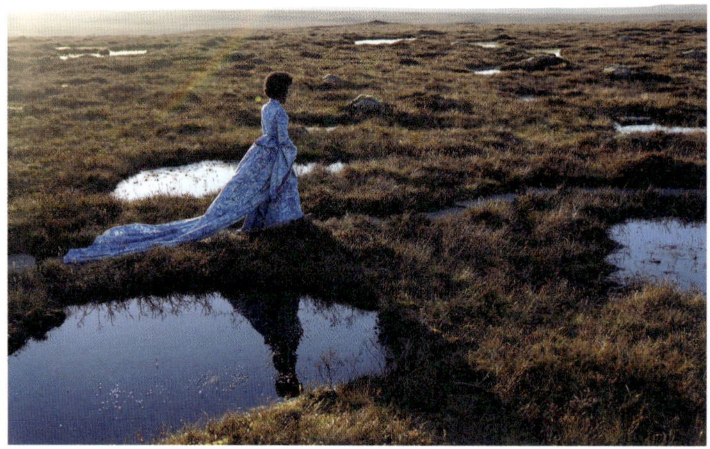

Zimbabwean-Scottish artist Sekai Machache in Scotland's Flow Country, a vast blanket bog and one of Europe's largest peatlands. Sekai explores the tension between stillness, growth, and decay, using bogs as a metaphor for the slow but steady evolution of identity.

Viewed more broadly, bogs offer a poignant metaphor for our modern impulse to accumulate, preserve, and protect – often without allowing for the natural processes of decay, change, or return. Without decomposition, there is no renewal. Fungi, nature's agents of breakdown, make this plain. In fact, fungi are often seen as enemies of preservation, degrading stone monuments, paintings, textiles, and ancient manuscripts.[68]

Bogs, by contrast, with their scarcity of fungi and slow biological rhythms, are extraordinary vessels of preservation. In their anaerobic embrace, they have held bodies, butter, and forgotten histories – symbols of stasis, memory, and silence.

And yet, fungi might teach us something different. Perhaps their presence – their resistance to stillness – is what keeps culture alive. By breaking things down, fungi ensure nothing stays fixed. As poet Seamus Heaney and painter T.P. Flanagan seemed to suggest, resilient cultures are not static. They adapt, reinvent, and transform. There was never just one way to bury butter in a bog – nor is there only one way to make use of what we recover.

So forgive me, but I'd suggest this: finish the butter you find in the bog, and plant the acorns back in the soil. Keep the culture alive. Cultural transmission is fragile – subject to time, change, and interpretation, especially when four thousand years and a peat bog stand between us and the past. Like fungi and plants adapting to the peculiar rhythms of the peatland, culture is not a fixed legacy but a living, ever-evolving cycle.

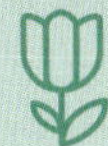

ACTIVITY & RECIPE

RECREATING 5TH-CENTURY BCE BOG BUTTER

Making butter in Ireland is a very superstitious process. Butter, derived from cows that were seen as sacred, carries with it a deep reverence and a mystical link to the supernatural. The act of churning butter was believed to call upon the blessings of deities and spirits from above and below, particularly during significant agricultural periods, uch as the beginning of the milking season.

So, come spring, gather your best butter-loving friends. Travel to your nearest bog, source some thick cream, and recreate some 5th-century BCE bog butter. Infuse this process with intention: Reflect on your forebears who may have engaged in this practice and think of future generations who might one day unearth your offering. Look to the ephemeral, mischievous water spirits and the chthonic beings who inhabit the bog.

Consider your place in the world and use the repetitive motion of churning butter to expel what you wish to be rid of. Allow the physical act to unblock your energy centres so you can flow.

Pass the bowl around and allow everyone to contribute to this physical, emotional, and spiritual release. The more you sweat, the better the outcome, just like the buttermilk leaching from the butter.

Once the butter has solidified, pause. Centre yourself: Be calm and dive into that inner core that connects you up, down, backward, forward, and deep into the eternal now. Then make the sacrifice.

EQUIPMENT

- Bowl
- Wooden spoon (According to legend, one should never use metal utensils to churn butter as it might spoil the milk or anger the spirits. Wooden churns are preferred, as they are more harmonious with nature.)
- Wooden vessel
- Blanket

INGREDIENTS

- 500ml/17fl oz/2 cups of double/heavy cream

METHOD

1. Pour the cream into a bowl. Beat as hard as you can until the cream starts to thicken (about 5 minutes).
2. The cream will then start to lose its billowy smoothness and become a little rough. After 10 minutes, it will start to separate.
3. Once the butter and buttermilk have completely separated, pour off all the buttermilk. (You can save this as a delicious marinade for cooking!).
4. Place your bog butter in a wooden vessel and wrap it with a blanket. This step is essential. You must protect it well, or it could be taken by the *púca*.

Tip: This is hard work, so pass the bowl around and share the load!

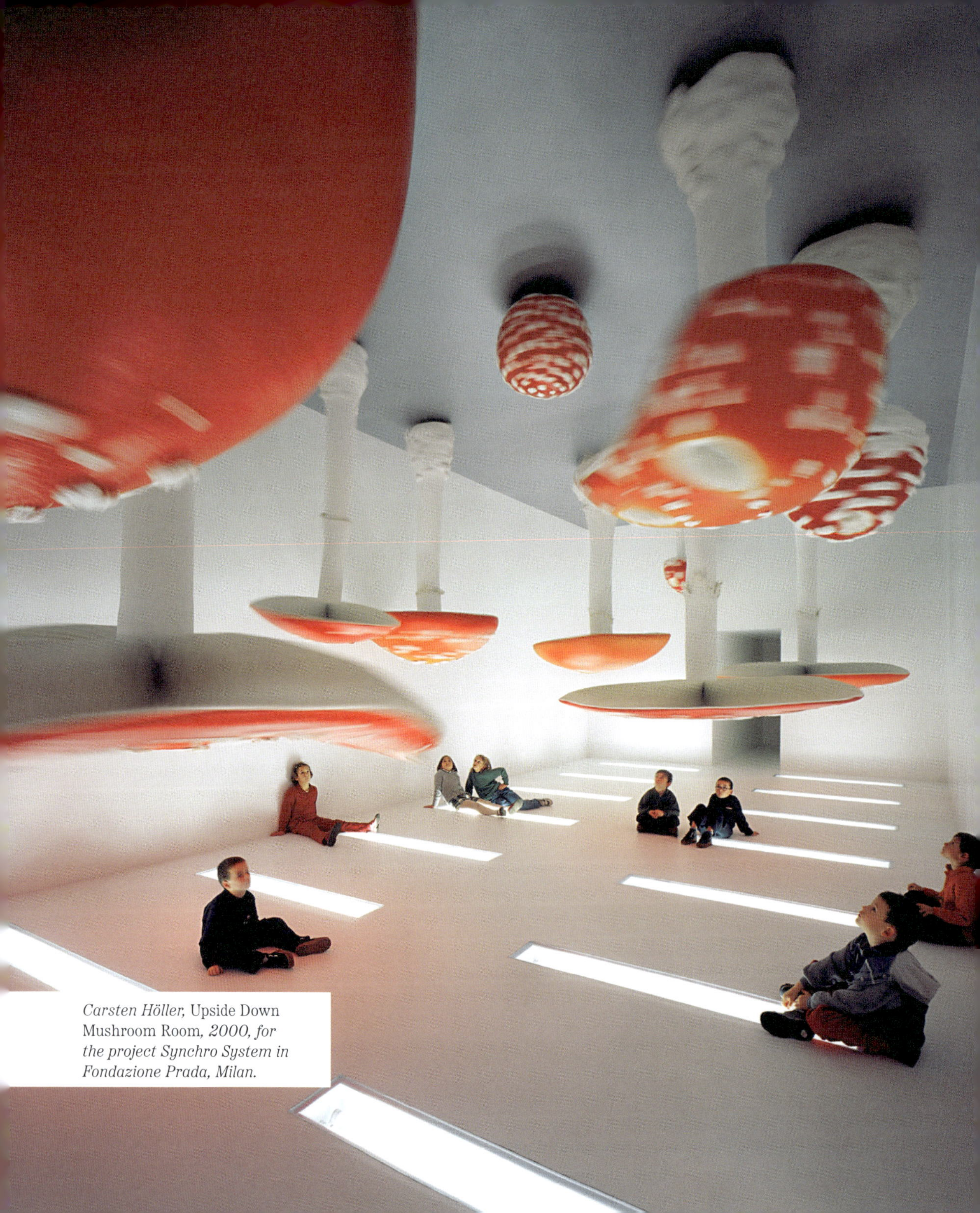

Carsten Höller, Upside Down Mushroom Room, *2000, for the project Synchro System in Fondazione Prada, Milan.*

4

IN & OUT: Transformation, Transportation, & Transcendence

"Then suddenly the mole felt a great awe fall upon him. An awe that turned his muscles to water held him and rooted his feet to the ground. With difficulty, he turned to look for his friend and saw him at his side, cowed, stricken, and trembling violently."

– *The Wind in the Willows*

Fungi are masters of transformation. Much like fire reduces wood to smoke and ash, fungi devour organic matter, metabolising it into entirely new forms. But unlike fire, fungi are ceaselessly generous. They transform what they touch, offering food, materials, medicines, knowledge, and inspiration to all they encounter. The mushroom-producing fungi are particularly remarkable in this respect. They burst forth from the earth, reshaping themselves into fantastical forms: from the bizarre Octopus Stinkhorn, *Clathrus archeri,* to the Mosaic Puffball, *Handkea utriformis*, and the Bleeding Polypore, *Hydnellum peckii*. Anyone who's ever bought a mushroom grow kit has witnessed this transformation firsthand. Saprotrophic mycelia colonise plain wood, break it down, and channel the nutrients into new, life-giving forms. Some fungi, like Morels, *Morchella* spp., even spring from ashes.

But mushrooms, the reproductive organs of fungi, are transient. They live their brief lives above the soil, their sole purpose to reproduce, spread spores, and decompose, often within days. This brief above-ground apparition has made mushrooms symbols of impermanence, albeit annual reminders of the hidden, ever-present fungal world below. They are also creatures of transition. Mushrooms tend to appear at transitional times of year: primarily autumn, but sometimes spring. They also emerge at transitional times of day: during dawn or dusk, when the world is neither fully awake nor fully asleep. Mushrooms are creatures of the in-between.

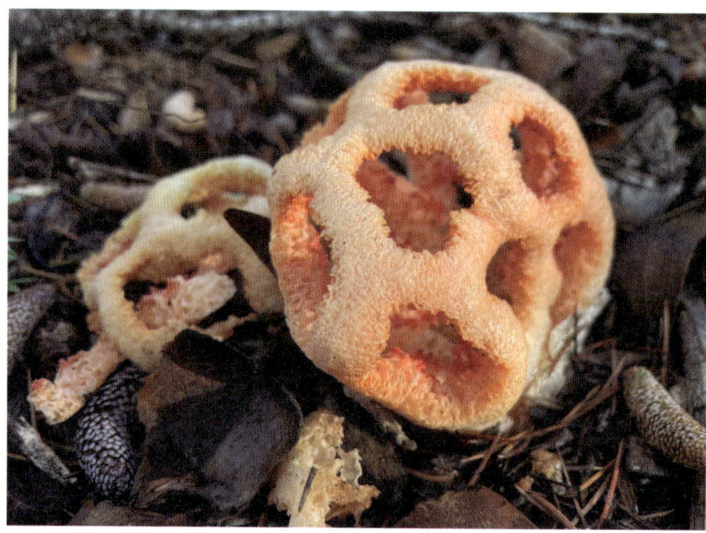

Red-cage Fungus, Clathrus ruber.

Given this, it's no surprise that many cultures have long associated mushrooms with ephemeral beings, like elves, fairies, and gnomes, and have regarded them as portals to other worlds. They're invisible but real, slipping between dimensions. These transitions they represent aren't just physical – they're psychological and spiritual. The mushroom offers not only a connection to the Earth but also a doorway to realms beyond our senses.

Magic mushrooms in particular have emerged as powerful tools for personal transformation. Across the globe, from sacred rituals to modern-day rave cultures, psychedelic mushrooms provide a profound invitation to alter our consciousness. They can twist our realities in unexpected ways. A psychedelic "trip" is a journey of transport. When taken with intention, mushrooms guide us out of our familiar state of mind, carrying us to new ways of seeing and experiencing the world.

But transformation doesn't always require psychedelics. For example, Mole in *The Wind in the Willows* and Simon in *Lord of the Flies* undergo moments of transcendence through direct, unmediated experience. These encounters are often overwhelming – too vast and intense for our mortal consciousness to fully absorb – and unfold through stages of apprehension, awe, and ultimately, exaltation.

Apprehension is the moment of encounter when we come face to face with something greater than ourselves, whether the vastness of the universe, the complexity of our psyche, or the interconnectedness of all beings. Then comes awe, wonder, even fear. We experience the relative greatness of what eco-philosopher Timothy Morton calls the "Hyperobject"[1] and realise our comparative insignificance. Finally, comes exaltation, where we experience a profound union with what we've encountered. The separation between the self and the world dissolves in an expansive, timeless experience of unity. This is the ultimate transcendence – where we, as conscious beings, become indivisible from existence, seeing, feeling, and being in a way that goes beyond ordinary human consciousness.

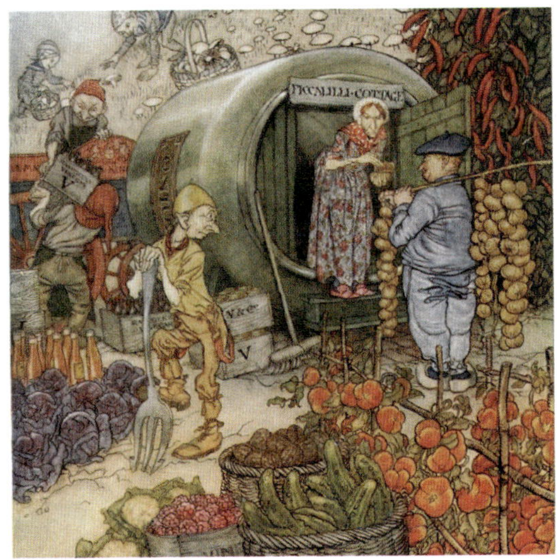

Mr. & Mrs. Vinegar at Home *in* English Fairy Tales *by Flora Annie Steel, illustrated by Arthur Rackham, 1918.*

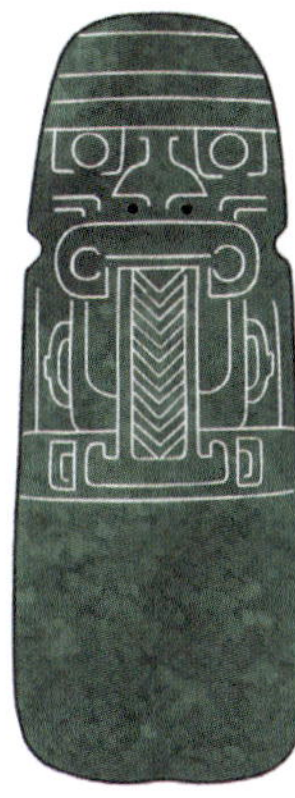

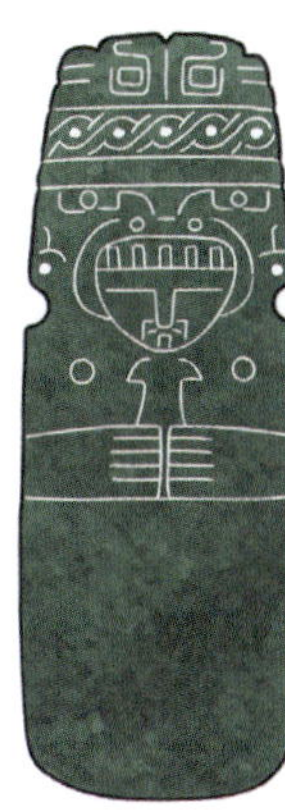

An illustration of a pair of anthropomorphic jade pendants, originally from a Mesoamerican coin axe. The figure on the right holds a mushroom – believed to be hallucinogenic.

Transformation has always been part of human existence. Our ancestors had countless techniques – chants, rhythms, fasting, rituals, and play – all designed to achieve self-transcendence. Play, especially, has been considered a sacred practice in many cultures, a means of stepping beyond the ordinary to connect with the divine. Children, in their instinctive joy, embody this spirit. They spin, roll, and imagine with abandon, finding ecstasy in the simplest actions.

This idea appears playfully with Disney's Dumbo and Timothy Q Mouse who seek a temporary transformation. But many fantasies and fairy tales revolve around transformation: frogs turn into princes, pumpkins become carriages, and servants rise as royalty. These stories mirror our own journeys, reflecting the challenges of embracing change and navigating uncertainty.

We are not alone in seeking transcendence from the ingestion of wild substances. As psychopharmacologist Ronald K Siegel notes, from jaguars chewing hallucinogenic vines to birds nibbling fermented fruit, animals, like us, seek altered states. So in this chapter, we leap with others of the animal kingdom into the unknown. We enter the Italian woods, where Porcini mushrooms and ancient legends await. We are pulled out of our minds and into the world around us, shrinking into miniature worlds and losing time and self. We dissolve into sensory deprivation tanks with dolphins on government-supplied LSD and uncover the influence of Siberian fungal folktales. Following Alice into Wonderland, we trace the origins of Lewis Carroll's hallucinogenic mushroom, then journey to the Himalayas, where Cordyceps fungi transform from mycelium to moth larvae and into a sacred aphrodisiac. Through rituals of connection, we harness the transformative power of dance and fungi, becoming agents of change, poised for metamorphosis.

FORAGING & PAYING ATTENTION

"Into the forest I go, to lose my mind and find my soul."

- John Muir

As I walked through the woods late one October night, I froze. Where I stood, and where I had just come from, was winter green and brown. But ahead of me, as far as I could see, everything was white with frost. An invisible boundary, made visible by frozen water, separated these two worlds. I stepped into the white landscape, waited, and stepped back out, nodding to myself, confirming that my sleep-deprived mind was not merely imagining things. So once more, I ventured into this Narnia, captivated by the elaborate ice crystals on the trees and the satisfying crunch of the solid ice beneath my feet.

This was the most enchanting manifestation of a microclimate I have ever experienced. But more than the beauty of it, I was struck by how the slight, almost imperceptible dip in the path, which I walked daily, had remained unnoticed until now. This tiny dip must have remained a degree or two colder than the surrounding woods, sparking this beautiful transformation. As I lingered in the chill air, I found myself whispering to the land, "This is my Porcini spot". I scanned my surroundings, touched the ground, and shook my head in awe. "Mushrooms . . ." I murmured, lost in thought.

Just as abruptly as this frozen world had begun, it ended. I stepped over the threshold to the other side, promising to return in autumn, eager to find the mushrooms that fruited annually in this very place.

***

Forests are realms of legendary transformation. They symbolise the Unknown, which, in the archetypal Hero's journey, one must enter to undergo profound physical and spiritual change. In them, good and evil, life and death, light and dark, exist. These tales navigate from rupture to rapture to return, leading to a renewed perspective on reality.

Stepping into a forest initiates an inner shift. The air changes, the canopy closes above, and the familiar path gives way to thickets and shadows. The forest calls us to be more attuned, more aware, and more alive.

The UK may have lost much of its wild landscapes, but in Europe, vast forests remain havens for wildlife - lynx, boars, wolves, and bears, guardians of the wild, still roam the land. While their presence

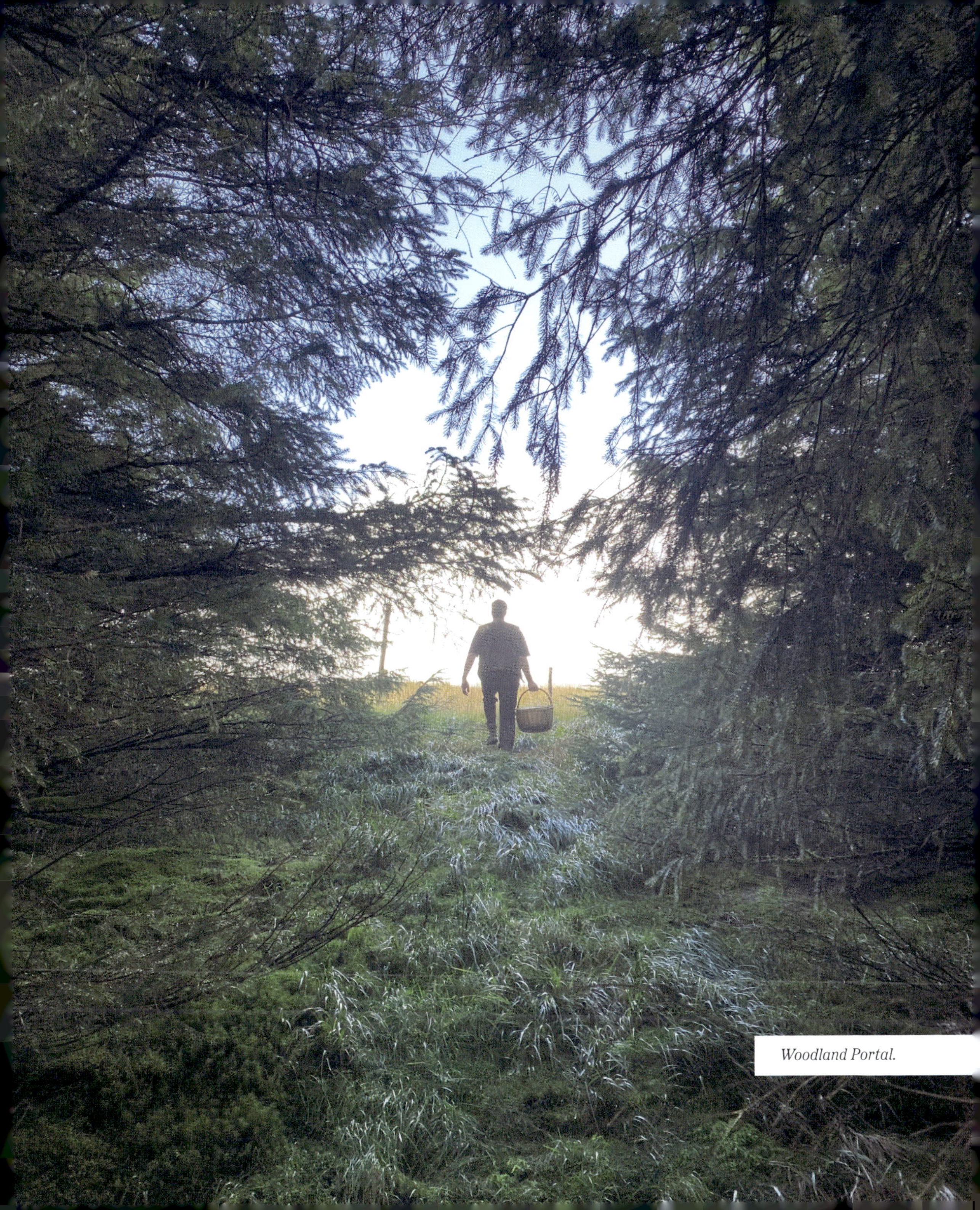

Woodland Portal.

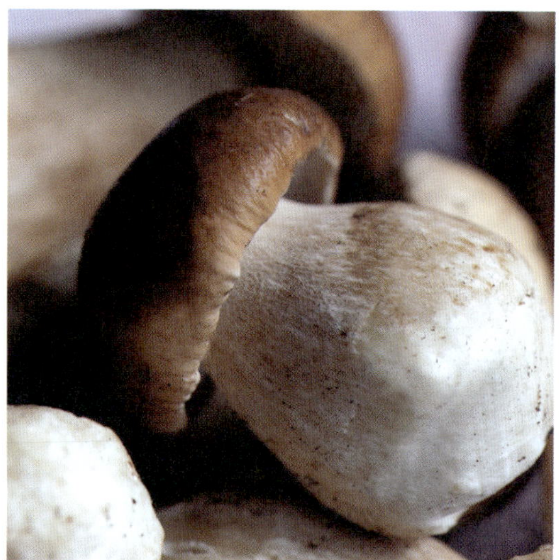

Porcini, meaning "piglets" in Italian, are prized edible mushrooms. Their Latin name, Boletus edulis, *"edible bolete", reflects their high status among foragers.*

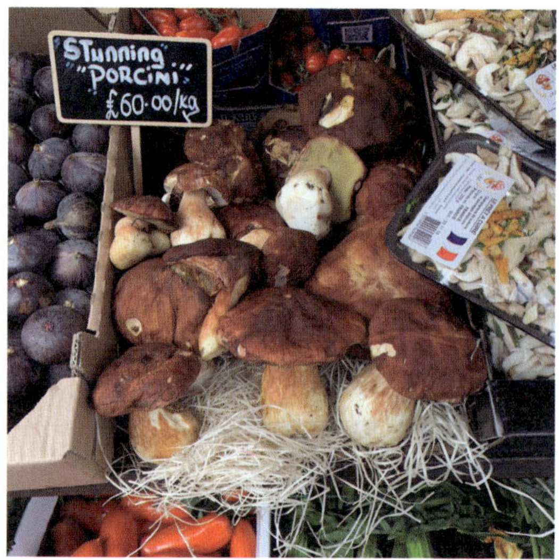

"Porcini are the mushroom that every hunter seeks. For some, notably the commercial collector, it is the only mushroom they seek." John Wright, The Forager's Calendar.

can pose risks if we're not cautious, they are more often mere inconveniences to the greater pursuit of autumn's crown jewel: the mushroom hunt.

Mushroom foraging is more than a tradition in many European cultures; it is a way of life. In Latvia, the obsession with mushroom foraging, or *sēņošana,* runs deep, passed down through generations. In Poland, mushrooming is a national sport, and the town of Grevena in Greece has earned the title of "mushroom capital". But among the foragers, Italians are particularly passionate about their mushroom harvests, from the Alps to the Apennines, where forests are home to many prized varieties, including the famous Porcini.

Porcini translates as "piglets" in Italian, and they are celebrated across Europe under various names. In France, they're called *cèpes* (trunk); in the UK, Penny Buns; in California, King Bolete; in Germany, *steinpilze* (stone mushroom); and in the Netherlands, *eekhoornjesbrood* (Squirrel's Bread). Their Latin name, *Boletus edulis,* literally means "edible Bolete", underscoring their esteemed status in the foraging world. As John Wright, author of *The Forager's Calendar*, notes, "Porcini are the mushroom that every hunter seeks. For some, notably the commercial collector, it is the only mushroom they seek."[2]

Porcini thrive in deciduous and coniferous forests. They form symbiotic relationships with trees like oak, beech, pine, and spruce, and prefer quiet, undisturbed woodlands. These mushrooms emerge in late summer to autumn and are common on the edges of well-established woodlands and plantations. Porcini are early-establishment mycorrhizal fungi, colonising tree roots within the first 20 years of a tree's life. The fungi take up to 20 years to fully establish and typically fruit most abundantly between

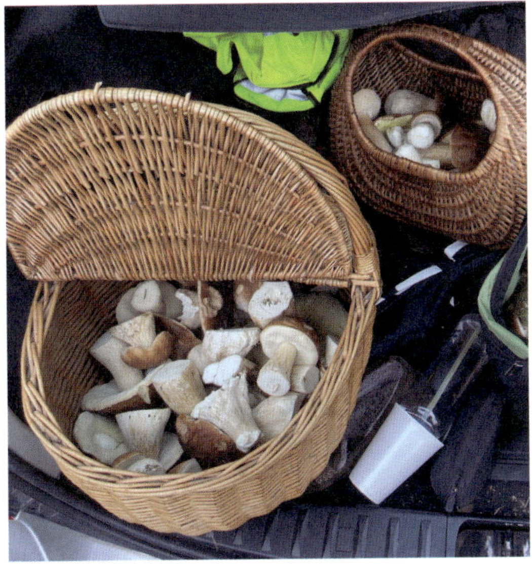

Baskets full of Porcini after an abundant harvest from Tom's secret Porcini spot!

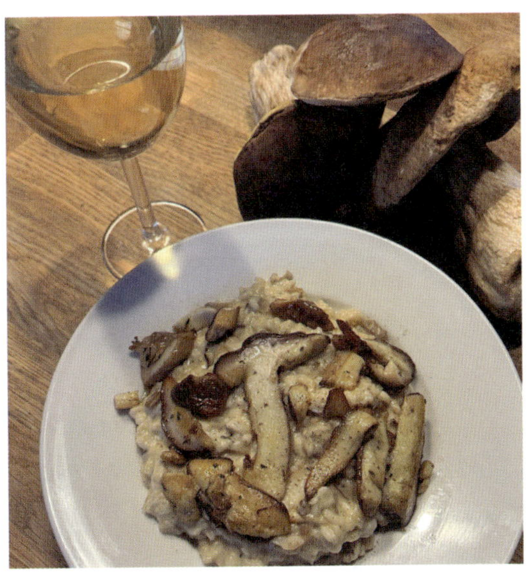

Tom Carter's freshly foraged Porcini risotto, served with Georgian orange wine. (Apparently a very good pairing . . . !).

25 and 45 years of the tree's life.[3] After this period, their presence declines as other mushrooms take over. Similar ecological preferences are shared by the Miller, *Clitopilus prunulus,* (which has a distinctive semen-like smell), Fly Agaric, and Peppery Bolete, *Chalciporus piperatus*, which often grow very close to Porcini.

In Italy, commercial foragers are often shepherds, well-versed in the rhythms of the land. They access mountain regions that are off-limits to tourists, where Porcini thrive in the transition zones between oak and chestnut trees.[4] For these foragers, the discovery of Porcini is more than just a harvest, it's a relationship with the land, learned over years of intimate knowledge of the mountains and forests.

The thrill of finding Porcini is addictive. In their early stages, they stand two to three inches tall and offer a rich umami flavour and firm texture, often shaved or sliced raw, much like truffles. As they mature, their aroma and taste intensify. Even older, larger specimens – if free from maggots or slugs – can be dried and powdered to enhance their flavour. My close friend Tom Carter, a farmer and porcini aficionado, turns these powders into wild stock cubes and "cep salt", blending dried porcini with sea salt. A small sprinkle on fish, risotto, or pasta transforms any dish into a masterpiece.

For some, the mushroom hunt is so intense that it becomes a near-sacred pursuit, leading to whispered stories of commercial foragers hauling hundreds of kilograms of Porcini after a hot summer and heavy autumn rainfall. However, seasoned foragers practice a strict code of ethics, ensuring that they harvest sustainably, leaving enough mushrooms to mature and sporulate for future seasons.

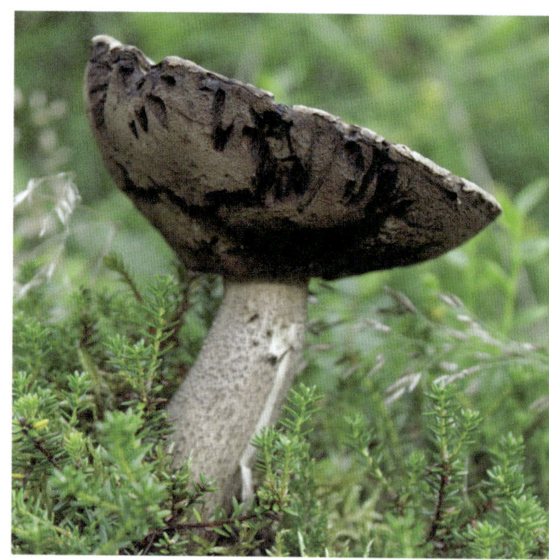

Brown Birch Bolete, identifiable by its dark brown scaly cap and grey-brown pores. To accurately identify mushrooms, it's best to get down to their level.

Among foragers, sharing the locations of our private foraging spots is a profound gesture of respect and friendship. Foragers are notoriously protective of their mushroom haunts, particularly commercial foragers who, I am told, wouldn't reveal their locations for love nor money. When Tom brought me to his sacred mushroom ground, I was blindfolded. I viewed this as a deep sign of mutual regard and understanding. Only true friends, those who honour the land and respect such confidentiality, are granted access to such special places.

We arrived a few days too late, and the heavy rainfall had already sparked busy insect and microbial activity. Still, some Porcini pushed through mossy overgrowths: golden caps upon a sea of green. Others fruited upside down from an overhang, curving their thick stems skyward.

Tom went ahead on his search, keen to return with a heavy basket, while I paused to examine a strange species. As you forage, you learn to recognise the fine nuances of the mushrooms' appearances, and this one was different. Yes, it had a thick stem, velvety cap, and distinctive sponge-like pores on its underside, but the classic white net pattern didn't mark its stem. Instead, it had dark brown scaly flakes, and its pores were a greenish-brown. It was a Brown Birch Bolete, *Leccinum scabrum*, cousin to the Porcini, though not as firm and tasty.[5]

To accurately identify mushrooms, it's best to get down to their level. Smells – citrusy, earthy, or musky – offer vital clues for identification. Tactility is also essential, and unlike plants, no mushroom poses a danger simply upon contact. Close observation is crucial: Do they have dense pores like Boletes or spiky "teeth" like Hedgehog mushrooms, *Hydnum* spp.? Are they squishy or hard? Do they turn blue upon bruising? On hands and knees, so close to the mushroom, we lose ourselves in the minutiae of the fungal fruiting body and its ecosystem.

This Porcini trip turned my world inside out. Amid the abundance of the woodland, I was overcome by a deep sense of remembrance that what we call outside is actually inside. I felt wholly enveloped by

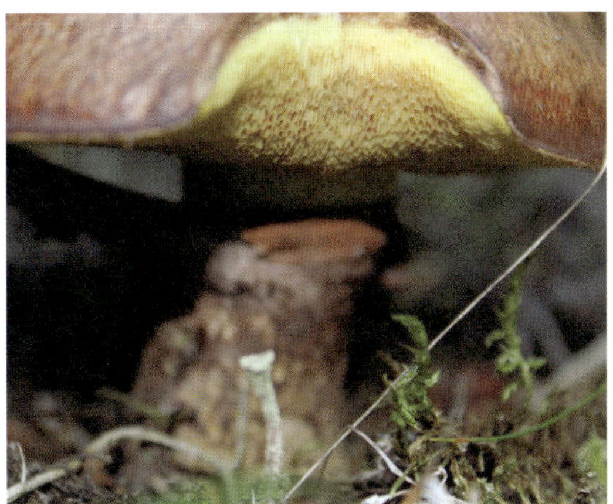

A macro view of a mature Icelandic Porcini! Foraging is a practice of paying attention; one must stay attuned to the broader context - seasons, climate, and environmental cues - while also observing the microcosm: subtle changes in colour, scent, and texture that help identify each mushroom.

nature, kneeling to inhale the soil's autumn aroma, yearning for the outside to permeate my inside and to feel more at home here. I remember my first foraging experience, where we ate the heads of wild chamomile, known as Pineapple Weed, *Matricaria discoidea*. Immediately, we were all transported to the familiar taste of fizzy slices of pineapple sweets. Next, we sampled Ribwort Plantain, *Plantago lanceolata*, whose fresh shoots burst with the well-known flavour of banana bonbons - the fluffy and foamy variety - synthesised from the now extinct Gros Michel bananas of Central America.

The revelation that these flavours, long associated with artificial sweetness, originated in nature sparked a twinge of melancholy within me. What a shame that my references for familiar smells and aromas are all synthetic. This experience shocked me into action. I wanted to pay attention to the world, to recognise the many beings and processes worthy of our attention - not just our passing attention, but our *whole* attention.

Foragers are masters at immersing themselves in the *umwelt,* or unique sensory world of another being. *Umwelt* in German means "environment" or "surrounding world", and refers to how an individual organism perceives and interprets its environment based on its sensory abilities and experiences. This is a world we can never know, but one that opens the doors of our imaginations. Exploring the world of fungi requires this imaginative leap, inviting us to perceive life through the peculiar lens of a mushroom. Taking the time to learn the nuances of who and what you seek is a gesture of both respect and humility - nature suffers no fools gladly, and it has far crueller ways of teaching the differences between seemingly identical mushrooms.

After spending the day on foot, eyes peeled for Porcini, I lay in bed that night with my eyes closed, scanning the forest of my mind for those golden earthly gifts. When foraging, you disappear into action. You scan the forest floor for flashes of colour among beds of brown soil or mossy green. When you're in this motion of doing and being, the world drops away. You become absorbed. If I could sustain that state forever, I would. It's peaceful and deeply satisfying.

Scientists say consciousness acts as a filtration system, discarding 99 per cent of sensory input to process the overwhelming information around us. To truly be present is to notice what our minds usually

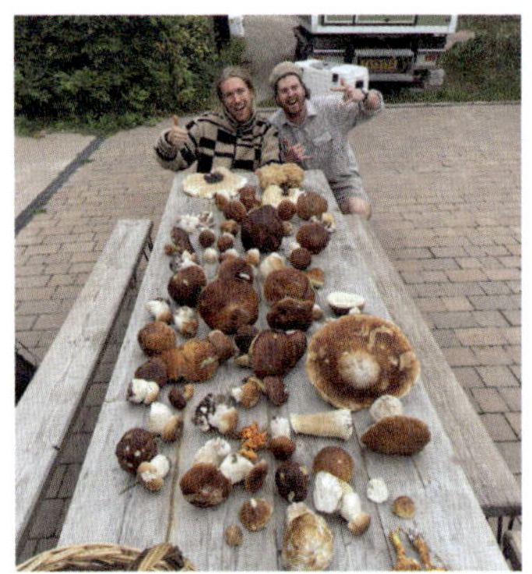

Tom Carter and Peter Chippy with their bounty of porcini, 2022.

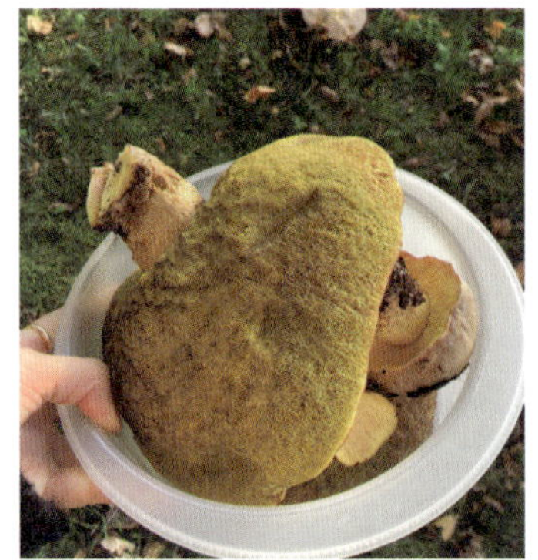

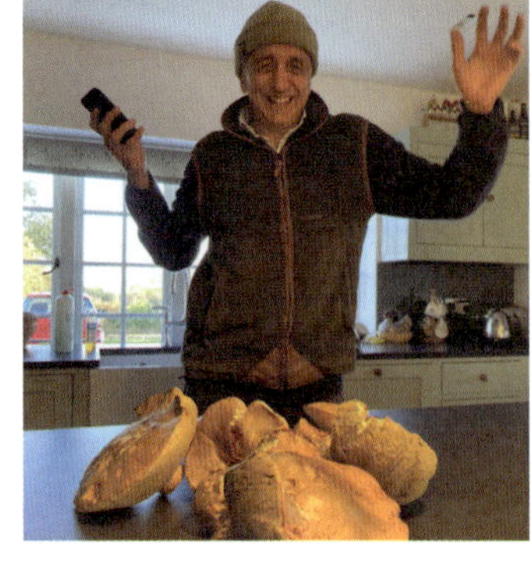

Massimiliano Casini foraging for porcini – the joy!

deem irrelevant. Aldous Huxley captures this in *The Doors of Perception* and *Island*, where mynah birds call the people of Pala to "Attention!" Foraging, for me, is a practice of just that – paying attention.

In many ways, foraging mirrors the experience of childhood, when everything is new and awe-inspiring. Babies discover the world with fresh eyes, seeing endless possibilities. As adults, we often lose this sense of wonder. Yet, by engaging with fungi, in all their diversity, we can reclaim it. Before scientists had tools like microscopes and telescopes to enhance perception, we had, and still have, the human capacity for attention and focusing. This attentiveness is inherently transformative. No longer passive observers, we become co-creators of the world we inhabit, embracing a responsibility that is as humbling as it is profound.

Neuroscientist and cultural historian Iain McGilchrist studies the brain's left and right hemispheres, revealing how each produces distinct interpretations of reality. The left hemisphere tends to reduce, categorise, and objectify, while the right hemisphere offers a more holistic, interconnected, and animate view of the world. The brain, split yet connected, is designed to pass the ball of our attention from right to left and back again: context-detail-context. Yet, McGilchrist argues that we live in an era where the left hemisphere has taken the ball and run.[6] The challenge, then, is to rebuild a dialogue between these two hemispheres to reclaim the full spectrum of life's beauty and complexity.

Foraging is a practice in this dialogue. Foragers must be aware of the broader context: the seasons, climate, and environmental cues, while also tuning into the microcosm: the subtle changes in colour, scent, or texture that help identify their desired mushroom.

In Italy, a legendary technique for finding Porcini is said to exist, cultural wisdom passed down through generations. I had heard tales of monks who only foraged during the waning moon, and foragers who would hunt Porcini ten days after a lightning strike. Eager to learn, I arranged a forage with my friend Juliette Casini and her father, Massimiliano, whose Italian family has a deep passion for mushrooms. She suggested I speak with her ninety-year-old great-uncle, Noberto, a legendary Porcini hunter. I was expecting some dramatic, esoteric tone or a fantastical secret or two, but the call was short. He left me with a single piece of advice: "*Fai attenzione*", "Pay attention".

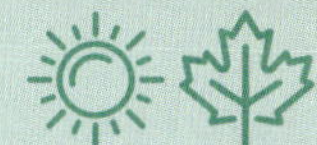

RECIPE

CASINI LINGUINE AI PORCINI

Casa Casini has hosted many unforgettable meals, but the Casini Linguine ai Porcini stands above them all. For the first time, here is the cherished family recipe from Juliette, Massimiliano, and Norberto.

SERVES 4

INGREDIENTS

- 350g/12½oz fresh Porcini mushrooms
- A healthy splash of olive oil
- 3 garlic cloves
- Parsley, finely chopped
- 400g/14oz linguine
- A handful of grated Parmesan
- Salt and pepper
- ½ glass of stock (if using dried mushrooms, use the water you used to rehydrate them as stock).

METHOD

1. Remove any debris from the mushroom with a knife or brush. (Do not wash.)
2. Roughly slice the porcini into thumb-size pieces. Some of the larger ones might have green-ish pores, in which case you'll need to cut the green off or it will be slimy.
3. Heat the olive oil in a pan over medium-high heat and add the garlic cloves. Fry for 2 minutes until they start to colour slightly.
4. Add your Porcini to the pan with a good crack of salt and black pepper. Sauté for 5–10 minutes, keeping them moving with a wooden spoon so that they cook equally and don't burn.
5. Once they have softened down, reduce the flame to as low as possible. Add half a glass of stock and a little of the chopped parsley, then cover and simmer for 30 minutes.
6. Meanwhile, cook your linguine as per instructions. Salt the water always!
7. Once cooked, drain off the water (but not too much) and add to the pan with the Porcini.
8. Gently mix together, adding a sizeable handful of Parmesan.
9. Pile onto plates. Top with a sprinkle of remaining parsley and a grating of parmesan. Buon appetito!

NOTES

- These Porcini are also delicious on toast. Even better with eggs on top!
- Whether Porcini taste better fresh or dried is a much-debated question, though the Casinis favour them fresh.

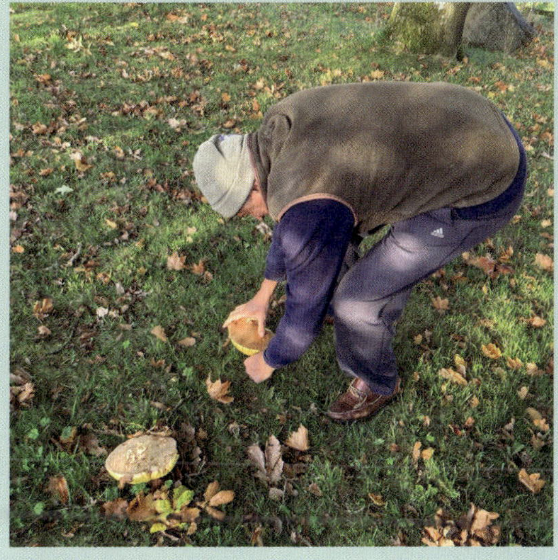

Massimiliano Casini foraging for Porcini.

CREATURELY INTOXICATION

"The impulse to change our consciousness is innate within us."

– Ronald K. Siegel

The fascination with altering consciousness is as old as humanity itself. Whether through ritual or recreation, humans have consistently sought to transcend their ordinary states of awareness.[7] Ronald K. Siegel, a psychopharmacologist, explored this obsession in his groundbreaking work *Intoxication: Life in Pursuit of Artificial Paradise*. He argued that the desire to alter our minds is as intrinsic to us as hunger, sleep, and sex – a "fourth drive" shared not just with other humans but with countless species across the animal kingdom.

Siegel proposed that the quest for intoxication is universal.[8] Many animals actively seek out mind-altering substances for pleasure, medicinal benefits, or even play. Wild elephants in Burma and India have been observed consuming opium-containing plants, while domesticated cats revel in catnip, whose active ingredient, nepetalactone, triggers euphoria and playful behaviour. Pigeons have a particular fondness for hemp seeds, which leave them "gay and crazy". Even squirrels, bears, foxes, and snails have been known to consume intoxicating mushrooms.[9,10] From butterflies to moose to humans, the impulse to alter one's consciousness is part of our evolutionary fabric.

Siegel's work did not stop at wild animal observation; he actively experimented on animals in laboratory settings. His experiments included giving LSD to pigeons and cocaine to monkeys, training the animals to articulate their experiences. Despite the unpredictable nature of the substances, many animals responded similarly to humans under the influence, entering what Siegel called an "artificial paradise". As most detested high-dose synthetic injections but enjoyed mild intoxicants in their natural form, Siegel believed that we have much to learn about safe drug use from our animal cousins. This reinforced his theory that the quest for intoxication, whether through drugs, alcohol, or other substances, is as universal as it is inescapable.

As the 20th century unfolded, Siegel's observations echoed in the broader cultural fascination with mind-altering substances. Following the mass production and distribution of LSD in the 1960s, many scientists and psychologists, eager to explore the therapeutic and mind-expanding possibilities of psychedelics, turned to both humans and animals as subjects of study.

One of the most bizarre of these studies came in 1971, when NASA funded experiments to investigate the effects of drugs on spiderweb construction. Inspired by Peter N. Witt's earlier work from 1948,

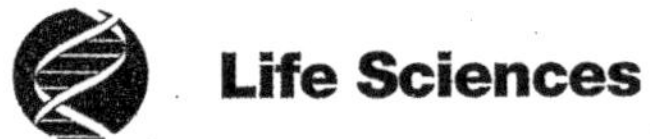

Vol. 19, No. 4, Pg. 82
April 1995

Life Sciences

Using Spider-Web Patterns To Determine Toxicity

Webs are visibly altered when spun by spiders exposed to chemicals.

Marshall Space Flight Center, Alabama

A method of determining the toxicities of chemicals involves recording and analysis of spider-web patterns. The method is based on the observation that spiders exposed to various chemicals spin webs that differ, in various ways, from their normal webs (see figure). Spider-web toxicity testing has potential as an alternative to toxicity testing on higher animals, which is expensive, time-consuming and becoming increasingly restricted by law.

The changes in webs reflect the degree of toxicity of a substance. The more toxic the chemical, the more deformed a web looks in comparison with a normal web. Inasmuch as the shape of a spider web resembles that of a crystal lattice in some respects, techniques of statistical crystallography are applied to obtain several quantitative measures of toxicity as manifested in the differences between photographs of webs spun under toxic and normal conditions.

The images of the cells are digitized and processed by an image-data-analysis program that computes various measures of the cellular structures of the webs, including numbers of cells and average areas, perimeters, and radii of cells. It appears that one of the most telling measures of toxicity is a decrease, in comparison with a normal web, of the numbers of completed sides in the cells: the greater the toxicity, the more sides the spider fails to complete.

This work was done by David A. Noever, Raymond J. Cronise, and Rachna A. Relwani of **Marshall Space Flight Center**. *For further information,* ***write in 48*** *on the TSP Request Card.* *MFS-28921*

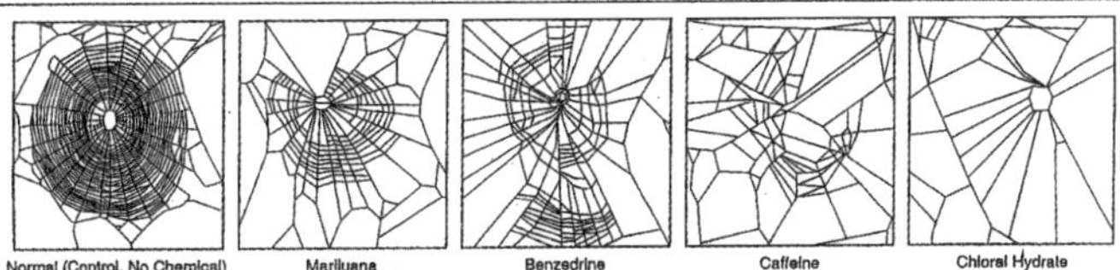

NASA's Spider Web Experiments. Webs spun by spiders under the influence of various substances, reveal how drugs can affect perception and behaviour across species.

NASA researchers dosed spiders with LSD, mescaline, caffeine, and other psychoactives to observe how they built webs. The results were predictably strange. Spiders on amphetamines built larger but less structured webs, while those under the influence of cannabis created smaller, more fragmented webs. Caffeine proved most disruptive, and LSD-spun webs were chaotically irregular,[11] revealing how drugs can disrupt even the most basic natural behaviours. Interestingly, low doses of LSD led to more regular, symmetrical webs,[12] hinting at the nuanced ways in which mind-altering substances affect perception and behaviour.

While such studies may seem outlandish today, they were once routine scientific endeavours. The 1960s and 1970s were a time of exploration into consciousness, and drugs were seen as a key to unlocking new levels of awareness. However, not all experiments were met with enthusiasm. The controversial research of John C. Lilly, an American neuroscientist, stirred even greater controversy.

In the 1950s, Lilly invented the isolation tank, giving humans the means to explore profound sensory deprivation. He famously called it a "doorway into the universe". Another such doorway for Lilly was LSD – a substance that quickly captivated him with its potential to expand consciousness.[13] His work, funded in part by NASA, extended to the study of interspecies communication, particularly with dolphins. His Dolphin House Research Centre was a unique coexistence environment, with the flooded lower levels serving as both the dolphins' headquarters and English classrooms. Lilly's research partner, Margaret Lovatt, even engaged in a highly publicised and controversial study in which she shared an isolation tank with a dolphin named Peter. The project, which involved dosing dolphins with government-supplied LSD, attracted significant media attention, particularly after reports surfaced of sexual behaviour between Lovatt and Peter.[14]

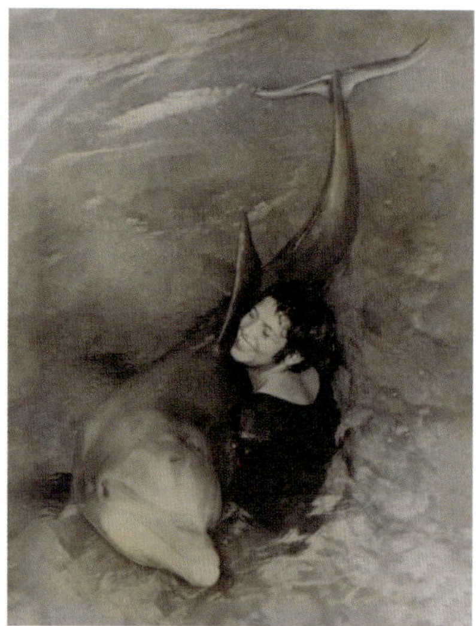

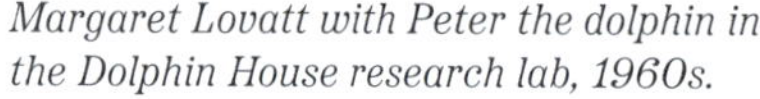

Margaret Lovatt with Peter the dolphin in the Dolphin House research lab, 1960s.

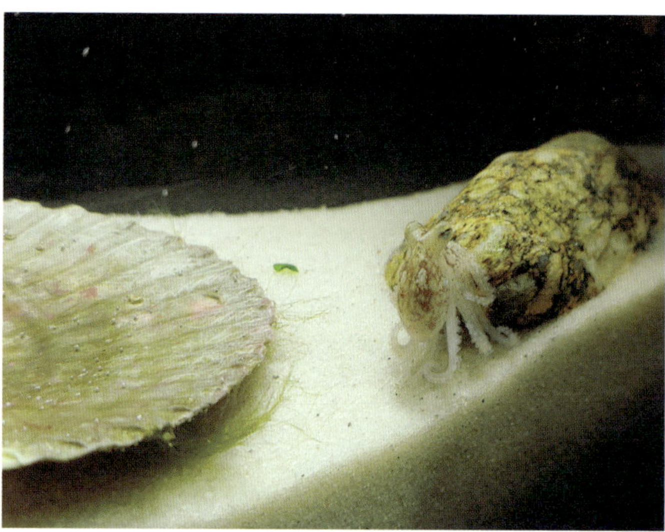

An octopus intoxicated with MDMA, exhibiting behaviour like that of a human under the influence of the "love drug".

Funding was cut abruptly in 1966, and the research facility closed. The dolphins were rehoused, with devastating consequences, including Peter's immediate suicide.[15] As Lilly noted, dolphins breathe consciously. If life becomes unbearable, they can simply choose to stop.[16]

Despite the outlandish nature of the research, Lilly and his team were not alone in their belief that animals, like humans, experience intoxication. Dolphins have been observed in the wild playing with pufferfish, which release neurotoxins that produce narcotic effects. Dolphins are known to bat the pufferfish around like a toy, before floating up to the surface in a daze.[17] This behaviour suggests that dolphins, much like humans, may understand the effects of intoxication and actively seek out substances to alter their consciousness.

Even today, research into animal intoxication continues to offer remarkable insights. Neuroscientist Gül Dölen has recently studied octopuses and their reactions to MDMA and magic mushrooms, adding a new chapter to the story of animal consciousness. Her experiments revealed that octopuses, already known for their complex behaviours and advanced neural systems, also exhibit profound behavioural changes when exposed to certain psychoactive substances. In perhaps the most legendary experiment of all time, Dölen's team introduced MDMA to an octopus via an "MDMA marinade," placed it in a tank, and waited.

Their setup featured a large tank divided into three chambers, each with doors for the octopus to navigate. In the initial control phase, no psychedelics were used. The third chamber contained an octopus, the second held a toy, and the first housed the primary participant – our octopus. Known for their curious yet solitary nature, the octopuses behaved predictably. Upon entering the first chamber, the octopus kept to itself, cautiously reaching into the second chamber to retrieve the toy while

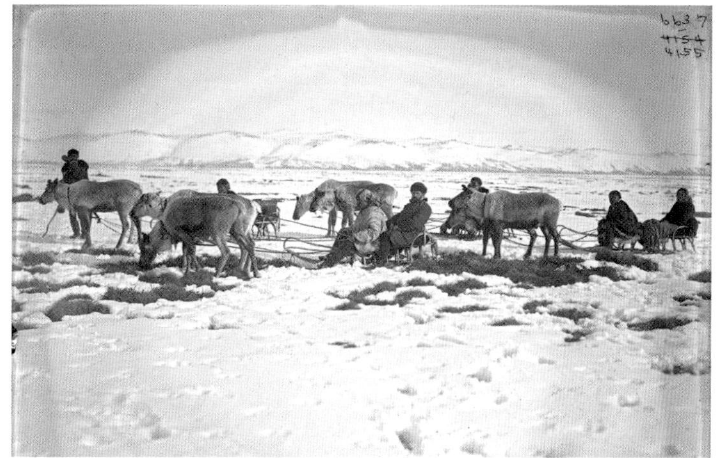

Russian-American ethnographers the Jochelsons travelling with the Koryak, semi-nomadic reindeer herders of Siberia, in 1901. The Koryak have a very intimate relationship with Fly Agarics. They have been known to drink reindeer urine after the animals consume the mushroom, as the psychoactive compounds remain active.

acknowledging the presence of the other octopus but showing no interest in interacting. The result was clear: curious, playful, and distinctly antisocial.[18]

The experiment took an intriguing turn in the second phase. Researchers soaked the octopus in a 0.01mg dose of MDMA. Upon entering the first chamber, the now-intoxicated octopus displayed a dramatic shift in behaviour. Like humans on the "love drug", it became hyper-affectionate, ignoring the toy and instead charging towards the other octopus, extending all eight arms in an overtly affectionate gesture. The sober octopus, overwhelmed by this unexpected display, shrank into the corner.

This experiment offers valuable insights into evolution, showing that, despite diverging over 650 million years ago, human and octopus neural systems share similarities. Both species respond to psychedelics that activate serotonin 2A receptors, enhancing emotional states and social interactions. However, much like with Witt's intoxicated spiders, we still lack understanding of the octopus's subjective experience. Further research is needed at the intersection of neurobiology, consciousness, and intoxication if we are to uncover not only the biochemical mechanisms of intoxication but also its deeper, evolutionary purpose.

Every creature that seeks out intoxication has its own way of pursuing, using, and processing intoxicants. Reindeer, for example, are known to seek out the Fly Agaric mushroom at great lengths, whose bright red cap contrasts starkly against the snowy tundra. While toxic to most animals, the mushroom's psychoactive compounds don't harm reindeer – in fact, they seem to love it. Their gut linings, like those of squirrels and guinea pigs, contain proteins that bind to the deadly toxins, neutralising their effects.[19] Remarkably, the mushroom's mind-altering agents survive the digestive process. For centuries, indigenous people like the Sámi in Siberia have used reindeer urine – after the animals have consumed the mushrooms – as a powerful hallucinogen.[20,21,22] The urine can be drunk up to six times without losing its potency. Likewise, reindeer reportedly go to great lengths to drink human urine after the humans have become intoxicated, passing the urine-bound psychoactive compounds among themselves.[23]

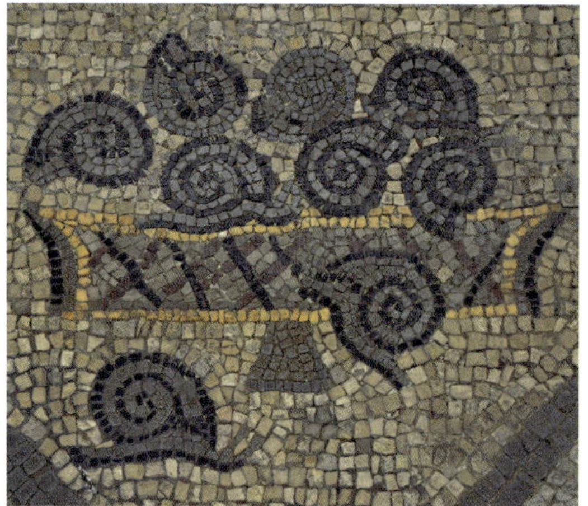

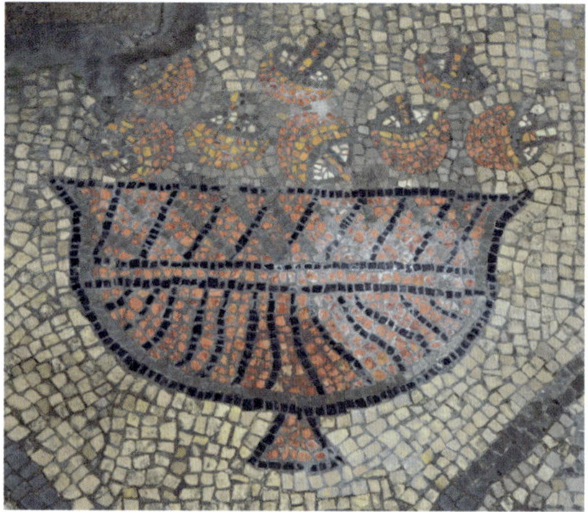

A floor mosaic in the Christian Basilica of Aquileia, Italy, showing mushrooms and snails, possibly indicating their combined use in clandestine psychedelic rituals.

"Reindeer, like men, suffer profound mental disturbances after eating the fly-agaric."

Gordon Wasson, Soma, 1968

Minus the urine, some speculate that these tales inspired the legend of Santa Claus: a figure dressed in red and white, flying through the sky with his red-nosed reindeer, much like the hallucinogenic effects of the Fly Agaric.

The idea that intoxicants can be consumed indirectly through animals is not new. The ancient Romans, for example, are believed to have consumed Fly Agaric's active ingredients by first feeding them to snails, then eating the snails themselves. This practice was documented in mosaics from the Christian Basilica of Aquileia in northern Italy, where both mushrooms and snails were depicted together in overflowing bowls, possibly indicating their combined use in religious ceremonies.[24] This may have been the Roman way of consuming safe and reliable hallucinogens.

The impact of intoxicants on snails' neurological states remains unclear. Snails have sensitive chemical receptors that help them distinguish edible fungi from toxic ones, but their perception differs from ours.[25] Did they evolve proteins to safely digest deadly amatoxins or are they left bewildered, confounded, and dazzled as we are? How do we tell when a snail is hallucinating? A Reddit user, LeapingGnOme, cast the question into the cosmos: "If you're a slug who does shrooms, let us know!" The consensus is that snails and slugs lack the cognitive capacity to experience "getting high" as we do, but they may still feel some euphoric effect, as they keep coming back for more!

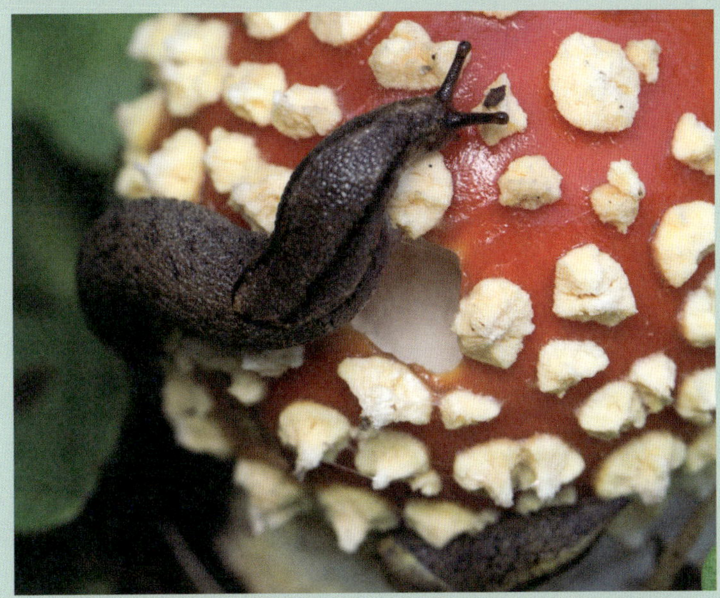

Reticulate Taildropper slugs in California, munching their way through an Amanita muscaria mushroom.

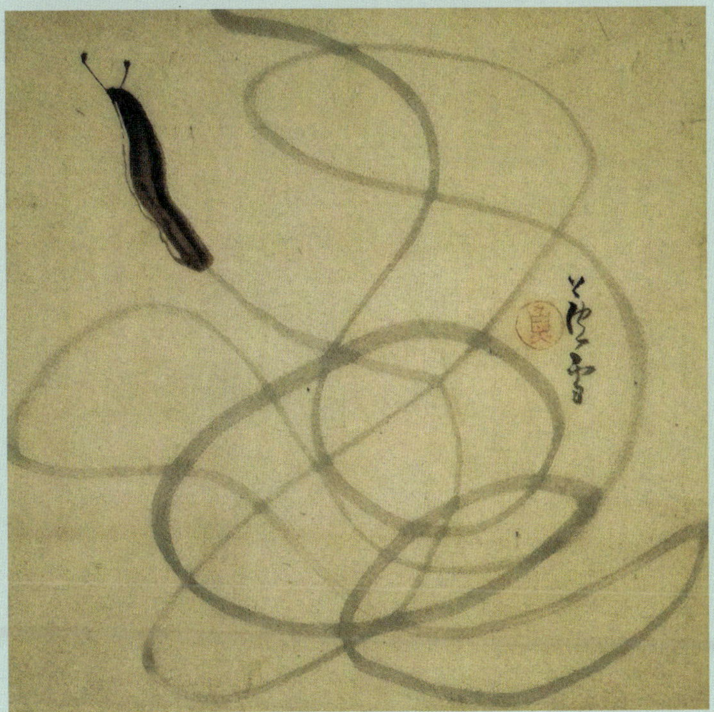

Nagasawa Rosetsu, Slug, *ink on paper, Edo period. We don't know whether snails and slugs are affected by the hallucinogenic properties of* Amanita muscaria. *My best advice is simply to follow their slime trails and watch for any unusual patterns of movement—although, realistically, the only change I could report is that they might become even more "sluggish," which isn't much help to anyone!*

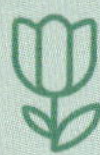

ACTIVITY

OBSERVING HALLUCINATING SNAILS

Since we can't definitively say how Fly Agaric mushrooms affect snails, it feels questionable to cultivate snails at home and feed them these mushrooms. However, it's not unusual to see slugs and snails consuming Fly Agarics in the wild. If you're lucky enough to witness this, stick around and observe the mollusc during and after its meal. Fresh Fly Agarics contain higher levels of ibotenic acid, an "excitotoxin" that stimulates both mental and physical activity (in humans). Dried mushrooms, on the other hand, are richer in muscimol, which mimics GABA neurotransmitters and has a calming effect. Take note of the mushroom's condition and pay attention to the snail's behaviour. While I wouldn't recommend taking the snail home for dinner, it has been done.

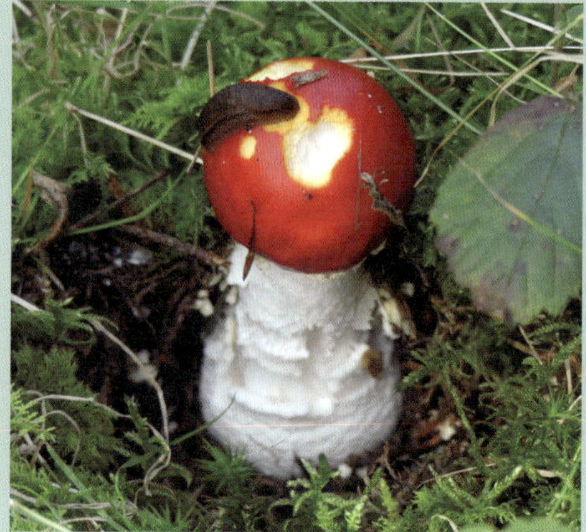

Slug on an intoxicating Fly Agaric mushroom. It remains unclear whether slugs and snails experience any psychoactive effects.

FAIRY TALES & FEVER DREAMS

"The key to the door of fairyland is now within anyone's reach . . ."

– George Andrews, Psilocybin[26]

Throughout the 19th century, European art and literature often paired mushrooms with enchanted landscapes, fairies, and otherworldly creatures. These fungi were more than decorative; they suggested thresholds to hidden realms, tiny portals to a world just beyond ordinary perception. Such depictions raise tantalising questions: Could the European fairy tradition conceal subtle encounters with mind-altering fungi? Did authors like Robert Kirk, Shakespeare, and Lewis Carroll draw from such experiences, consciously or not, in crafting their magical worlds?

To explore these questions, we must first revisit the enchanted beings that populate Western folklore.

Beneath the everyday, according to traditional tales, lies a "secret commonwealth," home to "wee bodies" – fairies, elves, gnomes, and pixies – whose lives mirror our own. They eat, sleep, dance, and love, yet their existence remains perilously close to our own. Mischief, danger, and fascination intermingle: fairies were said to abduct mothers to nurse fairy children, leave changelings in their place, or lead travellers astray into perilous landscapes. These accounts, meticulously recorded by 17th-century Scottish pastor Robert Kirk in *The Secret Commonwealth of Elves, Fauns, and Fairies*, treat Fairyland not as escapist fantasy but as a real, unpredictable, and potentially dangerous domain.

Kirk described fairies as composed of "a substance somewhat of the nature of a condensed cloud," evoking the delicate, diaphanous beauty of morning dew or spider silk. This evanescent quality resonates with the mushrooms often appearing at twilight, ephemeral and liminal, marking the threshold between the mundane and the magical.

The association between fairies and fungi runs deeper than mere coincidence. The Renaissance alchemist Paracelsus classified beings into four elemental species: undines of water, sylphs of the air, salamanders of fire, and gnomes of the earth. Gnomes, dwelling underground and intimately linked with soil and hidden groves, share a symbolic affinity with mushrooms, which thrive in damp, secretive niches. Certain species – Fairy Ink Caps, Dryad's Saddles, and Pixie Cups – bear names or mythological associations linking them directly to the fae.

In Victorian children's literature, fairies and mushrooms were often portrayed with whimsy and charm. Delicate sprites frolicked in Scarlet Elf Cups or leapt between mushroom caps, while Cecily Mary Barker's illustrations presented gentle, nature-loving fairies, cultivating a vision of innocence and delight.

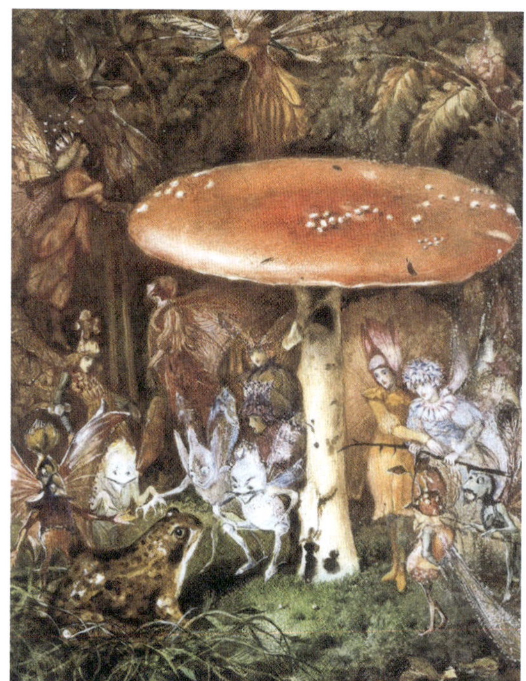

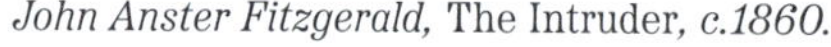

John Anster Fitzgerald, The Intruder, *c.1860.*

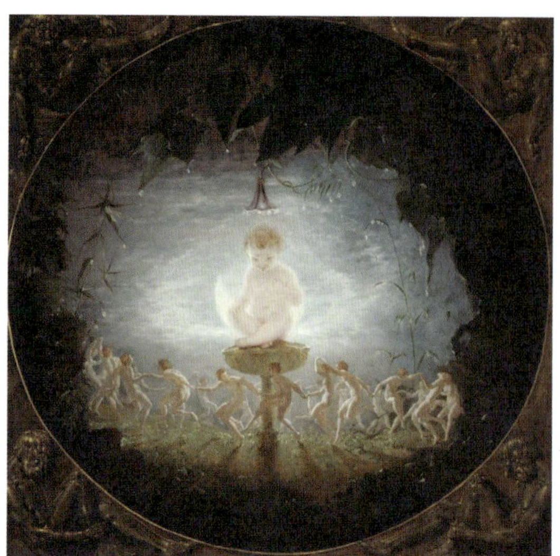

Richard Dadd, Puck, *1841. Oil on canvas.*

Yet, as historian Marina Warner observes, this sweetened portrayal diverges from the older, darker tales.[27] Fairies were once unpredictable and dangerous, capable of malice, abduction, or death. These cautionary narratives – found in the earliest Grimm tales and European folklore – remind us that encounters with the Otherworld were neither safe nor trivial.

Fairy Rings, naturally occurring circles of mushrooms, exemplify this duality. These formations have long inspired awe and superstition. In Holland, they were linked to the devil's churn; in Austria, they were attributed to dragons dancing in the grass. The mushrooms themselves, *Marasmius oreades,* sprout from concentric rings of mycelium, which deplete the soil beneath them, leaving a spectral footprint of the underground network. Across northern Europe, folklore describes fairies dancing atop these rings, a motif immortalised in Richard Dadd's depiction of Puck in *A Midsummer Night's Dream*. Linguistic echoes persist too: the Gaelic word pookies, once referring to mischievous spirits, now occasionally describes mushrooms in Irish slang.[28] Shakespeare himself immortalised these "midnight mushrooms" in *The Tempest*, hinting at their uncanny presence.

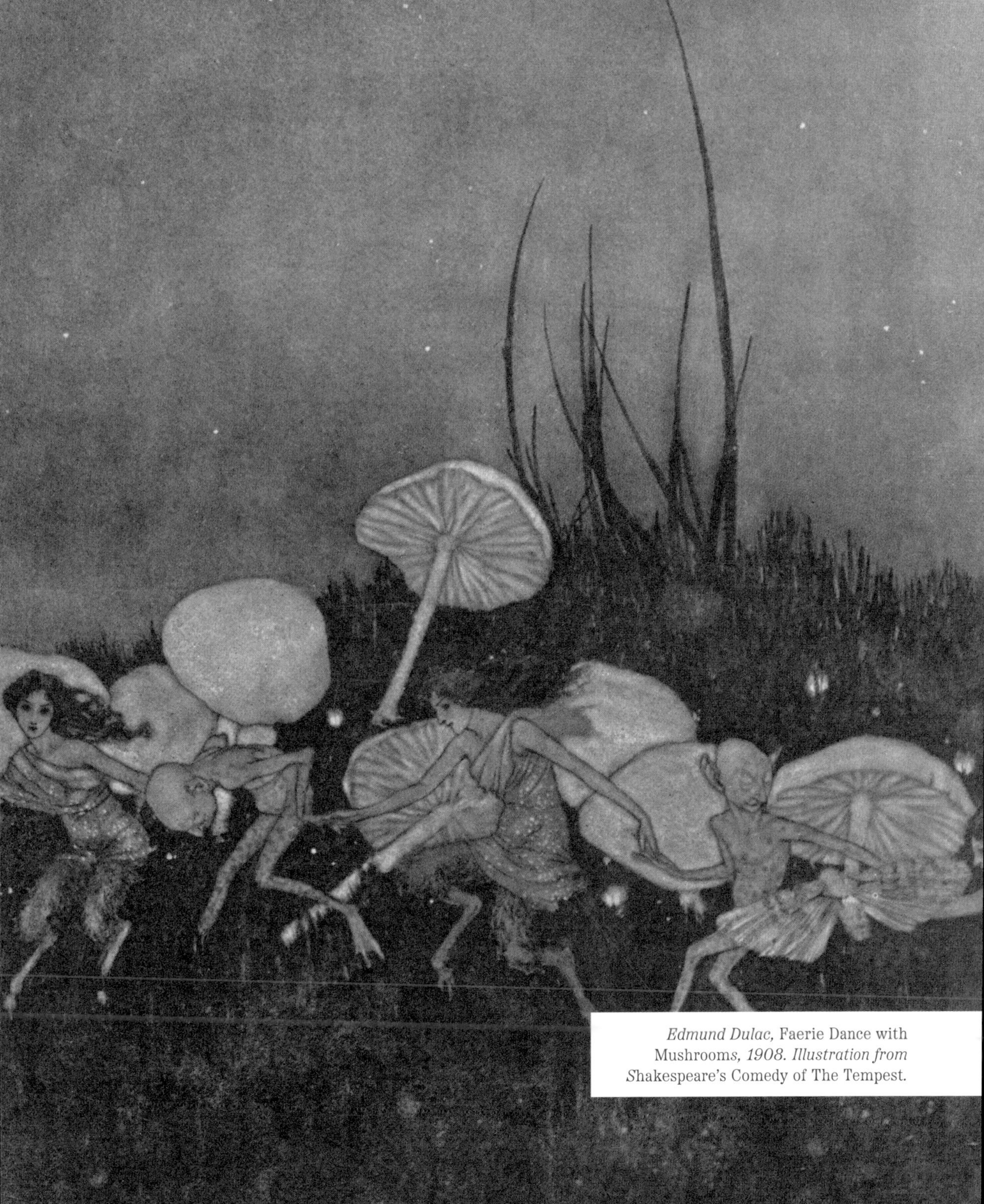

Edmund Dulac, Faerie Dance with Mushrooms*, 1908. Illustration from Shakespeare's* Comedy of The Tempest.

Ye elves of hills, brooks, standing lakes and groves,
And ye that on the sands with printless foot
Do chase the ebbing Neptune and do fly him
When he comes back; you demi-puppets that
By Moonshine do the green sour ringlets make,
Whereof the ewe not bites, and you whose pastime
Is to make midnight mushrooms . . .

– The Tempest, *Shakespeare, 1623*

Fairy Rings were also considered dangerous. In France, enormous toads were said to guard these circles, punishing trespassers. Celtic tradition warned mortals that stepping into such rings could trap them in Tír na nÓg, a timeless Otherworld. William Allingham's story of Little Bridget, abducted by fairies for seven years, is one such cautionary tale.[29]

These stories reflect a practical wisdom disguised as magic. Some mushrooms are toxic; others hallucinogenic. Folk narratives frequently warned against certain fungi, encoding knowledge about edible versus poisonous varieties. For example, the Fool's Funnel mushroom, with its poisonous qualities, was long associated with demonic influence or ill fortune.

Artists such as Henry Fuseli further entwined fungi and folklore. In *The Awakening of the Fairy Queen Titania* (1785), mushrooms and fae coexist in surreal landscapes, suggesting that these fungi were symbolic of altered perception and ethereal encounters.

This raises a recurring question: were these depictions mere metaphors, or did they encode knowledge of psychoactive fungi? Marina notes that fairy tales frequently link supernatural beings like Shakespeare's fairies to disruptions in consciousness, hinting at altered states, dreams, or hallucinatory visions. Throughout folklore, encounters with the otherworldly often coincide with experiences of delirium, ecstasy, or trance.

While mushrooms appear widely in folklore, hallucinogenic species like the Fly Agaric, *Amanita muscaria*, became emblematic only in the 19th century. Russian folktales, popularised in collections illustrated by Ivan Bilibin, prominently feature these fungi. In tales such as Vasilisa the Brave, Baba Yaga's forest teems with mushrooms that evoke otherworldly visions – red-and-white Fly Agarics alongside Liberty Caps, sometimes linked to magical or transformative experiences.

Tales of Baba Yaga, collected by figures like ethnographer Alexander Afanasyev, are rooted in circumpolar traditions, including Inuit and Siberian shamanism. They are rich with themes of transformation, nocturnal flight, and spiritual journeys – many explicitly connected to the Fly Agaric. The mushroom's psychoactive compounds, muscimol and ibotenic acid, can induce altered perception, euphoria, hallucinations, or, in high doses, nausea, severe illness, or a coma. Tales of Siberian shamans consuming Fly Agarics circulated in Europe by the 18th and 19th centuries, adding mystique and caution to the mushroom's cultural identity.

Polish General Joseph Kopék, stationed in the Kamchatka Peninsula in the 1830s, documented his experiences with the Fly Agaric. After ingesting the mushroom, he entered vivid visions of

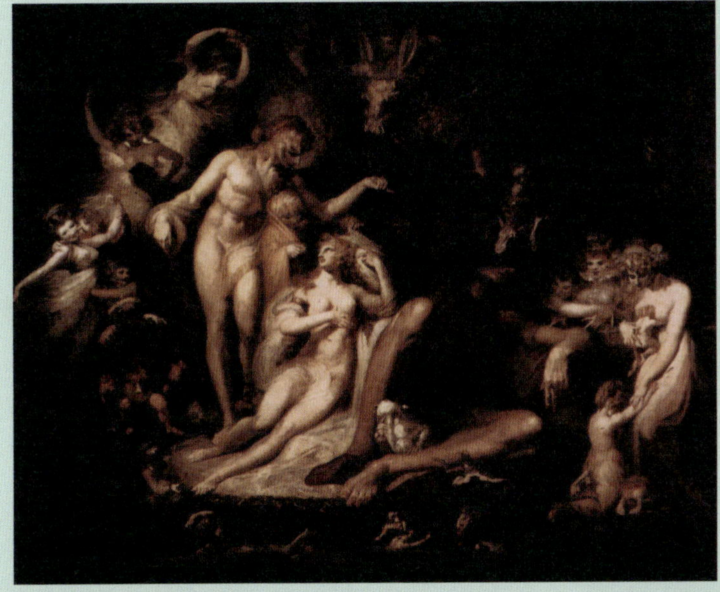

Henry Fuseli, The Awakening of the Fairy Queen Titania, *c.1785.*

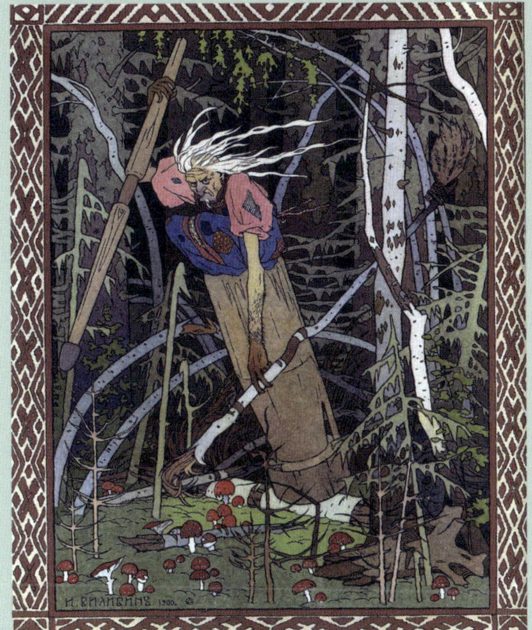

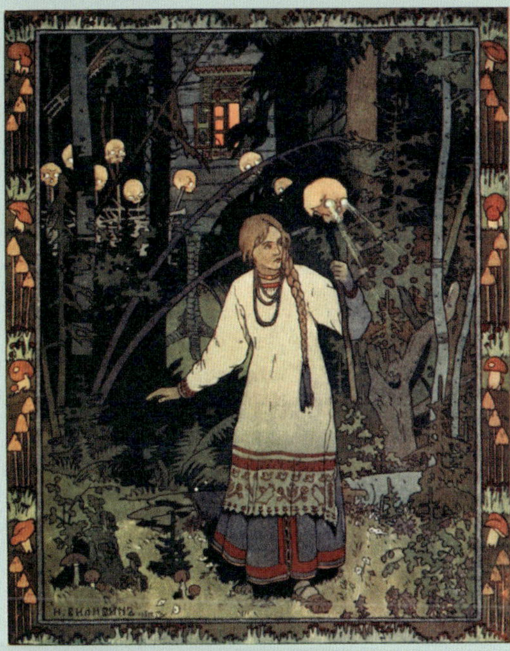

Ivan Bilibin, Baba Yaga & Wassilissa the Brave, *1900, featuring psychedelic Liberty Caps and Fly Agarics.*

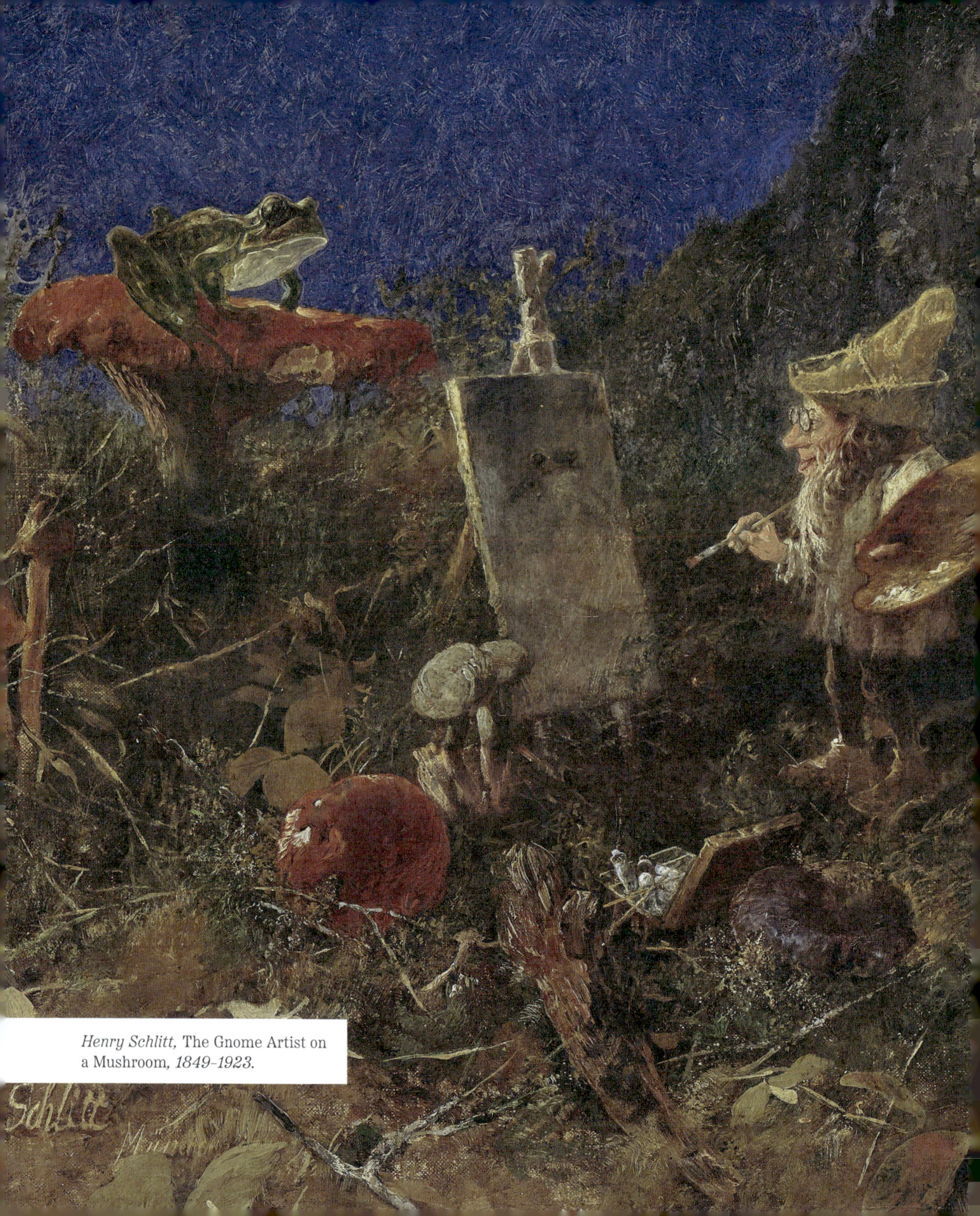

Henry Schlitt, The Gnome Artist on a Mushroom, *1849–1923.*

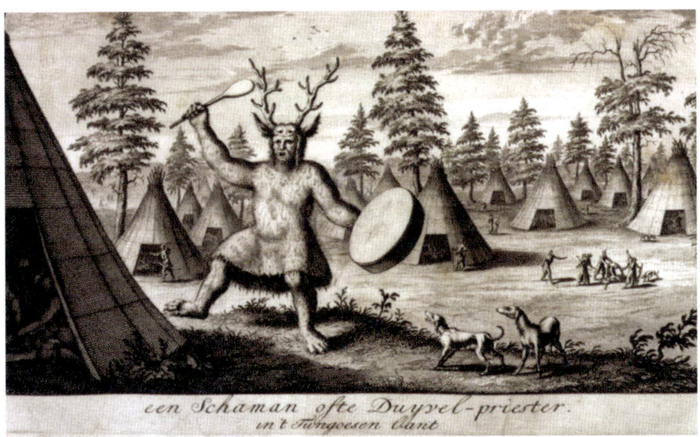

Siberian Shaman intoxicated with the Fly Agaric mushroom. Stories of shamanic rituals involving self-induced intoxication with this iconic red mushroom spread across Europe during the 18th and 19th centuries, cementing the Fly Agaric's reputation as the quintessential mushroom of transformation.

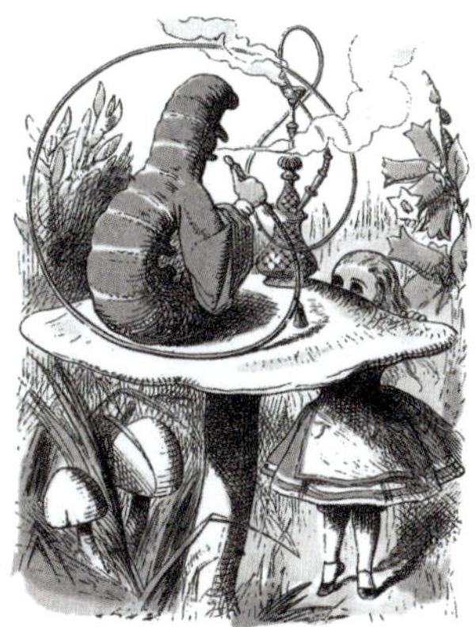

Advice from a caterpillar. *Illustration by Sir John Tenniel from the first edition of Lewis Carroll's* Alice's Adventures in Wonderland, *1865. Alas, there is nothing to suggest it is a Fly Agaric.*

otherworldly gardens, animated by luminous figures offering fruits and flowers. Later, a stronger dose revealed lost memories and prophetic imagery. For Kopék, these experiences were transformative, though contemporaries dismissed them as delirium or demonic influence.

The Fly Agaric's dual nature, both enchanting and hazardous, captured the Victorian imagination. This symbolic ambivalence is evident in Lewis Carroll's Alice's Adventures in Wonderland (1865). Alice encounters a caterpillar perched on a mushroom whose effects alter her size and perception. While Carroll's narrative resonates with psychedelic imagery, we don't know whether he knew of the Fly Agaric's psychoactive properties.

We do know that Carroll suffered from insomnia and migraines, and experimented with remedies that contained aconite and belladonna, likely affecting his imagination and dreams. His personal library included texts on hallucinogenic plants and fungi, also potentially influencing his creative output. Notably, though, Carroll's original illustration of the mushroom shows not the flaming red-and-white Fly Agaric, but an undistinguished toadstool. Nevertheless, the story's subsequent adoption into psychedelic culture has cemented this mushroom as a symbol of magical transformation.

Whether or not Carroll intended it, the association between mushrooms and magical transformation endures. The archetypal "fairytale mushroom" has become a cornerstone of modern psychedelic culture, offering a symbolic doorway into altered perception, curiosity, and wonder. Like the fairy rings of folklore, these stories remind us that the line between everyday reality and otherworldly experience is thin, and that a mushroom can mark the threshold of that liminal space.

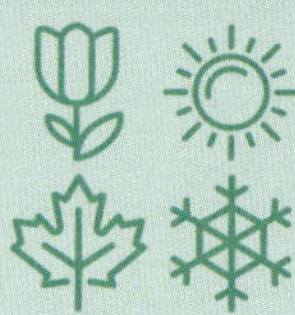

ACTIVITY

DISCOVERING MUSHROOMS IN LITERATURE

In José Montes-Baquer and Salvador Dalí's 1975 film *Impressions de la Haute Mongolie*, a Mongol princess feeds her subjects powdered mushrooms that induce vivid hallucinations and inspire them to paint.

Psychedelic mushrooms have long played a role in inspiring fantastical, feverish visions. Whether magic mushrooms inspired Dalí himself, we might never know, though famously, when asked, he admitted, "I don't do drugs. I am drugs."

Like so many of us, I was raised on the magic of mythological stories and fairy tales. These stories, like Dalí's film, often featured mushrooms, princesses, and, almost always, chimeras: hybrid creatures like sphinxes, hippogriffs, and mermaids, all dazzling amalgams, though fictional and implausible in real life.

Yet, in the natural world, we have a real-life chimera: cicadas and the parasitic fungus *Massospora cicadina*. The fungus synchronises with the cicadas' life cycle, remaining silent within them during their seventeen-year underground dormancy. Once the insects emerge – infected – the fungus expertly causes its abdomen to decompose while preserving and taking over its central nervous system. The cicadas become hypersexual, embarking on erratic flights, singing and flicking their wings, inadvertently spreading spores to other cicadas via their absent abdomen. The cicadas' bodies are nothing more than vessels for the fungus, a hostile blend of life and death.

Experts rightly describe these erratic actions not as cicada behaviours, but as fungal behaviours, a testament to this parasitic conquest and manipulation of another species. This living chimera, or zombie, isn't just a turn of phrase; it's how they're understood within the neuroscience community. Myth and science converge here, just as fungal spores invade their hosts.

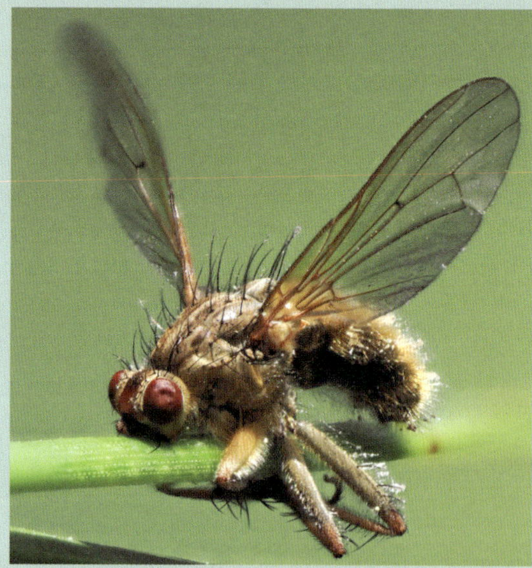

A real-life chimera: the Death Fly Fungus, Entomophthora muscae, *one of many entomopathogenic fungi that infect and manipulate insects.*

This motif of transformation through fungi, whether parasitic or hallucinogenic, resonates throughout mythology, folklore, and modern media alike. We see this with the post-apocalyptic Japanese anime *Sabikui Bisco*, the Cordyceps-inspired video game *The Last of Us*, and the cult-classic film *A Field in England*.

In old literature too. While rummaging through my parents' old bookshelves, I came across A.E.M. Bayliss's *Children's Fancies* (1925), full of whimsical references to fairy rings and transformation. I later discovered a haiku by Kobayashi Issa (1763–1827), which read:

Dear Children,
Be not deceived
By the red toadstools!

Sage advice.

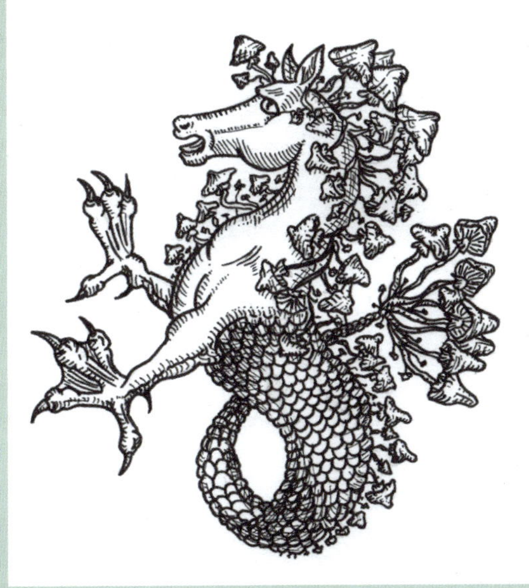

I. P. Adamatsky's mythical chimera: the Fungal Hyppocamp.

YOUR TASK

1. Revisit old films, books, or artworks with magical or mythological elements. Can you find any fungi? Which real-life mushroom might they represent, and what powers do they possess? I promise, there are more of these hidden mushrooms than we know.[30]
2. If you feel inspired by your finds, create your own mythological fungal creature. Write a story, draw, or sculpt your character. Is your creature chimeric with its host or does it stand alone? Can it trap people in an eternal sleep or perhaps grant visions of the future? Or might a single nibble change the rules of reality – grass becomes pink, gravity reverses, fungi dominate everything?
3. Get inspired by our twisted, timeless tales and the strange fungi that exist in the real world. But if you seek living-mushroom counsel, keep your wits about you, and never trespass into a fairy ring.

LORD SHIVA'S LIBIDO

"Tell us decisively which we ought to attend upon? The sloping sides of the mountains in the wilderness or the buttocks of a woman abounding in passion?"

– 5th century poet and sage Bhartrihari of Ujjain

In the vast landscape of world religions, few celebrate the pursuit of pleasure as a moral and divine pursuit. Yet in Hinduism, eroticism is seen as sacred. Ancient Indian civilisations regarded bodily pleasure as a vital gateway to the sublime and integral to life's spiritual journey.[31,32]

The Creation Hymn of the Rig Veda begins by acknowledging *kama* – sensual desire – as one of the fundamental forces of existence, a divine energy that drives all life. In Hindu philosophy, *kama* is recognised as one of the *purusharthas,* the four aims of human life, emphasising that sensory pleasures are crucial for individual well-being. This concept is echoed in the Mahabharata, where *kama* is personified as the God of love: Kama, a youthful, Eros-like figure armed with a bow made from sugar cane, strung with threads of longing, shooting flower-tipped arrows that incite boundless love.

Although not officially part of Hindu scripture, the *Kama Sutra* stands as the world's oldest and most comprehensive guide to sensuality, emotional fulfilment, and human relationships. Written by the Brahmin scholar Vatsyayana, it condenses millennia of wisdom on love, courtship, and eroticism across ancient northern India. The text is divided into seven chapters, addressing topics such as General Principles, Embraces (Foreplay), Sexual Unions, Courtship and Marriage, The Wives of Others, Courtesans, and The Arts of Seduction & Tonic Medicines.[33] Despite its explicit subject matter, the *Kama Sutra* offers a deeply philosophical perspective on love, transcending the purely physical to delve into the emotional and spiritual dimensions of relationships.[34]

In contrast, the Western world largely misunderstood the eroticism of Indian culture. Sir Richard Burton's controversial 1883 English translation of the *Kama Sutra* horrified Victorian sensibilities, leading to its widespread censorship and eventual ban. Pirated versions surfaced, often reducing the text to mere "Hindu pornography", stripping it of its philosophical depth and historical context. Over time, however, more authentic translations have emerged, shedding light on a rich and complex cultural tradition that celebrated eroticism as both art and spiritual practice.

Growing up in the UK, I was hugely influenced by my Sri Lankan grandfather, whose home was filled with erotic literature, art, and sculptures. Among them were miniature *Kama Sutra* paintings and a statue of Lord Shiva – a symbol of divine love and eroticism. Shiva, often represented by the *lingam* (a phallic symbol), is celebrated in Hindu scriptures for his passionate, millennia-long love affairs, particularly his sensual relationship with Parvati in the Himalayas.[35]

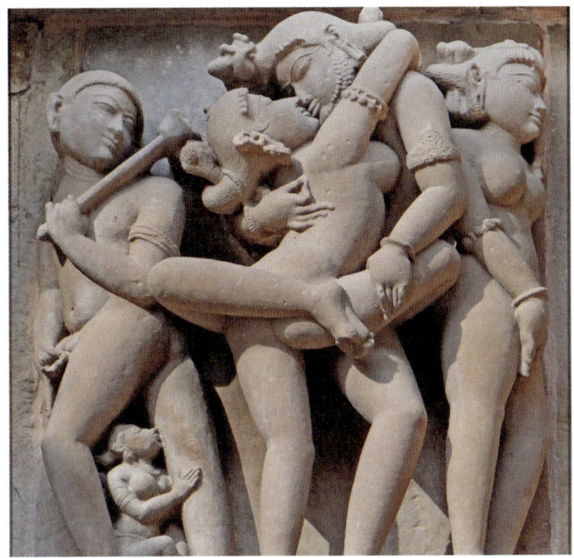

Erotic Indian figures carved into the walls of the Khajuraho Temples, reflecting themes of love and sensuality in ancient art.

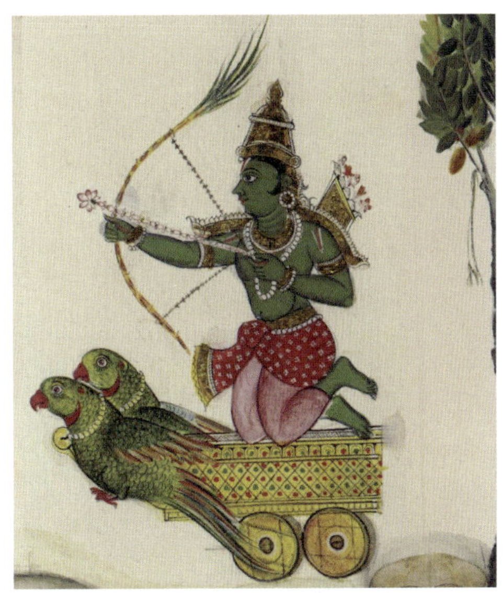

Kama, God of Love and Desire, shooting his flower-tipped arrows that inspire passion.

Shiva's stories encapsulate the tension in Hinduism between sensual indulgence and asceticism. In one ancient myth, after perfecting the art of love, Shiva retreats into meditation in the Himalayas. Parvati, frustrated by his neglect, sends the god Kama to disturb Shiva's deep meditation with his blossom-tipped arrows. Sexually awakened, yet in a fit of rage, Shiva burns Kama to ashes, turning him into Ananga, the "bodiless one".

The pursuit of erotic fulfilment was not only accepted but revered. The *Kama Sutra* even dedicates an entire chapter to remedies for rekindling passion. Among these unorthodox solutions are curious concoctions like a drink made from milk boiled with sugar and the testicles of a goat, as "an aphrodisiac provocative of sexual vigour." Another, more bizarre recipe involves smearing "insects from a tree" on one's genitals to create permanent swelling. But, as with the rest of the *Kama Sutra*, it's not so much the letter of these practices that matters, but the spirit of embracing and honouring sensuality.

Beyond the *Kama Sutra*, cannabis was also incorporated into erotic practices. Since the 2nd century CE, *bhang*, a honey-infused cannabis drink, has been used in India to calm the mind and enhance sensory awareness, facilitating both meditation and erotic arousal.[36] Devotees would consume the cannabis-infused drink ninety minutes before engaging in tantric sex, using mantras to invoke deities like Kali to achieve spiritual oneness.[37]

Another native remedy, the Cordyceps fungus, has long been used to boost vitality and stamina – in the bedroom and beyond. Although not directly mentioned in the *Kama Sutra*, Cordyceps have a rich history in traditional Chinese medicine for treating conditions such as low libido and fatigue. Its medicinal use was first recorded in a 15th-century text *An Ocean of Aphrodisiacal Qualities,* where the

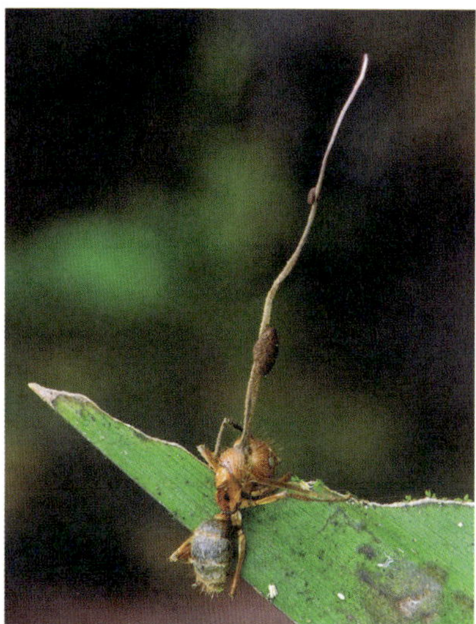

Ophiocordyceps unilateralis, *the "zombie fungus," infects ants, driving them to climb high and lock into a fatal "death bite," the perfect position for releasing its spores.*

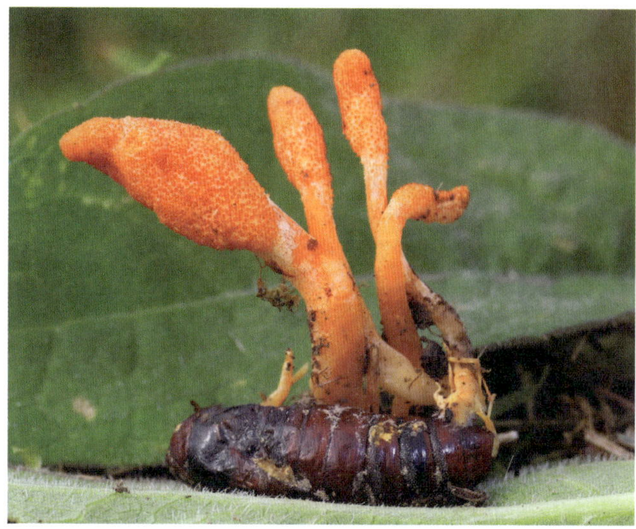

Scarlet Caterpillar Club fungus, Cordyceps militaris, *consuming a moth caterpillar. This parasitic fungus invades the host's body, taking over its nervous system and eventually killing it – sprouting orange fruiting bodies from the remnants to release spores.*

author, lama and physician Zurkhar Namnyi Dorje, describes Cordyceps as a valuable drug for "rotsa" ailments concerning sexual virility. As such, the alliance between cannabis and Cordyceps is rumoured to facilitate optimal conditions for reaching sexual climax.

Like the parasitic fungi that invade cicadas, Cordyceps are entomopathogenic, infecting insects and spiders to complete their life cycle. There are roughly 800 species of Cordyceps-like fungi, each targeting a specific host. *Cordyceps militaris*, known as the Scarlet Caterpillar Club fungus, infects moth and butterfly larvae, while *Ophiocordyceps unilateralis,* the Zombie fungus, infects ants. The latter forces its host to climb high, where it locks itself in place with a "death bite," creating the perfect conditions for the fungus to release its spores – ideally directly above an ant trail.

One of the most famous Cordyceps species, *Ophiocordyceps sinensis,* is known as "Himalayan Viagra". According to legend (or brilliant salesmen), Himalayan herders observed their yaks consuming this fungus and becoming instantly aroused. Traditional medicine attributes these effects to Cordyceps' ability to target the lungs, kidneys, and adrenals, organs linked to vitality and reproductive energy. Modern research suggests that Cordyceps may improve male reproductive function by increasing sperm count and motility and enhance female libido by up to eighty-six per cent, making it one of nature's most potent aphrodisiacs.[38]

Beyond their reputation for boosting sexual health, Cordyceps also offer powerful antiviral and anti-inflammatory benefits, while enhancing endurance by increasing ATP production. A 2010 study revealed that older adults who consumed Cordyceps showed significant improvements in exercise

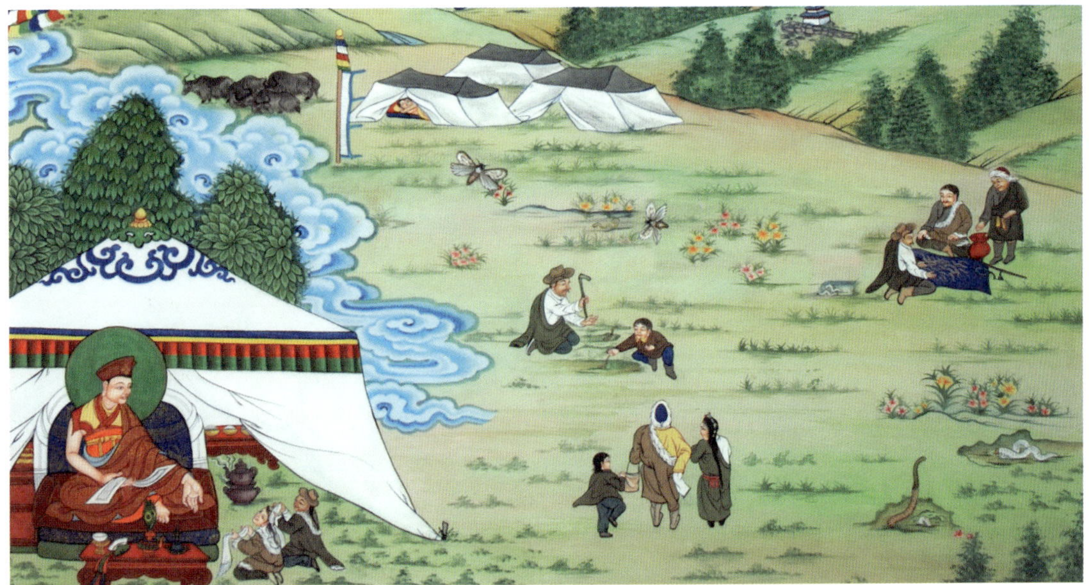

Contemporary thanka (traditional painting) of Cordyceps foragers in the Himalayas. Cordyceps have a long history in traditional Chinese medicine for treating low libido and fatigue. They are believed to boost vitality and stamina, "in the bedroom and beyond" . . .

performance.[39] Similarly, the 1993 Chinese women's running team set multiple Olympic world records, attributing their success not to steroids, as initially suspected, but to the energising, and legal, effects of Cordyceps and turtle blood! Unfortunately, a few years later it was revealed that cordyceps, turtle blood, *and* steroids had been used by the team. Alas!

On the Himalayan plateau, Cordyceps are known as *yartsa gunbu,* meaning "winter worm, summer grass", a nod to their seasonal transformation from caterpillar to mushroom. In 2005, explorer Bruce Parry was treated to a traditional brew made from these wild fungi. Sitting inside a black, waterproof tent made from yak hair, seventy-eight-year-old yak herder Penjo heated fresh yak butter in a frying pan and added a generous handful of freshly harvested *yartsa gunbu*. After a few minutes of sizzling, Penjo casually poured in half a bottle of whisky, allowing the fungi to soak up the alcohol and release their medicinal compounds. Just five minutes later, the brew was ready. Bruce took a tentative sip, expecting some instant surge of spiritual, or spiritual–or sexual–enlightenment. Predictably, nothing happened. He was later told that the true benefits of *yartsa gunbu* require consistent use over weeks, if not months. Still, the next morning Bruce swore he felt "like a new man", keeping the myth – and the desire for these fungi – very much alive.[40]

In the Himalayas, Cordyceps are harvested during a brief window each year and can fetch astronomical prices – up to $500 for just five grams.[41] The largest varieties are literally worth their weight in gold. Towns across India and China have experienced explosive economic growth due to this "fungal gold rush", igniting tensions among foragers over rights and sustainability. Demand far outstrips supply,

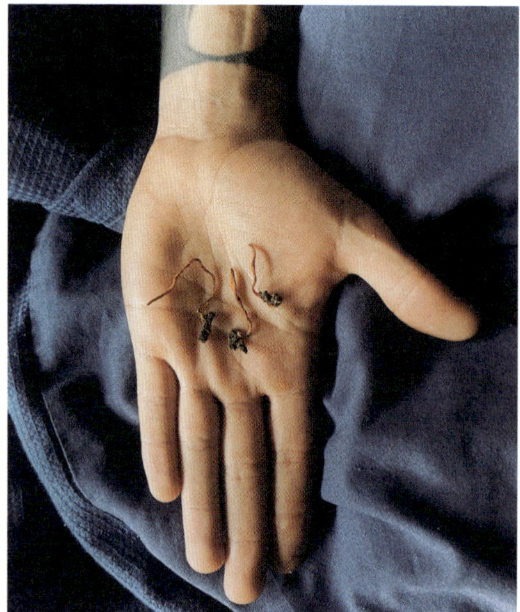

Testing hand foraged, UK-native wild Cordyceps to see if Himalayan legends hold true.

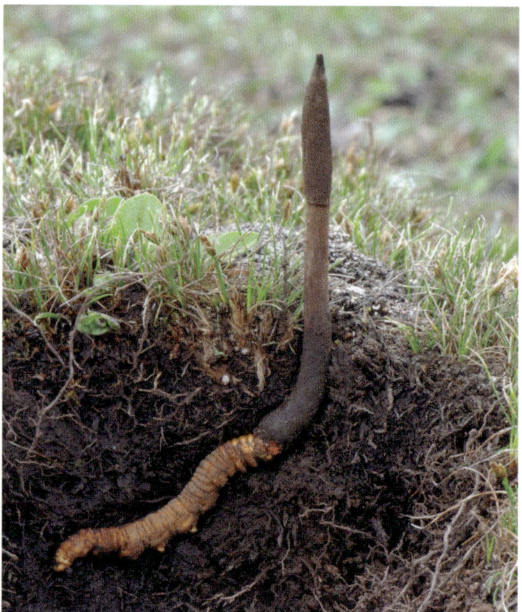

The insect-fungus complex: Yartsa gunbu *with the dark fungal fruiting body emerging from the ghost moth's head.*

and as wild specimens are harvested before they can disseminate spores, concerns about the fungus' long-term viability are mounting.[42] To address this and meet demand more quickly and affordably, Chinese farmers began cultivating *Cordyceps militaris*. After decades of trial and error, the method—now used worldwide—succeeded. A single tray of cultivated *C. militaris* can match a lifetime's harvest of wild *yartsa gunbu*, and though it lacks the adventure and lore, some farmed varieties reportedly contain higher levels of beneficial compounds like cordycepin and adenosine, making them equally, or even more, effective.[43]

But we don't need to farm our own or travel to the Himalayas to find Cordyceps; they live in the wild throughout Africa, Europe, and the Americas. Despite the difficulty of spotting them among tufts of grass, moss, and gorse, my partner and I found fifteen *Cordyceps militaris* on the moors of southwest England. The day was spent on our stomachs, crawling around as if we were fungal archaeologists, carefully excavating sacred treasures. We brought them home, cleaned them, collected spores, and used them all for a culinary experiment. Guided by insights from foragers and friends, we prepared them to see if the legends of their transformative powers held true. They did not disappoint.

But don't just take my word for it. I dare you to try them yourself. Invoke the spirit of Shiva, celebrate the strange and sacred journey through caterpillar to fungus to human, and honour the rich tradition where sexual pleasure meets spiritual transformation.

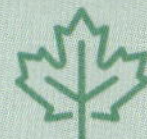

RECIPES

CORDYCEPS LOVE ELIXIRS

BRUCE'S RECIPE (BUTTER-FUNGUS-CATERPILLAR-WHISKY")

INGREDIENTS

- 2 heaped tbsp of yak butter
- 10g fresh wild Cordyceps/Yartsa gunbu (*Ophiocordyceps sinensis*)
- Half a bottle of whisky

METHOD

1. Heat the butter in a frying pan.
2. Add the cordyceps and let them simmer for 3–4 minutes.
3. Pour in the whisky and leave on a low heat for 4 minutes.
4. Pour into a mug and drink – insects and all.

SHIVA'S RECIPE

INGREDIENTS

- 10g Cordyceps (wild or cultivated)
- Boiling water
- 1 tsp honey

METHOD

1. "Powder the dried mushrooms and pour boiling water over them. When warm, add honey." – An anonymous man I met in a Chinese herbal shop in San Francisco.

The Layap People of Laya, in remote Bhutan, forage for Cordyceps in spring and summer, harvesting the fungus from high-altitude meadows for its medicinal value.

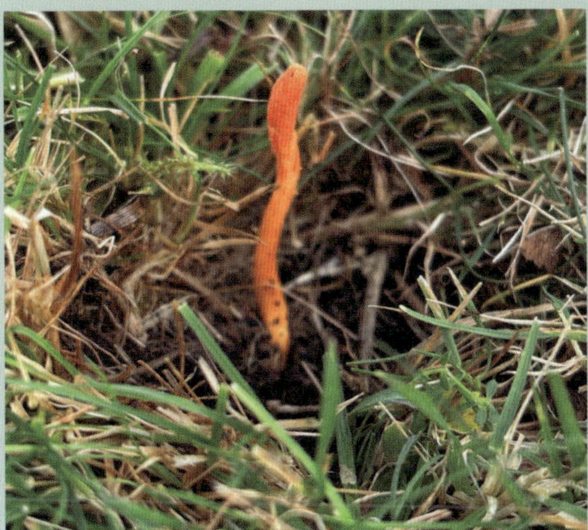

Wild Cordyceps, often called "Himalayan Viagra", can be worth their weight in gold. We wondered, does the same hold true for wild cordyceps foraged in the UK?

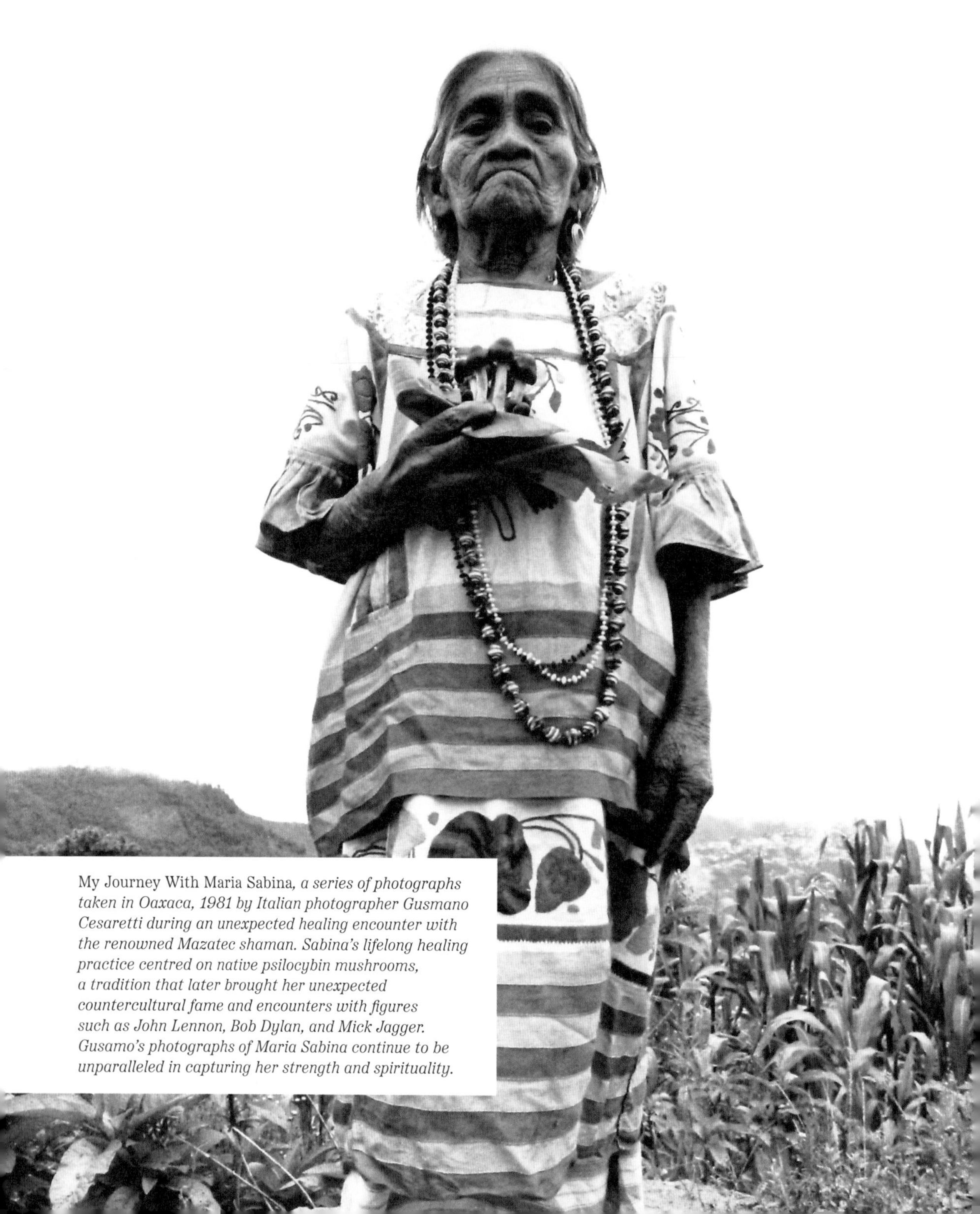

My Journey With Maria Sabina, *a series of photographs taken in Oaxaca, 1981 by Italian photographer Gusmano Cesaretti during an unexpected healing encounter with the renowned Mazatec shaman. Sabina's lifelong healing practice centred on native psilocybin mushrooms, a tradition that later brought her unexpected countercultural fame and encounters with figures such as John Lennon, Bob Dylan, and Mick Jagger. Gusamo's photographs of Maria Sabina continue to be unparalleled in capturing her strength and spirituality.*

MOVEMENT & RITUALS

This narrative includes graphic descriptions of the traumatic experiences of war veterans. Please skip this story if it may be distressing.

"Dance is the hidden language of the soul."

– Martha Graham, dancer and choreographer

At Breaking Convention 2023, I found myself shoulder to shoulder with mycologists, therapists, philosophers, and a scattering of silent veterans. We watched, transfixed, as a video played across the lecture hall screen: a man, mid-forties, sinewy and taut, lay on a mat in a softly lit room, an eye mask resting lightly across his face. No restraints. No medical bed. But his body shook as though trying to break through something invisible. His arms curled towards his chest, fingers gripping the air. His legs kicked violently. His breath, audible on the video, came in gasps.

This was a psilocybin-assisted therapy session, recorded in the Netherlands by the Psychedelic Somatic Institute (PSI). A body, writhing – not in pain, not quite – but in release.

The man, a US combat veteran, had spent nearly 20 years living in the aftermath of a bombing. He had survived, though his best friend had not. In therapy he spoke little about it. But the nightmares came frequently. Flashbacks. Emotional numbness. And that ever-present feeling of being elsewhere.

This was his fourth day in the PSI protocol. He had started with cannabis-assisted somatic sessions, letting his nervous system slowly edge closer to his long-held trauma. Now, under the effects of psilocybin truffles and the support of a trained therapist, he was allowing his body to express what words never could.[44,45]

The session was carefully crafted. In the PSI model, the aim isn't to create a ceremony full of awe and transcendence. The focus is on staying present, staying in the body, and processing biographical material. The dose of psilocybin is kept intentionally low – just enough to quieten the overactive, external self-looking down thinking that often blocks healing, without tipping into a fully altered state. This helps loosen the grip of *selective inhibition* – the learned tendency to suppress strong emotions like grief or rage in order to function in society. Instead of filtering or controlling the experience, or putting words to an emotion, the goal is to allow movement, often involuntary and autonomic, to emerge.

"Imagine walking down the street and tripping on the sidewalk", says Saj Ravzi, founder and Director of Education at PSI. "Without thinking, your body quickly reorganizes – muscles and balance adjust to prevent you from falling. Even with a mild threat like that, your nerves take over instantly, responding faster than you consciously can. That's the kind of fast, automatic response we're looking for."

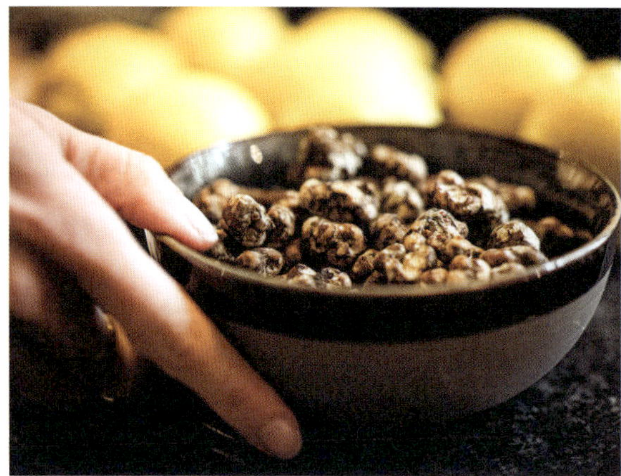

Psilocybin truffles are the underground sclerotia (hardened mycelial masses) of certain psychedelic mushroom species, such as Psilocybe mexicana *or* Psilocybe tampanensis, *that contain the psychoactive compound psilocybin. While technically not mushrooms, they produce similar psychedelic effects and are legal in some countries, including the Netherlands.*

In *The Body Keeps the Score*, psychiatrist Bessel van der Kolk outlines what this man was demonstrating on that floor: that trauma lives not in the mind or in the past, but in the body: in twitching muscle memory, disrupted breath, chronic tension, and the persistent inability to feel safe. Healing trauma isn't a matter of simply remembering it; it's about processing and moving it through.[46] Animals do this instinctively, shaking after a stressful event: physically releasing the experience so it can escape and the animal can move on. Our bodies know this too. Van der Kolk's approach, rooted in bodywork methodologies, suggests that shaking, dancing, humming, singing, yoga, or other somatic therapies can help release the emotions trapped within the body.

PSI operates on a similar principle. Founded by therapists and educators like Saj Razvi, their Psychedelic Somatic Interactional Psychotherapy (PSIP) method is designed not around managing symptoms, but dismantling the unconscious systems that keep trauma stuck. They believe that with the right preparation, psychedelics like ketamine, MDMA, cannabis, and psilocybin can serve as catalysts for introspection, somatic release, and, eventually, identity reconstruction.

Back in the Netherlands, the veteran's shaking began to slow. His hands unclenched. His breathing softened. The therapist, seated beside him, had barely moved, just offering subtle verbal encouragement: reminders of safety, of presence, of the now.

Later, in an integration circle, the veteran said he had "run out of his body". In the session, he had relived the moment before the blast with intense clarity: the shift in the air, a whistle in the distance – and for the first time, he hadn't turned away. A part of him ran, grief coming up from his feet, and another part observed, with compassion and understanding.

Clinical research into psilocybin for trauma has accelerated rapidly in recent years. In 2023, Compass Pathways completed a Phase 2 open-label study administering a 25mg dose of psilocybin (COMP360) to 22 individuals diagnosed with PTSD.[47] The results were striking: over 80 per cent showed significant symptom reduction within four weeks, and more than half were in remission after three months. Another study, underway at Johns Hopkins, is currently evaluating the effect of two

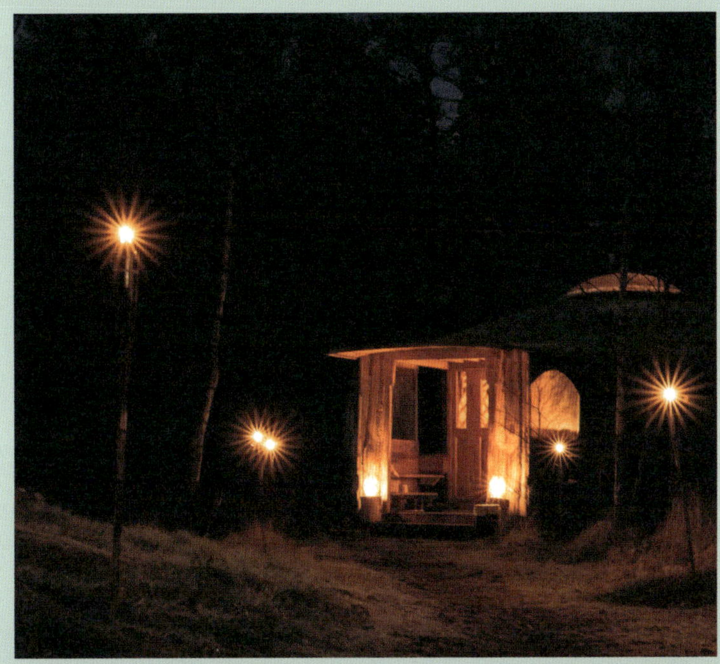

Psilocybin-assisted session in the Netherlands with Spinoza Ceremonies.

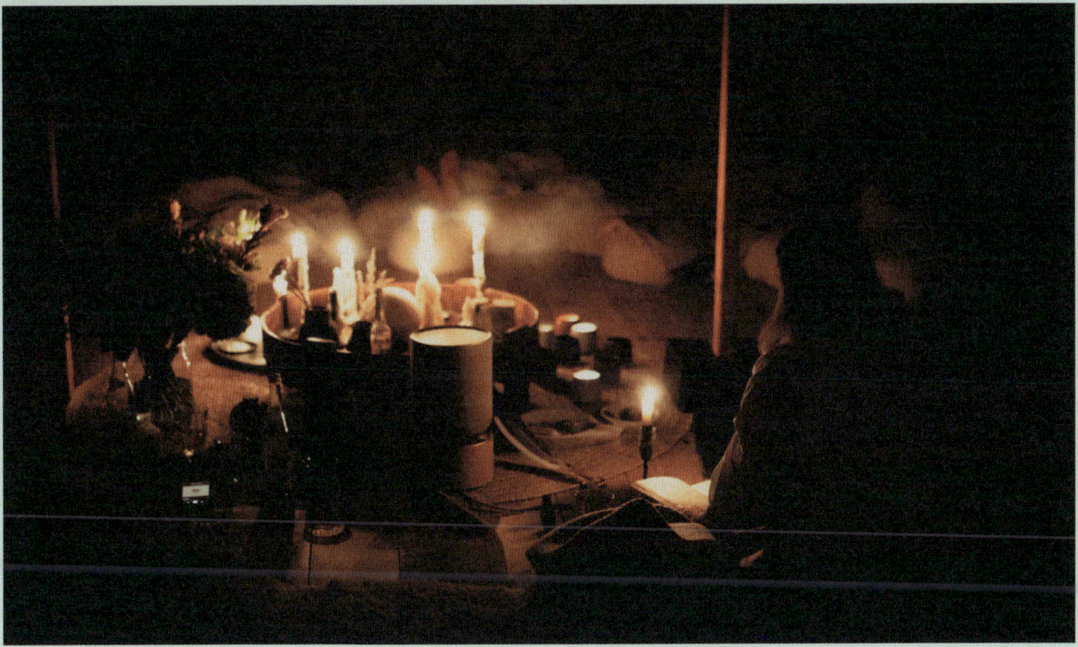

high-dose psilocybin sessions for trauma survivors,[48] while Yale,[49] the University of Washington,[50] and veteran-focused clinics in the UK are launching their studies[51] – often pairing psilocybin with somatic or cognitive processing therapies. Today, more than a dozen trials are underway worldwide, COMPASS is preparing for Phase 3, and organisations such as Veterans Walk & Talk and Heroic Hearts are lobbying for therapeutic access as psilocybin edges closer to legal use across Europe and Canada.

Against this backdrop, PSI's work in the Netherlands offers a markedly different paradigm. While many organisations use synthesised psilocybin, PSI pairs legal, natural psilocybin truffles with somatic trauma work that begins days before the dose. Cannabis is first used to gently reveal dissociation, to test the body's capacity to feel, to tremble, to speak. By the time psilocybin is introduced, the person is no longer sealed inside a defensive loop; their nervous system is in dialogue, opening the possibility for deeper reorganisation.[52] "The primary agent of transformation here is the movement that's taking place at the level of the nervous system", Saj explains. Where clinical protocols emphasise structure, PSI emphasises safety through spontaneity.

The results, while anecdotal, can be profound. In one case report published by PSI, a client with complex PTSD experienced a 98.5 per cent reduction in dissociative symptoms after only a handful of cannabis- and psilocybin-assisted PSIP sessions — evidence of genuine cognitive and somatic restructuring.[53] Still, Saj is clear about the limitations: "This isn't evidence-based science," he says. "It's anecdotal. It's what we find in our practices, and it's a model developed from direct clinical experience."[54] Yet for the veterans, assault survivors, and individuals carrying childhood trauma who come through PSI's doors, the transformations unfolding in their bodies often speak louder than any graph could. Bodies don't lie.

At Breaking Convention, the lecture ended. When the lights rose, the room lingered in a kind of quiet reverence. Not everyone understood what they had just seen, but many, I think, felt it. That something had shifted. That the trembling of a man on the floor was not madness or fragility, but the intelligence of a body reclaiming its truth.

And, ultimately, it is in places like PSI – in the quiet rooms of Amsterdam, where bodies shake, remember, and reorganise – another kind of healing is taking shape. Not as theory. Not as narrative. But as movement. As a soul dancing its way back into the body.

Later at Breaking Convention, I slipped into another lecture, one far less institutional and more chaotic. The speakers were artists, DJs, anthropologists , and dancers – guardians of the underground. They were there to remind us that the psychedelic renaissance didn't start in a lab, and it won't be saved by one. They spoke of raves, renegade rituals, moonlit fields, and strobe-lit warehouses. They critiqued the sterilisation of psychedelic healing, arguing that the clinical setting, with its reliance on synthesised psilocybin, questionnaires, and constant supervision, strips the magic from the mushroom.

"We've been doing this the whole bloody time!" one speaker laughed, to nods and scattered applause.

Ru Callender, a psychedelic undertaker and old-school raver, stood at the mic and gave us the sermon: "I believe that dancing in a field all night with your friends on ecstasy can be just as productive in healing as any supervised session in a clinical environment."[55]

And I didn't disagree. Because while clinical psilocybin therapy is giving us data – beautiful, promising data – it's also showing us what underground culture has long known: movement is medicine. Grief

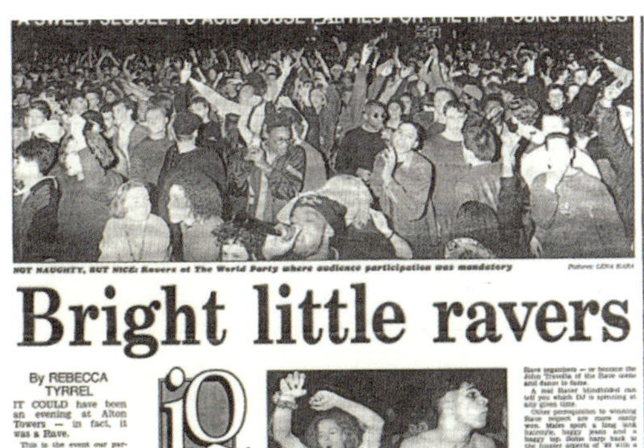
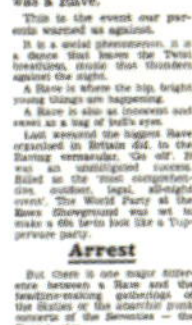
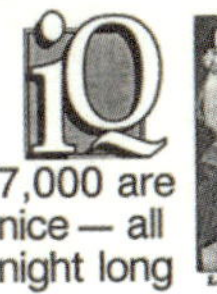
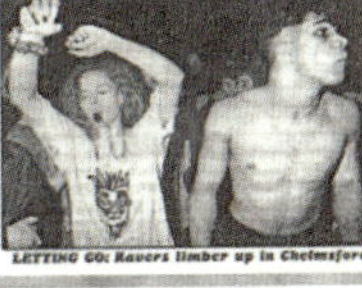
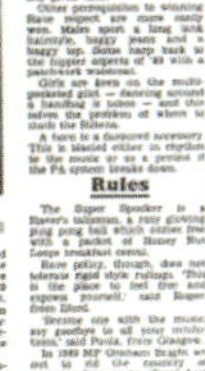

NOT NAUGHTY, BUT NICE: Ravers at The World Party where audience participation was mandatory

Bright little ravers

By REBECCA TYRREL

iQ

7,000 are nice — all night long

IT COULD have been an evening at Alton Towers — in fact, it was a Rave.

Arrest

LETTING GO: Ravers limber up in Chelmsford

Rules

Movement is medicine. Dance, music, and rhythm channel collective energy, allowing communities to release tension, express emotion, and connect deeply with one another.

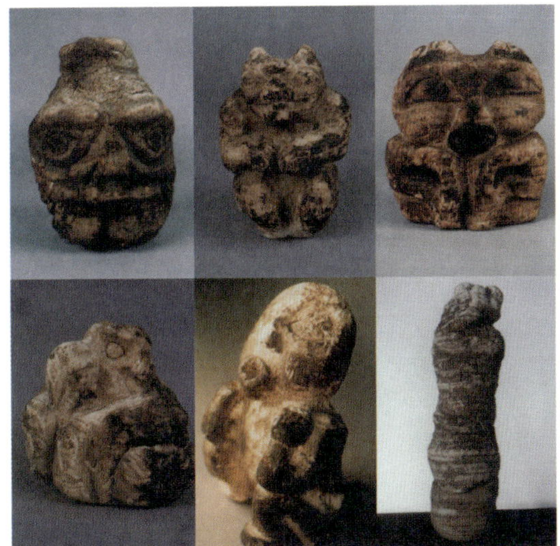

Masks made from the Agarikon Fungus, Laricifomes officinalis, *were created by Indigenous communities of the Pacific Northwest and placed on graves of as guardians in the afterlife.*

doesn't exit the body through insight alone. It exits through breath, through sweat, through wails that turn to laughter and legs that won't stop shaking.

I thought of heaving dance floors. Of ritual fires. Of my own childhood, huddled around unsanctioned ceremonies with cousins and friends, singing our way into oblivion.

Long before Western science named it "psychedelic therapy", we had ritual – intuitive technologies for transformation. Rituals arise instinctively during times of celebration, mourning, or transition. They mark rites of passage, such as birth, death, heartbreak, and harvest, each marked with movement, music, masks, fasting, and fire. These weren't performances; they were portals. Structured chaos, where emotion had permission to erupt, rearrange, and settle as something new.

In some traditions, a sacrifice was required. Something old had to burn so something new could rise. Among the Diné (Navajo), a horse might be slaughtered to guide the deceased through the afterlife.[56] In the high Himalayas, bodies became smoke, lifted skyward through ritual fire.

Every culture has had its version of this release. Not always gentle. Not always sober. But always held.

In the 1960s, anthropologists in the Wahgi Valley of New Guinea thought they'd discovered a new form of psychedelic ritual. The Kuma people were said to eat a hallucinogenic mushroom called *nonda*, triggering a kind of "mushroom madness".[57] Women donned warrior regalia and danced provocatively; men ran through villages howling. Some saw spirits. Others lost their speech.

Western scientists were enthralled – finally, a mushroom ritual outside Mesoamerica and Siberia. Expeditions followed and samples were analysed, and yet no trace of psychedelic compounds was found.

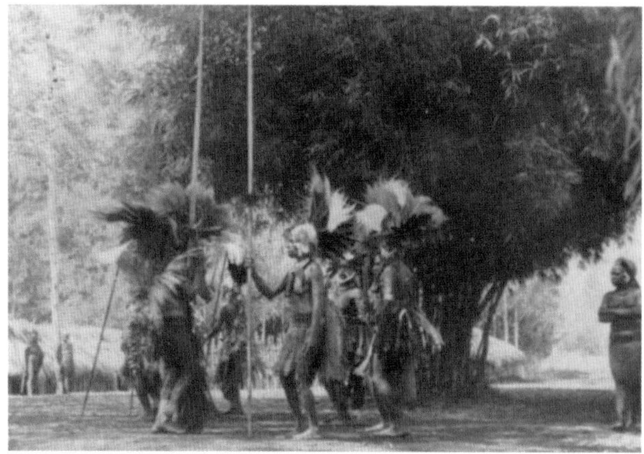

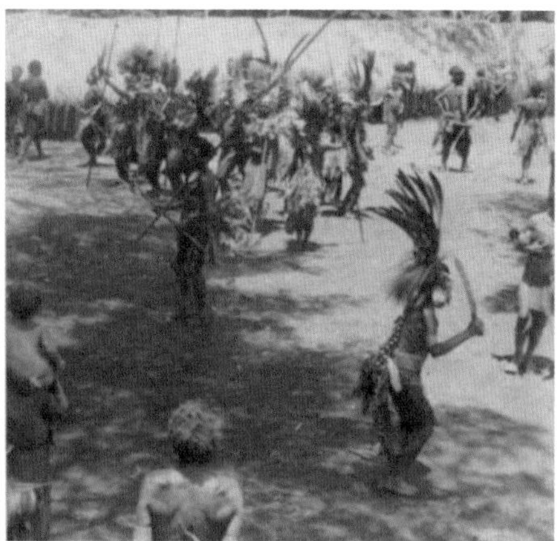

"Mushroom Madness" in the New Guinea Highlands. The Kuma people were said to consume a hallucinogenic mushroom called nonda, *triggering a form of "mushroom madness", though no psychoactive ingredients have ever been identified by scientists.*

The mushrooms were a placebo. But the ecstasy was real.

What the anthropologists had witnessed was not pharmacology, but cultural permission – a sanctioned rite of rebellion. The *nonda* mushroom created a space in which people could finally do what their bodies were asking for: to scream, to seduce, to break rank, to let go.

The Greeks called this *ekstasis*, "to stand outside oneself". These ecstatic states were not indulgences but sacraments, cultivated through ritual, song, dance, drumming, fasting, sleep deprivation, and even pain. Each method served the same purpose: to loosen the boundaries of ordinary consciousness so that the psyche could reorganise itself.

The historian of religion Mircea Eliade considered shamanism to be humanity's first ecstatic technology. He believed that altered states of consciousness were crucial for community healing and divination, though cautioned against the use of psychedelics, viewing them as a "vulgar" substitute for purer forms of trance.[58] Real transformation would come not from the substance, but from the ceremony: the costume, the drum, the mask that allowed the self to dissolve and reform in relation to the sacred.[59]

I thought of the Reishi mushroom masks carved in Nepal and some now housed at Kew – its expression ancient and unflinching.[60] Or the Agarikon masks of the Pacific Northwest, worn by shamans and placed over graves to guide the spirit and ensure safe passage between worlds. These masks were interfaces, technologies of protection and transmission. You wore the mushroom to commune with it. You wore the mask to become something more-than-human.[61]

The Dogon of West Africa, too, use mushroomed rituals, grounded in symbolism rather than ingestion. They rub carbonised mushrooms on their drums to "give them voice".[62] They dance, they sing, they surrender. Their rituals are wildly playful, supreme catalysts for creativity and connection. Like psychedelics, play deconstructs habitual ways of thinking and being, creating space for spontaneity and enabling a reconnection with one's primal self.

Diné activist Pat McCabe[63] speaks powerfully about this. In the West, she says, we dismiss such practices as "primitive," mistaking emotional expressiveness for immaturity. We teach children to contain their rage, their joy, their tears – to grow up. Yet some parts of us aren't meant to be contained. They're meant to move, to express, to be seen rather than managed into silence. Rituals create the conditions for this: a safe space to loosen the mind's grip and notice what lies underneath. They let us stretch beyond our usual boundaries and then return to ourselves with a little more clarity.

Psilocybin, in both clinical and ceremonial settings, seems to support this process. It softens mental control just enough for the body to speak. Tears surface without explanation. Laughter releases tension. Limbs tremble or unwind. What was stuck begins to move again. This is memory, held in the body, finding a way to reorganise.

Whether through mushroom placebos among the Kuma, psilocybin-assisted therapy in Amsterdam, or the anonymity of a crowded dancefloor, the effect is often the same: a somatic loosening. Each experience reminds us that healing begins when we stop bracing against ourselves.

The body already knows how to grieve, release, and begin again. It just needs the rhythm, the setting, and the invitation.

ACTIVITY

ECSTASY IN AN UNDERGROUND RAVE

You are invited to dance. Not for performance. Not to be seen. But to feel. Attend a rave. Go barefoot in a field. Lose yourself under stars or strobes. Meet the self you hide from in daylight. Let the music become your medicine. Let the movement carry what words cannot. Let it shake something loose.

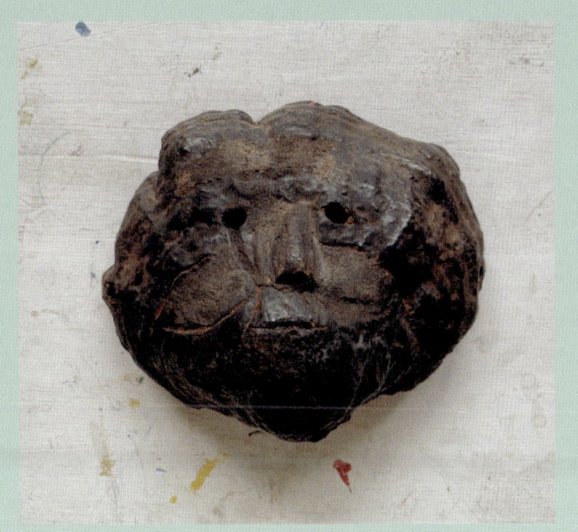

Sacred Agarikon Mask.

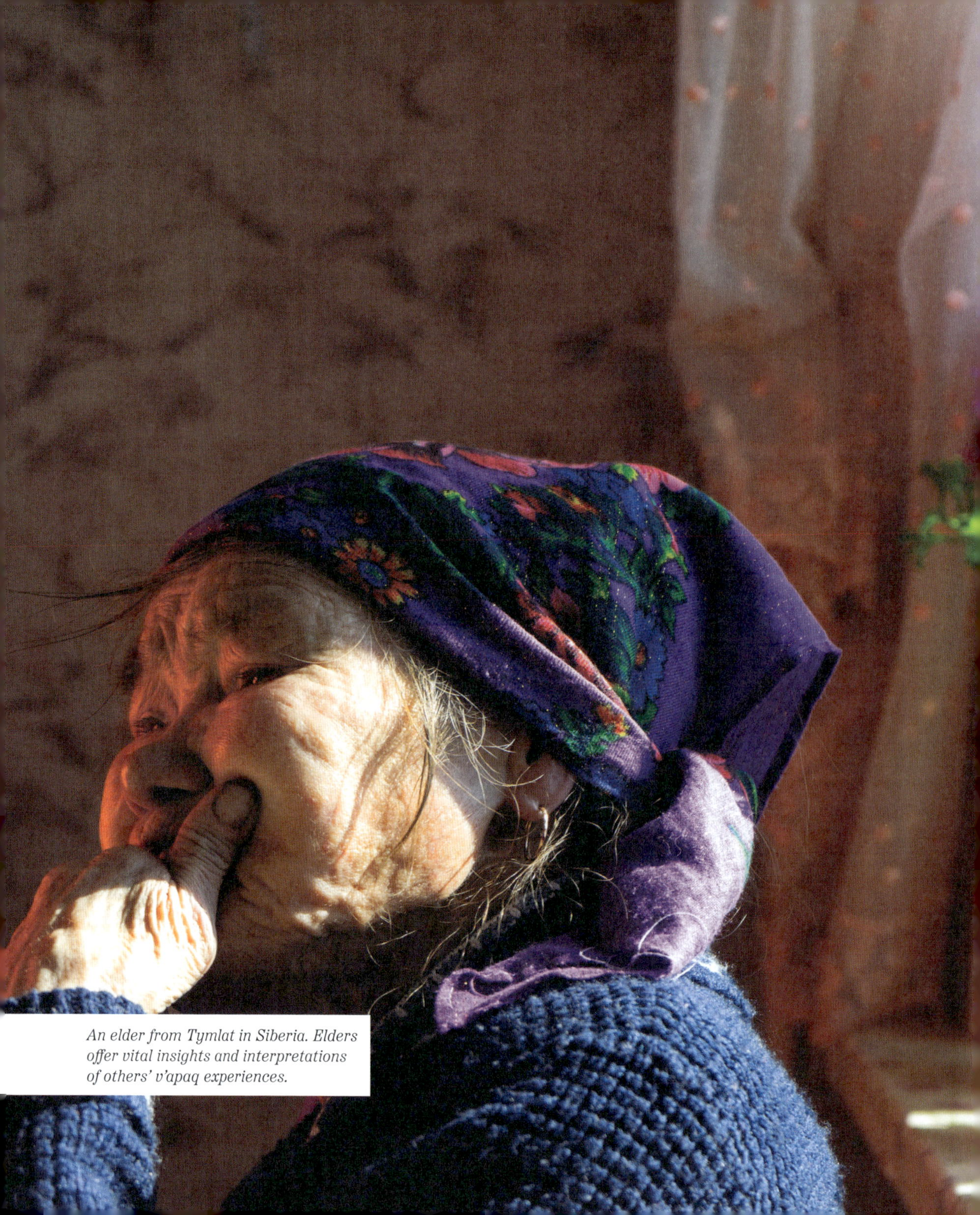

An elder from Tymlat in Siberia. Elders offer vital insights and interpretations of others' v'apaq experiences.

4.5

INTEGRATION: Hanging Up the Phone

Once you lose yourself in an altered state, how do you find your way back – and where, exactly, are you returning to?

Pat McCabe describes transformation as an outwards expansion followed by a return to one's roots – a journey that makes sense in cultures with intact initiation rituals with intact "psychedelic containers." But today, many of us face a widening gap in intergenerational knowledge. Without elders or community rituals to guide us, many find themselves navigating deep personal transformation without maps. We self-initiate through reinvented rites of passage, meditation, or psychedelics – sometimes with insight, sometimes with risk.

I've heard of people taking 10g of Fly Agaric without a sitter or flying to the Amazon for a weekend psilocybin retreat, returning to work on the red eye. Some take large doses without a clear intention, while others embark on intense solo trips without any support afterwards. But these practices don't give the mushrooms the safety nor the space they deserve.

Psychedelic-assisted practitioners emphasise one crucial point: the trip itself isn't the key. It's the work done before and after – the preparation and the integration – that determines the experience's impact.

Dr Raquel Bennett teaches that preparation involves confronting what we usually avoid – old wounds, guilt, relationships. It's helpful to set intentions, move the body, spend time in nature. And afterwards, during integration, the experience is absorbed. Sometimes it's blissful, sometimes jarring. Without this phase, says Bennett, psychedelic therapy is incomplete – unethical even.[1]

We undergo this cycle all the time. A mother greets her child from sleep with a smiling, "Welcome back!" Altered states – whether through sleep, sex, music, or psychedelics – are departures from the self. And we re-enter, changed.

Returning from a journey can feel disorientating, especially when the world around you hasn't changed at all. You've grown; others still see the old you. This disconnect complicates reintegration – not just for you, but for them too.

Paul Stamets once shared a story of a friend who wanted to take a psychedelic journey. Paul agreed, on one condition: the man's wife must also participate. Psychedelics can fast-track transformation,

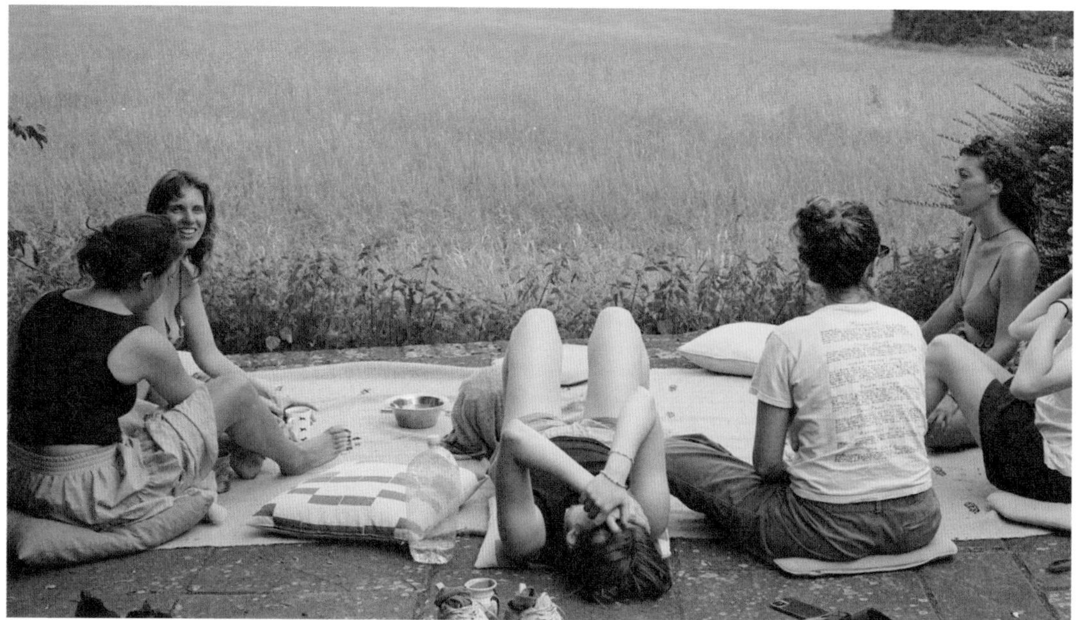

Integration Circle. Many people say that preparation and integration are just as crucial, if not more, than the psychedelic experience itself. Preparation involves confronting what we often avoid – old wounds, guilt, and unresolved relationships – while integration allows the experience to be absorbed and understood.

"ten years of therapy in six hours." But if loved ones remain behind, the divide can be painful. In the end, she declined, and Paul withdrew his offer. Integration, he knew, is relational.

The insights we receive from psychedelics often demand action – quit the job, end the relationship, start anew. But therapists caution for patience. During the "window of opportunity" after a journey, the brain is pliable and receptive to new patterns. Sometimes it's not about burning everything down but setting boundaries, repairing connections, or building new habits.

Integration can take many forms. For some, it's movement – yoga, running, swimming. Others turn to dance practices, or lose themselves in soil and seeds, letting composted thoughts feed new growth. Music from your psychedelic journey might help re-access that inner state. Anything that reconnects you to body and mind is worthwhile.

Community, too, is vital. Sharing stories in integration circles, being witnessed without judgement, helps release pressure and anchor the experience. It also fosters belonging, often sparking a drive towards justice and service. Many return from these journeys with a clearer sense of purpose and a deeper understanding of their responsibility towards others.

Nature, ever patient, remains one of our best allies. A daily walk, birdsong, a mountain climbed – all help ground us. They echo the awe we feel during journeys: reminders of our vastness and our fragility.

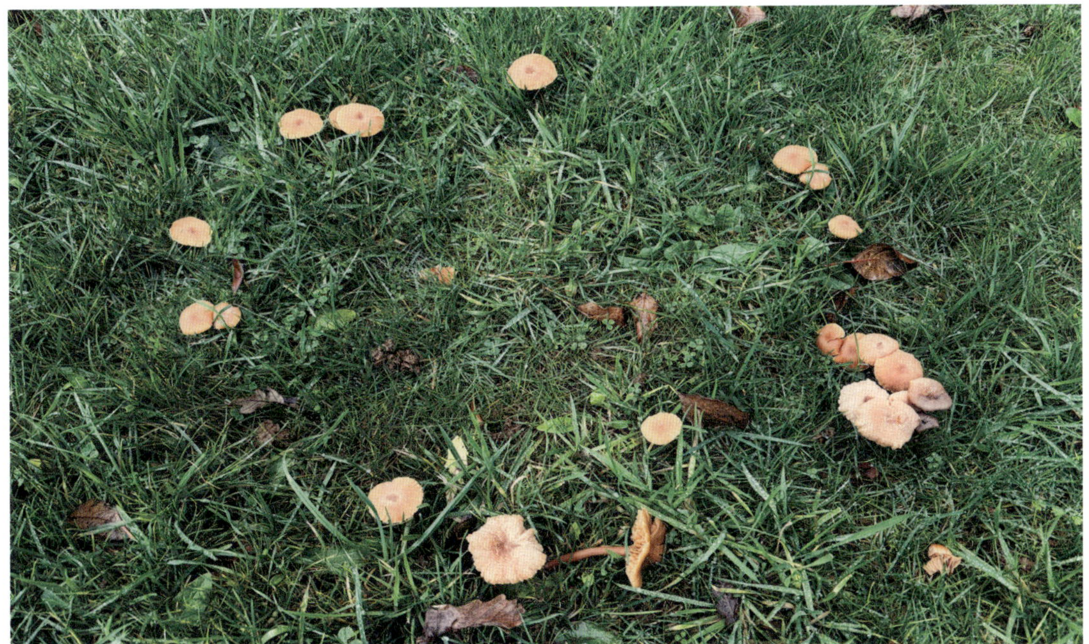

Fairy Ring Champignons grow from mycelium that expands outwards in a radial pattern. As the mycelium spreads, it fruits at the active outer edge, producing the characteristic ring of mushrooms each year.

Ultimately, integration is found in the everyday. Drinking water. Making dinner. Saying thank you. Sleeping deeply. Loving generously. As Bill Richards once said, he's still integrating his first psychedelic trip – 60 years on. The work is never really finished.

There's an adage in psychedelic circles: "Once you get the message, hang up the phone."[2] We must be careful not to chase the experience for its own sake. Repeated high-dose use can lead to escapism. The goal isn't endless tripping, it's transformation. The real challenge is living the insight, not just seeking it.

As Monica Gagliano puts it, "It's not the compound in your system. If they've been with you before, they stay forever."[3] Healing lives in the moments in between.

Perhaps the greatest gift of the mushroom is the reminder that the power is already within you. These journeys don't add anything new; they reintroduce you to yourself. And they never show you more than you're ready to see. Maria Sabina wisely encouraged, "Nothing that the mushrooms show should be feared."[4] Trust in that. Trust in you.

The tension between becoming and belonging is real. We yearn to evolve, yet long to be embraced as we are. Fungi show us how: Mycelia spread both outwards to explore, and among themselves to nourish and connect. In the next chapters, we'll follow this pattern – moving outwards to map the worlds beyond, then rooting inwards to cultivate what matters most.

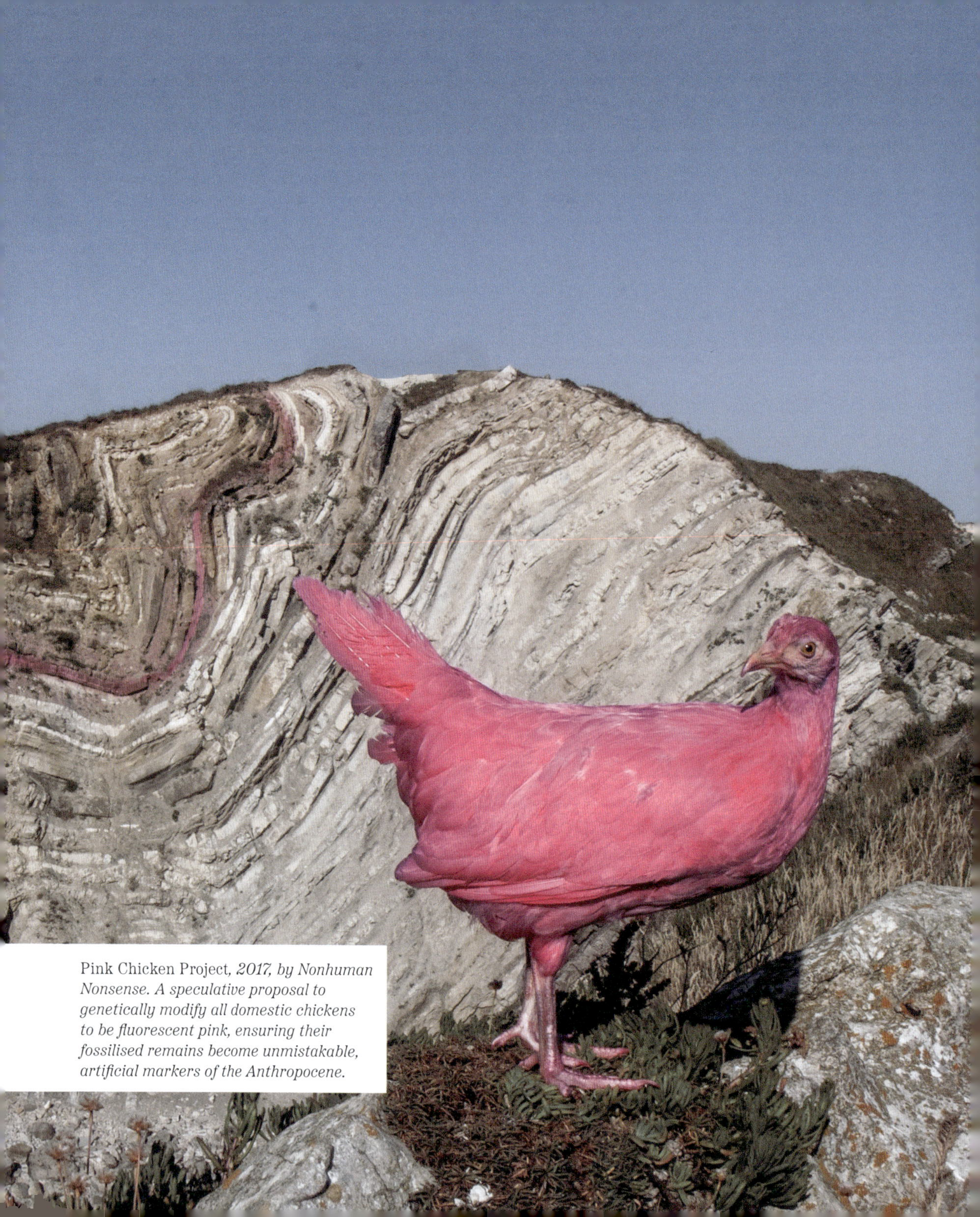

Pink Chicken Project, *2017, by Nonhuman Nonsense. A speculative proposal to genetically modify all domestic chickens to be fluorescent pink, ensuring their fossilised remains become unmistakable, artificial markers of the Anthropocene.*

5

INTER:
Being Ecological

"Ecology isn't something that's elsewhere. We are right there in the thick of ecological relations when we are eating a Big Mac."

– Timothy Morton, Eco-philosopher

We are living in the Anthropocene. Our presence is etched into the Earth's geological record – through plastic sediments, industrial soot, nuclear fallout, and the bones of about 2.5 trillion domestic chickens we've consumed over the last 50 years.[1] The speculative Pink Chicken Project, proposes genetically modifying the entire *Gallus gallus* domesticus species to a fluorescent pink.[2] When fossilised, these chickens would serve as unmistakable markers of our epoch.

Human debris permeates every layer of soil and sea. But fortunately for us, so do fungi. They branch through the Earth's crust and populate its oceans, atmospheres, and inhabitants, reminding us that ecology is not external to us. We are ecology.

In her design philosophy *Material Ecology*, architect Neri Oxman advocates for a shift from simply designing consumable products to actively engaging with the ecosystems they exist within. A burger isn't just food; as eco philosopher Timothy Morton points out, it's a dense ecological node: deforestation in the Amazon, methane from cattle, soy monocultures for feed, antibiotic overuse, carbon emissions, and, eventually, fungal decomposition in landfills.[3] Each object and action is nested within networks of cause, effect, and exchange.

During my Biodesign master's, we trained ourselves to think through these entanglements. We observed insect behaviour in slow motion, peered at cellular life through microscopes, and studied ancient fossils – each, stretching our perceptions of time and scale. Some bacteria, like *Clostridium* and *E. coli,* complete their life cycle in minutes, while rocks persist for eons. "Creating in the biological age", Oxman reminds us, "requires us to tune into these organisms" – to understand life from nonhuman perspectives.[4]

What would it mean to experience the world as a spore, an octopus, a bird? What can we learn about communication and exchange through the lens of fungi? These are not frivolous or purely imaginative exercises. They are part of a growing body of inquiry that is reshaping the frontiers of science. By exploring how sound influences form, how vibration affects health, and how chemical cues guide life underwater, researchers are challenging long-held assumptions about the forces that shape our worlds.

Just as every era is influenced by its dominant materials – the Stone Age, the Bronze Age – networks, both technological and biological, shape ours.[5]

One of the most striking models of networked interdependence is the Wood Wide Web – the underground fungal networks that share resources and signals between plants. They remind us that life forms are not isolated; they are constantly responding to one another. In this network, Mother Trees are imagined like *Avatar*'s Eywa: memory keepers and message relayers, forming a living internet.

Technology has always been connective: from fire and the wheel to electricity and artificial intelligence. Today, the internet, cargo ships, planes, satellites, and undersea cables form an invisible network of connections linking continents. These hyper-connected infrastructures shape how we communicate, collaborate, and navigate the planet. They offer new tools to explore previously inaccessible environments, such as space, the deep oceans, and soil, as well as new ways of understanding life.

Alongside these human-made technologies, biotechnologies are also reshaping our world. Synthetic biology and genetic engineering are redefining what's possible. We are editing genes, growing materials, hybridising nature. The boundaries between human and nonhuman, natural and synthetic, are dissolving. We are co-evolving with our creations: cyborgs of carbon, code, and culture.

But this isn't entirely new. Myth and story have long served as connective tissue, threading individuals into communities and communities into ecologies. Take alcoholic fermentation – an ancient practice rooted in local grains, wild yeasts, and shared rituals. Before microbiology unravelled the science, fermentation was seen as divine: Methe personified drunkenness, Ceraon presided over wine mixing, and Amphictyonis represented wine-fuelled diplomacy. Local brews, both mythic and microbial, united communities and lubricated relationships between nations.

Dionysus, god of wine, embodies the ecological essence of myth. Crowned with ivy and surrounded by satyrs, maenads, and animals, he blurs the line between nature and culture, reminding us to rejoin the web of life from which we've become estranged.

To be ecological is to be entangled. It is to acknowledge that every sip of wine, every movement, breath, and byte is part of a dynamic, environmental network. It is to know that we are nature in the universe, experiencing itself.

This chapter steps into that webbed worldview. We journey from space stations to oceanic depths, from fungal networks beneath forests to yeast cultures in our kitchens. We move across planetary and microscopic scales, exploring how humans have always been entangled through myth, ritual, technology, and ecology. We encounter extremophilic fungi on asteroids and in volcanic vents, listen to soil with bioacoustic tools, and consider how fermentation bridges the ancient and the engineered. Networked life challenges anthropocentric assumptions, reminding us that everything in life is ecological.

There is something like a mycorrhizal network that connects us, and our actions ripple across ecosystems.

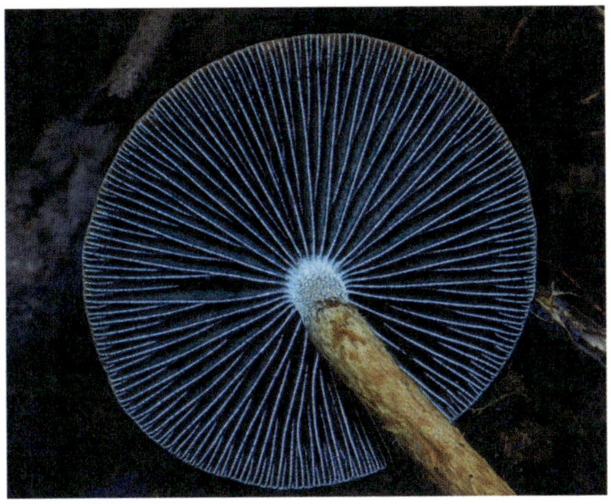

The underside of a biofluorescent Leratiomyces squamosus var. thraustus. *Gill edges and upper stem fluorescence under 365-nanometer UV light.*

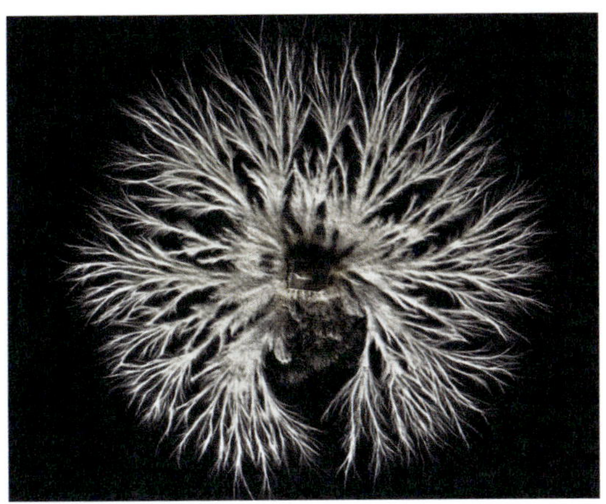

Psilocybe ovoideocystidiata *mycelium. With a time-lapse, you can capture the growth of the mycelium as it moves radically from the centre.*

TIME-LAPSE PHOTOGRAPHY

Time-lapse photography will be a valuable tool for many of the experiments in this chapter. It allows us to shift our perception, bending time and space to reveal things usually invisible to the naked eye. By compressing hours, days, or even weeks into seconds, we gain access to an entirely different pace of life.

When you watch a time-lapse of mycelium growth, slugs, bugs, and spiders flash in and out of the frame. It makes you realise how irrelevantly quick animal life is for a fungus! Patience is a key. Filmmaker and director Louie Schwartzberg, who has had a time-lapse camera running nonstop for over 40 years, reminds us that this, compressed into human timeframes, equates to approximately 16 fungal days. Let that reframe your sense of time.

For Louie, time-lapses are a gateway to wonder, curiosity, and the sacred. They let us step out of time according to what we know and witness the vitality of life beyond our usual perspective. Suddenly, fungi seem to move like animals. They become relatable, which helps build empathy between our species.

Louie also emphasised that expensive lenses and equipment aren't necessary. Any camera - an old phone, a starter DSLR, a macro lens - can work. These tools simply help us observe life on fungal time and reconnect with scales and rhythms beyond our own.

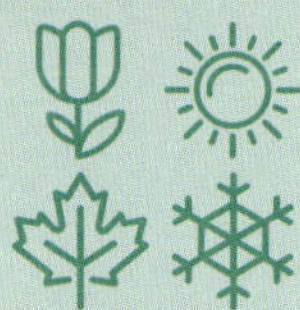

ACTIVITY

CREATING A TIME-LAPSE

METHOD

1. Choose a room without windows to avoid changing light conditions.
2. Use a plain backdrop to keep the focus on your subject.
3. Place your organism (e.g. mushroom or substrate) on a stable surface or stand.
4. Set up a constant light source (make sure it doesn't overheat).
5. Mount your camera securely on a tripod or solid base.
6. Charge your camera fully or use continuous power if available.
7. If possible, switch your camera to manual mode to lock in settings like aperture, shutter speed, and focus – this keeps your image sequence consistent.
8. Take a photo, then turn the camera off to conserve power.
9. Return at regular intervals to take more images. Repeat until you have enough photos.

NOTES

- If your camera has a built-in time-lapse mode, use it! Play with intervals based on how fast your subject changes. Reishi mushrooms might need just 2–3 photos per day, while fast-growing mycelium may benefit from one every hour. Be aware that frequent shooting can quickly drain battery life. You can use extended batteries or power adapters to prolong the camera's runtime.
- Of course, you can still have fun with slightly less metronomic accuracy, even if your camera doesn't have a time-lapse feature. Simply take a photo and return at regular and appropriate intervals for your subject matter to take more images. Repeat until you have enough photos.

AUTOMATING THE PROCESS WITH ARDUINO

- If you want to step up your setup, consider using an Arduino-powered system. With basic coding and some relays, you can automate the whole process: power the camera on and off, trigger the shutter at regular intervals, control a humidifier to maintain the right environment, and switch a light on and off.
- This is ideal for fungal time-lapses, where you want to control humidity, lighting, and shutter timing precisely. In one of my early experiments, I created a time-lapse of my Mycelium Boot in my bathroom using this setup. With help from Bristol-based videographer Richard Mann, who shared both code and equipment, I was able to bring the project to life.
- Although it requires some specialised gear, much of it can be borrowed or constructed from inexpensive components. And with AI or online communities, getting help with writing Arduino code is easier than ever.

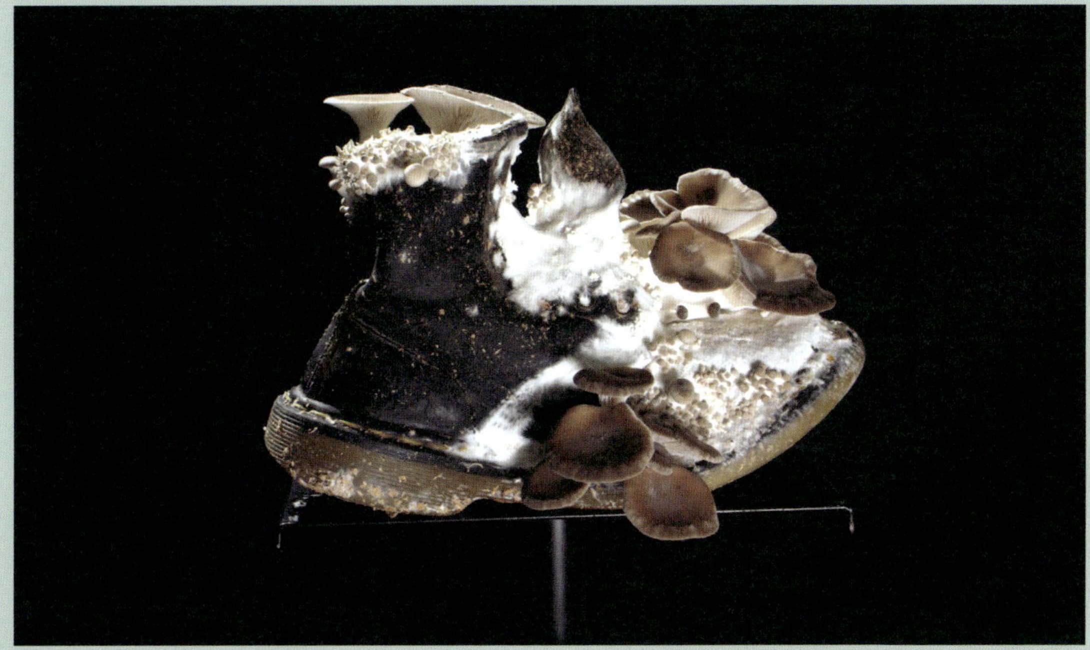

Mycelium Boot: DIY Fungal Kicks.

EDITING YOUR TIME-LAPSE VIDEO

Once you've captured your images, it's time to compile them into a video.

USE GIPHY (FOR QUICK GIFS)

1. Upload your images to GIPHY.com
2. Follow the prompts to create an animated GIF
3. Download and share!

USE ADOBE PREMIERE PRO (FOR HIGH-QUALITY VIDEO)

1. Open Premiere Pro and select New Project. Name it and choose a save location.
2. Go to File > Import, then select the first image in your time-lapse folder.
3. Check Show Options > Image Sequence, then click Import.
4. Drag the imported sequence into the Timeline.
5. Right-click the clip to adjust playback speed under Speed/Duration.
6. Use options like Reverse Speed or Time Interpolation to get the desired effect.
7. To export: Go to File > Export > Send to Adobe Media Encoder. In Media Encoder, press the green play button to render.
8. Find your final video at the chosen save location and watch!

SPACE

Christmas Eve, 1968. Apollo 8 made history. As the first crewed spacecraft to orbit the Moon, it sent back a now-iconic image: "Earthrise". The photo captured Earth, delicate and blue, floating in the blackness of space. Astronaut Jim Lovell summed up the moment: "The vast loneliness is awe-inspiring, and it makes you realise just what you have back there on Earth." It sparked global reflection on our planet's beauty and fragility, becoming a symbol of hope for both environmental and anti-war movements.

But the allure of space persisted, gradually drawing our focus towards Mars. Companies like SpaceX and Blue Origin began building towards interplanetary futures, envisioning life among the stars. Yet, as we dream of colonising other planets, we carry with us more than ambition – we carry microbes, too.

From the earliest missions, scientists took great care to prevent Earth microbes from contaminating space.[6] Equipment is sterilised and astronauts undergo rigorous hygiene routines. Yet, fungi always find a way. Moulds like *Aspergillus* and *Penicillium* have colonised spacecrafts and space stations, breaking down waste, damaging equipment, and adapting to microgravity.[7]

This led to the emergence of Astromycology, the study of fungi in space. Scientists have grown fungi outside the International Space Station (ISS), exposed lichen to extreme radiation, and launched spores into orbit. Many survived unharmed, some even thrived. Fungi's resilience makes them promising allies for life beyond Earth: they are our ultimate cosmic companions.

Elon Musk's drive with SpaceX is adding currency, but transforming Mars into a liveable habitat for humans has long fascinated artists and scientists. In 1961, American astronomer and planetary scientist Carl Sagan proposed engineering Venus by seeding its upper atmosphere with photosynthetic microorganisms. These algae and bacteria would convert carbon dioxide into oxygen, thus gradually transforming the dense, toxic, and scorching Venusian atmosphere. This idea became known as "terraforming", engineering an environment to make it more Earth-like and hospitable. Nearly 60 years later, London's Design Museum hosted "Moving to Mars",[8] an exhibition that explored the practicalities and ethics of colonising the Red Planet.

The designs were incredible; simple yet ingenious. Engineers, artists, biologists, and more, came together in an interdisciplinary collaboration to showcase speculative and practical designs, from closed-loop life systems to fungal-based architecture.

But the ethical implications of terraforming Mars remain a heated debate. Should we introduce Earth life to alien environments? The excitement of expansion to a new world meets unease. However, the history of humanity suggests that if it is possible to do, it will be done. We once planted a flag on the Moon. Today, we ask which organisms will join us in space. The answer, without a doubt, includes fungi.

Fungi offer practical and existential solutions to challenges in space, from nutrition and construction to clothing, medicines, and consciousness-expanding drugs. Mycodesigners, bioengineers, and agriculturalists are leveraging fungi's exhaustive capabilities to support space exploration and help make life on Mars a reality. But as always, it's essential to select the right fungus for your needs. Let's explore that now.

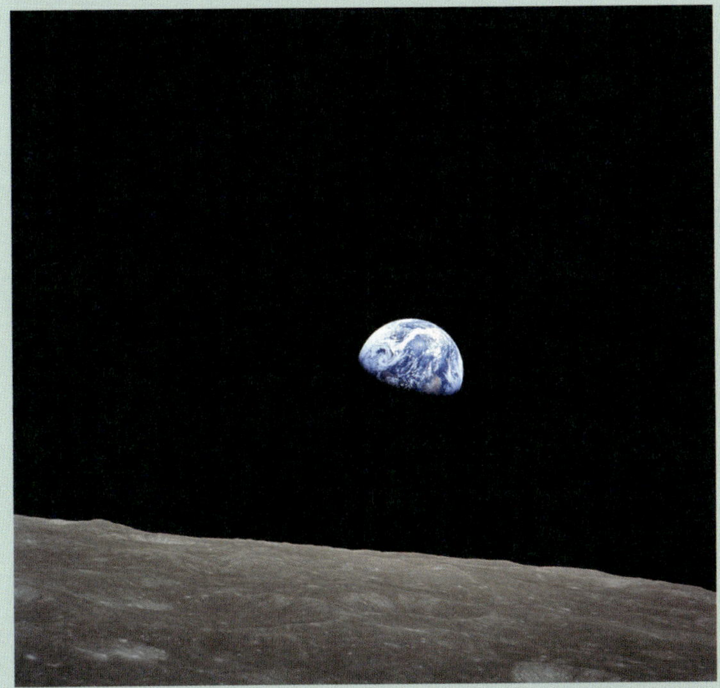

Earthrise, *1968. Apollo 8. Photographed during the first crewed mission to orbit the Moon, capturing Earth rising over the lunar horizon.*

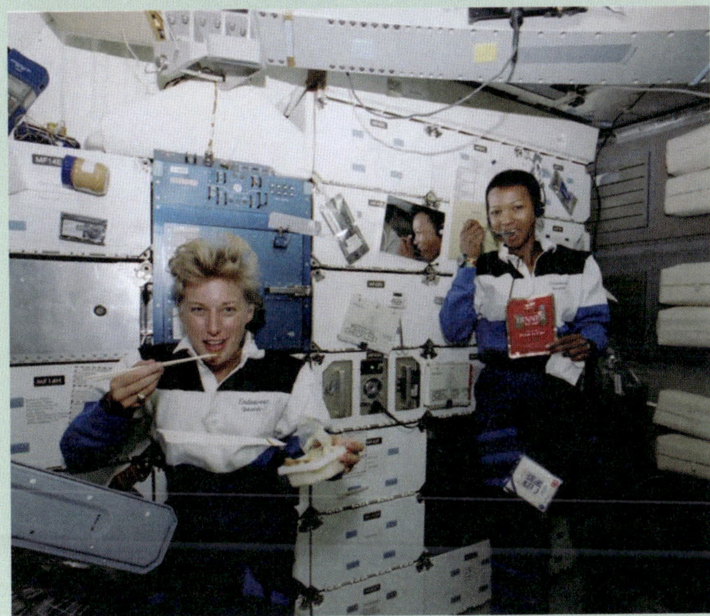

NASA Astronauts N. Jan Davis and Mae Jemison share a meal aboard Spacelab during a 1992 space shuttle mission. To ensure safety and prevent contamination, all food and equipment are sterilised before launch.

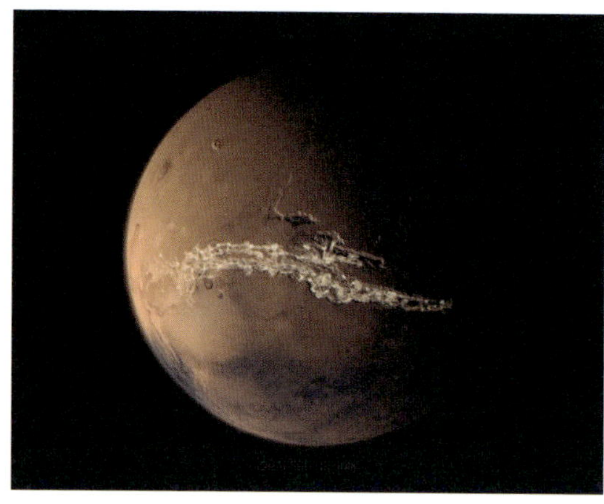

Mars City Scar, *Mars City Design. Future Martian cities may be built using locally mined regolith and metals. NASA has also proposed growing habitats in situ using 3D-printed, mycelium-based composites.*

FOOD

In space, where resources are scarce, closed-loop systems are crucial for survival. NASA's "Closed Life-Support Systems" integrate algae, bacteria, and fungi to recycle waste. The "Algatron" purifies urine using algae, while moulds and yeasts convert faeces into food or building materials.[9] Particularly adept in this field are *Pleurotus* species, like Oyster mushrooms, which can turn waste into high-protein, vitamin-D-rich food. They also contain lovastatin, which could help protect astronauts' bones from the effects of zero gravity.

Moreover, without soil, astronauts rely on hydroponic systems to grow nutrient-dense micro-greens. These systems benefit from mycorrhizal microfungi, such as *Rhizophagus irregularis*, which help roots absorb minerals and release gases that promote growth.[10] Some rock-inhabiting fungi (RIF), like *Aspergillus* and *Cladophialophora*, could also break down carbon-rich asteroids into fertile soil, potentially supporting Martian agriculture.[11]

CONSTRUCTION

Housing, too, is being reimagined. Transporting materials to Mars is prohibitively expensive, with a projected cost of about $10,000 per kilogram.[12] Instead, NASA proposes growing habitats in situ from 3D-printed mycelium-based composites. *Ganoderma* species, like Reishi, grow dense, fibrous mycelium with strong binding properties. These fungi can form affordable, lightweight composites, stronger than concrete and naturally resistant to fire and water. All you need are weightless spores, cultivated into mycelium and inoculated into regolith – the dust that coats other planetary surfaces.

Moreover, as some melanated species like Black Reishi and Black Pearl Oysters can absorb cosmic radiation without damaging their DNA, these species could be used to provide thermal and radiation protective structures grown in space.[13] Some researchers even propose incorporating engineered cyanobacteria into these structures to heal cracks as they expand when exposed to air, creating living, self-repairing Martian homes.

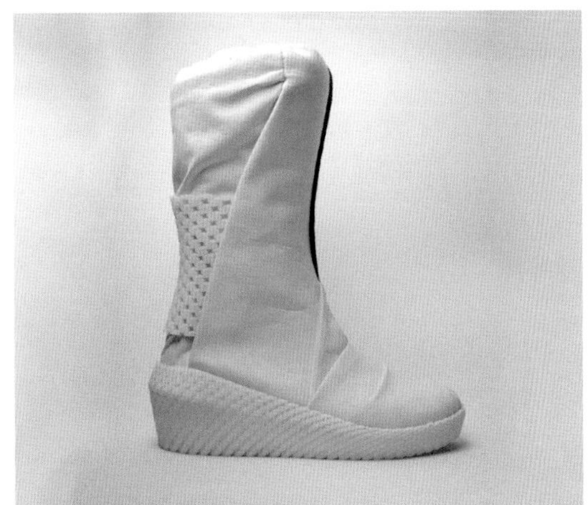

MARSBOOT prototype, a speculative reimagining of the classic Moon Boot, made from mycelium. Designed by Liz Ciokajlo in collaboration with mushroom-leather innovator Maurizio Montalti.

CLOTHING

In 2018, designer Liz Ciokajlo and mushroom-leather innovator Maurizio Montalti introduced the MARSBOOT, a reimagining of the Moon Boot, made from mycelium and human sweat. Grown from mycelium cultured in a nutrient broth of cotton and hemp, it is lightweight, durable, and resilient. In the future, astronauts might wear mycelium gear that shields them from harmful radiation. Given that planes are also exposed to elevated levels of gamma radiation, fungal-based flight wear may one day move into commercial aviation. The idea may sound speculative, but don't be surprised if it takes off.

MEDICINE

Beyond food and material design, fungi are also reshaping medicine and drug development in space. In 2016, NASA's Jet Propulsion Lab collaborated with USC to send *Aspergillus nidulans* to the ISS. Amazingly, the microgravity and radiation triggered changes in its genome and metabolism, resulting in the production of novel compounds never seen on Earth. This opens possibilities for discovering and producing new antibiotics in space, a critical need as resistance grows on Earth.[14]

PSYCHEDELICS

One of the most unexpected potential allies in space are psychedelics. Mycologist Paul Stamets advocates for psilocybin as a tool for astronaut wellbeing.[15] Long missions can lead to isolation, depression, and spiritual crises. Psilocybin enhances a sense of connection – to others, to nature, and to the universe. For astronauts facing the psychological void of deep space, this sense of unity could be essential.

The vision is radical: astronauts in fungal suits, living in mycelium homes, eating mushrooms, and exploring their consciousness via psychedelic fungi – a true myconaut era.

But fungi may have already beaten us in the space race. As natural terraformers, they possess remarkable resilience. The theory of *Panspermia* – the idea that life can travel between planets via meteoroids, comets, or space dust – includes hardy microorganisms like fungal spores. These spores

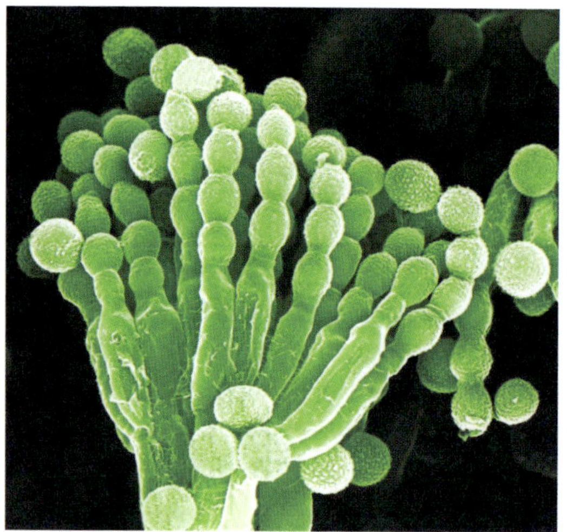

Penicillium *mould spores germinating in space. Microgravity and radiation can alter a fungus's genome and metabolism, leading to the production of novel compounds not found on Earth.*

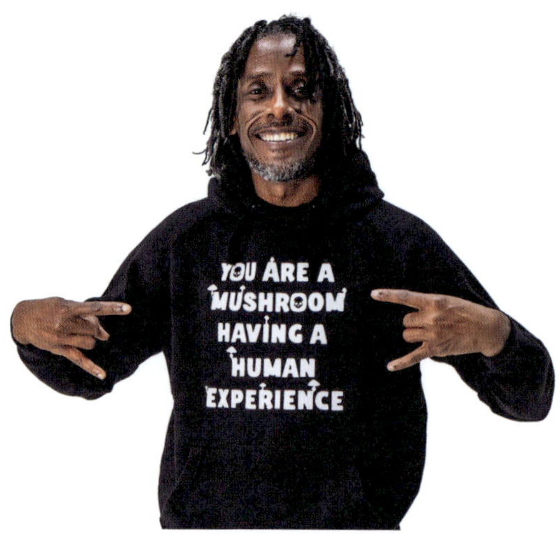

Darren Le Baron: "You are a mushroom having a human experience." A creative twist on the Panspermia hypothesis, which suggests that microscopic extraterrestrial fungi may have seeded life on Earth.

can survive extreme conditions: vacuum, radiation, extreme heat, and freezing temperatures, making them viable candidates for interplanetary transfer.[16] Mycorrhizal fungi played a critical role in Earth's early ecosystems, forming symbiotic relationships with the first land plants over 400 million years ago, enabling the colonisation of terrestrial environments.[17] If life can travel through space, fungi are strong contenders, both as carriers of life and facilitators of its flourishing on alien worlds.

This raises intriguing questions: Could Earth, and perhaps other planets, have been colonised by microscopic extraterrestrial fungi? And if so, what counts as "invasive" in the grand scheme of the cosmos?

Though invasiveness might seem insignificant on a galactic scale, its impact deeply resonates here on Earth. The rise of DIY mushroom grow kits has raised concerns about native biodiversity.[18] While it's great that people are exploring fungi cultivation at home, introducing non-native species can disrupt local ecosystems. For example, the common Grey Oyster Mushroom, *Pleurotus ostreatus*, is native to the UK, but many companies sell exotic or hybrid varieties, like the Yellow Oyster Mushroom, *Pleurotus citrinopileatus*, in grow-your-own kits. These non-native, commercially bred strains can readily outcompete local fungi, especially if composted, or even just grown on your windowsill.

A single troop of Oyster mushrooms can release 200-600 million spores per day,[19] and perennial mushrooms like Ganoderma species can produce up to 5 trillion spores annually.[20] Most spores germinate rapidly, and once a non-native fungus takes hold, it's nearly impossible to eradicate. Spores and mycelial networks spread invisibly and persist indefinitely – causing uncontrollable ecological disruption.

On the other hand, native fungi support ecosystems. They decompose organic matter, recycle nutrients, and nurture plant life. Native flora and fauna have co-evolved with local "funga," and are

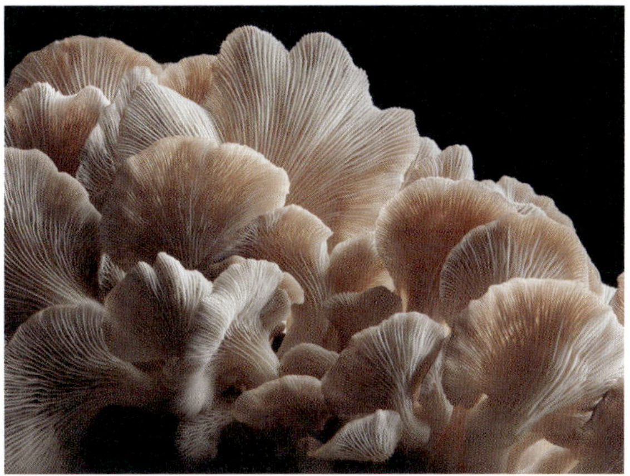

Oyster Mushrooms, Pleurotus *spp. can release between 200-600 million spores per day. Considering the vast number of spores produced by a single mushroom and the incredible global fungal biodiversity, we see that fungal DNA permeates our biome, confusing our understandings of native and invasive species.*

therefore better equipped to cooperate with or defend themselves against these organisms. This helps to maintain balanced ecosystems and healthy food chains. As we explore fungi for food, materials, and medicines, it's essential to prioritise native species and cultivate them responsibly.

The question of native vs. invasive fungi highlights a deeper question: How do we balance our curiosity and exploration with ecological responsibility?

While we marvel at the idea of fungi hitchhiking on asteroids or sunbathing on a wing of the ISS, we're quick to criticise the careless introduction of non-native species to places like the Moon or Mars. This double standard reflects the tension between scientific progress and environmental protection. I experienced this firsthand when strict New Zealand biosecurity laws resulted in the destruction of my archive of spore prints and dried plants. They were burned to protect native ecosystems – a stark reminder of how seriously some countries take biosecurity.

But *again*, this issue largely depends on your perspective. When you consider the sheer volume of spores produced by a single mushroom, and then place that in the context of global fungal biodiversity, you begin to see how deeply fungal DNA permeates our biome. Mushrooms are like invisible and uncontrollable rainstorms, constantly showering spores into the world, soaking everyone and everywhere in search of an ecological niche. When we pass through borders, we carry these spores on our shoes, bags, and bodies. We are, in essence, accomplices in sporulation and contamination. Then on a planetary scale, Earth itself is sporulating, "seeding the galaxy with its germplasm". Panspermia suggests life may have come from outer space. "Equally likely," Stamets notes, "Earth is inoculating the heavens."[21]

Yet, my focus remains localised – here on Earth. As we prepare for the possibility of life on Mars, we must not forget our duty to care for the Earth. Our survival is deeply tied to this planet, and it's unlikely we'll ever thrive elsewhere as we do here. The closed-loop systems we design for space may guide us towards sustainability here. MycoHAB in Namibia grows mushrooms on invasive bush species, and repurposes the spent mycelium blocks into carbon-negative "mycobricks" for housing. Likewise, companies like Ecovative use mycelium to create eco-friendly packaging, leather alternatives, and food at their New York State mushroom farm, "Spaceship Earth."

ACTIVITY

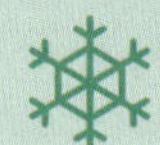

GROWING A MARTIAN GARDEN (ARTIFICIAL ENVIRONMENTS)

It's hard to fathom just how extreme life would be on Mars. Temperatures average -63°C (-81°F) and can swing by 133°C (271°F) between day and night. Towering dust storms, or "dust devils", driven by fierce winds can engulf the planet for months. With an atmosphere that's 95 per cent carbon dioxide and too thin to support liquid water, intense radiation from cosmic rays and solar flares bombard its surface. While fungi might fare better than humans, they still face steep challenges – particularly the lack of water.

Simulating Martian conditions is tricky, but possible. To start a simple experiment, follow this protocol.

PART 1: PREPARING MALT YEAST AGAR (MYA)

Malt yeast extract is a common growth medium for cultivating microorganisms. The malt and yeast provide readily available nutrients while the agar serves as a gelling agent to solidify the medium.

EQUIPMENT

- Lab gloves
- Digital scale (accurate to 0.1g)
- Microwave/autoclave-safe container (e.g. Pyrex beaker, Mason jar, or heatproof flask (500ml–1l)
- Measuring cylinder or graduated container
- Pressure cooker, autoclave, or microwave
- Petri dishes (typically 90mm)
- Heat-resistant gloves
- Still air box (SAB), laminar flow hood, or a clean workspace
- Parafilm tape (masking tape will suffice if you're just experimenting)

INGREDIENTS (MAKES 500ML OF MEDIUM, 20-25IN PLATES)

- 10g malt extract
- 2.5g yeast extract
- 7.5g agar powder
- 500ml/17fl oz/2 cups of distilled water

METHOD

1. Weigh out the specified amounts of malt extract, yeast extract, and agar powder.
2. In a clean, heatproof beaker, combine the ingredients with approximately 450ml/15fl oz/1¾ cups of distilled water (add dry to wet). Mix thoroughly, then add more water to reach a total volume of 500ml/17fl oz/2 cups.
3. Loosely screw on the lid – do **not** seal it tightly (to prevent pressure buildup).
4. Sterilise in a pressure cooker or autoclave at 121°C/250°F for 15–20 minutes.
5. Alternatively, microwave in short bursts, swirling between each wearing heat-resistant gloves.
6. Repeat until the mixture comes to a rolling boil and appears clear (no powder or cloudiness).

Careful not to let it overflow.

7. Cool the sterilised MYA solution to about 45–50°C/113–122°F before pouring the agar into Petri dishes.
8. In a sterile environment wearing gloves, pour the warm solution into sterile Petri dishes, filling them one-third to one-half full. Place the lids on top, slightly ajar to prevent condensation.
9. Let the agar solidify at room temperature (approximately 30–60 minutes). Place the lids on fully.
10. If not using immediately, label and store in the fridge, as Petri dishes can remain sterile for several weeks.

PART 2: CULTIVATING MYCELIUM IN AN ARTIFICIAL ENVIRONMENT

EQUIPMENT

- Fungus of choice (a cutting from a mushroom or liquid culture syringe)
- MYA plates
- Microporous tape
- Variable Artificial Environment:: Freezer, UV light, or lamp

METHOD

1. Choose a variable: temperature, light, moisture, CO^2, or UV.
2. Select a native Reishi, Oyster, Aspergillus, or a psychedelic mushroom (if legal in your country).
3. Inject a fifth of a liquid culture syringe onto each MYA plate. Alternatively, take a small cutting from the inside of a mushroom and place it on an agar plate. (This is a simple method for cloning mushrooms),
4. Seal with microporous tape and label.
5. Set one plate as a control, exposed to typical day/night cycles (fungi have endogenous circadian rhythms).
6. Place the other plates in extreme conditions: a freezer, under UV light, high CO (sealed with non-microporous tape), or adjusted Martian light cycles (24.6 hours).
7. Watch how the fungus adapts. You'll learn about their rhythms, preferences, and astonishing resilience. After all, they might just be going back home.

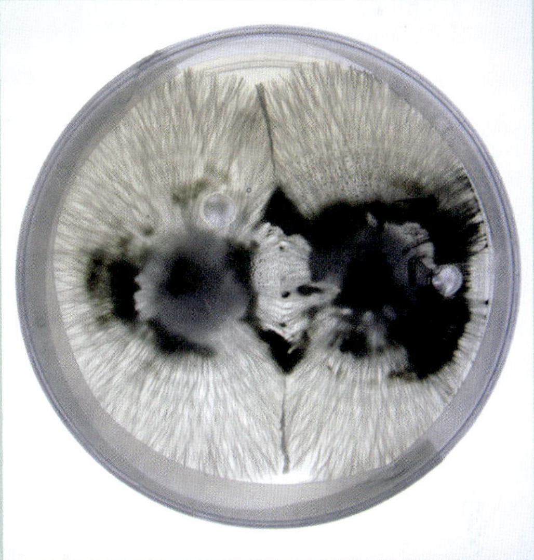

An unidentified species from Barbados spontaneously darkening in cold British weather. Species with darker spores and mycelium are generally better equipped to tolerate harsh conditions.

OCEANS

Marine fungi exist and we know almost nothing about them. And yet everywhere that researchers have taken the time to look, whether in hydrothermal vents, deep-sea sediments, Arctic ice, surface waters, salt marshes, sandy beaches, or even within animal bodies, they've consistently found them.[22]

In each of these niches and more, fungi perform essential ecological roles. Within whale guts, fungi help digest nutrients and bolster immune defences. In mangrove roots, mycorrhizal fungi enhance nutrient access and facilitate communication through expansive mycelium networks. On fishing gear and shipwrecks, saprotrophic fungi decompose carbon-rich materials, creating food sources and habitats for other marine life.

While most marine fungi are known to live on or within other organisms such as algae, corals, sponges, or even other fungi, many free-floating yeasts also drift independently through the water column. These tiny travellers play critical roles in global nutrient cycles and offer tantalising clues about the evolution of life and ecological resilience.[23]

Yet, the ocean is no easy place to live. Its conditions – high salinity, immense pressure, and low light – are extreme. But life itself began in this very crucible.

Water formed on Earth around 4.4 billion years ago.[24] The primordial oceans were rusty green and saturated with iron sediment. Around 600 million years later, around the scalding vents of the ocean floor and shielded from the Sun's radiation, life is thought to have sparked into being.[25] These marine "extremophiles" likely harnessed energy through chemosynthesis, drawing power from Earth's mineral-rich core. Approximately 3 billion years after that, the first single-celled fungi appeared in the oceans – the ancestor of all fungi (unless one subscribes to the Panspermia hypothesis).

From this one organism, marine fungi exploded, adapting to various oceanic niches and branching into freshwater and terrestrial ecosystems around 600 million years ago. Today, fungi are found in every water body, from sea to sky, highlighting the interconnectedness of Earth's water systems.

Perhaps unsurprisingly, the highest diversity of aquatic fungi can be found in biologically rich regions such as coral reefs and the Amazon River. American geneticist Craig Venter discovered this during the Sorcerer II Global Ocean Sampling Expedition in 2017, a journey that circumnavigated the globe to map the ocean's microbiome.[26] His team identified millions of new genes and almost a thousand new microbial genomes, painting a more complex picture of the ocean's microscopic world than we'd ever imagined.

Most marine fungi belong to the ascomycetes, the largest fungal phylum, which includes many yeasts and moulds, as well as land-dwelling species like truffles and morels. Chytrids are another group of marine fungi known for their unique ability to move using whip-like flagella. They are considered the most primitive of marine fungi.

A particularly rare and fascinating exception among underwater fungi is *Psathyrella aquatica,* the only known fully-submerged gilled mushroom (basidiomycete). Discovered in Oregon's Rogue River in

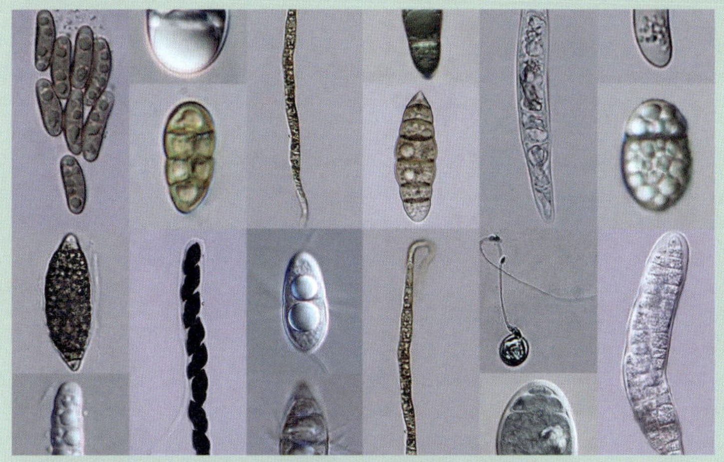

Microscopic marine fungi. Marine fungi are abundant, with around 2,000 species found to date.

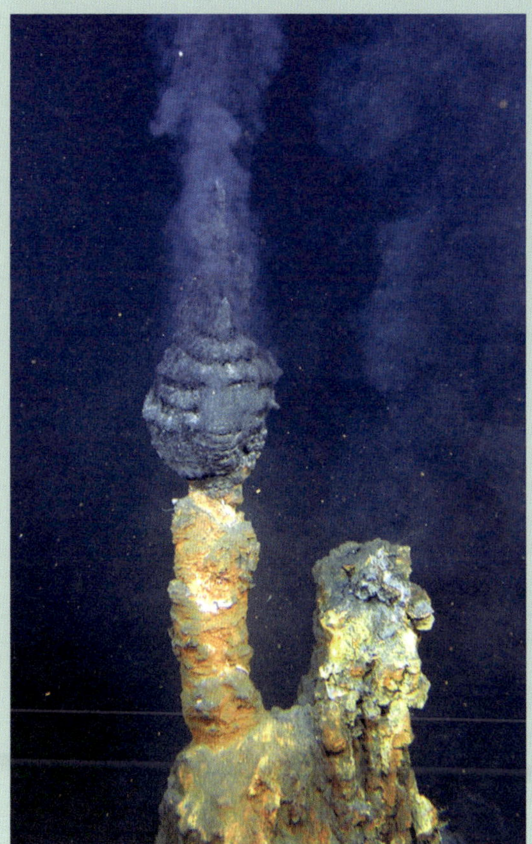

Hydrothermal vents. About 3.8 billion years ago, life is thought to have originated around these scalding ocean-floor vents, sheltered from the Sun's harsh radiation.

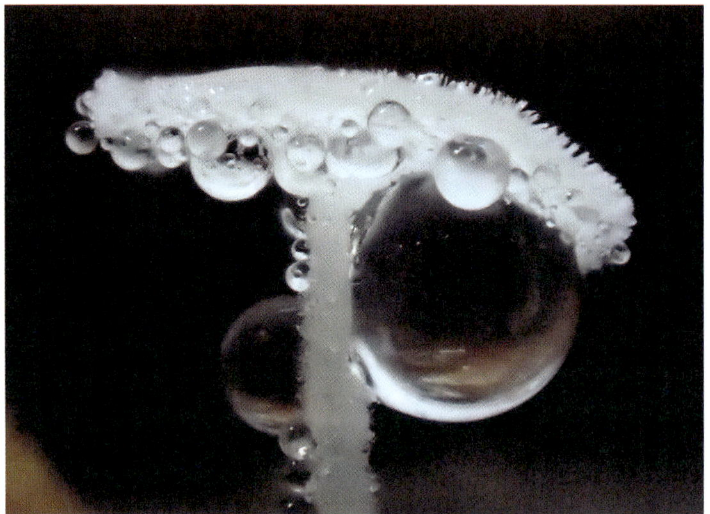

The Stalked Hairy Fairy Cup, Lachnum virgineum *– a water-loving fungus found along streams and rivers. It thrives on decaying organic matter in moisture-rich habitats, where water is key to its growth and spore dispersal.*

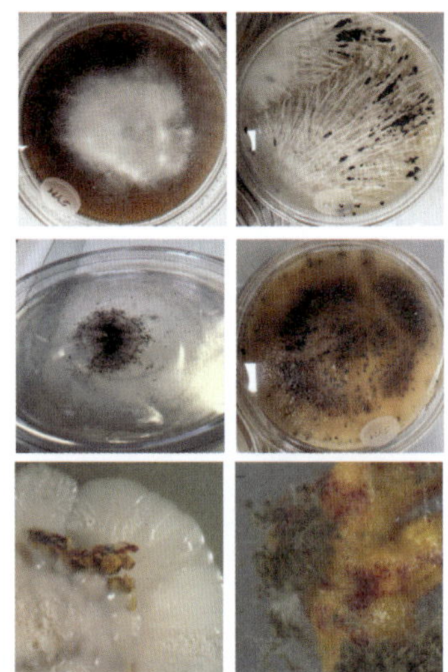

A series of marine fungi cultured on agar plates, including yeasts, moulds, and filamentous fungi.

2010, this species thrives in cold, fast-flowing freshwater, rooted to submerged wood or plant matter at the riverbed. Its spores are adapted to underwater conditions, possibly dispersed by water currents or aquatic invertebrates. Despite the overall abundance of aquatic fungi, scientists estimate that less than one per cent have been identified.

Most of what we know about marine fungi comes indirectly, from studying other organisms, like seagrasses, mangroves, and octopuses. I first encountered marine fungi in Galicia when researching these eight-armed creatures for my thesis. I was scheduled to visit Pescanova's new octopus aquaculture site, but due to pandemic restrictions, the meeting took place in an unlikely setting – a parking lot. My friend Paula and I drove to meet Pescanova researchers Ricardo and Pablo, hoping the rendezvous would be worthwhile (and safe).

The big black van was unsettling, but both men stood at its side beaming. And for good reason. Inside the van was a large tank, housing a mother octopus and her 100,000 eggs. She wasn't just any octopus; she was the first born, raised, and bred entirely in captivity – the world's first "closed-loop octopus". They named her Kat. Resting in a terracotta pot, she used her funnel to oxygenate her hanging eggs.

Ricardo and Pablo had also transformed the van's interior into a mobile lab, complete with two microscopes, cameras, and paralarvae swimming in jars. As Paula peered into the microscope, I climbed into the tank, goggles on, mesmerised by the iridescent bursts of chromatophores Kat fired in my direction, and thrilled when a single curious arm reached out to greet me.

It was a surreal, magical afternoon. My cheeks ached from smiling as I emerged from the tank, overwhelmed by their kindness and the presence of this magnificent creature.

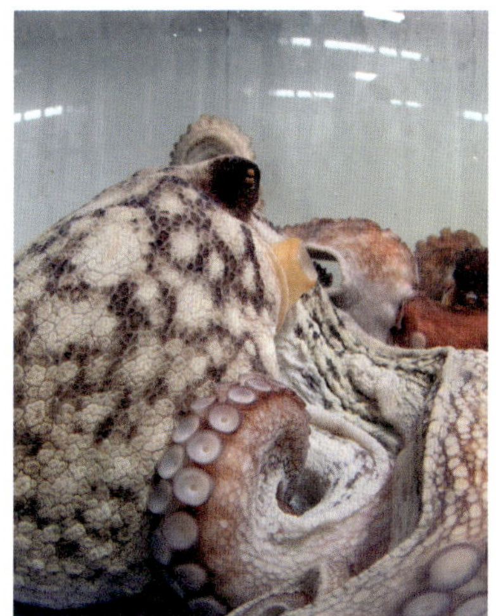

The first octopus to be born and bred in an aquaculture facility, having its skin swabbed for microbial testing.

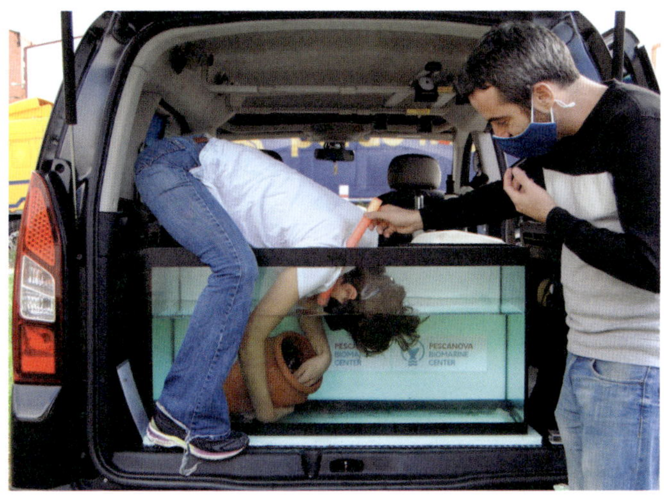

My first encounter with marine fungi: on the skin of an octopus. In octopus aquaculture, researchers are studying the effects of farming on the octopus microbiome to ensure their health and well-being.

Once dried off, I started asking questions: Why was Pescanova investing so heavily in breeding octopuses? Could these famously intelligent creatures adapt to life in captivity? What did Galicians, known for their love of octopus, think about eating farmed ones? Was aquaculture ever truly ethical? And why was it so hard to close the breeding loop?

Among the answers came a curious detail – Ricardo's team was studying the octopus microbiome. Through DNA extraction techniques, they were analysing the skin and gut microbiota of their octopuses, tracking changes throughout their lives.[27] Because the skin is an octopus's primary defence against pathogens, a robust microbiome is essential for survival. But moving from ocean to captivity alters their microbiomes, particularly for paralarvae,[28] so Pescanova is researching how to keep their octopuses and their microbes safe and healthy.

Research into octopus microbiomes has largely focused on bacteria, since most cephalopod studies use 16S rRNA gene sequencing – capturing bacteria, but not fungi, which require ITS sequencing. Still, it's worth asking: what roles do both bacteria and fungi play in octopus health? We know the development of the Hawaiian Bobtail squid is influenced by colonisation and signalling from a microbial symbiont.[29] Gut bacteria support digestion, immunity, and early survival, and skin microbes may help defend against pathogens like *Vibrio lentus*. Given their antimicrobial properties, skin-dwelling octopus fungi could be the source of novel antibiotics [30] – after all, Penicillin came from a fungus. The sea may hold similar breakthroughs. [31]

And yet, the paradox: farming animals in overcrowded, artificial environments often necessitates antibiotics, which contributes to global antibiotic resistance. Scientists remain aware of this contradiction – innovation and ethical tension often coexist.[32]

As researchers start to cotton onto the immense potential biotechnological applications of fungi, they're heading to the deep ocean. 200–1,000 metres below the surface, the twilight zone encompasses some of the least explored regions on Earth. Nearly pitch black and home to bioluminescent fish, vampire squid, and pressure-resistant microbes, it is alive with extremophilic fungi. Some can withstand temperatures as high as 122°C (250°F) and pressures 200 times greater than sea level. The Mariana Trench and oxygen minimum zones may also harbour life forms unlike any we've ever known, and like fungi in space, subject to extreme forces, these creatures could be the source of novel antibiotics, antivirals, antifungals, anti-aging creams, you name it. In the sediments of the South China Sea, mud-dwelling fungi have been found to produce compounds that inhibit a key enzyme of the human immunodeficiency virus (HIV).[33] Like fungi exposed to the harsh conditions of space, many of these extremophiles – fungal and otherwise – are emerging as promising sources for life-saving drugs.[34]

Marine fungi are also emerging as powerful allies in tackling ecological crises. Following the Deepwater Horizon oil spill, species like *Aspergillus, Penicillium*, and *Fusarium* surged in contaminated sediments, playing a key role in breaking down high-molecular-weight hydrocarbons and aiding natural bioremediation. Similarly, fungi floating in the Great Pacific Garbage Patch, including *Parengyodontium album*, have been shown to degrade polyethylene when it's first weakened by UV light.[35] In laboratory tests, *P. album* mineralised UV-pretreated PE at about 0.044 per cent per day, converting it primarily into CO_2. With over 400 billion kilograms of plastic entering our oceans annually, these findings suggest fungal bioremediation could be a critical tool in reducing pollution and restoring marine environments.

Many wonder how fungi survive underwater. They "breathe" by exchanging gases across their membranes through osmosis. Some are aerobic, others anaerobic, and yeasts can switch between the two. This flexibility has allowed certain fungi to move from water to land – and back again – over millions of years. It's not amphibious, but more akin to whales: once land-dwelling mammals, they returned to the sea. Unlike most life forms that stay put once they leave the ocean, fungi (and whales) are rare in their ability to adapt across such extremes.[36] Still, most fungi are highly specialised; freshwater, marine, and terrestrial species remain ecologically distinct, making the few that transition between realms especially remarkable.[37]

And yet fungi on land have an unexpected role in the water cycle.[38] As water evaporates, droplets form beneath mushroom gills. Their spores and the droplets are lofted skyward on gentle air currents, forming invisible vertical rivers. Spores are the largest biological particles that help form raindrops, collectively weighing as much as half a million blue whales each year.[39] As spores rise, they attract more water vapour, forming raindrops by the billions.[40] Clouds, especially cumulonimbus ones, serve as highways for fungal spores, spreading them across continents and ecosystems.

At least 16,000 fungal species release spores this way, helping to stimulate rainfall in rainforests and nurture moist environments necessary for fungal life. When spores land in soils, they germinate into hyphae – tiny filaments that act like sponges, storing and transporting water. When conditions are right, hyphae grow into tight bundles and inflate with a pulse of water, forming a mushroom[41] – sometimes in waterlogged soils, other times submerged in rivers.

From icy snowflakes to mangrove roots, from tears to tidal pools, fungi exist everywhere. As Pacific Island nations remind us, the ocean is in our blood, and we are stewards of its future. The resilience and versatility of marine fungi make them indispensable allies in preserving ocean health and sustaining life throughout the hydrologic cycle.

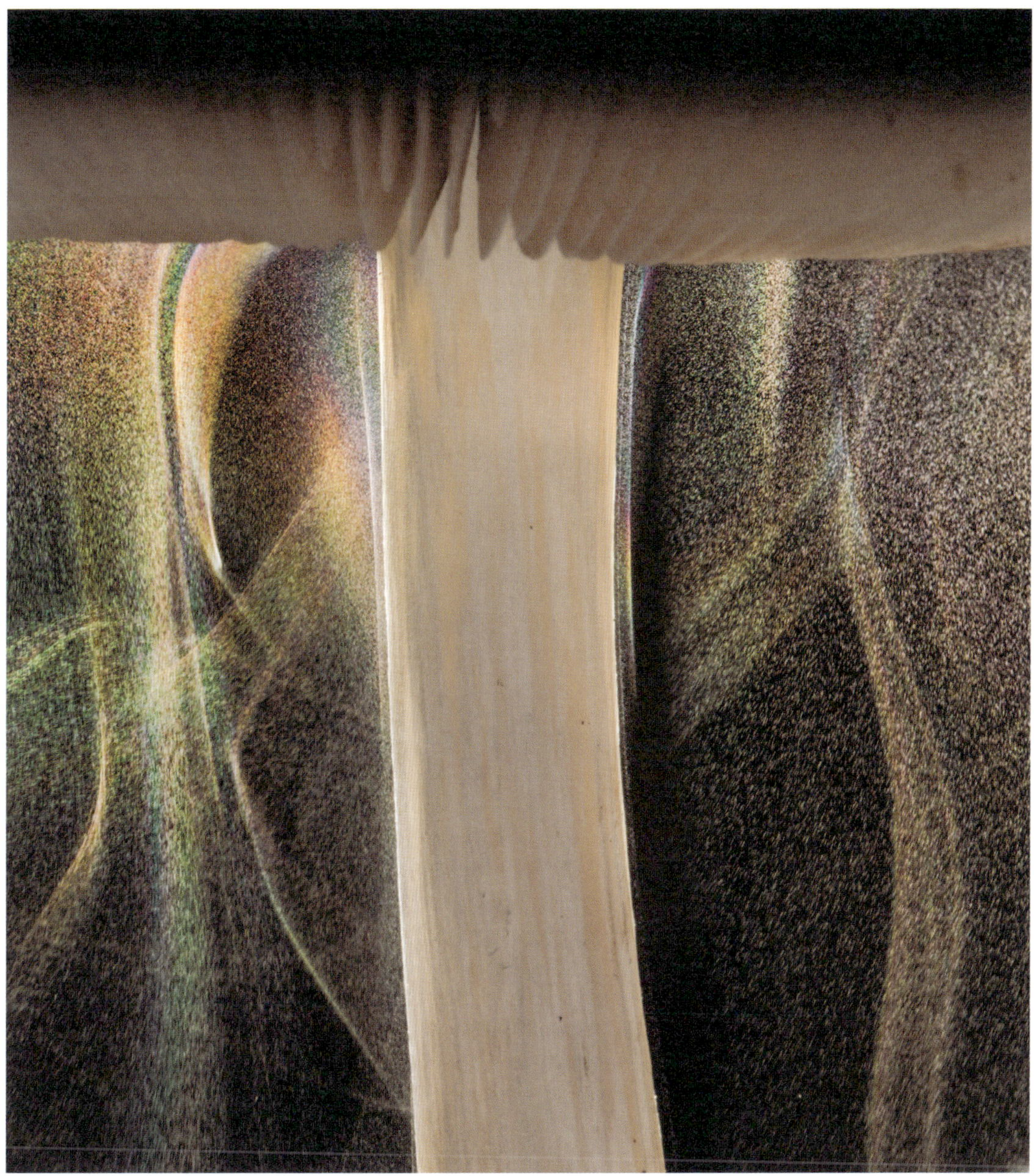

Spore rainbow. Fungal spores released from mushroom gills ride humid air currents, acting as microscopic seeds for water droplets. As they rise, they help form clouds and drive moisture through the atmosphere, shaping the water cycle.

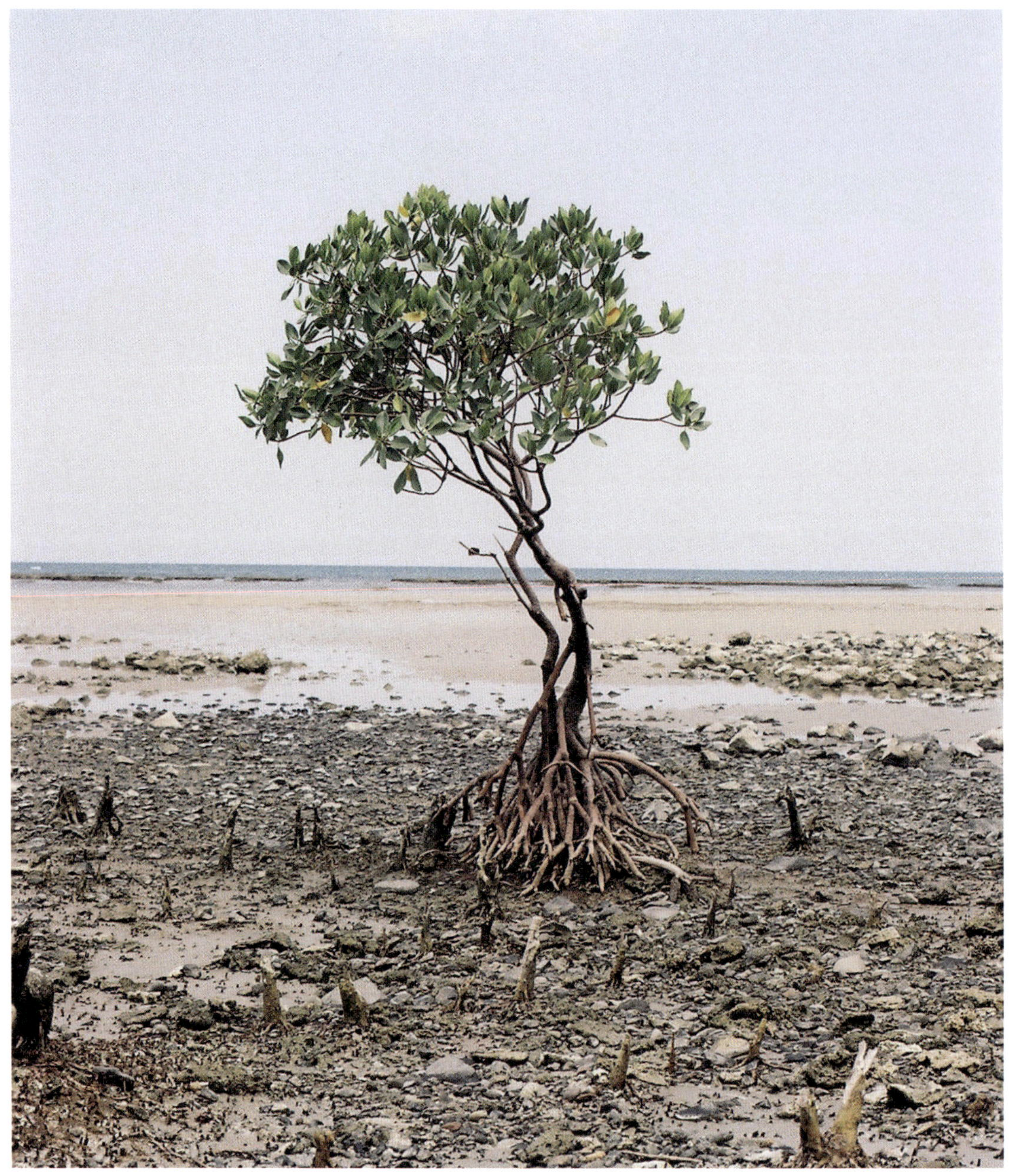

Mangroves in intertidal zones. Mangroves thrive in saltwater, supported by mycorrhizal fungi that help them adapt to the harsh intertidal environment.

ACTIVITY

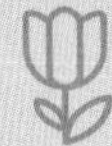

COLLECTING AQUATIC FUNGI THROUGHOUT THE WATER CYCLE

Our understanding of fungi in aquatic ecosystems and the water cycle is still emerging. Few people realise fungi *live* in water, let alone how to identify them.

Even scientific journals feature multiple papers asking the same question: *Who are the marine fungi?*

This hands-on citizen science project aims to change that by collecting, identifying, and sharing aquatic fungi observations on iNaturalist, a global biodiversity platform.

DRIFTWOOD SAMPLING

1. Choose a water body: sea, river, swamp, or estuary.
2. Collect a piece of driftwood. Place it in a Tupperware container with a paper towel soaked in the same water you found it in.
3. Seal the container for 2 weeks. Fungi will grow on the wood.
4. Examine with a microscope or magnifying glass. Photograph and identify using online databases.

MICROSCOPIC WATER SAMPLING

1. Collect rain, river, or puddle water (near moss is ideal).
2. Optional: Use methylene blue to dye your sample.
3. Observe under a microscope, you may even spot tardigrades (eight-legged water bears or moss piglets!)

CULTIVATING MARINE FUNGI

1. Filter your seawater sample (1l) and sterilise it in a pressure cooker (121 PSI for 1 hour).
2. Mix with agar-agar to make "ocean agar". (See Malt Yeast Agar Recipe on page 192 and substitute the distilled water with sterilised sea water.)
3. Place a tiny sample of your marine fungus onto the plate. Alternatively, swab a marine sponge, seaweed, snail, or shell with a cotton bud, and swipe it across the plate in an "s" shape.
4. Allow it to grow and see what happens!

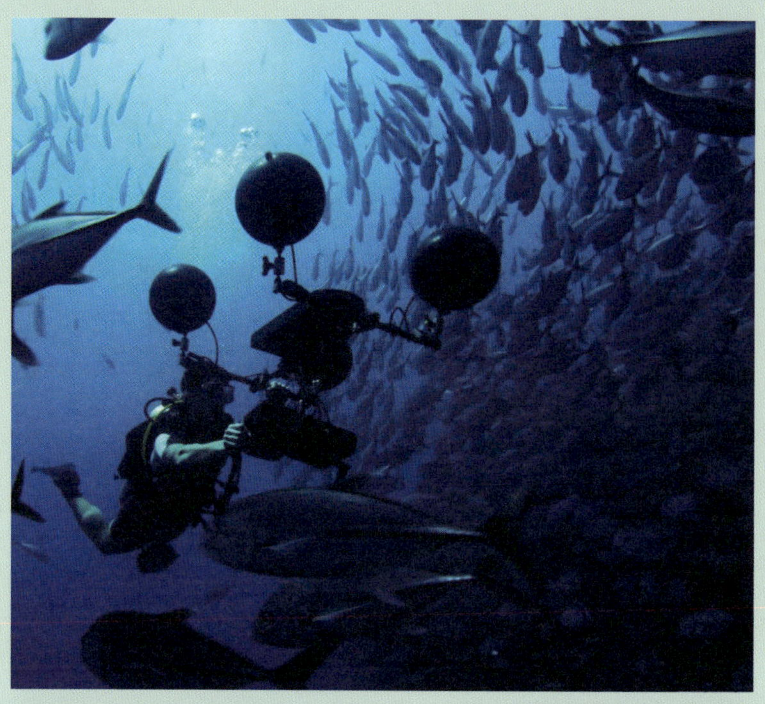

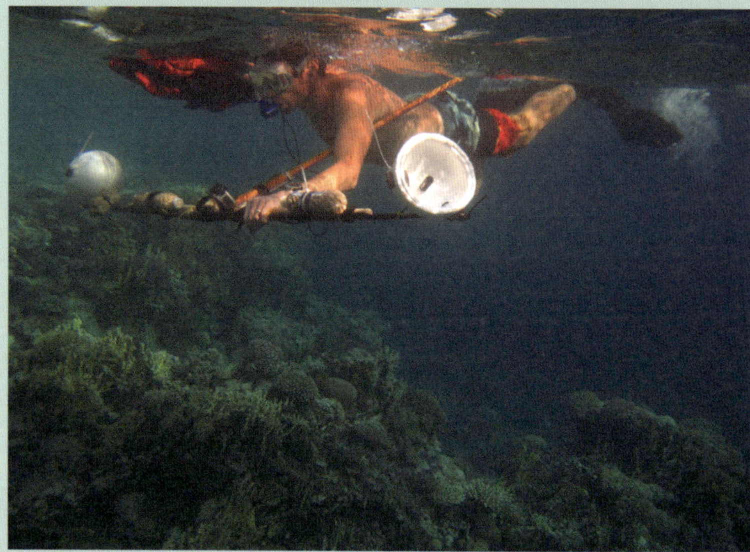

Marine biologist and fish ecologist Steve Simpson underwater with two different types of hydrophones. Hydrophones capture underwater sounds that are used to monitor and improve ecosystem health.

LAND & WATER: BIOACOUSTICS

As I float 20 metres from the shore, the lively hum of human activity surrounds me. But when I take a deep breath and dive beneath the surface, the noise above fades, and I'm immersed in the extraordinary symphony of the underwater world. Aquatic plants release tiny air bubbles, rocks groan under immense pressures, and marine creatures add their voices to the mix with pops, grunts, thuds, clicks, and moans. Although we cannot hear fungal presence in the oceans, they are all around us.

Sound travels faster and further underwater than in air, making it a vital sensory tool for marine life – and for scientists. Using bioacoustics, researchers are tuning into these underwater soundscapes to monitor and restore marine ecosystems.[42]

Marine biologists are deploying hydrophones (underwater microphones) across reefs, coastlines, and deep-sea habitats to record everything from animal vocalisations to the hum of passing boats. These recordings help track migration, feeding, and mating, and reveal how soundscapes shift over time. They offer a window into the health of marine ecosystems, what Steve Simpson, a marine biologist at the University of Exeter, calls "listening to the ocean's heartbeat".

Simpson is using these tools to help coral reefs recover. Healthy reefs are noisy, full of life, while degraded reefs fall silent.[43] By playing recordings of vibrant reefs in damaged areas, Simpson lures fish back to help restore them.[44] This "acoustic enrichment" creates a revitalising cycle: more fish mean more cleaning of algae, which gives coral a chance to regrow.[45] The results have been extraordinary, showing that sound can be a powerful tool for healing ecosystems.

Bioacoustics serves a dual purpose: It lets us listen to ecosystems in decline and use sound to restore biodiversity. Both approaches are reshaping conservation science, and our relationship with the natural world.

Soundscape ecologist Bernie Krause was one of the first to recognise nature's acoustic complexity. Over decades, he recorded more than 5,000 hours of wild soundscapes, capturing the voices of over 15,000 species.[46] His research revealed that these natural soundscapes, what he calls "biophanies", are not chaotic, but orchestrated. Each species claims its own acoustic niche, like instruments in a symphony.

In 2016, Krause debuted The Great Animal Orchestra, a groundbreaking auditory and visual installation that transformed his field recordings into an immersive journey through seven wild regions. It captured the unique dialects of humpback whales in the Pacific and the hustle of insects in the Amazon. But Krause also documented their decline, and let audiences sit in the silence of ecological loss.

His work isn't only for human ears. In 1985, Krause and Diana Reiss helped guide a lost humpback whale named Humphrey back to the ocean and to his family using songs from his kin. It was a landmark moment, showing bioacoustics' real-world potential in animal conservation.

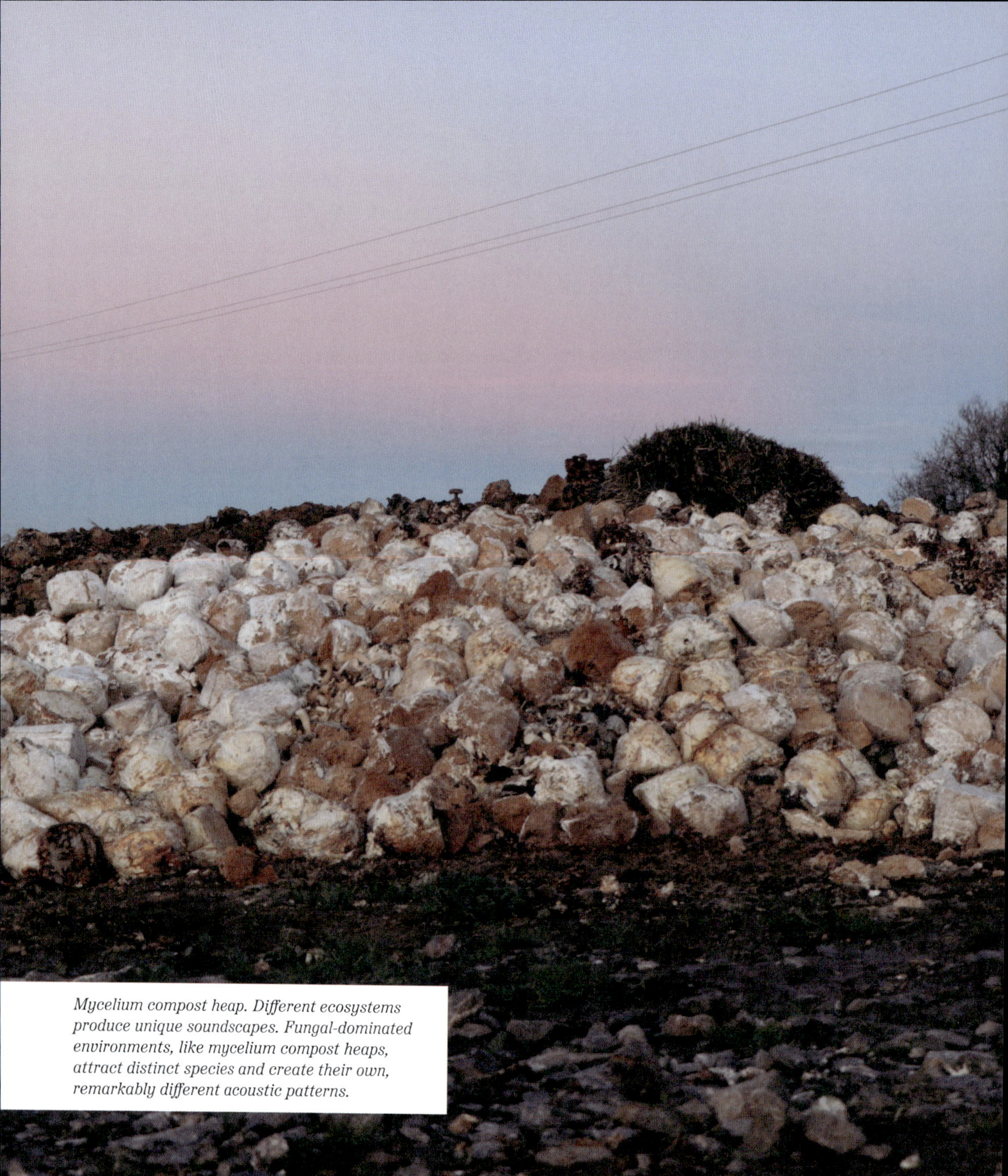

Mycelium compost heap. Different ecosystems produce unique soundscapes. Fungal-dominated environments, like mycelium compost heaps, attract distinct species and create their own, remarkably different acoustic patterns.

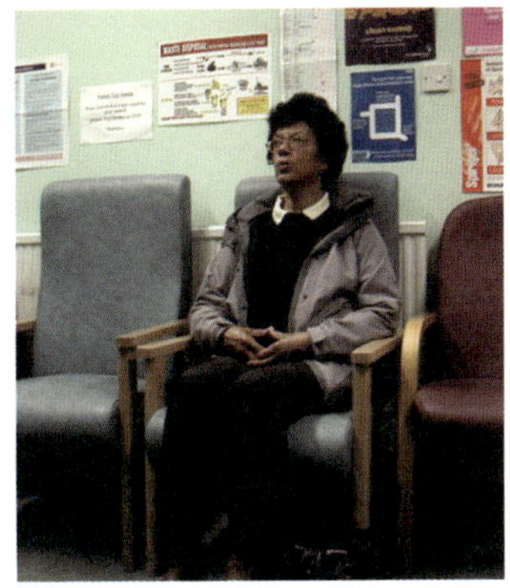
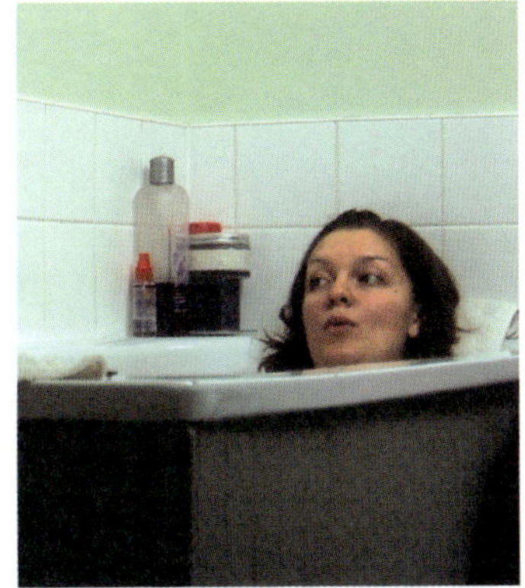
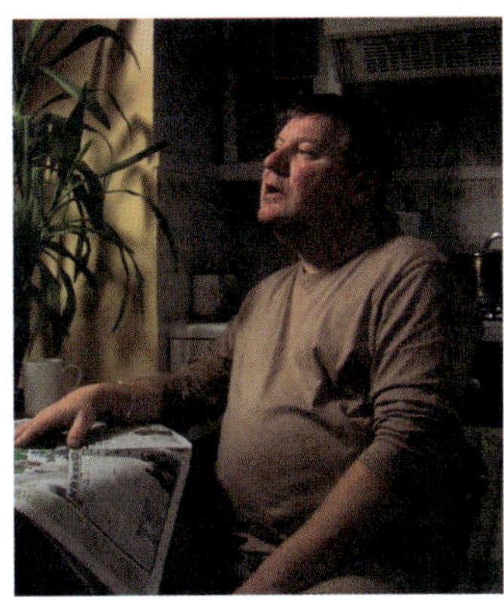

Dawn Chorus *(2007), Martin Coates. In his work, humans mimic slowed down bird calls. Recordings of these are then sped back up, transforming human voices into lifelike avian songs.*

Inspired by Krause, musician Cosmo Sheldrake carries this legacy into the realm of art and legislation. His piece *Song of the Cedars*, made from recordings in Ecuador's Los Cedros cloud forest, is part of a first of its kind legal effort – with writer Robert Macfarlane, mycologist Giuliana Furci, and legal scholar César Rodríguez – to recognise the forest as a co-author, aiming to grant moral authorship rights to an ecosystem.

Likewise, Sheldrake's 2020 album *Wake Up Calls* features endangered British birds, originally recorded as alarm clocks to turn morning routines into acts of environmental awareness.[47] His work slows down birdsong to make their rhythms more relatable to human ears, echoing sound artist Marcus Coates's *Dawn Chorus*, where humans mimic slowed bird calls that were then sped back up – transforming human voices into startling lifelike avian calls, complete with their jittery head movements.

These sonic experiments reveal the time-scaled disconnect between humans and other species. Birds sing in tempos that often feel alien, reminding us of poet Gary Snyder's insight: "As the crickets' soft autumn hum is to us, so are we to the trees, as are they to the rocks and the hills." We all move, breathe, and sing, just at different paces. By listening more closely or more slowly, we begin to bridge these divides, opening ourselves to the possibility that nonhuman voices carry meaning too.

Bioacoustics isn't limited to the ocean or the forest canopy, it also extends underground. In soil environments, where visual observation is nearly impossible, listening offers a non-invasive sensory window into ecosystem health. Soil is alive with life and sound. It is often overlooked despite being the foundation of every terrestrial ecosystem. Beneath a single footprint lies a familiar, yet essential web of organisms: earthworms, ants, beetles, fungi, roots, and microbial communities that quietly orchestrate the health of the biosphere. That is, quietly to us.

Recording these subterranean soundscapes is a growing frontier. Soil bioacoustics uses specialised microphones, particularly contact microphones placed directly into the ground, to detect the tiny, rustling movements of insects and other invertebrates. These recordings are revealing just how active

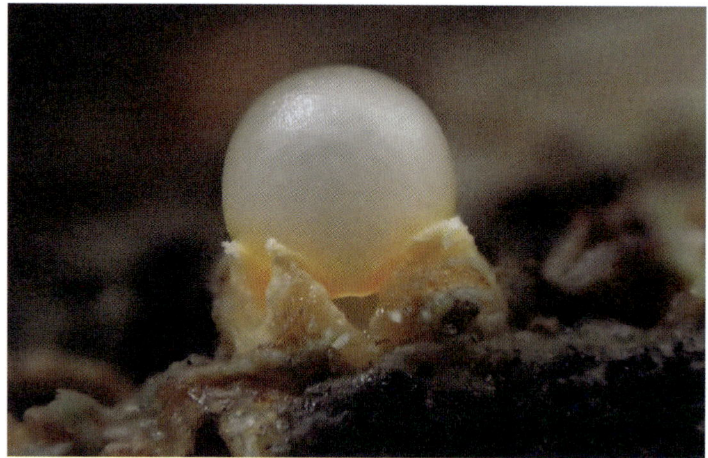

The Cannonball Fungus, Sphaerobolus stellatus, *famously pops when it launches its spore-filled peridioles. Similarly, Puffballs and Bird's Nest mushrooms release spores with audible pops and snaps, contributing to woodland soundscapes.*

and expressive some soils really are. By listening carefully, scientists can diagnose the health of soils, compare biodiversity between locations, and monitor restoration progress over time.[48]

One of the most pioneering initiatives in this area is the Swiss-based interdisciplinary project Sounding Soil. It invites farmers, ecologists, artists, and curious citizens to listen to the living ground beneath them. Their recordings capture the movements and communications of tiny creatures – springtails, oribatid beetles, centipedes – along with the subtle crackling of root growth and the dribble of water moving through porous layers. The project aims to reconnect people with the soil's ecological and cultural significance, offering tools and educational resources to help them listen and learn.[49]

Soil soundscapes vary widely depending on environment. For example, forest soils tend to be cooler, damper, and acoustically more muted than those in sunny meadows or vineyards. Even within a single farm, you might find dramatic differences between the soundscape of a compost pile and that of a conventionally tilled field. The latter often exhibits reduced biological diversity, and their soundscapes may be noticeably quieter or uniform. These variations reflect the complex interplay of soil structure, moisture content, organic matter, and, crucially, biological activity.

In designated conservation areas such as Sites of Special Scientific Interest (SSSIs), the soundscape of soil can be especially rich, serving as an audible indicator of biodiversity. A diverse soil community ensures functional redundancy, meaning multiple organisms perform similar roles, which is crucial for resilience in times of stress or species loss. Listening to soil in such areas can reveal subtle but telling signs of ecological health, as the presence and behaviour of flora, fauna, and funga underground generate distinctive acoustic signatures.

Advanced machine learning is now being used to classify and interpret these complex audio files, marking a significant shift in ecological monitoring.[50] Soil soundscapes, once difficult to analyse due to their low frequencies and overlapping biological and abiotic sounds, are now being decoded by sophisticated algorithms trained to recognise species-specific auditory markers. Variations in frequency,

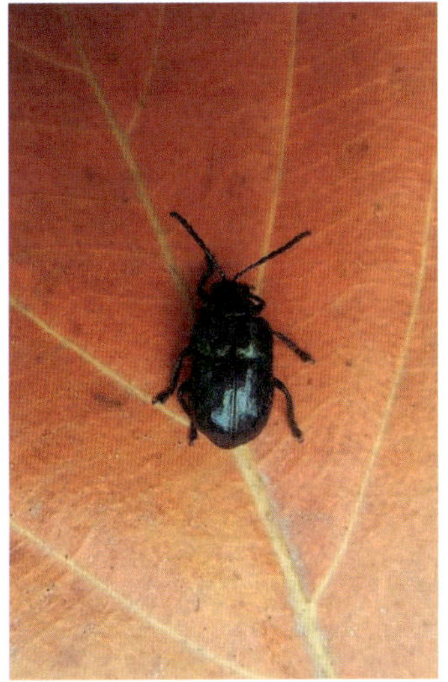
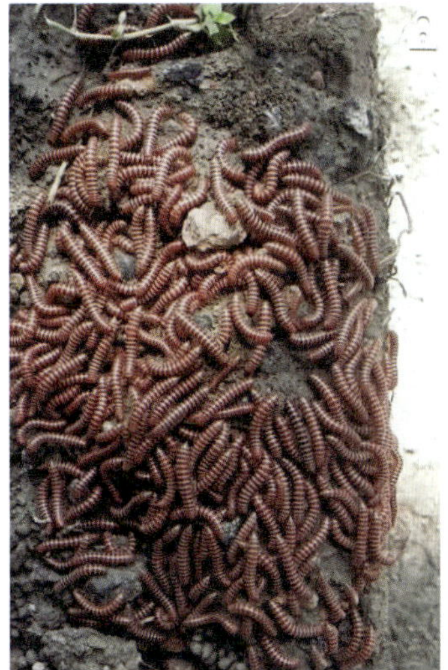
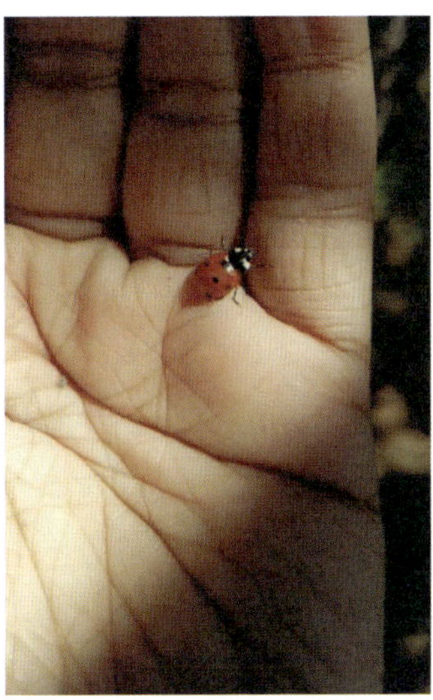

Whether beetles, millipedes, ladybirds, or fungal networks, all organisms contribute their own acoustic signatures to ecosystems. Recordings capture the movements of centipedes, spiders, ants, and the subtle crackling of roots growing and water moving through soil layers.

rhythm, and amplitude, such as the tunnelling of beetles, stridulation of ants, or rapid vibrations of millipede legs, all create identifiable patterns in audio recordings.[51]

Machine learning models are also being trained to detect behavioural patterns, such as foraging or mating, and monitor changes in activity over time. This allows researchers to track seasonal or even daily shifts in soil activity, which can then be correlated with environmental factors like moisture, temperature, or human disturbance.

Beyond animals, these algorithms could tell us what fungi are present and how they're connected, helping us to map their networks and perhaps contribute to organisations like SPUN (Society for the Protection of Underground Networks) who map, protect, and advocate for mycorrhizal fungal networks globally. Further, they could help us make informed decisions on how to boost agricultural productivity, guide soil restoration, and enhance tree-planting success by matching species with their ideal fungal partners.[52]

Go deeper still, and the world of microbes emerges, silent to the human ear, but now under investigation through bioacoustics and vibrational sciences. Microbially speaking, soil is the most diverse habitat on Earth, home to billions of microorganisms in just a single teaspoon. Their presence, absence, or activity tells us everything about a habitat's health, productivity, and potential to recover.

Traditional microphones can't capture microbial activity directly, but new research is exploring whether vibrations, a form of mechanical sound energy, can influence microbial growth. This idea might sound speculative, but recent experiments suggest it could revolutionise ecosystem restoration and sustainable agriculture.

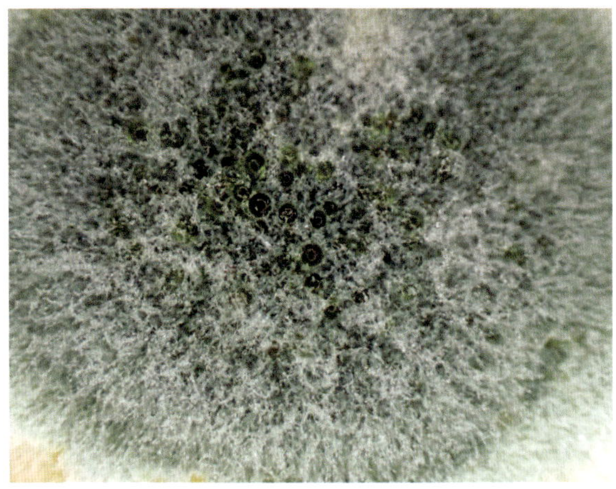

When exposed to daily doses of white noise, the fungus Trichoderma harzianum *showed increased biomass, spore production, and mycelial growth. This suggests that vibration could play a role in stimulating – or potentially hindering – microbial growth, opening up possibilities for using sound to influence internal and external microbiomes.*

At Flinders University in Australia, microbial ecologist Jake Robinson is exploring how sound affects soil microbiology. His work focuses on *Trichoderma harzianum*, a beneficial fungus used in biocontrol and plant health. Robinson's team exposed these fungi to low-level, daily doses of white noise, just 30 minutes a day.

The results were striking. Compared to fungi grown in silence, the sound-treated *Trichoderma* produced 1.7 times more biomass, with increased spore production and mycelial expansion. While these fungi lack ears or auditory organs, they seem capable of detecting and responding to vibration, possibly through mechanoreceptors in their cell walls or through electrically sensitive pathways that influence gene expression.

Robinson's findings are supported by other studies, including work by entomologist Richard Hofstetter, who demonstrated that moulds grown near running, constantly vibrating fridges grew more vigorously than those in still conditions.[53] These experiments might prove useful for food safety or crop transportation, but they also hint at an unprecedented, largely unexplored territory: The use of sound to heal or enhance microbiomes.

The implications would be huge. Vibrational sound therapies could potentially foster beneficial microbial communities in degraded soils, helping plants grow stronger and more resilient. They could even reduce reliance on chemical fertilisers or fungicides. In cities, where soil health is often poor and ecological function is compromised, this approach could restore balance without disturbing the soil physically.[54]

Robinson and his interdisciplinary collaborators, including quantum physicists, music therapists, and psychologists, also wonder how this might affect human health. Could the music we hear during childhood shape our microbiome, affecting cognitive development and immune health? Can enriching the earth with healthy soundscapes simultaneously restore ecosystems and diversify human microbiomes? Or has the earth always been doing this, we just never stopped to listen.

ACTIVITY

MYCELIAL SOUNDSCAPES

PART 1: LISTENING TO SOIL

EQUIPMENT[55]

- Contact Microphone (I used a C-Series & Acoustic Microphone with Neutrik ¼ inch jack + 2 probes from JRF Microphones)
- XLR impedance adaptor (also from JRF)
- Audio Interface (XLR to USB Signal Converter)
- Headphones
- Laptop

METHOD

1. Choose your site, perhaps a community allotment, wildflower meadow, orchard, or compost heap. Connect the microphone, adaptor, and audio interface to your computer. Plug the probe and headphones into the microphone and insert the probe into the soil.
2. Listen closely and try to stay still; above-ground movement can introduce unwanted noise.
3. Compare two sites: a healthy organic compost pile and a patch of chemically treated lawn, for example. What differences do you hear?
4. Record these sounds on QuickTime Player. Choose "New Audio Recording" and select your JRF microphone as the input. These can then be analysed and edited on Audacity or Adobe Audition and turned into ringtones, songs, or even dropped into DJ sets. The Sounding Soil project also accepts submissions to its acoustic map.

PART 2: PLAYING TO FUNGI

Alternatively, experiment with vibrational growth stimulation at home.

METHOD:

1. Brew two cups of herbal tea (peppermint works well).
2. Put the used tea bags into identical containers without lids and place both in a dark cupboard with minimal noise or vibrations.
3. Designate one container as your sound treatment sample. Every day, for 30 minutes, place it on a speaker and play your chosen sound. This could be classical music, white noise, ambient soundscapes, the radio, or your favourite pop song on repeat. The second container is your control; keep it in silence.
4. Visually monitor the microbial growth over 5–7 days. You might start to see a fuzzy mat of mycelium, slight discolouration, or differences in texture. Document your results through daily notes, photographs, or a time-lapse video.

Experiment with different teas and tempos. Does a fast beat encourage faster growth? Do minor keys slow things down? Might fungi prefer jazz to classical? Who knows? Let's see!

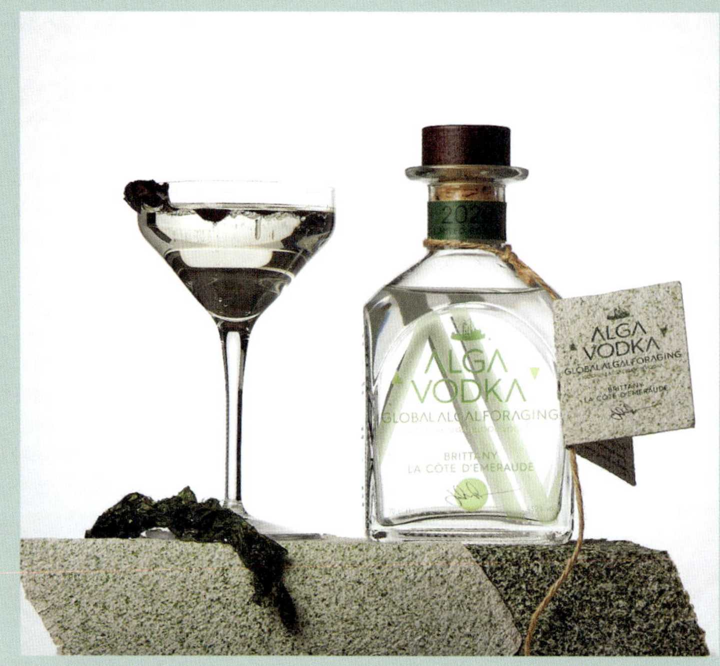

Blimey! Algae Vodka.
"Slippery Martini."

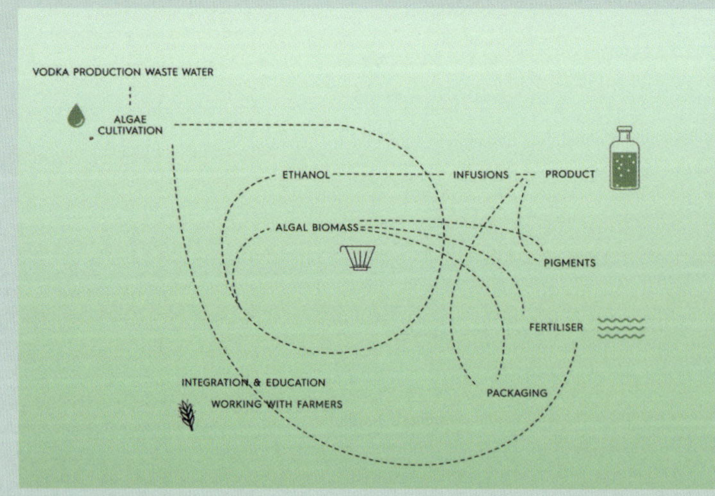

Algae Vodka System: High-starch microalgae are cultivated in traditional vodka production wastewater. The algae is then fermented and distilled to create vodka once again.

CIVILISATIONS & YEAST

In 2020, during the final stretch of my Biodesign Master's programme, I may have had my best idea yet. My cohort was part of a pioneering collaboration with Louis Vuitton Moët Hennessy (LVMH), who challenged us with a deceptively simple brief: "Design for Nature". Our mission was to create forward-thinking, nature-centric innovations for one of their Maisons – luxury brands that span watches and jewellery, fashion and leather, perfumes and cosmetics, and wines and spirits.

My focus landed on the latter. I wanted to explore this category through the lens of regenerative systems and ecological design, not just to create a product but to imagine a new way of producing it.

As I combed through biotechnology journals and sustainability articles, one particular buzzword caught my attention: algae biofuels. In these papers, I noticed something interesting: Terms like biofuel, bioethanol, and ethanol were often used interchangeably. Knowing that ethanol is the main ingredient in vodka, a lightbulb went off: Why not make vodka from algae?

That question became the foundation of what would evolve into *Blimey! Algae Vodka*, a speculative but scientifically grounded venture that envisions algae not only as a feedstock for biofuel, but as the base for a luxury, sustainable spirit.

But the idea was never just about a bottle of vodka. It was about systems thinking – a closed-loop, regenerative design where production waste becomes input for the next cycle. I wanted to address the environmental waste streams of traditional spirit manufacturing and offer a viable, beautiful, and delicious alternative.

Here's how it works. Traditional vodka production creates nutrient-rich wastewater high in nitrates and phosphates – two major contributors to destructive algal blooms in rivers and lakes. In the *Blimey!* model, this wastewater is repurposed to cultivate high-starch microalgae. These algae are then fermented and distilled into vodka, completing a sustainable loop that transforms trash into treasure.

The goal of this system was to tackle the root causes of destructive algal blooms, which are often fuelled by excess nutrients from fertiliser runoff and distillery waste. By turning these pollutants into raw materials for algae cultivation, the process becomes both preventative and productive. The result is a site-specific spirit that evolves with the local water chemistry, climate, and algae strain – each batch unique, each one a story of environmental regeneration.

But there was more. Leftover algal biomass – the thick, nutrient-dense byproduct – is transformed into artisanal goods, including compostable packaging, inks, and fertilisers. Collaborations with local farmers who needed fertiliser closed the loop, creating a micro-economy around algae that benefits both ecosystems and communities.

At the microbial core of this concept is yeast, specifically *Saccharomyces cerevisiae,* a single-celled fungus responsible for transforming sugars into alcohol through fermentation. This ancient organism, no bigger than a red blood cell, has shaped, and continues to shape, human civilisations in profound ways.

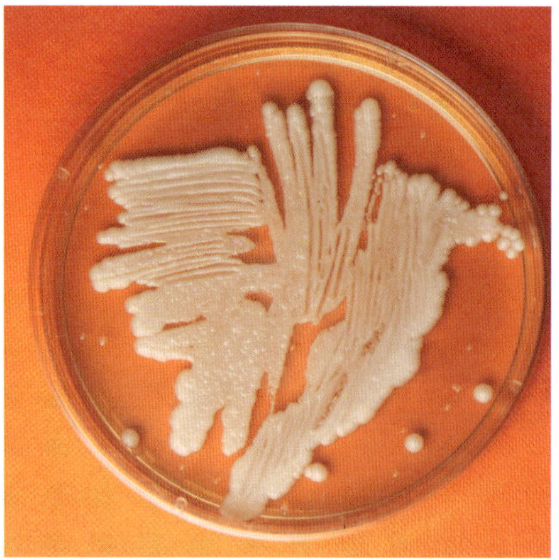

The yeast Saccharomyces cerevisiae *(known as brewer's yeast) is key to making bread, beer, and wine – staples of Western civilisation.*

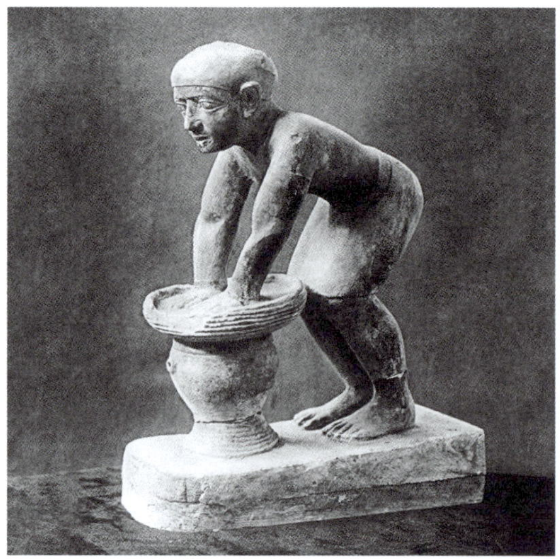

Figure of an ancient Egyptian brewer pressing out fermented bread in a basket. Beer drained into the pot beneath. This figure from the ancient Egyptian city of Saqqarah is in the Cairo Museum.

The word fermentation comes from the Latin *fervere*, meaning "to boil", a reference to the bubbling vats of grapes observed by the Romans. In French, it's *effervescence*; in Spanish, *agitación* – each capturing the process's energy and motion.

Yeast is the invisible force behind bread, beer, and wine – three foods so foundational they're often considered sacred. Without yeast, there would be no kefir, kombucha, soy sauce, sake, miso, or marmite, nor such diversity of cheeses, chocolates, and coffees. As poet John Ciardi put it, "Fermentation and civilization are inseparable."

Our relationship with yeast stretches back over 13,000 years. Archaeological evidence shows early fermented drinks made from palm sap in the Philippines, fruits in China, and honey in Africa.[56] These weren't just yummy, sugary beverages; they were nutritionally and culturally significant – not to mention often safer to drink than water.

What's remarkable is that fermentation was discovered independently by many cultures across the globe: pulque in Mesoamerica, kvass in Slavic regions, millet beer in Africa, and sake in Japan. These early brews likely arose spontaneously: rainwater mixing with sugary substances like grains, fruit, or honey, creating an ideal environment for yeasts. Over time, this ad-hoc partnership between human and fungus deepened into a co-dependence. Some anthropologists even propose that early humans transitioned from foraging to farming for bread and beer.

In ancient Mesopotamia, beer culture was deeply ingrained in daily life and spirituality. *The Epic of Gilgamesh*, one of the oldest written stories, tells of Enkidu, a wild man, becoming civilised by

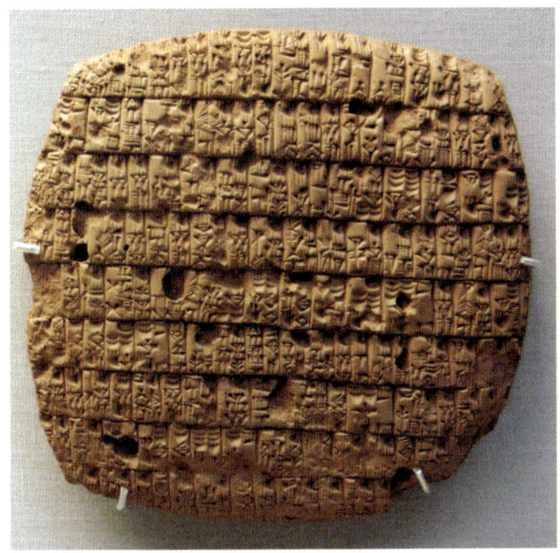

Cuneiform tablet recording beer allocation in Girsu, reign of Uruinimgina (2351–2342 BC). In Mesopotamia, beer was distributed as daily rations and wages. This early writing, from Sumer (modern day southern Iraq), uses a jar symbol to denote beer and track quantities issued to workers.

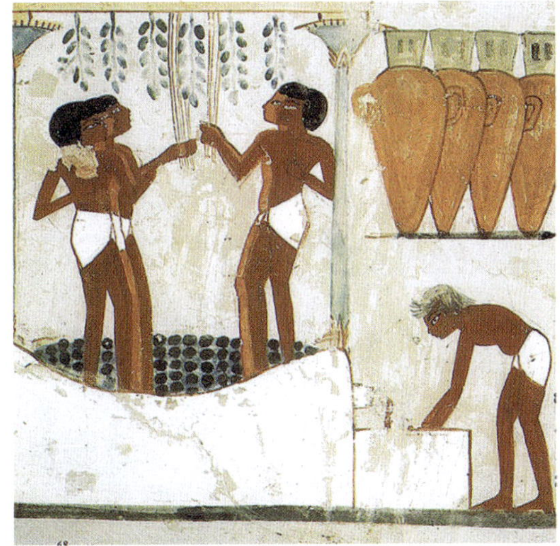

Paintings of the beer-making process in the tomb of the ancient Egyptian "Chief Beer Maker".

consuming bread and beer. Most interpret this as symbolising humanity's greatest leap from nature to culture. But others invert the dynamic, seeing it as the domestication of humans by a microscopic yeast.[57] Fermentation reminds us that culture is not something that is outside of nature; all societies are embedded in natural ecologies.[58]

Fermentation is inherently ecological: Where you live determines what plants grow and which local yeasts thrive. Every location has its own microbial terroir and aerobiome. Wild yeasts drift through the air, settle on sugars, and each species imparts distinct textures, aromas, and flavours to their ferment. Fermentation shows how natural ecosystems shape both social customs and cultural identity.

The Sumerians deified fermentation. Ninkasi, the goddess of beer, was honoured with a hymn that doubled as a brewing recipe, chanted aloud to pass knowledge down through generations.[59] In Babylon, beer was so important it had legal standing. King Hammurabi's Code decreed that beer rations be distributed by class: workers received two litres a day, civil servants three, priests five.[60] Remarkably, the need to record these rations helped drive the development of writing and mathematics, inadvertently advancing culture itself. Brewing was also held to extraordinarily high standards; diluting beer or producing a bad batch could get you drowned in your own vat.[61]

The ancient Egyptians continued and refined the tradition of beer-making. Known as *bousa*, their beer was thick, nutrient-dense, and relatively low in alcohol. It was brewed on a massive scale, distributed as wages, and consumed communally. The Egyptians even developed a rich vocabulary

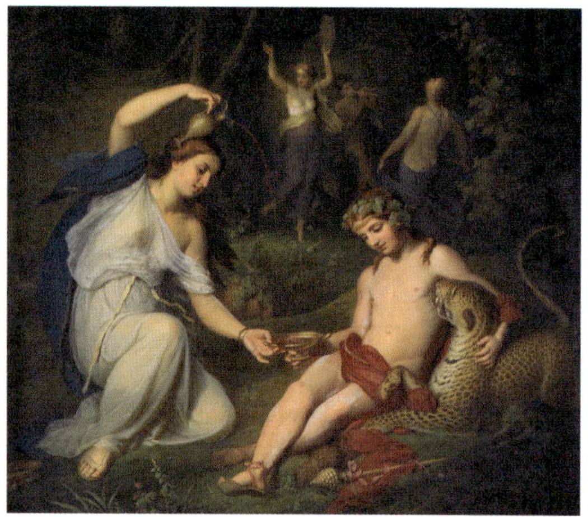

Dionysus (Bacchus in Roman mythology), was the god of domestication and wildness. He embodied both order and chaos, with wine perfectly capturing this duality as a force of both civility and abandon.

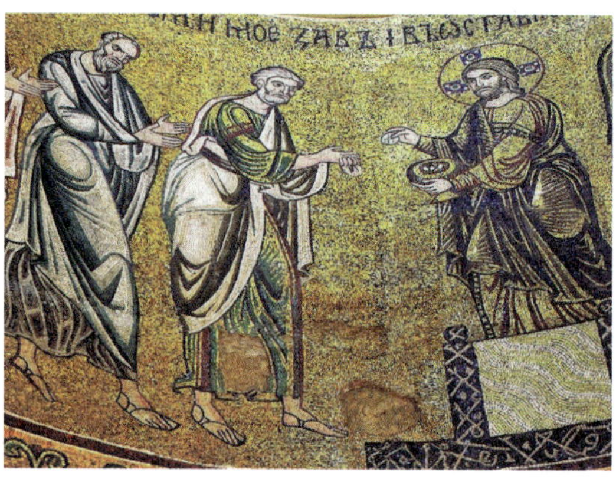

11th-Century Mosaic, St Sophia's Cathedral, Kiev. This mosaic reflects the religious tension over yeast during the Great Schism of 1054. The Eastern Church used leavened bread (symbolising divine transformation through yeast), while the Western Church preferred unleavened wafers (associating yeast with sin).

for beer, with names like "Friend's Beer", "Iron Beer", "Beer of Truth", and "Beer of the Protector", revealing its emotional and symbolic significance.

Beer also featured prominently in religious life. Hieroglyphs depict beer being offered to the gods and enjoyed during festivals such as the Festival of Drunkenness, held in honour of the fierce lion goddess Sekhmet. According to legend, when Sekhmet threatened to destroy humanity, she was pacified by drinking red-dyed beer mistaken for blood. After consuming several barrels, she passed out, sparing Egypt from her wrath.

Beer played an important role in death as well as life. Archaeologists have uncovered a 5,000-year-old brewery in an ancient necropolis, capable of producing nearly 6,000 gallons of beer.[62] Dedicated to the jackal god Khenti-Imentiu, the site later became linked with Osiris, god of the afterlife. Osiris, credited with giving humanity agriculture and culture, also taught them how to brew beer, the ultimate divine gift.

In Greece and Rome, wine was the drink of the elite, favoured by gods like Dionysus who "brought wild plants [and yeasts] into the house of civilisation."[63] Dionysus was god of both domestication *and* wildness, with wine sitting perfectly at this intersection as a force of both civility and abandon. "Wine is rudderless", Plato warned. Author Michael Pollan echoes this, noting that "the same wine that loosens the knots of inhibition and reveals nature's most beneficent face can also dissolve the bonds of civilisation and unleash ungovernable passions." [64]

As beer spread westward, its status fell. Against the backdrop of wine, beer became associated with "barbarians" – primitive, unrefined, un-Roman. Germanic tribes like the Toutons remained loyal to their brew, showing that cultural identity is shaped not just by who we are, but by who we are not.

But even as wine gained prestige, beer endured in the colder, northern fringes of Europe. During the Middle Ages, after the fall of the Roman Empire, monasteries became the guardians of fermentation. Monks brewed beer as sustenance and sacrament, using it to fund abbey operations. These spiritual centres preserved brewing knowledge throughout centuries of war and plague, unknowingly cultivating and selecting yeast strains that evolved and improved with time.

Throughout history and across cultures, yeast has played a paradoxical role in uniting and dividing societies. For many, alcohol is a unifying force – an occasion to gather, strengthen bonds, and enjoy life's pleasures. It has shaped global trade and cultural identities. But for others, alcohol embodies excess, vice, moral decay, and colonialism.

As European explorers, missionaries, and later American soldiers spread across the globe, they introduced indigenous cultures to the "luxuries" of civilisation – clothing, Christianity, technology, and alcohol, all in the name of progress. The arrival of alcohol often led to widespread over-use and social disintegration, a pattern that played out across the world – from the Arctic to Africa, Aotearoa to the Amazon. In these instances, alcohol became both a symbol of civilisation's reach and a catalyst for the erosion of native cultures and social systems.

Likewise, the tension around yeast is particularly pronounced in religion. The Great Schism of 1054, which split Christianity into Eastern Orthodox and Western Catholic branches, was partly fuelled by disagreements over the Eucharist.[65] The Eastern Church used leavened sourdough (fermented with yeast), while the Western Church preferred unleavened wafers. Known as the "azyme controversy", this theological divide was rooted in differing views on leaven: for the West, it represented corruption; for the East, it symbolised divine transformation.

This dynamic would shift dramatically in the 19th century with the advent of fermentation science. With his microscope, Louis Pasteur revealed that fermentation was not mystical but microbial. His discoveries led to the identification of key yeast species, including *Saccharomyces cerevisiae* (top-fermenting yeast, or "sugar fungus of beer") and *S. carlsbergensis* (bottom-fermenting yeast linked to Copenhagen's Carlsberg Brewery). This marked the transition of brewing from an arcane art to a controlled science.

Today we know that *S. cerevisiae* is just one member of a huge fungal family. *Brettanomyces* brings funky, earthy flavours to farmhouse ales; *Kluyveromyces marxianus* ferments dairy products like kefir; *Pichia pastoris* is used in bioengineering; and *Torulaspora delbrueckii* adds complexity to wines and bread.

The craft brewing revival embraces this diversity. Communities are reconnecting to their local histories and ecosystems via wild yeasts and ancient strains. Some brewers now isolate yeast from oak trees, fruit skins, or even the air in historic sites to capture hyper-local flavours. Microbiologist Keith Thomas revived yeast from a 19th-century shipwrecked beer, recreating a lost porter recipe. Meanwhile, Staffelter Hof, the world's oldest continuously operating winery, still ferments with living yeast cultures dating back centuries.

But the microbial frontier continues to evolve. Yeast is the subject of intensive research, with billions of dollars invested in its modification and potential applications across science and industry.[66] Its genome has been sequenced, and genetic engineering now allows us to programme yeast like software. Using CRISPR and Precision Fermentation, scientists can modify yeast to improve fermentation efficiency,

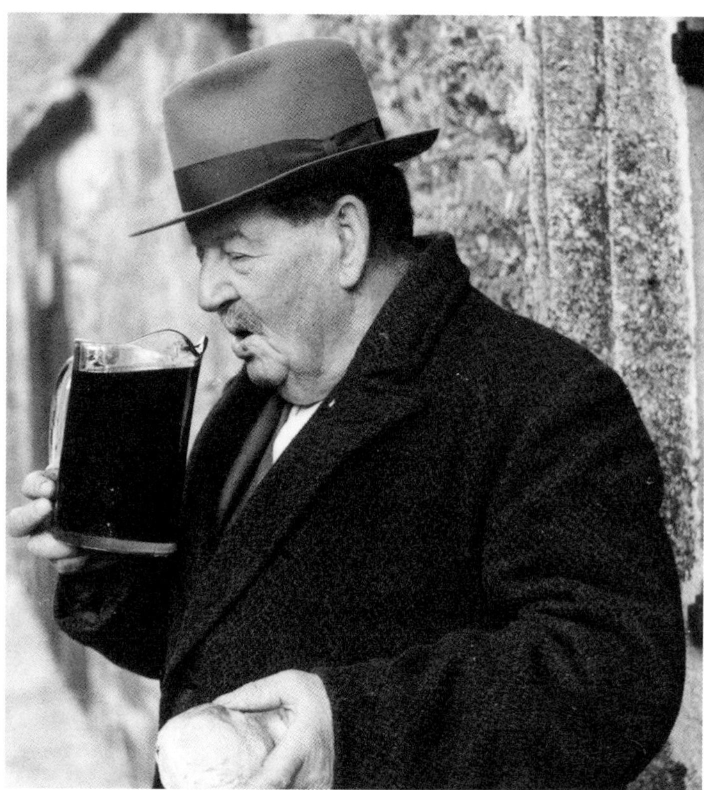

At the Ancient Order of Purbeck Marblers and Stonecutters' annual meeting in Corfe Castle, Dorset, 75-year-old quarryman Sam Bower holds a traditional loaf and quart jug, used for beer only on Shrove Tuesday.

increase ethanol yields, or produce new flavours, like cacao-free chocolate.[67] Heme proteins for plant-based meats (like the Impossible Burger) and even spider silk, extend yeast's powers even further.

And then, there's biofluorescent beer.

By inserting genes from a biofluorescent jellyfish, yeast can be made to glow under UV light. The result is both a novelty and a marvel, a drink that bridges microbiology and mixology. DIY kits from companies like The ODIN let home brewers experiment with CRISPR themselves, inserting Green Fluorescent Protein (GFP) into yeast cells.[68]

Though much contested, this blend of genetically modified science, art, and fermentation reveals the true essence of brewing. It's not just about creating intoxicants but about storytelling, ecosystems, and ethics.

As brewers, scientists, artists, and biohackers continue to push the boundaries of yeast, we must ask deeper questions: Who has access to these technologies? Who benefits? And what are we creating? Whether sipping algae vodka or biofluorescent beer, we are always, knowingly or otherwise, engaging in a broader conversation with microbes, one that shapes our civilisation.

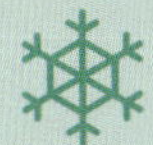

ACTIVITY

BREWING BIOFLUORESCENT BEER

METHOD

1. Check out the ODIN's website.
2. Browse through the options of DIY biotechnological possibilities: kits to genetically modify frogs, yeasts, bacteria, plants, salamanders, and human tissue.
3. If possible, and legal in your country, consider buying their kit to genetically engineer brewing or baking yeast to fluoresce. It's $179, but worth every cent.

For copyright reasons, I can't detail the process here, but I encourage you to explore this contested boundary between natural and artificial, and nature and culture, by creating biofluorescent beer – or bread – the enduring staples of civilisation.

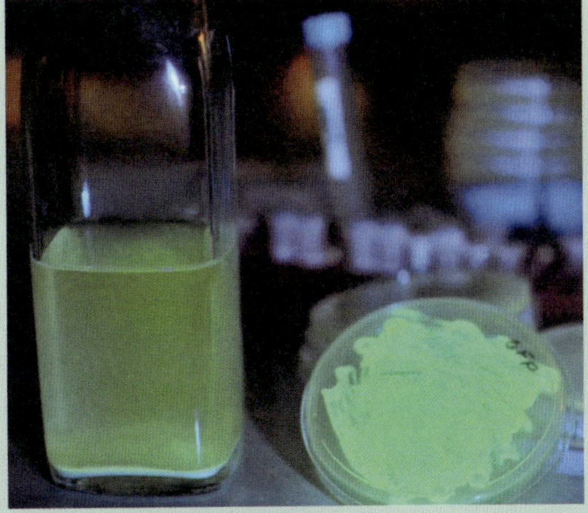

Biofluorescent beer made from genetically modified yeast.

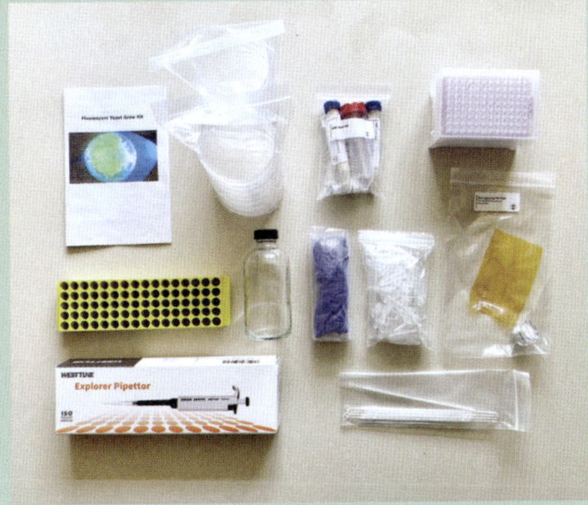

CRISPR kit used to genetically modify yeast with a GFP (green fluorescent protein), enabling biofluorescence in microbial cultures.

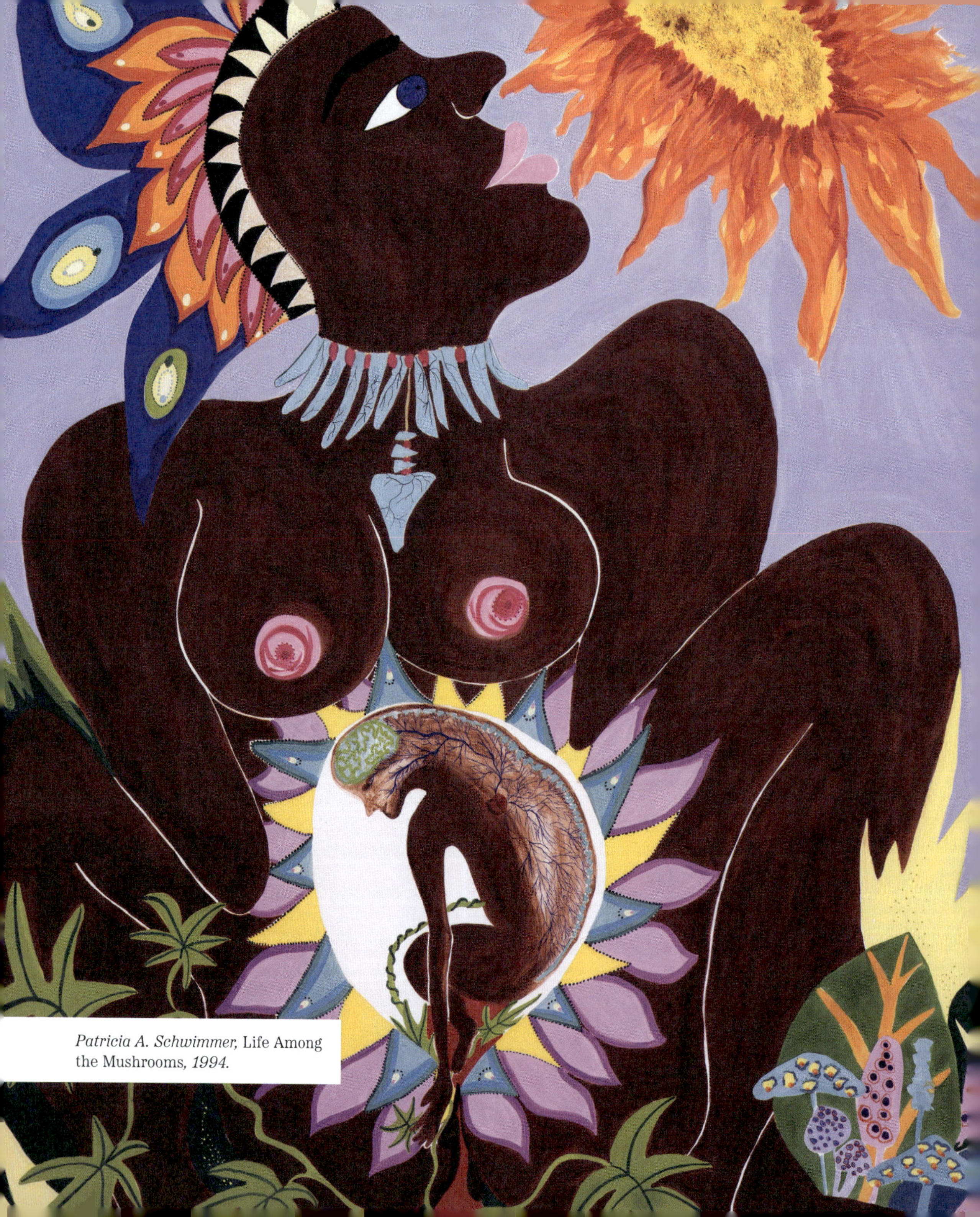

Patricia A. Schwimmer, Life Among the Mushrooms, *1994.*

6

INTRA: Craft, Continuity, & Communities of Care

"A cry of joy rings out across the tundra. Saša, the youngest, has just spotted a red shape at the side of the road, on the ground, interwoven with moss and lichen. With a cough of the engine, the muddy 4x4 screeches to a halt, and the two girls eagerly spring from their seats, followed by their mother, who wants to see the object of all the excitement with her own eyes: "muxomor, muxomor!" No doubt about it, it's a Fly Agaric. Standing around the bright red mushroom with white spots, Saša and Nastja wait for a sign from Svetlana Vasil'evna to make sure they're doing things "right". Their attentive faces are bent towards the soft, spongy soil of the marshy tundra, typical of the coasts of the Koryak district, in the north of the Kamchatka Peninsula. At their feet, other scarlet hats reflect the rays of the summer sun. After a few moments of silent, amused hesitation, Svetlana says, looking at her children: "If we want to pick them, now we have to dance."

– Anthropologist Amélie Barbier, "Talking with v'apaq", Terrain: Anthropologie & Sciences Humaines, 2021. This article is a translated account from her field study in Kamchatka, north-eastern Russia, from late July to early October 2019.[1]

In the village of Tymlat, northeast Russia, the Fly Agaric plays a significant role in daily life. Known as *muxomor* in Russian and *v'apaq* in the Čukotko-Koriak languages, it is believed to possess the power of omniscient vision. Inhabitants use the mushroom to address a wide range of ailments, and its collection, preparation, consumption, and visionary interpretation nurture and sustain community bonds.

According to Amélie Barbier's ethnographic observations, *v'apaq* serves as a conduit for the transmission of ecological and cosmological knowledge, evolving over time through intergenerational relationships. While historically the domain of men, the practices surrounding *v'apaq* are now largely overseen by women, especially respected elders.

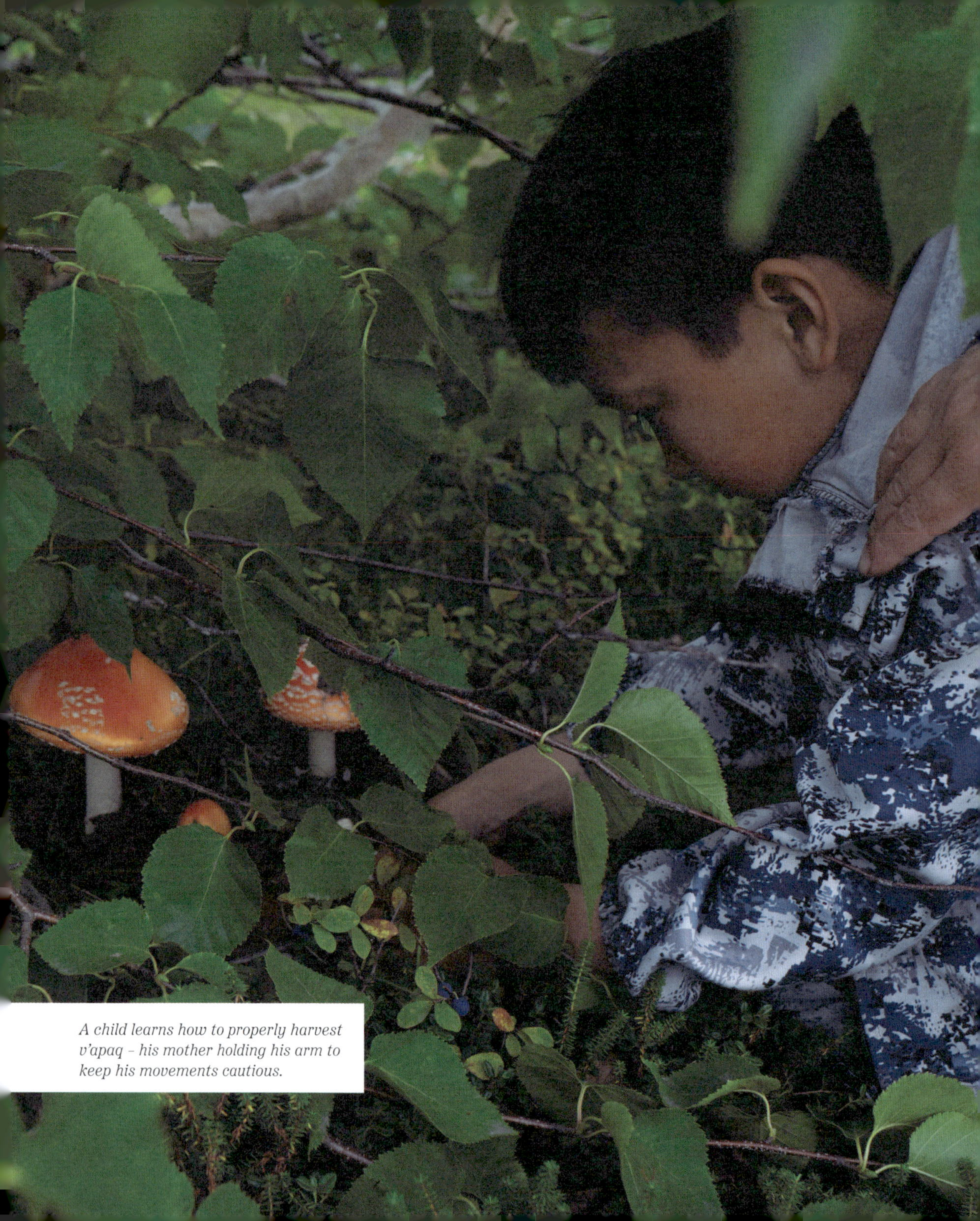

A child learns how to properly harvest v'apaq – his mother holding his arm to keep his movements cautious.

Humans are one of the only species to undergo menopause, and this has profound cultural implications. Older women – grandmothers, mothers-in-law, aunties – play key roles in safeguarding and passing on knowledge. Evolutionarily, we have "grandmothers" because culture, care, and community are survival traits.[2]

This ethos of care extends beyond people and into the living world. Whether gathering *v'apaq*, tending a garden, or cultivating microbes, we are drawn into biological time – a slower, cyclical rhythm that grounds us in presence. These quiet, attentive acts become ways of nurturing ourselves, others, and the ecosystems we inhabit. Artist Amartey Golding explores this beautifully, framing self-care not as isolation, but as ancestral and communal care: tending our roots to sustain the flame of connection.

In a world in crisis that demands speed and output, choosing rest, joy, and hope becomes an act of resistance. Especially in difficult times, love and community are not luxuries, they are our lifelines.

This culture of acceleration fractures not just ecologies but also traditions and imaginations. In Galicia, they speak of *la extinción de las artes*, the extinction of the arts, as local crafts and place-based knowledges fade. Braiding, pottery, foraging, weaving, storytelling, seafood gathering – these skills once stitched communities together and carried their values forward. Practised communally, they are living expressions of identity, passed through generations. Their loss reflects the broader severing of people from land, food, and one another.

But we are not isolated beings – we are multi-species collectives – *Homo holobionts* – living in constant collaboration with trillions of microbes. These intimate communities are shaped not only by food and ecology, but by history, kinship, class, race, and gender. Even our thoughts and kisses are more-than-human experiences. Microbes, like us, live in communities, as seen in ferments like tempeh and sauerkraut, where yeasts, moulds, and bacteria co-create flavour and form. The language of fermentation – "mother culture", "koji kin" – also evokes lineage and care. Fermentation is a craft of co-becoming: humans and microbes shaping one another over time.

While the nutritional benefits of fermented foods are well known, some of the most compelling microbiome research is emerging from foragers. Wild foods – game, nuts, berries, mushrooms, and herbs – offer microbial richness that is absent from industrial foods. Rewilding the gut reanimates old relationships between humans, land, seas, and microbes.

Fermentation revivalist Sandor Katz argues that industrial food systems isolate us from our nourishment.[3] Reclaiming ancestral knowledge – what grows where, how to ferment, when to harvest – restores agency and reconnects us to culture and place. Sharing this food becomes an act of continuity and care.

Across cultures, the hearth has symbolised warmth, connection, and the sacred centre of community. Meals are more than sustenance; they are how we express love, memory, and belonging. Nomadic peoples even carry fire across landscapes, using fungi like Amadou to transport embers, keeping both literal and symbolic flames alive. In food, in fire, in fermentation, we find craft, continuity, and care passed from hand to hand.

Mycology bridges science and traditional ecological knowledge (TEK), offering insight into reciprocity and regeneration. TEK teaches that what we give to the land, it gives back. Fermentation reflects this. To keep a sourdough starter alive, you must regularly discard part of the culture. That sacrifice sustains the rest. Indigenous foodways often reflect similar principles: take only what is needed, leave

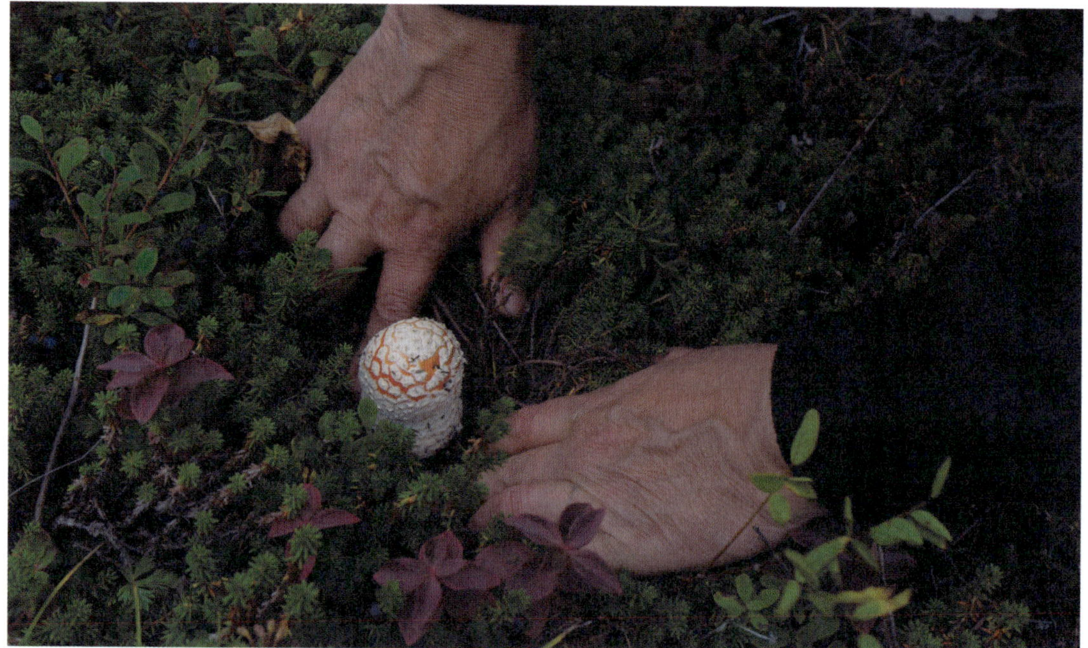

A forager collecting v'apaq. Often the community of the Koryak district sing, dance, and speak to the mushrooms before harvesting.

something behind, ensure the cycle continues. Even the act of foraging reflects this ethic. As gatherers walk, seeds and spores fall from their baskets, regenerating the landscapes from which they harvest. This is not extraction; it is mutual exchange.

To be alive, then, to be a steward, is to be in relation: porous, entangled, and co-created.

And so, in this chapter, we look to those who nourish culture as living collaboration. From Korea to Japan and Indonesia, we see how fermentation is often passed down the matrilineal line through hands-on learning. We rewild ourselves by gathering wild food, preparing ferments, and sharing ancestral stories to restore both biological and cultural diversity. We grow and fabricate mycomaterials, honouring those who actively resist the extinction of the arts. And finally, as the climate crisis and conflict displace people and disrupt ecologies, we return to the fundamentals of connection. Through taxonomies and traditions, through mycelium and memory, we find ways to connect to culture wherever we are.

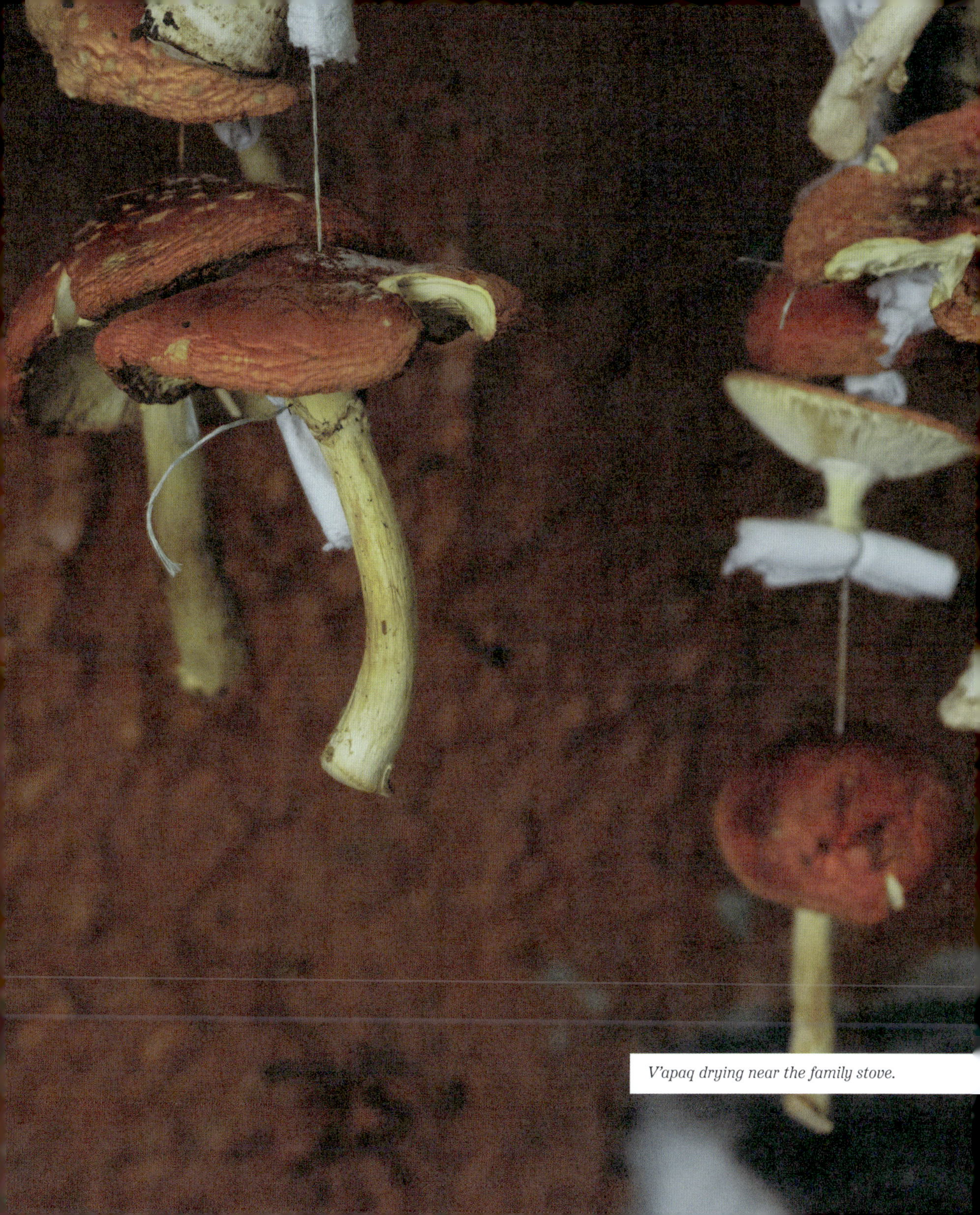

V'apaq drying near the family stove.

KIMCHI, KOJI, & KINSHIP

In Korean fermentation traditions, grandmothers often speak of *son-mat*, or "hand taste", reflecting the personal touch of the maker. Handmade kimchi carries the warmth, care, and individuality of its creator, infusing each batch with a unique feel and flavour that true enthusiasts can instantly recognise and sincerely appreciate.

This connection isn't just emotional, it's microbial. Each grandmother's skin and oral microbiome is transferred to the salted vegetables during preparation (via touch and breath), subtly shaping the flavour and texture of the kimchi. Some are even said to have "better kimchi hands", meaning their microbes yield tastier results. Microbial variations arise from factors like season, weather, diet, geography, and even a walk outdoors. The process is beautifully unpredictable, a living collaboration between human and environment. It's a quiet blend of art and science that honours family, place, ecology, and culture.

Fermentation is more akin to farming or shepherding than cooking.[4] It's dynamic and variable, as we're collaborating with other living beings. Fermentation likely began out of necessity or by accident, as microbes naturally present in the environment settled on food and broke down carbohydrates and proteins. When this process is uncontrolled, it's referred to as "rotting". But when it produces something delicious, we call it "fermentation".[5]

At its core, fermentation is about creating the right conditions for specific microbes to thrive. While many fermented foods rely primarily on bacteria, others, such as cheese, bread, chocolate, and soy sauce, depend largely on fungi. All ferments, however, rely on communities of microbes that work via ecological succession. It might first be a mould, followed by bacteria and later a unicellular yeast – or any other combination or sequence. Microbial cultures interact with one another and establish their own ecological niches. Whether using bacteria or fungi, first or last, fermentation requires patience and precision. Too much salt can halt microbial activity, while too little can lead to spoilage.

This tradition typically emerged in regions with harsh winters, where preserving food was essential for survival. But fermentation is universal; every culture has its fermented foods, from Peruvian manioc flour to Icelandic fermented shark and Sri Lankan *meekiri* (fermented buffalo milk).

Kimchi is a staple of Korean cuisine. It literally means "salted fermented vegetables" and is still found on a Korean's family table, breakfast, lunch, and dinner. But kimchi is more than just food, it's a symbol of identity and heritage. The tradition of *kimjang*, or making and sharing kimchi, dates back to 3000 BCE. This annual communal event involves fermenting vegetables like napa cabbage and daikon (radishes) with seasonings like *gochugaru* (Korean chilli pepper), garlic, ginger, and salted seafood. In both North and South Korea, *kimjang* is an official "Intangible Cultural Heritage" and an ancient, collaborative art.[6]

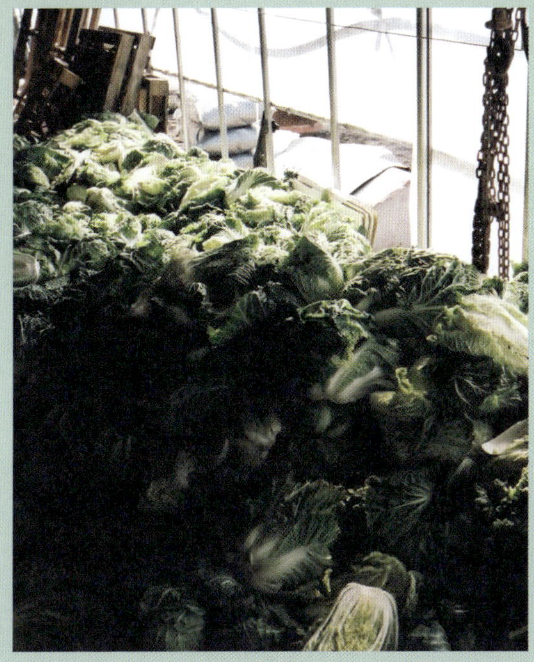

Kimchi combines napa cabbage and daikon with seasonings like gochugaru (Korean chilli pepper), garlic, ginger, and salted seafood. Its fermentation varies with the seasons and according to region.

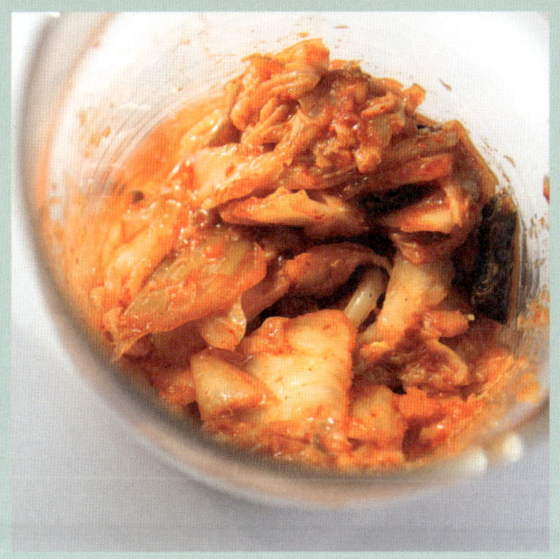

Kimchi, literally "salted fermented vegetables", is a staple of Korean cuisine. Often made by mothers and grandmothers, it is deeply embedded in Korean culture – both socially and microbially.

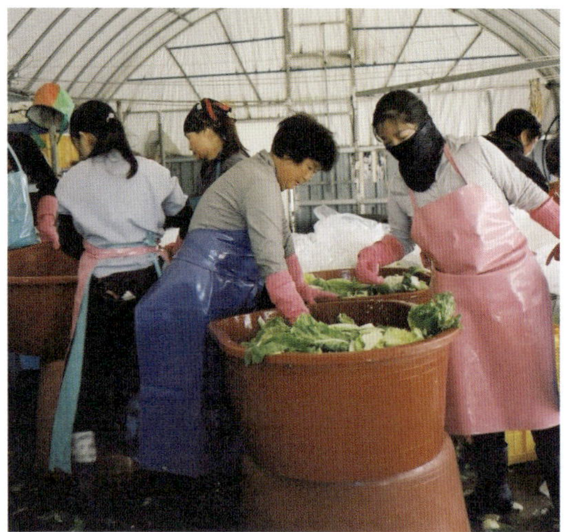

Women preparing kimchi during the annual communal event, Kimjang.

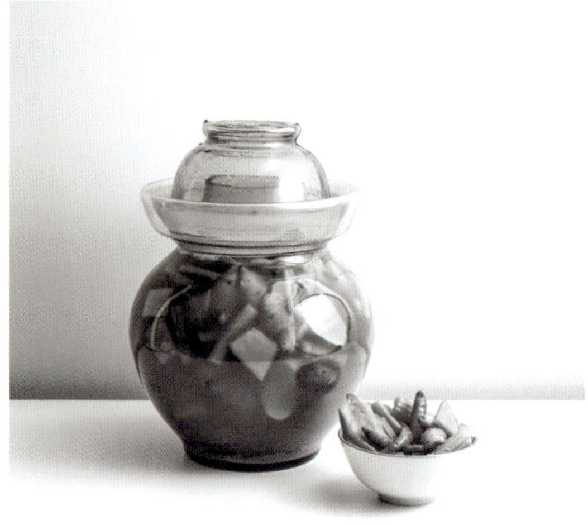

Mother Culture Vase. Like a family heirloom, fermentation passes down unique cultures of bacteria and yeast through generations. These "mother cultures" connect families, carrying the living legacy of their ancestors in every batch.

Kimchi's flavour comes from a balance of *Lactobacillus* bacteria first, and yeast fermentation second.[7] While the science of microbes wasn't necessarily understood, through meticulous experimentation, Koreans learned how to harness the power of fermentation. A second-generation kimchi farmer from East Branch Farms in New York explained that the goal is to celebrate and preserve the vegetable. Over time, various kimchi methods and recipes emerged, and historical texts, such as *Tongguksesigi*, describe how kimchi recipes adapted to the seasons. Summer kimchi captures intense, vibrant flavours, while winter kimchi, made after the first frost, is sweeter, or more accurately, less bitter.

Traditionally, winter kimchi was stored in large earthenware jars called *onggi*, buried underground to keep them cool and slow fermentation. Regional variations also play a role; kimchi from Gangwon Province typically includes fish, while Chungcheong Province kimchi favours pork-based recipes. Gwangju, located in the southwest, is renowned for its bold, intensely fermented kimchi, often regarded as the best in Korea. Quirky family variations and modern twists can be found everywhere, in local markets and supermarkets worldwide. People from all around the world are reimagining traditional ferments for new audiences, from Mac Kimchi at the Edinburgh Fermentarium, a Reddit user's "Sprite Kimchi", and California's Mother-in-Law's artisanal kimchi.

MICROBIAL MOTHERS

Mothers and mothers-in-law play an essential role in Korea's culinary traditions. Korean mothers regarded teaching their daughters how to make kimchi from a young age as a necessary part of family education. Young women were expected to know how to make twelve variations before they were married. Likewise, when a bride married into her new family, it was customary for her to learn their traditional family recipes, often from the mother-in-law. As one of the most revered culinary skills in any Korean household, learning the in-laws' kimchi recipe was particularly important.[8] In late autumn, women relatives or neighbours would sit in a circle trimming enormous Korean cabbages, cleaning and pickling them, then sprinkling salt and seasonings between their leaves. This distinctive scene is a part of family life and can be seen in Korea alone.

The matrilineal legacy extends to the microbes we inherit. While we acquire microbes from our fathers, siblings, friends, and even pets, our first and most critical microbial "seeding" occurs during birth through the vaginal canal and soon after through breastfeeding, courtesy of our mothers. Fermentation echoes this maternal transmission: just as we inherit microbes from our mothers and their mothers, families pass down unique microbial cultures through their ferments. These "heirloom" or "mother cultures", often maintained for centuries, carry the living fingerprints of ancestors, connecting generations through food.

A 120-year-old pickle jar from rural Sichuan, China, for example, has been passed down through five generations of women.[9] When a woman in the family marries, she receives a jar of pickles with the mother-in-law's brine, which keeps the microbial community alive and solidifies family ties. Contemporary Korean fermenters often say their ancestors live on within these shared cultures, highlighting the deep intergenerational bond sustained through the microbial world.

When sharing a microbial culture with friends or family, you often take a portion from the mother culture. This culture requires careful attention – it needs regular feeding and harvesting to thrive. Maintaining a SCOBY (Symbiotic Culture of Bacteria and Yeast) for kombucha, for example, involves feeding it brewed tea and sugar while regularly removing SCOBY layers to eat, create new batches, or share. This delicate balance of give and take creates a symbiotic relationship, fostering mutual growth and sustenance. As these microbial communities are cultivated, shared, and cultivated again, they support human communities in productive and creative endeavours, teaching us ancient skills and providing us with live foods and drinks. Kimchi, kombucha, pickles, and more remind us that we are not just what we eat, but who we eat. "Kimchi", I am told, "teaches us".

Microbes have helped civilisations shape their cultural identities. These tiny organisms, along with the foods and medicines they produce, have sustained communities for thousands of years. This practice of self-creation, or autopoesies, has endured because the microbes literally keep us alive: they preserve our food and, therefore, our existence. Communities have carried these microbial cultures across vast distances, transporting their heritage in jars or envelopes of spores.[10] The idea that we can take our culture with us wherever we go is both inspiring and comforting.

Many of the microbes we cultivate today can be traced back to our ancestors, great-great-grandmothers and beyond. While some connections come from their hands, as with kimchi, others come from their saliva, as in the case of sake. This traditional Japanese rice wine relies on the filamentous fungus *Aspergillus oryzae*, known as koji, followed by lactic acid bacteria and yeast. While modern sake production avoids such practices, the traditional method of sake-making, known as *kijōzō*, uses the saliva of an unmarried woman to initiate fermentation.[11] Though virtually extinct in modern mainstream sake production, accounts suggest this method, and its ceremonial significance, persisted in some regions, such as Okinawa, as late as the early 20th century.[12]

I first learned about this unusual method from the bizarre but fantastic Japanese manga series *Moyasimon: Tales of Agriculture,* where a character recreates his grandmother's sake recipe. The secret ingredient? Saliva. In a modern twist, he chews steamed rice, spits it into the fermentation vat, and lets the microbes work their magic.

Saliva contains amylase, the same starch-breaking enzyme found in koji, kickstarting fermentation by converting starches into sugars for yeast to turn into alcohol. This enzymatic process underpins ancient fermentation traditions across the globe. In Ecuador, for example, women chew corn and spit it into pots to ferment *chicha*, a traditional maize beer. The act of spitting honours Pachamama, the Earth Mother, as a gesture of reciprocity and respect. Similar practices exist in Ghana, Zambia, Malawi, and Cameroon where women historically chewed grains and root vegetables to initiate the fermentation of local brews such as *pito* or *akpeteshie*. These ferments are cultural expressions, woven into rituals, ceremonies, and social bonds.

Fermentation offers a radical perspective on our relationship with microbes. Vessels function like external digestive systems, harbouring microbes similar to those in our mouths and guts. These microbes secrete familiar enzymes such as protease, amylase, and lipase, which break down proteins, starches, and fats, respectively, making food easier to digest. Beyond enhancing flavour and nutrition, these microbes also support gut health by acting as prebiotics, which nourish our existing beneficial microbes, and probiotics, which help diversify and strengthen the preexisting gut microbiome.

Unlike humans, fungi don't have mouths or digestive tracts. Instead, they release enzymes into their environment to break down food, which they then absorb and use. As Merlin Sheldrake explains, "Animals put food in their bodies, whereas fungi put their bodies in the food." We, in turn, harness their capabilities by putting their bodies into our food and then into our bodies, creating an ingenious, mutually beneficial relationship: they eat our food, we eat them, they continue to eat our food within us.

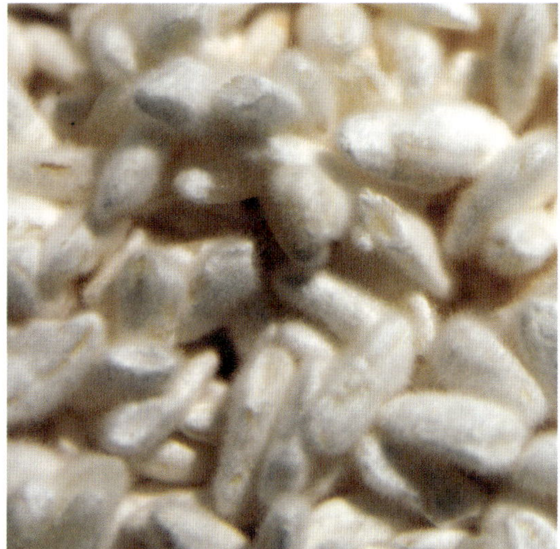

"Kōji kin" fermenting steamed rice. Rice contains insoluble fibres that koji breaks down into more digestible and bioavailable molecules, creating a distinct, apricot-like aroma.

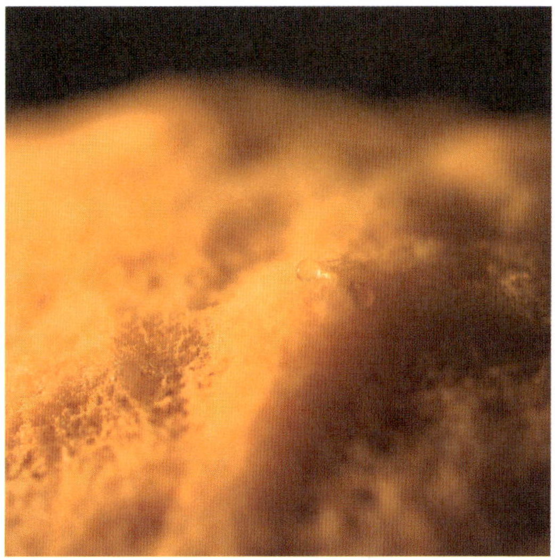

The Red Bread Mould, Neurospora intermedia, *is used in Indonesian cuisine, grown on soy by-products, cassava, or "peanut presscake". It shows that fermentation extends far beyond traditional ingredients like grapes, barley, and rice, and opens up a world of diverse microbes to explore.*

KOJI KIN

While we cultivate relationships with microbial mothers, we also establish connections with microbial kin. Koji kin, from the mould *Aspergillus oryzae*, is responsible for making Japanese sake, miso, shoyu, rice vinegar, mirin, katsobushi, and shochu. They are regarded in the highest esteem and shared as gifts between families, friends, and researchers. Koji is typically cultivated on steamed rice or legumes like soybeans, sprinkled over its surface, and left to produce enzymes that break down the substrate.

Haruko Uchishiba, founder of London-based The Koji Fermentaria, explains that "Koji is not just an ingredient. It's a symbol of harmony between nature and culture, tradition and the Japanese spirit. Koji is the gateway to the Japanese soul." Japanese mythology holds that miso was a gift from the gods, bringing health, happiness, and long life. Likewise, the first written record of Japanese sake points to its revered and spontaneous origins.

For millennia, koji has been selectively bred to thrive in warm, humid conditions, ideally at a temperature around 30°C (86°F) with 70 to 80 per cent humidity. Koji cultivation is practised throughout East Asia, but its precise use has evolved in very different ways, resulting in huge regional diversity. In China, koji is cultivated with wild spores on raw and milled grain to produce bold, expressive, and rich flavours. In Japan, it is grown in a controlled manner to create gentle, balanced, and harmony-focused

The sacred rice offered to the gods began to sprout mould.
With it, we brewed sake, and gathered to celebrate.
The freshly made sake was presented to the brewer,
who then offered it back to the gods.
– Translation from Harimanokuni no Fudoki c. 713 AD

flavours. The Danish Michelin-star restaurant and fermentation lab, Noma, regards koji as an invaluable microbial ally, "the best kind of magic."[13]

Working with koji requires exceptional craftsmanship and care. To make miso, a paste of cooked soybeans (sometimes with coconut, peanuts, or other seeds) is inoculated with koji and salt, then left to ferment for months or even years. The timing and season significantly impact the fermentation process – summer miso matures in three to four months, whereas winter miso takes longer. Soy sauce, another koji-based product, undergoes a similar process, resulting in its familiar yet striking umami flavour and complex aroma.

Interestingly, soy contains phytoestrogens, plant-based chemicals that mimic oestrogen in the body. Studies suggest that Asian women experience fewer menopausal symptoms, possibly due to their high consumption of fermented soy products like sake, miso, and soy sauce.

My exploration of koji led me from London's Koji Fermentaria to New York's Blue Hill at Stone Barns. Here, researchers are working with another mould, *Neurospora intermedia*, gifted by gastro-scientist Vayu Hill-Maini at UC Berkeley. While mushroom farmers and bakers regard this mould as a nuisance, Blue Hill's team uses its rapid growth to create delicious and experimental dishes. This is unsurprising as Blue Hill is another world-renowned Michelin-starred restaurant and farm, known for growing some of the most delicious vegetables in the world. From mushroomy flour to sweet rice custard and *oncom* (a fermented soy by-product), the possibilities with *Neurospora* are endless.[14]

Taking inspiration from Indonesian cuisine, they're also experimenting with *Neurospora*-inoculated plant-based milks to create cheese-like products. Andrew Luzmore, Blue Hill's lead researcher, and his team are even inoculating stale bread with Neurospora to make "cheesy" fried toast. While the dish has been well-received by politicians and celebrity guests, its uncooked, bright pink, fuzzy appearance often catches people off guard, but only occasionally ruins their appetites.

Neurospora serves as a reminder that we can ferment so much more than the traditional grapes, barley, rice, and soybeans – and work with so many more different microbes! In *The Art of Fermentation,* Sandor Katz writes, "Let's ferment acorns, turnips, sorghum, or whatever food surpluses we can access or create! Make the most of surplus. It's dignifying and endlessly creative."

While the fermentation revival is thriving, it may take time for Westerners to embrace the art of cultivating and eating mouldy foods, let alone see these microbes as our ancestral kin. Yet, with patience and practice, working with live foods attunes us to their stories: the lineages, traditions, and histories they carry. As Koji for Life reminds us, koji's growth is like the circle of life. "We can learn a great deal by projecting ourselves onto the microbial world."

RECIPE & ACTIVITY

CULTIVATING KOJI KIN
THE KOJI FERMENTARIA

This activity is adapted from The Koji Fermentaria's excellent workshop. You'll steam rice, inoculate it with koji kin (*Aspergillus oryzae* spores), incubate it for 24 hours, then carry it on your body for another 12–24 hours, using your natural warmth and humidity to support its growth. By the end, you'll have a fluffy, living koji cake that can be used fresh or dried and powdered.

Koji cultivation is the first step in making miso, soy sauce, and sake. This recipe focuses on stage one: creating enzymes from rice and koji.

EQUIPMENT

- Steamer (preferably bamboo)
- Digital scales (accurate to 0.01g)
- Fine-mesh sieve
- Hot-water bottle
- Tray
- Drying rack
- Canvas cloth
- Cheesecloth
- Incubator or warm box (proofing box, plastic container, etc.),
- Optional: baking parchment and a small plastic food bag

INGREDIENTS

- 0.1g koji spores, *Aspergillus oryzae*
- 100g/3½oz long-grain rice (or barley, wheat, acorns, even mushrooms!)
- Filtered, non-chlorinated water
- Sprinkle of sea salt or kosher salt

PREPARE THE SUBSTRATE

1. Rinse thoroughly, then soak in warm (50°C/122°F) water for 24 hours. Drain.
2. Steam in batches, one ladle at a time. Wait for each to turn translucent before adding the next. Steam for ~50 minutes until the grains are soft inside and firm outside (achieving a "Haribo texture", also known as *Gaiko-Nainan*).
3. Cool to room temperature, as spores are rather heat sensitive.
4. Clean your tools and workspace thoroughly.

INOCULATE

1. Use 0.1% of the rice's raw weight in spores (up to 2 to 3 times is okay).
2. Spread the rice on canvas. Sprinkle spores as evenly as possible with a fine-mesh sieve, then gently fold. Work fast to prevent the rice from cooling.
3. Optional: add a sprinkle of salt to deter unwanted bacteria.

INCUBATE

1. Form a mound with the inoculated rice, then wrap it in canvas.
2. Place it on a drying rack over a hot-water bottle in a warm, humid space (e.g., an incubator or container with a damp cloth).
3. Replace the hot water as needed. Ideal conditions are 30°C/86°F and 80% humidity.
4. Check periodically for growth and contamination. You may need to adjust the temperature, humidity, or substrate to optimise growth.

HARVEST & DE-KOJI (DEHYDRATE)

1. After 36–48 hours, the rice should be bound together with white, cottony mould and smell delicious and sweet, like overripe apricots.
2. Break up the cake and spread it on the canvas. Draw a spiral pattern in the koji to aerate.

STORAGE

1. You can use the koji cake immediately or store it in an airtight container in the fridge for up to a week.
2. Alternatively, you can dehydrate it at 40°C/104°F for 24 hours to store for future use.
3. You can brush off the spores for reuse. Label your batches to track the most effective cultures!

RECIPE IDEAS

- Fresh Koji Cake: Great for snacking or as a carbohydrate base for a meal
- Koji Powder: Dry and grind into powder. Add a spoonful to soups, stews, or smoothies.
- Shio Koji (Koji Marinade): Blend fresh/dried koji with salt and water (ratio: 5 parts koji: 1 salt: 5 water).
- Use as a marinade for meat, fish, tofu, or vegetables. It's delicious!

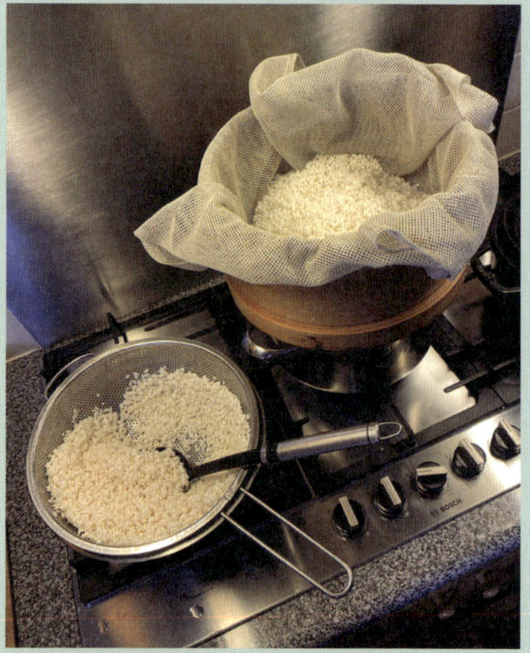

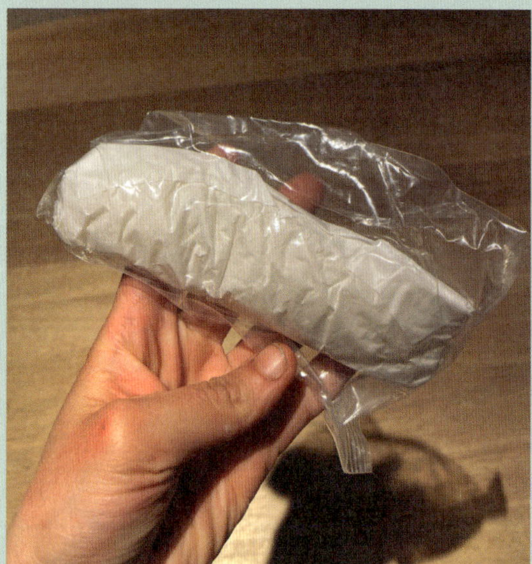

We slept with this packet in our pyjama pockets (or near enough), using our natural body temperature to incubate the koji kin.

REWILDING THE MICROBIOME

***"Mud. Mud. Glorious Mud.
Nothing quite like it for cooling the blood.
So follow me, follow down to the hollow,
And there, let us wallow, in glorious mud."***

– Hippoporamus, *Flanders and Swann, 1957*

(Sung to me by my grandfather when I was young.)

Amou Haji was often dubbed the "dirtiest man in the world".[15] For decades, he lived in solitude in southern Iran, avoiding soap and water out of fear that it would make him ill. His diet was extreme – rotten meat and puddle water, and he even smoked animal dung. Though villagers urged him to wash, he refused until finally taking a bath after more than 60 years. Just months later, at the age of 94, he fell ill and died.

Microbiologists speculate that Haji's unique microbial exposure contributed to his longevity. This idea supports the "Old Friends" hypothesis, which proposes that humans co-evolved with certain microbes critical to immune development.[16] These microbes, often environmental, play a crucial role in training our immune systems to distinguish between harmful and harmless agents. Modern disconnection from these microbes, the theory suggests, influences our susceptibility to disease and contributes to rising rates of immune system overreactions, such as allergies, asthma, and autoimmune diseases.[17]

For much of human history, regular contact with soil, animals, and diverse natural environments shaped our immune systems. But industrialisation, urban living, antibiotics, and our obsession with cleanliness have created a sterile world. These changes have dramatically reduced our exposure to beneficial microbes, particularly in polluted urban areas where harmful pathogens outnumber helpful ones. [18] Even Louis Pasteur, father of germ theory, is said to have recanted on his death bed, famously acknowledging that healthy, biodiverse environments are more important than eliminating germs in maintaining good health.

This loss of microbial diversity extends to our food and soil. Decades of industrial agriculture have depleted the earth's nutrients through the use of pesticides and intensive mono-cropping. Since the early 1900s, about 75 per cent of plant genetic diversity has been lost. Today, just three crops – rice, wheat, and maize – account for 60 per cent of global calories.[19]

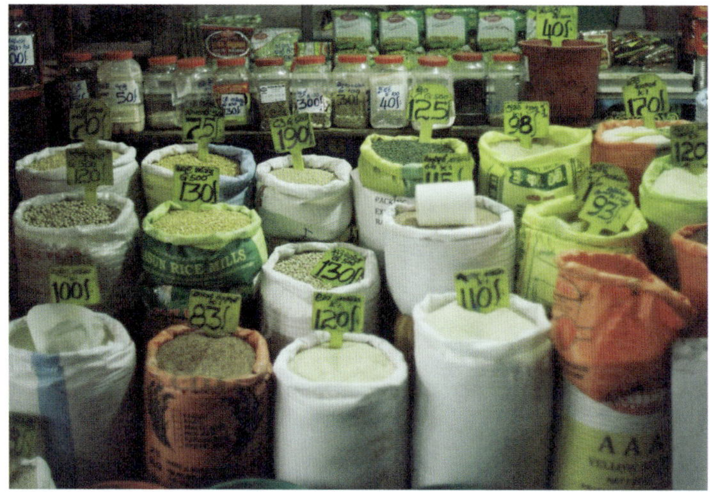

Three crops – rice, wheat, and maize – supply 60 per cent of global calories, and overall nutrient density has declined. In many regions outside the Western world, traditional diets still include a wide variety of grains and legumes, such as those seen in Sri Lanka.

Wild foods, on the other hand, retain their ancestral genetic makeup, nutrient complexity, and microbial richness. Botanist Wolfgang Stuppy, previously of Kew's Millennium Seed Bank, explores wild edible species for their resilience to climate change, specifically drought resistance and rising temperatures.[20] For example, *Avena fatua,* the wild ancestor of oats, resists disease better than its modern counterpart.[21] Likewise, Einkorn wheat, the earliest cultivated wheat, contains less of the problematic gluten found in today's heavily hybridised varieties – gluten that some scientists believe is harming our guts.[22] These wild species may hold the key to future food security.

Archaeological records indicate that when humans transitioned from a nomadic lifestyle to farming around 10,000 BCE, both dietary and gut microbial diversity sharply declined. Intrigued by this shift, professional forager and nutritionist Mo Wilde and fellow forager Matt Rooney launched a bold experiment: eat old wild food for a year, drawn entirely from the British Isles.[23]

Their wild menu of over 400 species included game, fish, mushrooms, berries, legumes, grains, roots, nuts, seaweeds, and weeds. Every three months, they tracked their gut microbiota, weight, and health markers. The experiment yielded outstanding results. Mo lost 31kg (68lbs) – weight she swore she could never shake – had improved gut microbiome responsiveness, and returned to a healthy BMI. Matt reversed his Type 2 diabetes in just ten days.[24] Their experiment inspired multiple iterations of the Wildbiome Project, a citizen science initiative now involving 120 people, including me.

We meticulously logged our wild meals using a food-tracking app, wore blood sugar monitors, and submitted stool samples, blood, body measurements, hair, and nails for testing. Each of us repeated these tests every month during the three-month programme, which ran from April to June 2025.

The 2023 Wildbiome study, supported in part by Professor Tim Spector and the nutrition science company ZOE, included 24 volunteers. Half ate wild food for one month, the other half for three. ZOE developed a unique "Microbiome (MB) score" to assess the balance between beneficial and harmful bacteria, found to be a better health predictor than diversity alone.

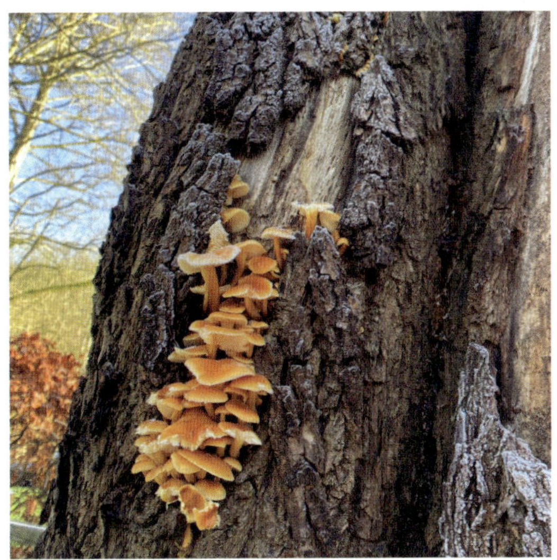

Velvet Shanks, Flammulina velutipes, *are one of the few mushrooms that can withstand frost, offering a reliable food source throughout winter.*

At the start of the Wildbiome challenge, the average MB score for wild food eaters was 52. After three months, it rose to 65. In contrast, the control group eating store-bought food hovered at 52. Of the 24 original participants, 16 were overweight or obese. By the end, all but one had lost weight. Ten people began with normal blood pressure; by the end of the study, that number doubled. While these results are impressive, they only raise further questions about how place, environment, ancestry, and diet shape our indigenous microbiomes and what a different microbiome might mean for us.

North American and European studies typically identify around 1,000 microbial species in the human gut. But this represents a narrow slice of global variation. It's estimated that over 2,000 species remain unclassified, especially among populations in East Africa and South America. Western microbiomes – shaped by diet, antibiotics, and environment – are often used as the default standard, but this risks overlooking essential microbial differences tied to heritage, geography, and lifestyle. While the Wildbiome Project version II expanded sixfold and spanned Europe and the Americas, there is still room for more inclusive microbiome research that reflects the diversity of global populations.

Still, I was keen to help us learn more and see whether eating wild would sort out my long-persisting gut issues. To prepare, I brushed up on my foraging skills and started gathering food in late November, when several berries, nuts, mushrooms, and weeds were still abundant. Later in the season, while I foraged for trumpet chanterelles, walnuts, and hairy bittercress, I wondered how far I'd go for protein: deer, boar, rabbits, fish, birds, or even insects? In the end, I expanded my diet to include all of them – not just out of curiosity, but because I had to. I was told in advance, "If you've got protein, you won't go hungry. After that, it's up to you to get creative."

Adopting a wild food diet demanded more than just creativity in the kitchen; it required total adaptability. When nature provided in abundance, I had to act fast, preserving everything I could. I smoked, dried, salted, fermented, froze, and pickled my finds – not only to prevent waste but to bring

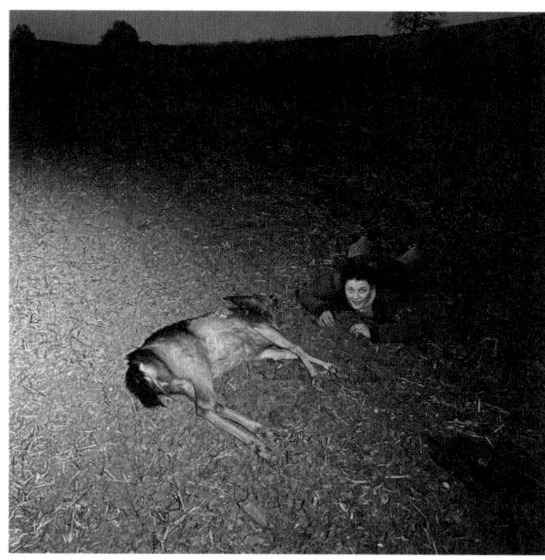

With my brother's guidance, I shot and butchered this deer. She became the foundation of my wild diet, and I made sure to use every part – from nose to tail – as a way of honouring the life I took. For the first time, I truly felt part of the food chain, and that reality was not always easy.

out the layered textures and flavours unique to wild foods. Some weeks were especially plentiful, like when I had to eat deer . . . for an entire week. Determined not to waste a morsel, I ate or used every part: nose to tail. So in truth, it stretched the whole three months, just long enough to sit with the emotional weight of killing a wild animal.

Foraging this way made me hyper-aware of time. In the most obvious way, I became guided by the seasons as available foods shifted with the sun and the earth. Winter roots gave way to spring shoots, and in summer, berries and blossoms burst forth. I practised delayed gratification daily. I'd spot the early signs of a tender Chicken of the Woods, but wait days for the perfect moment to harvest – always hoping no one got there first. Making something as basic as acorn flour was a laborious, multi-day ritual. Every task was a lesson in patience.

Nature began to shape my routine: foraging by day, preserving at dusk, hunting at dawn or night. I paid attention to the wind's direction and the moonlight. I looked for rabbits and listened for the calls of pigeons. I felt, in some strange way, like an insect whose antenna had suddenly come to life.

In just three months, I changed. I spent most of my time outdoors, hands in the soil, climbing trees for catkins, throwing traps into rivers, tracking animals through cold woodlands. My sensory awareness grew: the sweetness of wild carrots, the eye-watering heat of horseradish, the transformative effect of frost on flavour. My body became loud, thanking me with a generous "mmmm" for every salty sea beet leaf. I discovered that 12 willow buds contain the equivalent of an aspirin, and that guelder-rose really does help with period pain. At one point, I even gave up traditional soaps in favour of alternatives derived from plants and wild boar to support my skin microbiome – until my sister staged an intervention.

My relationship with nature shifted from pleasure to dependence. The natural world became my pantry, my pharmacy, my teacher. For the first time, I realised I was within the food chain. Flowers were for me, but also for the bees and the beetles. I couldn't take them all. I didn't want to take them all.

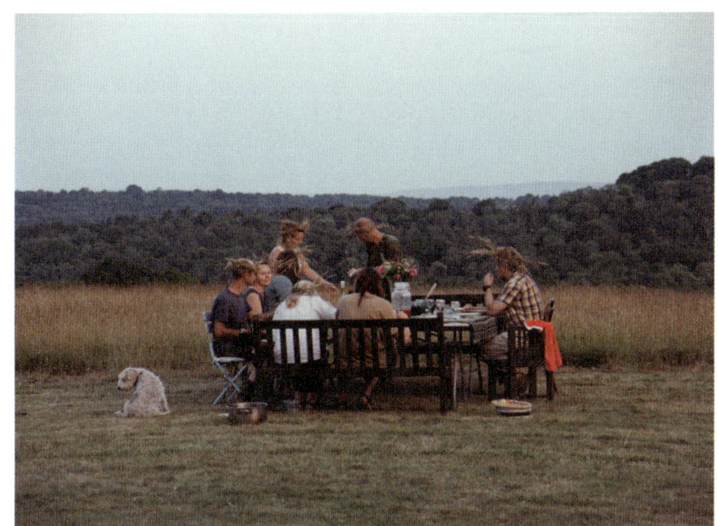

Wildbiome Summer Solstice Gathering. Every couple of weeks, Wildbiome participants gathered to forage, prepare, cook, and feast together. These gatherings grounded us and reminded us why we were doing this: to reconnect with the earth, our food, our medicine, and one another.

I printed off Robin Wall Kimmerer's *Honorable Harvest* and read it daily.[25] It begins:

> *Know the ways of the ones who take care of you, so that you may take care of them.*
> *Introduce yourself. Be accountable as the one who comes asking for life.*
> *Ask permission before taking. Abide by the answer.*
> *Never take the first. Never take the last.*

I was enmeshed within relationships of accountability and responsibility, so I gave thanks. Daily.

As the weeks passed, a few threads began to spiral outwards from this experience: access to healthy food, location, and the value of community. A harsh truth emerged early on: Much of Britain's wild food is polluted. I began the project in Bristol, but the more I foraged, the less I wanted to eat this food. I was picking Jelly Ear mushrooms near sewage pipes, razor clams from murky estuaries, and three-cornered leeks from busy roadsides. Rivers and their fish were off limits – too contaminated – and legally, I couldn't dig up roots without a landowner's permission.

Eventually, I moved back home to West Sussex in southern England, expecting the countryside to offer cleaner, healthier food. I was wrong. I quickly learned that in modern agriculture, "clean" often means heavily sprayed with chemicals – an invisible hazard that was hard to escape.

Living inland, I relied on what was available: common hogweed, wild garlic, spring mushrooms, and local game like deer, rabbits, and pigeons. Had I been by the coast, my diet would have looked very different, rich in sea beets, samphire, wild kale, fish, and shellfish. To fill the nutritional gaps, I travelled to the coast every ten days or so to harvest fresh greens from clifftops and public footpaths, and seaweeds from the ocean's generous bounty.

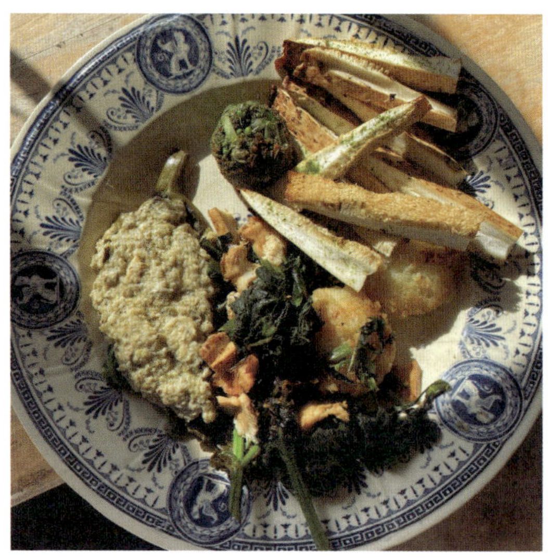

A typical Wildbiome lunch: blanched nettles and sea beet leaves, grilled dryad's saddle mushrooms, alexander-root patties, fermented greens, nettle, hazelnut, and venison protein balls, and as always, a little bit of grey-brown mush (repurposed mushroom soup . . . !)

The impact of location on diet led us to revive non-monetary systems of trade and support. This was important. Our goal wasn't self-sufficiency and detachment from food systems, but reconnection – reviving ancient forms of exchange, trading game for fish, mushrooms for berries, or chestnuts for acorns. Some trades crossed borders – a friend in Scotland swapped hazelnuts for reindeer fat from Norway.

But these networks became more than just practical. Every couple of weeks, Wildbiome participants gathered to forage, prepare, cook, and feast. We'd clean barrels of alexander roots together, share stories, laugh, and cry – often over unbelievably delicious wild pemmican (a traditional, long-lasting mix of dried meat and fat, sometimes with berries). Eating wild can be isolating; few people live off foraged food, and meals are supposed to be social. It was easy to feel like we were slipping out of modern society; we certainly stepped outside of the food system. These gatherings grounded us. They reminded us why we were doing this.

As Fergus the Forager once said, "Eating wild can connect us to nature, the changing seasons, and our immediate surroundings. But it is impoverished if it does not connect us to each other." Our meet-ups made that connection real.

To help deepen my foraging practice, I established a solid web of mentors, many of whom are close friends, each with unique skills. Every so often, I received gifts: bouquets of nettles, baskets of blewit mushrooms, and spears of fresh fish, which were kind – but strange!

Nutritionist Elena Yates taught me the medicinal uses of wild plants as we roamed Bristol's woodland in search of yarrow and ribwort plantain. Tom Carter, a skilled hunter, took me out during calm nights under the stars, using an infrared torch to hunt various game. Joey, my partner, provided unwavering love and support, joining me on weekend foraging trips and helping me find even the most inconspicuous mushrooms. Mark Hubbard, who works at a local farm, taught me how to butcher meat – a surreal but necessary shift for someone who had long been a vegetarian. The list of those who helped me goes on.

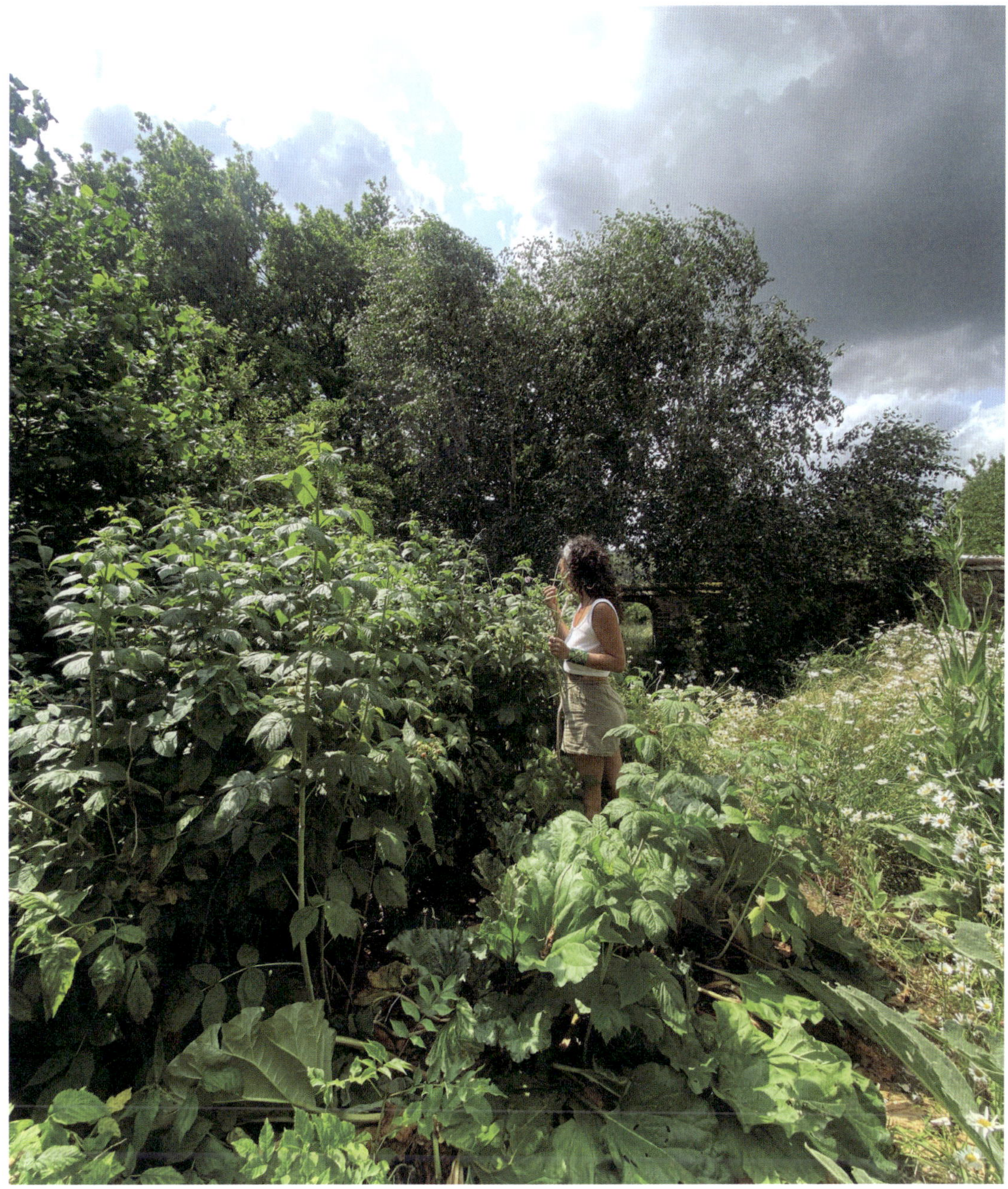

Juju Maschietto foraging from the wild walled garden at the peak of summer.

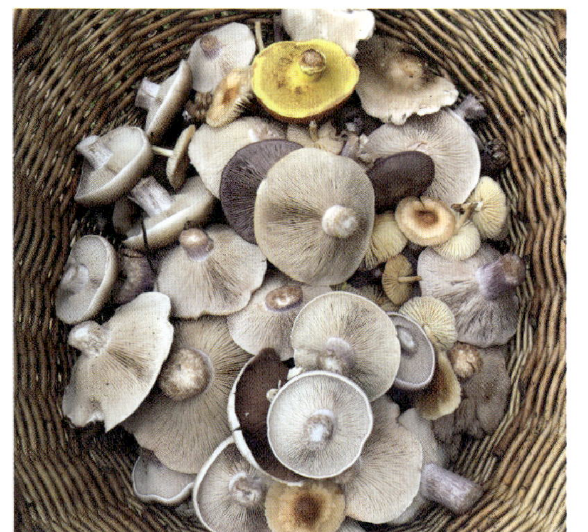

Wild foraged basket with Field Blewits, Collybia personata*; Wood Blewits,* Collybia nuda*; Field Mushrooms,* Agaricus campestris*; and a single bolete.*

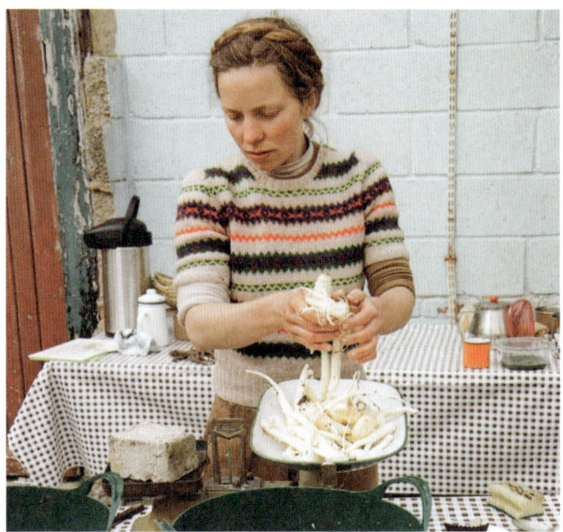

Hetty, weighing out portions of alexander roots we had foraged that morning. She uses half a brick as her measuring tool.

Before my challenge began, Mark and I butchered a deer together. To our surprise, it wasn't as wild as we had imagined. We found undigested cultivated wheat and corn inside her stomach. So, we wondered, what is wild?! Is it even possible to find truly wild food? The more I discussed this with others, the blurrier the concept became. "Wild" could mean uncultivated, uninhabited, inhospitable, untamed. It is anything and everything free from human influence. But few places on Earth meet that definition anymore.

Oddly, the richest "wild" foraging grounds are often places touched by human activity (or disturbance): hedgerows, roadsides, playgrounds, old gardens. These "edges" are where wild species thrive. Many so-called wild species, like nettles and chestnuts, were once planted, introduced by the Romans or later settlers. Feral plants, once cultivated, have since become untamed, as seen with Japanese knotweed or crab apples. Complicating things further, foragers practise "guerrilla gardening", intentionally allowing seeds and spores to fall from their baskets, encouraging future growth – in some places, like Trentino, Italy, using a perforated basket to spread spores is required by law. Do these count as wild? And what about my brother's wild, walled garden: untouched for years and abundant with wild food? Most raspberries grow inside the dilapidated raised beds, but some fall outside. Are these the only ones I'm allowed? Ultimately, wildness exists on a spectrum; it's subjective and was left to the forager's better judgement.

As I dug, picked, and pulled from the earth each day, the significance of soil became impossible to ignore. Soil isn't just dirt. It's a dynamic mix of biology and geology, rich with bacteria, fungi, archaea, protists, and viruses. Its microbiome directly impacts what grows, how we digest food, and even how we breathe.

I learned about the aerobiome – the invisible microbial community floating in the air. When rain hits a pavement, particles rise, releasing that earthy smell we call petrichor. Much of it originates

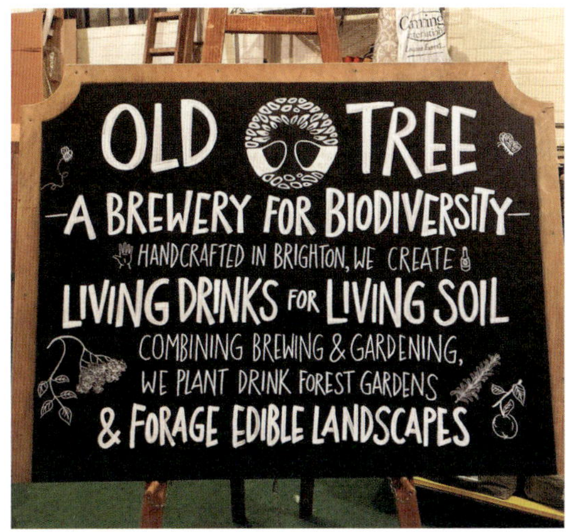

Old Tree: A Brewery for Biodiversity.

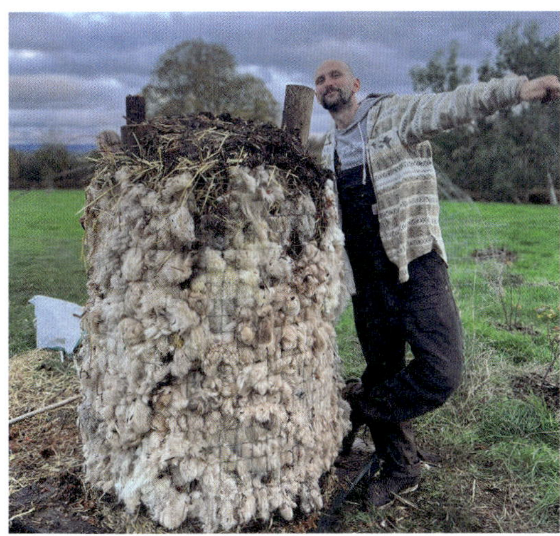

Old Tree Tom at Three Pools Permaculture Farm with his make-shift Johnson Su fungi-dominant bioreactor.

from the soil. These microbes have antimicrobial properties that help protect us, whether in or out of the soil.[26]

The soil also affects the skin microbiome of the foods we eat. No matter how thoroughly we scrub, every root and shoot carries the soil's microbial imprint straight into our guts. Soil, in many ways, is the original probiotic.

Elena had a more flexible interpretation of what I meant by "soil". On one walk together, her dog Jasper happily ate a lump of sheep dung. She shrugged. Cow and sheep manure, she explained, help condition the soil, suppressing harmful microbes and seeding healthy ones. That benefit extends to Jasper's gut. In fact, many primates eat faeces for similar microbial reasons. While humans and higher primates evolved to avoid it due to disease risk, modern medicine is circling back. The growing demand for Faecal Microbiota Transplants (FMTs), where stool from a healthy donor is transplanted into a patient's gut to repopulate their microbiome with healthy, diverse microbes, reflects this ancient microbial logic. Given that FMTs are being explored for inflammatory bowel conditions, metabolic issues, and even neurological disorders like autism, Parkinson's, multiple sclerosis, and bipolar disorder,[27] evidently, one person's healthy brain function may, quite literally, begin in another's well-balanced gut.

This idea – that microbes shape us from the inside out – extends far beyond medicine. It's also at the heart of how we grow food, ferment drinks, and steward ecosystems. Old Tree Brewery, my wild mead suppliers, beautifully illustrates this. Founded by Old Tree Tom, the brewery sees fermentation as a form of ecological alchemy. They craft live kombucha from wild herbs and brew "soil teas" – living compost infusions rich in native microbes that rejuvenate ecosystems.

Old Tree's kombucha is delicious, but it's also alive, shaped by its microbial environment. When the brewery relocated from a Brighton basement to a new site in Lewes, their brews began to fail.

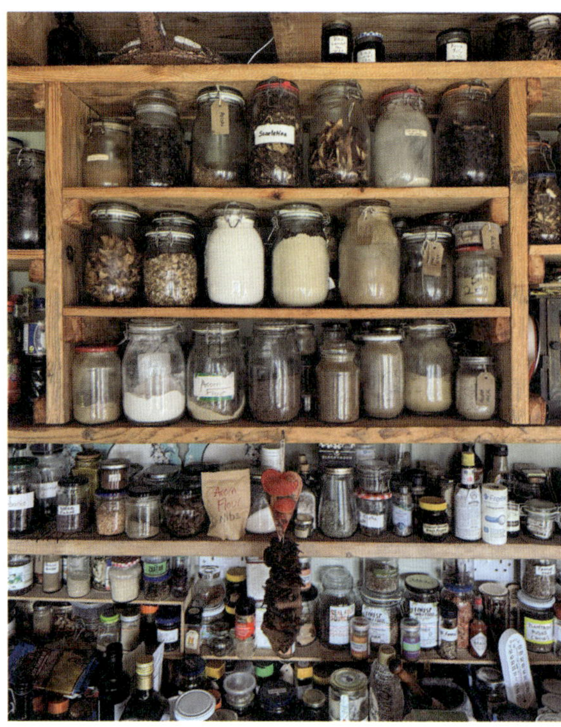

Mo Wilde's Wild Spice Cabinet, 2020.

The culprit? Airborne bakery yeasts from the neighbouring business. It took four months for the cultures to adapt and thrive again – a powerful lesson in how local microbiomes influence everything.

Their soil teas are made from fungal-dominant compost using a Johnson-Su Bioreactor, fed with twigs, leaves, and organic carbon. This system mimics the forest floor, encouraging slow and low-maintenance fungal growth. A single thimbleful of compost tea, when diluted and sprayed, nourishes soil like a probiotic smoothie.

These teas combat antibiotic-resistant bacteria, prevent plant diseases like blight, and promote underground fungal networks that enhance plant resilience. Old Tree treats soil like a human gut: complex, dynamic, and dependent on beneficial microbes. It's a holistic, ecological vision – fermentation not just as food, but as medicine for the planet.

Old Tree's vision – and the Wildbiome community's ethos – champions a future where soil, microbes, and people thrive together. They call it the "archaic fermentation revival". I call it [environ]mental health: the profound, reciprocal relationship between ecological and human well-being.

Together, we are crafting a new kind of ecosystem, one that's not bound by geography or profession. We forage wild food, we compost, we trade. We spray fermented teas onto the land to keep our microbial "old friends" alive. In doing so, we're rediscovering something ancient yet urgently needed: what we feed the earth ultimately feeds us.

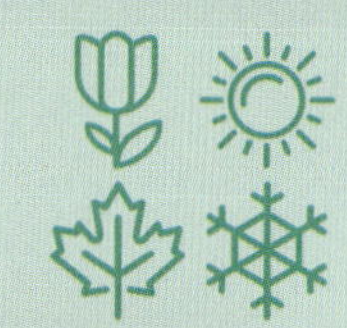

RECIPE

WILD SPICE RACK

In *The Wilderness Cure*, Mo Wilde writes that the single most impactful thing you can do for long-term health is to eat more herbs, especially wild ones. Throughout history, humans have gone to extreme, and often unethical, lengths to source rare spices and exotic flavours. Yet many forget that we all have access to a rich palette of native herbs and spices, wild ingredients that once filled our ancestors' spice racks.[28,29]

In the UK alone, the wild landscape offers horseradish, mustard, garlic, sumac, bay, rosemary, and, of course, sea salt. Local plants provide not only delicious flavour but also deep cultural and ecological connection.

The Wildbiome Community taught me everything I know about flavour. Here's a glimpse of my own Wild Spice Rack, a collection of native substitutes for common kitchen spices:

- **Salt:** Sea salt
- **Pepper:** Alexanders seeds or pepper dulse
- **Garlic:** Wild garlic (grind and mix with salt for wild garlic salt, it's amazing)
- **Mustard:** Garlic mustard seeds
- **Paprika/Citrus:** Staghorn sumac seeds
- **Allspice/Bitter orange:** Common hogweed seeds
- **Wasabi:** Scurvygrass
- **Clove:** Wood avens roots
- **Chilli:** Water pepper seed
- **Ginger/Clove:** Magnolia petals
- **Almond:** Cherry blossom
- **Spice blend:** Powdered ruffle lichen, *Parmotrema perlatum*, still used in garam masala today
- **Saffron:** Saffron Milkcap mushroom

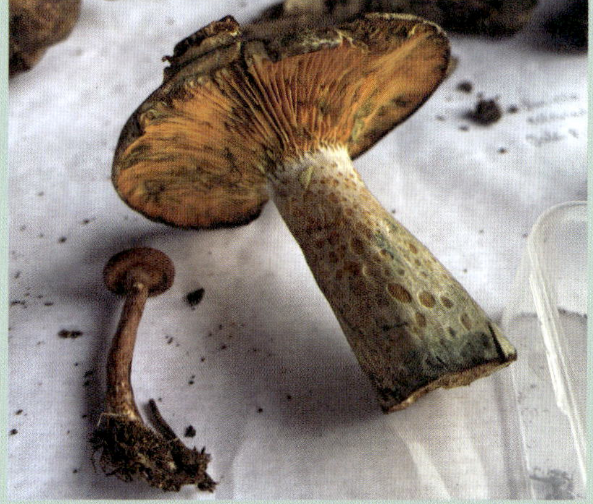

Saffron Milkcap, Lactarius deliciosus. *Among mushrooms, the Milkcaps are perhaps the most generous in flavour variety, with the Curry, Coconut, Peppery, and Saffron Milkcaps each contributing to a dynamic wild pantry.*

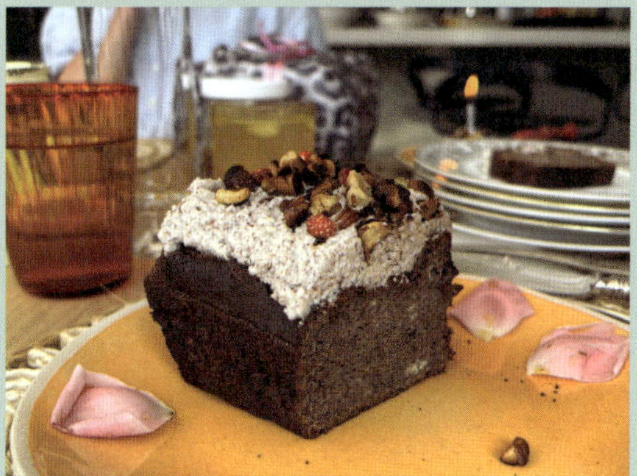

Wild birthday cake! Made with acorn flour, chestnut flour, catkin flour, deer tallow, hazelnut oil, duck eggs, honey, dried rose hips, wild sumac, and sea salt. Recipe from Gemma Hindi @earthwildlondon – watch this space!

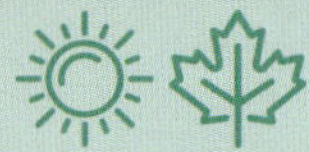

RECIPE

WILD MUSHROOM JERKY

Over my three-month journey, mushrooms proved invaluable. When a mushroom fruits, it often fruits in abundance, making dehydration an ideal method for preserving its flavour. Ground into powders or turned into jerky, they enrich everything from soups and stews to pancakes and biltong.

Mushroom jerky is my favourite: crunchy, nutritious, and the perfect vehicle for showcasing wild herbs and spices. (Bear in mind, taste buds adapt! These flavours can seem very different when you're not on a wild food diet!)

You'll find the marinades under each heading, and the method for all three at the bottom of the opposite page.

EQUIPMENT

- Dehydrator or a well-ventilated warm area
- Grinder (for powders)
- Baking tray
- Airtight container

INGREDIENTS

- 300g/10½oz fresh mushrooms
- Base Marinade (for all varieties):
  - 10ml apple cider vinegar
  - Pinch sea salt
  - Large pinch alexanders seeds
  - 7.5ml hazelnut oil or tallow
  - Optional: 1 tsp fermented honey water

SAFFRON MILKCAP JERKY

Source: *Lactarius deliciosus* (found in pine forests, late summer-autumn).

MARINADE ADDITIONS

- 1½ tsp ground and dried wild rosemary
- 2 stalks dried mugwort, 1½ tsp juniper berries, or a splash of dry gin
- 1½ tsp ground water pepper leaves or seeds
- 1½ tsp pine needle ash or 1 tsp infusion
- 3 tsp birch or maple syrup
- **Flavour:** fruity, piney, nutty-spicy, resinous

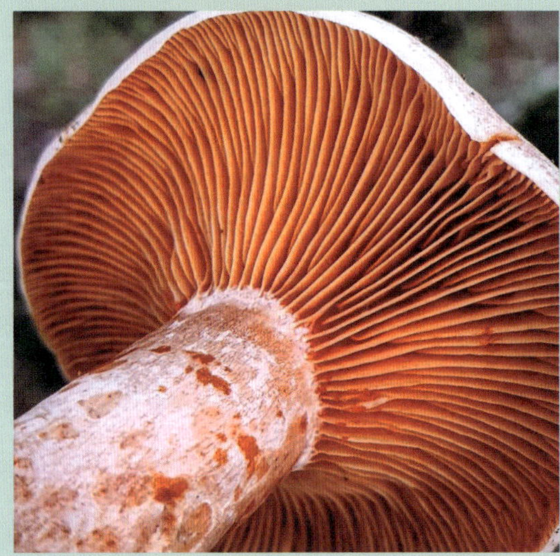

Saffron Milkcap.

DRYAD'S SADDLE JERKY

Source: *Polyporus squamosus* (early spring, on decaying hardwood)

MARINADE ADDITIONS

- ½ tsp black mustard seeds
- 2 pinches pepper dulse
- 1½ tbsp dried fennel fronds
- 2 bay leaves
- 2 dried cow parsley heads
- 1 tsp dried horseradish root or leaf
- **Flavour:** nutty, mild, cucumbery when fresh; meaty when dried
- **Note:** Use young mushrooms for the best texture.

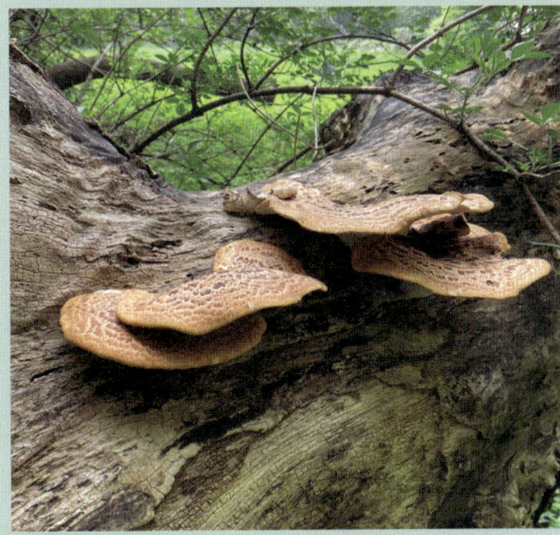

Dryad's Saddle.

MAITAKE JERKY

Source: *Grifola frondosa* (found at the base of old oaks and sometimes beech trees.)

MARINADE ADDITIONS

- ½ tsp wild thyme
- ½ tsp hawthorn berry vinegar
- ½ tsp mustard seeds
- **Optional:** a pinch of water pepper
- **Flavour:** deeply umami, rich, meaty

METHOD FOR ALL

1. Slice the mushrooms to ½cm/¼in-thick or tear into petals.
2. Roast lightly (12 minutes; ~20 for Dryad's Saddle).
3. Blend the marinade ingredients into a paste.
4. Massage into mushrooms; marinate for approx. 8–12 hours.
5. Dehydrate until cracker dry.
6. Store in an airtight container for up to a month.

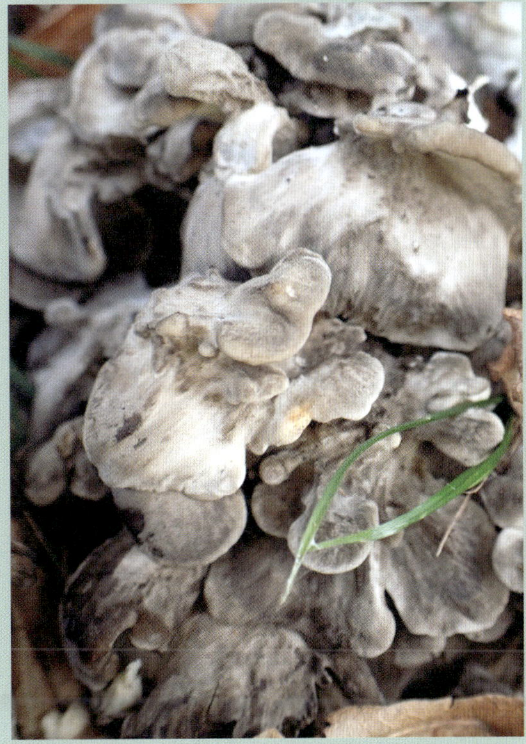

Maitake.

LIST OF WILD FOODS

FUNGI

Amethyst Deceiver, *Laccaria amethystina*
Artist's Bracket, *Ganoderma applanatum*
Beefsteak, *Fistulina hepatica*
Birch Polypore, *Fomitopsis betulina*
Coconut Scented Milkcap, *Lactarius glyciosmus*
Curry Milkcap, *Lactarius camphoratus*
Dryad's Saddle, *Cerioporus squamosus*
Giant Puffball, *Calvatia gigantea*
Golden Chanterelles, *Cantharellus cibarius*
Hedgehog, *Hydnum repandum*
Honey Fungus, *Armillaria* spp.
Horn of Plenty, *Craterellus cornucopioides*
Jelly Ear, *Auricularia auricula-judae*
Lion's Mane, *Hericium erinaceus*
Maitake, *Grifola frondosa*
Mousseron, *Marasmius oreades*
Oyster Mushroom, *Pleurotus ostreatus*
Peppery Bolete, *Chalciporus piperatus*
Peppery Milkcap, *Lactarius piperatus*
Porcini, *Boletus edulis*
Saffron Milkcap, *Lactarius deliciosus*
Scarlet Elf Cup, *Sarcoscypha coccinea*
Shaggy Parasol, *Chlorophyllum rhacodes*
St George's Mushroom, *Calocybe gambosa*
Summer Truffle, *Tuber aestivum*
True Parasol, *Macrolepiota procera*
Tuberous Polypore, *Polyporus tuberaster*
Turkey Tail, *Trametes versicolor*
Velvet Shank, *Flammulina velutipes*
Winter Chanterelle, *Craterellus tubaeformis*
Witches' Butter, *Tremella mesenterica*
Wood Blewits, *Clitocybe nuda* (also *Lepista nuda*)

PLANTS

Alexanders, *Smyrnium olusatrum*
Apple Mint, *Mentha suaveolens*
Ash, *Fraxinus excelsior*
Beach Rose, *Rosa rugosa*
Beech, *Fagus sylvatica*
Bitter Dock, *Rumex obtusifolius*
Black Mustard, *Rhamphospermum nigrum*
Blackthorn, *Prunus spinosa*
Bracken Fern, *Pteridium aquilinum*
Cherry, *Prunus avium*
Cleavers, *Galium aparine*
Common Borage, *Borago officinalis*
Common Burdock, *Arctium minus*
Common Duckweed, *Lemna minor*
Common Hawthorn, *Crataegus monogyna*
Common Hogweed, *Heracleum sphondylium*
Common Lime, *Tilia × europaea*
Common Plum, *Prunus domestica*
Common Sorrel, *Rumex acetosa*
Common Thistle, *Cirsium vulgare*
Cow Parsley, *Anthriscus sylvestris*
Cowslip, *Primula veris*
Crab Apples, *Malus sylvestris*
Dandelion, *Taraxacum officinale*
Elder, *Sambucus nigra*
European Larch, *Larix decidua*
Fennel, *Foeniculum vulgare*
Feral Rhubarb, *Rheum × hybridum*
Field Elm, *Ulmus minor* (seed from)
Fool's Watercress, *Apium nodiflorum*
Garlic Mustard, *Alliaria petiolata*
Golden Saxifrage, *Chrysosplenium* spp.
Goosegrass, *Galium aparine* (alias)
Gorse, *Ulex europaeus*
Great Reed Mace (Cattail), *Typha latifolia*
Great Yellow Cress, *Rorippa amphibia*
Greater Stitchwort, *Stellaria holostea*
Ground Ivy, *Glechoma hederacea*
Ground Elder, Aegopodium podagraria

Guelder-rose, Viburnum opulus
Hairy Bittercress, *Cardamine hirsuta*
Hazel, *Corylus avellana*
Hedge Mustard, *Sisymbrium officinale*
Herb Robert, *Geranium robertianum*
Himalayan Balsam, *Impatiens glandulifera*
Hops, *Humulus lupulus*
Japanese Flowering Cherry, *Prunus serrulata*
Lady's Mantle, *Alchemilla vulgaris*
Leatherleaf Mahonia, *Mahonia bealei*
Lemon Balm, *Melissa officinalis*
Lesser Calamint, *Calamintha nepeta*
Lesser Celandine, *Ficaria verna*
Lesser Knapweed, *Centaurea nigra*
Lilac, *Syringa vulgaris*
Magnolia, *Magnolia* spp.
Marsh Pennywort, *Hydrocotyle vulgaris*
Marsh Samphire, *Salicornia europaea*
Marshmallow, *Althaea officinalis*
Milk Thistle, *Silybum marianum*
Mugwort, *Artemisia vulgaris*
Nettle, *Urtica dioica*
Navelwort, *Umbilicus rupestris*
Orache, *Atriplex* spp.
Orange Daylily, *Hemerocallis fulva*
Oxeye Daisy, *Leucanthemum vulgare*
Pendulous Sedge, *Carex pendula*
Peppermint, *Mentha × piperita*
Pine Needles, *Pinus* spp.
Prickly Pear, *Opuntia ficus-indica*
Primrose, *Primula vulgaris*
Purple Dead Nettle, *Lamium purpureum*
Red Campion, *Silene dioica*
Red Clover, *Trifolium pratense*
Red Dead Nettle, *Lamium purpureum*
Ribwort Plantain, *Plantago lanceolata*
Rock Samphire, *Crithmum maritimum*
Rose, *Rosa* spp.
Rosemary, *Salvia rosmarinus*
Rowan, *Sorbus aucuparia*
Saffron, *Crocus sativus*
Scots Pine, *Pinus sylvestris*
Sea Beet, *Beta vulgaris* subsp. *maritima*
Sea Blite, *Suaeda maritima*
Sea Cabbage, *Brassica oleracea* var. *oleracea*
Sea Kale, *Crambe maritima*
Sea Leeks, *Allium ampeloprasum* var. *porrum*
Sea Purslane, *Atriplex portulacoides*
Sea Rocket, *Cakile maritima*
Sea Samphire, *Salicornia* spp.
Sea Sandwort, *Honckenya peploides*
Shepherd's Purse, *Capsella bursa-pastoris*
Silver Birch, *Betula pendula*
Smooth Golden Fleece, *Urospermum dalechampii*
Sowthistle, *Sonchus* spp.
Spear Thistle, *Cirsium vulgare*
Spoon-leaved Scurvy Grass, *Cochlearia officinalis*
Staghorn Sumac, *Rhus typhina*
Staghorn Plantain, *Plantago coronopus*
Sweet Vernal Grass, *Anthoxanthum odoratum*
Three-cornered Leek, *Allium triquetrum*
Tree Mallow, *Lavatera arborea*
Valerian, *Valeriana officinalis*
Water Pepper, *Persicaria hydropiper*
Watercress, *Nasturtium officinale*
Water Mint, *Mentha aquatica*
Wild/Feral Apple, *Malus sylvestris*
Wild Celery, *Apium graveolens*
Wild Chives, *Allium schoenoprasum*
Wild Garlic, *Allium ursinum*
Wild Mustard, *Sinapis arvensis*
Wild Parsnip, *Pastinaca sativa*
Wild Radish, *Raphanus raphanistrum*
Wild Sage, *Salvia verbenacea*
Wild Thyme, *Thymus serpyllum*
Willow, *Salix* spp.
White Clover, *Trifolium repens*
White Dead Nettle, *Lamium album*
White Mustard, *Sinapis alba*
Wood Avens, *Geum urbanum*
Wood Sorrel, *Oxalis acetosella*
Yellow Archangel, *Lamium galeobdolon*
Yellow Rocket, *Barbarea vulgaris*

BERRIES

Bilberry, *Vaccinium myrtillus*
Blackberry, *Rubus fruticosus*
Cherry Plum, *Prunus cerasifera*
Damson, *Prunus domestica* subsp. *insititia*
Elderberry, *Sambucus nigra*
Gooseberry, *Ribes uva-crispa*
Haw, *Crataegus monogyna*
Juniper, *Juniperus communis*
Mulberry, *Morus* spp. (commonly *Morus nigra* or *Morus alba*)
Raspberry, *Rubus idaeus*
Rose Hip, *Rosa* spp.
Rowan, *Sorbus aucuparia*
Sea Buckthorn, *Hippophae rhamnoides*
Sour Cherry, *Prunus cerasus*
Strawberry, *Fragaria vesca* (wild), *Fragaria × ananassa* (cultivated)
Wild Cherry, *Prunus avium*

TREE SAPS & RESINS

Birch sap, *Betula* spp.
Pine resin, *Pinus* spp.
Spruce resin, *Picea* spp.
Sycamore sap, *Acer pseudoplatanus*

SEEDS

Acorns, *Quercus* spp.
Alexanders, *Smyrnium olusatrum*
Bitter Dock, *Rumex obtusifolius*
Black Mustard, *Brassica nigra*
Common Hogweed, *Heracleum sphondylium*
Curly Dock, *Rumex crispus*
Lesser Knapweed, *Centaurea nigra*
Scot's Lovage, *Ligusticum scoticum*
Spignel, *Meum athamanticum*
Sunflower Seeds, *Helianthus annuus*

NUTS

Beech, *Fagus sylvatica*
Cobb (Cobnut – a type of cultivated hazel), *Corylus avellana*
Hazel, *Corylus avellana*
Monterey Pine, *Pinus radiata*
Stone Pine, *Pinus pinea*
Walnut, *Juglans regia*
Hazelnut Milk, (from *Corylus avellana*)
Hazelnut Oil, (from *Corylus avellana*)

MEAT

Boar, *Sus scrofa*
Muntjac Deer, *Muntiacus reevesi*
Pheasant, *Phasianus colchicus*
Rabbit, *Oryctolagus cuniculus*
Roe Deer, *Capreolus capreolus*
Canada Goose, *Branta canadensis*
Mallard Duck, *Anas platyrhynchos*
Wood Pigeon, *Columba palumbus*

INSECTS

Aphids, *Aphidoidea*
Carpenter Ants, *Camponotus* spp.
Common Snails, *Cornu aspersum*
Ermine Moths, *Yponomeutidae*
Grasshoppers, *Caelifera*
Miscellaneous (Maggots, *Diptera;* Beetles, *Coleoptera*; Caterpillars, *Lepidoptera*)
Wasps, *Vespidae*

FISH

Brown Trout, *Salmo trutta*
Gurnard, *Chelidonichthys* spp.
Mackerel, *Scomber scombrus*
Rainbow Trout, *Oncorhynchus mykiss*
Sardines, *Sardina pilchardus*
Sea Bass, *Dicentrarchus labrax*
Skate, *Raja* spp.
Smooth Hound, *Mustelus mustelus*

SEA CREATURES

Limpet, *Patella vulgata*

Mussels, *Mytilus edulis*

Octopus, *Octopus vulgaris*

Oysters, *Ostrea edulis*

Razor Clams, *Ensis* spp.

Scallops, *Pecten maximus*

Winkles, *Littorina littorea*

MICROBES/FERMENTS

Elderflower Wine

Koji, *Aspergillus oryzae*

Kombucha

Lilac Wine

Mead

Neurospora, *Neurospora crassa*

SCOBY

Vinegar (Raw, Plum, Apple Cider)

Walnut Wine

SEAWEEDS

Bladderwrack, *Fucus vesiculosus*

Bootlace (Sea Spaghetti), *Himanthalia elongata*

Carragheen (Irish Moss), *Chondrus crispus*

Dulse, *Palmaria palmata*

Toothed Wrack, *Fucus serratus*

Green Algae (Sea Lettuce), *Ulva lactuca*

Kelp (Oarweed), *Laminaria digitata*

Laver, *Porphyra* spp.

Pepper Dulse, *Osmundea pinnatifida*

Red Hornweed, *Ceramium virgatum*

Sargassum, *Sargassum* spp.

Sea Spaghetti, *Himanthalia elongata*

Serrated Wrack, *Fucus serratus*

Soldier's Red String Weed, *Solieria chordatls*

Spiral Wrack, *Fucus spiralis*

Sugar Kelp (Oarweed), *Saccharina latissima*

Wakame, *Undaria pinnatifida*

ANIMAL PRODUCTS

Duck Egg, *Anas platyrhynchos* (Mallard Duck)

Goose Egg, *Anser anser* (Domestic Goose)

Hen Egg, *Gallus gallus domesticus*

Honey, *Apis mellifera* (Western Honeybee)

Quail Egg, *Coturnix coturnix*

Tallow (Venison), *Cervus elaphus* (Red Deer)

Tallow (Boar), *Sus scrofa* (Wild Boar)

Tallow (Duck), *Anas platyrhynchos* (Mallard Duck)

Tallow (Goose), *Anser anser* (Domestic Goose)

MISC

Sea Salt

MYCOMATERIALS

Károly rose early for the hunt, slipping into his shoes, grabbing his bag, axe, and taser.[30] The morning air was crisp, the forest calling as it always did. This was no seasonal rite, it was a rhythm lived through every month, passed down through generations. His father, grandfather, and great-grandfather had all walked this path. His axe, now weathered and worn, carried the marks of all their hands.

Together with his dog, Károly crossed the meadow, spotting Field mushrooms in their usual troops but not stopping to harvest. They pressed on, the scent of damp earth growing stronger as they entered the dense forest of Romania's Carpathian Mountains, home to the Tinder fungus, *Fomes fomentarius*.

In Romania, this Polypore fungus grows primarily on mature beech trees. While it's found across the northern hemisphere, only a few select regions yield the highest quality conks. The best are the smaller fruits, harvested year after year from the same trees. In the village of Corund in eastern Transylvania, the craft of harvesting Amadou dates back to at least 1840. The fungus is processed into Amadou, a felt-like material used to craft wallets, accessories, and hats – including Paul Stamets' iconic Amadou cap, handcrafted by Karoly himself. Today, however, Károly is the last in his lineage of Amadou artisans.

After harvesting the mushrooms, Károly returned home and began shaving them into thick slices. He sat outside with his father, smoking and chatting under the warm autumn sun. They placed the shavings into a bath and boiled them overnight before pounding them into the dense, felt-like material that is the hallmark of their craft. It's a slow, meticulous process, but one that reflects a deep understanding of the environment and the properties of the mushroom itself. This is a craft that requires both skill and community – it's labour-intensive, but it's also a way of life.

Károly and his father come from a long lineage of mushroom craftsmen. They were not the first, and we hope they will not be the last.

As word of their craft spread, the world of mycodesign and mycomaterials began to take off. From large biotech firms in the Netherlands, US, and Italy, such as MOGU and Bolt Threads, to community labs like Barcelona's FAB LAB and Guatemala's Fungi Academy, mycomaterials have become a new trend. Universities now have dedicated lab facilities for experimenting with fungi, and I even had the opportunity to work in a studio-come-laboratory on a working mushroom farm, focused on creating fungi-based packaging.

But there's a key difference between modern mycodesign and the Transylvanian craft: while they reshape the mushroom itself, we grow the mycelium.

Mycelium, the vegetative structure of fungi, is a brilliant natural adhesive; it weaves through its substrate and binds materials together in unique and unconventional ways. It can form lightweight, compostable, fire- and water-resistant structures that are both functional and beautiful in a rustic, organic manner. Mycodesigners have used mycelium to create a huge variety of products, from packaging and leather alternatives to insulation and soundproofing. Some have even created kayaks, surfboards, shoes, helmets, and 3D-printed furniture by printing a nutrient scaffold that the fungus grows into, or by using bio-inks that contain live fungal cells. These are not built, but grown.

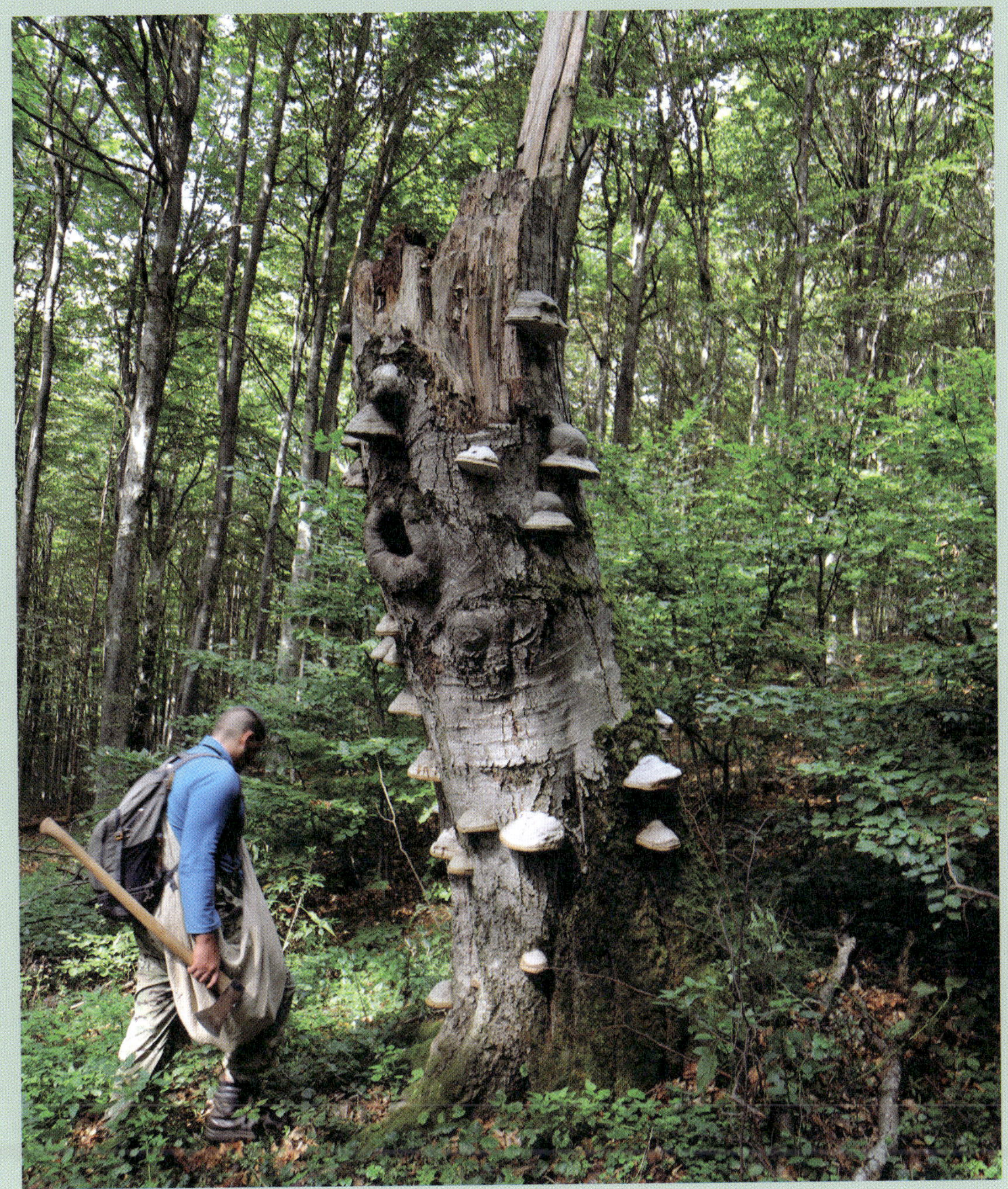

Károly Maté hunting for the Tinder Fungus, Fomes fomentarius, *in eastern Transylvania.*

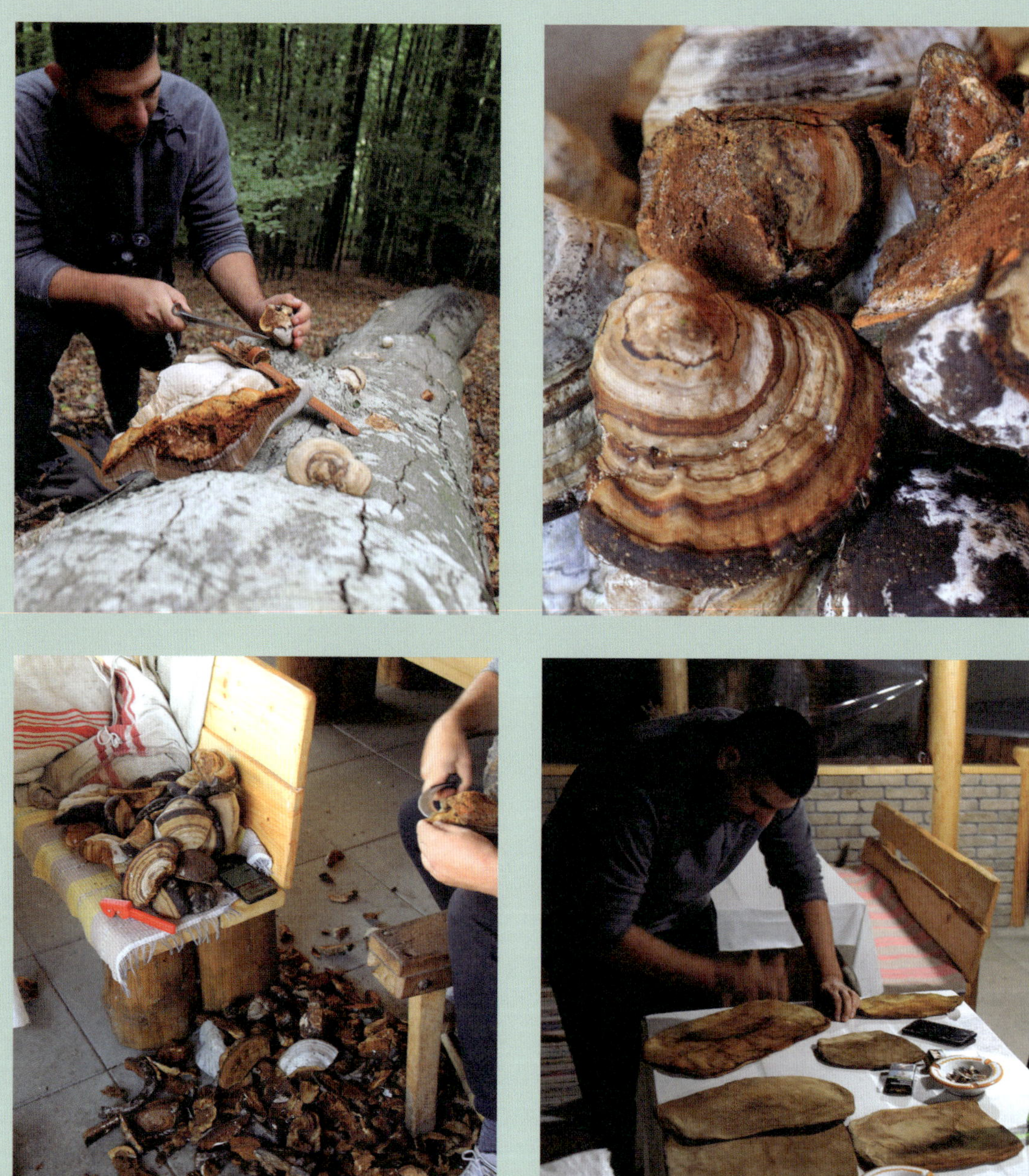

Amadou leather-making sequence: Find, Harvest, Prepare, Process.

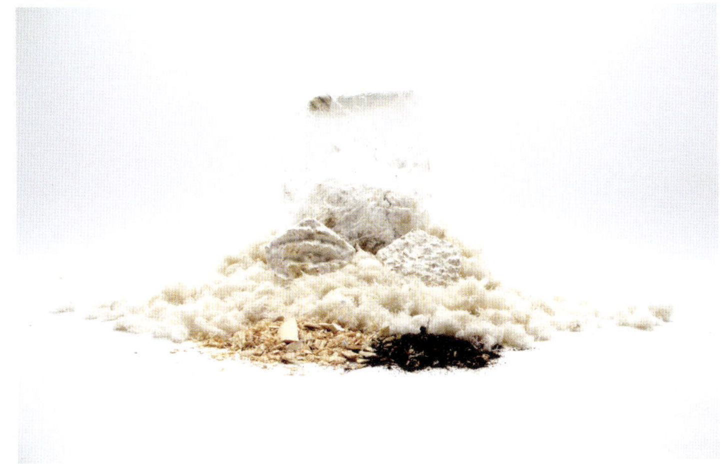

Prototyping mycelium panels grown from local waste streams, including sawdust, coffee grounds, and textile waste.

Because we are working with living organisms, mycodesign is inherently collaborative. This is something I love as an artist – mycelium brings its own touch to the finished product. We can set the stage for it to grow into the shape we envision, but the precise outcome is always a surprise. Mycelium doesn't always cooperate – there's the risk of contamination, strange colouration, or sometimes no growth at all. But that unpredictability is part of the fun.

To work with fungi, one needs patience. But eventually, you develop so-called "farmer's intuition", an embodied understanding that comes only from experience. The smell of the substrate might be off, the material might feel too wet or too dry, or sometimes, everything is just right. Over time, you learn to read the mycelium's needs, and this makes all the difference.

But to begin experimenting, most mycodesigners start with Oyster mushrooms. They are forgiving and thrive on a wide range of materials. In my Biodesign master's programme, my team and I focused on regeneration, so Oysters were our go-to mushroom. We grew mycelium on local waste streams: textile offcuts, coffee grounds, and even pistachio shells. We learned that Oysters thrived on carbon-rich substrates, such as sawdust and cardboard. They also loved textiles, managed well on coffee grounds, and could even handle the salty pistachio shells. But all in moderation – too much was overwhelming and led to contamination.

At the end of our experiments, we created acoustic and insulation panels by inoculating a medley of substrates with Oyster mycelium. These panels were inspired by MOGU, a mycomaterials company that pioneered mycelium-based products.

As we worked, we were continually struck by the Oysters' remarkable adaptability – a kind of biochemical learning in action. They managed to break down surprisingly resistant materials, cigarette butts and printing inks in particular, by experimenting with a broad array of enzymes, like trying keys in countless locks. When one enzyme "fit", the fungi reinforced its use, gradually refining their response. This process wasn't instantaneous; it took time and multiple iterations. We began with substrates they already thrived on, then slowly introduced more complex ones – like orange

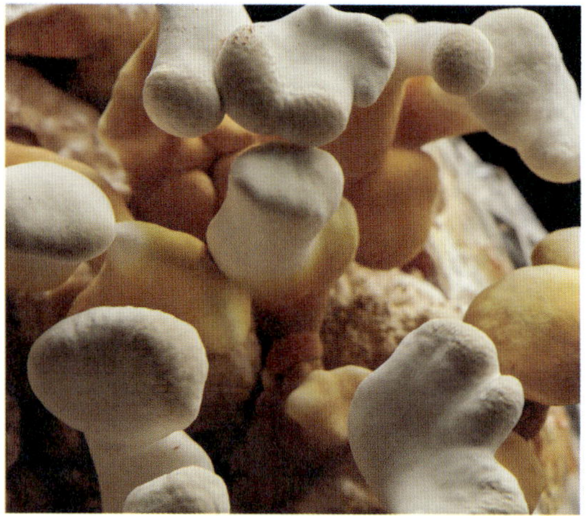

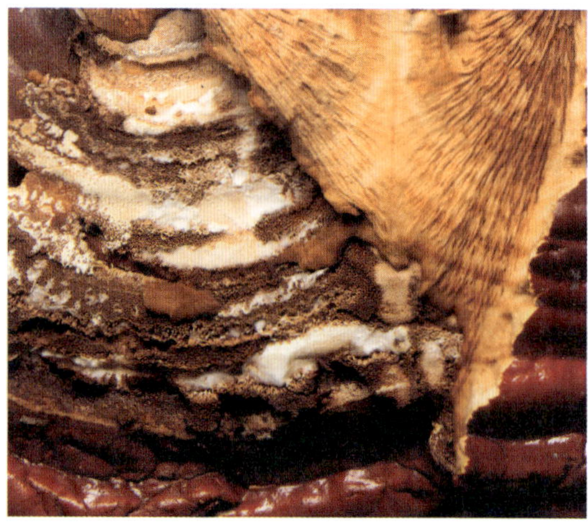

The fruiting body's structural properties offer valuable clues about the mycelium's properties and its best uses. Reishi is a particularly leathery, tough mushroom, and this translates to the mycelium, making it an ideal species for biodesign and mycomaterials. The cross section of a Reishi mushroom shows hyphal growth, suede-like mycelium, and its glossy patina.

peel – allowing them to adapt incrementally. Over time, they became more efficient, as if building a kind of metabolic muscle memory.[31]

Is this learning? Not in a conscious or neural sense, but it is adaptive, responding to success and feedback; selective, phasing out ineffective enzymes; and responsive, adjusting to local environmental conditions. Knowing this, mycodesigners can train and guide fungi towards specific outcomes.

Likewise, different fungi prefer to grow in different environments, and each species produces distinct types of mycomaterials. So designers select their fungal partners based on the qualities they want to achieve. For strength and durability, *Ganoderma* species like Reishi and Artist's Bracket are ideal. These fungi form dense, woody conks on mature trees like Károly's Tinder fungus, and their tough mycelium lends itself to applications like mushroom leather and building materials. On the other hand, Oyster mushrooms have softer fruiting bodies and lighter, more flexible mycelium. Fascinatingly, the structural qualities of the fruiting body are often reflected in the mycelium, revealing a neat interplay between these two forms of fungal life.

The fungi's colour can also provide insight. Oysters come in many colours: pink, yellow, blue, grey, and pearlescent, while *Ganoderma* species range from yellow to red, purple, brown, black, and even dark green. These colour changes are not only aesthetic, but they can also signal the fungi's maturity. Most mycelium starts off-white, but over time, progresses through different hues. Their textures and finishes vary too, ranging from suede-like to leather-like, and from matte to glossy. *Ganoderma* translates to "shiny skin", and many species have a natural glossy sheen – the appropriately named Lacquered Bracket, especially so. You, the designer, can choose which species to use and when to stop their growth, making it a dynamic collaboration with the living organism.

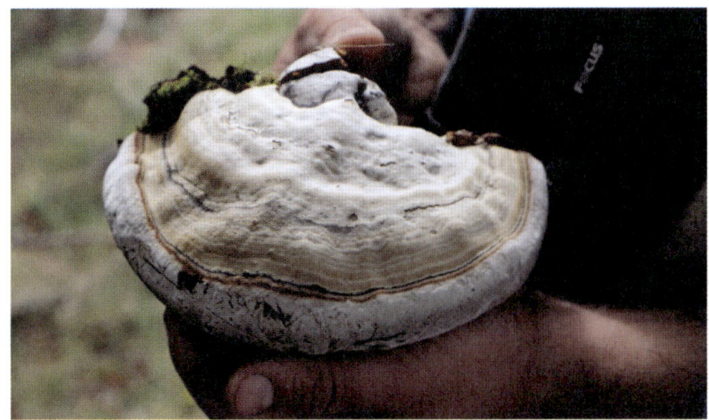

Károly and Amadou. Traditional crafts, made with head, heart, and hands, have a resilience that is hard to break.

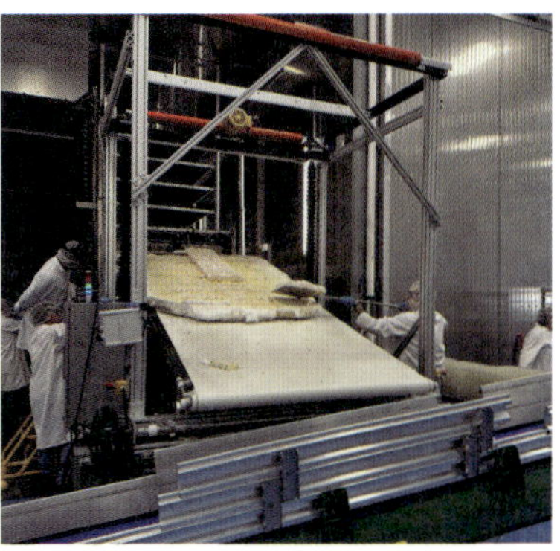

Ecovative, a US-based industrial-scale mycelium farm, produces innovative mycelium-based products, including leather alternatives, packaging, and even fungi-based bacon.

Working with fungi is magical. I remember Mondays at my studio-lab: checking on the progress of my mycelium creations, seeing who had grown, who had failed, and who had gone AWOL over the weekend. Most of the time, I had the freedom to experiment with shapes and designs. I created vases, bowls, busts, lampshades, podiums, pillars, mushroom-shaped statues, and fruiting picture frames. My main task, though, was developing mycelium packaging.

The company I worked with had created a prototype of hemp-based mycelium packaging, but my designated task was more ambitious – to design packaging for their full product range. I measured, scaled the design, and used Rhino software to model it in 3D. After preparing a mould, I inoculated it with Reishi mycelium and allowed it to grow for a week. A final two days outside the mould and they formed a thick white mycelial layer, a little like camembert rind. After drying and lacquering, I had created 100 per cent compostable, eco-friendly packaging.

Almost . . . Things didn't quite go to plan. Before drying, the packaging held the products perfectly, but afterwards, they no longer fit. Despite careful scaling, the final box was too small. It was a setback, but it was also a learning experience. Mycelium packaging, though sustainable, can be labour- and resource-intensive. The time, energy, and materials required for each box were far greater than expected, and it turned out to be less sustainable than traditional cardboard – their original packaging to which they swiftly returned.

A more scalable approach might have been to start small, like my colleague did, focusing on a single product rather than an entire bundle. As I worked on this project, I realised that the technology behind mycelium packaging can be complex and requires dedicated resources to be feasible at scale. Companies like Biomyc, based in Sofia, have made strides in creating next-generation mycelium-based products; however achieving widespread scalability still requires significant mechanisation and the use of AI.

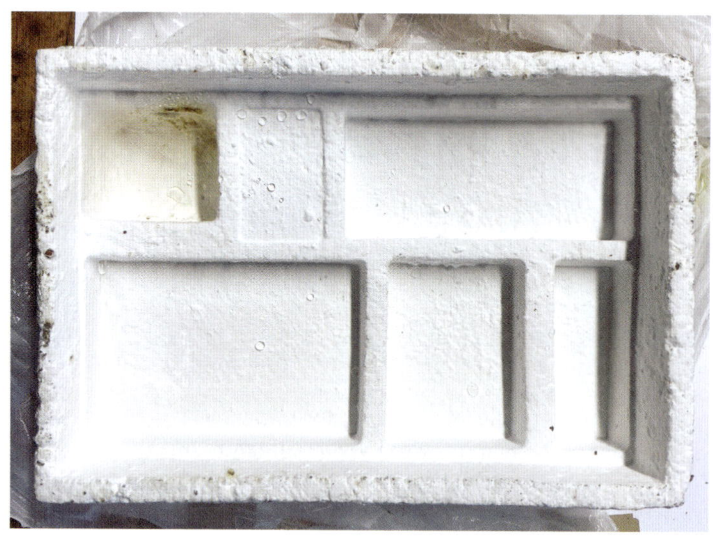

Mycelium packaging crafted with Reishi, a fungus known for its durability and strength, offering a sustainable packaging alternative. (In theory!)

Enter Ecovative. Founded as early as 2007, Ecovative is a pioneer in mycelium-based products and exemplifies the future of mycodesign. Their industrial-scale mycelium farm uses AI sensors and machine learning to control the growth of mycelium, ensuring optimal conditions for producing mycelium-based materials, from leather alternatives to packaging and even fungi-based bacon. Ecovative's collaboration with high-profile brands like Calvin Klein and Tommy Hilfiger has made them a leader in the space, and by open-sourcing their patents, they demonstrate a clear commitment to making fungal biotechnology more accessible and mainstream.

Ecovative's AirMycelium is grown under tightly controlled conditions to produce strong, smooth mycelial sheets without fruiting. Initial incubation occurs at 24–30 °C (75–86°F) with greater than 80 per cent humidity and high CO_2 (>5,000 ppm), to encourage rapid colonisation. In the finishing phase, the temperature is lowered to 15–25 °C, CO_2 is raised to 10,000–60,000 ppm, and humidity is kept above 90 per cent. Directed airflow (~100 CFM) and minimal light exposure help guide vegetative hyphal growth. These conditions promote dense, branched mycelium ideal for material applications, while suppressing mushroom formation. Growth typically takes 4–14 days. The substrate includes carbohydrates, protein, lignin, and fat, supporting robust development. This process enables the formation of pliable, uniform sheets suited for packaging, leather-like materials, and structural products.[32,33]

Ecovative's ethos centres on balancing three forms of intelligence: artificial, mycelial, and human. First, Ecovative uses AI sensors to monitor environmental conditions, processing data into patterns and networks that provide machine-derived insights.[34] Algorithms analyse mycelium behaviour in ways human cognition simply can't. By using machine learning, Ecovative gains precise control over mycelium growth environments, ensuring consistent and effective results.

But engineer and data scientist Orkan Telhan, who is responsible for the AI-fungal-human interface, has a keen sensitivity. Not only does Ecovative use AI and sensing technologies, but they are eager to interface these with their farmers' intuition. His interface enhances the farmers' ability to respond to their fungi in real time, transforming their capacity for care in unprecedented ways.

Finally, they honour the sophistication of mycelium – its complex, responsive behaviour that we cannot yet replicate. But we can work with it. So, weaving these three "intelligences" together: human, machine, and fungal, Ecovative is achieving unprecedented communication across species and extraordinary material developments.

Orkan's view on AI is more complex than the typical focus on productivity and efficiency. He envisions creating systems that allow mycelium and AI to communicate, potentially giving rise to new hybrid forms of life that aren't driven by human needs. This approach suggests a future where technology and nature collaborate in ways we haven't yet fully imagined.

In late 2024, talking with Orkan felt sobering. Just a few years earlier, the fungi-based industry was thriving, driven by the pandemic's push for sustainability and a renewed connection to nature. Fungi became symbols of innovation and regeneration. But now, there's a sense that the "Mushroom Boom" has peaked, as consumer preferences shift back to plastics, foam, and traditional animal products. Bolt Threads, one of Ecovative's largest competitors, has even paused production of Mylo, its mycelium-based leather alternative, due to financial challenges and difficulties securing funding amid shifting market priorities.

Orkan acknowledges this shift but remains steadfast in his commitment. He believes every mycelium-based alternative – whether packaging, leather, or bacon substitutes – creates a ripple of positive change. Replacing harmful materials like polystyrene and reducing reliance on animal products, Orkan argues, is a matter of life and ethics.

Yet, a stark contrast exists between modern biotech and traditional crafts. Genuinely impactful mycelium leather production requires AI, a system that is efficient but fragile. If the tech fails, the system can collapse, and with it, the knowledge. Technology holds us in an empowering and debilitating bind. On the other hand, traditional crafts like Amadou making, made with head, heart, and hands, have a resilience that is harder to break. The knowledge is embodied and adaptable. It encourages first-hand experience with wild nature and can surely withstand the test of time.

Artists and designers like Mari Koppanen and Harvey Shaw aim to preserve and adapt this craft, reimagining Amadou for contemporary use. Cultures and crafts must evolve to survive. Rather than letting them fade into nostalgia, perhaps it's time to reinvent and reintegrate. The future of Amadou could be brilliant, and I'd love to see what it becomes.

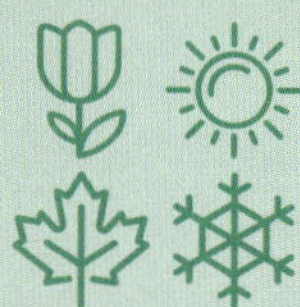

ACTIVITY

CRAFTING A MYCELIUM SCULPTURE

In 2022, Lauren Nasrallah, Sam Rowbotham, and I set out to grow a mycelium chair. Mycelium is the underground root-like structure of fungi, and when cultivated properly, it can be shaped into a variety of forms, from functional objects to beautiful sculptures. This activity introduces you to the fascinating world of mycofabrication, where nature and creativity meet. You'll learn how to grow your own mycelium sculpture – a sustainable and biodegradable art piece that showcases the power of nature's design. (The chair was ambitious; bowls are a safer place to start.)

EQUIPMENT

- A mould (a bowl, box, or 3D printed shape)
- A large mixing bowl
- Cling film or wax paper
- Tray for setting the sculpture
- Scales
- Measuring jug
- Isopropyl alcohol spray
- 2 plastic grow bags
- Gloves
- Pressure cooker
- Dehydrator or oven

INGREDIENTS

- 2kg/4½lb organic substrate (hard wood chips or sawdust from oak and/or beech).
- 80g/2¾oz xanthan gum
- 1 pre-bought inoculated grow block (Oyster or Reishi)
- 1.2l/40½fl oz/5 cups of water (enough to hydrate the substrate)
- Optional: 600g/21oz spent coffee grounds
- Optional: Wax or lacquer for finishing

METHOD

PREPARE YOUR SUBSTRATE

1. Begin by selecting your substrate. Hard wood chips and sawdust are ideal, as they provide a nutritious environment for mycelium to grow. If using sawdust, soak it in water for a few hours to soften it, then drain. Coffee grounds can also be added for extra nutrients, especially if using oyster mushrooms. The ideal water content is 70 per cent.
2. Mix thoroughly in a large bowl.
3. To sterilise your substrate and boost mycelium growth, place your mixed substrate into a grow bag, seal it with tape (leave a little space for air to escape), and pressure cook at 121 PSI for 30 minutes. Afterwards, let it cool to room temperature. Inoculate with Oyster or Reishi grow block..
4. Break up your pre-bought substrate block while it's still in the bag, then open and empty it into the mixing bowl.
5. Wearing sterile gloves, use your hands to evenly mix the contents of this bag with your hard wood substrate mix.
6. If you are planning on sculpting your design, add the xanthan gum, which will help bind the mixture together. Add a little more water to balance out the water content.

MOULD YOUR SCULPTURE

1. Prepare your mould – this could be a silicone shape, a simple plastic, glass, or metal bowl, or even a custom-made form from cardboard. If you're aiming for a specific shape (like a bowl or figure), ensure the mould can hold the mixture without spilling over. Line the inside of the mould with cling film or wax paper to prevent the mixture from sticking.
2. Transfer your mycelium substrate mixture into the mould, pressing it down gently to compact the material. Shape it into whatever form you like, but try not to make it too thin or wobbly!

INCUBATE AND GROW

1. Place your mould on a tray and cover it loosely with cling film or place it in a grow bag to maintain moisture. Leave it in a warm, dark spot (around 18–24°C/65–75°F) for 5–7 days. During this time, the mycelium will begin to run through the substrate, binding it together and taking the shape of the mould.
2. Check on your sculpture daily to ensure it's not contaminated (mint-green Trichoderma is the usual culprit). The mycelium will start to form a dense, white mat as it colonises the entire substrate.

DRY AND FINISH

1. After about 7 days, your mycelium sculpture should be fully grown. At this point, you can either expose it to light and let mushrooms fruit from it, or take it out the bag and dry it in a dehydrator or an oven at 40°C/104°F. Once dry, the sculpture should be firm and solid.
2. For added durability and finish, you can seal your dried sculpture with a thin layer of wax or non-toxic lacquer. This step helps protect it from moisture and extends its lifespan.

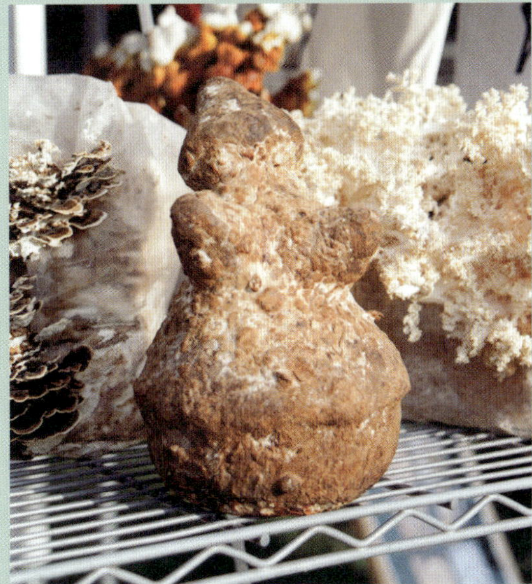

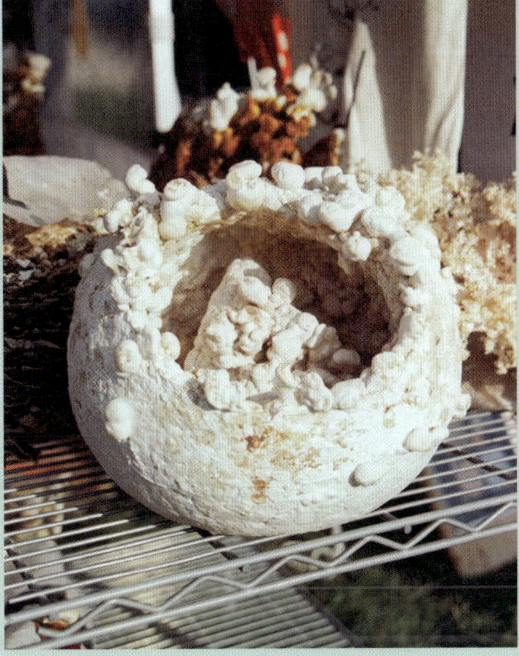

"Happy Mycelium Woman" and "Egg," sculpted with UK native Hoof Fungus.

PHYLOGENETIC FAMILY TREES: A Dream of Nova Scotia

Daydream

My heart is not on Highland
Nor that tanned Bermuda island
And remembering Ceylon is hard for me.
And my heart is not on Bay Street
Where the moguls run 'round bare feet
When you've been there once that's all there is to see.
And my love is not in England
I don't like a Queen and King land
Pomp and circumstance are far too much for me.
And Europe's just too distant
One can't get there in an instant
The price for freedom's much too high a fee.
Give me taste of salt and windswept
Lifting fog and lilting sunset
Sailing down Back Harbour, out but back for tea.
Berry picking on the hillside
Boats moored carefree, low and high tide
And the sound of gulls, that's where I want to be.
I can feel the mist rise slowly
And the plaintive loon call lowly
Oh! I pray one day I can afford the fee.
Just to buy a one-way ticket
Far from crowded city thicket
Down to Chester, Nova Scotia, by the sea.

– Christopher Ondaatje

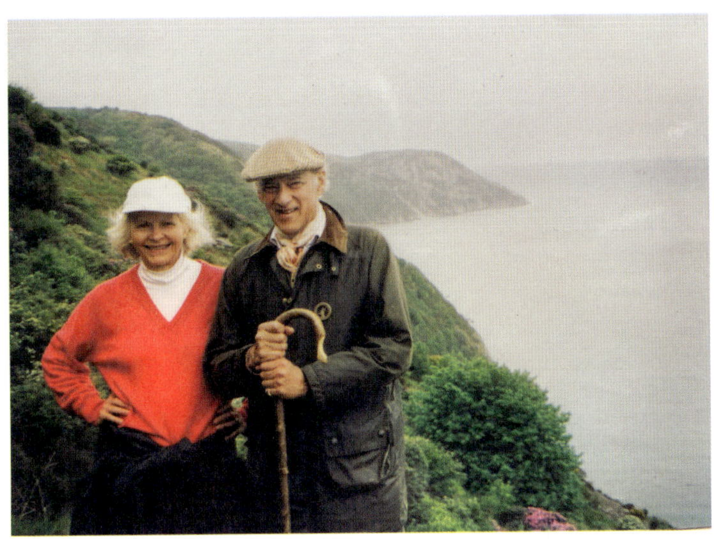

My grandparents in Chester, Nova Scotia, a place that came to be known as home.

To this day, I recall a recurring childhood dream: My family and I sailed towards a mystical island hidden in fog. As we approached, loons paddled away and moored boats rocked gently in our wake. To my young imagination, the island was a treasure trove of sea glass, berries, mushrooms, and more – a magical world I longed to return to upon waking.

Years later, I found myself on a boat, headed for a low dock on a pebbled beach in Chester, Nova Scotia. Stepping onto the island, something shifted. This place, so vivid in my memories, was not just the figment of a dream. It was real – connected to my family, my heritage, and my story. Chester was where my extended maternal family had created childhood memories, shared dreams, and forged a deep connection with the land across generations.

The sense of belonging that runs through my veins is inseparable from Canada, a country defined by migration, displacement, and the quest for identity. My family's story is complex: my grandfather was born in Ceylon (now Sri Lanka) to an eccentric, privileged family of mixed Dutch, Sinhalese, and Tamil descent. After his parents' separation and his father's financial ruin, he left school at 17 and, in 1956, migrated to Canada, seeking a new life.

My grandmother's story is equally entwined with the history of displacement. A Latvian, she lived through the Soviet occupation of her homeland in 1940. After fleeing to Germany, she eventually found refuge in Canada, where she married my grandfather in 1959. Together, they raised three children, including my mother, the youngest of the three siblings. Under the principle of *jus soli* (right of the soil), my mother and her siblings were born Canadian citizens. Yet, *jus sanguinis* (right of blood) reveals a mosaic lineage: 49 per cent Baltic, 23 per cent Scandinavian, 20 per cent Southeast Asian, and 10 per cent mixed. Ancestry DNA testing has illuminated the genealogical ties of millions, painting a complex global family tree. But according to these calculations, we are 0 per cent Canadian.

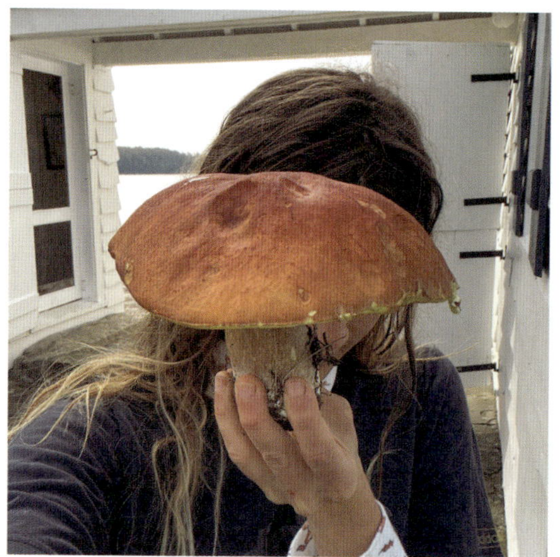

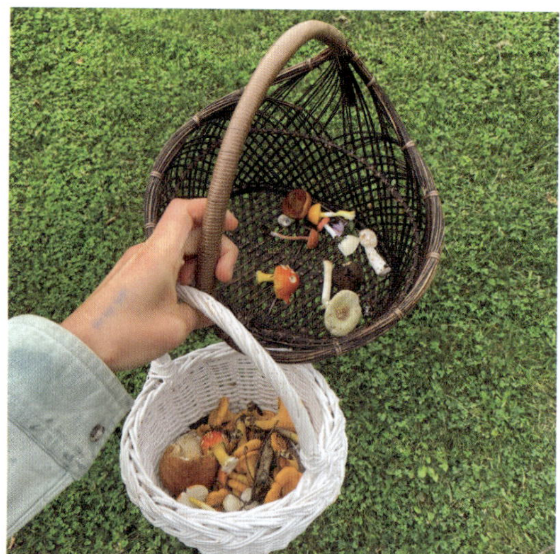

A huge Porcini, foraged by my grandmother, and a basket full of fungi!

But belonging goes deeper than blood or soil. For those navigating diaspora or enduring the scars of conflict, cultural identity is often carried through intangible means – stories, songs, dances, culinary traditions, and spiritual connections. Belonging is an ever-evolving dance, shaped by the land's stories, by the struggles of survival, and by the histories we inherit. For me, belonging is nurtured through my family's traditions: Gordon Lightfoot's songs, annual lobster feasts, and summers spent in Nova Scotia.

Every summer, my extended family gathered on the island for two weeks of blueberry picking, wild swimming, and safariing in the zebra-striped "bumper car" to spot deer, herons, owls, seals, and even Hilton, the infamous great white shark. My grandparents realised their dreams on that island. My grandfather vowed his family would never endure his hardships, creating a life of agency, freedom, and belonging. My grandmother aspired to raise a healthy and joyous family – a mission she embraced with boundless love and laughter. We were spoiled with marshmallows, wonderfully inappropriate songs, and epic tales of Sri Lankan leopards.

This island is where I first learned to forage, my eyes glued to the ground alongside an army of cousins as our grandmother, a passionate mycophile, guided us in search of Chanterelles.

When my cousin Gillian suggested a trip to Chester in September 2023, after six years away, I couldn't resist. I convinced my boss that this two-week trip would double as essential fungi research for ongoing projects, and he encouraged me to go. Just before I arrived, my grandfather emailed, "No mushrooms here this year. Perhaps when you come."

I arrived to find the island far from barren. Hurricane Franklin had swept through the area, bringing an incredible abundance of mushrooms. Among the wood stacks, deer-grazed meadows, dying trees, and pine forests, the land was alive with edible, poisonous, hallucinogenic, and medicinal fungi. My grandparents' home became a mushroom hunter's dreamscape, filled with diverse ecological niches

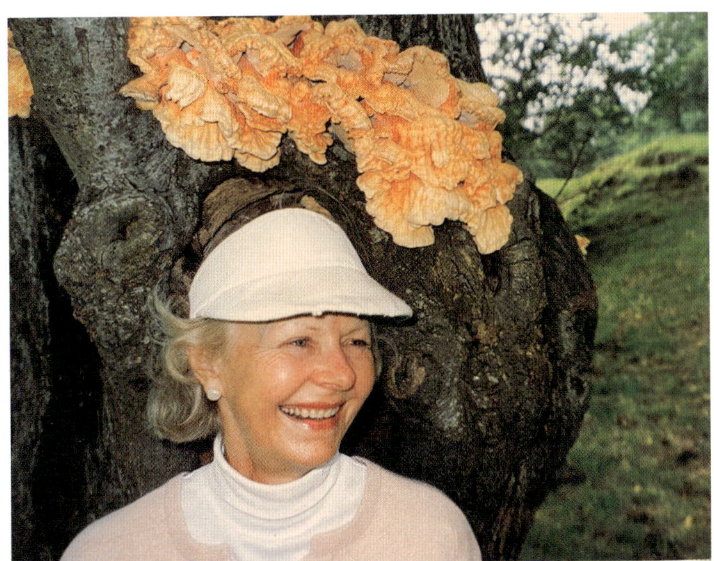

A photograph of my grandmother with a Chicken of the Woods from her Nature Nurtured Diary. She wrote: "Major discovery of the weekend: Chicken of the Woods found growing on an oak tree in Hamlet's field."

for foraging. I found colossal Birch Polypores, my first Caesar's Mushroom, and Turkey Tails sprouting from tree stumps. My grandmother, overjoyed to see my discoveries, joined me in exploring the island's thickets of birch, pine, and fir. She was, in fact, the huntress of this magnificent Cep.

My grandma has always cared deeply for the Earth. Throughout her life, she has cultivated gardens across the globe, meticulously documenting their evolution in journals titled "Nature Nurtured". Her gardens – secret gardens, water gardens, rose gardens, wildflower gardens, and vegetable patches – reflect her personal mood and that of the earth. Her Devonian water garden, in particular, was magnificent, with llamas, lichen-covered statues, and water lilies – an oasis of inspiration and care. "Halliday's Field" promised Ceps each autumn and the occasional Parasol was a delight. The day my grandparents found a Chicken of the Woods on an oak tree featured in three separate scrapbooks, with details of how they whizzed it into an egg-white omelette with fresh herbs from the garden. I never knew how much one could crave rain and its abilities to transform a beautiful garden into an Earthly paradise.

Mushrooming was my grandmother's first love, a skill passed down through generations. In her garden diary, she documents her return to Latvia after the fall of the Soviet Union, observing both the landscape and the cultural shifts brought about by occupation:

"Well, here we are! On the Riga train . . . I didn't sleep at all, but woke up early to the misty, forested landscape – beautiful groves of white birches. Strained to see mushrooms, but no luck. / Riga feels so different from anywhere else I've ever been . . . an unexpected elegance . . . / Note: Latvia has the lowest birth rate in the entire Soviet Union . . . / Note: In Leningrad, the Russians were the oppressed; in Latvia, they are the oppressors."

In those pages, she laments the weaponisation of hunger, the loss of sovereignty, and the erasure of culture. Yet the land and people remain resilient, an enduring reminder of the strength of place

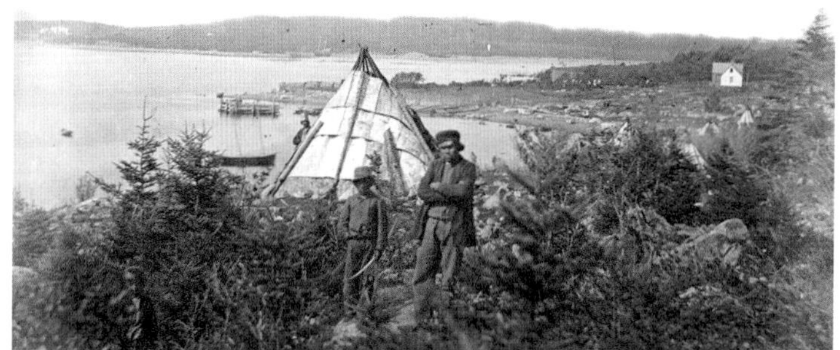

Mi'kmaq people at Tufts Cove, Nova Scotia, Canada, 1871 – four years after the Confederation of Canada, when the provinces of Ontario, Quebec, Nova Scotia, and New Brunswick united to form the Dominion of Canada within the British Empire.

and memory. She writes, "Their love for the land is perhaps the most formidable force of all – both destructive and regenerative." It was in these same landscapes, now defaced by war and the machinery of occupation, that my grandmother found solace and strength.

It was also here, on the island, that I first learned the story of the Mi'kmaq people – the Indigenous inhabitants of this land, long ago displaced by settlers. Strangely, through cookbooks, my grandmother taught me the history of French Catholics, Irish, Scots, and English settlers who forcibly displaced the Mi'kmaq, causing irreparable damage to their spiritual and cultural connection to the land.[35] Their hair was cut, language suppressed, and families separated. Biodiversity plummeted and bison were hunted to extinction so as to undermine Indigenous resilience, spirit, and livelihoods.

Traditionally, the Mi'kmaq practised a semi-nomadic, hunter-gatherer lifestyle intimately tied to the land's offerings. Their language, shaped by nature's musical sounds, speaks of sustainability and respect. The Mi'kmaq word *nenuite'tg* (ne·nu·i·deetk), for example, refers to the concept of taking only what is necessary and with respect,[36] ensuring the long-term sustainability of all life. By contrast, the English word "harvest" fails to capture the gratitude and relational element.[37] Despite centuries of violence and oppression, their language, culture, and resilience endure.

In recent years, there has been a resurgence of Indigenous-led movements, as communities work to reclaim ancestral food systems and ecological knowledge.[38,39] Central to this effort is the push to decolonise agriculture, led by figures like Sean Sherman, the Sioux Chef. Sherman is reintroducing native foods to Indigenous communities, using everything from wild-harvested antelope, grouse, geese, and porcupines to foraged mushrooms, wild prairie turnips, and locally grown heirloom corn and beans. Sherman's efforts with the North American Traditional Indigenous Food Systems (NATIFS) initiative aim to educate Indigenous chefs on the use of seasonal foods and traditional cooking methods. At the same time, it empowers Indigenous communities by fostering a deeper connection to their land and promoting food sovereignty within a broad, kin-centric ecological framework.

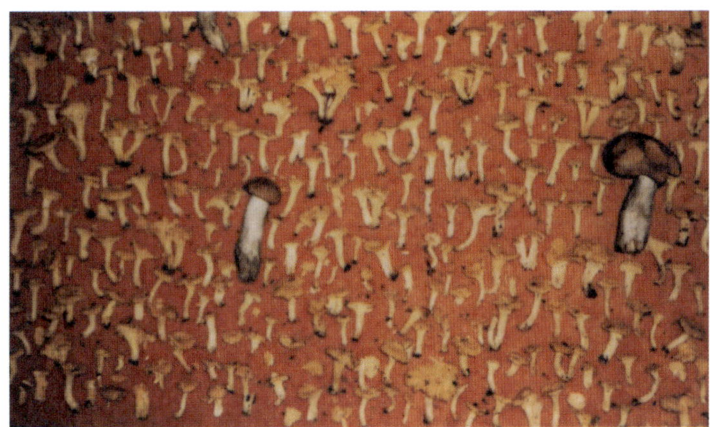

Ceps and Chanterelles.
A particularly successful forage!

Likewise, Soul Fire Farm, co-founded by Leah Penniman in upstate New York, is an Afro-Indigenous farm that champions social and political resistance through agroecology.[40] In *Farming While Black*, Penniman connects regenerative farming to Black Indigenous traditions, with techniques like raised beds and multi-species polycultures rooted in practices from the Ovambo of Namibia and Nigeria. The farm serves as both an educational space and a symbol for combatting systemic racism in food systems.[41] Leah explains that when black people witness the beauty of interwoven wild and cultivated biodiversity, it's essential that they know they're not merely borrowing from a past legacy, but creating a future shaped by their ancestors' invaluable contributions.[42] The act of rewriting these narratives holds equal importance to the practices themselves.

Closer to home, Situ'lɨsk, a permaculture farm near Atuomkuk/Wentzell Lake, serves as a hub for culture, language revitalisation, and ecological education. These initiatives are part of a broader movement to regenerate the land, heal communities, and honour the wisdom of Indigenous peoples who have been stewards of these lands for millennia.

Much like my grandmother, I have forgotten much of the knowledge passed down through generations, especially in the realm of foraging and herbal medicine. But this collective forgetting, as Monica Gagliano writes, is not a permanent loss. "None of it could ever be forgotten. These vast vegetal archives will always be open for consultation."[43] The memories, the teachings, are always accessible, waiting to be rediscovered.

After an afternoon spent discussing family ancestry and legacy, my grandma and I ventured outdoors for a lengthy forage. We kept to the island's periphery, searching with calm determination. We made it almost the whole way round without spotting a single mushroom, but just as we began the final homeward stretch, we found a stunning golden troop of Chanterelles.

These mushrooms shone with a soft orange hue, their texture hearty, and their interiors hollow and white. With their signature ribbed folds cascading beneath the smooth funnel-shaped caps, they felt like fingers wrinkled by the earth's moisture. As we crouched down to gather them, we were met with a gentle aroma, reminiscent of fresh apricots.

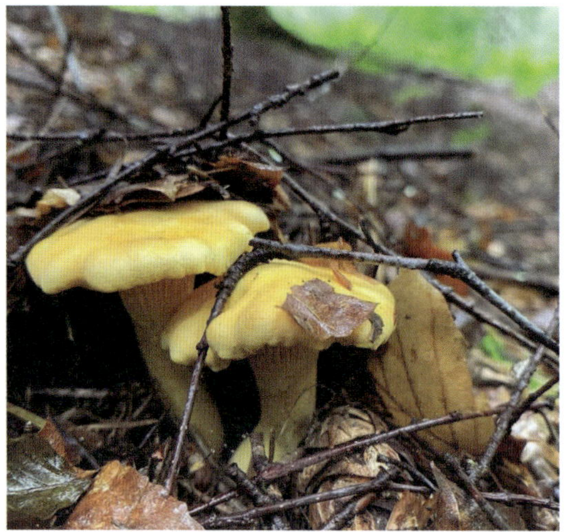

Chanterelles in Edinburgh's Botanical Gardens. With the ecological parallels and historical ties between Nova Scotia and Scotland, I sought to analyse the variations between these two mushrooms.

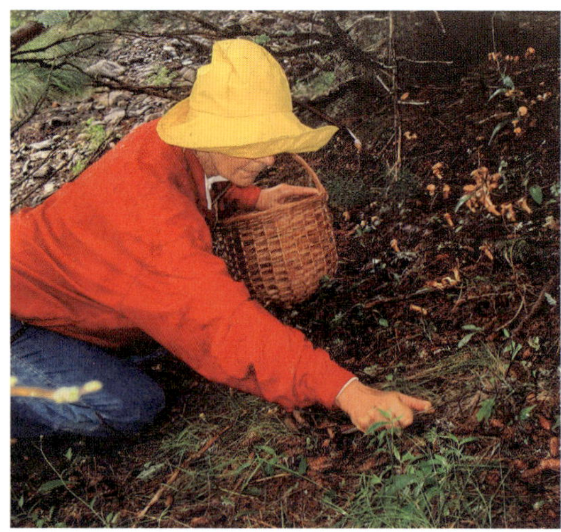

Grandma Ondaatje foraging for Chanterelles in Chester, Nova Scotia.

We picked a few for dinner, while I dried three for future exploration. Our conversations sparked curiosity about the evolutionary paths of fungi – whether they, too, experience displacement through urbanisation, climate change, or even war, impacting their ecological distribution. Known for my knack for keeping dried plants and mushrooms from my travels, I was determined to find my Chanterelle from Edinburgh's Botanical Gardens, collected during my first visit in 2017. Given the ecological parallels and historical ties between Nova Scotia and Scotland, I wanted to analyse variations between these two mushrooms. All I needed to do was remember where I'd left the Chanterelle!

That evening, I reached out to two people: Rachel Swenie, a fungal ecologist at the University of Tennessee specialising in Chanterelle evolutionary biology, and David Satori, a mycologist with a quiet passion for DNA sequencing.

DNA technologies are transforming our understanding of species, and fungi are no exception. Although the evolutionary lineage of fungi is not well-documented, as their soft tissues don't fossilise well, traditional classifications have shifted with the advent of DNA sequencing, offering new insights into fungal evolution.

DNA sequencing has revealed that what was once broadly classified as *Cantharellus cibarius* (Golden Chanterelle) actually comprises multiple distinct species spread across different regions. Some, like *C. amethysteus* (Amethyst Chanterelle), were previously recognised as separate species based on their distinctive morphology. However, many others were grouped together under *C. cibarius* until genetic analysis uncovered their differences. These subtle distinctions often require detailed microscopic study or DNA sequencing to identify.

David explained: "Each fungus has DNA regions that show variability among species. The ITS region is widely used to compare fungi and determine the similarity between them." By sequencing these regions (or "barcodes"), scientists can quantify base pair similarities, though comparing entire genomes provides deeper insights into species-specific traits like enzyme production and evolutionary history. So I found my mushroom, sequenced the ITS regions of both my Chanterelles, and discovered that they belonged to different species. Good. I was glad for the genetic diversity. As expected, the Scottish Chanterelle was the European Golden Chanterelle, *Cantharellus cibarius*. The Nova Scotian mushroom, however, was the less common *Cantherellus camphoratus*, which, amazingly, was first described in Chester, Nova Scotia, in 1979!

To see how "related" they were, I found a recent phylogenetic tree of all known Chanterelle species. My two Chanterelles occupied different clades, or evolutionary branches. Notably, though the European Chanterelle is widespread across the temperate northern hemisphere, it showed very low genetic diversity (less than one per cent), while the Nova Scotian Chanterelle exhibited greater genetic diversity compared to its cousins.

While these experiments shed light on the evolutionary links among organisms and genes, they represent merely one part of a larger narrative. The environment always plays its hand. For example, a single mycelial network can yield two mushrooms on either side of a tree; despite sharing identical DNA, each may express itself differently depending on its unique microclimate. Microclimactic differences, such as temperature fluctuations or humidity levels, can influence a mushroom's colour, while dry conditions often lead to reduced size or slower growth.

Even more amazingly, epigenetics can induce cellular changes in fungi without altering their DNA sequences. These temporary changes in gene expression can be heritable and can enable fungi to adapt to environmental stressors. Temperature, humidity, soil conditions, pollution, and anthropogenic spread significantly influence fungal growth and distribution, particularly as climate change alters their ecological landscape.[44,45] The environment can shape both primary and secondary metabolites, their physical forms, the species with which they partner, and even the timing of their spore dispersal. The dynamic interplay between environment and fungi inspires fascinating questions about adaptability and expression.

Of course, this narrative parallels the human experience. Both humans and non-humans flourish in ideal circumstances and adapt when necessary. The challenges faced by indigenous peoples in Canada and around the world echo deep struggles for survival and recognition amid systemic pressures. Who indigenous peoples are today reflects the identities they have been forced to adopt. Aldo Leopold poignantly stated, "One of the penalties of ecological education is that one lives alone in a world of wounds."[46] This idea resonates within socio-ecological contexts, prompting us to consider how healing happens in the face of destruction, especially when harm is compounded by historical injustice. This becomes even more complex when those causing harm today are themselves carrying the wounds of past harm – my own family included.

While I hold Canadian citizenship and legal residency, my connection to the land comes with an uncomfortable privilege. It's an unsettling reminder that Indigenous and First Nations communities, whose relationship with the land is rooted in millennia of history, continue to face systemic displacement. The question of who truly belongs is far more complicated than a simple narrative of

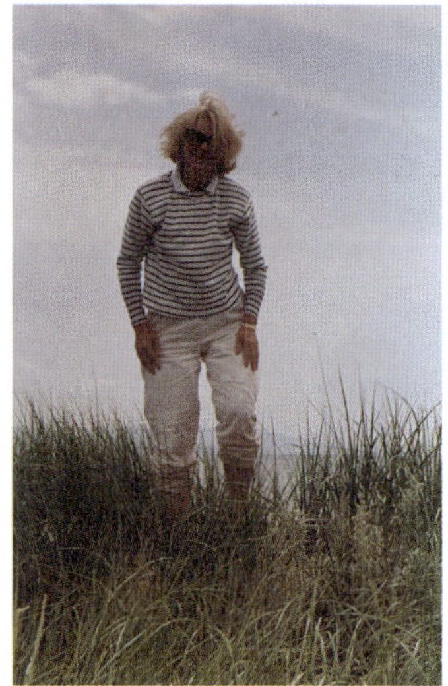

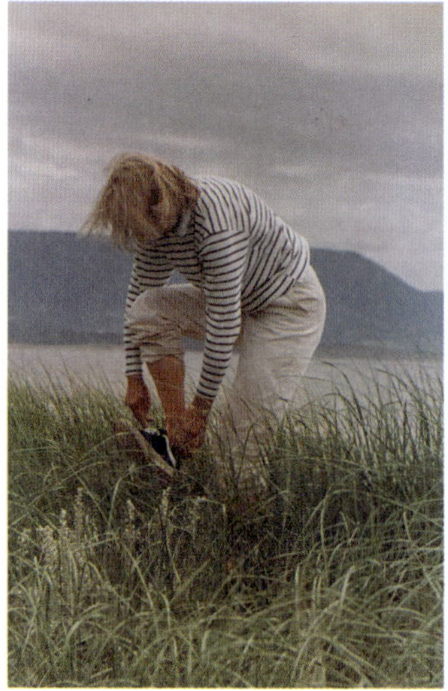

Grandma Ondaatje foraging before she lost her shoe.

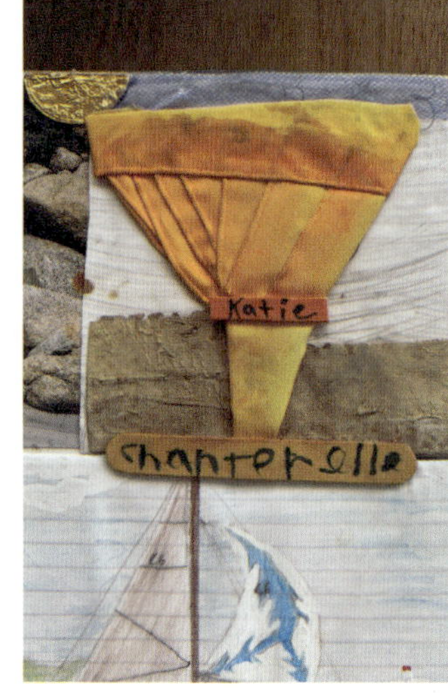

An artwork I created for my grandparents as a thank you for the summer spent in Chester.

land ownership. Who gets to claim a place, and how far back should we trace history to determine rightful connection?

Our identities, shaped by multiple origins, defy binary categories like “one culture versus another” or “connection versus disconnection”. Our experiences blend, and our roots are nourished by diverse histories, not just bloodlines. New, hybrid land-based cultures can emerge from this blending, allowing us to explore ways in which different identities can coexist and flourish. The stories we share become anchors; the roots we plant offer nourishment for future generations. Our legacies extend beyond soil and blood – they grow through ecosystems, shared experiences, and the dreams we weave together.

The day my physical connection to Nova Scotia disappeared was heart-wrenching. The land was sold without warning, and my cousins and I left without saying goodbye. But culture lives within us. My mind, body, and epigenetics carry the memory of that island. The same holds true for fungi. When transplanted into new environments, fungi express themselves differently: adapting while retaining genetic traces of their past. These memories are encoded in their DNA, reflecting the resilience of both nature and culture.

Though I couldn’t bid farewell in waking life, a dream offered me the closure I sought. The dream was calm yet clear; all my family were there and we knew we were leaving. A melancholy hung in the usual morning fog, tinged with an undercurrent of hope. We had gathered to celebrate my cousin Gillian’s wedding and all the years filled with laughter, growth, and love. I wandered the land, foraging for Chanterelles, sometimes alone, and at other moments, arm in arm with my grandmother. It was both achingly peaceful and soul-stirring.

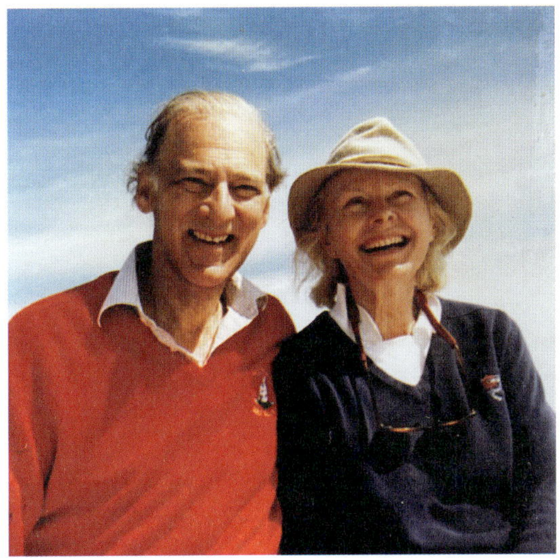

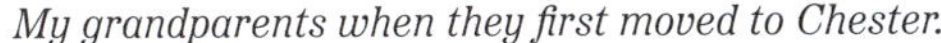

My grandparents when they first moved to Chester.

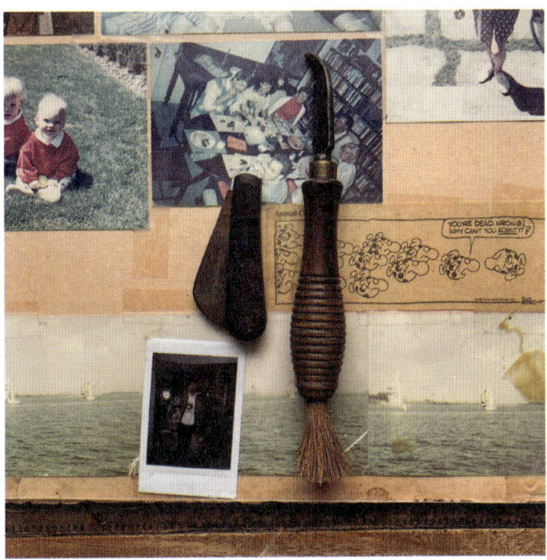

My grandmother's foraging knife.

I cannot begin to fathom the anguish of being uprooted from one's land and home, driven by war, climate, or other forces that fracture ties to one's roots. The mingled scents of familiarity, the faces of loved ones, and the silhouettes of trees and animals are suddenly ripped away.

As migration continues to rise due to climate change, drought, disease, war, and economic opportunity, we grapple with questions of belonging. Historically, we have displaced one another, but surely, we must recognise that walls only serve to deepen wounds. Were it not for my grandparents' ability to migrate, their identities and mine would be profoundly different. But did their freedom come at a cost to others?

Daniel Godinez Nivon, a multi-disciplinary artist who partners with Central American Indigenous communities, reminds me that our greatest power lies in our dreams. He encourages us to share our dreams as a source of comfort, assuring us we are not alone. Unity in dreaming builds the energy necessary to convert those dreams into reality.

Fungi hold their histories within their DNA, prompting me to wonder: Do fungi dream? We know they sleep . . . Can they teach us lessons about belonging and resilience? All I know is that my family's souls remain intertwined with that island, just as my Turkey Tail mushroom tinctures made on my last visit still taste like Nova Scotia – especially when drunk with apple juice! In this, I find enough. As my grandma often reminds me, "The past is merely the prologue."

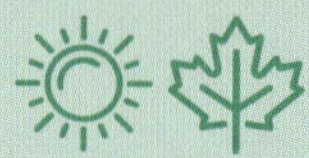

RECIPE

GRANDMA ONDAATJE'S SOUR CREAM OF CHANTERELLE SOUP, FROM CHESTER CHOWDER

In 1982, at only 18 years old, my mum wrote her first cookbook, *Chester Chowder: A Potpourri of Nova Scotia Recipes*. She cycled around the small seaside town to collect recipes from local friends and families, with hand-drawn illustrations by her sister and the funds donated to the young people of Bonny Lea Farm. Chanterelles find their way into several recipes, and here, I give my grandma's Sour Cream of Chanterelle Soup.

In Nova Scotia, Chanterelles are fairly plentiful in July and August. If you can find some, try them in this soup – absolutely delicious!

INGREDIENTS

- 225g/½lb Chanterelles
- 3 tbsp butter
- 1 tbsp flour
- 4 cups chicken or fish bouillon
- 1 egg yolk
- 1 cup sour cream
- 2 tbsp fresh dill

METHOD

1. Clean and slice large Chanterelles. Leave small ones whole. Sauté in butter. Sprinkle with flour. Add bouillon; simmer for 30 to 40 minutes. Beat together the egg yolk, sour cream, and dill. Place in a soup tureen. Pour the hot soup over the cream, stirring constantly. Serves 6.

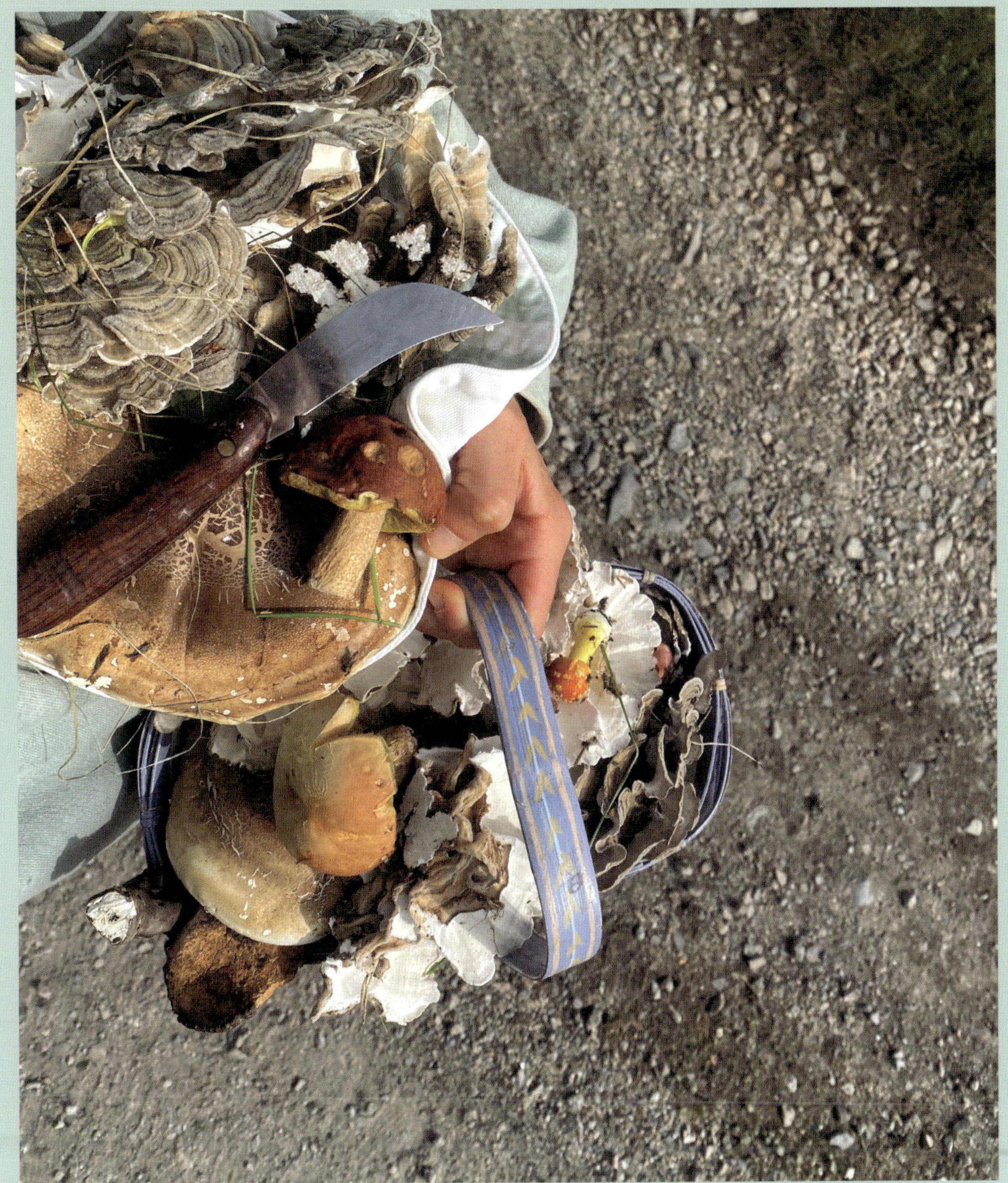

Basket full of mushrooms in Chester, Nova Scotia: Turkey Tail, Birch Polypore, Porcini, and a Yellow Dust Amanita!

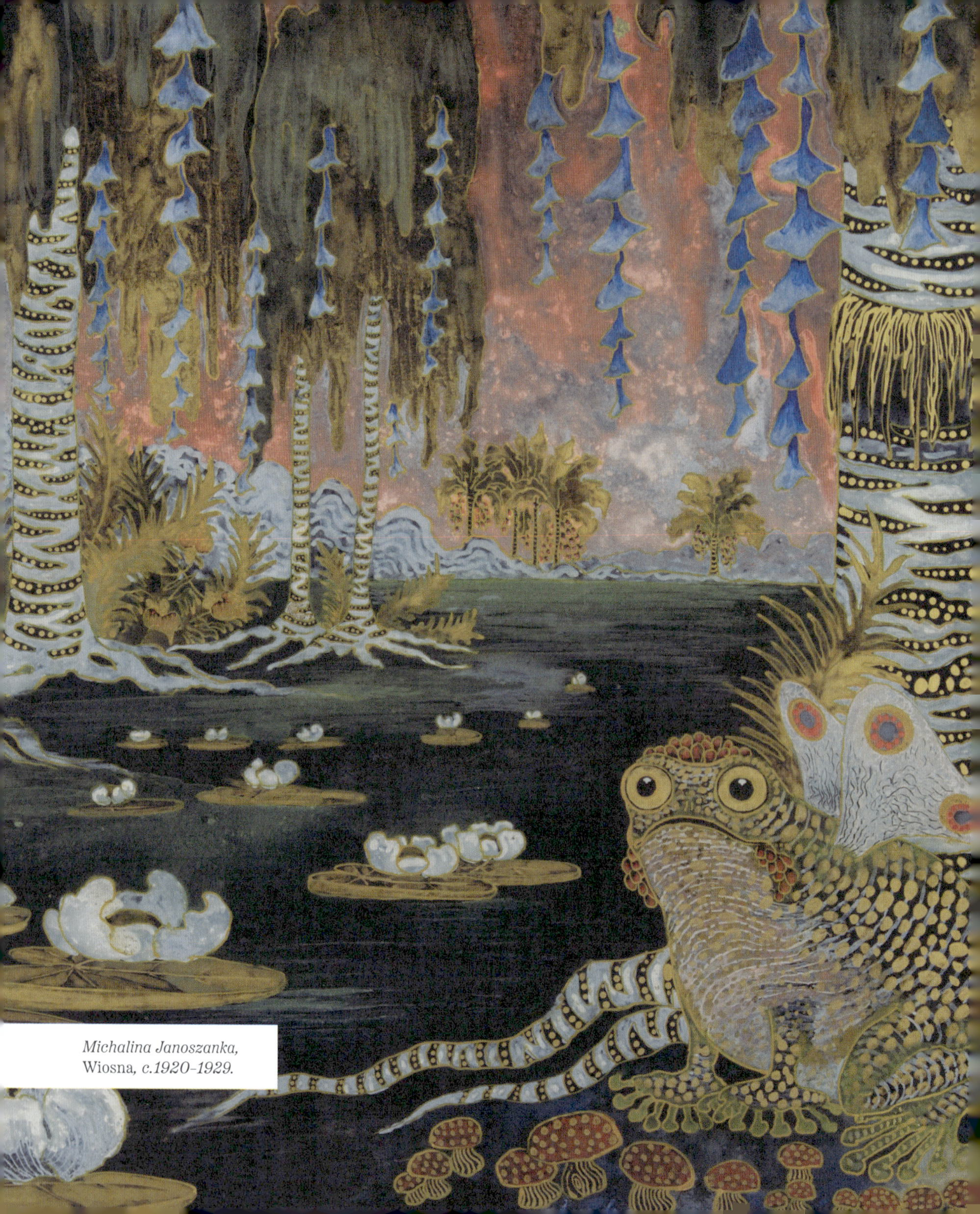

Michalina Janoszanka,
Wiosna, *c.1920–1929.*

7

INCONSISTENCIES: Mystery & Paradox

"How wonderful that we have met a paradox. Now we have some hope of making progress."

– Niels Bohr

In Greek mythology, the primordial deities were not human-like gods with colourful personalities; they were abstractions: Nyx (Night), Tartarus (the Underworld), Eros (Love and Desire). From Chaos, the original void, and Gaia (Mother Earth), complexity emerged: gods, heroes, monsters, and elemental forces. The cycle of chaos to order and back again, what we now call entropy, is a foundational myth of both science and storytelling. These layered, ambiguous stories reflect something true about life: it is inherently paradoxical.

As humans, we are paradoxical beings. We seek certainty but are driven by curiosity. We create order yet thrive in the unknown. From childhood, we are primed to wonder. Einstein once advised that to become more intelligent, one should "read fairy tales"[1] because they open us up to mystery. Imagination is not the opposite of knowledge; it is its catalyst.

Fungi, perhaps more than any other life form, confront us with this kind of catalytic strangeness. They are so utterly unlike us – alien in form, behaviour, and ecology – that we reach for metaphor to understand them. The "Wood Wide Web", fungal "economies", or fungi as "ecosystem architects" are attempts to translate their world into ours. We anthropomorphise them to bring them closer, yet they resist simplification and categorisation.

Fungi blur the lines between individual and collective, life and death. Some species clean up lithium mines or break down plastics; others emit invisible toxins. Some heal us; some consume us. Lichens are part algae, part fungi. Truffles shift between sex expressions. Mycorrhizal fungi live inside and around plant roots so thoroughly that it's unclear where the plant ends and the fungus begins. These relationships dissolve boundaries we assumed were fixed – between species, sexes, identities. They call into question the very frameworks we use to define life.

We often think of science as the tool to make sense of such complexity. But science itself contains paradox. Quantum physics reveals that energy exists as both waves and particles, depending on the observer. Entanglement suggests that two things can be connected across space and time. These ideas challenge not only our understanding of the world but the notion that science offers clear, singular truths. Yuval Noah Harari and others note that the deeper we explore science, the more it requires faith.

Movements like Radical Mycology and Queer Ecology embrace these complexities. They challenge the idea that knowledge must come from institutions or professionals. Amateur mycologists, intuitive experimenters, even those guided by dreams or psychedelics, are making meaningful contributions to the sciences. Perhaps we should not be surprised. After all, folk practices, like applying mouldy bread to wounds, paved the way for penicillin.[2] Informal knowledge is not lesser knowledge and not all science is peer-reviewed.

Science and art are also not opposites, but rather complementary ways of seeing.[3] The boundary between them is porous. Scientists often draw inspiration from music, myth, or metaphor. Mycologist Beatrix Potter was as much a storyteller as a scientist. Understanding fungi may require philosophy, poetry, fluid dynamics, and spirituality. Each field offers a different lens through which to view these multifaceted organisms.

Fungi also challenge us to rethink the idea of intelligence. In one video, "The Blob",[4] a carbon-rich lipid moves through a fungal network, approaches a junction, and takes one path. Then it stops, changes speed, reverses, and splits down both forks. Is it deciding? Not in any human sense. But it's responding, reevaluating. There is agency here, though not the kind we typically recognise. And this activity ripples outward, influencing ecosystems on a planetary scale.

This is why fungi are so compelling. They reveal the living, improvisational nature of the world beneath our feet and all around us. Soil biology is the study of countless organisms navigating complexity in real-time. These organisms don't follow scripts. They respond, adapt, invent. Like us, they are improvising through uncertainty. And that makes them deeply relatable, even if we cannot fully comprehend them.

It's tempting to hope that fungi will save us – from environmental collapse, from disease, from ourselves. There's a growing narrative of "myco-evangelism" that casts fungi as gods and heroes in our crisis story. But this belief overlooks the fact that no species can save us from unsustainable behaviour. Fungi are not saviours. They are participants: creative, chaotic, and neutral. They can dismantle what no longer serves, but they do not rebuild in our image.

And so we return to paradox and ambiguity. Fungi challenge binary thinking: good and bad, male and female, alive and dead, art and science. They ask us to think in terms of both/and instead of either/or. They urge us to be comfortable with contradiction.

In this spirit, the stories that follow explore and celebrate fungal paradoxes. The antifungal properties of Shiitake mushrooms and the violent mycelial mimicry of *Squamanita paradoxa*. Lithium – both a life-saving psychiatric drug and an environmentally taxing mineral – becomes a lens for examining the paradoxes of technological progress and the role of fungi in our future. Fungal sex, identity, and reproduction reveal an ecology of fluidity, resisting simple definitions. And the selective breeding of fungi pushes at the edges of what life can be, inviting us to reconsider what it means to intervene in nature.

As we navigate these worlds, we must resist the urge to make them neat. The living world is not orderly, but wild, layered, contradictory. As the biologist J B S Haldane once said, "The universe is not only stranger than we suppose, it is stranger than we can suppose." That is the wonder. Not that everything makes sense, but that we continue to seek meaning in the mess.

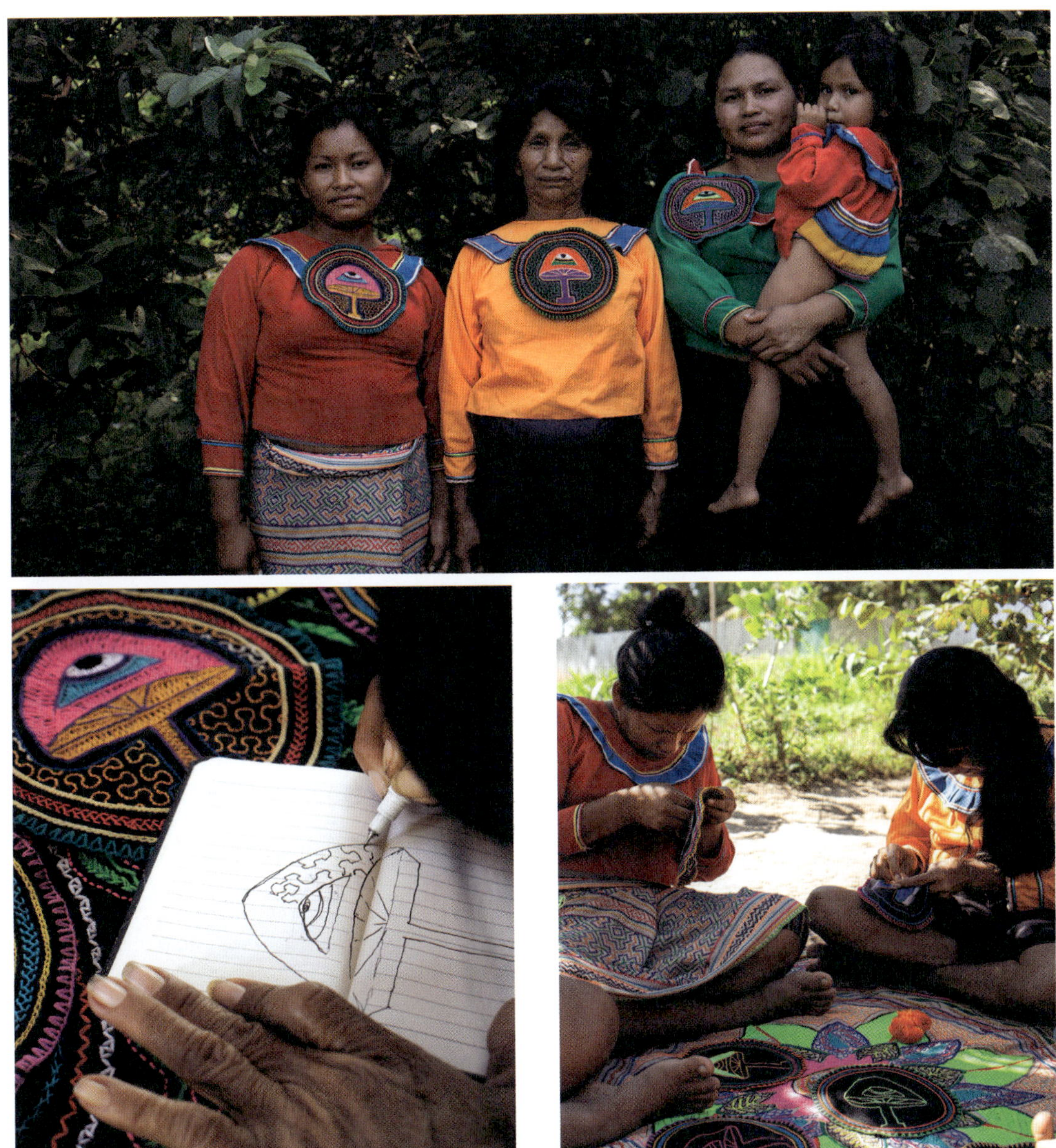

These visionary embroideries are hand stitched by Shipibo-Conibo women of the San Francisco village in Pucallpa, Peru. Their sacred Kene designs represent the inner energy of all living beings, and some are inspired by visions of the Kono Nete, or "Mushroom World". Although Psilocybe mushrooms were not traditionally used as a sacred medicine in the same way as Ayahuasca, they are consumed and honoured today as sources of resilience, vitality, and guidance. Each pattern carries ancestral wisdom that protects and nurtures the wearer.

ANTIFUNGAL FUNGI & FUNGAL PARASITES

"Fungi practice cannibalism all the time."

– *Lawrence Millman,* Fungpiedia

A few years ago, a friend of mine ran up to a medicinal mushroom stand at Medicine Festival, desperately seeking a remedy for a recent outbreak of candida. She had plans to meet her "ex" later that evening and needed a quick fix for her fungal infection. Without hesitation, the tincture expert recommended only one thing: a substantial dose of Shiitake.

Shiitake mushrooms, *Lentinula edodes*, are native to East Asia and are widely revered for both their culinary and medicinal properties. These mushrooms have been a staple in Oriental cuisine for centuries, regarded as a delicacy with a rich, earthy flavour that enhances soups, sauces, and even sweets and fizzy drinks.[5] In Japan, they were once reserved exclusively for royalty, earning them the moniker "King of mountain treasures". Shiitake were even so valuable that they triggered "Shiitake wars" among farmers,[6] and ancient cultivation sites were kept secret for national security reasons.[7]

Globally, Shiitake ranks as the second most widely cultivated mushroom, after the Button mushroom, *Agaricus bisporus*. Its cultivation dates to the 12th century in China, and by the 14th century, it was introduced to Japan, where it became a highly valued crop. Traditional cultivation involved rubbing Shiitake spores into wounds on logs and waiting for the mushrooms to fruit – a process dependent on luck or perhaps the prayers of Buddhist monks.[8]

In 1940s Kyoto, agriculture student Kisaku Mori revolutionised Shiitake farming with a method that remains in use today. His technique involved drilling holes in logs, inserting wood plugs inoculated with mycelium, sealing the logs with wax, and then waiting for a year or two. After being submerged in cold water, the logs were struck with hammers to stimulate mycelial growth – a process known as the "soak and strike". This process mimics natural stressors like falling branches or heavy rain, triggering the fungus to initiate fruiting as a survival response. This innovation allowed Shiitake cultivation to become more predictable, ensuring a steady supply of mushrooms that are still harvested in Japan and worldwide.

In Japanese culture, the growth of Shiitake mushrooms is said to parallel a boy's journey to manhood.[9] Traditionally, families inoculate logs at a boy's birth, and the mushrooms mature alongside him. Upon reaching adulthood, the boy inherits the logs and the fortune and good health they bring.

Traditional Chinese Medicine values Shiitake for their ability to "activate the blood", and recent research confirms their potential to treat high blood pressure and lower cholesterol.[10] Shiitake's

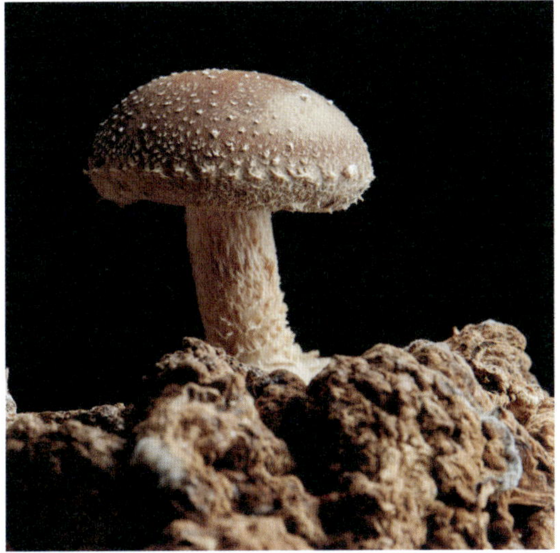

Shiitake, from the Japanese "take" (mushroom) and "shii" (the tree on which the mushrooms grow in the wild).

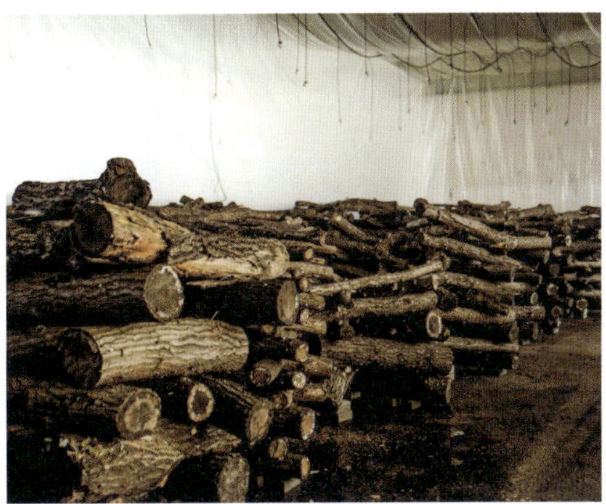

Shiitake log cultivation, a technique refined in 1940s Kyoto, involves inoculating logs with mycelium, leaving them for one to two years, then submerging them in cold water. The logs are then struck with hammers to stimulate mycelial growth in a process known as "soak and strike".

anti-cancer properties have also been extensively researched in Japan since the 1960's.[11]

Like other medicinal mushrooms, Shiitake contain a wide variety of secondary metabolites with antioxidant, anti-inflammatory, and antimicrobial properties.[12] One such compound, Lentin, even demonstrates potent antifungal effects.[13] [14] This apparent contradiction – an antifungal fungus – arises from the fierce competition fungi face in their ecosystems, where they battle for resources both among themselves and against parasitic foes. A single log can host over fifty fungal species, and soils are alive with countless more. To survive, Shiitake produce antibacterials, antivirals, and antifungals, that help them survive in these crowded environments – whether in logs, soil, or even within our bodies.

Shiitake's antifungal compounds offer a powerful tool in fighting mycotoxins and fungal infections. This makes them an ideal recommendation in cases of mushroom poisoning and incidentally, for my friend dealing with candida. Unlike refined carbohydrates, which promote micro-fungal growth in our bodies, Shiitake contain beta-glucans and other polysaccharides that are indigestible to humans but beneficial to our immune system and gut microbiota.[15] When consumed, Shiitake mushrooms help restore balance, supporting the immune system in managing fungal overgrowth, and potentially preventing infections.

This extends to plants and animals. Asian fruit farmers use Shiitake's antifungal properties to protect crops like apples and strawberries from fungal threats. [16] Shiitake extracts enhance biocontrol methods, safeguarding plant wounds from contamination. Likewise, other fungi, such as yeasts, are included in cow feeds to enhance rumen fermentation and fibre breakdown.[17] Their antifungal properties help stabilise the microbial balance, thereby preventing the growth of harmful pathogens. This supports

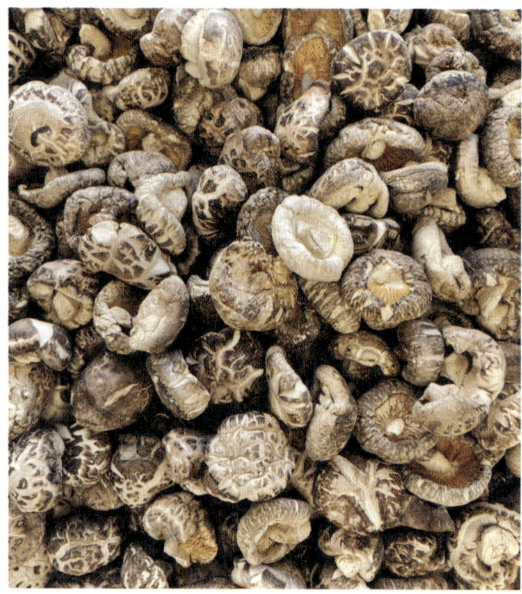

Dried Shiitake in a Japanese Market. Though it may seem paradoxical, Shiitake's antifungal compounds offer a powerful tool in fighting mycotoxins and fungal infections.

better feed efficiency, digestion, and immune health, promoting improved milk production and overall cow health by regulating fungal activity in the rumen.

The relationship between fungi and animals is paradoxical, rooted in our shared evolutionary history. Both belong to the Opisthokonta supergroup, first proposed in 2002, which encompasses organisms that had a single posterior flagellum at some stage in their evolutionary history.[18] This common ancestry reveals that fungi are more closely related to animals than to plants or other eukaryotes. This evolutionary kinship may be the reason that we are particularly responsive to the compounds fungi produce, whether beneficial or harmful. Fungi can be our closest allies, helping to treat infections, reduce antimicrobial resistance, and produce some of the strongest antibiotics, such as penicillin. But other fungi are more akin to enemies, producing deadly mycotoxins or pathogenic enzymes to which we are equally susceptible. This duality is inherent in the fungal kingdom: fungi are both healers and hazards, depending on the context, dose, preparation, and the host's immune system.

A good friend of mine has long struggled with eczema, an immune disorder that causes red, irritated skin patches. From an immunological perspective, eczema is characterised by an overactive immune response and skin barrier dysfunction. He had read about the immunomodulatory effects of Shiitake and asked me for advice. To be clear, I am no doctor. I encouraged him to consult one and to do further research, but we discussed some potential options. To avoid overwhelming his immune system – or counteracting his immunosuppressant medications – I suggested he first adopt a diet rich in Shiitake mushrooms[19] before considering supplements. Another, more unusual option I mentioned, was to take an occasional bath in Shiitake mycelium, which contains antimicrobial compounds that might help soothe the skin.[20]

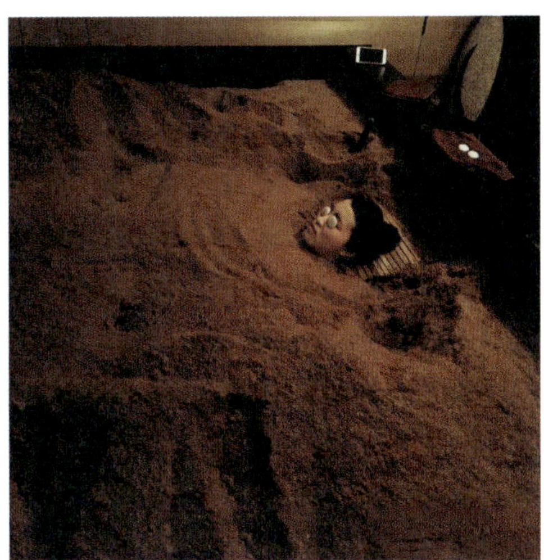

Hakkō *enzyme bathing: bathing naked in decomposing wood chips.* Hakkō *means fermentation in Japanese, and those who immerse themselves in these mycelium-infused beds are, in essence, being fermented alive.*

He was curious but sceptical, and asked me to try first. So, in the summer of 2024, I took home several bags of spent Shiitake substrate – the woody, myceliated material left behind once the mushrooms have fruited and been harvested. After crumbling up and drying the spent substrate in sunlight to enhance its vitamin D content, I added it to my bathwater. I left it to soak for a while to extract all the bioactive compounds, then climbed in. Soaking in the resulting mycelium bath, I felt not only relaxed (and a little weird) but rejuvenated, emerging slightly caramelised in scent and hue.

This practice resembles the traditional Japanese art of bathing naked in decomposing wood chips, known as Hakkō. In Japanese, Hakkō means fermentation, and those who submerge themselves in these cedar, rice bran, and living myceliated beds are essentially being fermented alive. These baths reach temperatures of 40°C (104°F) and promote skin health by releasing microbial enzymes that break down contaminants and activate the skin's natural healing processes.

As I luxuriated in the rich, enzymatic waters of my Shiitake bath being activated, decomposed, and cleansed in ways beyond my wildest imagination, the teachings of Augustus De Morgan's poem, *Siphonaptera*,[21] came to mind:

> ***"Great fleas have little fleas upon their back to bite 'em.***
> ***And little fleas have lesser fleas, and so ad infinitum."***

Fungi, like fleas, demonstrate similar patterns of interdependence and coexistence, verging on self-phagism. Many species engage in parasitic relationships with one another. The *Hypomyces* genus, for example, includes species like the Bolete Eater, which envelops Porcini mushrooms in a white layer that turns spongy and sulphurous as it ages. Similarly, the Lobster Mushroom parasitises certain inedible mushrooms, like Milkcaps and Russulas, transforming them into edible delicacies, their scent and appearance now resembling that of a lobster.

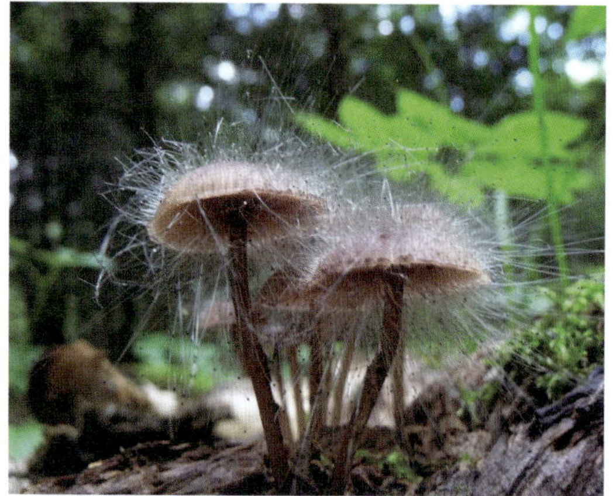

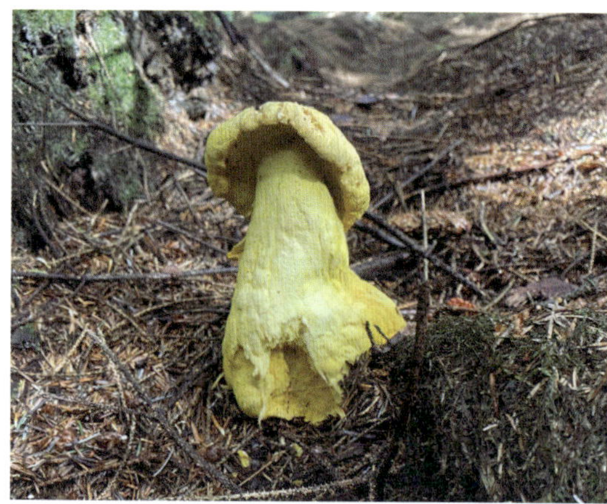

The Bolete Eater, Hypomyces chrysospermus, *is a parasitic fungus that infects Bolete mushrooms, transforming the host's appearance to a whitish, golden-yellow.*

These are the mycoparasitic fungi: the fungi that parasitise other fungi. But fungal-to-fungal encounters are not always competitive. The Piggyback Rosegill, *Volvariella surrecta*, for example, grows on the cap of the Clouded Funnel, *Clitocybe nebularis*, without harming its host, using it as a perch rather than as food. The Rosegill emerges from a white volva, often held in perfect position by the depression in the Funnel's cap. It only emerges once its host has grown and sporulated, allowing for mutual proliferation. In the wild, this rare interplay looks completely fantastical – a beautiful mushroom fruiting from the cap of another, resembling a "piggyback" ride – and highlights the many peculiar ways in which fungi can interact with one another.

Even rarer are the Strangler fungi, *Squamanita* spp., which entirely override their mushroom hosts by invading and consuming their tissues at the mycelial level. *Squamanita paradoxa*, the Powdercap Strangler, exemplifies this process: its mycelium infiltrates the host mushroom's mycelium, gradually replacing and transforming it. This results in a striking genetic and physical takeover, where the remnants of the original host remain visible only as a golden base beneath the newly formed, shaggy white tissue of the Strangler fungus.

This survival and reproduction strategy seems counterintuitive. The Piggyback and Lobster fungi, though parasitic, still allow their hosts to grow and reproduce. This makes sense, since their survival depends on them. In contrast, Stranglers break this mutualistic narrative. By consuming their hosts before their hosts can sporulate, the Stranglers ultimately contribute to their own demise. In doing so, they challenge the conventional rules of natural selection in the fungal world – or at least the ones we assume to be true.

But really, we shouldn't be surprised. Mycologists know one thing for sure: in the fungal kingdom, there's always an exception to the rule. If fungi are to play a crucial role in restoring our internal and external ecosystems, as many believe, we must first understand their complexities and paradoxes. After all, we don't want to end up on the wrong side of them. Or, more accurately, have the wrong ones end up inside us!

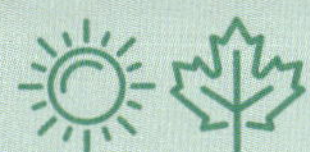

ACTIVITY

DISSECTING PARASITIC FUNGI

1. To experience the world of antifungal fungi and mycoparasitic fungi, head to a damp, wooded area and keep an eye out for a few interesting species. Look for Bolete Eaters, Lobster Mushrooms, Piggyback Rosegills, or Stranglers. *Tremella* species, known for their moisture-retaining and antifungal properties, are often the easiest to find. With over 170 species, *Tremella* thrives on dead branches of deciduous trees like maple, oak, and birch, and can be found year-round. They form slimy, indistinct films as they search for fungal hosts, then invade, triggering mycelial growth and producing gelatinous, fruiting bodies.
2. Once you spot a specimen, collect it – the entire mushroom if possible. Use a scalpel to slice a thin section, ideally both parts (if they can be separated), and examine them under a microscope. Look for variations in colour, spore structures, and mycelial branching patterns.
3. If a microscope isn't available, you can cut the mushroom in half to observe the differences between species. A hand-held microscope, macro lens, or even the naked eye can also reveal interesting details, particularly with the larger mushrooms. Without a microscope, consider searching for the rare but locally common Parasitic Bolete, *Pseudoboletus parasiticus*, which often reveals tangled mycelia.
4. Finally, if you encounter a *Squamanita*, be thorough in documenting your find, as they are incredibly rare. Take photos of the entire specimen, its gills, the surrounding environment, and nearby species. Upload it to iNaturalist and inform a mycologist. Your discovery will not go unnoticed!

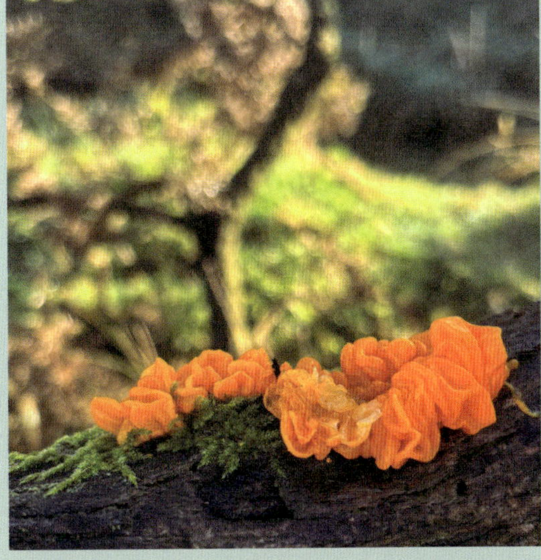

Tremella spp.

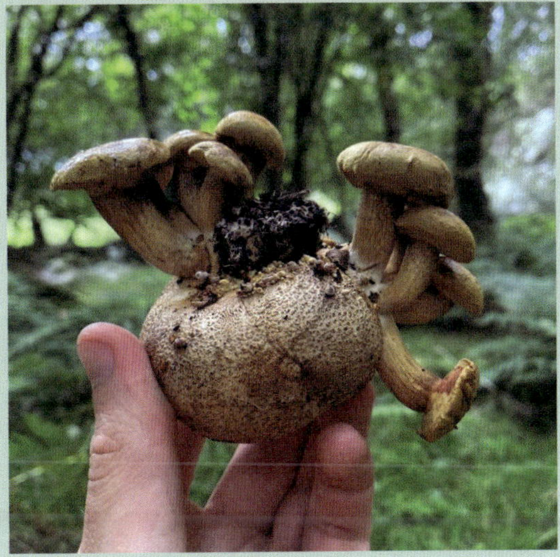

Parasitic Bolete, Pseudoboletus parasiticus.

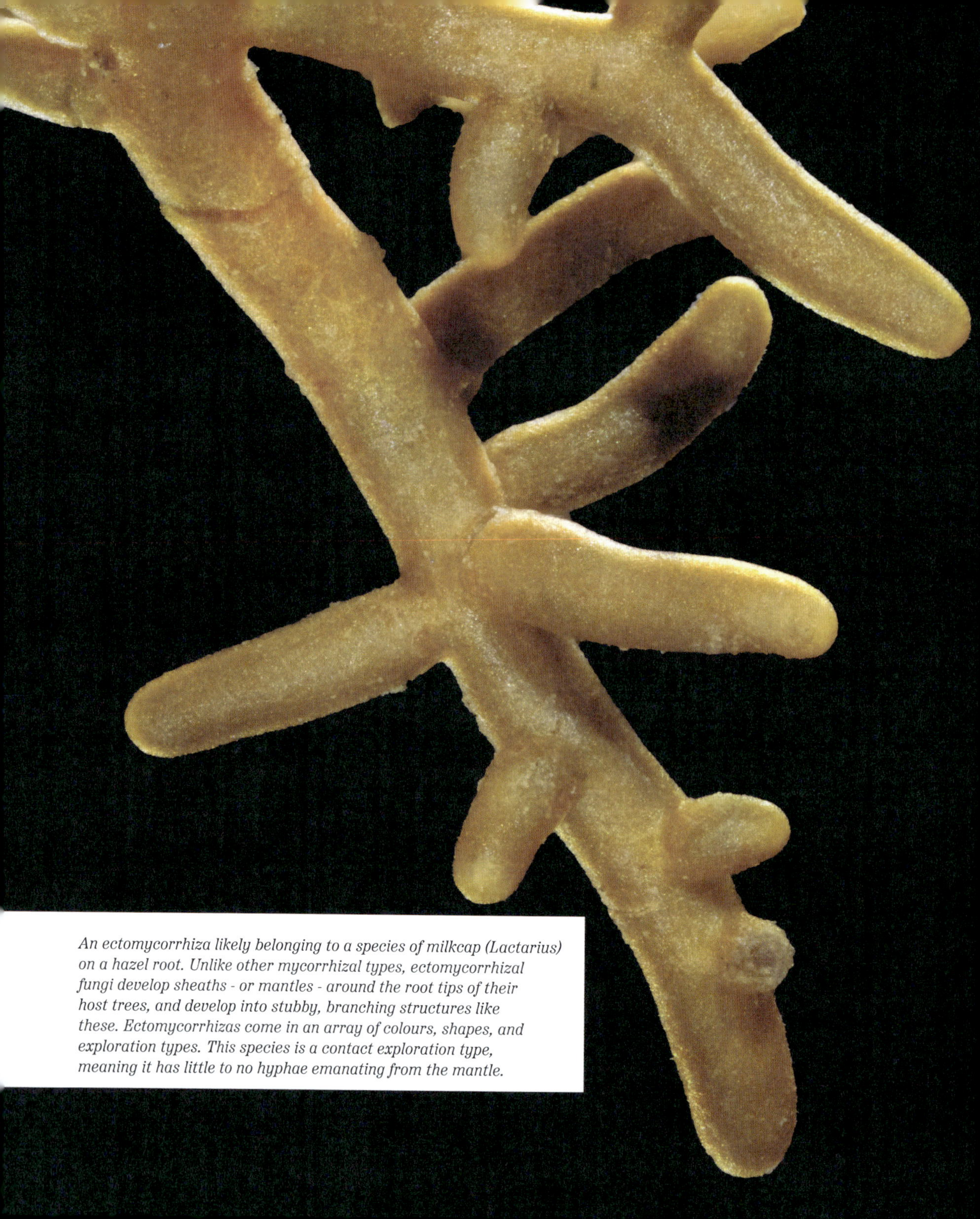

An ectomycorrhiza likely belonging to a species of milkcap (Lactarius) on a hazel root. Unlike other mycorrhizal types, ectomycorrhizal fungi develop sheaths - or mantles - around the root tips of their host trees, and develop into stubby, branching structures like these. Ectomycorrhizas come in an array of colours, shapes, and exploration types. This species is a contact exploration type, meaning it has little to no hyphae emanating from the mantle.

QUEER & DECOLONIAL MYCOLOGY

Mycology can be understood as queer, both in the organisms it studies and in the communities that form around it.[22] Mushroom festivals and forays often embody a distinctly queer spirit: they resist rigid institutional structures, operate without strict hierarchies, and thrive through collaboration. The cultural suspicion of fungi – what some call *mycophobia* – has long mirrored anxieties about queerness, since both are linked to countercultural identities and unconventional ways of being. In recent years, "Queer Mycology" has emerged as a lively current within cultural and ecological thought, drawing energy from queer ecology, radical mycology, and decolonial science. Many practitioners describe the sense that fungi themselves unsettle normative categories, reshaping how humans think, relate, and imagine their place in the world. It is an experience widely shared across mushroom communities, where queerness and mycology intertwine in both practice and philosophy.[23]

Fungi themselves embody this queerness – not as aberrations from the norm but as expressions of Nature's variety. Consider cicadas. When infected and controlled by *Massospora* fungi, they display both male and female mating behaviours, singing to attract females and flicking their wings to lure males. in effect, the fungi make them bisexual. Other species, like *Fusarium*, exhibit morphologically fluid forms, shifting between yeast and filamentous states depending on environmental conditions. For queer mycologists, such examples remind us that "queerness" is simply a contemporary word for an ancient, recurring tendency in nature.[24]

The fungal "Queendom" also offers a stunning example of sexual diversity. Some species form multiple partnerships while others avoid sexual reproduction altogether. Many, like truffles, reproduce with two primary mating types (+ and -) and can either give or take genetic material depending on context – becoming hermaphroditic as a reproductive strategy.[25] But fungi like the Splitgill mushroom, *Schizophyllum commune*, go even further, exhibiting over 23,000 potential mating types (not just male/female or positive/negative), each with its own compatibility rules. This polysexuality ensures its survival and adaptability, making it a fungal embodiment of resilience and fluidity. As such, *Schizophyllum commune* has been adopted as the ultimate fungal queer icon.

Fungal reproduction – unpredictable, contextual, and in constant flux – teaches us this: Nature does not favour dichotomies; it favours diversity, mutation, and experimentation.

One such experiment altered the course of eukaryotic evolution forever. An ancient eukaryotic-like cell, or host cell, engulfed a bacterium. Instead of digesting it, however, the two formed a mutually beneficial relationship: the bacterium supplied the host with energy, while the host provided the bacterium with a stable environment and access to nutrients. This endosymbiotic theory, proposed by Lynn Margulis in the 1960s, was a radical departure from conventional evolutionary thought that saw nature as a battleground of competition between individuals. Instead, Margulis suggested that life, in

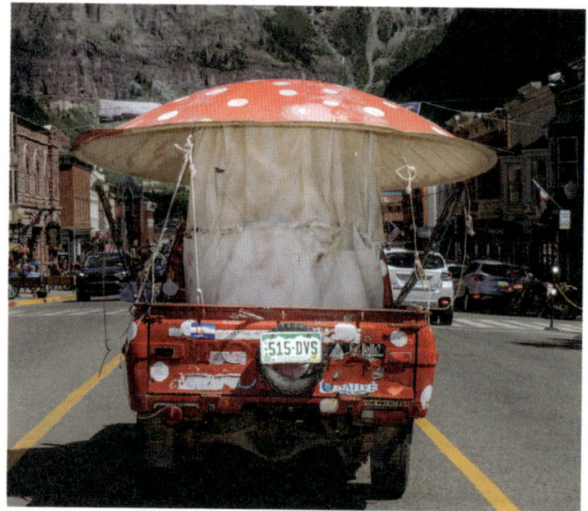

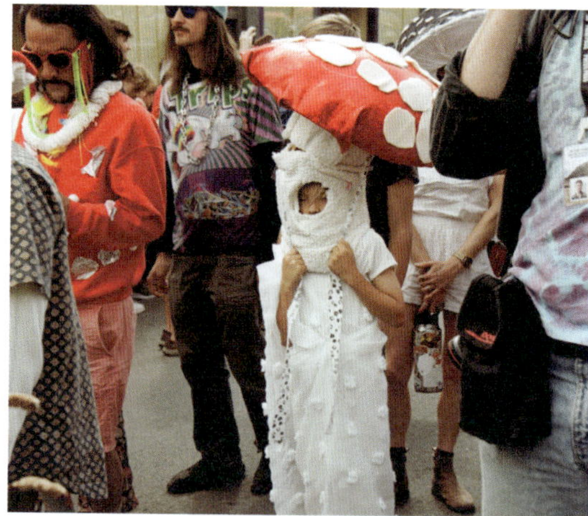

The Telluride Mushroom Festival. An annual event celebrating all things fungi through workshops, forays, cooking demonstrations, and educational talks, set in Colorado's scenic Rocky Mountains.

its complexity, is the result of ancient *symbioses* (the mutual engagement between two organisms) and *endosymbioses* (where one organism becomes absorbed by another.) Her theory has been bolstered by genetic evidence and is now widely regarded as true.

Margulis even extended this idea, suggesting that many organisms, including humans, exist as holobionts – complex, multi-species systems in which microbes and the host organisms live in mutually beneficial relationships. Examples of such biological cooperation are abundant, with animal microbiomes and mycorrhizal networks being two of the most celebrated and well-known. In these worlds, the line between one and the other, inside and outside, often blurs. Consider an endomycorrhizal plant root. From the outside, we see the plant material, perhaps with few external mycorrhizal filaments. Phase the material out, using advanced imaging techniques, and we find an extraordinarily dense mesh of mycelium, illustrating the depth of fungal integration within the root. Endosymbiotic relationships have evolved independently 60–80 times, suggesting this kind of partnership is not only effective but evolutionarily compelling – a good idea that keeps happening.

Queer mycologists often use these examples to highlight that nature is inherently fluid and collaborative. Likewise, narratives around the hyperconnected Wood Wide Web (WWW) and symbiotic multi-species microbiomes further support the queer-ecological perspective.

Yet, the scientific community remains critical of the overly romanticised narratives that often accompany discussions of symbiosis. Our gut and skin ecosystems are rife with competition, tension, and exploitation. Likewise, the concept of the mycorrhizal WWW was taken too far when it gave the impression that entire forests are interconnected by a unified mycelium, which isn't true. Mycologist David Satori explains that most mycorrhizal species span only a few square meters, and there are thousands of genetically distinct individuals doing their own thing[26] – not to mention the notorious photosynthetic-less "hackers" and the innumerable parasites of the system.

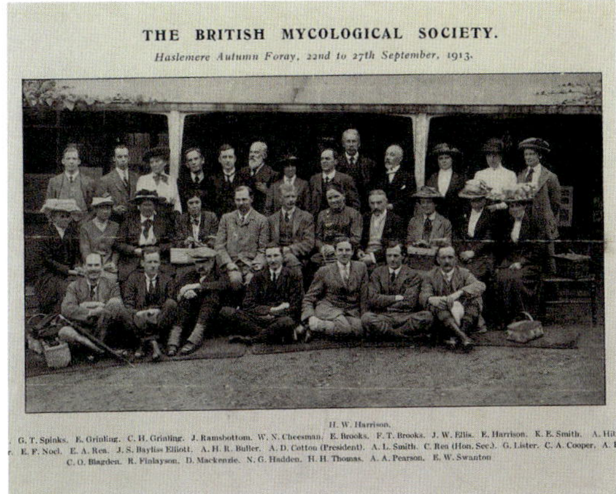

British Mycological Society at the Haslemere Fungus Foray, 1913.

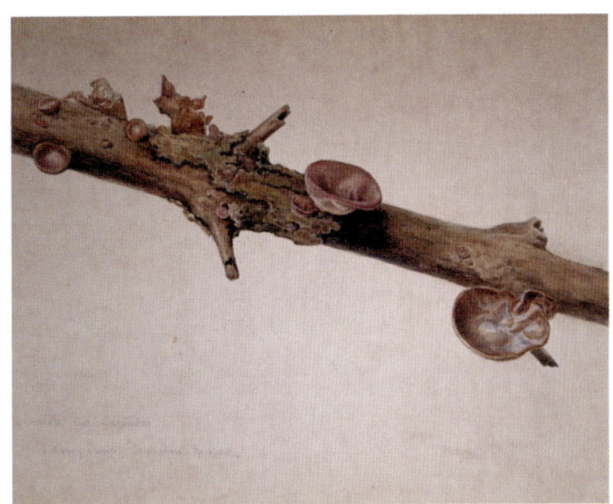

Beatrix Potter's Illustrations of a Wood Ear, Auricularia auricula-judae

True collaboration, as evolutionary biologist Toby Kiers observes, is more like an alloy of competition, conflict, *and* cooperation. Much like family or community dynamics, ecological relationships are rarely simple or harmonious, but they are, as queer ecologists rightly point out, fluid, entangled, and biodiverse.

The culture surrounding mycology also offers parallels to queer communities. Often dismissed as "strange" and "peripheral", mycology was overlooked by mainstream science for millennia. Aristotle, like most ancient thinkers, treated them as plants. In his *Historia Plantarum* (4 BCE), he referred to mushrooms, truffles, and similar organisms as *phyta atelē*, or "imperfect plants." He gave them this name because, unlike "perfect" plants, they had no visible flowers, fruits, or seeds.

This misconception continued throughout the 14th century when Swedish botanist Carl Linnaeus admitted that fungi were difficult to categorise, with poorly understood reproduction, so he described the group as "confused and chaotic." Even until the 20th century, these so called "strange plants" were deemed unworthy of "polite botany." Mycologist Mary Elizabeth Banning (1822–1903) captured this outsider status, describing fungi as "vegetable outcasts – like beggars by the wayside dressed in gay attire; they ask for attention but claim none."[27]

This marginalisation meant mycology became a refuge for outsiders, including those who rejected traditional scientific hierarchies or those who were rejected by them. It became a field where women – Catharina Dörrien, Élise-Caroline Bommer, and Beatrix Potter – though labelled "eccentrics," could make significant contributions[28,29] Potter's fungal illustrations, for example, showcased not only her scientific acumen but her storytelling and aesthetic appreciation of the fungal world.

As for contemporary mycology, those who study the subject often call themselves "amateur mycologists" – literally "lovers" in Latin. This is largely because there are few places to formally study mycology, meaning people have to take matters into their own hands: developing unconventional ways of learning and sharing knowledge, via comics and magazines, foraging walks, fungi festivals, and clandestine underground meetings. (I'm thinking of the psychedelic cultivators "O T Oss and O N

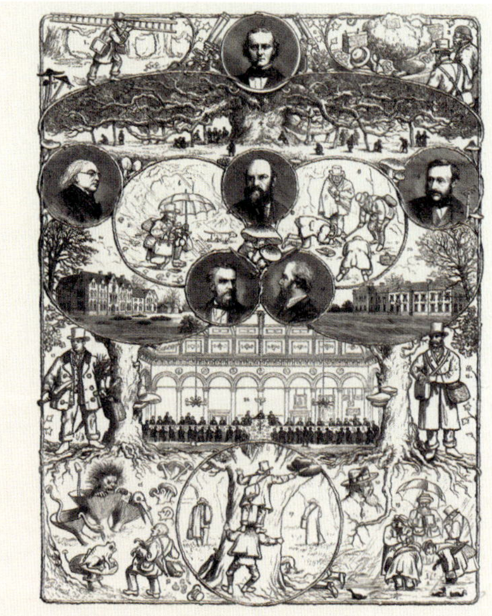

In October 1880, the Hereford Fungus Eaters held Britain's first fungal foray.

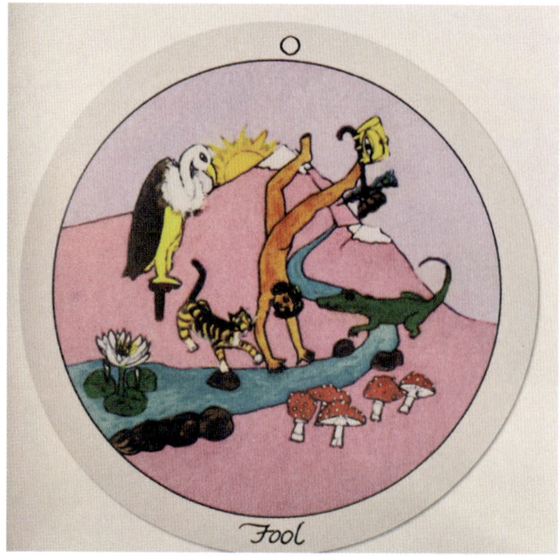

The Fool *Tarot card by Karen Vogel and Vicki Noble. The Fool's openness, trust in the unknown, and willingness to move through flux–as a gender fluid figure–echo themes of queerness, re-enchantment, and decolonial approaches to knowledge where myth and science intersect.*

Oeric" (the pseudonyms of Terence and Dennis McKenna).) These books became underground staples and the events became seasonal traditions, keeping the study of fungi alive even on the margins.

A defining moment in mycology's history took place in England in 1868, when the Hereford Fungus Eaters held their first fungal foray. This group of mycologists, passionate about edible species, launched what became an annual gathering for fungal enthusiasts. The aim was simple: to create a collaborative space for learning, whether for beginners or experts. This initiative helped popularise mycology in Britain, establishing a passionate, quirky – *and queer* – mycological community that thrives to this day.

Likewise, in the US, the insanely creative and inspiring Telluride Mushroom Festival took root in 1980 when a handful of fungi-loving friends decided on a whim to make it happen. Among them was Gary Lincoff, a mycologist who inspired countless people to pause their lives and devote themselves to mushrooms. Lincoff was adamant that mycology should be open to everyone – whether six or ninety-six – and his vision helped diversify the mycological community. He, like many others, embodied the spirit of radical mycology: open-source, punk in ethos, and fuelled by the mantra "spores not wars."

Today, people and their animals flock to the festival for forays, workshops, lectures, poetry slams, yoga, the costume parade, and the legendary Puff Ball Dance Party. Attendees come to celebrate fungi, learn together, and battle for glory in the fiercely contested "best-dressed mushroom" competition – where costumes are as scientifically precise as they are wildly imaginative.

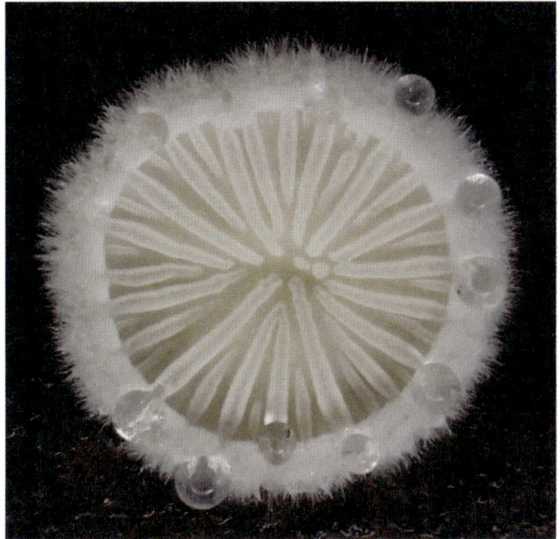

The Splitgill, Schizophyllum commune, *has over 23,000 mating types. Photographer Steve Axford calls it "The most promiscuous fungus we know."*

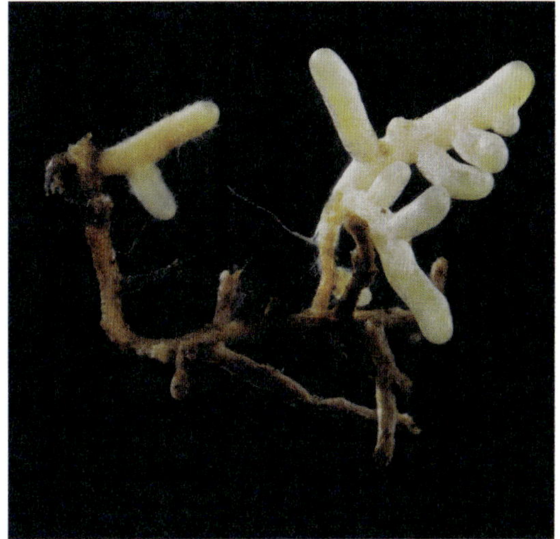

An ectomycorrhiza of a species of bolete, likely Xerocomellus *on an oak root. These ectomycorrhizae are almost as diverse in appearance as the mushrooms they produce. It is possible to identify this species using DNA barcoding techniques.*

On a walk with Susy, an amateur mycologist known as "Queer as Funghi," they described queer mycology not as a fixed discipline but as a dynamic interaction that embraces diverse, non-normative methods of learning – the parade being a perfect example. Susy leads walks for children and adults with special educational needs, encouraging them to touch, smell, listen, sing, and dream alongside fungi. These sensory, creative approaches often deepen participants' connection to and understanding of fungi beyond traditional scientific frameworks.

Though fungi are one of the most species rich organisms on the planet, we still don't see a proportional representation of mycologists within the ecological sciences. Yet, mycology remains as radical and interdisciplinary as ever. Artists, chefs, ecologists, psychologists, philosophers, shamans, architects, geneticists, comedians, all come together to celebrate fungal diversity. Some study fungi as biological organisms, while others use them as malleable metaphors to explore broader cultural and ecological ideas. As Dr Patty Ononiwu Kaishian, Curator of Mycology at the New York State Museum, points out, science should be dynamic and inclusive, reflecting the rich diversity of human culture. She emphasises that the word "science" comes from the Latin *scire*, meaning "to know," and that science is not one singular, fixed way of knowing. It is one of many methods of engaging with the world. Knowledge, she argues, is inseparable from culture, and science, at its best, is a tool for collective, intergenerational, and cross-cultural understanding. Through shared inquiry, we gradually chip away at the vast mystery of life.[30]

Like all sciences, mycology cannot be disentangled from culture. Colonialism and racism, for example, are embedded in botanical taxonomy. The fungus Jew's Ear, *Auricularia auricula-judae*, carries the weight of anti-Semitic stereotypes and a legend about Judas Iscariot and elder trees. In a step towards decolonising knowledge, this fungus has been renamed *Jelly Ear*. This shift reflects a growing movement within the sciences to acknowledge that scientific understanding is never neutral, but deeply shaped by cultural, political, and historical contexts. A more lighthearted example is the recent naming of a yellow sponge-like mushroom "*Spongiforma squarepantsii*".

"Had nature any outcast face
Could she a son condemn
Had nature an Iscariot
That mushroom – it is him."
– *Emily Dickinson,* The Mushroom, *1874*

The decolonisation of science also requires recognising the enormous contributions of Indigenous knowledge systems, and ethically integrating them into a broader scientific discourse. A beautiful example of the non-European and even non-human foundations of science is Quinine, derived from the Chinchona, or "Fever Tree." Quinine bark, used to treat malaria, was "discovered" by French explorers after they learned of its healing properties from Spanish colonisers in what is now Venezuela, who had themselves learned about it from Indigenous peoples, who are said to have observed mountain lions self-medicating with the bark. Unfortunately, neither the Venezuelans nor the mountain lions were credited with the findings. However, ancient figures like Pliny, Aristotle, and Dioscorides frequently credited animals for scientific discoveries, notably citing wounded goats for discovering the antiseptic properties of dittany. Science, as it turns out, is both multi-cultural and multi-species.

Decolonising science is also about dismantling extractive practices, like "helicopter science," where researchers parachute into a country, extract data, and leave with little accountability or reciprocity. This modern-day form of colonialism is still widespread. In contrast, organisations like SPUN (Society for the Protection of Underground Networks) are reimagining how science can be done more ethically and collaboratively. SPUN maps global mycorrhizal networks using machine learning and environmental data to help governments make better environmental decisions. It also supports local researchers all over the world, from Mexico to Madagascar, with grants to pursue fungi-focused projects that meet local needs, such as advocating for watershed protection or policy change. The data remains locally owned, but it also feeds into SPUN's global models, creating a mutual benefit without appropriation.

This grassroots network, now active in over 100 countries, is growing into a vibrant, transnational community – one I hope the early mycologists would applaud. Explorers share methods, build local capacity, and nurture a culture of care for the fungal world.

SPUN, Susy, Patty, and others are working to conduct more ethical, accountable, and accurate scientific inquiry, recognising the importance of situating their work within broader sociocultural contexts. Susy continues to inspire new ways of interacting with fungi, while Patty actively diversifies museum spaces. SPUN leads by example, integrating decolonial approaches into its system and culture. Meanwhile, fungi forays continue to bring together both amateur and professional mycologists to explore, identify, and celebrate the biocultural diversity of fungi.

ACTIVITY

GET INVOLVED!

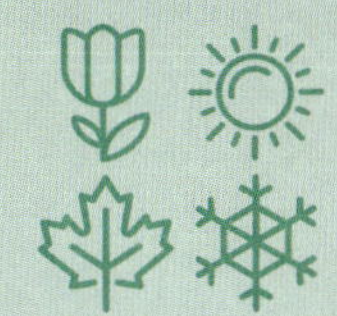

Dominant cultural narratives shape our understanding of identity, society, and science. Occasionally, a scientific discovery disrupts these ideas, say a hermaphroditic truffle or a mushroom with 23,000 mating types, forcing us to rethink what we consider "natural". These moments challenge not only scientific thinking but also ripple through culture, politics, and self-perception.

For the past 300 years, the dominant scientific view portrayed nature as a battleground of competition, using Darwin's (misinterpreted) "survival of the fittest" to justify exploitation, colonisation, and control. Later, the idealised "Wood Wide Web" emerged as a metaphor of connection and care, complete with a "Mother Tree". These narratives, deeply gendered and politically charged, often reflect human desires more than they describe nature.

But not all shifts in understanding are immediate or permanent. The reclassification of fungi from plants to their own kingdom in the mid-20th century was met with scepticism and resistance, as was the initial backlash against the Wood Wide Web, which later captivated the public. Perhaps Western culture, starved of connection, was ready for the idea.

Today, fungi as "queer" occupy a similar space in the cultural conversation, embraced not only for their biological quirks but for what they represent: something flexible, entangled, and defiantly non-normative.

But all metaphors drawn from nature are limited; they are human attempts to extract meaning from the more-than-human. And mushrooms? They're just the fruiting bodies – short-lived reproductive structures. Reducing a fungus to its mushroom is like reducing a human to their genitals.

If we want to think outside the box, we need to move beyond the mushroom.

With this in mind, your task is threefold:

1. Engage with the fungi community. Join a foraging walk, attend a fungi festival, or dive into online spaces where fungi enthusiasts gather. Along the way, you'll encounter fungi in all their bizarre glory – slimy, scaly, warty, smelly, fluffy, and luminous. You'll learn by touching, squishing, sniffing, listening, and watching as spores and aromas float on the breeze. In these moments, you might find yourself blending with the forest itself, becoming part-fungal, part-soil, part-human.

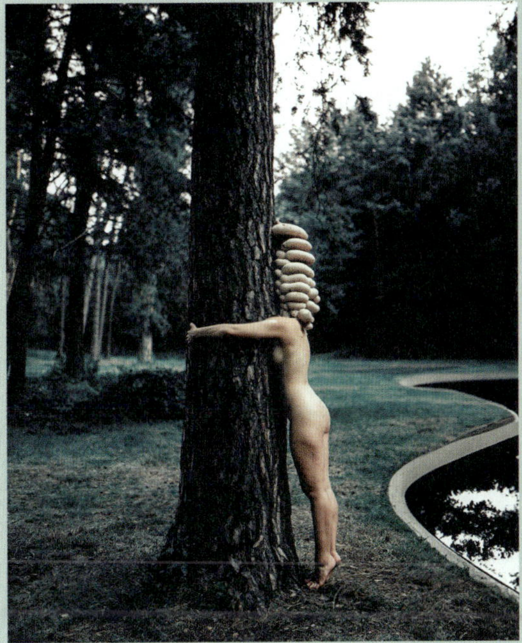

Bring Us the Fungus, Tree Hugger, *2023.*

2. Reflect on your own experience of queerness and decoloniality, both in relation to the natural world and to your identity. What does it feel like to see nature in terms of fluid partnerships, reciprocity, and accountability? How might your experiences with fungi challenge or expand your own understanding of gender, sexuality, and the legacies of colonialism? Find a fungus that resonates with your values – something that surprises, challenges, or queers your perception of nature and invites you to rethink the relationship between culture, ecology, and history.
3. Bring your insights to life through creative writing, art, performance, or another medium that speaks to you. Move beyond intellectual understanding and manifest queer, decolonial, and radical mycology in a tangible way – whether it's cultivating a fungal "forest garden" rooted in local, Indigenous knowledge, writing a poem about permeability from a mycelial perspective, or creating an artwork that portrays fungi, quietly breaking through the cracks of colonialism.

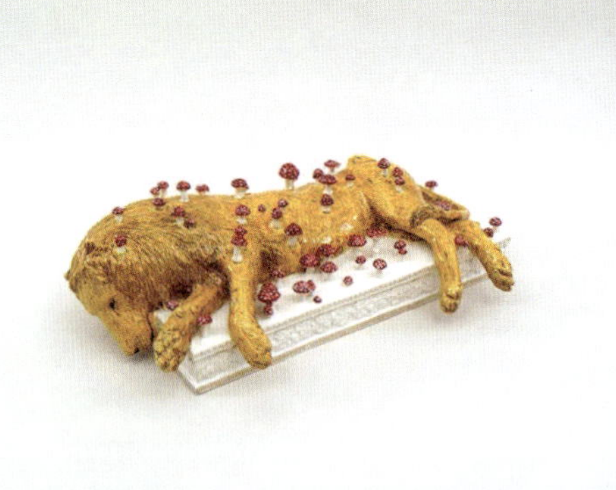

Claire Partington, The Red Lion, *2021. Part of the "Britainton" exhibition, this work critically reexamines Britain's historical self-image as portrayed in art. The lion, a powerful symbol of the British Empire, rests in slumber as nature reclaims its place in the nation's visual history. Once a symbol of conquest and land seizure, Partington's lion now lies dormant and subdued – immobilised by mycelium, its imperial force relegated to the past.*

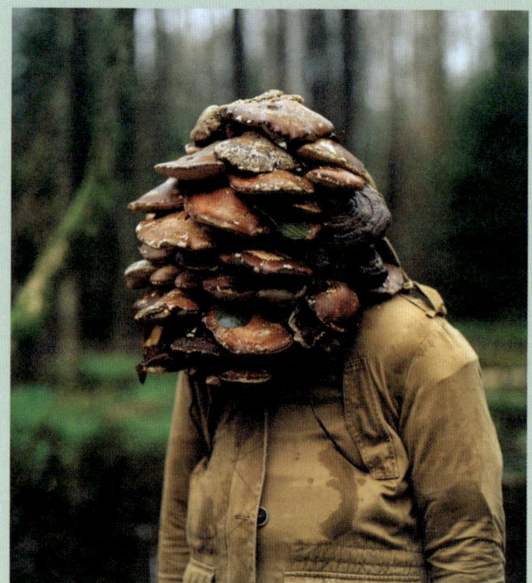

Eyes as Big as Plates, *#Ragnhild (Norway 2022).*

MYCOREMEDIATION

"Mushrooms can show us how to live in the ruins of modernity."

– *Anna Tsing,* The Mushroom at the End of the World

Fungi are the Earth's natural miners. Through their mycelial networks, fungi break down rocks, decompose organic matter, and absorb essential minerals and metals, facilitating nutrient cycling in ecosystems. They are primarily after nitrogen, vital for synthesising proteins and nucleic acids – the building blocks of life. But they also seek phosphorus, potassium, rare and trace metals, all while reshaping the landscape and fusing ecosystems together. In their ability to mine and make good of our waste, fungi offer us invaluable lessons in navigating toxicity.

In her book *Let's Become Fungal!* Yasmine Ostendorf-Rodríguez explores the pervasive presence of toxicity in modern life.[31] From industrial pollution to the widespread use of synthetic chemicals, we are surrounded by a constant bombardment of environmental contaminants. We are complicit in this toxicity, embedded in systems that depend on unsustainable consumption and waste – whether it's the clothes we wear, the food we eat, the computers and phones we buy, or the energy we consume. In this context, our pursuit of material comfort and convenience often comes at a high ecological and ethical price. This is the paradox of toxicity: the price we pay for progress.

British sculptor Gabriella Gormley explores this paradox through her personal experience with Lithium. In her beautiful article *Lithium: My Irreplaceable Element,*[32] Gabriella reveals her tripartite relationship with lithium: as a global commodity, a stabilising medical treatment, and an erratic force in her ceramic practice.

Prescribed for bipolar disorder six years ago, Gabriella is keenly aware of lithium's broader global impact. Often hailed as the "metal of the future" due to its role in renewable energy, lithium is a vital component in modern electronics and batteries. However, Gabriella reflects that its extraction and processing are not as "clean" as they're made out to be.

She explains that most of the world's lithium is sourced from Chile's Atacama Desert, the driest place on Earth. Yet, lithium extraction is highly water-intensive, requiring millions of litres of water to produce just one ton of lithium.[33] In a region already facing water scarcity, this process depletes vital groundwater, disrupting local ecosystems and displacing indigenous communities. It also destabilises the land, contaminates rivers with toxic brine, and accelerates soil degradation, causing irreversible damage to local biodiversity including shrimp, flamingos, and microorganisms.[34] As Gabriella points out, "Our reliance on coal and oil is under scrutiny, and rightly so, but the idea that lithium presents a singular solution, without consequence, is misguided. The exploitation of the land and the disruption

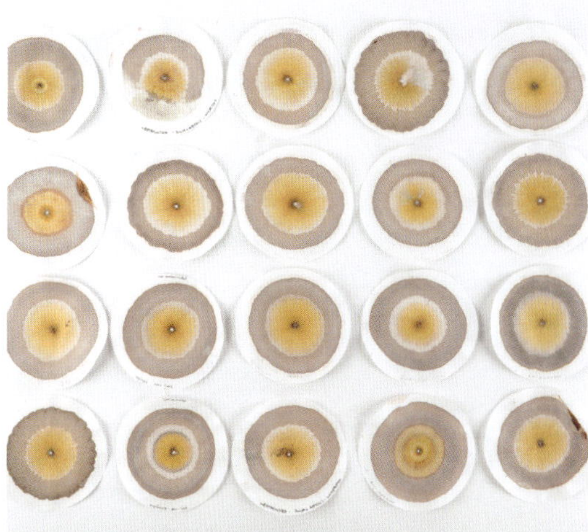

"Soil Chromas" offer a visual insight into underground ecosystems, highlighting key factors such as soil structure, fertility, biological diversity, organic matter, humus content, mineral availability, and toxicity levels.

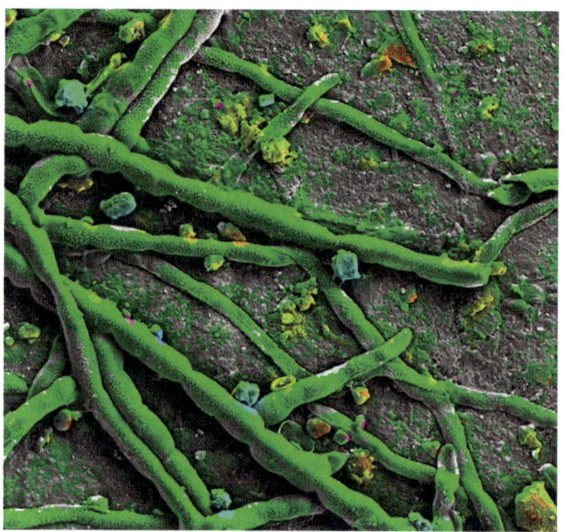

Hyphae *mining nitrogen from the soil, shown by the green colouration.*

of ecosystems were wrong then, and they are wrong now." Lithium has become just another commodity masked as an eco-friendly solution to our global crises.

As demand for lithium grows, so too does its price, reaching a record $80,000 per ton in December 2022. This surge has sparked geopolitical competition, with countries like the US and Russia vying for control of lithium-rich regions, including areas in Ukraine.[35,36] New mining operations are also emerging worldwide, from revived tin mines in Cornwall, UK[37] to Chinese mines at the foot of the Himalayas.[38]

Lithium's primary use is in electronics, but its history and applications stretch beyond this. For decades, it has been used in medicine, most notably as a treatment for bipolar disorder. Rediscovered as a mood stabiliser in the 1940s, lithium remains the only non-synthetic psychiatric drug. Its connection to natural sources is significant: spa towns like Baden-Baden in Germany and Lithia Springs in Georgia once thrived on lithium-rich mineral springs, and areas with higher lithium concentrations in drinking water report lower suicide rates.[39] Interestingly, lithium's mood-boosting properties were even included in the original formula for 7UP!

Beyond psychiatry, lithium is a key ingredient for those who work with glass and ceramics. At temperatures above 1000°C (1832°F), lithium can cause glaze cracks and a phenomenon called "flashing", where the clay burns to a brilliant orange. Gabriella has explored these reactions in her work, experimenting with varying amounts of lithium to create erratic and striking outcomes.

After six years of treatment, Gabriella has consumed over 1.5 kilograms of lithium. She continues to navigate her relationship with this element, balancing her multifaceted dependence on it and the

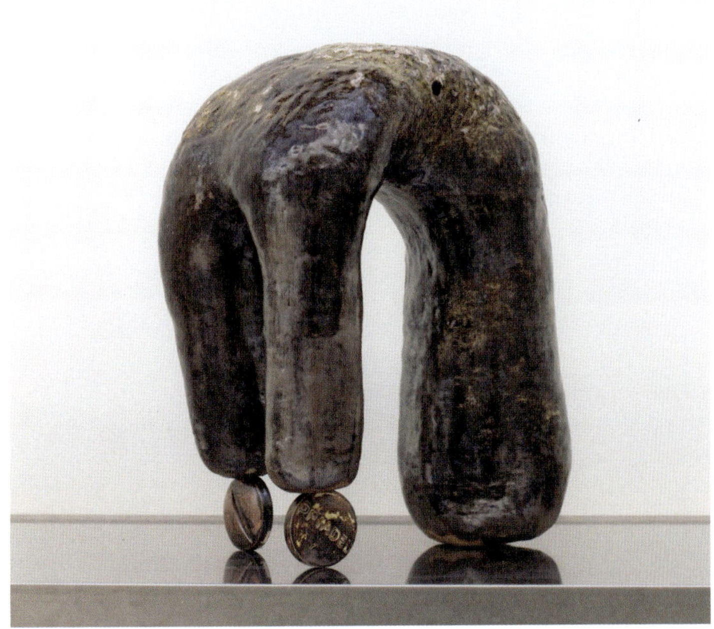

A sculpture by Gabriella Gormley (2018), made with a lithium glaze that acts as a "wild flux" ingredient.

responsibility that comes with it. Her concern is that as our global reliance on lithium grows, there is little accountability for its political, social, and ecological consequences.

This raises a crucial question: what happens when all the lithium is extracted? How do we responsibly manage the growing amounts of toxic waste, including the lithium batteries flooding the market?

As always, we turn to nature. Plants, fungi, and bacteria can degrade or remove toxins from polluted environments in a process known as bioremediation. With regards to lithium, lab studies show that fungi like *Aspergillus versicolor* and the yeast *Kluyveromyces marxianus* can bioabsorb lithium from water,[40] while *Aspergillus niger* not only tolerates high lithium levels but also boosts its organic acid production in response.[41]

This is key to how fungi extract metals from solid matrices such as ores, soils, or e-waste. Fungi, especially filamentous moulds like *Aspergillus niger*, naturally secrete organic acids, such as oxalic and citric acid, when under stress. These acids lower the pH of their environment, dissolve metal oxides, and chelate (bind to) metal ions, making them more soluble and easier to recover. In practical applications, *A. niger* has been used to leach lithium, cobalt, nickel, and copper from spent lithium-ion batteries, recovering up to 100 per cent of lithium and cobalt using biogenic acids.[42] In case you were wondering, nearly all commercial citric acid used in soft drinks is made through the fermentation of *A. niger*.

Fungi are nature's "molecular disassemblers".[43] With acids they can remove heavy metals from the environment by concentrating and stabilising them, and with enzymes they can break down complex toxins into simpler, less harmful compounds. Many do this naturally, but we can encourage such processes of "mycoremediation" by introducing spores or mycelium into contaminated sites, either in one-off or repeated treatments.

In the wild, fungal enzymes break down lignin and cellulose, the main structural components of wood and two of the most complex materials in nature. Since these natural polymers share structural similarities with petroleum-based compounds like diesel, oil, herbicides, and industrial dyes, mycelium is uniquely equipped to tackle them effectively.

The fungi that specialise in this process are twofold: the white rotters (which break down lignin) and the brown rotters (which break down cellulose). White-rot fungi, such as Oysters, Maitake, Turkey Tail, and Reishi, are particularly adept at breaking down nature's toughest compounds and recalcitrant, toxic compounds.

White-rot fungi produce specialised enzymes, like lignin peroxidase, that cleave irregular lignin bonds. They then release a torrent of free radicals that target and rupture these structures in a non-specific manner. This gives them flexibility, allowing them to break down a wide array of stubborn hydrocarbons, making them powerful agents of mycoremediation, capable of decomposing oil spills, cigarette butts, nappies, industrial dyes, and more.[44]

In a 1998 groundbreaking study, Paul Stamets inoculated diesel-soaked wood chips with Oyster mycelium, which successfully absorbed and metabolised the oil. [45] Over six weeks, the toxic, lifeless site transformed into an "oasis of life", covered in healthy Oyster mushrooms, attracting plants, insects, birds, and mammals. This ecological cascade reveals fungi as pioneer species, often the first to colonise disturbed environments. By breaking down complex nutrients, fungi produce organic matter that is more readily available to other life forms. They also fix nitrogen, retain moisture, and neutralise pollutants, stabilising ecosystems and facilitating the arrival and survival of other species.

What's more, even dead fungi can contribute to environmental restoration. The decaying remnants of fungal networks, known as fungal necromass, have been shown to immobilise toxic elements and stabilise contaminated soils.[46] While the exact mechanisms remain unclear, researchers suggest that bioabsorption plays a key role: Metal ions bind to the chitin in fungal cell walls, effectively reducing the toxin's mobility. Studies indicate that fungal necromass may even be more effective than living fungi in certain forms of ecological remediation.[47]

One of the most striking examples of mycoremediation involves using fungi to extract radioactive contaminants. In the Chernobyl Exclusion Zone, the white-rot fungus *Schizophyllum commune* was deployed on contaminated soils and waterways, where it actively absorbed radioactive strontium and cesium within its hyphae.[48] Moreover, several melanised fungi, including *Cladosporium sphaerospermum, Wangiella dermatitidis*, and *Cryptococcus neoformans*, have exhibited growth towards radiation sources. Researchers suggest that these fungi use melanin to convert radiation into energy, similar to how plants use sunlight.[49] This unique ability positions fungi as promising agents for bioremediation of radioactive waste, offering a natural way to stabilise contaminated sites.

Despite its promise, mycoremediation remains a complex and evolving field. Traditional methods of remediation, such as chemical treatment, incineration, and excavation (aka "dig and dump"), offer quick fixes but fail to address the root causes of contamination. These methods can also cause further harm to ecosystems: fighting pollution with more pollution. By contrast, mycoremediation is a slower process, but it offers a more holistic, sustainable solution.

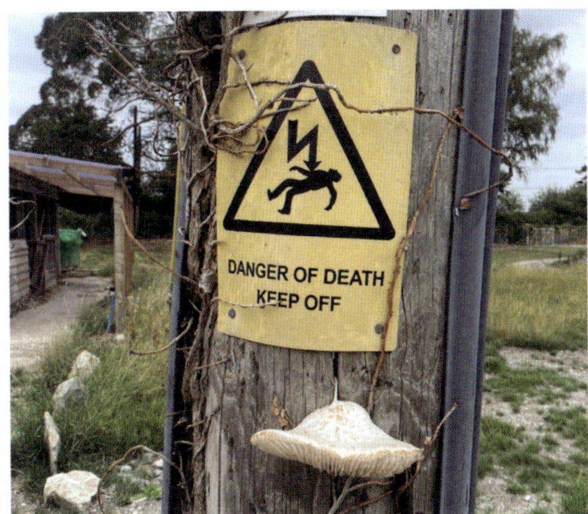

The brown-rot fungus Neolentinus lepideus, *commonly known as the "Train Wrecker," gets its name from its ability to decompose creosote-treated railway ties. The name reflects its destructive impact on wooden railway sleepers, which, like utility poles, were often treated with creosote to prevent fungal decay.*

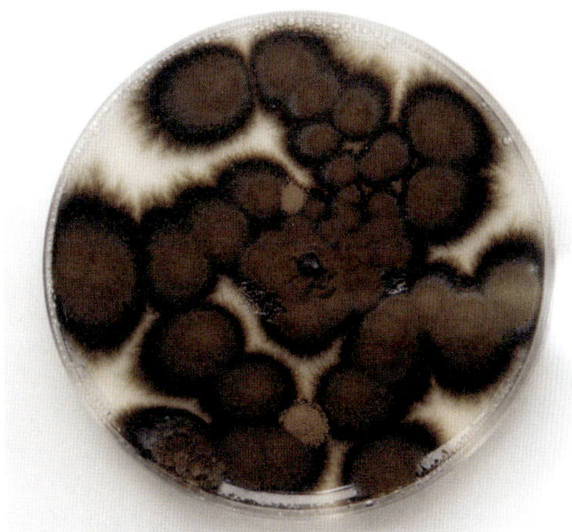

Fungi like Cladosporium sphaerospermum *exhibit radiotrophism, growing towards radiation sources. Researchers suggest these melanised fungi use melanin to convert radiation into energy, much like plants use sunlight.*

One of the greatest challenges to large-scale mycoremediation is time. While chemical methods can be completed in a matter of days, fungal-based remediation may take weeks or even months. Furthermore, introducing non-native species of fungi to certain environments can be tricky and potentially disruptive to local ecosystems.

Expert Daniel Reyes suggests that the future of mycoremediation might not lie in the fungi themselves, but in the acids and enzymes they produce. Companies are now cultivating fungi in controlled environments, exposing them to stimuli that encourage the secretion of specific compounds, which they then extract and use to treat polluted sites. By building enzyme libraries, companies can select the right enzymes to target specific pollutants, ensuring faster and more predictable results. This method bypasses the need for fungi to "figure out" which enzymes to use, as humans will have already identified the most effective ones.

I am sceptical of all of this, though perhaps I am naïve. From my perspective, the promise that fungi will "save the world" is brilliant in so much as it brings fungi to the table. No doubt they offer promising avenues for environmental cleanups and restoration. But the idea that we will continue this level of resource extraction and environmental destruction while relying on fungi to clean up our mess is both troubling and frustrating. It also reduces fungi to merely "tools" that serve a purpose for us rather than seeing them as wildlife with intrinsic value.

Mycoremediation offers a way to actively support ecosystems at critical tipping points. It allows us to step in, give nature a push where needed, and help accelerate the processes of repair, healing, and regeneration. But the first step, surely, is to stop doing the things we already know are harming

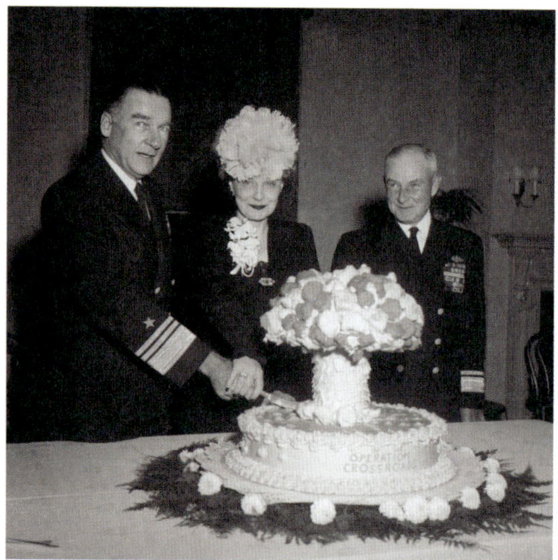

Admiral Blandy and his wife cut an Operation Crossroads mushroom cloud cake in November 1946. The operation conducted two US nuclear tests at Bikini Atoll earlier that year—the first detonations since the bombing of Nagasaki in August 1945.

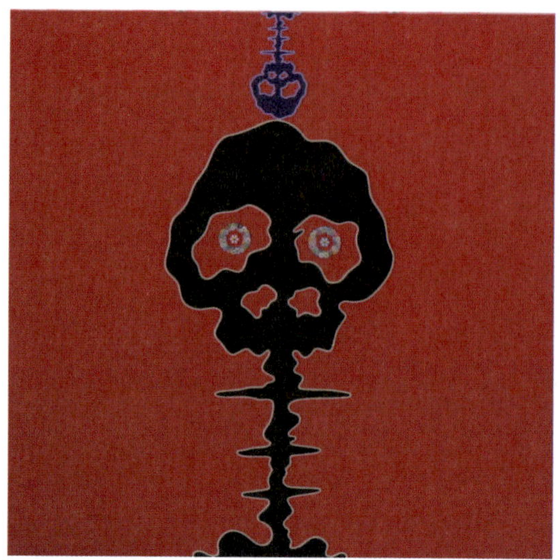

Takashi Murakami, Mushroom Bomb, *2001. The mushroom cloud was never meant to symbolise regeneration. Yet, in a bleak twist of irony, we now turn to actual mushrooms to remediate the very ecological scars our technologies have inflicted.*

ecosystems. That alone gives them a better chance to begin restoring and regenerating effectively. And often, it's surprising just how quickly life can return. Think of succession after a glacier retreats: what begins as bare rock becomes forest in just a few decades.

Two truths exist at the same time, and it's not always easy to hold them both. Zoomed in on the here and now, human activity is driving ecological collapse, and we seem unwilling or unable to change course. This is awful and hard to really think about. But, equally, on a massively zoomed-out scale, we know that life will continue. Nature responds to catastrophe with regeneration. Earth's history is punctuated by mass extinctions, wildfires, and ice ages, and yet, each time, life returns, often with renewed complexity. Tsunamis or volcanic eruptions can devastate ecosystems, but the speed at which they heal is astonishing: ecological succession gives way to seasonal succession, layers of life growing and dying upon one another. After the Permian-Triassic extinction, or the "Great Dying," around 90 per cent of species vanished. Oceans stagnated, landscapes burned, and ecosystems collapsed. And still, life came back. It always does.

Alongside our paradoxical relationship with toxic materials – lithium for batteries, oil for transportation, pesticides and plastics for food – we face a deeper paradox: how to hold both the urgency of the present and the indifference of deep time. Every life and ecosystem matters profoundly. And yet, in the end, life will go on, with or without us.

If the future of Earth isn't human, it will almost certainly be fungal. The rotters are endlessly ingenious, poised to inherit the Earth – and all our toxic gifts.

ACTIVITY

DIGESTING TOXIC WASTE WITH OYSTER MUSHROOMS

Humans excel at creating toxic compounds but are terrible at cleaning them up. Fungi, on the other hand, are naturally adept at turning toxicity into opportunity. The objective of this activity is to test the ability of Oyster mycelium to break down various pollutants.

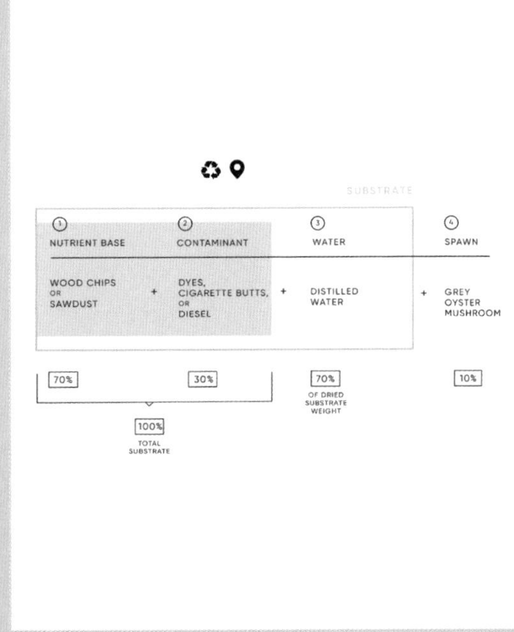

Ratios of substrate to choice contaminant to spawn.

EQUIPMENT

- Pressure Cooker
- Scales
- Mason jar or mushroom grow bag
- Grinder

INGREDIENTS

- 70% sawdust (preferably hardwood like oak or beech)
- 30% contaminant of choice (e.g., cigarette butts, spent ink cartridges, oil-contaminated soils)
- 10% Oyster grain spawn (you can buy them, or make your own)
- 70% diluted water

METHOD

1. Forage for a contaminant. Keep it in a container for easy management.
2. Dry and grind your contaminant into smaller pieces to increase the surface area. This step is key for enhancing mycelium's ability to break down the material.
3. Create a base substrate by mixing 70% sawdust with your dried and ground contaminant (~30% based on the material). The sawdust will act as a nutritional foundation to support the mycelium during the breakdown process.
4. Weigh your mixture (sawdust + contaminant). Add 70% of the weight of the mixture in water to achieve optimal moisture content.
5. Place the mixture into a mason jar or mushroom grow bag and sterilise in a pressure cooker at 121 PSI for 1 hour to eliminate unwanted microorganisms.
6. Once the sterilised substrate has cooled, inoculate it with Oyster grain spawn (10% of the total post-sterilised weight). Thoroughly mix the spawn into the substrate.

7. Seal the bag or place the lid on the jar.
8. Monitor the growth of the mycelium as it starts to colonise the substrate. Take a clone of the most virulent mycelium or mushroom and culture it on agar to keep working with it. Gradually increase the ratio of contaminants to sawdust in subsequent experiments to train the mycelium to focus on the breakdown of the pollutants.
9. Measure the success of the process by observing the degradation of the pollutants over time. Record any changes in colour, texture, or weight of the contaminants to assess how effective the mycelium is at digesting them.

▵ **Note:** Mycelium requires time to "remember" how to metabolise new types of contaminants. Be patient and gradually introduce the toxins in higher concentrations.

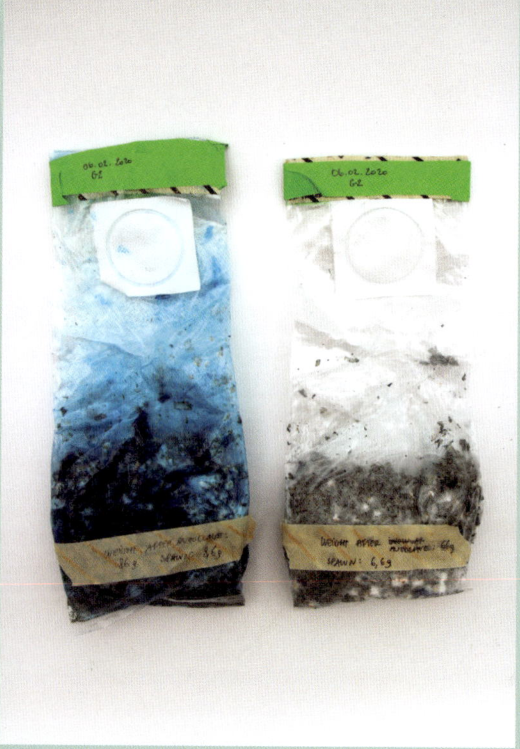

Oyster mycelium growing in (and possibly remediating) smashed ink cartridges.

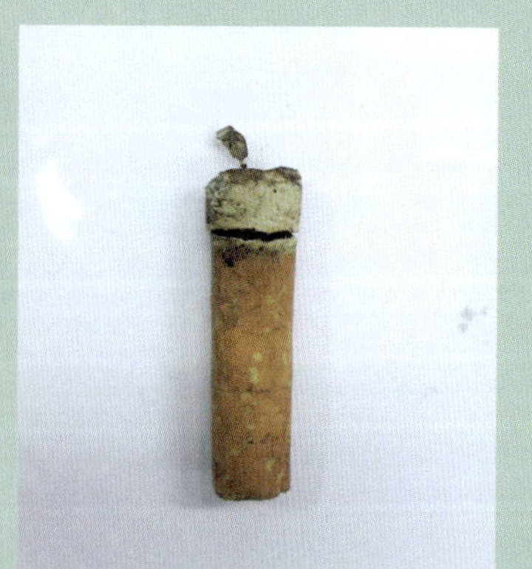

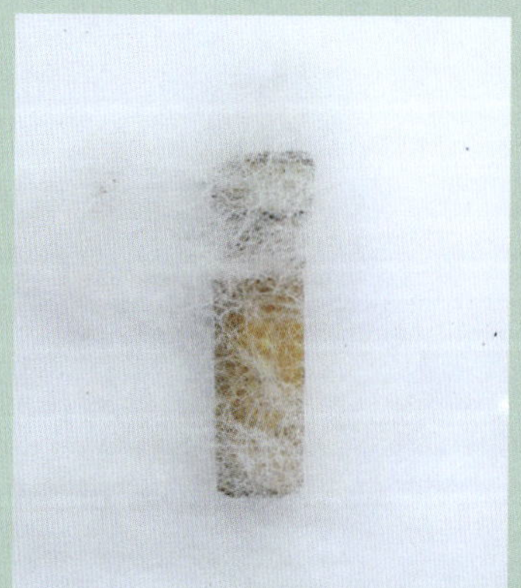

Oyster mushrooms digesting a cigarette butt in a 2020 experiment: Day 1; Day 7; Day 14. Native Oyster species are being employed for just this in Brazil's Mata Atlântica (Atlantic Forest).

SELECTIVE BREEDING: FUTURE FUNGI

We don't know what secrets lie unexpressed within the genome of a fungus. Wild fungi are manifestations of millions of years of evolution – we all are. Evolution is shaped by chance and randomness, but time gives it the appearance of intention and purpose. Consider the "blue halo" effect observed on flower petals that seems perfectly designed to help bees locate pollen. And how ingenious of a Lion's Mane mushroom to grow its teeth downwards to maximise spore dispersal and prevent contamination. The organisms that exist today are those best adapted to their ecological niches and environmental context. But within the genomes of every species lies a bank of hidden genes, traits, and phenotypes, waiting for the right moment to emerge.[50]

Humans have meticulously tapped into the vast genetic reservoirs of plants and animals through the process of selective breeding. The beloved carrot, for example, was originally white but bred to be a brilliant orange as an ode to King William of Orange (1650–1702). Likewise, the astonishing diversity of dog breeds, from Chihuahuas to Mastiffs and every colour, size, and temperament in between, has been bred by human determination and the chance recombination of genotypes and phenotypes. It is a dialogue between breeder and infinite possibility, selecting for criteria like sweetness, beauty, easy control, intoxication, and more.[51]

In contrast, the fungal kingdom remains largely unexplored. While certain fungi, particularly psychedelics, have been selectively bred for traits like shape, colour, and potency, inbreeding often reduces genetic diversity, with some species even risking extinction. A promising alternative is to promote sexual reproduction by crossing genetically distinct strains: unlocking genetic potential and enhancing biodiversity. This emerging field is gaining interest from hobbyists, farmers, and academics alike, and I am fortunate to live with and love one of these passionate, pioneering individuals.

Joey Leahy is the Lab Manager at Bristol Fungarium, who devotes his life to growing mushrooms and expanding their genetic diversity. He spends his days, evenings, and weekends contemplating the untapped potential of fungi. So when Natural England approached the Fungarium with a request to isolate a Lion's Mane "monokaryon", Joey eagerly accepted the challenge.

Monokaryon mycelia contain a single haploid nucleus in each cell, similar to a human gamete.[52] Without a complete genome, many fungi cannot produce mushrooms, just as an egg or sperm alone cannot create a foetus. To create a mushroom, two compatible monokaryotic mycelia must pair up. If compatible, they fuse almost immediately and form dikaryotic mycelium, which contains two nuclei – one from each parent. From here, their lengthy courtship begins. Eventually, in response to environmental changes or triggers, this dikaryotic mycelium will fruit into a genetically complete mushroom.

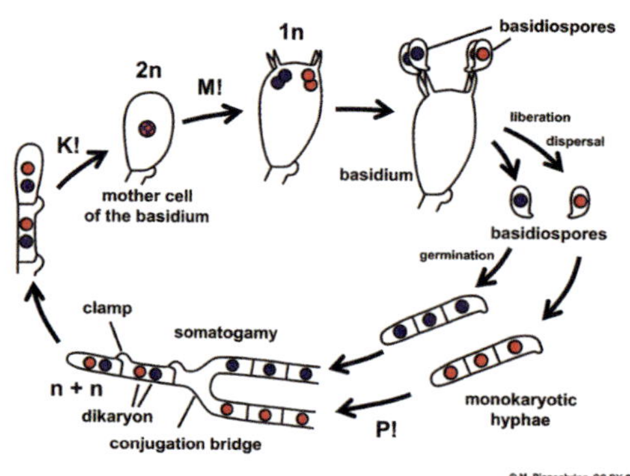

Reproductive cycle of basidiomycete fungi: Spores germinate to form monokaryotic mycelia with one nucleus per cell. When two compatible mycelia fuse, they form dikaryotic mycelia containing two nuclei per cell. Under suitable conditions, these develop into fruiting bodies (mushrooms), where nuclear fusion and meiosis produce haploid spores. The spores disperse and germinate, restarting the cycle.

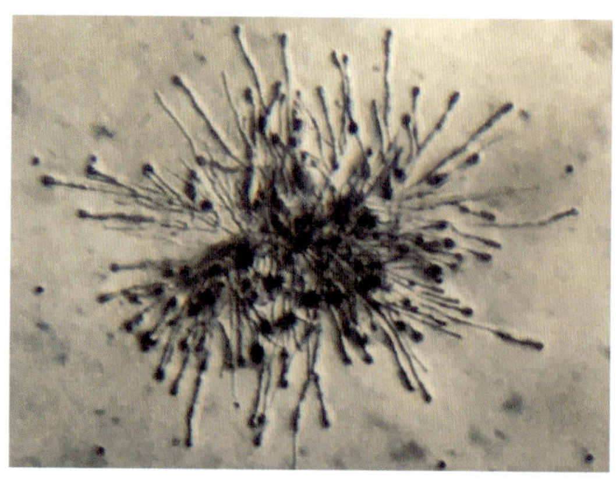

Spores germinating into monokaryotic mycelia. A spore is a microscopic reproductive unit that germinates into hyphae, carrying half the genetic material needed for full reproduction. In this sense, a spore acts like a "half-seed", until hyphae from two spores meet and fuse to create dikaryotic mycelium.

Within this mushroom's basidia (spore organelle), the two haploid nuclei fuse, exchanging genetic material to produce a new, diploid nucleus. This nucleus divides into four genetically distinct spores, each ready to be released and begin the reproductive cycle anew.

With Lion's Mane mushrooms specifically, the growth patterns of monokaryons and dikaryons are strikingly different: monokaryons grow in straight, radial lines, relentlessly seeking potential mates, while dikaryons, being paired, adopt a more exploratory, winding fashion, reinforced by thicker mycelial threads.

Joey's task for Natural England involved several intricate steps. First, he allowed Lion's Mane spores to drop and collected them. He then applied diluted spore solutions onto agar plates enriched with dark wastewater from wood chips – the mushrooms' preferred substrate. Once the spores germinated, the hyphae broke down the nutrients in the wastewater, causing the surrounding agar to turn transparent. Joey then jumped in to isolate the monokaryotic hypha before it could find a mate, and transferred it to a new agar plate to establish a fresh network of a single monokaryotic Lion's Mane mycelium.

At the time of writing, Joey has isolated 15 genetically distinct monokaryons, each carrying half a genome sequence. While 15 might not seem like many, the process is convoluted and fraught with challenges: contaminants can intrude, "ambiguous mycelium" can disguise itself, and the slightest delay can let monokaryons fuse and form dikaryons.

To encourage crossbreeding, Joey places two monokaryons on the same agar plate roughly 3cm apart. If they successfully mate, you can see "clamp connections" under a microscope – small lumps on the sides of hyphae, which facilitate the movement of nuclei between cells by "hopping" over via the

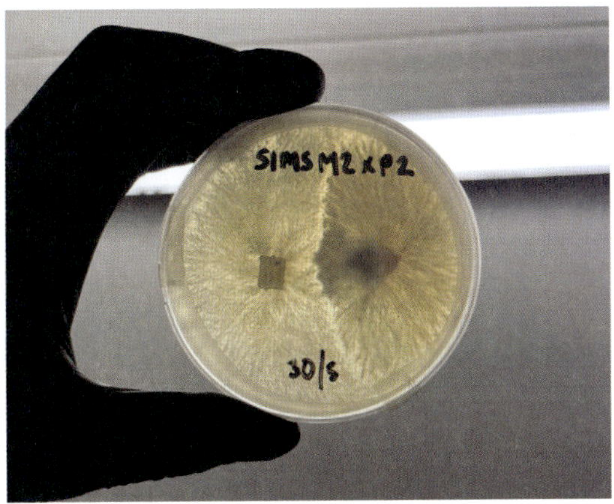

To encourage crossbreeding, Joey places two monokaryon mycelia (from the same species) on the same agar plate roughly 3cm apart. If they are compatible, they will fuse. If not, a "barrage zone" will form where the secrete enzymes and toxins to ward one another off.

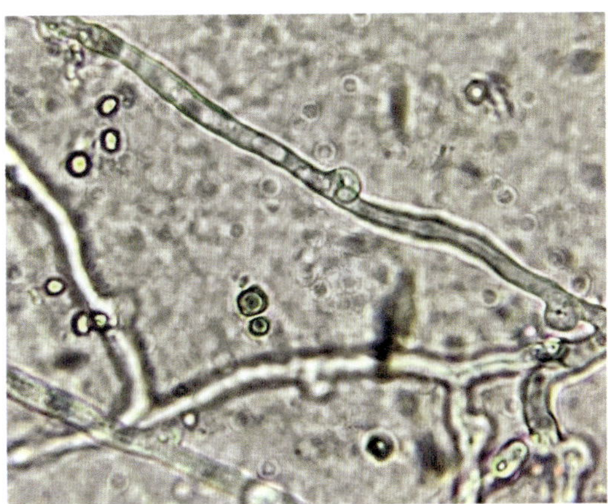

A clamp connection. A specialised structure formed in certain fungi during cell division. It facilitates the movement of nuclei between cells by "hopping" over the septa via the clamp, rather than passing through, ensuring genetic stability and healthy cell division.

scepta via the clamp, rather than passing through them, ensuring healthy cell division. When the clamp connections appear, these dikaryons are known as "crosses".

Once a cross is established, traditional processes of mushroom cultivation can take place: transferring your mycelium from agar to liquid culture, then to grain, and finally to substrate. However, *unlike* traditional mushroom cultivation processes, the mushrooms that emerge will never have been seen before on Earth. The first crosses to produce mushrooms, known as F1 (filial generation one), are fascinating because they exhibit unique characteristics compared to commercially cultivated Lion's Mane. Some mushrooms show no bruising; others have a dense, chewy texture. Some have replaced their usual black tea-like scent for a more floral aroma, while others display soft rosy hues or unusual upward-growing teeth. Some form perfectly round, shaggy pom poms, while others resemble cauliflowers.

However, it's the F2 generation and beyond that hold the most exciting potential. The spores from F2 mushrooms are more likely to express recessive genes that have lain dormant for generations, offering a unique opportunity to explore hidden traits. This raises many questions: what ancient characteristics are hidden within the genomes of these fungi? Could diving into their genetic histories teach us about the past? Given the sparse fungal fossil record, since fungi lack hard structures and decompose quickly, we have little insight into when Lion's Mane first evolved or the environments it adapted to. Did it once have darker hues? Did it once colonise a broader spectrum of trees than the beech and occasional ash it favours today? These questions remain unanswered, but the potential to uncover them by studying new genetic crosses is tantalising.

Joey is currently establishing a Lion's Mane monokaryon collection – an invaluable genetic diversity database akin to a spore library or seed bank.[53] He collects spores from a wide range of

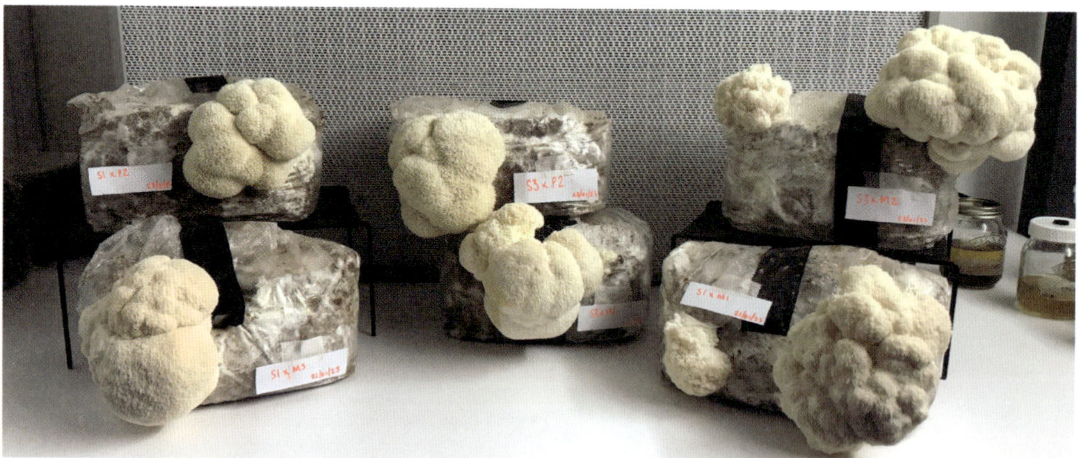

First-generation of crossbred Lion's Mane! Cultivators selectively breed for traits like morphology, growth, metabolites, yield, stress tolerance, and hidden recessive traits, which may appear in later generations. Initially a cross between commercial and native strains, Joey now focuses exclusively on native strains to enhance local biodiversity and express diverse native genes.

commercially available species and those shared within the mushroom community. As Joey puts it, "It's an amazing quirk of fungi: with very little effort we can take clones of mushrooms. From a single specimen, you can generate hundreds of strains with radically different traits, both morphological and physiological. You can even grow the exact same mushroom again and get a fresh spore print." Lion's Mane spores also have an exceptionally low germination rate, so to be in possession of Lion's Mane mycelia is quite incredible.

His collection aims to safeguard strains for future research, though the exact applications are yet to be determined. This is a form of "bioprospecting" – the search for fungal species that can yield valuable medicinal drugs, biochemicals, pigments, enzymes, and more. Joey is particularly focused on finding strains with greater vigour, pest resistance, higher therapeutic compounds, and unique sensory traits such as an unusual flavour or aroma. "It's a dialogue between you and the infinite ways a mushroom can be a mushroom", he says, highlighting the potential for discovery in fungal breeding.

These libraries and collections are essential. It's why places like Kew Fungarium, which holds the world's most extensive collection of fungi, exist: to preserve the past and present diversity of fungi and seek out undiscovered species to ensure that entire branches of fungal life aren't lost to extinction.

The ecological potential of these libraries is immense, especially when considering genera like *Hericium*. This genus includes the classic Lion's Mane, *Hericium erinaceus*; Coral Tooth, *H. coralloides*; Tiered Tooth, *H. cirrhatum;* and Bear's Head, *H. americanum.* All these species are now incredibly rare. Lion's Mane, in particular, is strictly protected under the Wildlife and Countryside Act (1981), making it illegal to pick. It's thanks to this protection that sightings of this mushroom have increased in recent years. While Lion's Mane seems to be making a quietly confident comeback, Comb Tooth is perhaps the

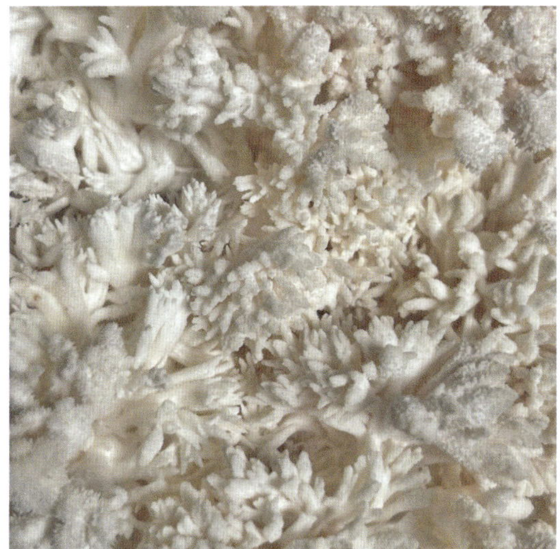

F2 Lion's Mane mushroom. Spores from F2 mushrooms are more likely to express dormant recessive genes, revealing traits like unique growth structures, smells, colours, density, and/or bioactive compounds.

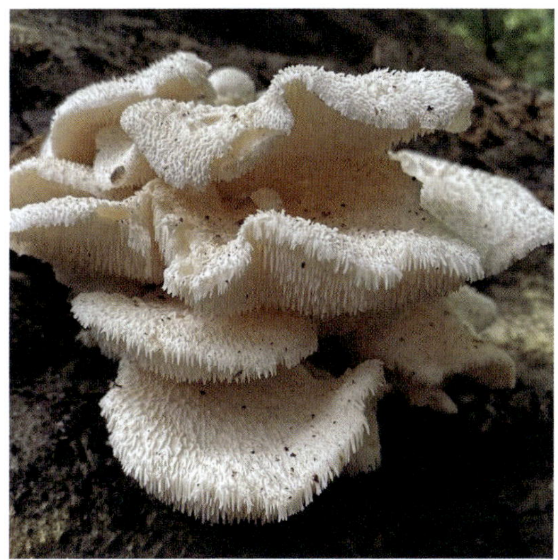

Tiered Tooth, Hericium cirrhatum. *A very rare mushroom in Britain, primarily found in southern England, with occasional occurrences in central and southern mainland Europe. Loss of old-growth forests and over-collecting pose threats to its survival.*

rarest and most deserving of Biodiversity Action Plan (BAP) priority status.[54] Natural England is on a mission to tap into the genetic histories and mating processes of these mushrooms to encourage their presence in the wild.

Our understanding of *Hericium* mating behaviour, however, is limited and sometimes contradictory. Swedish mycologist Nils Hallenberg proposed that Coral Tooth may be homothallic, capable of reproducing from a single spore, while haploid fruiting has also been observed in Lion's Mane.[55] UK expert Lynne Boddy stresses the need for more research to determine whether these fungi tend towards inbreeding or outbreeding, though current evidence leans towards the latter.[56] This is encouraging, as sexual reproduction via outbreeding fosters genetic recombination and diversity.

Biodiversity is not just about the number of species in any given ecosystem, but the genetic diversity within those species – an essential component of their overall conservation. We have seen this in the case of *Penicillium camemberti*, the fungus responsible for producing various soft cheeses like Camembert and Brie.[57] After years of selective breeding, this species has become infertile, a phenomenon known as genetic bottlenecking.[58] Scientists are now revisiting genetic databases with 19th-century Penicillium species to crossbreed with modern strains and hopefully restore the genetic diversity necessary for reproduction. Similarly, in the animal kingdom, Belgian artist Koen Vanmechelen has been crossbreeding chickens from different countries since 1999, creating a collection of chickens with "unrivalled genetic diversity that reverses the logic of industrial chicken farming."[59] Could a similar

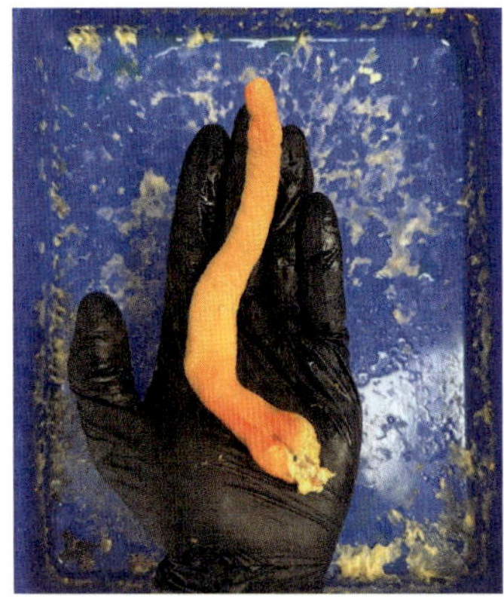
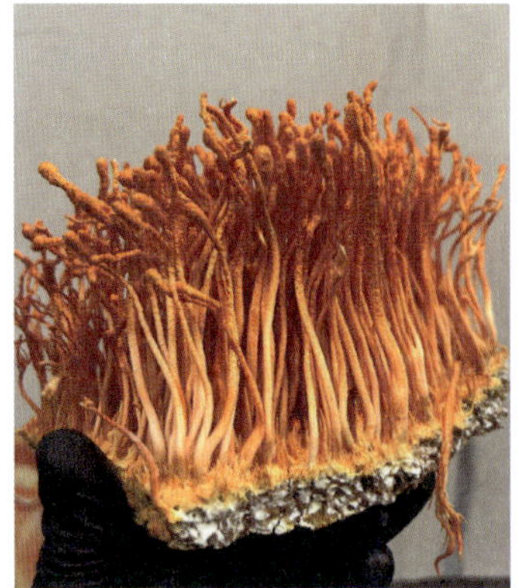
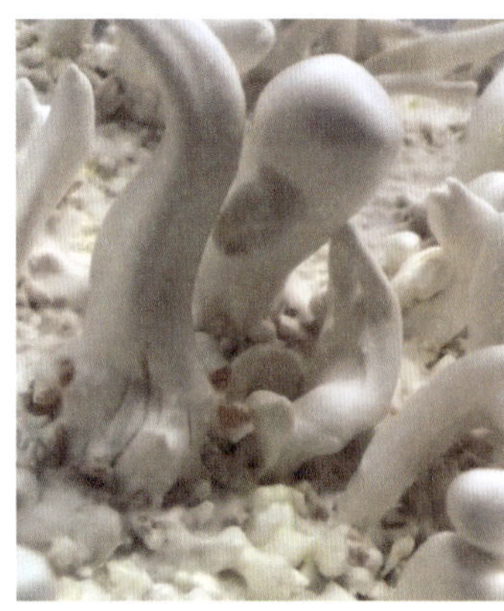

Cordyceps mushrooms selectively bred for different traits. Left: Ryan Paul Gates (US) selects for size. Centre: Lawrence Kaizan (UK) preserves the long, thin wild form. Right: Joey Leahy (UK) has cultivated albino Cordyceps, a recessive trait that typically appears after multiple generations of selective breeding, revealing unusual genotypes and phenotypes. These examples show how breeding can dramatically alter the same species over generations, largely depending on the cultivator's preferences.

approach work for Lion's Mane? Might genetic data guide conservation efforts by providing baseline genetic diversity? Could crossbreeding amplify the expression of ancient, dormant genes to better equip them to adapt to a changing world?

Some scientists take an even more direct approach, subjecting fungi to extreme environmental pressures, such as sending them into space or bombarding them with radiation[60] to induce mutations. Others are genetically modifying mushrooms for improved shelf life or visual appeal. For example, the White Button mushroom, *Agaricus bisporus*, has been genetically modified to resist browning using the CRISPR–Cas9 gene-editing technique. The plant pathologist Yinong Yang deftly deleted a few base pairs in the mushroom's genome to reduce the activity of an enzyme responsible for browning. Remarkably, the USDA (United States Department of Agriculture) approved this modified mushroom without requiring the typical regulatory scrutiny, making it the first CRISPR-edited organism to be sold without restriction.[61]

Though different from genetically modified organisms (GMOs), creating crosses and hybrid species raises pressing ecological and ethical considerations. While the process holds the potential to develop novel expressions of an organism, it also risks disrupting ecosystems and competing with native species. However, first and foremost Joey now works exclusively with native strains, aiming to maximise the expression of local genetics in the environment. Within this focus, he also argues that he isn't doing anything that nature doesn't do daily: spores from countless varieties of fungi are constantly drifting through air currents, rivers, and animal fur. When given the opportunity, their mycelia can fuse to create entirely new genetic recombinations. They do this all the time; the only difference is that in the wild, it's unmediated and unpredictable.

"Nature", Joey explains, "thrives on diversity." Every day in his lab, he observes instances of "hybrid vigour", where the offspring of two genetically distinct species combine and produce larger and more

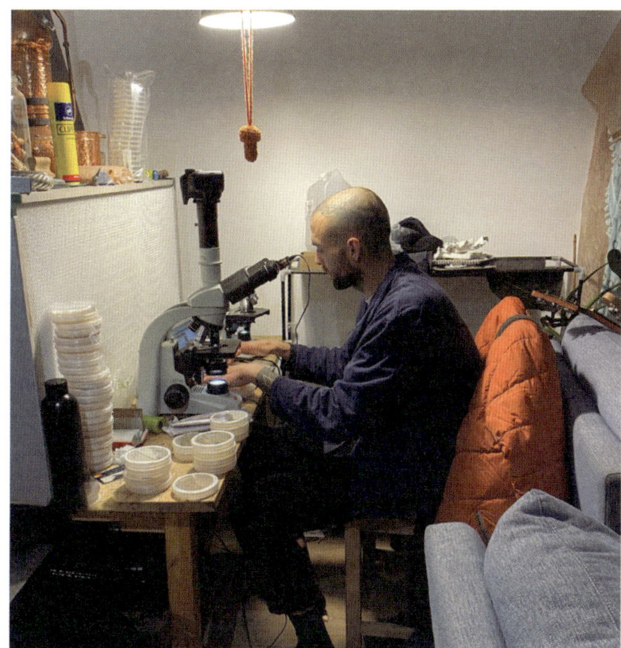

Joey Leahy in his home laboratory checking for clamp connections.

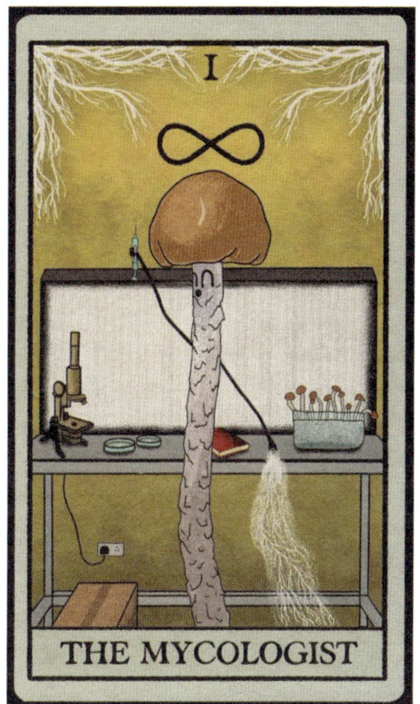

The Mycologist, *William Brown, Fungalphabet.*

vigorous strains. The process literally appears to be fuelled by energy and excitement. Joey simply creates the conditions for these fungi to mate, speeding up natural processes, selecting for specific traits, and resurfacing ancient characteristics.

But this inquiry extends beyond a single mushroom species. What about Oyster Mushrooms, Turkey Tail, or Reishi? Each carries the potential to unravel its complete genetic story. This "dark genetic matter" encompasses dormant genes and expressions within organisms we've already identified. But what of the dark genetic matter of the dark matter fungi – those we have yet to discover? The possibilities are, at least to my mind, literally unfathomable.

Every fungus, macro or micro, holds vast untapped potential. Viewing fungi this way, as overflowing with hidden stories, is a joyous and inspiring perspective to have on the world. Engaging with dark matter, dark ecologies, and latent genotypes represents a pathway to expanding diversity, not creating genetic bottlenecks. Joey and I, cheese lovers, and hopefully many others, will continue to experiment, cross-breed, cross-pollinate, and ask questions, and maybe one day, he and I will create our own little experimental Fungarium.

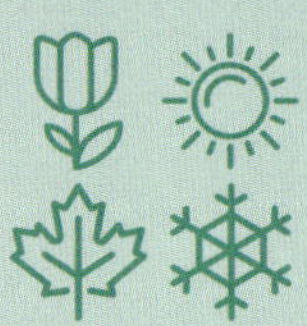

ACTIVITY

ISOLATING MONOKARYOTIC MYCELIUM

JOEY LEAHY

PART 1: SPORE DROP

EQUIPMENT

- Toothpick
- Metal rack or cup
- Foil
- Still air box (SAB) or flow hood
- Lion's Mane mushroom (*Hericium erinaceus*)

METHOD

1. Choose a Lion's Mane mushroom that you particularly like. Remember, it's illegal to collect specimens from the wild (even a single tooth), so it's best to cultivate your own at home and take a sample from there.
2. Cut a 5 x 5cm (2 x 2 inch) chunk from the fruiting body.
3. Insert a toothpick through the chunk and balance it on a sterile metal rack or cup, placing the foil beneath.
4. Place inside a SAB or flow hood to reduce air flow and minimise contamination risks.
5. Let it rest for one hour to allow any insects or contaminants to drop from the mushroom.
6. Replace the sheet of foil and leave the apparatus for 48 hours. (Sometimes the spores don't drop straight away so be patient and wait till you see white spores on the foil).
7. Gently move the mushroom and rack to the side and keep the foil with spores.

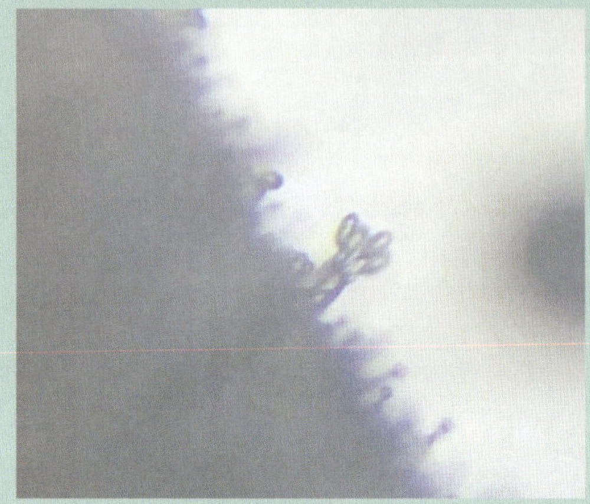

Four genetically distinct Lion's Mane spores emerging from a basidia.

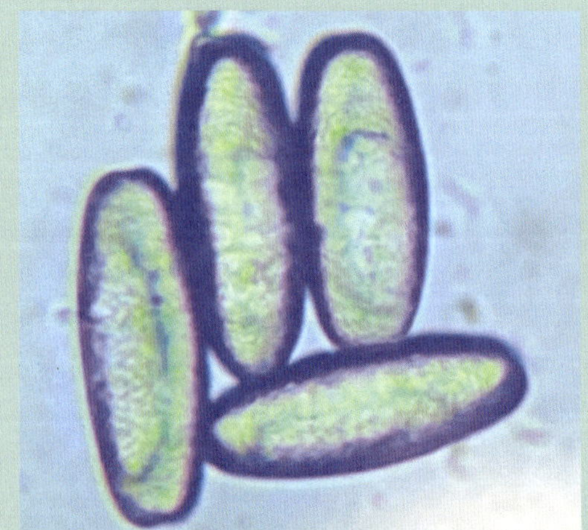

Lion's Mane spores, x40 magnification.

PART 2: ISOLATING MONOKARYONS

EQUIPMENT

- MYA plate (supplemented with dark wastewater from soaked wood chips) (*see page 192 for protocol*)
- Sterile pipette
- Sterile cotton bud
- 25ml distilled or bottled water
- 5 small vials or test tubes
- Scalpel
- 99% rubbing alcohol
- Lab gloves
- Microscope slides
- Still air box or flow hood
- Microscope
- Lion's Mane mushroom spores

METHOD

1. Label five small vials (1x, 2x, 3x, 4x, 5x) and fill each with 5ml sterilised distilled water.
2. Use a sterile cotton bud to collect spores from the Lion's Mane spore drop and add them to the "1x" vial. Mix the vial thoroughly to disperse the spores.
3. Using a sterile pipette, transfer 1ml of the "1x" spore solution to the "2x" vial. Repeat this dilution process through to the "5x" vial. Each dilution significantly reduces the spore concentration, making later isolation more manageable.
4. Drop 1ml from the "5x" vial onto the MYA plate and close the lid. Monitor closely for 24 hours.
5. As soon as transparent spots appear (indicating spore germination), use a sterile scalpel to scrape a small amount of mycelium onto a microscope slide for inspection. Only a tiny amount is needed.
6. If you can't see clamp connections, it's likely a monokaryon! Take another small sample from the same transparent spot and transfer it to a new MYA plate.
7. Double-check to confirm it's a monokaryon by taking three random samples from the plate. You can also use growth patterns to help identification: Monokaryons grow in straight, thin lines, while dikaryons show thick, swirling patterns. Any unusual growth may indicate contamination, so monitor closely.
8. Check the original MYA plate for more transparent spots and repeat the isolation process if necessary.
9. Once two clean monokaryons are isolated, place them on opposite sides of a new Petri dish and let them grow towards each other. If they fuse, the mycelium will become thicker and more winding.
10. After fusion, proceed with standard cultivation methods: liquid culture, grain inoculation, and substrate transfer. Remember, the F2 generation is where genetic variation becomes most interesting. If you find a mushroom with desirable traits (e.g., flavour or colour), you can stabilise it by crossing it back with the original monokaryon (a tried and tested method).

Keep exploring, isolating, and crossing to diversify your gene pool. Experiment with different strains and connect with the mushroom community – you never know who, or what mushrooms, might be out there!

EPILOGUE

If you're reading these words from a book, you've already contributed to its microbial story. Your skin, breath, sweat, and the tiny microorganisms you've picked up throughout your day – whether from a pet, lunch, or a crowded bus ride – have left their mark. These microbes are the same ones we wash off our hands or that fade into the walls of our homes, sometimes causing deterioration, sometimes just lingering as silent witnesses.

All books, from ancient scrolls to paperbacks, are living microbial time capsules. Their surfaces host an invisible community of fungi, bacteria, viruses, skin cells, and traces of the cosmetics we use. When we run our fingers along the lines of text, fold the corners of pages, or fall asleep with a book in hand, we are leaving behind our own microbial signature.

Religious texts are especially rich in these signatures as they are subject to extraordinary forms of engagement. Holy books, cherished and revered, are read, passed hand to hand, kept in breast pockets, whispered into, wept upon, subject to devotional kissing, hidden in caves, and carried across continents.[1] Each of these intimate acts leaves its mark. Ancient bibles, some dating as far back as 4 AD, still bear the microbial fingerprints of their scribes. [2] The York Gospels even carry human DNA on nearly 20 per cent of their pages, particularly where sacred oaths were sworn.[3] Traces of *Propionibacterium* (linked to acne) and *Staphylococcus* (associated with infections) were abundant, simultaneously threatening these historical artefacts and adding to their archaeological importance.

Because microbes are sensitive to their environment, the specific species found on a manuscript can point to its geographic origin, socio-ecological conditions, and even cultural exchanges. For example, a 12th-century Gospel of Luke was written on parchment made from the skins of eight and a half calves, ten and a half sheep, and half a goat, giving us a glimpse into livestock management practices in Medieval England. Another manuscript, found in southern Europe, contained traces of *Anobium punctatum* dung, a beetle species native to northern Europe, suggesting it was made in England before travelling to Italy. The materials used – leathers, inks, and plant-based dyes – carry their own DNA, revealing the blend of local and exotic resources that fuelled trade. In this way, the microbes and materials on a manuscript can trace its journey through time and space, creating a record of human interaction and movement.

DNA sequencing of such works can reveal astonishing details about environments and the people who handled them: their health, ailments, diet, ancestry, and even hair and eye colour. Microbiologist James Kinross notes, "Each time you turn a page, hundreds of microbes exchange between your skin and the paper . . . pressed like dormant microscopic flowers."[4] Books are microbial and cultural records, revealing human interaction far beyond what the text conveys.

Forensic microbiologists and mycologists take this idea one step further.[5] Microbial traces can help reconstruct events, uncover hidden histories, and even point to past crimes. Books might carry

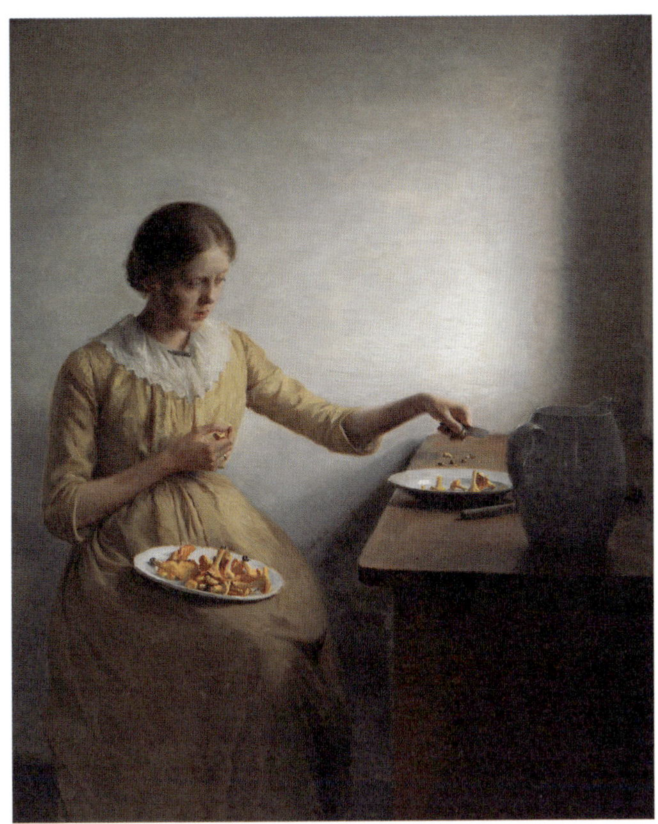

Peter Ilsted, A Young Girl Preparing Chanterelles, *1892. Oil on canvas.*

particles of blood or dust from war zones. They may have been hidden away during times of conflict, smuggled across borders, or deliberately contaminated as a form of bioterrorism, as with poisoned letters. Forensic microbiology becomes a kind of cultural detective work, uncovering not just who read or wrote a book, but what happened around it.

Though your physical copy of this book may seem identical to mine, its microbial community is entirely unique to you: shaped by the places you've taken it, the bookshelves it has sat upon, and the experiments conducted alongside its open pages. From this perspective, your book is a living entity, an evolving record of your shared journey. If every book harbours its own unique biological community, then scaled up or down, every page, shelf, and library has a microbiome, as dynamic as a coral reef or forest floor.

Next time you pick up a book in a bathroom or leave one behind on holiday, consider the unseen ecosystem you're engaging with and reshaping. Who else might be hiding between the lines? What microbial stories are yet to be told? The possibilities, like the mycelial networks soon to cover these pages (see Bonus Recipe, page 311), are vast and entangled.

ACTIVITY

CREATURES & CULTURES' LIVING LIBRARY

1. If you're curious about the microbial life you've added to this book, use a cotton bud to swab its cover or pages, culture them on an MYA plate (see page 192 for protocol), then watch them grow.
2. I'd love for you to send in your samples so I can create a visual library of the microbes that joined us on this exploration together. You'll most likely find bacteria like *Staphylococcus*, *Streptococcus*, and *Lactobacilli*, and fungal moulds, mildews, and yeasts. Don't worry, I won't make cheese from your samples. Unless, of course, you'd like me to! In that case, there's a template consent form on page 314 for anyone adventurous enough to donate their body-rubbed microbial profile in exchange for a slice of book-reader cheese.

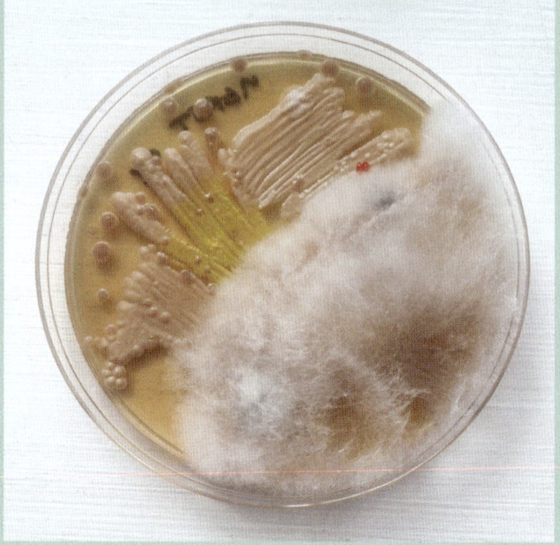

Though paper provides poor nourishment and moisture for most microorganisms, books, newspapers, maps, and more can still become valuable microbial time capsules. So, swab your book to discover who's living in yours!

BONUS RECIPE

FUNGAL PAGES

"Fungi might make mushrooms, but first they must unmake something else."

– Merlin Sheldrake, *Entangled Life*[6]

This final experiment reminds us that knowledge isn't something we passively consume, it's something we absorb, digest, decompose, and recompose into new life and ideas. My hope is that this book won't simply sit as a stagnant vessel of information and curiosities but will become part of the fantastic fungal world it explores.

There are many ways to approach this activity, but here is a loose protocol for turning your book into a mushroom.

EQUIPMENT

- Scales
- Mushroom grow bag with filter patch
- Ladle
- Tape
- Optional: Pressure Cooker

INGREDIENTS

- This book
- Native Oyster mushroom grain spawn
- Water

METHOD

1. Weigh the book.
2. Place it in a mushroom bag, then add 70% of its weight in filtered water.
3. Optional: Seal the bag and sterilise it in a pressure cooker at 121 PSI for 20 minutes. (This would increase the mushrooms' chances of fruiting but kill all the other microbes in the book.)
4. Let it cool to room temperature.
5. Using a heaped ladle, sprinkle oyster mushroom grain spawn throughout its pages. Close the book and seal the bag with tape.
6. Keep the book in a dark space at room temperature for a month (or until the book is fully colonised by white mycelium and starts to show little "pins" or balls of mycelium).
7. After a month, cut a 10cm/4in slit in the top of the bag to expose the book to air and move the bag into a light room.
8. Within a week, small mushrooms should emerge.
9. Harvest. Cook. Eat. Digest both the fungi and the ideas that shaped them.

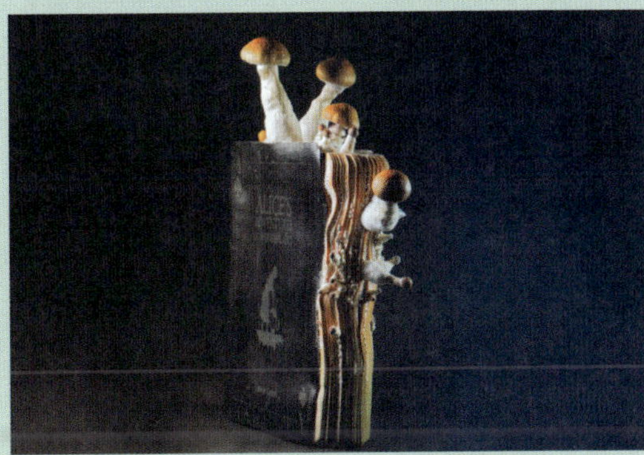

Alice in Wonderland Digested by Fungi *by Igor Siwanowicz.*

APPENDIX

Best Foraging Practice

Foraging can be a rewarding way to connect with nature and gather wild foods, but it requires knowledge, respect, and caution to ensure safety and sustainability. First and foremost, accurate identification is crucial – never eat a wild mushroom or plant unless you are 100 per cent certain of its identity. Many edible species have toxic lookalikes, so use reputable field guides, apps, or seek expert advice. Be wary of AI-generated fungi ID books, as several have been released and contain errors.

When harvesting, take only what you need and leave plenty for wildlife and future growth. Avoid disturbing the surrounding habitat. Some foragers recommend cutting mushrooms at the base to protect the underground mycelium, and this works well for many species. But for others, like porcini, cutting leaves a large wound at the base of the fruiting body, which I believe makes the fungus more vulnerable to disease. A gentle twist-and-pull from the base usually works well, with minimal mycelial damage and little trace – though I acknowledge this goes against common practice. Regardless of method, avoid over-harvesting any one area. A simple guideline helps: never take more than half, never take the first, and never take the last.

When foraging with an ultraviolet light, be mindful that UV rays can damage living cells. Prolonged exposure is harmful to animals, fungi, and likely all plants as well, so keep the light on only as long as necessary.

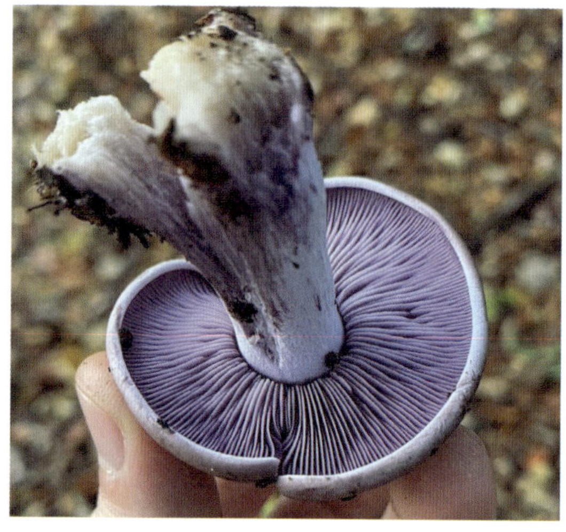

Wood Blewit, Collybia nuda.

Always be mindful of the law. Many parks and reserves prohibit foraging or require permits, so check local regulations before collecting. Respect private property boundaries and ask permission when necessary.

Most importantly, forage ethically and educate yourself continuously. Responsible foraging helps support biodiversity, community traditions, mental well-being, and your own safety. Two final tips: foraging into the sun is difficult, so wear a cap, and of course, have fun!

TEMPLATE CONSENT FORM

FOR PARTICIPATION IN MICROBIAL CLONING PROJECT

I, the undersigned, [Name], hereby give my informed consent to Kit Ondaatje Rolls to clone the bodily microbes from the sample I have provided, for the creation of "Book-Reader Cheese" or "Sourdough Bread", as detailed below.

By signing this document, I confirm my understanding and agreement to the following terms:

SELECTION (PLEASE TICK YOUR PREFERENCE)

- ☐ Soft Cheese
- ☐ Hard Cheese
- ☐ Sourdough Bread

Note: Unfortunately, gluten-free alternatives are not available at this time due to the complexity of preparation.

TERMS AND CONDITIONS

1. **Offer Expiration:** This offer expires one year after the publication of this book – on July 14, 2026.
2. **Process Duration:** I understand that the microbial cloning process may take several months to complete, and I will be kept updated on the progress.
3. **Consumption Warning:** I acknowledge that I will **not** consume the resulting cheese or bread, as it may pose health risks due to its experimental nature. I agree not to ingest any of the products or otherwise interact with them in a way that could cause harm.
4. **Liability Disclaimer:** I understand and accept that Kit Ondaatje Rolls is **not** liable for any consequences or harm that may result from the consumption or interaction with the "Book-Reader Cheese" or "Sourdough Bread".
5. **Confidentiality and Use of Data:** I understand that my personal data, including my name and the microbial sample provided, will be handled with care and confidentiality, and will only be used for the purposes of this project. My data may be used for research or publication, but my identity will remain anonymous unless I grant permission otherwise.
6. **Participation Is Voluntary:** I acknowledge that my participation in this project is completely voluntary, and I may withdraw at any time without consequence.

PARTICIPANT INFORMATION

Name (Printed): ___________________________

Email: ___________________________________

Signature: ________________________________

Date: ____________________________________

RETURN INFORMATION

To organise the postage of your microbial sample, please send your signed form to:
kitondaatjerolls@gmail.com

RETURN ADDRESS

[Insert Address]

This form is an essential part of the project, and I acknowledge that by signing it, I consent to participate under the above conditions. Should I have any questions or concerns, I will contact Kit Ondaatje Rolls directly for clarification.

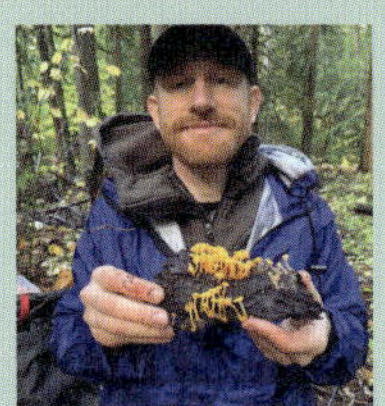
Alan Rockefeller

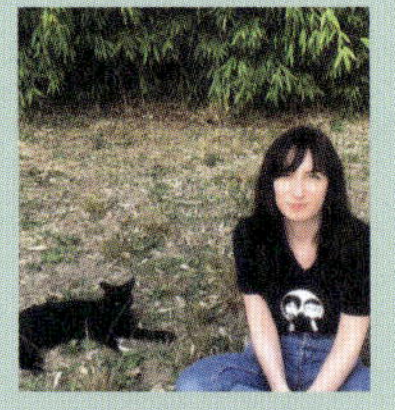
Amélie Barbier

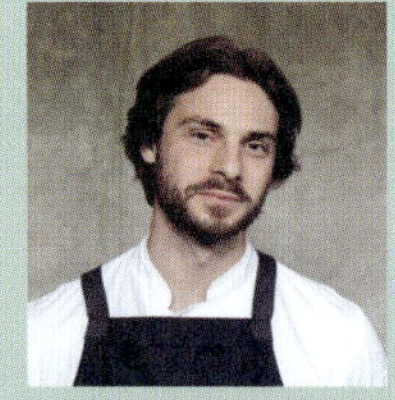
Andrew Luzmore

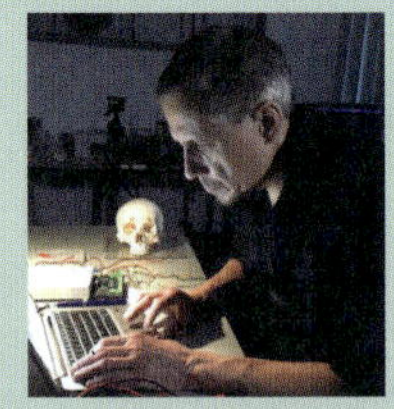
Andy Adamatzky

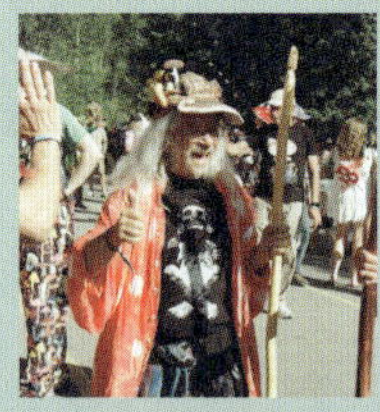
Art Goodtimes

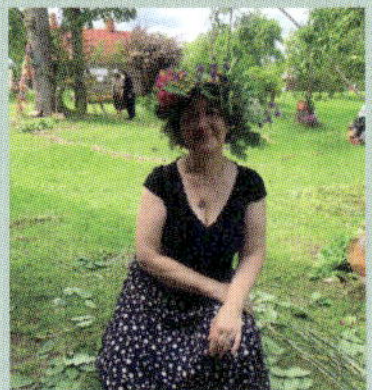
Baiba Baika

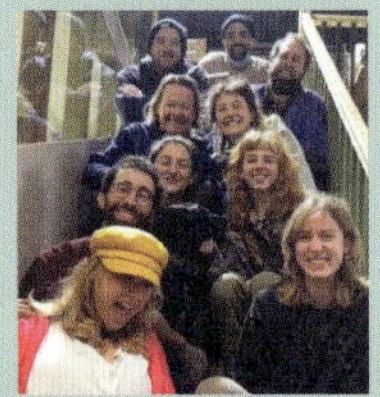
Bristol Fungarium

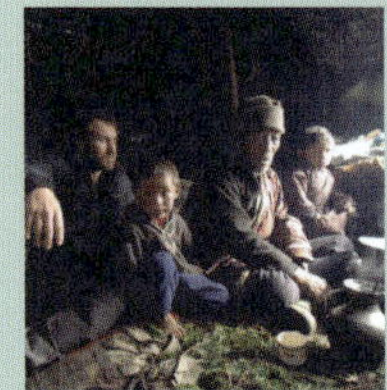
Bruce Parry & The Layap People

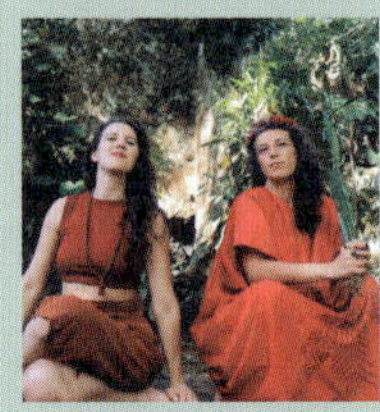
Bruna Piazza & Juju Maschietto

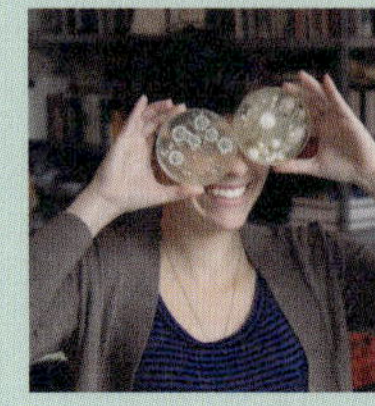
Christina Agapakis

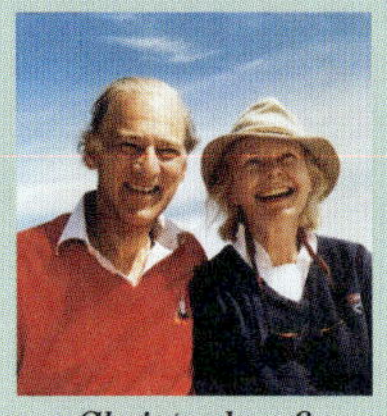
Christopher & Valda Ondaatje

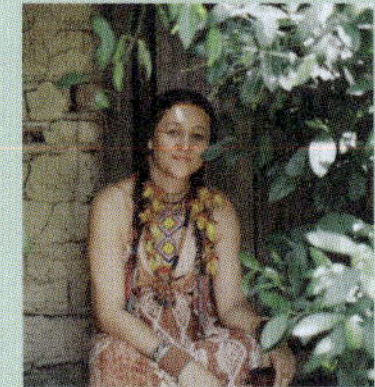
Cristina Tukuá

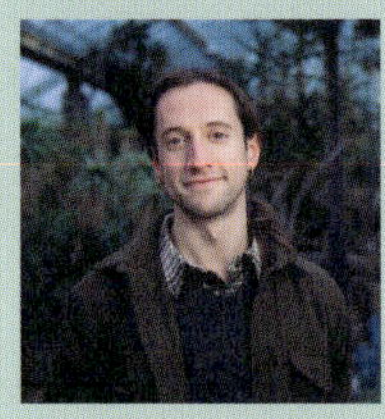
David Satori

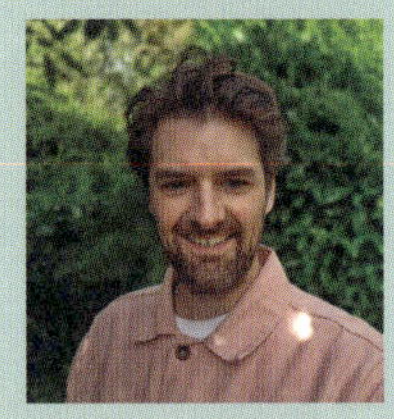
Dr Johnny Drain

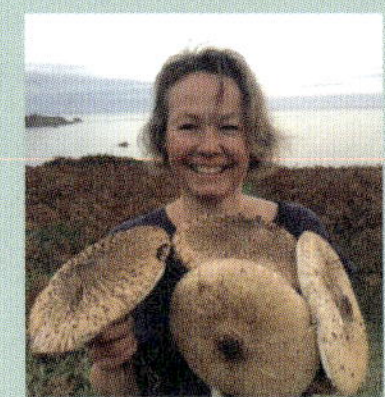
Elena Yates

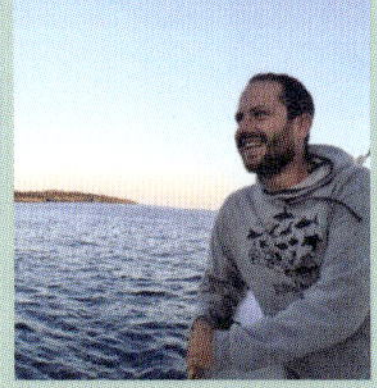
Fabio Favoretto

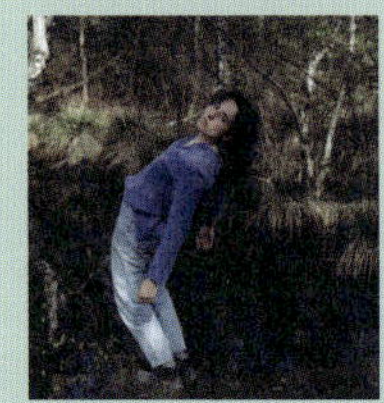
Gabriella Gormley

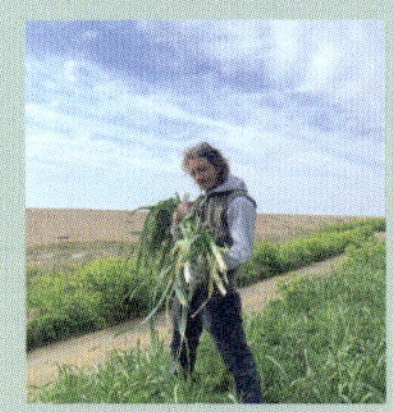
George Linklater

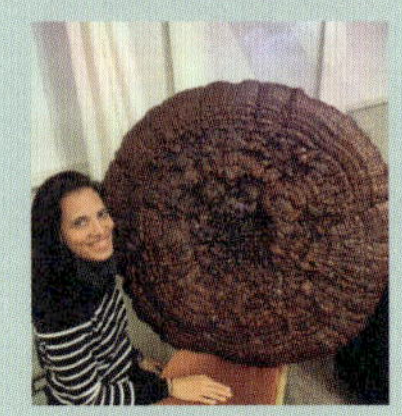
Hania Opienski

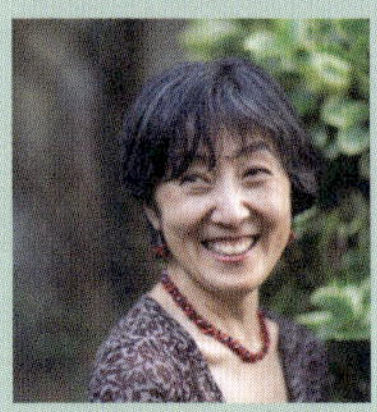
Haruko Uchishiba

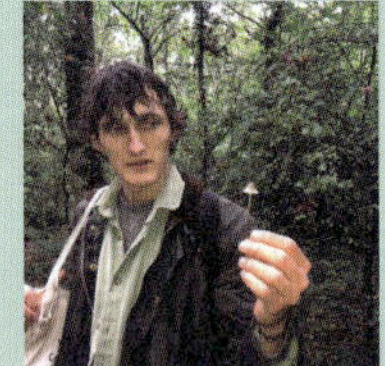
Harvey Shaw

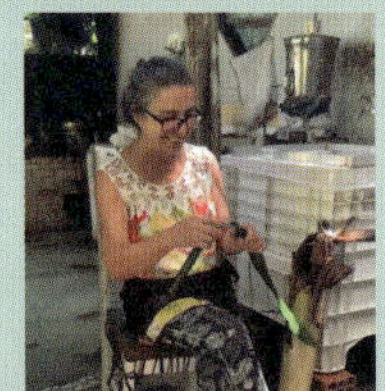
Carmen, Papel de Quintal

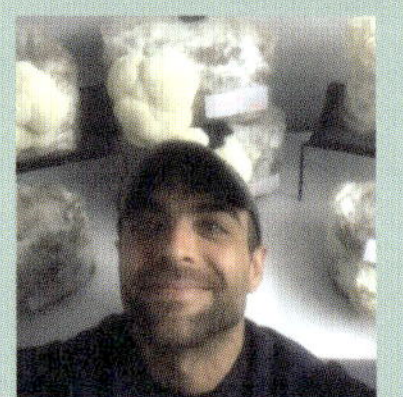
Joey Leahy

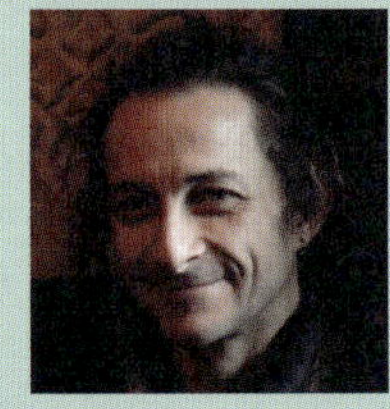
Julian Vayne

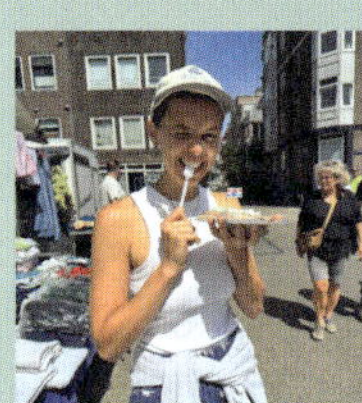
Juliette Casini

Acknowledgements

This book's journey began at COP26, where Bianca Gerlinger generously offered me the opportunity to speak on SHE Changes Climate's *Creative Sisters and Brothers* panel. Surrounded by incredible artists and ecologists from different cultures, the experience sparked the idea for this work, and it hasn't strayed far from those first mind-maps. Tate, thank you for your unwavering support as I navigated bringing this book to life while we searched for jobs. It felt endless and I am forever grateful – we did it! Bristol Fungarium, I learned so much during my time with you and thank you for letting me create my lab/studio on your working mushroom farm! It was a dream come true. Juju and Bruna, you opened my mind and body to a new way of engaging with the world, a way that I deeply craved but had never experienced. Your teachings guided me throughout the research and writing of this book. Gabi, thank you for nurturing the Brazilian community through dance, yoga, and birthday parties. You move with love and I can't wait for all that's to come. Tom, thank you for encouraging me to take the leap and flip FLOP. There's nothing that foraging, swimming, or a sauna sing-along can't mend. To my family, your support throughout this entire project has been amazing. I am so lucky to have you all, and our time together (with Fig!) means the world to me. Sam, in particular, thank you for keeping me alive with all the meat and fish while I finished this book on the Wildbiome project. Ginny, your story was the first I wrote, and you are often in my thoughts. Gran, Bumps, and all the Ondaatje Mahaney Ruperts, you've shaped me into who I am; wild and yet hopefully somewhat rooted. We all share this and how lucky we are. When's the next reunion?!

To every single person I interviewed for this book, Andy Adamatzky, Christina Agapakis, Hanouf Al-Alawi, Mackenzie Amara, Rachel Armstrong, Baiba Baika, Amélie Barbier, Bristol Fungarium, Tom Carter, Juliette Casini, Massimiliano Casini, Noberto Casini, Sam Dalrymple, Tom Daniel, Johnny Drain, Catherine Euale, Fabio Favoretto, Kazzala Goodweather, Gabriella Gormley, WhiteFeather Hunter, John Hunnex, Lily Johnson, Robert Kesseler, Satish Kumar, Kit Lavender, Joey Leahy, George Linklater, Andrew Luzmore, Juju Maschietto, Maurizio Montalti, Malu Moreira, Lauren Nasrallah, Karen O'Toole, Sidnee Ober-Singleton, Christopher Ondaatje, Valda Ondaatje, Hania Opienski, Neri Oxman, Sergio Pajé, Bruce Parry, Bruna Piazza, Martin Powell, Jem Purry, Saj Ravzi, Jake Robinson, Alan Rockefeller, June Rolls, Sam Rowbotham, David Satori, Sayen Scantlebury, Louie Schwartzberg, Harvey Shaw (with acknowledgement to Károly Maté and his family), Merlin Sheldrake, Jonathan Swift, Orkan Telhan, Cristina Tukuá, Ricardo Tur Estrada, Haruko Uchishiba, Julian Vayne, Melissa Waddingham, Marina Warner, Isabel Whitworth, Mo Wilde, and Elena Yates, Kit and Jem, thank you for your generosity in sharing your time and wisdom. It's more than inspiring to witness the passion that unfolds when people are given the space to speak – especially when talking about fungi! Ludovico Einaudi, I am sorry your interview never made it into the book. It was brilliant, but it had nothing to do with fungi! My fault.

To those who shared photographs for this book, Andy Adamatzky, Amélie Barbier, Bring Us The Fungus, Bristol Fungarium, William Brown, Tom Carter, Juliette Casini, River Cousin, Lisa Cutcliffe, Sebastian Enriquez (Revolucion Fungi), Moisés Hernández, Karoline Hjorth & Ritta Ikonen (Eyes as Big as Plates), Joey Leahy, Sekai Machache, the MA Biodesign Cohort, Jana Nicole, Christopher Ondaatje, , Alan Rockefeller, Eleonora Rombolà, David Satori, Harvey Shaw, George Sturby, Damon Tighe, Luis Undritz, Melissa Waddingham, The Wild Room and Mischa de Stroumillo, Phil Winter, Rich Wright, Elena Yates, and Marc Violo, your photographs are beautiful and have brought this book to life. Also to Helen Robinson for creating the Creatures & Cultures Compass: thank you for being patient and creating such a wonderful illustration of what I had only envisioned in my mind. And to Gabriella Turner and Isabella Horspool, thank you both so much for accompanying me on two last-minute interviews in Brazil, and for translating such memorable interviews. I only wish I had understood more when we were there!

Josh, thank you for embracing the challenge of editing this book. Your extensive knowledge of mythology, alchemy, and anthropology was invaluable – I can think of no one better to bounce ideas off while I was writing and editing the first draft. The way you could find the exact page in the exact book from a half-formed thought I'd shared was both brilliant and a little terrifying – what a mind! You're an extraordinary teacher, writer, and poet. Thank you for your guidance in keeping me on track and reining in the tangents! To my dad, Charles Rolls, for reviewing this book with such little notice and for telling me I needed more time, and to my mum, Jans Ondaatje Rolls, for going through all the recipes. To David Satori for doing the most thorough mycological check on the book. You added so many exciting references and nuances to the text, I am in awe of your academic, artistic, and humanistic capabilities! Thank you! To Beth and Claire, my mushroom adventures began with you. Finally, to Joey, my friend, mushroom adventurer, running superstar, and cook! Thank you for tolerating my frequent bouts of writer's hibernation and helping me to love well, eat well, and go to bed on time! I can't wait for more adventures.

And finally to the fungi. How strange and significant you are. May our understanding and appreciation of you grow with every passing day.

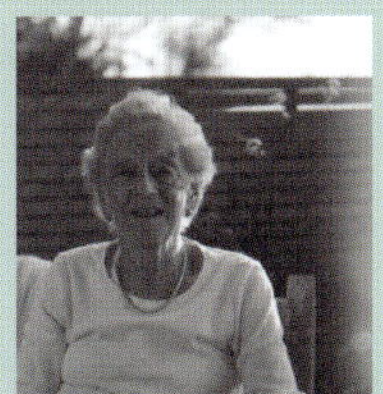
June Rolls

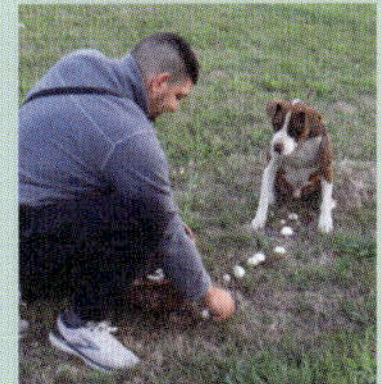
Karoly Maté

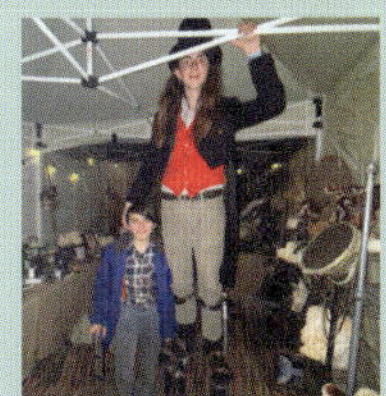
Kit Lavender & Jem Purry

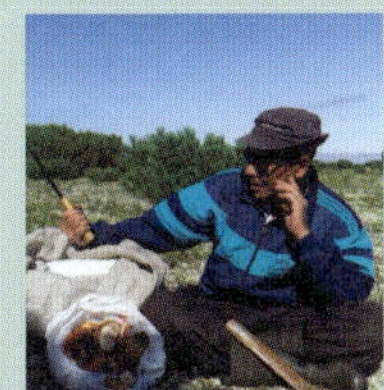
Koryak Community

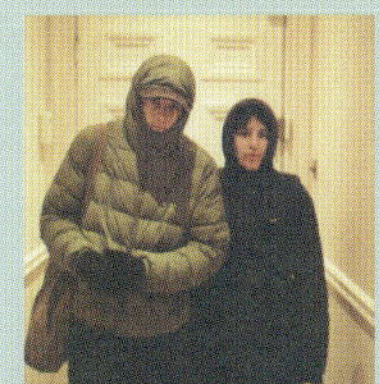
Lauren Nasrallah & Sam Rowbotham

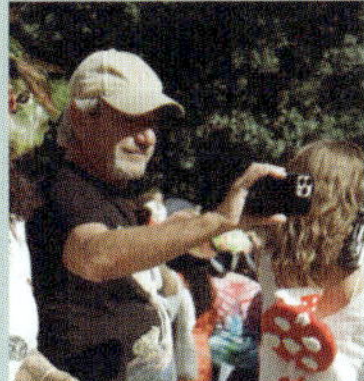
Louie Schwartzberg

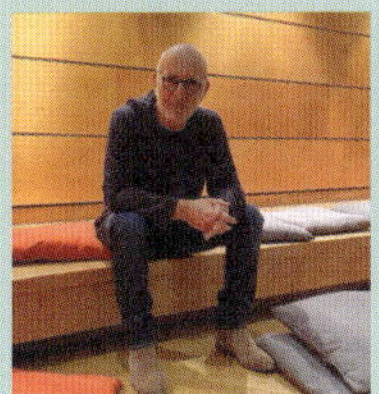
Ludovico Einaudi

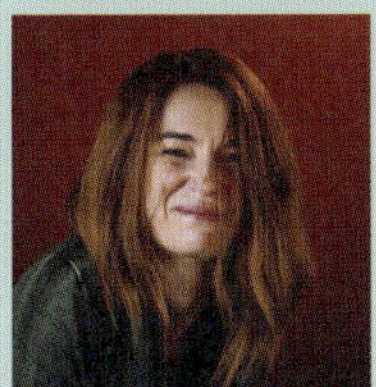
Mackenzie Amara

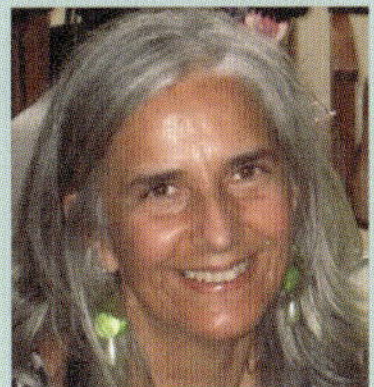
Malu Moreira

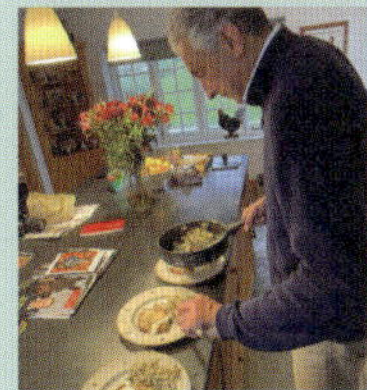
Massimiliano Casini

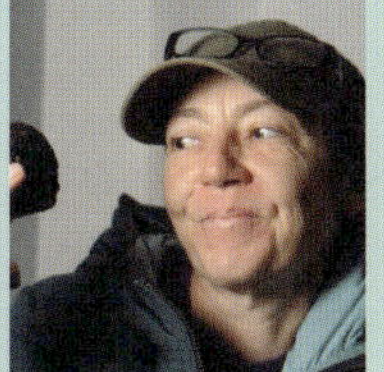
Melissa Waddingham

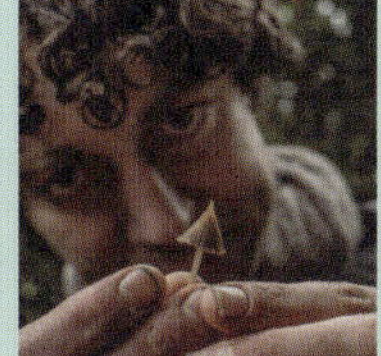
Merlin Sheldrake

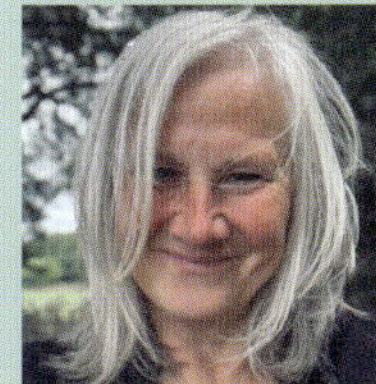
Mo Wilde

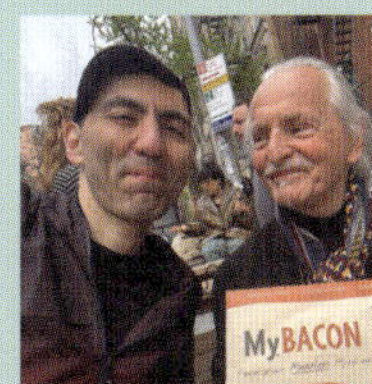

Orkan Telhan Estrada

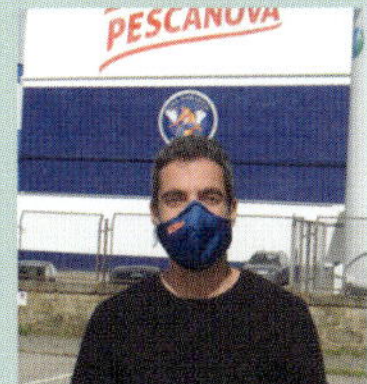

Ricardo Tur

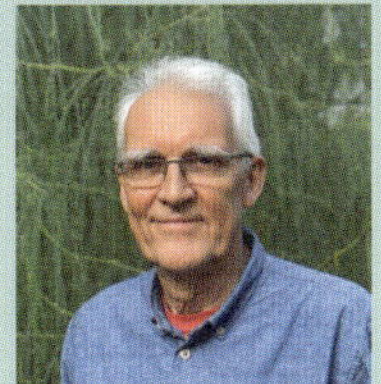
Rob Kesseler

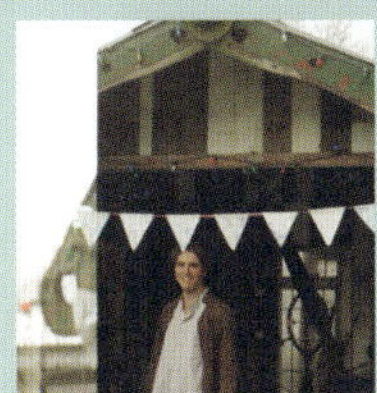
Sam Dalrymple

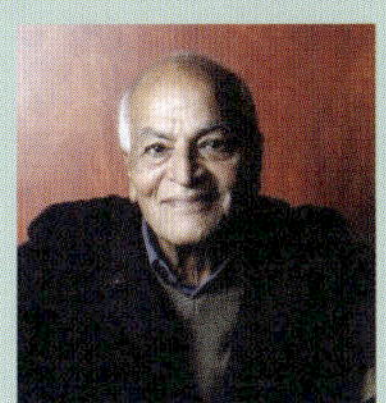
Satish Kumar

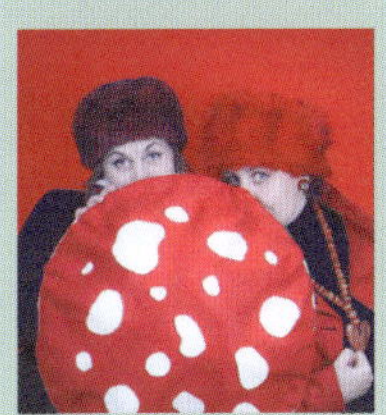
Seed SistAs

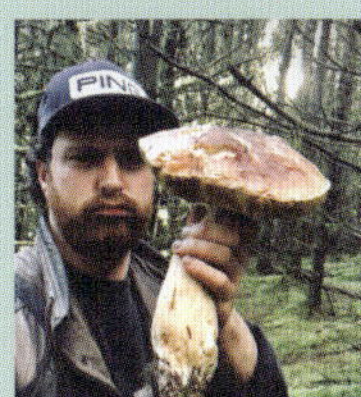
Tom Carter

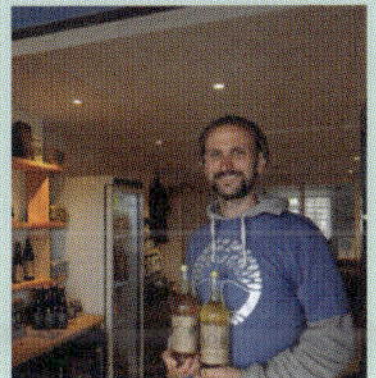
Tom Daniell

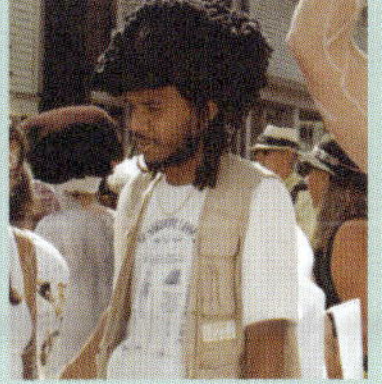
Will Padilla-Brown

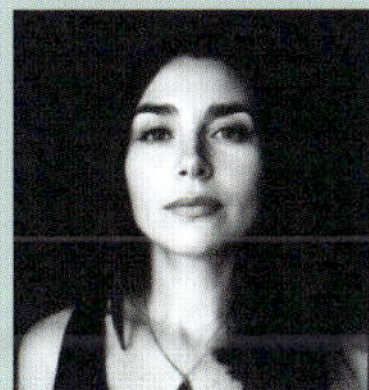
White Feather Hunter

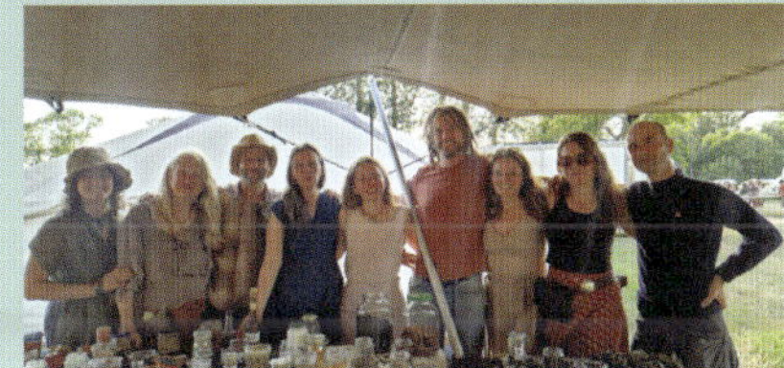
Wildbiome Participants

About the Author

Kit Ondaatje Rolls is a London-based biodesigner and fungi researcher whose work bridges art, ecology, and culture. Her fascination with fungi began while studying Social Anthropology at the University of Edinburgh, where she experimented with making leather alternatives from discarded orange peel in her free time. While searching for a natural binder, she discovered BIOHM and NATURA Labs, who encouraged her to grow Oyster mycelium on citrus waste. After months of "training" the mushrooms, she realised the mycelium alone might make a better leather alternative—though she still loves oranges!

Kit went on to join the first cohort of Central Saint Martin's Master's in Biodesign, specialising in regenerative system design. Her final project, *Blimey! Algae Vodka*, won the MA Biodesign, Maison/0, and LVMH "One Nature, One Future" award, and was exhibited at the IUCN Congress in 2021. She has since spoken at COP26 with SHE Changes Climate, and was a keynote speaker at ChangeNOW 2022 in Paris.

After graduating, she ran her own a lab/studio at Bristol Fungarium, developing mycelium-based packaging and sharing knowledge about the cultural history and modern benefits of medicinal mushrooms. She later joined the Wildbiome Project, a citizen science study in which 120 foragers across the UK, Europe, and North America ate only wild food for 1-3 months. Kit completed the full three months, surviving on game, wild greens, seed flours, and, naturally, plenty of mushrooms.

Today, Kit works with The Fungi Folks, co-runs FFUNGA: Functional Mushrooms, and is helping to establish London's native fungi library - stepping stones towards her long-term vision of a National Fungi Museum.

Kit's wide-ranging experience across the fungi world - from fashion and food to soil health and supplements - uniquely positions her to write a book that is expansive, finely detailed, and enriched with personal insight. This is her second book.

Endnotes

PROLOGUE

1 Blair Hedges, S, et al, "A molecular timescale of eukaryote evolution and the rise of complex multicellular life," BMC Evolutionary Biology, 4(2), 2004, pp.1–9.

2 Lofgren, A A, & Stajich, J E, "Fungal biodiversity and conservation mycology in light of new technology, big data, and changing attitudes," *Current Biology*, 31(19), 2021, pp.pR1312–R1325

3 Niskanen, T, et al, "Pushing the Frontiers of Biodiversity Research: Unveiling the Global Diversity, Distribution, and Conservation of Fungi," *Annual Review of Environment and Resources*, 48, 2023

4 Vajda, V, & Mcloughlin, S, "Fungal Proliferation at the Cretaceous-Tertiary Boundary," *Science*, 303(5663), 2004, p.1489

5 Remy, W, et al, "Four hundred-million-year-old vesicular arbuscular mycorrhizae," *Proceedings of the National Academy of Sciences of the United States of America,* 91, 1994, pp.11841–11843

6 Martinez, N D, & Marshmann, G L, "How fungi build planet-altering 'road' networks," *Nature*, 2025

7 Stamets, P, *Mycelium Running,* Ten Speed Press, Berkley, 2005, p.96, 98, & 113

8 Yates, I E, "Evidence for Fusarium endophytes in cultivated and wild plants," *Microbial Endophytes*, 2000

9 Kuo, H-C, et al, "Secret lifestyles of Neurospora crassa," *Scientific Reports*, 4, 2014

10 Tsunoda, K, et al, "Changes in Concentration of Ibotenic Acid and Muscimol in the Fruit Body of Amanita muscaria during the Reproduction Stage," *Food Hygienic Studies of Toxigenic Basidiomycotina. II,* 34(1), 1990

11 "Meet the researcher helping to feed 60 million people by fighting Rice Blast Fungus," *Norwich Research Park*, 2022, www.norwichresearchpark.com/meet-the-researcher-helping-to-feed-60-million-people-by-fighting-rice-blast-fungus

12 Neabore, L K, "Wake-up Call: Rapid Increase in Human Fungal Diseases under Climate Change," *Environmental Health Perspectives,* 132(4), 2024

13 Maliye, C C & Lohit, Y T, "Mushroom Sprouting out of a Living Frog," *Reptiles & Amphibians*, 2024

14 Cooke, M, *The Seven Sisters of Sleep: The Celebrated Drug Classic*, Prism Press, Dorset, 1997, p.259

15 Schultes R E, Hofmann A, & Rätsch C, *Plants of the Gods*, Healing Arts Press, Vermont, 1992, p.36, 70, 75

16 Arora D, *Mushrooms Demystified: A Comprehensive Guide to the Fleshy Fungi*, Ten Speed Press, California, 1986, pp.694–695

17 Iapichino, M, "A precise relationship among Buller's drop, ballistospore, and gill morphologies enables maximum packing of spores within gilled mushrooms," *Mycologia*, 113(2), 2021, pp.300–311

18 "Pilobolus and the lungworm," *The Cornell Mushroom Blog*, December 14, 2006, blog.mycology.cornell.edu/2006/12/14/pilobolus-and-the-lungworm/

1 DOWN: REVOLTING REVOLUTIONS

1 Buller, A H R, "The Fungus Lore of the Ancient Greeks and Romans (Presidential Address)," 1914

2 Koji children are initiated in a cave for nine years, then another nine if they choose, which most do.

3 Bonser, W, "Magical Practices against Elves," *Folklore*, 37(4), 1926

4 Rajput, A, Sharma, R, & Bharti, R, "Pharmacological activities and toxicities of alkaloids on human health," *Materials Today: Proceedings,* 48(5), 2022, pp.1407–1415

5 Lawrey, J D, "Dictyonema huaorani (Agaricales: Hygrophoraceae), a new lichenized basidiomycete from Amazonian Ecuador with presumed hallucinogenic properties," *The Bryologist*, 117(4), 2014, 386–394

6 Hunter, W F, "Mooncalf Menstrual Meat (MMM)," *Continuum: Journal of Media & Cultural Studies,* 37(5), 2023

7 Heinrich, K, "The Malleus Maleficarum," Internet Archive, 1508, archive.org/details/b3136245x/page/n9/mode/2up

8 The Seed Sistas, *Poison Prescriptions: Power Plant Medicine, Magic & Ritual*, Watkins Publishing, 2022

9 "Seed SistAs - Discovering the Ancient Through Native Power Plants," *Entheogenesis Australis – Entheo TV,* 2024, www.youtube.com/watch?v=ywdfdewoF78

10 Chassar, M, "Ergot: the story of a parasitic fungus," *Wellcome Foundation*, 1958, wellcomecollection.org/works/t7rqnn2f

11 Private Interview with midwife Cristina Tukua of the Guarani people in Brazil, 2023

12 Private interview with Mexican artist Daniel Godinez Nivon who works with the Triqui community, 2023

13 Smakosz, A, et al., "The Usage of Ergot (Claviceps purpurea (fr.) Tul.) in Obstetrics and Gynecology: A Historical Perspective," *Toxins*, 13(7), 2021, p.492

14 Gabbai, Lisbonne, Pourquier. "Ergot poisoning at Pont St. Esprit." *British Medical Journal*, 15(2), 1951
15 Acid Farmers, Mike Jay. <mikejay.net/the-acid-farmers/>
16 "6. Psychedelics Live Show: Part 2," *The Drug Science Podcast*, 2019
17 "Bicycle Day – What can we learn from the past? Erika Dyke PhD," *Psychedelics Today,* (VITAL Training Programme), 2024
18 Prisma, *Death Doesn't Exist: The Mother on Death, Sri Aurobindo on Rebirth*, Prisma, 2022
19 Muraresku, B, *The Immortality Key*, St. Martin's Press, New York, 2020
20 Wasson, RG, Hofmann, A, & Ruck, C, *The Road to Eleusis: Unveiling the Secret of the Mysteries,* Harcourt Brace Jovanovich, 1978
21 Blanchette, R, "Historic Wonders of the Fungal World: The Evil Demon Hand and Fungus Digitatus," *University of Minnesota,* 2017
22 *Baltic Healing: Returning to Your Mother's Womb*, Baika, B, & Lotscher, A, 2024 [film], vimeo.com/ondemand/baltichealing
23 "What happens to our bodies after we die," *BBC Future*, 2015, www.bbc.com/future/article/20150508-what-happens-after-we-die
24 Metcalf, J, "Microbial community assembly and metabolic function during mammalian corpse decomposition," *Science*, 351(6269), 2015, pp.158–162
25 Keenan, S W, Emmons, A L, & DeBruyn, J M, "Microbial community coalescence and nitrogen cycling in simulated mortality decomposition hotspots," *Ecological Processes*, 12(45), 2023
26 ESS Feed, "The Global Truffle Market in 2025 Trends Opportunities and Challenges," 2025, essfeed.com/the-global-truffle-market-in-2025-trends-opportunities-and-challenges-the-global-truffle-market-in-2025-trends-opportunities-and-challenges/
27 Jacobs, R, *The Truffle Underground: A Tale of Mystery, Mayhem, and Manipulation in the Shadowy Market of the World's Most Expensive Fungus*, Melville House, UK, 2020
28 Khalifa, S A M, et al, "Truffles: From Islamic culture to chemistry, pharmacology, and food trends in recent times," *Trends in Food Science & Technology*, 91, 2019, pp.193–218
29 Private interview with the UK's leading truffle expert Melissa Waddingham, 2025
30 Pacioni, G, et al, "Truffles contain endocannabinoid metabolic enzymes and anandamide," *Phytochemistry,* 110, 2015 pp.104–110
31 University of California - Irvine, "'Love hormone' helps produce 'bliss molecules' to boost pleasure of social interactions," *Science Daily*, 2015
32 Morgunova, M, et al, "Black and white truffles as a source of neuroactive biogenic amines," *Natural Product Research*, 1–4, 2024
33 Vahdatzadeh M, Deveau A, & Splivallo R, "The Role of the Microbiome of Truffles in Aroma Formation: a Meta-Analysis Approach." *Applied Environmental Microbiology*. 81(20), 2015, pp.6946–6952
34 Piattoni, F, et al, "Viability and morphology of *Tuber aestivum* spores after passage through the gut of *Sus scrofa*," *Fungal Ecology*, 9, 2014, pp.52–60
35 Takaki, K, et al, "Effect of Electrical Stimulation on Fruit Body Formation in Cultivating Mushrooms," *Microorganisms,* 2(1), 2014, pp.58–72

2 UP: SPIRIT & SUBJECTIVITY

1 Hunter, P, "The fungal grid," *EMBO Reports*, 24(5), 2013, p.3
2 Gregory, P H, "Electrostatic Charges on Spores of Fungi in Air," *Nature*, 1957. Also in: Buller, A H R, "Researches on fungi." Volume VI, *CABI Databases*, 1935
3 Clark-Cotton, M, Jacobs, K C, Lew, D J, "Chemotropism and Cell-Cell Fusion in Fungi," Microbiology and Molecular Biology Reviews. 86(1), 2022
4 Adamatsky, A, "Language of fungi derived from their electrical spiking activity," *Royal Society Open Science,* 9(4), 2022
5 Hemenway, P, *The Secret Code*, TASCHEN, 2020, p.116
6 Roob, A, *Alchemy & Mysticism*, TASCHEN, 2023, p.84
7 Cosmic Core, "Article 188: Botany/Mycology – Part 11 – The Geometry of Moss, Algae & Fung,i" www.cosmic-core.org/free/article-188-botany-mycology-part-11-the-geometry-of-moss-algae-fungi/
8 All Things Fungi Festival, Chris Timmerman, [Talk] 2025
9 Wolfe, D A, *Chaga: King of the Medicinal Mushrooms*, North Atlantic Books, 2012
10 Rogers, R, *The Fungal Pharmacy: The Complete Guide to Medicinal Mushrooms and Lichens of North America,* North Atlantic Books, 2011

11 Lin Yutang, *The Importance of Understanding*, Heinemann, 1961
12 "Penglai: Island of Immortality and Mythological Marvel," *Chinese Weird Tales*, weirdtales.me/what-is-penglai/
13 "Tracing The History of Hallucinogens in China," Talking Drugs, 2022, www.talkingdrugs.org/the-history-of-hallucinogens-in-china/
14 Strassberg, *Chinese Bestiary: Strange Creatures from the Guideways Through Mountains and Seas*, University of California Press, 2008
15 Smith, D, "LING ZHI, Ganoderma lucidum, the Chinese Mushroom of Immortality," *North American Mycological Association,* namyco.org/ling-zhi-ganoderma-lucidum-the-chinese-mushroom-of-immortality/
16 Willard, T, *"Reishi Mushroom: Herb of Spiritual Potency and Medical Wonder,"* Chapter 1: The Emperor's Search, *Lubrecht & Cramer Ltd,* 1995, pp.7–24
17 Lawrence, S, *The Magic of Mushrooms: Fungi in Folklore, Superstition and Traditional Medicine* (Royal Botanic Gardens, Kew), Welbeck, 2022, p.12
18 Ware, J R, *Alchemy, Medicine, and Religion in the China of A.D. 320: The Nei P'ien of Ko Hung,* M.I.T. Press, 1967, pp.68–96
19 "Reishi Mushroom Market Size To Reach $13.60 Billion By 2030," Grand View Research, 2024, www.grandviewresearch.com/industry-analysis/reishi-mushroom-market-report
20 Thuy, N H L, et al., *"Pharmacological Activities and Safety of Ganoderma lucidum Spores: A Systematic Review," Cureus*, 15(9), 2023
21 Gregory, P H, "Electrostatic Charges on Spores of Fungi in Air," *Nature*, 1957
22 All Things Fungi Festival, Sidnee Ober-Singleton: Biofluorescence Night Walk, 2024
23 "How do fungi communicate?" MIT Technology Review, 2023, www.technologyreview.com/2023/04/24/1071363/fungi-fungus-communication-explainer/
24 Buffi, M, et al, "Electrical signaling in fungi: past and present challenges," *Microbiology Reviews*, 49, 2025
25 "Fungi: Web of Life" Screening with Merlin Sheldrake, St George's, Bristol, 2025
26 Fukasawa, Y, Savoury, M, & Boddy, L, "Ecological memory and relocation decisions in fungal mycelial networks: responses to quantity and location of new resources," *The ISME Journal*, 14(2), 2020, pp.380–388
27 Money, N P, "Hyphal and mycelial consciousness: the concept of the fungal mind," *Fungal Biology*, 125(4), 2021, pp.257-259
28 Martinez, N D, & Marschmann, G L, "Revealing how fungi build planet-altering 'road' networks," Nature, 2025
29 Galvez, L O, et al., "A travelling-wave strategy for plant-fungal trade," *Nature*, 2025
30 Fischer M S, Glass N L, "Communicate and Fuse: How Filamentous Fungi Establish and Maintain an Interconnected Mycelial Network." *Frontiers of Microbiology*, 10(619), 2019
31 Sikes, B A, "When do arbuscular mycorrhizal fungi protect plant roots from pathogens?", *Plant Signaling Behaviour*, 5(6), 2010, pp.763–765
32 Roy, B A, "Floral mimicry by a plant pathogen," *Nature*, 362, 1993, pp.56-58
33 de Freitas Soares, F E, Sufiate, B L, & de Queiroz, J H, "Nematophagous fungi: Far beyond the endoparasite, predator and ovicidal groups," *Agriculture and Natural Resources*, 52(1), 2018, pp.1-8
34 Fascinated by Fungi Podcast, Gordon Walker, Episode 14: Fungal Communication, 2023
35 Kapsali, V, *Biomimetics for Designers*, Thames & Hudson, London, 2016, pp.158-159
36 Tero, A, et al, "Rules for biologically inspired adaptive network design." *Science*, 327(5964), 2010, pp.439–442
37 Queen's University. "Slime mold mimics Canadian highway network." ScienceDaily, 2012
38 Adamatzky, A, & Jones, J, "Road planning with slime mould: If Physarum built motorways it would route M6/M74 through Newcastle," *International Journal of Bifurcation and Chaos,* 20, 2010, pp.3065–3084.
39 Adamatzky, A, & Alonso-Sanz, R, "Rebuilding Iberian motorways with slime mould," *Biosystems*, 105(1), 2011, pp.89-100
40 Tero, A, et al, "Rules for Biologically Inspired Adaptive Network Design," *Science*, 327(5964), 2010, pp.439–442
41 Adamatzky, A, *Physarum Machines: Computers from Slime Mould,* University of the West of England, 2010
42 Adamatzky, A, & Ganida, A, "Living mycelium composites discern weights via patterns of electrical activity," *Journal of Bioresources and Bioproducts,* 7(1), 2022, pp.26–32
43 Adamatzky, A, Gandia, A & Chiolerio, A, "Towards fungal sensing skin." *Fungal Biology Biotechnology,* 8(6), 2021
44 "Bio-processors – Creating electrical components from slime mould," *University of Plymouth*, YouTube, 2020, www.youtube.com/watch?v=OCbxOoRmNak
45 Kumar Mishra, et al., "Sensorimotor control of robots mediated by electrophysiological measurements of fungal mycelia," *Science Robotics*, 9(93), 2024

46 Lex Fridman, "Michael Levin: Biology, Life, Aliens, Evolution, Embryogenesis & Xenobots | Lex Fridman Podcast #325," YouTube, 2022
47 Private Interview with Andrew Adamatzky, 2025
48 Adamatzky, A, *Fungal Machines: Sensing and Computing with Fungi*, Springer, 2023
49 Adamatzky, A, "Language of Fungi Derived from Their Electrical Spiking Activity," *Royal Society Open Science*, 9(4), 2022
50 MOLD Magazine, "MIT OpenAg Releases the Personal Food Computer 3.0, a STEM-Friendly Collaboration with Educators," 2018, thisismold.com/space/farm-systems/mit-openag-releases-the-personal-food-computer-3-0-a-stem-friendly-collaboration-with-educators
51 Helene Steiner, "Project Florence," www.helenesteiner.com/project/project-florence
52 "Mr E. Brande, on a Poisonous Species of Agaric," *The Medical and Physical Journal*, 3(11), 1800, pp.41-44
53 Letcher, A, *Shroom: A Cultural History of the Magic Mushroom*, Faber & Faber, 2007
54 Hofmann, A, Heim, R, & Tscherter, H, "Présence de la psilocybine dans une espèce Européenne d'agaric, le Psilocybe semilanceata," *Comptesrendus*, 257, 1903, pp.10-12, www.samorini.it/doc1/alt_aut/ek/hofmann2.pdf
55 Wasson, R G, "Seeking the Magic Mushroom," *Life Magazine*, 1957
56 "Psilocybin (Magic Mushrooms)," drugscience.org.uk
57 Korman, A, Johnson, M W, & Griffiths, R, "Psilocybin for Depression: How Do We Get to the Next Level?," *Frontiers in Psychology*, 2021
58 Davis, A K, Barret, F S, & May, D G, "Effects of Psilocybin-Assisted Therapy on Major Depressive Disorder," *JAMA Psychiatry*, 2021, 78(5), pp.481-489
59 Carhart-Harris, R, et al., "Trial of Psilocybin versus Escitalopram for Depression," *The New England Journal of Medicine*. 2021, 384(15) pp.1402-1411
60 Barba, T, et al, "Psychedelics and sexual functioning: a mixed-methods study," *Scientific Reports*, 2024, *14*(1), pp.1–16
61 Ross, S, et al., "Rapid and sustained symptom reduction following psilocybin treatment for anxiety and depression in patients with life-threatening cancer: a randomized controlled trial," *Journal of Psychopharmacology*, 2016, 30(12), pp.1165–1180
62 Agin-Liebes, G, & Davis, A K, "Psilocybin for the Treatment of Depression: A Promising New Pharmacotherapy Approach," *Current Topics in Behavioral Neurosciences*, 2022, 56, pp.125–140
63 Gosling, T, Lagan, B, & Hayward, E, "Magic mushrooms enter mainstream as treatment for depression," *The Times*, 2025, www.thetimes.com/world/europe/article/the-magic-of-mushrooms-is-psilocybin-really-a-cure-for-depression-dvtrwlpf7
64 "Microdosing: Fact or Fiction? – UC Davis Psychedelic Summit 2023," *UC Davis Health*, YouTube, 2023
65 "56. Microdosing Psychedelics with Dr James Fadiman," *The Drug Science Podcast*, 2022
66 "Elon Musk Does It. Sergey Brin Does It. Your Boss Might Do It. Welcome to the Workplace Shroom Boom," *WIRED*, 2023, www.wired.com/story/microdosing-workplace-shroom-boom/
67 "6. Psychedelics Live Show: Part 2," *The Drug Science Podcast*, 2019
68 Private Interview with Alan Rockefeller, 29.09.25
69 Wild Food UK, "Liberty Cap"
70 Sheldrake et al, R, McKenna, T, & Abraham, R, *Chaos, Creativity, and Cosmic Consciousness*, Park Street Press, Vermont, 2001, p.17
71 McKenna, T, *Food of the Gods*, Ebury Press, 1999
72 Hofmann, A., *LSD, My Problem Child: Reflections on Sacred Drugs, Mysticism and Science*, Multidisciplinary Association for Psychedelic Studies, 1979
73 Wasson, R G, Doniger W, *Soma: Divine Mushroom of Immortality*, New York, 1968, archive.org/details/wasson-1968-soma/page/8/mode/2up
74 Zare, M, & Williams, M T, "Muslim Women and Psychedelics: A Look at the Past, Present, and Future," *International Journal of Mental Health and Addiction*, 22(2), 2023, pp.1–16
75 de Rios, M D, & Stachalek, R, "The Duboisia genus, Australian aborigines and suggestibility," *Journal of Psychoactive Drugs*, 31(2), 1999, pp.155–61
76 le Baron, D, "Psychedelics in Africa: The Untold Story Revisited," *Medicine Festival*, 2024 (talk)
77 Nemu, D, "Getting High with the most high: Entheogens in the Old Testament," *Journal of Psychedelic Studies*, 3(2), 2019, pp.117-132
78 Muraresku, B, *The Immortality Key: The Secret History of the Religion with No Name*, St Martin's Press, 2020
79 McKenna, T, "Opening the Doors of Creativity" (Lecture)

80 Woolfe, S, "Ancient Motifs in Psychedelic Experiences," 2013, www.samwoolfe.com/2013/09/ancient-motifs-in-psychedelic.html
81 Apostolia Papadamaki, "Anamnesis - Remembering our Ancient Future," *Medicine Festival* 2024 (Talk)
82 Eglash, R, *African Fractals: Modern Computing and Indigenous Design*, Rutgers University Press, 1999
83 Woolfe, S, "The Psychedelic Nature of Islamic Art and Architecture," *Medium*, 2018, samwoolfe.medium.com/the-psychedelic-nature-of-islamic-art-and-architecture-7a011e27a888
84 French, A, & Walden, K, *Modernity and the Construction of Sacred Space*, De Gruyter, Oldenbourg, 2024, pp.9-10
85 Maillart-Garg, M, & Winkelman, M, "The 'Kamasutra' temples of India: A case for the encoding of psychedelically induced spirituality," *Journal of Psychedelic Studies,* 3(2), 2019, pp.81-103
86 Huxley, A, *The Doors of Perception and Heaven and Hell,* Vintage, London, 2004, p.5
87 Hancock, G, "Psychedelics and the Quest for Life After Death: A Lost Key to Prehistory?," *Breaking Convention*, 2023
88 Schultes, R E, & Hofmann, A, *The Botany and Chemistry of Hallucinogens* (2nd ed.). Charles C Thomas, 1997

3 CENTRE: FLOW & BALANCE

1 Browne, C, *Entering Time: The Fungus Man Platters of Charles Edenshaw*, TALONBOOKS, 2016, p.112
2 The British Columbian Quarterly, "Review: Entering Time: The Fungus Man Platters of Charles Edenshaw," *BC Studies,* 209, 2021, pp.142-145, bcstudies.com/book_film_review/entering-time-the-fungus-man-platters-of-charles-edenshaw/
3 See page 219-223 for more information of v'apaq in Siberia
4 Schultes R E, Hofmann A, & Rätsch C, *Plants of the Gods,* Healing Arts Press, Vermont, 1992, p.82
5 Woven Science, 2025, www.woven.science
6 Myers, W, *Biodesign*, Thames & Hudson, 2018, pp.28-31
7 Flourishing Diversity, "Listening Sessions," 2025, flourishingdiversity.com/listening-sessions
8 Tree, I, *Wilding*, Picador, 2018, p.47
9 Chainey, D D, & Winsham, W, *Treasury of Folklore: Woodlands & Forests*, Batsford, UK, 2021
10 Gooley, T, *How to Read a Tree*, Hodder & Stoughton, 2023
11 Renault, H, "Harnessing lignin evolution for biotechnological applications," *Current Opinion in Biotechnology*, 56, 2019, pp.105-111
12 Sheldrake, M, *Entangled Life*, Penguin Random House, UK, 2018
13 The Heart of England Forest, "English Oak," heartofenglandforest.org/english-oak
14 Ekstrom, A L, et al, "Deadwood manipulation and type determine assemblage composition of saproxylic beetles and fungi after a decade," *Journal of Environmental Management*, 372(123416), 2024
15 Niemela, T, Wallenius, T, & Kotiranta, H, "The Kelo Tree, A Vanishing Substrate Of Specified Wood-Inhabiting Fungi," *Polish Botanical Journal*, 47(2), 2002, pp.91-101
16 Woodland Trust, "Ancient oaks in the English Landscape," ati.woodlandtrust.org.uk/reports/published-research/ancient-oaks-in-the-english-landscape/
17 Wainhouse, M, & Boddy, L, "Making hollow trees: Inoculating living trees with wood-decay fungi for the conservation of threatened taxa, A guide for conservationists," *Global Ecology and Conservation*, 33, 2022
18 Boddy, L, *Fungi and Trees: Their complex relationships*, Arboricultural Association, 2021
19 Mitchell, R J, et al, "Oak associated biodiversity in the UK (OakEcol)," *Environmental Information Data Centre*, 2019
20 All Things Fungi Festival, "David Satori: Britain's Ancient Celtic Rainforests," 2024 (Talk)
21 Shrubsole, G, *The Lost Rainforests of Britain*, William Collins, UK, 2022
22 Tallantire, P A, "The early-Holocene spread of hazel (Corylus avellana L.) in Europe north and west of the Alps: an ecological hypothesis." *The Holocene*, *12*(1), 2002, pp.81-96
23 Coppins, A M, & Coppins, B J, "Atlantic Hazelwoods – a neglected habitat?". *Botanical Journal of Scotland*, *55*(1), 200, pp.149-160
24 Ondaatje Rolls, K, *Homeostatic Toes: The Arts as Catharsis*, 2018
25 Scott, K, *Fungarium*, Big Picture Press, 2020
26 Zonca, V, *Lichens: Toward a Minimal Resistance*, Polity, 2022
27 St Clair, K, *The Secret Lives of Colour*, Penguin Putnam Inc, 2024
28 "Lichens," NatureSpot, www.naturespot.org/gallery/lichens
29 "Mushroom and Lichen Dyers United," *Facebook forum*, www.facebook.com/groups/mycopigments/

30 Casselman, K L, *Craft of the Dyer: Colour from Plants and Lichens,* Northeast, University of Toronto Press, Toronto, 1980
31 "Chlorociboria aeruginosa - Turquoise Elfcup," *First Nature*, www.first-nature.com/fungi/chlorociboria-aeruginosa.php
32 Dominique Cardon, *Natural Dyes: Sources, Tradition, Technology and Science,* Archetype Publications Ltd, London, 2007
33 "The Use of lichens for dyeing," The British Lichen Society, 2024
34 Whitworth, I, et al, "Foraging for Colour," *The Journal for Weavers, Spinners and Dyers*, 288, Winter 2023
35 *"Global Medicinal Mushroom Market Size and Trends," Coherent Market Insights*, 2025, www.coherentmarketinsights.com/industry-reports/global-medicinal-mushroom-market
36 Powell, M, *Medicinal Mushrooms: The Essential Guide*, Mycology Press, 2013, p.6
37 Hobbs, C, *Christopher Hobbs's Medicinal Mushrooms: The Essential Guide: Boost Immunity, Improve Memory, Fight Cancer, Stop Infection, and Expand Your Consciousness*, Storey, 2021, pp.97–101
38 Powell, M, *Medicinal Mushrooms: The Essential Guide*, Mycology Press, 2013, p.6
39 "Fu Ling Poria: A TCM Herb for Strengthening the Spleen and Calming the Mind," *Jongji Medical Group Online*, 2025, www.hjmedicalgroup.com/en/post/fu-ling-poria-a-tcm-herb-for-strengthening-the-spleen-and-calming-the-mind
40 Private interview with biochemist and Traditional Chinese Medicine herbalist Martin Powell, 2024
41 Chen, J, et al., "Maitake Mushroom (Grifola frondosa) Extract Induces Ovulation in Patients with Polycystic Ovary Syndroms: A Possible Monotherapy and a Combination Therapy After Failure with First-Line Clomiphene Citrate," *The Journal of Alternative and Complementary Medicine,* 16(12), 2010. pp.1295–1299
42 Powell, M, *Medicinal Mushrooms: The Essential Guide*, Mycology Press, 2013, p.6
43 Powell, M, *Medicinal Mushrooms: The Essential Guide*, Mycology Press, 2013, p.8
44 Roy, M, et al, *"Pharmacological and therapeutic inventory of fungi in cancertherapy--A comprehensive review," AIMS Molecular Science,* 12(1), 2025, pp.67–98
45 van Steenwijk, H P, Bast, A, & de Boer A, "Immunomodulating Effects of Fungal Beta-Glucans: From Traditional Use to Medicine," *Nutrients*. 2021, 13(4), p.1333
46 Stamets, P, et al., "Extracts of Polypore Mushroom Mycelia Reduce Viruses in Honey Bees," *Scientific Reports*, 8, 2018
47 Güneşdoğdu, M, Gedik, G, & Abaci, S H., "Biocontrol effect of Fomes fomentarius mushroom against Varroa destructor," *Medycyna Weterynaryjna*, 2025
48 Rogers, R, *The Fungal Pharmacy: Medicinal Mushrooms and Lichens of North America: The Complete Guide to Medicinal Mushrooms and Lichens of North America*, North Atlantic Books, 2011
49 Private interview with Bristol Fungarium, 2025
50 "Medicinal Mushrooms: Hania Opienski | CNM Specialist Podcast – Full Episode," *College of Naturopathic Medicine,* YouTube, 2023, www.youtube.com/watch?app=desktop&v=jhK4psXuSRM
51 Rogers, R D, *Medicinal Mushrooms: The Human Clinical Trials*, Independently Published, 2020, pp.52–56
52 Hobbs, C, *Christopher Hobbs's Medicinal Mushrooms: The Essential Guide: Boost Immunity, Improve Memory, Fight Cancer, Stop Infection, and Expand Your Consciousness*, Storey, 2021, pp.97–101
53 Bonaz, B, Sinniger, V, & Pellissier, S, "The Vagus Nerve in the Neuro-Immune Axis: Implications in the Pathology of the Gastrointestinal Tract," *Frontiers in Immunology*, 8(1452), 2017
54 "Lion's Mane Mushroom," *Alzheimer's Drug Discovery Foundation*, 2016, www.alzdiscovery.org/uploads/cognitive_vitality_media/Lions-Mane-Cognitive-Vitality-For-Researchers.pdf
55 Szućko-Kociuba, I, "Neurotrophic and Neuroprotective Effects of Hericium erinaceus," *International Journal of Molecular Sciences,* 24(21), 2023
56 "Dementia: Your questions answered and lion's mane mushrooms in the lab," *BBC Radio 4,* 2025
57 Nakazato, H, et al, "Efficacy of immunochemotherapy as adjuvant treatment after curative resection of gastric cancer," *The Lancet*, 343(8906), 1994, pp.1122_1126
58 Maehara, Y, et al, "Biological mechanism and clinical effect of protein-bound polysaccharide K (KRESTIN®): review of development and future perspectives," *Surgery Today*, 42(1), 2011, pp.8–28
59 Lin, X, et al, "Microbial Community Structure and Activity Linked to Contrasting Biogeochemical Gradients in Bog and Fen Environments of the Glacial Lake Agassiz Peatland," *Applied and Environmental Microbiology*, 78(19), 2012, pp.7023–7031
60 Irish Museum of Archaeology
61 Aldhouse-Green, H, *Bog Bodies Uncovered: Solving Europe's Ancient Mystery*, Thames & Hudson Ltd, London, 2015, p.69 and 109
62 Tolkien, J R R, *The Lord of the Rings: The Two Towers,* George Allen & Unwin Ltd, UK, 1954, Chapter 7

63 Irish Museum of Natural History
64 Private interview with bog butter expert Karen O'Toole in the Irish Museum of Natural History, 2024
65 Synnott, C, "Records of Bog Butter Finds in the memoirs of the Irish Ordnance Survey, 1830 to 1839," *Ulster Journal of Archaeology,* 62, 2003, pp.143–160
66 "Bog butter and the Céide Fields: archaeology as inspiration for contemporary art - Gareth Kennedy," *The Heritage Council,* YouTube, 2018, www.youtube.com/watch?v=O_QvEzY4R3c
67 "The Bog Wood Story," *Celtic Roots*, shop.celtic-roots.com/pages/the-bog-wood-story
68 Sterflinger, K, "Fungi: Their role in deterioration of cultural heritage," *Fungal Biology Reviews*, 24(1–2), 2010, pp.47–55

4 IN & OUT: TRANSFORMATION, TRANSPORTATION, & TRANSCENDENCE

1 Morton, T, *Hyperobjects: Philosophy and Ecology after the End of the World (Posthumanities),* University of Minnesota Press, 2013
2 Wright, J, *The Forager's Calendar: A Seasonal Guide to Nature's Wild Harvests,* Profile Books Ltd, UK, 2020, pp.237–240
3 Private conversation with farmer and Porcini enthusiast Tom Carter (2025) who learned from expert Simon Evans. Tom explains that Porcini take up to 20 years to establish, then fruit most abundantly between 25 and 45 years of a tree's life – possibly longer, though he's unsure, as most of the plantations where they thrive are logged around 40-45 years.
4 Private interview with the Casini family, 2025
5 "Brown Birch Bolete," Wild Food UK, www.wildfooduk.com/mushroom-guide/brown-birch-bolete/
6 McGilchrist, I, *The Master and his Emissary: The Divided Brain and the Making of the Western World*, Yale University Press, 2012
7 Inglis, B, *The Forbidden Game*, Charles Scribner's Sons, New York, 1975
8 Seigel, R, *Intoxication: The Universal Drive for Mind-Altering Substances*, Rochester, Vt., Park Street Press, 2005
9 *The Bear* (1988) (Film)
10 "*The Bear* (1988) (film) – Amanita Muscaria Scenes," *Не почтовая МАРКА*, www.youtube.com/watch?v=o_7za9D4kk8
11 Noever, D A, "Using Spider Web Patterns to Determine Toxicity," Life Sciences, 19(4), 1995, p.82
12 Walker, M, *Why We Sleep: The New Science of Sleep and Dreams*, Penguin, 2018, p.30
13 "The Man Who Talked to Dolphins While High on LSD," *KiraTV*, 2023, www.youtube.com/watch?v=0PJVb4OQVUs
14 "The Dolphin Who Loved Me," *The Guardian*, 2014, www.theguardian.com/environment/2014/jun/08/the-dolphin-who-loved-me
15 "The Man Who Talked to Dolphins While High on LSD," *KiraTV*, 2023, www.youtube.com/watch?v=0PJVb4OQVUs
16 Lilley J C, Man and Dolphin, Doubleday, 1961
17 "Dolphins purposely 'getting high' on pufferfish - Dolphins - Spy in the Pod: Episode 2," *BBC*, YouTube, 2014, www.youtube.com/watch?v=msx3BAhIeQg
18 Edsinger, E, & Dölen, G, "A Conserved Role for Serotonergic Neurotransmission in Mediating Social Behavior in Octopus," *Current Biology*, 28(19), 2018, pp.3136-3142
19 Park, B, "Squirrels and Amanitas," *The Mycophile*, 59(1), 2019, p.5, www.biodiversitylibrary.org/item/274999#page/5/mode/1up
20 Wasson, R G, & Doniger, W, *Soma: Divine Mushroom of Immortality,* New York, 1968, p.25
21 Since Wasson's publication of *Soma*, firsthand accounts of this practice have become rare. However, evidence shows Western ethnographers reenacting it (Shaman's Drum: "In Search of Mukhomor, the Mushroom of Immortality" Salzman, J, et al, 1996, p.46) – an example of our desire to romanticize and preserve "primitive" rituals. It's as though we need other cultures to be strange and exotic, so we recreate them ourselves, often infusing them with a sense of authenticity that we wish to be true. In doing so, we almost breathe life back into these rituals, keeping them alive in our own image.
22 Salzman, J, et al., Shaman's Drum: "In Search of Mukhomor, the Mushroom of Immortality." 1996, p.46
23 Wasson, R G, & Doniger, W, *Soma: Divine Mushroom of Immortality,* New York, 1968, pp.75–76
24 Fabbro, F U, "Mushrooms and Snails in Religious Rituals of Early Christians: Archeological Evidence at the Ancient Basilica of Aquileia," *Journal of Psychoactive Plants & Compounds*, 1999, pp.1129-7301
25 Speiser, B, & Rowell-Rahier, M, "Effects of Food Availability, Nutritional Value, and Alkaloids on Food Choice in the Generalist Herbivore Arianta arbustorum (Gastropoda: Helicidae)," *Oikos*, 62(3), 1991, pp.306–318
26 Andrews, G, "Psilocybin," 1977

27 Private interview with Marina Warner, January 2025
28 Jay, M, "Mushrooms in Wonderland," 2003, mikejay.net/mushrooms-in-wonderland/
29 Jay, M, "Mushrooms in Wonderland," 2003, mikejay.net/mushrooms-in-wonderland/
30 A few to get you started: Lewis Carroll, *Alice's Adventures in Wonderland*; Sylvia Plath, *Mushrooms*; Charlotte Perkins Gilman, *The Yellow Wallpaper*; Shirley Jackson, *We Have Always Lived in the Castle*; H P Lovecraft, *The Whisperer in Darkness*; Sergey Anufriev & Pavel Peppershtein, *Mythogenic Love of Castes*; H G Wells, *The Purple Pileus*
31 Dalrymple, W, *Nine Lives: Searching for the Sacred in Modern India*, Bloomsbury Publishing, 2009
32 "In Our Time, The Kama Sutra," *BBC Radio 4*, 2012, www.bbc.co.uk/programmes/b01bb9c9
33 Vatsyayana, *The Kama Sutra of Vatsyayana, Translated by Richard Burton,* 1992 (e-book), www.gutenberg.org/files/27827/27827-h/27827-h.htm
34 Danielou, A, *The Complete Kama Sutra: The First Unabridged Modern Translation of the Classic Indian Text*, Park Street Press, 1994
35 Dalrymple, W*, Nine Lives: Searching for the Sacred in Modern India,* Bloomsbury Publishing, 2009
36 "A global history of weed and sex," *Leafly*, 2020, www.leafly.com/news/canada/global-history-of-weed-and-sex
37 Robinson, R, *The Great Book of Hemp*, Park Street Press, 1995, p.95
38 Jiraungkoorskul K, Jiraungkoorskul W, "Review of Naturopathy of Medical Mushroom, Ophiocordyceps Sinensis, in Sexual Dysfunction," *Pharmacognosy Reviews,* 10(19), 2016
39 Chen, S, et al, "Effect of Cs-4 (Cordyceps sinensis) on exercise performance in healthy older subjects: a double-blind, placebo-controlled trial," *Journal of Alternative Complementary Medicine*, 16(5):, 2010, pp.85–90
40 "Tribe, Layap," BBC Two, 2007
41 Personal Interview with a Chinese Herbalist in San Fransisco, 2024.
42 Winkler, D, "Yartsa Gunbu (Cordyceps sinensis) and the Fungal Commodification of Tibet's Rural Economy", *Economic Botany*, 62(3), 2008, pp.291–305
43 Lu, Y, et al, "Metabolic profiling of natural and cultured Cordyceps by NMR spectroscopy," *Scientific Reports,* 9(1), 2019
44 "Psychedelic Somatic Institute: The PSIP Model," ed. Saj Razvi, *LPC*, 2020
45 "Psychedelic Psilocybin Magic Truffle Veteran Retreat," *Films for Action*, 2022
46 van der Kolk, B, *The Body Keeps the Score*, Penguin, 2015
47 "Compass Pathways announces durable improvement in symptoms through 12 weeks in open-label phase 2 study of COMP360 psilocybin in post-traumatic stress disorder," Compass Pathways, 2024, s204.q4cdn.com/927483861/files/doc_news/Compass-Pathways-announces-durable-improvement-in-symptoms-through-12-weeks-in-open-label-phase-2-study-of-COMP360-psilocybin-in-post-L385Z.pdf
48 "A Study of Psilocybin for PTSD," Johns Hopkins University, *ClinicalTrials.gov*, 2025, clinicaltrials.gov/study/NCT06407635
49 "Open-Label Psilocybin Study in Transdiagnostic Population," Yale University, *ClinicalTrials.gov*, 2025, clinicaltrials.gov/study/NCT06442423
50 "Psilocybin clinical trial for Alcohol Use Disorder & PTSD: PsiloStudy," *UW Medicine*, 2025, ntap.psychiatry.uw.edu/psilostudy/
51 Biscoe, N, et al, "Psilocybin-assisted psychotherapy for the treatment of PTSD in UK armed forces veterans: A feasibility study protocol," *European Journal of Trauma & Dissociation*, 7(4), 2023
52 "Psilocybin Mushroom Therapy (part 2)," *Psychedelic Somatic Institute*, 2021, www.psychedelicsomatic.org/post/psilocybin-mushroom-therapy-part-2
53 Psychedelic Somatic Institute, 2025, www.psychedelicsomatic.org/
54 "Saj Razvi – A Match Made in Heaven: A psychobiological pathway to pair with the psychedelic medicine," *Breaking Convention,* YouTube, 2023, www.youtube.com/watch?v=hbDpYXO1UiA
55 "Rupert Callender – Raving in the Grave," *Breaking Convention*, YouTube, 2023, www.youtube.com/watch?v=HAUPt6eCYCI
56 "Navajo Death Rituals," Navajo Code Talkers, 2014, navajocodetalkers.org/navajo-death-rituals/
57 Reay, M, ""MUSHROOM MADNESS" IN THE NEW GUINEA HIGHLANDS," *Oceania*, 31(2), 1960, pp.137–139
58 Russian anthropologist A V Šapovalov proposes a contrasting viewpoint: he argues that the use of psychedelics, specifically *Amanita muscaria* in Siberia, was part of an ancient "trance system," which was eventually replaced by visionary practices that no longer relied on psychotropic substances (Šapovalov, 2001).
59 Hofmann, A, *LSD, My Problem Child: Reflections on Sacred Drugs, Mysticism and Science,* Multidisciplinary Association for Psychedelic Studies, 1979

60 Blanchette, R, "Historic Wonders of the Fungal World: the evil demon hand and Fungus digitatus," *University of Minnesota,* 2017

61 Blanchette, R A, et al., "Nineteenth Century Shaman Grave Guardians Are Carved Fomitopsis officinalis Sporophores," *Mycological Society of America,* 84(1), 1992, pp.119–124

62 Chevalier, J, & Gheerbrant, *Dictionnaire des Symboles,* Éditions Robert Laffont/JUPITER, 1982, p.205

63 "Listening Session with Pat McCabe (Weyakpa Najin Win, Woman Stands Shining)," *Flourishing Diversity*, 2021, flourishingdiversity.com/events/listening-session-with-pat-mccabe/

4.5 INTEGRATION: HANGING UP THE PHONE

1 "Dr. Raquel Bennett - Therapeutic Ketamine: Models and Mechanisms in Psychiatry and Psychotherapy," *Yale Psychedelic Science Group,* YouTube, 2019, www.youtube.com/watch?v=Av7tptlNp3M

2 Watts, A, *The Joyous Cosmology: Adventures in the Chemistry of Consciousness*, Vintage Books, 1962

3 Gagliano, M, *Thus Spoke the Plant*, North Atlantic Books, US, 2018

4 María Sabina, "The Life," *University of California Press,* content.ucpress.edu/title/9780520239531/9780520239531_sabina.pdf

5 INTER: BEING ECOLOGICAL

1 FAOSTAT: Meat, chicken – Producing Animals/Slaughtered, www.fao.org/faostat/en/#data/QCL, Data showing a rise from ~20 billion annually in 1975 to ~70 billion in 2025.

2 "Nonhuman Nonsense," *The Pink Chicken Project*, nonhuman-nonsense.com/pink-chicken-project

3 Cohen, J J, *Prismatic Ecology: Ecotheory Beyond Green*, Univ Of Minnesota Press, 2014, p.295

4 "Neri Oxman: Biology, Art, and Science of Design & Engineering with Nature | Lex Fridman Podcast #394," Lex Friedman, YouTube, 2023, www.youtube.com/watch?v=XbPHojL_61U

5 Antonelli, P, et al., *Neri Oxman: Mediated Matter: Material Ecology*, The Museum of Modern Art, New York, 2020

6 McGuirk, J, & Nahum, A, *Moving to Mars: Design for the Red Planet*, Design Museum Publishing, 2019

7 Viktorov, A N, et al, "Residential colonization of orbital complex 'Mir' environment by penicillium chrysogenum and problem of ecological safety in long-term space flight," *Aerospace and Environmental Medicine*, 32(5), 1998, pp.57–62

8 Moving to Mars Exhibition, 2019

9 "The Closed Life-Support System," *National Aeronautics and Space Administration*, 1966, ntrs.nasa.gov/api/citations/19670025254/downloads/19670025254.pdf

10 Liu, G, et al., "Simulated microgravity and the antagonistic influence of strigolactone on plant nutrient uptake in low nutrient conditions," *Microgravity*, 4(20), 2018

11 Shevtsov, J, "Making Soil for Space Habitats by Seeding Asteroids with Fungi," *NASA*, 2021, www.nasa.gov/general/making-soil-for-space-habitats-by-seeding-asteroids-with-fungi/

12 Greenblatt, J, & Anzaldua, A, "How space technology benefits the Earth," *The Space Review*, 2019, www.thespacereview.com/article/3768/1

13 Shunk, G K, et al, "A Self-Replicating Radiation-Shield for Human Deep-Space Exploration: Radiotrophic Fungi can Attenuate Ionizing Radiation aboard the International Space Station," b*ioRxiv*, 2021

14 Blachowicz, A, et al., "The International Space Station Environment Triggers Molecular Responses in Aspergillus niger," *Frontiers in Microbiology*, 13, 2022

15 "6 ways mushrooms can save the world | Paul Stamets | TED," *TED*, 2008, www.youtube.com/watch?v=XI5frPV58tY

16 Wainwright, et al, "Are Microbes Currently Arriving to Earth from Space?" *Journal of Cosmology*, 7, 2010, pp.1692–1702

17 Redecker, D, Kodner, R, & Graham, L E, "Glomalean Fungi from the Ordovician," *Science*, 289(5486), 1920

18 "Mushroom-growing boom could cause biodiversity crisis, warn UK experts," *The Guardian*, 2024, www.theguardian.com/science/article/2024/may/31/mushroom-growing-boom-could-cause-biodiversity-crisis-warn-uk-experts

19 Baars, J J P, Hendrickx, P M, & Sonnenber, A S M, "Prototype of a Sporeless Oyster Mushroom," Applied Plant Re-search Mushroom Research Unit, 2004

20 Stamets, P, *Mycelium Running*, Ten Speed Press, Berkley, 2005, p.17

21 Stamets, P, *Mycelium Running*, Ten Speed Press, Berkley, 2005, pp.134–135

22 Gladfelter, A S, James, T Y, & Amend, A S, "Marine Fungi," *Current Biology*, 29(6), 2019, pp.191–195
23 "Marine Fungi – Ettinger, C, PhD," *Mushroom Revival Podcast*, 2021, podcasts.apple.com/mx/podcast/marine-fungi-cassie-ettinger-phd/id1462757524?i=1000509484977
24 Gamaleldien, H, "Onset of the Earth's hydrological cycle four billion years ago or earlier," *Nature Geoscience*, 17, 2014, pp.560–565
25 Martin, W, et al, "Hydrothermal vents and the origin of life," *Nature Reviews Microbiology*, 6, 2008, pp.805–814
26 "Global Ocean Sampling Expedition (GOS)," *J. Craig Venter Institute*, www.jcvi.org/research/gos
27 Costas-Imbernón, D, et al, "The skin microbiome as a new potential biomarker in the domestication and health status of Octopus vulgaris," *Frontiers in Marine Science*, 11, 2024
28 Roura, A, "You Are What You Eat: A Genomic Analysis of the Gut Microbiome of Captive and Wild *Octopus vulgaris* Paralarvae and Their Zooplankton Prey," *Frontiers in Physiology*, 8, 2017
29 McAnulty, S J, et al, ""Failure To Launch": Development of a Reproductive Organ Linked to Symbiotic Bacteria," *Host-Microbial Iteractions*, 14(1), 2023
30 Keeler, E, "Deep-sea hydrothermal vent sediments reveal diverse fungi with antibacterial activities," *Microbial Ecology*, 97(8), 2021
31 "Ocean fungi from twilight zone could be source of next penicillin-like drug," *The Guardian*, 2024, www.theguardian.com/environment/2024/jan/16/ocean-fungi-from-twilight-zone-could-be-source-of-next-penicillin-like-drug
32 Kinross. J, *Dark Matter: The New Science of the Microbiome*, Penguin Life, UK, 2024
33 Zhou, X, et al, "Aspernigrins with anti-HIV-1 activities from the marine-derived fungus Aspergillus niger SCSIO Jcsw6F30," *Bioorganic & Medicinal Chemistry Letters*, 26(2), 2016, pp.361–365
34 Scales, H, *The Brilliant Abyss*, Bloomsbury Sigma, London, 2021, Chapter 7
35 Vaksmaa, A, et al, "Biodegradation of polyethylene by the marine fungus Parengyodontium album," *The Science of the Total Environment*, 934(172819), 2024
36 Thewissen, et al, "From Land to Water: the Origin of Whales, Dolphins, and Porpoises," *Evolution: Education and Outreach*, 2, 2009, pp.272–288
37 "Dr Sally Fryar – Marine and Aquatic Fungi," *The Queensland Mycological Society*, YouTube, 2022, www.youtube.com/watch?v=zyaoSsCYJzg
38 Taylor, J W, et al, "Fungi as key players in ecosystem functioning: Drivers of rain formation and nutrient cycling," *Fungal Biology Reviews*, 28(4), 2014, pp.151–156
39 Nizeti, J, Kaufmann, G, & Slee, M, "Fungi: Web of Life," Stranger Than Fiction Films, 2023
40 Huffman, J A, et al, "High concentrations of biological aerosol particles and ice nuclei during and after rain," *Atmospheric Chemistry and Physics*, 13(10), 2013, pp.5221–5234
41 Lindemann, S R, et al, "Soil fungal networks and their role in water transport." *Nature Communications*, 8(15811), 2017
42 "Sounds in the Ocean: Environmental and Anthropogenic," *NOAA Fisheries, www.fisheries.noaa.gov/national/science-data/sounds-ocean-environmental-and-anthropogenic*
43 BBC Earth Explore, "Fish Sounds: Do fish talk to each other?" *YouTube*, 2018, www.youtube.com/watch?v=POITHO2VVrw&pp=0gcJCfwAo7VqN5tD
44 Simpson, S, et al, "Acoustic enrichment can enhance fish community development on degraded coral reef habitat," *Nature Communications*, 10(5414), 2019
45 TEDx Talks, "The secret soundtrack of the sea | Steve Simpson | TEDxExeter," *YouTube*, 2022, www.youtube.com/watch?v=fZIffZ9oRxw
46 Pallamidessi, J, "Bernie Krause – The Great Animal Orchestra," *YouTube*, 2021, www.youtube.com/watch?v=btrinTDDjnQ
47 "A conversation across time and space: the power of birdsong," *The Guardian*, 2020, www.theguardian.com/environment/2020/dec/15/cosmo-sheldrake-the-power-of-birdsong-aoe
48 Sueur, J, et al, "Rapid acoustic survey for biodiversity appraisal," *PLoS ONE*, 9(12), 2014, e115524
49 "Sounding Soil – healthy soil makes noise," *The Biovision Foundation*, www.biovision.ch/en/project/sounding-soil/
50 Sethi, S, et al, "Characterizing soundscapes across diverse ecosystems using a universal acoustic feature set." *Proceedings of the National Academy of Sciences of the United States of America*, 117(29), 2020, pp.17049-17055
51 Robinson, J, et al, "Monitoring soil fauna with ecoacoustics," *Proceedings of The Royal Society of London Series B: Biological Sciences*, 291(2030), 2024

52 "The Sound of the Underground," The Friends of Westonbirt Arboretum, 2024, www.fowa.org.uk/blog/the-sound-of-the-underground
53 Hofstetter, R W, Copp, B E, & Lukic, I, "Acoustic noise of refrigerators promote increased growth rate of the gray mold Botrytis cinerea." *Journal of Food Safety*, *40*(6), 2020
54 Robinson, J, M, Breed, M F, & Beckett, R, "Probiotic Cities: microbiome-integrated design for healthy urban ecosystems," *Science & Society*, 42(8), 2024, pp.942–945
55 If you're in Switzerland, the Sounding Soil project rents equipment and accepts submissions to its sound map. Alternatively, you can rent or borrow equipment from universities or sound hire services.
56 McGovern, P E, et al, "Fermented beverages of pre- and proto-historic China," *Proceedings of the National Academy of Sciences of the United States of America,* 101(51), 2004
57 Paulette, T, "Fermentation in Ancient Mesopotamia, Beer, Bread, and More Beer," *Fermentology*, 2020
58 Cohen, J J, *Prismatic Ecology: Ecotheory Beyond Green,* University of Minnesota Press, 2014 (Ch: Black Ecology, Levi R. Bryant, pp.291-310)
59 "The Hymn to Ninkasi, Goddess of Beer," *World History Encyclopedia*, 2022, www.worldhistory.org/article/222/the-hymn-to-ninkasi-goddess-of-beer/
60 Hornsey, I S, "A History of Beer and Brewing," *The Royal Society of Chemistry*, 2003
61 "SYSK Selects: How Beer Works," Stuff You Should Know [podcast], 2017
62 Gershon, L, "World's Oldest 'Industrial-Scale' Brewery Found in Egypt," *Smithsonian Magazine*, 2021, www.smithsonianmag.com/smart-news/worlds-oldest-industrial-scale-brewery-found-egypt-180977026/
63 Pollan, M, *The Botany of Desire*, Random House, New York, 2001
64 Pollan, M, *The Botany of Desire*, Random House, New York, 2001
65 Nelson, R, "A eucharist of sourdough or wafer? What a thousand-year-old religious quarrel tells us about fermentation," *The Conversation*, 2024, theconversation.com/a-eucharist-of-sourdough-or-wafer-what-a-thousand-year-old-religious-quarrel-tells-us-about-fermentation-212698
66 Money, N P, *The Rise of Yeast: How the Sugar Fungus Shaped Civilization,* Open University Press Oxford, 2018
67 Planet A Foods, planet-a-foods.com
68 THE ODIN, www.the-odin.com

6 INTRA: CRAFT, CONTINUITY, & COMMUNITIES OF CARE

1 Barbier, A, "Parler Avec v'Apaq," *Terrain: Anthropologie & Sciences Humaines,* 2021
2 Dalton, D, "How evolutionary biology can explain why human and a few marine mammal females are the only ones that are menopausal," *Journal of Theoretical Biology*, 543, 2022
3 Katz, S, *The Art of Fermentation,* Chelsea Green Publishing Co, 2021
4 Cooper, S, *The Fermentation Kitchen: Recipes and Techniques for Kimchi, Kombucha, Koji and More*, DK Red, 2024
5 Redzepi, R, & Zilber, D, *The Noma Cookbook*, Artisan Publishers, NY, 2018
6 "Culture, Kinship and Kimchi," *Montclair State University*, 2022
7 Seo, S-H, et al, "Effect of Fungi on Metabolite Changes in Kimchi During Fermentation," *Molecules*, 25(21), 2020
8 Mother-in-Law's Kimchi, milkimchi.com/pages/about-us
9 "Sichuan Paocai (Infinite Pickle Jar)," *Day With Mei*, 2025, www.daywithmei.com/sichuan-paocai-infinite-pickle-jar/
10 South Korea's first astronaut, Yi So-yeon, even brought specially prepared, microbe-free kimchi aboard the ISS in April 2008, sharing the space-safe version with her international crewmates.
11 The Untold History of Women in Sake Brewing, Deeper Japan, deeperjapan.com/journal/untold-history-of-women-in-sake-brewing
12 "Sake in Japanese Food Culture (No. 2)," Kikkoman Food Forum, www.kikkoman.com/en/culture/foodforum/the-japanese-table/29-2.html
13 Redzepi, R, & Zilber, D, *The Noma Guide to Fermentation*, Artisan, New York, 2018, p.32
14 Rekdal, V M, et al, "Neurospora intermedia from a traditional fermentation food enables waste-to-food conversion," *Nature Microbiology,* 9, 2024, pp.2666–2683
15 "Amou Haji," *Wikipedia*, 2025, en.wikipedia.org/wiki/Amou_Haji
16 Lowry, C A, et al, "The Microbiota, Immunoregulation, and Mental Health: Implications for Public Health," *Current Environmental Health Reports,* 3(3), 2016, pp.270–286

17 Kinross, J, *Dark Matter: The New Science of the Microbiome,* Penguin Life, UK, 2024, Track 5, 35:00
18 Rook, G A W, Lowry, C A, & Raison, C L, "Microbial 'Old Friends', immunoregulation and stress resilience," *Evolution, Medicine, and Public Health*, 2013(1), 2013, pp.46–64
19 "What is Happening to Agrobiodiversity?," *Food and Agriculture Organization,* www.fao.org/4/y5609e/y5609e02.htm
20 Kessler, R, & Stuppy, W, *Seeds: Time Capsules of Life*, Papadakis, 2024
21 Tucker, M, "Seeds of life: The plants suited to climate change," *BBC News*, 2019, www.bbc.co.uk/news/extra/HVJMVYKmjp/seeds-of-life
22 Kinross, J, *Dark Matter: The New Science of the Microbiome*, Penguin Life, UK, 2024, Track 5 33:30
23 Wilde, M, *The Wilderness Cure*, Simon & Schuster UK, 2022
24 "The Wildbiome Project Results," *Mo Wilde,* monicawilde.com/the-wildbiome-project-results/
25 Wall Kimmerer, R, *Braiding Sweetgrass*, Milkweed Editions, 2015
26 "Invisible friends in the air we breathe?," *Jake M Robinson*, 2024, www.jakemrobinson.com/blog/invisible-friends-in-the-air-we-breathe
27 Li Y, Wang Y , Zhang T, Fecal Microbiota Transplantation in Autism Spectrum Disorder, Neuropsychiatric Disease and Treatment, 18, 2022, pp.2905–2915
28 "Wild Spices of the UK," *Galloway Wild Foods*, 2016, gallowaywildfoods.com/wild-spices-of-the-uk/
29 "Edible Seeds & Wild Spice Conversion Chart," *Mo Wilde*, 2013, monicawilde.com/wild-spice/
30 Informed by mycodesigner Harvey Shaw, who spent a month in Transylvania with Károly and his family, 2024
31 Sheldrake, M, *Entangled Life: How Fungi Make Our Worlds, Change Our Minds and Shape Our Futures*, Penguin Publishing, 2018, p.203
32 Google Patents, "Method of Producing a Mycological Product and Product Made Thereby," Ecovative LL, US20200024577A1, United States, patents.google.com/patent/US20150033620A1/en
33 Meya, V, & Mengel S, "Patent landscape analysis for materials based on fungal mycelium: a guidance report on how to interpret the current patent situation," *Fungal Biology and Biotechnology,* 11, 2024
34 "Biodesign Meets Ai: Making Space for More-Than-Human Intelligences," *Normal Phenomena*, 2024, normalphenomena.life/editorial/biodesign-meets-ai-making-space-for-more-than-human-intelligences/
35 Nightengale, M, *Out of Old Nova Scotia Kitchens,* Nimbus Publishing Ltd, 1989
36 "Mi'gmaq/Mi'kmaq Online Talking Dictionary," Mi'kmaq Online, mikmaqonline.org/
37 "Mi'kMaq identity – Mi'kmaq: First Nation people (6/6)," *OpenLearn from The Open University*, YouTube, 2013, www.youtube.com/watch?v=iGIw25_ML3U
38 "Re-Rooting Agroecology as a Social Movement," *Oxford Real Farming Conference*, 2025, www.youtube.com/watch?v=qQQjfDuPgXU
39 "Roots of Resistance: Farming in Palestine," *Oxford Real Farming Conference*, 2025, www.youtube.com/watch?v=FSMLpY5iGKE
40 Penniman, L, *Farming While Black,* Chelsea Green Publishing Co, 2018
41 Steinauer-Scudder, C, "The Seeds of Ancestors: A Day at Soul Fire Farm," *Emergence Magazine*, 2019
42 "Leah Penniman "Farming While Black" author, Soul Fire Farm cofounder & Heinz Award honoree (S05E03), *We Can Be Podcast,* 2024
43 Gagliano, M, *Thus Spoke the Plant*, North Atlantic Books, US, 2020, Ch 7
44 Bidartondo, M I, et al, " State of the World's Fungi 9. Climate change: Fungal responses and effects," *Royal Botanic Gardens KEW,* 2018
45 "State of the World's Plants and Fungi 2023: Tackling the Nature Emergency: Evidence, gaps and priorities," *Royal Botanic Gardens KEW,* 2023, pp. 28 and 33
46 Leopold, A, *A Sand County Almanac*, Oxford University Press, 1949

7 INCONSISTENCIES: MYSTERY & PARADOX

1 "Pacifica Graduate Institute, Altered States Conference: Navigating Uncertainty by Jean Houston," YouTube, 2019, www.youtube.com/watch?v=W9V8N2T3Tsc&pp=ygUSI2FsdGVyZWRzdGF0ZXMyMDE5
2 "S1E8. Hexing Herbs and the Witches of Medieval Europe," Plants of the Gods, 2021
3 "Fungi Cosmology," *Labverde*, 2025, www.labverde.com/fungi-cosmology

4 "The Blob." Video from Merlin Sheldrake's Lab at the VU (Vrije Universiteit) in Amsterdam and its Physics Institute, Amorph. Shown during Old Tree Soil's event, "Merlin Sheldrake in Conversation," 27 May 2025

5 Jones, K, *Shiitake: The Healing Mushroom*, Inner Traditions/Bear, 1995

6 Lawrence, S, *The Magic of Mushrooms; Fungi in folklore, superstition and traditional medicine (Royal Botanic Gardens Kew),* Headline Publishing Group, 2002, p.96

7 Jones, K, *Shiitake: The Healing Mushroom*, Inner Traditions/Bear, 1995

8 Jones, K, *Shiitake: The Healing Mushroom*, Inner Traditions/Bear, 1995

9 "SHIITAKE: Trails to Oishii Tokyo," *NHK World Japan*, 2023, www3.nhk.or.jp/nhkworld/en/shows/2054160/

10 Hobbs, C, *Medicinal Mushrooms*, Storey, 2021

11 Smith, et al, *Medicinal Mushrooms: Their Therapeutic Properties and Current Medical Usage with Special Emphasis on Cancer Treatments,* University of Strathclyde & Cancer Research, 2002, p.35

12 Xu, X, et al, "Chemical Composition, Antioxidant and Anti-Inflammatory Activity of Shiitake Mushrooms (Lentinus edodes)." *Journal of Fungi*, 10(8), 2024, p.552

13 Hearst, R, et al, "An examination of antibacterial and antifungal properties of constituents of Shiitake (*Lentinula edodes*) and Oyster (*Pleurotus ostreatus*) mushrooms," *Complementary Therapies in Clinical Practice*, 15(1), 2009, pp.5–7

14 Ngai, P H K., & Ng, T B, "Lentin, a novel and potent antifungal protein from shitake mushroom with inhibitory effects on activity of human immunodeficiency virus-1 reverse transcriptase and proliferation of leukemia cells," *Life Sciences*, 73(26), 2003, pp.3363–3374

15 Rogers R D, *Medicinal Mushrooms: The Human Clinical Trials*, 2020, pp.59-66

16 Tolaini, V, et al, "Lentinula edodes enhances the biocontrol activity of Cryptococcus laurentii against Penicillium expansum contamination and patulin production in apple fruits," *International Journal of Food Microbiology*, 138(3), 2010, pp.243–249

17 Chaucheyras-Durand, F, et al, "Live yeasts enhance fibre degradation in the cow rumen through an increase in plant substrate colonization by fibrolytic bacteria and fungi," *Journal of Applied Microbiology*. 120(3), 2016, pp.560-70

18 Steenkamp, E. T, Wright, J, & Baldauf, S L, "The protistan origins of animals and fungi." *Molecular Biology and Evolution,* 19(7), 2002, pp.754–763

19 Make sure to cook Shiitake mushrooms very well as raw or undercooked Shiitake can lead to a toxic condition known as "flagellate dermatitis," which causes severe itching that can persist for several weeks.

20 Jones, K, *Shiitake: The Healing Mushroom*, Inner Traditions/Bear, 1995, p.13

21 Augustus De Morgan, *A Budget of Paradoxes*. Longmans, Green, and Company, 1872, pp.376–377

22 Kaishian, P, & Djoulakian, H, "The Science Underground: Mycology as a Queer Discipline," *Catalyst: Feminism, Theory, Technoscience,* 6(2), 2020

23 Efird, E, "Queer Mycology's Meta-Analysis: Fungi Roll Queer Studies to the Edge of Theory," The University of Edinburgh, 2025

24 "Queer Ecologies by Jasmine Qureshi," *All The Elements Voices*, 2024 (podcast)

25 Nakamura, A, et al, "Cultivation and mating of the truffle Tuber japonicum in plantations of ectomycorrhizal Quercus serrata seedlings," *Mycology*, 91(2), 2025

26 "The Role of Woodland Mycorrhizal Fungi," *WoodlandsTV*, 2024, www.youtube.com/watch?v=IOBuzzhv4OE

27 "The Maryland Naturalist," *The Natural History Society of Maryland*, 3(1), 1987, p.51

28 "Women of Science Spotlight: Mary Banning," *The New York State Museum*, nysm.nysed.gov/women-of-science/mary-banning

29 "Beatrix Potter (1866-1943)," *The Linnean Society*, www.linnean.org/the-society/history-of-science/beatrix-potter-the-tale-of-the-linnean-society

30 "Patricia Ononiwu Kaishian: Queer Mycology (MAWDC 6/4/23)," *Mycological Association of Washington DC*, YouTube, 2023, www.youtube.com/watch?v=e4hSPjlmiV8

31 Ostendorf-Rodríguez, Y, *Let's Become Fungal!,* Astrid Vorstermans & Pia Pol, Valiz, Amsterdam, 2023, p.120

32 Gormley, G, "Lithium: My Irreplaceable Element," *KÅRK magazine*, 2022

33 Simpson, J G, et al., "Liquid metal battery storage in an offshore wind turbine: Concept and economic analysis," *Renewable and Sustainable Energy Reviews*, 149, 2021

34 "The side effects of lithium mining," *Wellcome Collection,* 2021, wellcomecollection.org/stories/the-side-effects-of-lithium-mining

35 Tabuchi, H, "Before Invasion, Ukraine's Lithium Wealth Was Drawing Global Attention," *The New York Times*, 2022, www.nytimes.com/2022/03/02/climate/ukraine-lithium.html

36 “What minerals does Ukraine have – and why does Donald Trump want them?,” *Sky News*, 2025, news.sky.com/story/what-minerals-does-ukraine-have-and-why-does-donald-trump-want-them-13316629
37 Cornish Lithium Plc, cornishlithium.com/
38 Faget, J, “Portuguese at loggerheads over lithium,” *DW*, 2021, www.dw.com/en/portugal-war-over-lithium-behind-the-mountains/a-59064217
39 Parnell, J, “Lithium with your tonic, Sir?,” *Geoscientist*, 2023, geoscientist.online/sections/features/lithium-with-your-tonic-sir/
40 Yücel, HG, et al, “A comparative investigation of lithium(I) biosorption properties of *Aspergillus versicolor* and *Kluyveromyces marxianus*,” *Water Science & Technology*, 81(3), 2020, pp.499–507
41 Lobos, A, et al, “Tolerance of three fungal species to lithium and cobalt: Implications for bioleaching of spent rechargeable Li-ion batteries,” *Journal of Applied Microbiology,* 131(2), 2021, pp.743–755
42 Bahaloo-Horeh, N, & Mousavi, SM. “Enhanced recovery of valuable metals from spent lithium-ion batteries through optimization of organic acids produced by Aspergillus niger.” *Waste Management*, 60, 2017, pp.66–679
43 Stamets, P, *Mycelium Running*, Ten Speed Press, Berkley, 2005, p.86
44 Stamets, P, *Mycelium Running*, Ten Speed Press, Berkley, 2005, p.86
45 “6 ways mushrooms can save the world | Paul Stamets | TED,” YouTube, 2008, www.youtube.com/watch?v=XI5frPV58tY
46 Maillard, F, “Fungal necromass presents a high potential for Mercury immobilization in soil,” *Chemosphere*, 311(1), 2023
47 Kiers, T E, et al., “Mycorrhizal mycelium as a global carbon pool,” *Current Biology*, 33(11), 2023, R560-R573
48 Traxler, L C, “The potential of Schizophyllum commune for mycoremediation at the Chernobyl exclusion zone,” *Faculty of Biological Sciences*, 2022
49 Dadachova, E, & Casadevall, A, “Ionizing radiation: how fungi cope, adapt, and exploit with the help of melanin.” *Current Opinion in Microbiology*, 11(6), 2008, pp.525–531
50 Gervais, N C, & Shapiro, R S, “Discovering the hidden function in fungal genomes,” *Nature Communications*, 15(8219), 2024
51 Pollan, M, *The Botany of Desire*, Random House, New York, 2001
52 Allaby, M, *A Dictionary of Plant Sciences,* Oxford University Press, 1998
53 *
54 Boddy, L, & Wald, P, “Creolophus (=Hericium) cirrhatus, Hericium erinaceus and H. coralloides in England,” *English Nature Research Reports*, 492, 2002, pp.5–12
55 Hallenberg, N, “Hericium coralloides and H. alpestre (Basidiomycetes) in Europe,” *Mycotaxon*, 18(1), 1983, pp.181–189
56 Boddy, L, “Ecology of Hericium cirrhatum, H. coralloides and H. erinaceus in the UK,” *Fungal Ecology*, 4(2), 2011
57 Barbieri, F, “If Camembert were to disappear too . . .,” *Fungi Film Festival,* 2024
58 “Magic Mushroom Genomes Reveal Route to ‘Designer’ Fungi,” *Technology Networks: Drug Discovery*, 2023, www.technologynetworks.com/drug-discovery/news/magic-mushroom-genomes-reveal-route-to-designer-fungi-381745#
59 Rosenthal, M, *Food: Bigger Than the Plate*, V&A, 2019, p.56
60 Dong, Y, “Edible and medicinal fungi breeding techniques, a review: Current status and future prospects,” *Current Research in Food Science,* 5, 2022, pp.2070–2080
61 Waltz, E, “Gene-edited CRISPR mushroom escapes US regulation,” *Nature*, 532(293), 2016

EPILOGUE

1 Lawler, A, “Ancient DNA offers clues to physical origins of Dead Sea Scrolls,” *National Geographic,* 2020, www.nationalgeographic.com/history/article/ancient-dna-offers-clues-physical-origins-dead-sea-scrolls
2 Gibbons, A, “Goats, bookworms, a monk’s kiss: Biologists reveal the hidden history of ancient gospels,” *Science Magazine,* 2017, www.science.org/content/article/goats-bookworms-monk-s-kiss-biologists-reveal-hidden-history-ancient-gospels
3 Teasdale, M D, et al, “The York Gospels: a one thousand year biological palimpsest,” *bioRxiv*, 2017, p.5
4 Kinross, J, *Dark Matter,* Penguin Life, 2023
5 Hawksworth, D, & Wiltshire P E J, “Forensic mycology: current perspectives,” *Research and Reports in Forensic Medical Science*, 5, 2015, pp.75-83
6 Sheldrake, M, *Entangled Life: How Fungi Make Our Worlds, Change Our Minds & Shape Our Futures*, Penguin Publishing, 2018, p.7

Picture Credits

Page 10 Map © Mycostories
Page 13 (left) Agricultural Research Service/Wikimedia Commons, (right) Rajarshi Rit/Wikimedia Commons
Page 15 Lohit Y.T./WWF India
Page 18 1. Cobalt Crust Fungus (Terana caerulea) (Elena Yates); 2. Blackening Polypore (Meripilus sumstinei) (Elena Yates); 3. Leafy Brain (Phaeotremella foliacea) (Elena Yates); 4. Scarlet Elf Cup (Sarcoscypha coccinea) (Elena Yates); 5. Fan-shaped Jelly Fungus (Dacryopinax spathularia) (Elena Yates); 6. Red Cage Fungus (Clathrus ruber) (Damon Tighe); 7. Turkey Tail (Trametes versicolor) (Elena Yates); 8. Reishi (Ganoderma lucidum) (Kit Ondaatje Rolls); 9. Octopuss Stinkhorn (Clathrus archeri) (Elena Yates); 10. Witches Butter (Tremella mesenterica) (Elena Yates); 11. Fairy Fingers (Clavaria fragilis) (Elena Yates); 12. Variable Oysterling (Crepidotus variabilis) (Elena Yates); 13. Hairy Nuts Disco (Lanzia echinophila) (Jasper Sharp); 14. Mosaic Puffball (Mosaic Puffball) (Elena Yates); 15. Bird's Nest Fungus (Nidulariaceae spp.) (Elena Yates); 16. Tripe Fungus (Auricularia mesenterica) (Kit Ondaatje Rolls)
Page 21 Helen Robinson
Page 25 (top) Diagram of basic interdepencies: Graham Caine, (bottom) David Satori
Page 27 Gift of Felix M. Warburg and his family, 1941 courtesy of the Metropolitan Museum of Art, USA
Page 28 (left) W. Schild. Die Maleficia der Hexenleut/Wikimedia Commons, (right) Elena Yates
Page 30 1487033 Sturgis McKeever, Georgia Southern University, Bugwood.org
Page 31 GroCycle Mushroom Farm, UK
Page 35 (left) Novartis company archives, (right) Sandoz A.G, Institute of Medical History, University of Bern, estate of Albert Hoffman
Page 36 (left) Wellcome Institute, (right) Wikimedia Commons (PD-US)
Page 42 (top) Boyer/Roger Viollet/Getty Images, (bottom) Elena Yates
Page 43 Loop Biotech
Page 47 Christina Agapakis & Sissel Tolaas
Page 49 Mischa de Stroumillo and The Wild Room
Page 50 Mischa de Stroumillo and The Wild Room
Page 51 Mischa de Stroumillo and The Wild Room
Page 53 (left) The FUNgi Guy & Jesper Launder, (right) David Satori
Page 54 (left) David Satori, (right) Vinayaraj V.R./Wikimedia Commons
Page 56 Imre Potyó
Page 59 Alan Rockefeller
Page 61 (top) Harvey Shaw, (bottom) Paul Hanny/Gamma-Rapho/Getty Images
Page 62 Wikimedia Commons (PD-US)
Page 63 (left) Horai Mountain by Matsudaira Sadanobu (PD-US), (right) Emily Munster
Page 64 Magu, Goddess of Longevity, Anonymous (PD-US)
Page 69 Alan Rockefeller
Page 71 (right) Wim van Egmond/Officina Corpuscoli. Caption by Maurizio Montalti
Page 72 Alan Rockefeller
Page 74 Graph from paper on Fungal Language Complexity, Mohammad Mahdi Dehshibi and Andy Adamatzky, University of West of England
Page 75 Andy Adamatzky
Page 80 (top left) Gift of Mr. and Mrs. Frederick S. Wait, 1907, Metropolitan Museum of Modern Art, (top centre) The Trustees of the British Museum, released as CC BY-NC-SA 4.0. Image from Wikimedia Commons, (top right) 2025 River Cousin
Page 81 (bottom) Anonymous 2022
Page 82 Alan Rockefeller
Page 85 Alan Rockefeller

Page 87 Ramin Rahmani Nejad Asil/Wikimedia Commons
Page 88 (left) Kat Harrison, (right) Illustration by Ernst Haeckel 1834-1919 (PD-US)
Page 89 (left) MinistryOfJoy/iStock Photo, (right) Eunika Sopotnicka/iStock Photo
Page 90 Grab from Instagram Reel @dakotawint
Page 91 Caroline Lena Becker/Musee du quai Branly/Wikimedia Commons
Page 96 Jana Nicole
Page 98 Argillite plate attributed to Charles Edenshaw Field Museum of Natural History, Chicago cat. 17952
Page 99 Igor Siwanowicz
Page 102 Wikimedia Commons
Page 103 (left) Rich Wright
Page 104 (left) Phil Winter
Page 105 (right) David Satori
Page 106 (left) Jasper Sharp
Page 109 (top) W.Carter/Wikimedia Commons, (bottom) Umberto Salvagnin/Flickr
Page 110 Wikimedia Commons
Page 111 Carolina Kyvik, Marie Melcore, Kit Ondaatje Rolls, Cassie Quinn, Eleanora Rombola (MA Biodesign 2021)
Page 112 Eleanora Rombola
Page 113 Eleanora Rombola
Page 115 (top) Mushroom Colour Atlas created by Julie Beeler, www.mushroomcoloratlas.com, (centre) Elena Yates
Page 117 Bristol Fungarium
Page 120 (left) Wikimedia Commons (PD-US), (right) Bristol Fungarium
Page 123 Bristol Fungarium
Page 127 Damon Tighe
Page 128 Estate of John Craxton
Page 129 L. Smith/Shetland Museum and Archives
Page 132 Sekai Machache
Page 134 Carsten Höller | Upside Down Mushroom Room, 2000. Synchro System, Fondazione Prada, Milan, 2000 courtesy the artist and Fondazione Prada, Milan © Attilio Maranzano
Page 136 Damon Tighe
Page 137 (left) Arthur Rackham/Wikimedia Commons (PD-US)
Page 140 (left) Mischa de Stroumillo and The Wild Room, (right) Jans Ondaatje Rolls
Page 141 (right) Tom Carter
Page 144 (left) Tom Carter, (centre, right) Juliette Casini
Page 145 Juliette Casini
Page 147 NASA
Page 148 (left) The John Lilly Estate
Page 149 Image # 4155 American Museum of Natural History
Page 150 Wikimedia Commons (PD-US)
Page 151 (top) Ken-ichi Ueda, iNaturalist Photo 5533453/Wikimedia Commons, (bottom) Wikipedia Commons
Page 154 (left) The Intruder – John Anster Fitzgerald/Wikimedia Commons (PD-US), (right) Alamy
Page 155 Mary Evans Picture Library
Page 157 (top) Kunst Museum/Wikimedia Commons (PD-US), (bottom) Ivan Bilibin/Wikimedia Commons
Page 158 Wikimedia Commons (PD-US)
Page 159 Alamy
Page 161 I.P. Adamatzky
Page 163 (left) Jean-Pierre Dalbéra/Flickr, (right) Wikimedia Commons (PD-US)
Page 164 (left) Daniel Winkler, (right) Bob Leccinu/Robert Kozak/Shutterstock
Page 165 image courtesy of Daniel Winkler
Page 166 (right) Daniel Winkler
Page 167 (left) Bruce Parry

Page 168 Gusmano CESARETTI
Page 170 George Sturby
Page 171 George Sturby
Page 173 (left) Clipping from the Daily Mail 1991, (right) Robert A. Blanchette, Brian D. Compton, Nancy J. Turner, Robert L. Gilbertson
Page 174 Dr. Marie Olive Reay 'Mushroom Madness' in the New Guinea Highlands
Page 176 Amélie Barbier
Page 178 Gabriella Gormley
Page 180 Pink Chicken Project 2017
Page 183 Alan Rockefeller
Page 187 (top) NASA/Bill Anders, (bottom) NASA
Page 188 Mars City Design, www.marscitydesign.com
Page 189 Officina Corpuscoli/Maurizio Montalti
Page 190 (left) Wellcome Institute/David Gregory and Debbie Marshall, (right) Darren Le Baron
Page 191 Bristol Fungarium
Page 195 (top) Dayarathne M.C. et al. 2020, (bottom) NOAA
Page 196 (left) Damon Tighe, (right) Maria del Carmen González
Page 197 (right) Paula Camiñera
Page 199 Agorastos Papatsanis
Page 202 Steve Simpson
Page 204 Bristol Fungarium
Page 205 Marcus Coates
Page 206 Damon Tighe
Page 207 Saumya Singh
Page 210 (top) Paul Cochrane
Page 212 (right) Print Collector/Getty Images
Page 213 (left) Getty Images/PHAS, (right) Wikimedia Commons (PD-US)
Page 214 (left) Bacchus with Leopart by Johann Wilhelm Shutze/Sothebys/Wikimedia (PD-US), (right) Wikimedia Commons (PD-US)
Page 216 Monty Meth/Topical Press Agency/Getty Images
Page 217 (top) The Odin/www.the-odin.com
Page 218 Patricia A. Schwimmer/Bridgeman Art Library
Page 220–223 Amélie Barbier and the Koryak Community
Page 225 (top) Lexie Park (Eat Nünchi) | www.eatnunchi.com
Page 226 (left) Lexie Park (Eat Nünchi) | www.eatnunchi.com
Page 229 (right) Jesper Svedberg
Page 236 Sam Rolls
Page 241 (right) Tom Carter
Page 242 Mo Wilde
Page 244 Lisa Cutcliffe
Page 252 Harvey Shaw
Page 253 Kit Ondaatje Rolls, Carolina Kyvik, Eleonora Rombola, Cassie Quinn, Marie Melcore (MA Biodesign)
Page 254 (left) Bristol Fungarium
Page 255 (left) Harvey Shaw, (right) Ecovative/My Forest Foods
Page 263 Christopher Ondaatje
Page 264 Joseph S. Rogers/Wikimedia Commons (PD-US)
Page 265 Sofia Barnes and Matthew Fratini
Page 266 (left) David Satori, (right) Christopher Ondaatje
Page 268 (left, centre) Christopher Ondaatje
Page 272 Muzeum Narodowe w Krakowie/Wikimedia Commons (PD-US)

Page 275 Sebastian Enriquez @revolucionfungi with acknowledgement to the Shipibo-Konibo women portrayed
Page 277 (left) Bristol Fungarium, (right) TrueShiitake www.obchod.trueshiitake.cz
Page 279 Ikoi Spa, New Zealand, www.ikoispa.co.nz
Page 280 (left) Mushroom Observer.org/Wikimedia Commons
Page 281 (top) Elena Yates, (bottom) David Satori
Page 282 David Satori
Page 284 (left) Caroline Tompkins
Page 285 (left) British Mycological Society, (right) Beatrix Potter artwork courtesy of the The Armitt Museum & Library
Page 286 (left) Bridgeman Art Library, (right) The Fool card from the Motherpeace Tarot Deck first published 1981. Co-created by Karen Vogel and Vicki Noble. www.motherpeace.com
Page 287 (left) Damon Tighe, (right) David Satori
Page 289 Bring Us The Fungus (@bringusthefungus)
Page 290 (top) Claire Partington, (bottom) Karoline Hjorth & Riitta Ikonen
Page 292 (left) MA Biodesign 2019, (right) Rob Kessler
Page 293 Gabriella Gormley
Page 296 (left) Harris & Ewing Studio/Wikimedia Commons, (right) Glen Koenig/Los Angeles Times via Getty Images
Page 298 (bottom) Moisés Hernández & Luis Undritz
Page 300 (left) Wikimedia Commons, (right) Joey Leahy
Page 301 Joey Leahy
Page 302 Joey Leahy
Page 303 (left) Joey Leahy, (right) David Satori
Page 304 (left) Ryan Paul Gates, (centre) Lawrence Kaizon, (right) Joey Leahy
Page 305 (right) William Brown, Fungalphabet
Page 306 (top) Joey Leahy
Page 309 Peter Ilsted/Statens Museum for Kunst/Wikimedia Commons (PD-US)
Page 311 Igor Siwanovicz
Page 312 David Satori
Page 314 Merlin Sheldrake image by Tomas Munita, Gabriella Gormley by Kasper Glendorf Palsnov, and David Satori by Sebastian Kettley © RBG Kew.

All other images © Kit Ondaatje Rolls

The publisher has made every reasonable effort to trace and obtain permission from copyright holders for all images reproduced in this book. Any omissions will be rectified if notice is given to the publisher.

Index

Note: page numbers in **bold** refer to information contained in captions.

C

D

E

F

M

N

O

P

Q

R

S

T

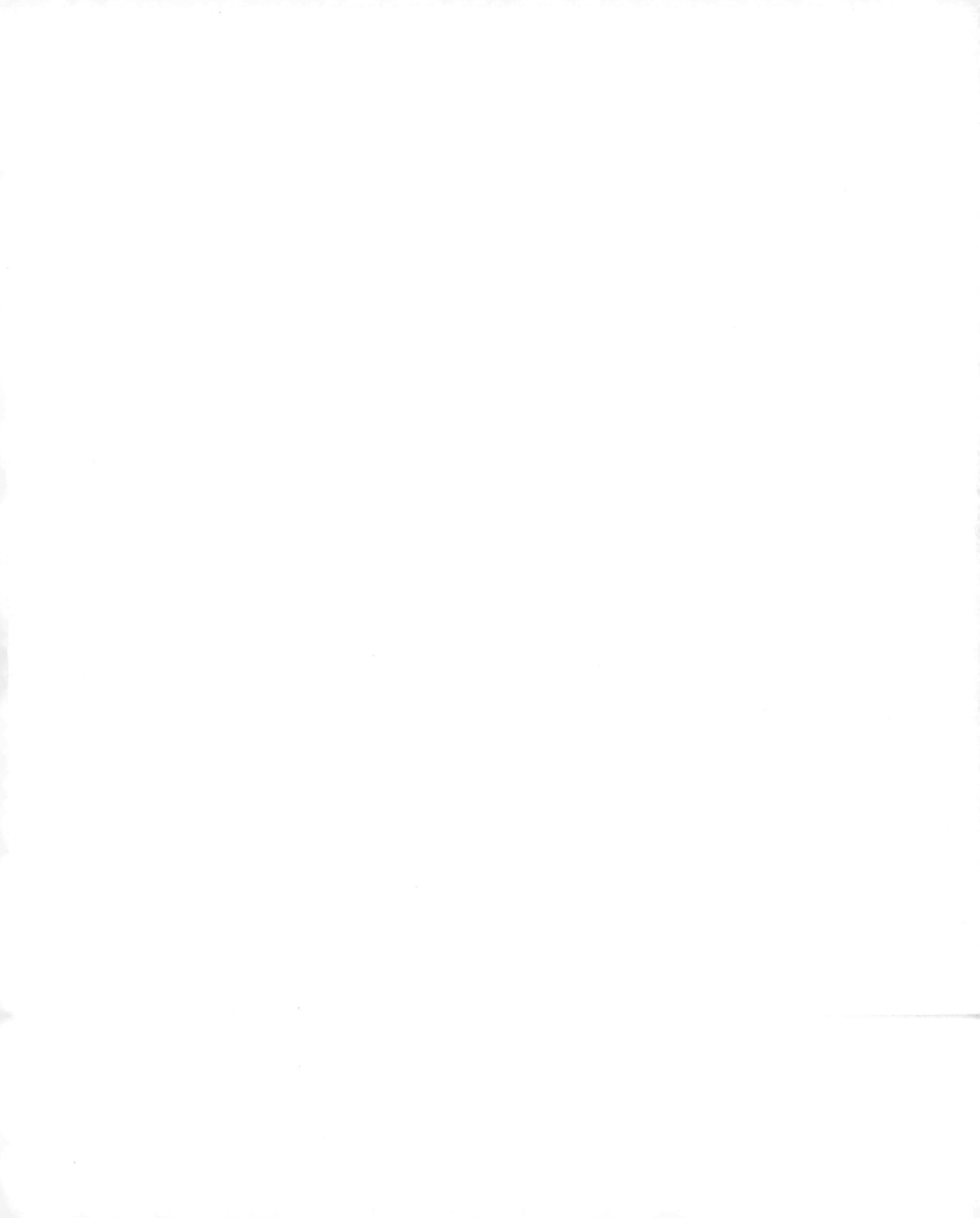

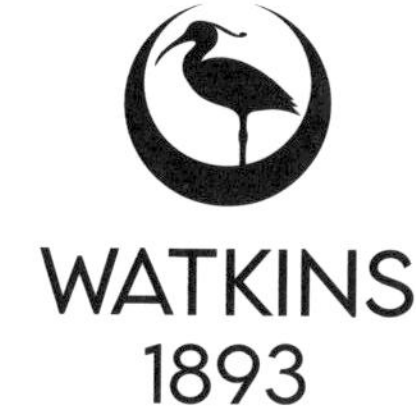

The story of Watkins began in 1893, when scholar of esotericism John Watkins founded our bookshop, inspired by the lament of his friend and teacher Madame Blavatsky that there was nowhere in London to buy books on mysticism, occultism or metaphysics. That moment marked the birth of Watkins, soon to become the publisher of many of the leading lights of spiritual literature, including Carl Jung, Rudolf Steiner, Alice Bailey and Chögyam Trungpa.

Today, the passion at Watkins Publishing for vigorous questioning is still resolute. Our stimulating and groundbreaking list ranges from ancient traditions and complementary medicine to the latest ideas about personal development, holistic wellbeing and consciousness exploration. We remain at the cutting edge, committed to publishing books that change lives.